Gilera Scooters
Service and Repair Manual

by Phil Mather

(4163 - 272 - 6AK2)

Models covered

Gilera Runner 50	49.3 cc	1997 to 2001
Gilera Runner 50 DD	49.3 cc	1999 to 2001
Gilera Runner 50 SP	49.3 cc	1999 to 2011
Gilera Runner Purejet 50	49.3 cc	2003 to 2007
Gilera Runner FX125	123.5 cc	1998 to 2001
Gilera Runner VX125	124.2 cc	2001 to 2008
Gilera Runner ST125	124.2 cc	2008 to 2011
Gilera Runner FXR180	175.8 cc	1998 to 2001
Gilera Runner VXR180	181.7 cc	2001 to 2002
Gilera Runner VXR200	197.7 cc	2003 to 2008
Gilera Runner ST200	197.7 cc	2008 to 2011
Gilera DNA 50 GP eXperience	49.3 cc	2000 to 2008
Gilera DNA 125	124.2 cc	2001 to 2003
Gilera DNA 180	181.7 cc	2001 to 2003
Gilera Ice	49.4 cc	2001 to 2004
Gilera SKP/Stalker*	49.4 cc	1997 to 2009

*Does not include Stalker Naked model

© Haynes Publishing 2011

A book in the **Haynes Service and Repair Manual Series**

ISBN 978 0 85733 545 6

British Library Cataloguing in Publication Data
A catalogue record for this book is available from the British Library

Printed in the USA.

Haynes Publishing
Sparkford, Yeovil, Somerset BA22 7JJ, England

Haynes North America, Inc
861 Lawrence Drive, Newbury Park, California 91320, USA

Haynes Publishing Nordiska AB
Box 1504, 751 45 UPPSALA, Sweden

Contents

LIVING WITH YOUR SCOOTER

Introduction

Daily (pre-ride checks)

MAINTENANCE

Routine maintenance and servicing

Contents

REPAIRS AND OVERHAUL

Engine, transmission and associated systems

Chassis components

Electrical system

Wiring diagrams

REFERENCE

Index

The Gilera Story

by Julian Ryder

Today, the name Gilera means a range of smart scooters styled with the usual Latin flair, but fifty years ago it was found on the tanks of the most powerful, most successful Grand Prix racers of their time. If you remember the shock waves caused by the launch of the Honda CB750 back at the end of the 1960s, you may think that Honda originated the high-revving four-cylinder engine. Not so. It was Gilera. And it was one of their beautiful four-cylinder 500 cc racers bikes that was first to lap the Isle of Man Mountain Circuit at over 100 mph. The marque dominated the world championship in the first half of the 1950s, winning the 500 title every year from 1950 to 1955 with the single exception of 1951. That was down to the genius of Geoff Duke and the slow but fine-handing single-cylinder Manx Norton. However, Duke saw which way racing was going and moved to Gilera. The British press accused Duke of treachery but he took the next three world titles, along the way he and the Gilera became one of the truly great man-machine combinations in the entire history of racing.

The Gilera story starts in 1909

The Gilera story actually starts way back in 1909 when a young mechanic called Giuseppe Gilera started making his own bikes in Milan. Things got serious when he moved to Arcore in 1920 and entered his bikes in the ISDT and some of the long-distance races so popular – and dangerous! – at the time, such as the Milan – Taranto.

The seeds of greatness were sown in the mid 1930s when Gilera acquired the rights to the Rondine engine from an aircraft company. This in-line four cylinder was water-cooled and supercharged but the chassis was pretty primitive. With the assistance of one of the original designers of the Rondine motor, the bike was totally redesigned for the 1948 season. The motor was pivoted backwards so that it was now only inclined 30-degrees forward. As forced induction was not allowed

in post-War racing, the supercharger was dispensed with and with it went the need for water cooling. The result was really the first recognisably modern racing multi, and it weighed just 290 pounds and measured just 15 inches across the crankcases.

From 1949 until the factory pulled out of racing in 1957, Gilera won 33 GPs and six world titles, but perhaps the event they are indelibly linked with happened on the Isle of Man in 1957. Geoff Duke thought he'd set a 100 mph lap in 1955 only to see it rounded down to 99.97 mph. When Duke was injured at the start of the '57 season he recommended Bob McIntyre to Gilera, and the Scot totally dominated the event. He blitzed the Junior (350 cc) TT in record time then in the eight-lap Senior (500 cc) race lapped over the magic ton four times. When Gilera stopped racing, MV Agusta took over with another in-line four designed, incidentally, by the same man who first designed the Gilera four, Piero Remor.

Why did Gilera stop racing? Officially it was the expense of racing but it seems just as likely that the death of the inspirational team manager, Giuseppe Gilera's son Ferruccio was the reason. Certainly Raymond Aisncoe, historian of the classic racing Gileras, pinpoints Ferruccio's death as the event that extinguished the spark of vitality in the owner after which the fortunes of the company gradually slid downhill.

The mighty fours also had a proud history in record breaking. Pre-War the great Piero Taruffi (engineer, Italian 500 cc champion, international tennis player, Summer and Winter Olympian, Mille Miglia and Targo Floria winner, factory Mercedes and Ferrari driver) had set an absolute record of 170.37 mph and a one-hour record of 127 miles using the supercharged bike. He set over 50 records on two, three and four wheels, many of them using Gilera power. In 1957 McIntyre used the 350 cc motor to set a one-hour record of 141.37 miles. The fours did race again, when in 1963 Geoff Duke persuaded the factory to let him use the use the old bike with himself as team manager with John Hartle, Derek Minter and Phil Read as riders. Hartle finished third at the end of the year but it was a quixotic enterprise.

In the real world of selling bikes to customers, things were not good. By 1960 the scooter boom was in full swing and Gilera was in trouble. However, the company's network of over 5000 service and retail outlets was a very attractive proposition for Piaggio, manufacturers of the ubiquitous Vespa, and in 1969 the 80-year old Giuseppe Gilera sold his company. He died in 1971.

Piaggio invested heavily in small two-strokes, with considerable success. There was an array of very successful 50 cc mopeds and motorcycles as well as some truly sporty 125s including the CX with single-sided swinging arm and single fork leg. There was even a return to GPs with a brace of 250 cc reed-valve twins. There was also some success with off-road singles in the Paris-Dakar and other desert rallies. Also on the four-stroke front, the old Saturno model from the 1950s was resurrected as a stylish modern 500 cc single but was a commercial irrelevance. The 558 cc Nordwest from 1991 was, however, well ahead of its time. It used an overbored Saturno motor in a supermoto package, but it wasn't enough. Piaggio closed the Arcore factory in 1993.

The Gilera brand was now transferred to the sort of scooter that underpins Piaggio's success. In the vital Italian scooter market with its hyper-sensitivity to fashion, if you get it right you sell by the boat-load. Get it wrong and you have a large stock of boat anchors on your hands. Gilera usually get it right, and in a canny piece of marketing that traded on the marque's history they went racing again in 2001. Piaggio had bought Spanish company Derbi and their successful 125 cc GP racers, so they badged one up as a Gilera, hired young Manuel Poggiali from San Marino as the rider and won the world title.

If you want to sell scooters in Italy having an Italian speaking teenage world champion riding a bike painted in the same colours as your scooter is a pretty good way to go about it.

The question for the immediate future is whether Piaggio will look to exploit the legacy of Gilera's golden classic-era success by moving their efforts up to the bigger classes. That could sell a lot of scooters.

Acknowledgements

Our thanks are due to Fowlers Motorcycles of Bristol who supplied the scooters featured in the photographs throughout this manual. We would also like to thank NGK Spark Plugs (UK) Ltd for supplying the colour spark plug condition photos, Draper Tools for many of the workshop tools photographed and Julian Ryder for writing the introduction 'The Gilera Story'.

Special thanks are due to Piaggio UK Ltd for supplying service literature, technical support and model photographs, and to Piaggio VE SpA, Italy, for permission to reproduce artwork from their publications.

About this Manual

The aim of this manual is to help you get the best value from your scooter. It can do so in several ways. It can help you decide what work must be done, even if you choose to have it done by a dealer; it provides information and procedures for routine maintenance and servicing; and it offers diagnostic and repair procedures to follow when trouble occurs.

We hope you use the manual to tackle the work yourself. For many simpler jobs, doing it yourself may be quicker than arranging an appointment to get the scooter into a dealer and making the trips to leave it and pick it up. More importantly, a lot of money can be saved by avoiding the expense the shop must pass on to you to cover its labour and overhead costs. An added benefit is the sense of satisfaction and accomplishment that you feel after doing the job yourself.

References to the left or right side of the scooter assume you are sitting on the seat, facing forward.

We take great pride in the accuracy of information given in this manual, but manufacturers make alterations and design changes during the production run of a particular model of which they do not inform us. No liability can be accepted by the authors or publishers for loss, damage or injury caused by any errors in, or omissions from, the information given.

Illegal copying

Frame and engine numbers

The frame serial number (or VIN (Vehicle Identification Number) as it is often known) is stamped into the frame, and also appears on an identification plate; your owner's manual will give exact details of its location. The engine number is stamped into the rear of the transmission casing at the back of the engine.

Both of these numbers should be recorded and kept in a safe place so they can be furnished to law enforcement officials in the event of a theft.

The frame and engine numbers should also be kept in a handy place (such as with your driving licence) so they are always available when purchasing or ordering parts for your scooter.

Each model type can be identified by its engine and frame number prefix – refer to *Model specifications and service schedules* in Chapter 1.

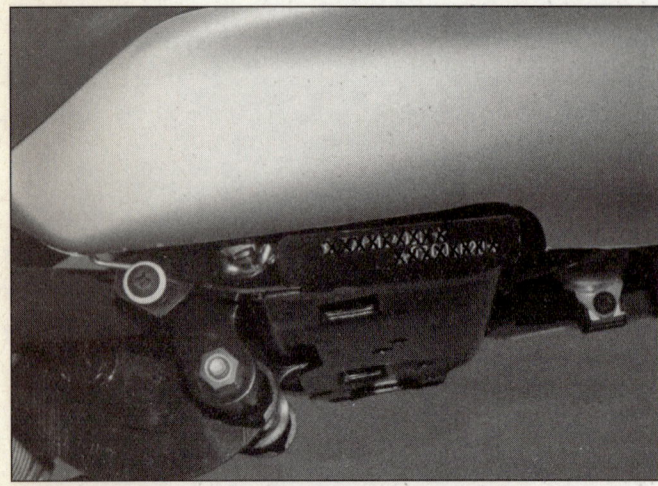

The frame number is stamped into the frame . . .

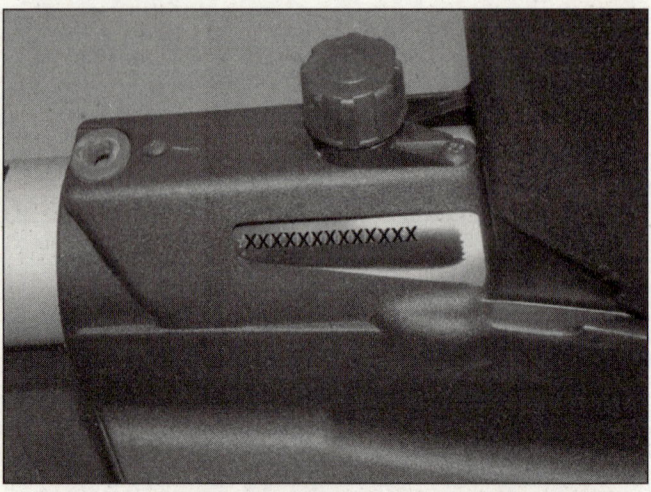

. . . and is sometimes behind a removable panel

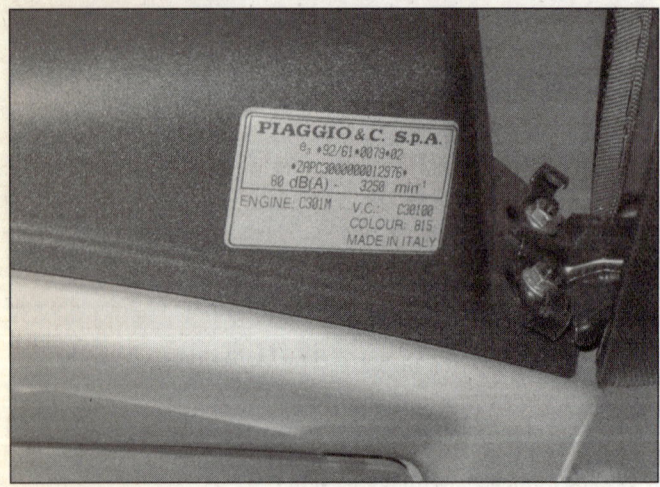

The frame number also appears on the identification plate

The engine number is stamped into the transmission casing at the back of the rear hub

Buying spare parts

When ordering replacement parts, it is essential to identify exactly the machine for which the parts are required. While in some cases it is sufficient to identify the machine by its title e.g. 'Runner 50', any modifications made to components mean that it is usually essential to identify the scooter by its year of production, or better still by its frame or engine number prefix.

To identify your own scooter, refer to the engine and frame number prefix information in *Model specifications and service schedules* in Chapter 1.

To be absolutely certain of receiving the correct part, not only is it essential to have the scooter engine or frame number prefix to hand, but it is also useful to take the old part for comparison (where possible). Note that where a modified component has superseded the original, a careful check must be made that there are no related parts which have also been modified and must be used to enable the replacement to be correctly refitted; where such a situation is found, purchase all the necessary parts and fit them, even if this means replacing apparently unworn items.

Purchase replacement parts from an authorised Gilera (Piaggio/Vespa) dealer or someone who specialises in scooter parts; they are more likely to have the parts in stock or can order them quickly from the importer. Pattern parts are available for certain components; if used, ensure these are of recognised quality brands which will perform as well as the original.

Expendable items such as lubricants, spark plugs, some electrical components, bearings, bulbs and tyres can usually be obtained at lower prices from accessory shops, motor factors or from specialists advertising in the national motorcycle press.

Professional mechanics are trained in safe working procedures. However enthusiastic you may be about getting on with the job at hand, take the time to ensure that your safety is not put at risk. A moment's lack of attention can result in an accident, as can failure to observe simple precautions.

There will always be new ways of having accidents, and the following is not a comprehensive list of all dangers; it is intended rather to make you aware of the risks and to encourage a safe approach to all work you carry out on your bike.

Asbestos

● Certain friction, insulating, sealing and other products - such as brake pads, clutch linings, gaskets, etc. - contain asbestos. Extreme care must be taken to avoid inhalation of dust from such products since it is hazardous to health. If in doubt, assume that they do contain asbestos.

Fire

● Remember at all times that petrol is highly flammable. Never smoke or have any kind of naked flame around, when working on the vehicle. But the risk does not end there - a spark caused by an electrical short-circuit, by two metal surfaces contacting each other, by careless use of tools, or even by static electricity built up in your body under certain conditions, can ignite petrol vapour, which in a confined space is highly explosive. Never use petrol as a cleaning solvent. Use an approved safety solvent.

● Always disconnect the battery earth terminal before working on any part of the fuel or electrical system, and never risk spilling fuel on to a hot engine or exhaust.
● It is recommended that a fire extinguisher of a type suitable for fuel and electrical fires is kept handy in the garage or workplace at all times. Never try to extinguish a fuel or electrical fire with water.

Fumes

● Certain fumes are highly toxic and can quickly cause unconsciousness and even death if inhaled to any extent. Petrol vapour comes into this category, as do the vapours from certain solvents such as trichloro-ethylene. Any draining or pouring of such volatile fluids should be done in a well ventilated area.
● When using cleaning fluids and solvents, read the instructions carefully. Never use materials from unmarked containers - they may give off poisonous vapours.
● Never run the engine of a motor vehicle in an enclosed space such as a garage. Exhaust fumes contain carbon monoxide which is extremely poisonous; if you need to run the engine, always do so in the open air or at least have the rear of the vehicle outside the workplace.

The battery

● Never cause a spark, or allow a naked light near the vehicle's battery. It will normally be giving off a certain amount of hydrogen gas, which is highly explosive.

● Always disconnect the battery ground (earth) terminal before working on the fuel or electrical systems (except where noted).
● If possible, loosen the filler plugs or cover when charging the battery from an external source. Do not charge at an excessive rate or the battery may burst.
● Take care when topping up, cleaning or carrying the battery. The acid electrolyte, even when diluted, is very corrosive and should not be allowed to contact the eyes or skin. Always wear rubber gloves and goggles or a face shield. If you ever need to prepare electrolyte yourself, always add the acid slowly to the water; never add the water to the acid.

Electricity

● When using an electric power tool, inspection light etc., always ensure that the appliance is correctly connected to its plug and that, where necessary, it is properly grounded (earthed). Do not use such appliances in damp conditions and, again, beware of creating a spark or applying excessive heat in the vicinity of fuel or fuel vapour. Also ensure that the appliances meet national safety standards.
● A severe electric shock can result from touching certain parts of the electrical system, such as the spark plug wires (HT leads), when the engine is running or being cranked, particularly if components are damp or the insulation is defective. Where an electronic ignition system is used, the secondary (HT) voltage is much higher and could prove fatal.

Remember...

✗ **Don't** start the engine without first ascertaining that the transmission is in neutral.
✗ **Don't** suddenly remove the pressure cap from a hot cooling system - cover it with a cloth and release the pressure gradually first, or you may get scalded by escaping coolant.
✗ **Don't** attempt to drain oil until you are sure it has cooled sufficiently to avoid scalding you.
✗ **Don't** grasp any part of the engine or exhaust system without first ascertaining that it is cool enough not to burn you.
✗ **Don't** allow brake fluid or antifreeze to contact the machine's paintwork or plastic components.
✗ **Don't** siphon toxic liquids such as fuel, hydraulic fluid or antifreeze by mouth, or allow them to remain on your skin.
✗ **Don't** inhale dust - it may be injurious to health (see Asbestos heading).
✗ **Don't** allow any spilled oil or grease to remain on the floor - wipe it up right away, before someone slips on it.
✗ **Don't** use ill-fitting spanners or other tools which may slip and cause injury.
✗ **Don't** lift a heavy component which may be beyond your capability - get assistance.

✗ **Don't** rush to finish a job or take unverified short cuts.
✗ **Don't** allow children or animals in or around an unattended vehicle.
✗ **Don't** inflate a tyre above the recommended pressure. Apart from overstressing the carcass, in extreme cases the tyre may blow off forcibly.
✔ **Do** ensure that the machine is supported securely at all times. This is especially important when the machine is blocked up to aid wheel or fork removal.
✔ **Do** take care when attempting to loosen a stubborn nut or bolt. It is generally better to pull on a spanner, rather than push, so that if you slip, you fall away from the machine rather than onto it.
✔ **Do** wear eye protection when using power tools such as drill, sander, bench grinder etc.
✔ **Do** use a barrier cream on your hands prior to undertaking dirty jobs - it will protect your skin from infection as well as making the dirt easier to remove afterwards; but make sure your hands aren't left slippery. Note that long-term contact with used engine oil can be a health hazard.
✔ **Do** keep loose clothing (cuffs, ties etc. and long hair) well out of the way of moving mechanical parts.

✔ **Do** remove rings, wristwatch etc., before working on the vehicle - especially the electrical system.
✔ **Do** keep your work area tidy - it is only too easy to fall over articles left lying around.
✔ **Do** exercise caution when compressing springs for removal or installation. Ensure that the tension is applied and released in a controlled manner, using suitable tools which preclude the possibility of the spring escaping violently.
✔ **Do** ensure that any lifting tackle used has a safe working load rating adequate for the job.
✔ **Do** get someone to check periodically that all is well, when working alone on the vehicle.
✔ **Do** carry out work in a logical sequence and check that everything is correctly assembled and tightened afterwards.
✔ **Do** remember that your vehicle's safety affects that of yourself and others. If in doubt on any point, get professional advice.
● **If** in spite of following these precautions, you are unfortunate enough to injure yourself, seek medical attention as soon as possible.

Note: *The daily (pre-ride) checks outlined in your owner's manual covers those items which should be inspected on a daily basis.*

Engine oil level check – four-stroke models

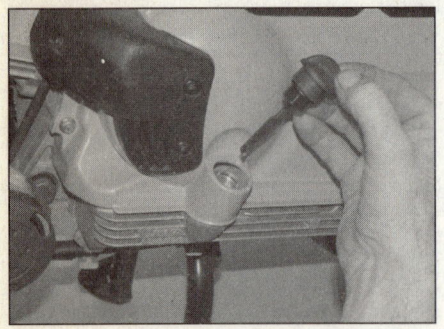

Before you start:
✔ Support the machine in an upright position on its centre stand. Make sure it is on level ground.
✔ Make sure you have a supply of the correct oil available.
✔ Check the oil level when the engine is cold. Wait at least 5 minutes if the engine has just been run.

Scooter care:
● If you have to add oil frequently, you should check whether you have any oil leaks. If there is no sign of oil leakage from the joints and gaskets the engine could be burning oil due to worn piston rings or failed valve stem seals.

1 The engine has a dipstick on the oil filler cap. Unscrew the cap and wipe the dipstick on some clean rag, then insert the clean dipstick back into the engine and screw the cap fully in.

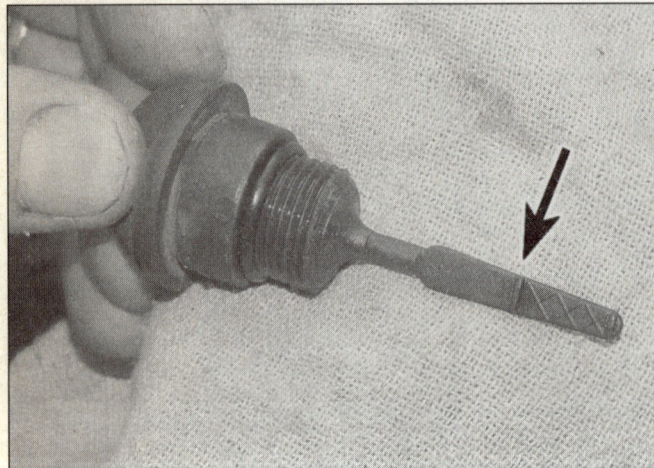

2 Unscrew the cap – the oil level should be up to the MAX line (arrowed).

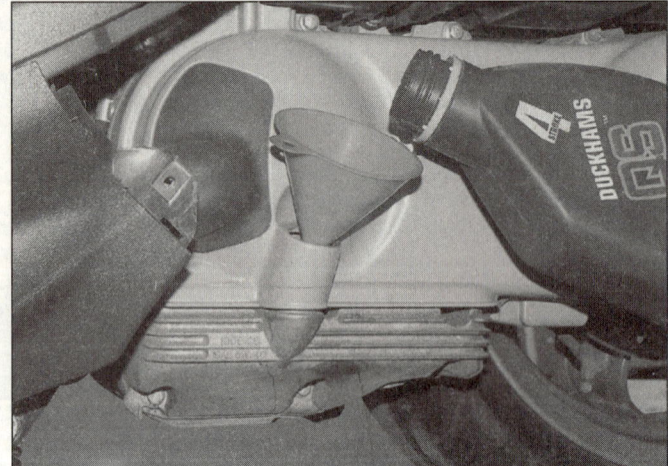

3 If necessary, top up with SAE 5W40 API SJ engine oil, to bring the level up to the MAX line. Do not overfill.

Fuel and two-stroke oil checks

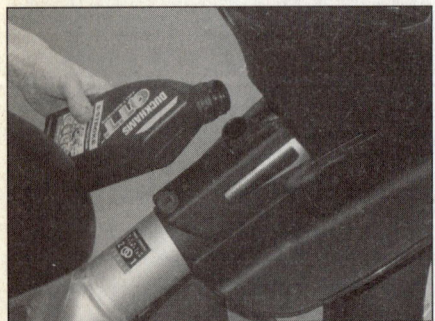

Two-stroke oil:
● On all two-stroke models check that the oil level warning light extinguishes immediately after the engine is started. If the light stays on or if it comes on whilst the scooter is being ridden, the oil tank requires topping-up.
● Do not rely on the oil warning light to tell you that the oil tank needs topping-up. Get into the habit of checking the level of oil in the oil tank at the same time as you fill up with fuel.
● If the engine is run without oil, even for a short time, engine damage and very soon engine seizure will occur. It is advised that a bottle of two-stroke oil is carried in the storage compartment for such emergencies.

Fuel:
● This may seem obvious, but check that you have enough fuel, to complete your journey. If you notice signs of leakage – rectify the cause immediately.
● Ensure you use the correct grade unleaded petrol (gasoline), minimum 95 octane. Note that the use of unleaded fuel will increase spark plug life and have obvious benefits to the environment – its use is essential on models fitted with a catalytic converter.

1 Top-up the oil tank with a synthetic two-stroke oil designed for motorcycle oil injection systems.

Coolant level check – liquid-cooled models

 Warning: DO NOT leave open containers of coolant about, as it is poisonous.

Before you start:
✔ Make sure you have a supply of coolant available (a mixture of 50% distilled water and 50% corrosion inhibited ethylene glycol anti-freeze is needed).
✔ Always check the coolant level when the engine is cold.
Caution: Do not run the engine in an enclosed space such as a garage or workshop.

✔ Support the scooter in an upright position whilst checking the level; make sure it is on level ground.

Scooter care:
● Use only the specified coolant mixture. It is important that anti-freeze is used in the system all year round, and not just in the winter. Do not top the system up using only water, as the system will become too diluted.
● Do not overfill the reservoir tank, which is located behind the front panel on Runner models and inside the storage compartment on DNA models. If the coolant is significantly above the UPPER or MAX line at any time, the surplus should be siphoned or drained off to prevent the possibility of it being expelled under pressure.

● If the coolant level falls steadily, check the system for leaks (see Chapter 1). If no leaks are found and the level continues to fall, it is recommended that the machine is taken to a Gilera dealer for a pressure test.

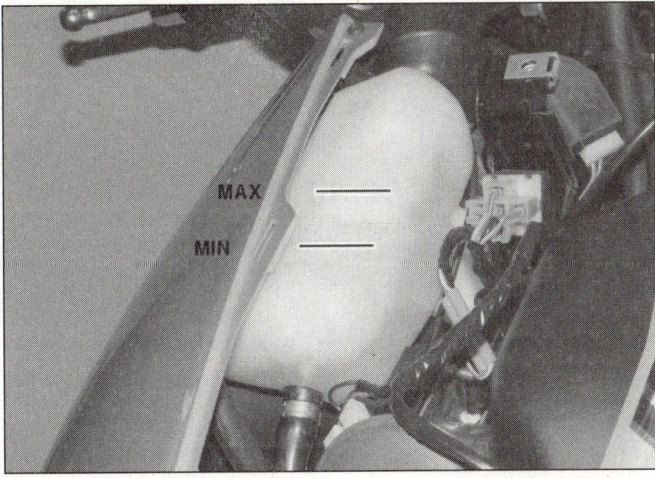

1 On Runner models, remove the front panel to check the coolant MAX and MIN level lines.

2 On Runner RST and ST models, remove the front cover inspection panel to view coolant level lines on reservoir.

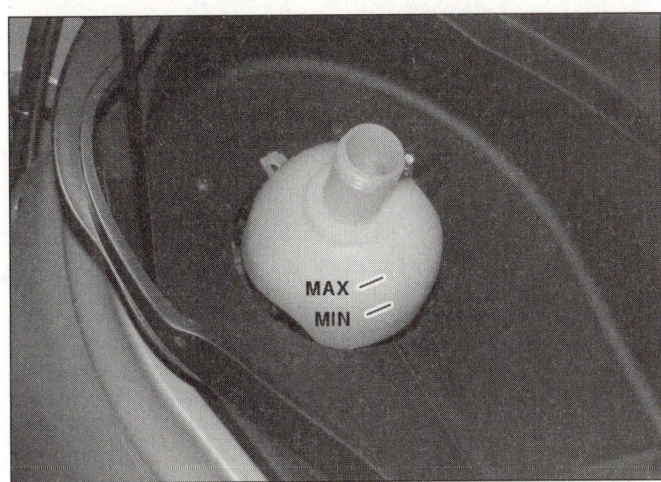

3 On DNA models, remove the coolant reservoir cover to check the coolant level.

4 Top-up if necessary with the specified coolant mixture.

Brake fluid level check – disc brakes

⚠️ **Warning: Brake hydraulic fluid can harm your eyes and damage painted surfaces, so use extreme caution when handling and pouring it and cover surrounding surfaces with rag. Do not use fluid that has been standing open for some time, as it absorbs moisture from the air which can cause a dangerous loss of braking effectiveness.**

Before you start:

✔ Support the scooter in an upright position.
✔ Make sure you have a supply of DOT 4 hydraulic fluid.
✔ Wrap a rag around the reservoir to ensure that any spillage does not come into contact with painted or plastic surfaces.

Scooter care:

● The fluid in the brake master cylinder reservoir will drop slightly as the brake pads wear down.
● If the fluid reservoir requires repeated topping-up this is an indication of an hydraulic leak somewhere in the system, which should be investigated immediately.
● Check for signs of fluid leakage from the hydraulic hoses and components – if found, rectify immediately.
● Check the operation of the brake before riding the scooter; if there is evidence of air in the system (spongy feel to lever), it must be bled as described in Chapter 7.

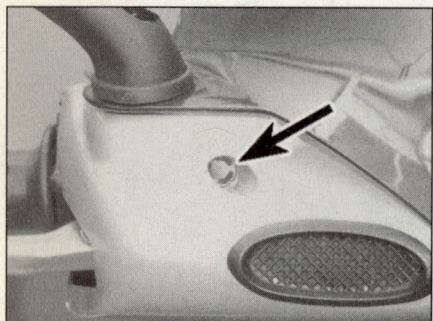

1 On Runner models, the brake fluid level is visible through the window in the handlebar cover (arrowed). If necessary, remove the reservoir cover or the handlebar cover (see Chapter 8) to check the level.

2 On SKP/ Stalker models the window is in the front of the reservoir (arrowed).

3 On DNA and Ice models, the window is in the side of the reservoir.

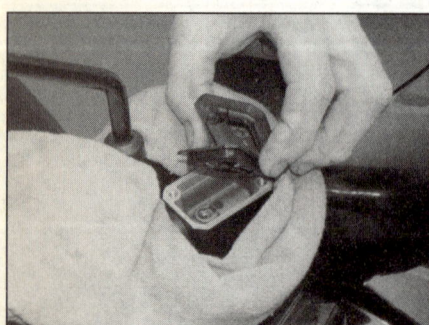

4 If the level is below the MIN level line, remove the two reservoir cover screws and remove the cover, the diaphragm plate and the diaphragm. On Runner models, first remove the front handlebar cover (see Chapter 8).

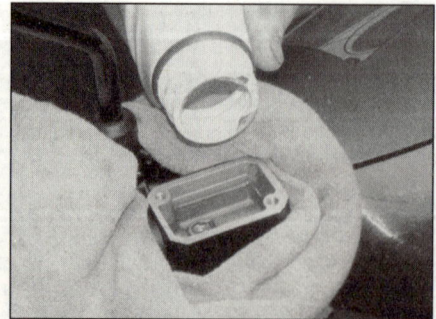

5 Top-up with new clean hydraulic fluid of the recommended type, until the level is above the MIN mark. Do not overfill and take care to avoid spills (see **Warning** above).

6 Ensure that the diaphragm is correctly seated before installing the plate and cover, then tighten the screws securely.

Tyre checks

The correct pressures:

● The tyres must be checked when **cold**, not immediately after riding. Note that low tyre pressures may cause the tyre to slip on the rim or come off. High tyre pressures will cause abnormal tread wear and unsafe handling.
● Use an accurate pressure gauge.
● Proper air pressure will increase tyre life and provide maximum stability and ride comfort.
● Refer to *Model specifications* in Chapter 1 for the correct tyre pressures for your scooter.

Tyre care:

● Check the tyres carefully for cuts, tears, embedded nails or other sharp objects and excessive wear. Operation of the scooter with excessively worn tyres is extremely hazardous, as traction and handling are directly affected.
● Check the condition of the tyre valve and ensure the dust cap is in place.

● Pick out any stones or nails which may have become embedded in the tyre tread. If left, they will eventually penetrate through the casing and cause a puncture.
● If tyre damage is apparent, or unexplained loss of pressure is experienced, seek the advice of a tyre fitting specialist without delay.

Tyre tread depth:

● At the time of writing UK law requires that tread depth on machines over 50 cc must be at least 1 mm over 3/4 of the tread breadth all the way around the tyre, with no bald patches (see *MOT Test Checks* in the *Reference* section). Many riders, however, consider 2 mm tread depth minimum to be a safer limit.
● For machines with an engine size not greater than 50 cc, UK law states that tread depth may be less than 1 mm if the tread pattern is clearly visible across the whole of the tread breadth all the way around the tyre.
● Many tyres now incorporate wear indicators in the tread. Identify the triangular pointer on the tyre sidewall to locate the indicator bar and replace the tyre if the tread has worn down to the bar.

1 Check the tyre pressures when the tyres are **cold** and keep them properly inflated.

2 Measure tread depth at the centre of the tyre using a tread depth gauge or ruler.

3 Tyre tread wear indicator bar and its location marking (usually either an arrow, a triangle or the letters TWI) on the sidewall (arrowed).

Suspension and steering checks

● Check that the front and rear suspension operates smoothly without binding.

● Check that the rear suspension is adjusted as required.

● Check that the steering moves smoothly from lock-to-lock.

Legal and safety checks

Lighting and signalling:

● Take a minute to check that the headlight, tail light, brake light, instrument lights and turn signals all work correctly.
● Check that the horn sounds when the switch is operated.
● A working speedometer graduated in mph is a statutory requirement in the UK.

Safety:

● Check that the throttle grip rotates smoothly and snaps shut when released, in all steering positions.
● Check that the stand return spring holds the stand securely up when retracted.
● Check that both brakes work correctly when applied and free off when released.

Chapter 1
Routine maintenance and servicing

Contents

Degrees of difficulty

Easy, suitable for novice with little experience 	**Fairly easy**, suitable for beginner with some experience	**Fairly difficult**, suitable for competent DIY mechanic 	**Difficult**, suitable for experienced DIY mechanic 	**Very difficult**, suitable for expert DIY or professional 

Introduction

1 This Chapter is designed to help the home mechanic maintain his/her scooter for safety, economy, long life and peak performance.

2 Deciding where to start or plug into the service schedule depends on several factors. If the warranty period on your scooter has just expired, and if it has been maintained according to the warranty standards, you may want to pick up routine maintenance as it coincides with the next mileage or calendar interval. If you have owned the machine for some time but have never performed any maintenance on it, then you may want to start at the nearest interval and include some additional procedures to ensure that nothing important is overlooked. If you have just had a major engine overhaul, then you may want to start the maintenance routine from the beginning. If you have a used machine and have no knowledge of its history or maintenance record, you may desire to combine all the checks into one large service initially and then settle into the maintenance schedule prescribed.

3 Before beginning any maintenance or repair, the machine should be cleaned thoroughly, especially around the engine and transmission covers. Cleaning will help ensure that dirt does not contaminate the engine and will allow you to detect wear and damage that could otherwise easily go unnoticed.

4 Certain maintenance information is sometimes printed on decals attached to the scooter. If the information on the decals differs from that included here, use the information on the decal.

5 All the four-stroke engined scooters covered in this manual are fitted with the four-valve, liquid-cooled LEADER (Low Emission ADvanced Engine Range) engine.

Note 1: The daily (pre-ride) checks detailed at the beginning of this Manual cover those items which should be inspected on a daily basis. Always perform the pre-ride inspection at every maintenance interval (in addition to the procedures listed).

Note 2: The intervals listed on the following pages are the intervals recommended by the manufacturer for each particular operation during the model years covered in this manual. Your owner's manual may have different intervals for your model.

Note 3: An initial (one-off) service will be performed by a Gilera dealer after the first 600 miles (1000 km) from new. Thereafter, the scooter should be serviced according to the intervals specified in the service schedules which follow.

Gilera SKP/Stalker

Model identification

Engine . . . . .49.4 cc single cylinder air-cooled two-stroke
Transmission. . . . . Variable speed automatic, belt driven
Ignition. . . . . Electronic
Suspension:
   Front. . . . . Upside-down telescopic forks
   Rear . . . . .Swingarm and monoshock
Brakes . . . . .Single disc (front), drum or disc (rear)
Engine no. prefix. .C131M (C401M 2005-on)
Frame no. prefix . . . . ZAPC 130 (ZAPC 401 2005-on)
Wheelbase. . . . . .1230 mm
Overall length . . . . .1760 mm
Overall width. . . . . .720 mm
Seat height . . . . .810 mm
Kerb weight . . . . 87 kg
Fuel tank capacity:
   Total . . . . 6.0 litres
   Reserve . . . . 1.5 litres
Introduced. 1997

Servicing specifications and lubricants

Spark plug type. . . . . .Champion RN2C
Spark plug electrode gap . . . . 0.6 to 0.7 mm
Idle speed . . . . .1800 to 2000 rpm
Tyre size:
   Front. 120/90-10
   Rear 130/90-10
Front tyre pressure. . . . . .17.5 psi (1.2 Bar)
Rear tyre pressure:
   Rider only . . . . 24 psi (1.6 Bar)
   Rider and passenger . . . . 29 psi (2.0 Bar)
Fuel type . . . . Unleaded petrol (gasoline) min 95 octane
Engine oil type . . . . Synthetic two-stroke oil for injector
                                               systems, API TC or higher
Engine oil tank capacity:
   Total . . . . 1.2 litres
   Reserve . . . . 0.4 litre
Gearbox oil type . . . . 80W90 API GL3 gear oil
Gearbox oil quantity. . . . . approx. 75 cc
Brake fluid. . . . . DOT 4
Air filter oil . . . . .50% air filter oil and 50% petrol (gasoline)
Variator . . . . Lithium soap grease (NLGI 3)
Speedometer drive gear . . . . Lithium soap grease (NLGI 3)
Brake levers . . . . Calcium soap grease (NLGI 1-2)
Control cables. . . . . .Motor oil or cable lubricant

Service intervals - Gilera SKP/Stalker

Note: *Always perform the Daily (pre-ride) checks before every service interval – see the beginning of this Manual*

	Text section in this Chapter	Every 5000 km (3000 miles) or 12 months	Every 10,000 km (6000 miles) or 2 years	Every 15,000 km (9000 miles) or 3 years
Air filter – clean	1	✔		
Battery – check	2	✔		
Brake system – check	3	✔		
Brake cable – check and lubrication	4	✔		
Brake fluid – change	5		✔*	
Brake hose – renew	6			✔*
Brake levers – lubrication	7	✔		
Brake pads/shoes – wear check	8	✔		
Drive belt – check	11	✔		
Drive belt – renew	11		✔	
Gearbox oil level – check	14	✔		
Gearbox oil – change	15		✔	
Headlight aim – check and adjustment	16		✔	
Idle speed – check and adjustment	17		✔	
Nuts and bolts – tightness check	18		✔	
Oil pump drive belt – renew	19			20,000 km/ 12,000 miles
Secondary air system – clean (models with catalytic converter)	20		✔	
Spark plug – gap check, adjust or renew	21	✔		
Speedometer cable and drive gear – lubrication	23		✔	
Steering head bearings – check and adjustment	24		✔	
Suspension – check	25		✔	
Throttle cable/oil pump – check and adjustment	26	✔		
Variator and clutch – check	28		✔ variator	✔ clutch
Wheels and tyres – general check	29	✔		

* The brake fluid must be changed every 2 years and the brake hose renewed every 3 years, irrespective of mileage.

Gilera ICE

Model identification

Engine	.49.4 cc single cylinder air-cooled two-stroke
Transmission	Variable speed automatic, belt driven
Ignition	Electronic
Suspension:	
Front	Telescopic forks
Rear	Swingarm and monoshock
Brakes	Single disc (front), drum (rear)
Engine no. prefix	C 301M
Frame no. prefix	ZAPC 300
Wheelbase	1220 mm
Overall length	1710 mm
Overall width	680 mm
Seat height	880 mm
Kerb weight	92 kg
Fuel tank capacity:	
Total	6.5 litres
Reserve	1.2 litres
Introduced	2001

Servicing specifications and lubricants

Spark plug type	Champion RN2C
Spark plug electrode gap	0.6 to 0.7 mm
Idle speed	1700 to 1900 rpm
Tyre size	120/90-10
Front tyre pressure	19 psi (1.3 Bar)
Rear tyre pressure	26 psi (1.8 Bar)
Fuel type	Unleaded petrol (gasoline) min 95 octane
Engine oil type	Synthetic two-stroke oil for injector systems, API TC or higher
Engine oil tank capacity:	
Total	1.6 litres
Reserve	0.4 litre
Gearbox oil type	80W90 API GL3 gear oil
Gearbox oil quantity	approx. 75 cc
Brake fluid	DOT 4
Air filter oil	50% air filter oil and 50% petrol (gasoline)
Speedometer drive gear	Lithium soap grease (NLGI 3)
Brake levers	Calcium soap grease (NLGI 1-2)
Control cables	Motor oil or cable lubricant

Service intervals - Gilera Ice

Note: *Always perform the Daily (pre-ride) checks before every service interval – see the beginning of this Manual*

	Text section in this Chapter	Every 5000 km (3000 miles) or 12 months	Every 10,000 km (6000 miles) or 2 years	Every 15,000 km (9000 miles) or 3 years
Air filter – clean	1		✔	
Battery – check	2	✔		
Brake system – check	3	✔		
Brake cable – check and lubrication	4	✔		
Brake fluid – change	5		✔*	
Brake hose – renew	6			✔*
Brake levers – lubrication	7	✔		
Brake pads/shoes – wear check	8	✔		
Drive belt – renew	11			✔
Gearbox oil level – check	14	✔		
Gearbox oil – change	15			✔
Headlight aim – check and adjustment	16		✔	
Idle speed – check and adjustment	17		✔	
Nuts and bolts – tightness check	18		✔	
Oil pump drive belt – renew	19			20,000 km/ 12,000 miles
Secondary air system – clean (models with catalytic converter)	20			✔
Spark plug – renew	22	✔		
Speedometer cable and drive gear – lubrication	23		✔	
Steering head bearings – check and adjustment	24		✔	
Suspension – check	25		✔	
Throttle cable/oil pump – check and adjustment	26	✔		
Variator and clutch – check	28		✔ variator	✔ clutch
Wheels and tyres – general check	29	✔		

* The brake fluid must be changed every 2 years and the brake hose renewed every 3 years, irrespective of mileage.

Gilera Runner 50, Runner 50 DD, Runner 50 SP

Model identification

Engine . . . . 49.3 cc single cylinder liquid-cooled two-stroke
Transmission. . . . . Variable speed automatic, belt driven
Ignition . . . . Electronic
Suspension:
  Front . . . . Upside-down telescopic forks
  Rear . . . . .Swingarm and monoshock
Brakes:
  Runner 50 .Single disc (front), drum (rear)
  Runner DD/SP. . . . . Single disc (front and rear)
Engine no. prefix. . . . . C 141M (M 461M – 50 SP RST)
Frame no. prefix . . . . .ZAPC 140 (ZAPC 461 – 50 SP RST)
Wheelbase. . . . . 1290 mm (1270 mm – 50 SP RST)
Overall length . . . . 1780 mm (1840 mm – 50 SP RST)
Overall width. . . . . 720 mm (750 mm – 50 SP RST)
Seat height . . . . .815 mm
Kerb weight:
  Runner 50 . . . . .98 kg
  Runner DD/SP. . . . . .93 kg
  Runner 50 SP RST . . . . .103 kg
Fuel tank capacity
  Runner 50, 50 DD, 50 SP . . . . .8.5 lit (1.5 lit reserve)
  Runner 50 SP RST .7.0 lit (1.7 lit reserve)
Introduced:
  Runner 50 1997
  Runner DD/SP 1999
  Runner 50 SP RST (restyle) 2005

Servicing specifications and lubricants

Spark plug type. . . . . Champion N84, N1C or RN1C
Spark plug electrode gap . . . . 0.5 mm
Idle speed . . . . .1800 to 2000 rpm
Tyre size – Runner 50, 50 DD, 50 SP
  Front 120/70-12
  Rear 130/70-12
Tyre size – Runner 50 SP RST
  Front 120/70-14
  Rear 140/60-13
Tyre pressures – Runner 50, 50 DD, 50 SP
  Front . . . . 23 psi (1.6 Bar)
  Rear . . . . 25 psi (1.8 Bar) (passenger – 29 psi (2.0 Bar))
Tyre pressures – Runner 50 SP RST
  Front . . . . 25 psi (1.7 Bar)
  Rear . . . . 29 psi (2.0 Bar) (passenger – 32 psi (2.2 Bar))
Fuel type . . . . Unleaded petrol (gasoline) min 95 octane
Engine oil type : . . . . Synthetic two-stroke oil
for injector systems, API TC or higher
Engine oil tank capacity
  Runner 50, 50 DD, 50 SP . . . . .1.8 lit (0.4 lit reserve)
  Runner 50 SP RST . . . . .1.6 lit (0.6 lit reserve)
Coolant type . . . 50% distilled water and 50% ethylene glycol anti-freeze
Cooling system capacity . . . . .approx. 0.9 litre
Gearbox oil type . . . . 80W90 API GL3 gear oil
Gearbox oil quantity. . . . . approx. 75 cc
Brake fluid. . . . . .DOT 4
Air filter oil . . . . .50% air filter oil and 50% petrol (gasoline)
Variator . . . . Lithium soap grease (NLGI 3)
Speedometer drive gear . . . . Lithium soap grease (NLGI 3)
Brake levers . . . . Calcium soap grease (NLGI 1-2)
Control cables. . . . . .Motor oil or cable lubricant

Service intervals - Gilera Runner 50, Runner 50 DD, Runner 50 SP

Note: *Always perform the Daily (pre-ride) checks before every service interval – see the beginning of this Manual*

	Text section in this Chapter	Every 5000 km (3000 miles) or 12 months	Every 10,000 km (6000 miles) or 2 years	Every 15,000 km (9000 miles) or 3 years
Air filter – clean	1	✔		
Battery – check	2	✔		
Brake system – check	3	✔		
Brake cable (Runner 50) – check and lubrication	4	✔		
Brake fluid – change	5		✔*	
Brake hose – renew	6			✔*
Brake levers – lubrication	7	✔		
Brake pads/shoes – wear check	8	✔		
Cooling system – check	9	✔		
Coolant – change	10			✔**
Drive belt – check/renew	11			✔
Gearbox oil level – check	14	✔		
Gearbox oil – change	15		✔	
Headlight aim – check and adjustment	16		✔	
Idle speed – check and adjustment	17		✔	
Nuts and bolts – tightness check	18		✔	
Oil pump drive belt – renew	19			20,000 km/ 12,000 miles
Secondary air system – clean (models with catalytic converter)	20			✔
Spark plug – renew	22	✔		
Speedometer cable and drive gear – lubrication	23		✔	
Steering head bearings – check and adjustment	24		✔	
Suspension – check	25		✔	
Throttle cable/oil pump – check and adjustment	26	✔		
Variator and clutch – check	28			✔
Wheels and tyres – general check	29	✔		

* The brake fluid must be changed every 2 years and the brake hose renewed every 3 years, irrespective of mileage.

** The coolant must be changed every 3 years, irrespective of mileage.

Gilera Runner Purejet 50

Model identification

Engine . . . . 49.3 cc single cylinder liquid-cooled two-stroke with 'Purejet' fuel injection

Transmission. . . . . Variable speed automatic, belt driven

Ignition . . . . Electronic

Suspension:

  Front . . . . Upside-down telescopic forks

  Rear . . . . Swingarm and monoshock

Brakes . . . . Single disc (front and rear)

Engine no. prefix. . . . . ZAPC 361M (ZAPC 462 – RST)

Frame no. prefix . . . . ZAPC 3610 (C452M – RST)

Wheelbase. . . . . 1290 mm (1280 mm – RST)

Overall length . . . . 1800 mm (1840 mm – RST)

Overall width. . . . . 720 mm (750 mm – RST)

Seat height . . . . .830 mm

Weight (dry). . . . . 89 kg (112 kg – RST)

Fuel tank capacity:

  Total . . . . 12.0 litres (7.0 litres – RST)

  Reserve . . . . 3.0 litres (1.7 litres – RST)

Introduced. . . . . 2003 (2005 RST restyle)

Servicing specifications and lubricants

Spark plug type. . . . . Champion RG6 YCA

Spark plug electrode gap . . . . .0.6 to 0.7 mm

Idle speed . . . . 2000 rpm

Tyre size – 2003/4:

  Front 120/70-12

  Rear 130/70-12

Tyre size – RST

  Front 120/70-14

  Rear 140/60-13

Front tyre pressure. . . . . 23 psi (1.6 Bar)

Rear tyre pressure . . . . 25 psi (1.8 Bar)

Fuel type . . . . Unleaded petrol (gasoline) min 95 octane

Engine oil type . . . . Synthetic two-stroke oil for injector systems, API TC or higher

Engine oil tank capacity

  2003/4 . . . . .1.8 lit (0.4 lit reserve)

  RST . . . . .1.6 lit (0.6 lit reserve)

Coolant type . . . 50% distilled water and 50% ethylene glycol anti-freeze

Cooling system capacity . . . . .approx. 0.9 litres

Gearbox oil type . . . . .80W90 API GL3 gear oil

Gearbox oil quantity. . . . . approx. 75 cc

Brake fluid. . . . . .DOT 4

Air filter oil. . . . . .50% air filter oil and 50% petrol (gasoline)

Speedometer drive gear . . . . Lithium soap grease (NLGI 3)

Brake levers . . . . Calcium soap grease (NLGI 1-2)

Control cables. . . . . .Motor oil or cable lubricant

Service intervals - Gilera Runner Purejet 50

Note: *Always perform the Daily (pre-ride) checks before every service interval – see the beginning of this Manual*

	Text section in this Chapter	Every 5000 km (3000 miles) or 12 months	Every 10,000 km (6000 miles) or 2 years	Every 15,000 km (9000 miles) or 3 years
Air filter – clean	1		✔	
Battery – check	2	✔		
Brake system – check	3	✔		
Brake fluid – change	5		✔*	
Brake hose – renew	6			✔*
Brake levers – lubrication	7	✔		
Brake pads – wear check	8	✔		
Cooling system – check	9	✔		
Coolant – change	10			✔**
Drive belt – renew	11			✔
Fuel system – renew filter	13		✔	
Gearbox oil level – check	14	✔		
Gearbox oil – change	15			✔
Headlight aim – check and adjustment	16		✔	
Nuts and bolts – tightness check	18		✔	
Oil pump drive belt – renew	19			20,000 km/ 12,000 miles
Secondary air system – clean	20			✔
Spark plug – renew	22	✔		
Speedometer cable and drive gear – lubrication	23		✔	
Steering head bearings – check and adjustment	24		✔	
Suspension – check	25		✔	
Throttle cable/oil pump – check and adjustment	26	✔		
Variator and clutch – check	28		✔ variator	✔ clutch
Wheels and tyres – general check	29	✔		

* The brake fluid must be changed every 2 years and the brake hose renewed every 3 years, irrespective of mileage.

** The coolant must be changed every 3 years, irrespective of mileage.

Gilera Runner FX125 and FXR180

Model identification

Engine . . 123.5 cc and 175.8 cc single cylinder liquid-cooled two-stroke
Transmission . . . . Variable speed automatic, belt driven
Ignition . . . . Electronic
Suspension:
   Front . . . . Upside-down telescopic forks
   Rear . . . . Swingarm and adjustable monoshock
Brakes . . . . Single disc (front), drum or disc (rear)
Engine no. prefix:
   FX125 . . . . MO 71M
   FXR180 . . . . MO 81M
Frame no. prefix – FX125:
   Front disc, rear drum brake model . . . . ZAPM 070
   Front and rear disc brake model . . . .(MY 99)ZAPM 070
Frame no. prefix – FXR180:
   Front disc, rear drum brake model . . . . ZAPM 080
   Front and rear disc brake model . . . .(MY 99)ZAPM 080
Wheelbase . . . . .1303 mm
Overall length . . . . .1780 mm
Overall width . . . . .720 mm
Seat height . . . . .815 mm
Kerb weight . . . . .115 kg
Fuel tank capacity (1998 model):
   Total . . . . 9.0 litres
   Reserve . . . . 1.5 litres
Fuel tank capacity (1999-on models):
   Total . . . . 12.0 litres
   Reserve . . . . 3.0 litres
Introduced 1998

Servicing specifications and lubricants

Spark plug type . . . . Champion RN2C
Spark plug electrode gap . . . . 0.6 to 0.7 mm
Idle speed . . . . .1400 to 1600 rpm
Tyre size:
   Front 120/70-12
   Rear (1998 model) 130/70-12
   Rear (1999-on models) .130/60-13
Front tyre pressure . . . . 20 psi (1.4 Bar)
Rear tyre pressure:
   Rider only . . . . 23 psi (1.6 Bar)
   Rider and passenger . . . . 29 to 32 psi (2.0 to 2.2 Bar)
Fuel type . . . . Unleaded petrol (gasoline) min 95 octane
Engine oil type . . . . Synthetic two-stroke oil for injector
                              systems, API TC or higher
Engine oil tank capacity:
   Total . . . . 1.8 litres
   Reserve . . . . 0.4 litres
Coolant type . . . 50% distilled water and 50% ethylene glycol anti-freeze
Cooling system capacity .approx. 1.7 litres
Gearbox oil type . . . . 80W90 API GL3 gear oil
Gearbox oil quantity . . . . approx. 80 cc
Brake fluid . . . . DOT 4
Air filter oil . . . . .50% air filter oil and 50% petrol (gasoline)
Variator . . . . Lithium soap grease (NLGI 3)
Speedometer drive gear . . . . Lithium soap grease (NLGI 3)
Brake levers . . . . Calcium soap grease (NLGI 1-2)
Control cables . . . . .Motor oil or cable lubricant

Service intervals - Gilera Runner FX125 and FXR180

Note: *Always perform the Daily (pre-ride) checks before every service interval – see the beginning of this Manual*

	Text section in this Chapter	Every 5000 km (3000 miles) or 12 months	Every 10,000 km (6000 miles) or 2 years	Every 15,000 km (9000 miles) or 3 years
Air filter – clean	1		✔	
Battery – check	2	✔		
Brake system – check	3	✔		
Brake cable – check and lubrication	4	✔		
Brake fluid – change	5		✔*	
Brake hose – renew	6			✔*
Brake levers – lubrication	7	✔		
Brake pads/shoes – wear check	8	✔		
Cooling system – check	9	✔		
Cooling system – draining, flushing and refilling	10			✔**
Drive belt – renew	11			✔
Fuel system – renew filter	13			20,000 km/ 12,000 miles
Gearbox oil level – check	14	✔		
Gearbox oil – change	15		✔	
Headlight aim – check and adjustment	16		✔	
Idle speed – check and adjustment	17	✔		
Nuts and bolts – tightness check	18		✔	
Oil pump drive belt – renew	19			30,000 km/ 18,000 miles
Spark plug – gap check and adjustment	21	✔		
Spark plug – renew	22		✔	
Speedometer cable and drive gear – lubrication	23		✔	
Steering head bearings – check and adjustment	24		✔	
Suspension – check	25		✔	
Throttle cable/oil pump – check and adjustment	26		✔	
Variator and clutch – check	28			✔
Wheels and tyres – general check	29	✔		

* The brake fluid must be changed every 2 years and the brake hose renewed every 3 years, irrespective of mileage.

** The coolant must be changed every 3 years, irrespective of mileage.

Runner VX125

Runner ST125

Gilera Runner VX125, ST125, VXR180/200 and ST200

Model identification

Engine . . . . 124.2 cc, 181.7 cc, 197.7 cc single cylinder
liquid-cooled four-stroke
Transmission . . . . Variable speed automatic, belt driven
Ignition . . . . Electronic
Suspension:
  Front . . . . Conventional telescopic forks
  Rear . . . . .Swingarm and adjustable twin shock
Brakes . . . . Single disc (front and rear)
Engine no. prefix:
  VX125 . . . . M241M (M461M – RST)
  VX125 RST Euro 3, ST125 . . . . M463M
  VXR180 . . . . M242M
  VXR200 . . . . .M242M 101 (M462M – RST)
  VXR200 RST Euro 3, ST200 . . . . M464M
Frame no. prefix
  VX125, VXR180/200 . . . . .ZAP M240
  VX125 RST . . . . .ZAP M461
  VX125 RST Euro 3, ST125 . . . . .ZAP M463
  VXR200 RST . . . . .ZAP M462
  VXR200 RST Euro 3, ST200 . . . . .ZAP M464
Wheelbase . . . . 1350 mm (1340 mm – RST)
Overall length . . . . 1900 mm (1890 mm – RST)
Overall width . . . . .750 mm
Seat height . . . . 815 mm
Weight (dry) . . . . 132 kg (137 kg – RST)
Fuel tank capacity:
  VX125, VXR180/200 . . . . .12.0 lit (3.0 lit reserve)
  VX125 RST, VXR200 RST . . . . .7.0 lit (1.7 lit reserve)
  VX125 RST, VXR200 RST Euro 3, ST125/200 . . .8.5 lit (1.7 lit reserve)
Introduced:
  VX125 and VXR180 2001
  VXR200 2003
  VX125 RST and VXR200 RST – restyled models 2005
  ST125 and ST200 2008

Servicing specifications and lubricants

Spark plug type . . . . NGK CR 8EB
Spark plug electrode gap . . . . 0.7 to 0.8 mm
Idle speed . . . . .1600 to 1700 rpm
Valve clearances (COLD engine):
  Intake . . . . 0.10 mm
  Exhaust . . . . 0.15 mm
Tyre sizes – VX125, VXR180/200
  Front 120/70-12
  Rear 130/70-12
Tyre sizes – VX125 RST, VXR200 RST, ST125, ST200
  Front 120/70-14
  Rear 140/60-13
Tyre presssures – VX125, VXR180/200
  Front . . . . 20 psi (1.4 Bar)
  Rear . . . . 23 psi (1.6 Bar) (passenger – 26 psi (1.8 Bar))
Tyre presssures – VX125 RST, VXR200 RST, ST125, ST200
  Front . . . . 25 psi (1.7 Bar)
  Rear . . . . 29 psi (2.0 Bar) (passenger – 32 psi (2.2 Bar))
Fuel type . . . . Unleaded petrol (gasoline) min 95 octane
Engine oil type . . . . .SAE 5W40 API SJ synthetic oil
Engine oil quantity . . . . approx. 1 litre
Coolant type 50% distilled water and 50% ethylene glycol anti-freeze
Cooling system capacity
  VX125, VXR180/200 . . . . .approx. 0.9 litres
  VX125 RST, VXR200 RST, ST125, ST200 . . . . . . .approx. 2.1 litres
Gearbox oil type . . . . 80W90 API GL3 gear oil
Gearbox oil quantity . . . . approx. 150 cc
Brake fluid . . . . DOT 4
Air filter oil . . . . .50% air filter oil and 50% petrol (gasoline)
Brake levers . . . . Calcium soap grease (NLGI 1-2)
Control cables . . . . .Motor oil or cable lubricant

Service intervals -
Gilera Runner VX125, ST125, VXR180/200 and ST200

Note: *Always perform the Daily (pre-ride) checks before every service interval – see the beginning of this Manual*

	Text section in this Chapter	Every 6000 km (3750 miles) or 12 months	Every 12,000 km (7500 miles) or 2 years	Every 18,000 km (11,250 miles) or 3 years
Air filter – clean	1	✔		
Battery – check	2	✔		
Brake system – check	3	✔		
Brake fluid – change	5		✔*	
Brake hose – renew	6			✔*
Brake levers – lubrication	7		✔	
Brake pads/shoes – wear check	8	✔		
Cooling system – check	9	✔		
Cooling system – draining, flushing and refilling	10		✔**	
Drive belt – check	11	✔		
Drive belt – renew	11		✔	
Engine oil and filter change	12	✔		
Fuel system – clean accelerator pump mechanism	13	✔		
Gearbox oil level – check	14	✔		
Gearbox oil – change	15			24,000 km/ 15,000 miles
Headlight aim – check and adjustment	16		✔	
Idle speed – check and adjustment	17		✔	
Nuts and bolts – tightness check	18		✔	
Secondary air system clean – RST Euro 3 models	20		✔	
Spark plug – gap check and adjustment	21	✔		
Spark plug – renew	22		✔	
Steering head bearings – check and adjustment	24		✔	
Suspension – check	25		✔	
Throttle cable – check and adjustment	26		✔	
Valve clearances – check and adjustment	27	First check***		24,000 km/ 15,000 miles
Variator – check	28		✔	
Wheels and tyres – general check	29	✔		

* The brake fluid must be changed every 2 years and the brake hose renewed every 3 years, irrespective of mileage.

** The coolant must be changed every 2 years, irrespective of mileage.

*** The valve clearances must be checked after the first 6000 km (3750 miles), then at 24,000 km (15,000 mile) intervals.

Gilera DNA 50 GP eXperience

Model identification

Engine	49.3 cc single cylinder liquid-cooled two-stroke
Transmission	Variable speed automatic, belt driven
Ignition	Electronic

Suspension:

Front	Telescopic forks
Rear	Swingarm and monoshock
Brake	Single disc (front and rear)
Engine no. prefix	C 271M
Frame no. prefix	ZAP C2700
Wheelbase	1330 mm (1350 mm – RST)
Overall length	1940 mm (1970 mm – RST)
Overall width	700 mm (780 mm – RST)
Seat height	770 mm (810 – RST)
Weight (dry)	112 kg

Fuel tank capacity:

Total	9.0 litres
Reserve	1.2 litres
Introduced	2000 (2005 – RST restyle model)

Servicing specifications and lubricants

Spark plug type	Champion RN2C (RN1C – RST)
Spark plug electrode gap	0.6 to 0.7 mm
Idle speed	1700 to 1900 rpm

Tyre size:

Front	120/70-14 (120/70-15 – RST)
Rear	140/70-14
Front tyre pressure	26 psi (1.8 Bar)
Rear tyre pressure	29 psi (2.0 Bar)
Fuel type	Unleaded petrol (gasoline) min 95 octane
Engine oil type	Synthetic two-stroke oil for injector systems, API TC or higher

Engine oil tank capacity:

Total	1.3 litres
Reserve	0.4 litres
Coolant type	50% distilled water and 50% ethylene glycol anti-freeze
Cooling system capacity	approx. 0.9 litres
Gearbox oil type	80W90 API GL3 gear oil
Gearbox oil quantity	approx. 100 cc (85 cc – RST)
Brake fluid	DOT 4
Air filter oil	50% air filter oil and 50% petrol (gasoline)
Brake levers	Calcium soap grease (NLGI 1-2)
Control cables	Motor oil or cable lubricant

Service intervals - Gilera DNA 50 GP eXperience

Note: *Always perform the Daily (pre-ride) checks before every service interval – see the beginning of this Manual*

	Text section in this Chapter	Every 5000 km (3000 miles) or 12 months	Every 10,000 km (6000 miles) or 2 years	Every 15,000 km (9000 miles) or 3 years
Air filter – clean	1			✔
Battery – check	2	✔		
Brake system – check	3	✔		
Brake fluid – change	5		✔*	
Brake hose – renew	6			✔*
Brake levers – lubrication	7	✔		
Brake pads – wear check	8	✔		
Cooling system – check	9	✔		
Cooling system – draining, flushing and refilling	10			✔**
Drive belt – renew	11			✔
Gearbox oil level – check	14	✔		
Gearbox oil – change	15		✔	
Headlight aim – check and adjustment	16		✔	
Idle speed – check and adjustment	17		✔	
Nuts and bolts – tightness check	18		✔	
Oil pump drive belt – renew	19			20,000 km/ 12,000 miles
Secondary air system – clean	20			✔
Spark plug – renew	22	✔		
Steering head bearings – check and adjustment	24		✔	
Suspension – check	25		✔	
Throttle cable/oil pump – check and adjustment	26	✔		
Variator and clutch – check	28		✔ variator	✔ clutch
Wheels and tyres – general check	29	✔		

* The brake fluid must be changed every 2 years and the brake hose renewed every 3 years, irrespective of mileage.

** The coolant must be changed every 3 years, irrespective of mileage.

Gilera DNA 125 and 180

Model identification

Engine . . . 124.2 cc, 181.7 cc single cylinder liquid-cooled four-stroke
Transmission . . . . Variable speed automatic, belt driven
Ignition . . . . Electronic
Suspension:
   Front . . . . Telescopic forks
   Rear .Swingarm and adjustable twin shock
Brakes . . . . Single disc (front and rear)
Engine no. prefix:
   DNA125 . . . . M261M
   DNA180 . . . . M281M
Frame no. prefix:
   DNA125 . . . . .ZAP M260
   DNA180 . . . . .ZAP M281
Wheelbase . . . . .1355 mm
Overall length . . . . .1940 mm
Overall width . . . . .700 mm
Seat height . . . . 770 mm
Weight (dry) . . . . .137 kg
Fuel tank capacity:
   Total . . . . 9.0 litres
   Reserve . . . . 1.2 litres
Introduced 2001

Servicing specifications and lubricants

Spark plug type . . . . NGK CR 8EB
Spark plug electrode gap . . . . 0.7 to 0.8 mm
Idle speed . . . . .1600 to 1700 rpm
Valve clearances (COLD engine):
   Intake . . . . 0.10 mm
   Exhaust . . . . 0.15 mm
Front tyre size 120/70-14
Rear tyre size 140/60-14
Front tyre pressure . . . . 29 psi (2.0 Bar)
Rear tyre pressure:
   Rider only . . . . 32 psi (2.2 Bar)
   Rider and passenger . . . . 36 psi (2.5 Bar)
Fuel type . . . . Unleaded petrol (gasoline) min 95 octane
Engine oil type . . . . .SAE 5W40 API SJ synthetic oil
Engine oil quantity . . . . approx. 1 litre
Coolant type . . 50% distilled water and 50% ethylene glycol anti-freeze
Cooling system capacity . . . . .approx. 0.9 litres
Gearbox oil type . . . . 80W90 API GL3 gear oil
Gearbox oil quantity . . . . approx. 150 cc
Brake fluid . . . . DOT 4
Air filter oil . . . . .50% air filter oil and 50% petrol (gasoline)
Brake levers . . . . Calcium soap grease (NLGI 1-2)
Control cables . . . . .Motor oil or cable lubricant

Service intervals - Gilera DNA 125 and 180

Note: *Always perform the Daily (pre-ride) checks before every service interval – see the beginning of this Manual*

	Text section in this Chapter	Every 6000 km (3750 miles) or 12 months	Every 12,000 km (7500 miles) or 2 years	Every 18,000 km (11,250 miles) or 3 years
Air filter – clean	1		✔	
Battery – check	2	✔		
Brake system – check	3	✔		
Brake fluid – change	5		✔*	
Brake hose – renew	6			✔*
Brake levers – lubrication	7		✔	
Brake pads – wear check	8	✔		
Cooling system – check	9	✔		
Cooling system – draining, flushing and refilling	10		✔**	
Drive belt – check	11	✔		
Drive belt – renew	11		✔	
Engine oil and filter change	12	✔		
Fuel system – renew filter / clean accelerator pump mechanism	13	✔		
Gearbox oil level – check	14	✔		
Gearbox oil – change	15			24,000 km/ 15,000 miles thereafter
Headlight aim – check and adjustment	16		✔	
Idle speed – check and adjustment	17	✔		
Nuts and bolts – tightness check	18		✔	
Spark plug – gap check and adjustment	21	✔		
Spark plug – renew	22		✔	
Steering head bearings – check and adjustment	24		✔	
Suspension – check	25		✔	
Throttle cable – check and adjustment	26		✔	
Transmission filter – clean	**see 1**	3000 km/1800 miles		
Valve clearances – check and adjustment	27	First check***		24,000 km/ 15,000 miles thereafter
Variator – check	28	✔		
Wheels and tyres – general check	29	✔		

* The brake fluid must be changed every 2 years and the brake hose renewed every 3 years, irrespective of mileage.

** The coolant must be changed every 2 years, irrespective of mileage.

*** The valve clearances must be checked after the first 6000 km (3750 miles), then at 24,000 km (15,000 mile) intervals.

1.2a Remove the screws securing the filter cover – DNA shown

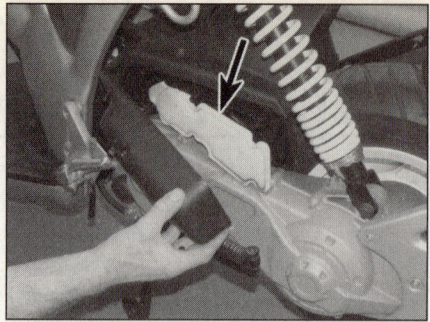

1.2b . . . then remove the cover and filter element (arrowed) – Ice shown

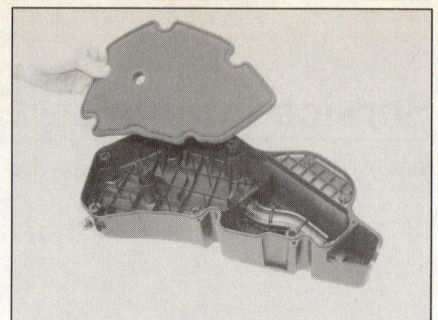

1.3 Filter element on Runner and DNA models

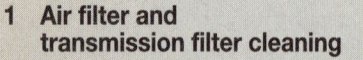

1 Air filter and transmission filter cleaning

Caution: If the machine is continually ridden in continuously wet or dusty conditions, the filter should be cleaned more frequently.

Air filter

1 Remove the body panels as required on your model to access the air filter housing, located above the transmission casing on the left-hand side of the engine (see Chapter 8).
2 Undo the screws securing the air filter cover and detach the cover (see illustrations).
3 Remove the foam filter element and wash it in hot soapy water, then blow it dry using compressed air (see illustration). Never wring the filter dry as it may tear.
4 Soak the filter element in a 50/50 mixture of

a dedicated air filter oil (Gilera recommend the Selenia product) and petrol (gasoline), then lay it on an absorbent surface and gently squeeze out the excess liquid. Make sure you do not damage the filter by twisting it.
5 Allow the filter to dry for a while, then fit it back into the housing and install the cover, making sure that the cover seal is in good condition.
6 If the filter element is excessively dirty and cannot be cleaned properly, or is torn or damaged in any way, fit a new one.
7 If the filter housing is fitted with a drain plug, undo the plug and release any trapped fluid (see illustrations)

Transmission filter

8 If applicable, undo the screws securing the filter cover to the drive belt cover and lift it off, then lift out the filter element (see illustrations). On all 50 cc models, and Runner FX and FXR

models, lever the filter cover out with a small screwdriver; the filter element is secured by a small metal clip (see illustrations). Clean and dry the element as described above, but do not oil it.

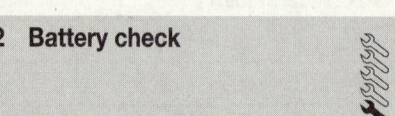

2 Battery check

Caution: Be extremely careful when handling or working around the battery. The electrolyte is very caustic and an explosive gas (hydrogen) is given off when the battery is charging.

Conventional battery

1 Remove the battery cover and partially lift the battery out of its holder (see Chapter 9). Check the electrolyte level which is visible

1.7a Some filter housings have a drain plug (arrowed)

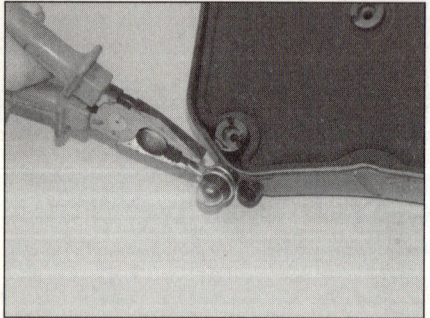

1.7b Release the spring clip with pliers to remove the plug

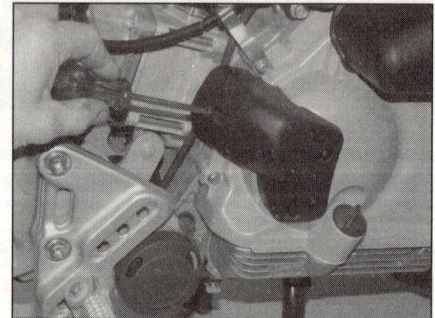

1.8a Remove the filter cover screws – DNA shown . . .

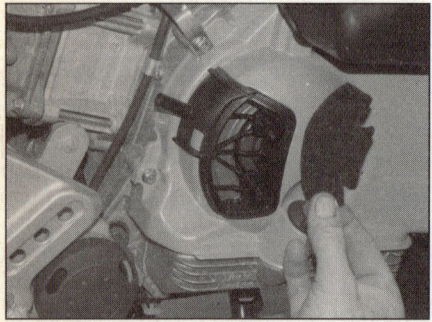

1.8b . . . and lift out the filter element

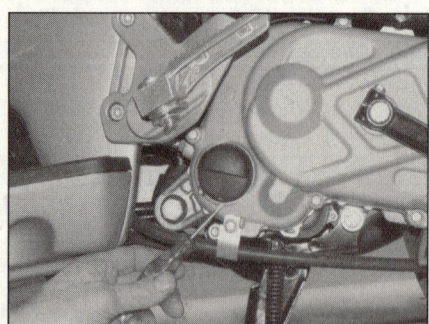

1.8c Lever the cover off with a small screwdriver – Ice shown

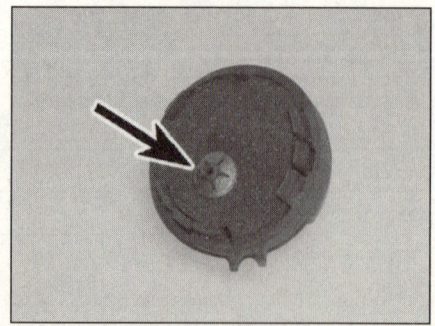

1.8d The filter element is secured by a small clip (arrowed)

through the translucent battery case – it should be between the UPPER and LOWER level marks **(see illustration)**.

2 If the electrolyte is low, disconnect the battery terminals (see Chapter 9) and move the battery to the workbench. Remove the cell caps and fill each cell to the upper level mark with distilled water. Do not use tap water (except in an emergency), and do not overfill. The cell holes are quite small, so it may help to use a clean plastic squeeze bottle with a small spout to add the water.

3 Install the battery cell caps, tightening them securely, then install the battery (see Chapter 9).

Maintenance-free battery

4 On models fitted with a sealed battery, no maintenance is required. **Note:** *Do not attempt to remove the battery caps to check the electrolyte level or battery specific gravity. Removal will damage the caps, resulting in electrolyte leakage and battery damage.* All that should be done is to check that its terminals are clean and tight and that the casing is not damaged or leaking. See Chapter 9 for further details.

3 Brake system checks

1 A routine general check of the brake system will ensure that any problems are discovered and remedied before the rider's safety is jeopardised. Refer to Sections 4 to 8.

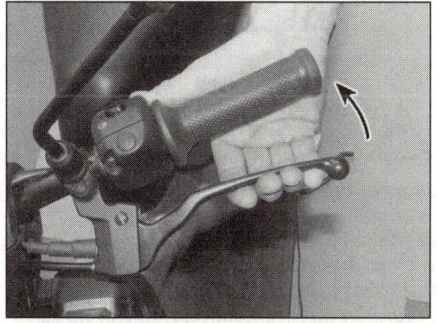

4.1 Checking brake lever freeplay

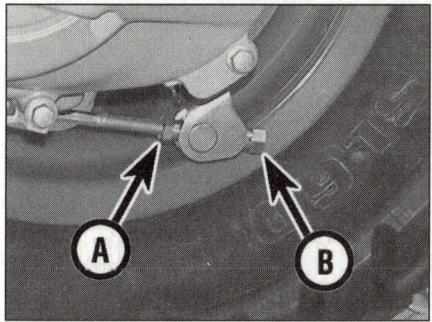

4.2 Loosen the locknut (A) and turn the adjuster (B) as required

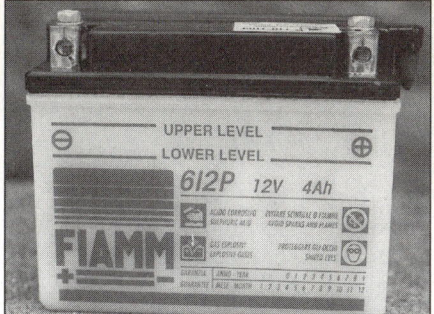

2.1 Battery electrolyte level must be between level marks

2 Check the brake cables and levers for looseness, improper or rough action, excessive play, bends, and other damage. Replace any damaged parts with new ones (see Chapter 7).

3 Make sure all brake fasteners are tight. Check the brake shoes (drum brake) and pads (disc brake) for wear (see Section 8) and on disc brake models make sure the fluid level in the reservoirs is correct (see *Daily (pre-ride) checks*). Look for leaks at the hose connections and check for cracks in the hoses. If the lever is spongy, bleed the brakes (see Chapter 7).

4 Make sure the brake light operates when each brake lever is pulled in. The brake light switches are not adjustable. If they fail to operate properly, check them (see Chapter 9).

4 Brake cable adjustment, check and lubrication – drum rear brake

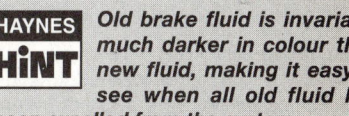

Adjustment

1 Check that there is not an excessive amount of freeplay in the brake lever before the brake takes effect **(see illustration)**. The wheel should spin freely when the brake is not activated, but the brake should come on when the lever is just pulled in. The actual amount of freeplay is not specified and is a matter of personal taste.

2 To take up freeplay in the lever, loosen the locknut and turn the adjuster nut on the lower end of the cable until the excess is taken out

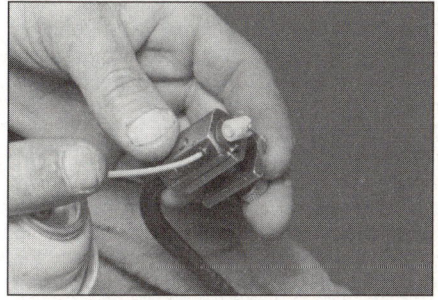

4.4a Lubricating a cable with a pressure lubricator. Make sure the tool seals around the inner cable

(see illustration). Don't forget to tighten the locknut when the cable has been adjusted. If the brake is binding without the lever being pulled, turn the adjuster nut in the opposite direction to provide some freeplay.

Check and lubrication

3 Since the cable is exposed to the elements, it should be lubricated periodically to ensure safe and trouble-free operation.

4 To lubricate the cable, disconnect its upper end from the handlebar lever (see Chapter 7). Lubricate the cable with a pressure adapter, or if one is not available, using the set-up shown **(see illustrations)**.

5 Check along the length of the outer cable for splits and kinks, and at the ends of the inner cable for frays. Check that the inner cable slides smoothly and freely in the outer cable. Renew the cable if necessary (see Chapter 7).

5 Brake fluid change – disc brake

1 Brake fluid will degrade over a period of time. It should be changed at the prescribed interval or whenever a master cylinder or caliper overhaul is carried out. Follow the procedure described in the brake bleeding section in Chapter 7.

> **HAYNES HiNT**
> *Old brake fluid is invariably much darker in colour than new fluid, making it easy to see when all old fluid has been expelled from the system.*

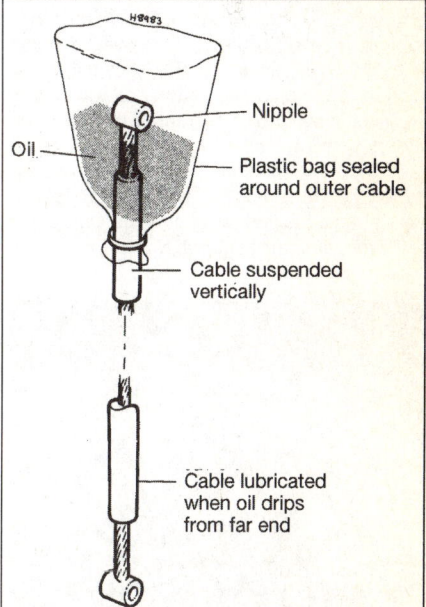

4.4b Lubricating a cable with a makeshift funnel and motor oil

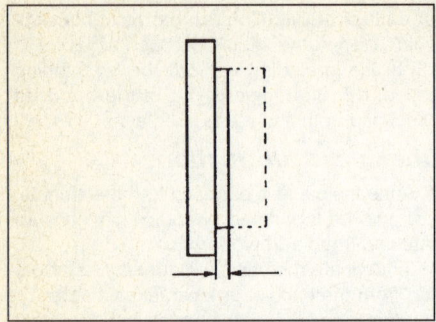

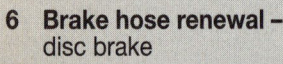

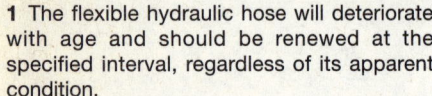

8.1 Brake friction material minimum wear limit

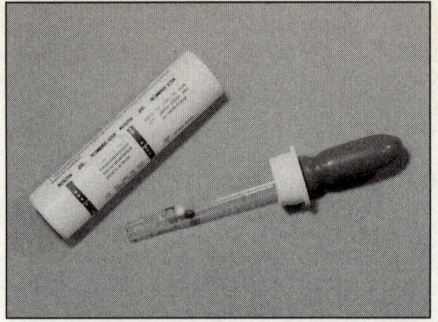

9.7 An antifreeze hydrometer is required to check coolant strength

6 Brake hose renewal – disc brake

1 The flexible hydraulic hose will deteriorate with age and should be renewed at the specified interval, regardless of its apparent condition.
2 Refer to Chapter 7 and disconnect the brake hose from the master cylinder and caliper. Always replace the banjo union sealing washers with new ones.

7 Brake lever pivot lubrication

1 Since the lever pivots are exposed to the elements, they should be lubricated periodically to ensure safe and trouble-free operation.
2 In order for the lubricant to be applied where it will do the most good, the lever should be removed and a calcium soap-based grease applied (see Chapter 6). However, if chain or cable lubricant is being used, it can be applied to the pivot joint gaps and will usually work its way into the areas where friction occurs. If motor oil or light grease is being used, apply it sparingly as it may attract dirt (which could cause the controls to bind or wear at an accelerated rate). **Note:** *One of the best lubricants for the control lever pivots is a dry-film lubricant.*

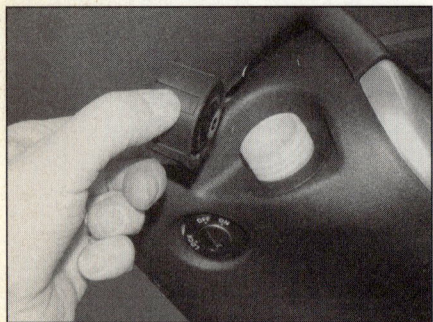

10.1 Remove the coolant reservoir cap slowly

8 Brake shoes/pads wear check

1 The brake shoes and pads are not marked with wear indicators – the only sure way of knowing the extent of wear is to remove the disc brake pads, or remove the rear wheel to access the shoes on drum brake models, and check visually (see Chapter 7). If the amount of friction material remaining on either the shoes or the pads is below the service limit (1.5 mm) they must be renewed **(see illustration)**. **Note:** *Always renew brake shoes and pads as a pair, never individually.*

9 Cooling system check – liquid-cooled engine

⚠ **Warning: The engine must be cool before beginning this procedure.**

1 Check the coolant level (see *Daily (pre-ride) checks*).
2 The entire cooling system should be checked for evidence of leaks. Examine each coolant hose and pipe along its entire length, noting that you will need to remove much of the bodywork to access the hoses. Look for cracks, abrasions and other damage. Squeeze each flexible hose at various points. They should feel firm, yet pliable, and return to their original shape when released. If they have become hardened, replace them with new ones.
3 Check for evidence of leaks at each cooling system joint. Tighten the hose clips carefully to prevent future leaks. On two-stroke engined models the water pump is located inside the crankcases; check the drain hole in the left-hand crankcase half for signs of leaks (see Chapter 3). On four-stroke engined models the water pump is mounted externally on the alternator cover; check below the pump for signs of leakage. If the internal seal in the water pump fails, coolant will leak out from the bottom of the alternator cover.
4 Check the radiator for leaks and other damage. Leaks in the radiator leave tell-tale

scale deposits or coolant stains on the outside of the core below the leak. If leaks are noted, remove the radiator (see Chapter 3) and have it repaired or fit a new one.
Caution: Do not use a liquid leak stopping compound to try to repair leaks.
5 Check the radiator fins for mud, dirt and insects, which may impede the flow of air through the radiator. If the fins are dirty, remove the radiator (see Chapter 3) and clean it using water or low pressure compressed air directed through the fins from the back. If the fins are bent or distorted, straighten them carefully with a screwdriver. If the air flow is restricted by bent or damaged fins over more than 30% of the radiator's surface area, renew the radiator.
6 Check the condition of the coolant in the reservoir. If it is rust-coloured or if accumulations of scale are visible, drain, flush and refill the system with new coolant (see Section 10).
7 Check the antifreeze content of the coolant with an antifreeze hydrometer **(see illustration)**. Sometimes coolant looks like it's in good condition, but might be too weak to offer adequate protection. If the hydrometer indicates a weak mixture, drain, flush and refill the system (see Section 10).
8 Start the engine and let it reach normal operating temperature, then check for leaks again.
9 If the coolant level is consistently low, and no evidence of leaks can be found, have the entire system pressure checked by a Gilera dealer.

10 Coolant change – liquid-cooled engine

⚠ *Warning: Allow the engine to cool completely before performing this maintenance operation. Also, don't allow antifreeze to come into contact with your skin or the painted or plastic surfaces of the scooter. Rinse off spills immediately with plenty of water. Antifreeze is highly toxic if ingested. Never leave antifreeze lying around in an open container or in puddles on the floor; children and pets are attracted by its sweet smell and may drink it. Check with local authorities (councils) about disposing of antifreeze. Many communities have collection centres which will see that antifreeze is disposed of safely. Antifreeze is also combustible, so don't store it near open flames.*

Draining

1 Cover the coolant reservoir cap with a heavy cloth and release it slowly **(see illustration)**. If you hear a hissing sound as you unscrew it (indicating there is still pressure in the system), wait until it stops.
2 Position a suitable container beneath the engine on the right-hand side at the front.

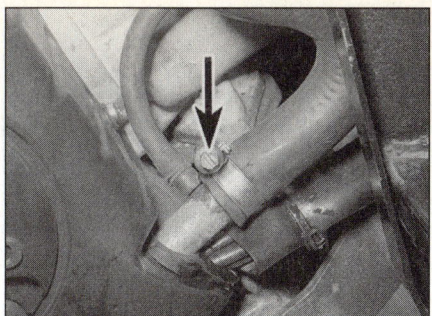

10.2a Loosen the clip (arrowed) and detach the coolant hose

10.2b Detach the lower coolant hose on externally mounted water pumps

10.16 Cooling system bleed screw

Either loosen the clip securing the coolant hose to the pipe on the side of the engine, then detach the hose, or loosen the clip on the lower hose on the water pump and detach the hose **(see illustrations)**. Allow the coolant to completely drain from the system.

Flushing

3 Flush the system with clean tap water by inserting a garden hose in the reservoir filler neck. Allow water to run through the system until it is clear and flows cleanly out of the detached hose. If there is a large amount of rust or sediment in the water, remove the radiator and flush it out separately (see Chapter 3).

4 Reconnect the coolant hose to the pipe or water pump and secure it with its clip (see Step 2).

5 Fill the cooling system via the reservoir filler with clean water mixed with a flushing compound. Make sure the flushing compound is compatible with aluminium components, and follow the manufacturer's instructions carefully. Fit the reservoir cap.

6 Start the engine and allow it to reach normal operating temperature. Let it run for about five minutes.

7 Stop the engine. Let it cool for a while, then remove the reservoir cap.

8 Drain the system once again.

9 Fill the system with clean water and repeat the procedure in Steps 6 to 8.

Refilling – four-stroke engined models

10 Attach the coolant hose to the water pump and secure it with its clip.

11 Fill the system all the way up to the MAX level mark in the reservoir filler neck with the proper coolant mixture (see this Chapter's Specifications). Install the reservoir cap. **Note:** *Pour the coolant into the reservoir slowly to minimise the amount of air entering the system.*

12 Start the engine and allow it to idle for 2 to 3 minutes. Flick the throttle twistgrip part open 3 or 4 times, so that the engine speed rises, then stop the engine.

 Warning: Make sure that the scooter is on its centre stand and that the rear wheel is off

the ground before starting the engine. If necessary, place a support under the engine to prevent the rear wheel contacting the ground.

13 Let the engine cool then remove the reservoir cap. Check that the coolant level is still up to MAX level mark. Top-up the reservoir if necessary, then refit the cap.

14 Check the system for leaks.

Note: *Do not dispose of the old coolant by pouring it down the drain. Instead pour it into a heavy plastic container, cap it tightly and take it into an authorised disposal site or garage – see* **Warning** *at the beginning of this Section.*

Refilling – two-stroke engined models

15 Attach the coolant hose to the pipe and secure it with its clip.

16 Remove the engine cover (see Chapter 8). Fully loosen the bleed screw and attach one end of a suitable length of rubber tube to it **(see illustration)**. Place the other end into the coolant reservoir.

17 Fill the system all the way up to the MAX level line on the reservoir with the proper coolant mixture (see this Chapter's Specifications). **Note:** *Pour the coolant into the reservoir slowly to minimise the amount of air entering the system.* As you fill the reservoir, air will bubble up from the rubber tube attached to the bleed screw.

18 When the system is full and no more air is coming out of the tube, tighten the bleed screw and install the reservoir cap.

19 Start the engine and allow it to idle for 2 to 3 minutes. Flick the throttle twistgrip part open 3 or 4 times, so that the engine speed rises, then stop the engine. Loosen the bleed screw to allow any air trapped in the system to come out, then tighten the screw.

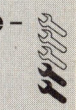 *Warning: Make sure that the scooter is on its centre stand and that the rear wheel is off the ground before starting the engine. If necessary, place a support under the engine to prevent the rear wheel contacting the ground.*

20 Let the engine cool then remove the reservoir cap. Check that the coolant level is

still up to MAX level line. Top-up the reservoir if necessary, then refit the cap.

21 Check the system for leaks.

Note: *Do not dispose of the old coolant by pouring it down the drain. Instead pour it into a heavy plastic container, cap it tightly and take it into an authorised disposal site or garage – see* **Warning** *at the beginning of this Section.*

11 Drive belt inspection and renewal

1 Referring to Chapter 2D, remove the drive belt cover, then inspect the belt as described and renew it if necessary. In the event of premature belt wear, the cause should be investigated. **Note:** *The drive belt must be renewed at the specified service interval.*

12 Engine oil and filter change – four-stroke engine

 *Warning: Be careful when draining the oil, as the exhaust pipe, the engine, and the oil itself can cause severe burns.*

1 Oil and filter changes are the single most important maintenance procedure you can perform on a four-stroke engine. The oil not only lubricates the internal parts of the engine, but it also acts as a coolant, a cleaner, a sealant, and a protector. Because of these demands, the oil takes a terrific amount of abuse and should be replaced at the specified service interval with new oil of the recommended grade and type. Saving a little money on the difference in cost between a good oil and a cheap oil won't pay off if the engine is damaged.

2 Before changing the oil, warm up the engine so the oil will drain easily. Stop the engine and turn the ignition OFF. Put the scooter on its centre stand, and position a clean drain tray below the engine.

3 Unscrew the oil filler plug from the left-hand side of the engine to vent the crankcase and to act as a reminder that there is no oil in the engine **(see illustration)**.

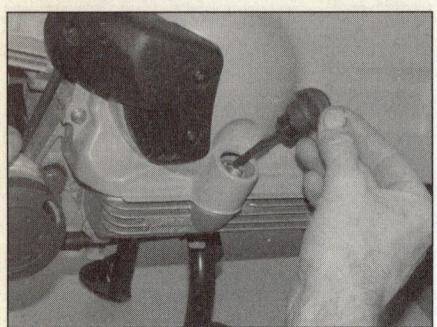

12.3 Remove the oil filler plug

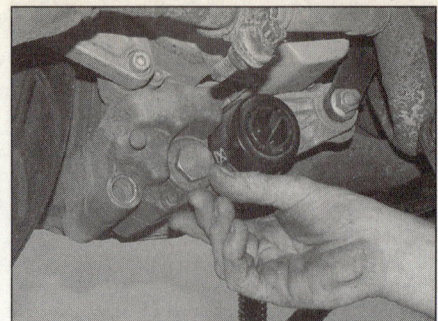

12.4a Unscrew the oil drain plug . . .

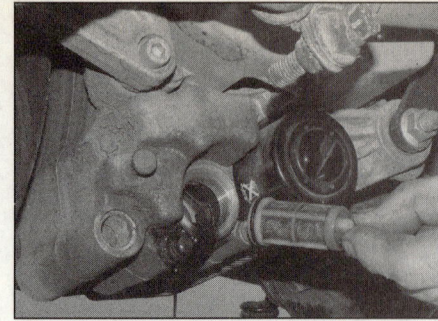

12.4b . . . then withdraw the gauze strainer

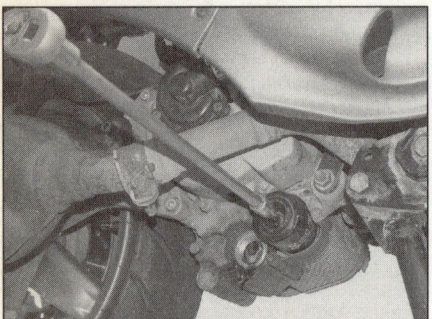

12.5a Unscrew the oil filter

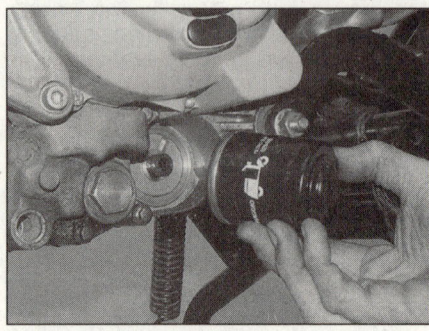

12.5b Lubricate the seal on the new filter and tighten it securely

4 Unscrew the oil drain plug below the alternator cover on the right-hand side of the engine and allow the oil to flow into the drain tray **(see illustration)**. Withdraw the gauze strainer and clean it in solvent to remove any debris caught in the mesh **(see illustration)**. Check the gauze for splits or holes and renew it if necessary.

5 Unscrew the oil filter and tip any residual oil into the drain tray **(see illustration)**. Smear clean engine oil onto the seal of the new filter, then install the filter and tighten it securely by hand **(see illustration)**.

6 Install the strainer, fit a new sealing washer or O-ring to the drain plug if necessary, then install the plug and tighten it to 24 to 30 Nm.

7 Refill the engine to the proper level using the recommended type and amount of oil (see *Daily (pre-ride) checks*); you may find that due to a certain amount of oil remaining in the engine, only 600 to 650 cc will be required.

Install the filler plug and tightening it by hand. Start the engine and let it run for two or three minutes. Shut it off, wait five minutes, then check the oil level. If necessary, add more oil to bring the level up to between the level marks on the dipstick. Check around the drain plug and the oil filter for leaks.

 **HAYNES HiNT** *Saving a little money on the difference between good and cheap oils won't pay off if the engine is damaged as a result.*

8 The old oil drained from the engine cannot be re-used and should be disposed of properly. Check with your local refuse disposal company, disposal facility or environmental agency to see whether they will accept the used oil for recycling. Don't pour used oil into drains or onto the ground.

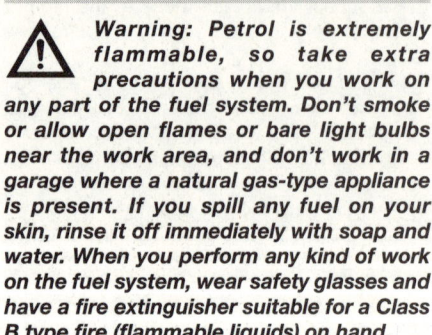

OIL CARE

Note: It is antisocial and illegal to dump oil down the drain. To find the location of your local oil recycling bank, call 08708 506 506 or visit www.oilbankline.org.uk

13 Fuel system filter renewal and carburettor cleaning

⚠ *Warning: Petrol is extremely flammable, so take extra precautions when you work on any part of the fuel system. Don't smoke or allow open flames or bare light bulbs near the work area, and don't work in a garage where a natural gas-type appliance is present. If you spill any fuel on your skin, rinse it off immediately with soap and water. When you perform any kind of work on the fuel system, wear safety glasses and have a fire extinguisher suitable for a Class B type fire (flammable liquids) on hand.*

Renew filter

1 Runner Purejet 50, FX125, FXR180, VX125, ST125, VXR180/200 and ST200 models, and DNA125/180 models, have an in-line fuel filter which must be renewed at the specified service interval **(see illustration)**. Trace

13.1a In-line fuel filter

13.1b Location of the fuel filter on Purejet 50 models

13.1c In-line filter is located on right-hand side of fuel tank on Runner VX/VXR RST and ST models

13.4 Keep the accelerator pump mechanism (arrowed) clean

the fuel hose from the carburettor to locate the filter; on Purejet 50 models, the filter is located on the right-hand side underneath the floor panel section of the side panel **(see illustration)**. Remove the bodypanels as necessary to access the filter (see Chapter 8).
2 To remove the old filter, first clamp the hose between the fuel tank and the filter to prevent fuel leakage – use any of the methods shown in *Tool Tips* in Chapter 4. Loosen the clips securing the fuel hoses to each end of the filter, being prepared to catch any residual fuel, and detach the hoses **(see illustration 13.1a or b)**. Withdraw the filter from its mounting (where fitted), noting which way up it fits.
3 Install the new filter in its mounting, making sure it is the correct way up – there should be an arrow marked on the body denoting the direction of fuel flow. Attach the fuel hoses and secure them with the clips. If the old clips are corroded or deformed, fit new ones.

Accelerator pump mechanism (four-stroke engine)

4 The exterior mechanism of the carburettor accelerator pump should be kept clean and free of road dirt **(see illustration)**.
5 Clean away any grit with a small paintbrush. If necessary, wash the carburettor carefully with hot soapy water, ensuring no water enters the carburettor body, and dry with compressed air. Oil deposits can be removed with a rag soaked in a suitable solvent. Take care to ensure the idle speed setting is not disturbed during cleaning.
6 If the scooter has not been used for a long period, a sticky residue may form in the

carburettor, jamming the throttle slide and accelerator pump assembly. Disassemble the carburettor and clean the components with a suitable solvent or carburettor cleaner (see Chapter 4).
Note: *If the carburettor is being disassembled, read through the entire procedure and make sure that you have obtained a new gasket set first.*

14 Gearbox oil level check

1 Place the scooter on its centre stand on level ground. The Ice, Runner FX125, FXR180, VX125, ST125, VXR180/200 and ST200 models and all DNA models are fitted with an integral filler cap and dipstick **(see illustration)**. The SKP/Stalker and all 50 cc Runner models have an oil level plug **(see illustration)**. Unscrew the filler cap or plug from the gearbox casing. Discard the filler plug sealing washer as a new one should be used on reassembly.
2 On models with a dipstick, use a clean rag or paper towel to wipe off the oil. Two different dipstick level markings are used on Gilera scooters – on DNA 50 GP models the lower mark on the dipstick denotes the correct level; on all other models, the second mark from the bottom denotes the correct level **(see illustration)**. Ensure the dipstick is screwed all the way back into the casing when the level reading is being taken. **Note:** *It is important to have the right information for*

checking the gearbox oil level on your specific machine. If in any doubt, consult a Gilera dealer for details.

 Warning: Do not risk under-filling or over-filling the gearbox as a transmission seizure or dangerous oil leakage may result.

3 On models with a level plug, the oil level should come up to the lower threads so that it is just visible on the threads **(see illustration)**.
4 If the oil level is below the appropriate line on the dipstick, or below the level of the plug threads, top the gearbox up with the recommended grade and type of oil (see Specifications at the beginning of this Chapter). Use a pump-type oil can to top up gearboxes with a level plug **(see illustration)**. Do not overfill.
5 Install the filler cap and tighten it securely by hand, or fit a new sealing washer to the level plug and tighten it securely.

15 Gearbox oil change

1 Remove the rear wheel (see Chapter 7).
2 Position a clean drain tray below the gearbox. Unscrew the filler cap or level plug (as applicable) to vent the gearbox and to act as a reminder that there is no oil in it.
3 Unscrew the oil drain plug and allow the oil to flow into the drain tray **(see illustration 14.1b)**. Discard the sealing washers on the drain and level plugs as new ones should be used.

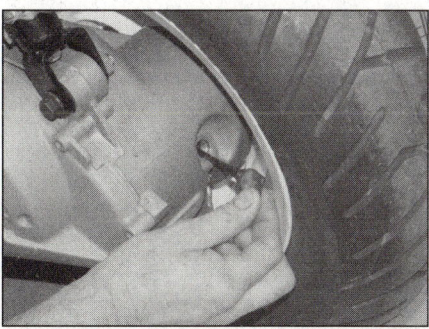

14.1a Gearbox oil filler cap and dipstick

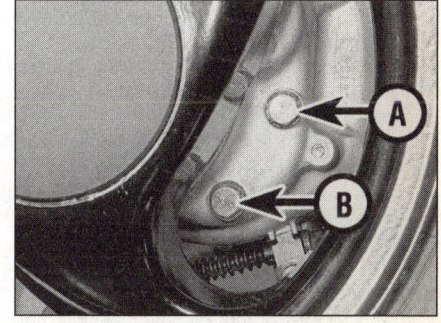

14.1b Gearbox oil level plug (A) and drain plug (B)

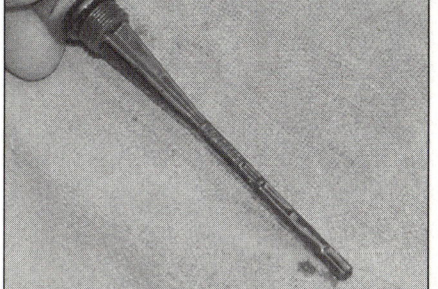

14.2 Ensure the correct mark is used when checking the oil level

14.3 Oil should be just level with the threads

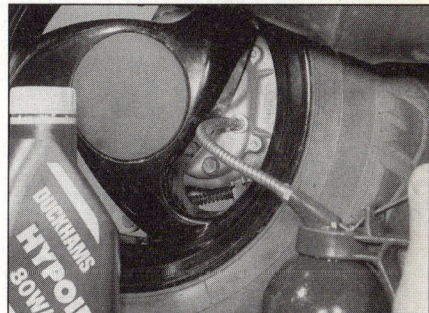

14.4 Topping-up the oil with a pump can

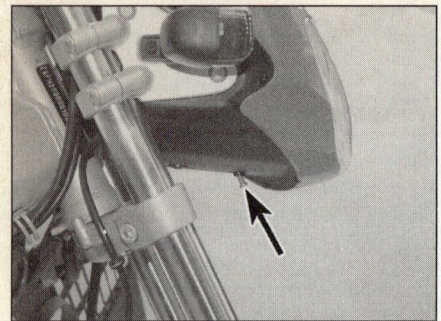

16.2a Headlight adjuster screw (arrowed)
on DNA models . . .

16.2b . . . on Runner models . . .

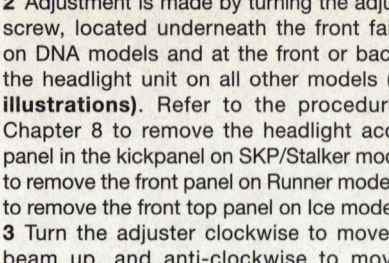

2 Adjustment is made by turning the adjuster screw, located underneath the front fairing on DNA models and at the front or back of the headlight unit on all other models **(see illustrations)**. Refer to the procedure in Chapter 8 to remove the headlight access panel in the kickpanel on SKP/Stalker models, to remove the front panel on Runner models or to remove the front top panel on Ice models.
3 Turn the adjuster clockwise to move the beam up, and anti-clockwise to move it down.

17 Idle (tickover) speed check and adjustment

Note: *The idle speed cannot be adjusted on Runner Purejet models. If the idle speed is incorrect, have the ECM system checked by a Gilera dealer with the appropriate diagnostic equipment (see Chapter 4).*
1 The idle speed should be checked and adjusted when it is obviously too high or too low. Before adjusting the idle speed, make sure the valve clearances (four-stroke engined models) and spark plug gap are correct. Also, turn the handlebars back-and-forth and see if the idle speed changes as this is done. If it does, the throttle cable may not be adjusted or routed correctly, or may be worn out. This is a dangerous condition that can cause loss of control of the scooter. Be sure to correct this problem before proceeding.
2 The engine should be at normal operating temperature, which is usually reached after 10 to 15 minutes of stop-and-go riding. Place the scooter on its centre stand and make sure that the rear wheel is clear of the ground. No tachometer is fitted to enable the idle speed to be compared with that specified, but ensure that at idle (twistgrip closed) the engine speed is steady and does not falter, also that it is not too high otherwise the automatic transmission will engage.
3 The idle speed adjuster screw is located on the carburettor **(see illustrations)**. On Ice models, first remove the plug in the right-hand side of the engine top cover to access the adjuster **(see illustration)**. On DNA models, remove the engine top cover (see Chapter

16.2c . . . on Ice models . . .

16.2d . . . and on SKP/Stalker models
(kickpanel removed for clarity)

16 Headlight aim check and adjustment

Note: *An improperly adjusted headlight may cause problems for oncoming traffic or provide poor, unsafe illumination of the road ahead. Before adjusting the headlight aim, be sure to consult with local traffic laws and regulations.*
1 The headlight beam can adjusted vertically. Before making any adjustment, check that the tyre pressures are correct and the suspension is adjusted as required. Make any adjustments to the headlight aim with the machine on level ground, with the fuel tank half full and with an assistant sitting on the seat. If the bike is usually ridden with a passenger on the back, have a second assistant to do this.

4 When the oil has completely drained, fit the drain plug using a new sealing washer, and tighten it securely. Avoid overtightening, as damage to the casing will result. On four-stroke models, tighten the drain plug to 15 to 17 Nm.
5 Refill the gearbox to the correct level using the recommended type and amount of oil (see Section 14). Install the filler cap and tighten it securely by hand, or fit a new sealing washer to the level plug and tighten it securely.
6 Check the oil level again after riding the scooter for a few minutes and, if necessary, add more oil. Check around the drain plug for leaks.
7 The old oil drained from the gearbox cannot be re-used and should be disposed of properly. Check with your local refuse disposal company, disposal facility or environmental agency to see whether they will accept the used oil for recycling. Don't pour used oil into drains or onto the ground.

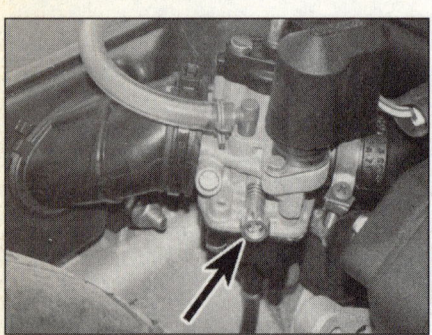

17.3a Idle speed adjuster on slide-type
carburettor (arrowed) . . .

17.3b . . . and on CV-type carburettor
(arrowed)

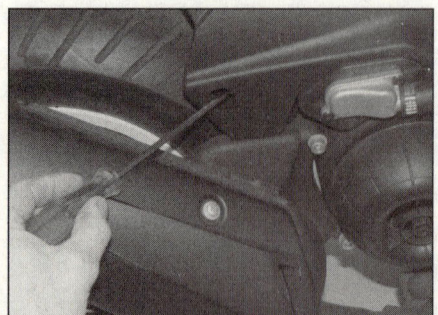

17.3c On Ice models, adjuster is accessible
through aperture in engine cover

17.3d On SKP/Stalker models, displace the hugger to access the adjuster (arrowed)

8). On SKP/Stalker models, displace the rear hugger **(see illustration)**. With the engine idling, turn the screw clockwise to increase idle speed, and anti-clockwise to decrease it.

4 Snap the throttle open and shut a few times, then recheck the idle speed. If necessary, repeat the adjustment procedure.

5 If a smooth, steady idle can't be achieved, the fuel/air mixture may be incorrect or the carburettor may need overhauling (see Chapter 4). **Note:** *On four-stroke engined models, some constant vacuum (CV) carburettors have a cut-off valve on the right-hand side of the body. If the valve diaphragm is faulty the engine will die at low revs (see Chapter 4).*

6 With the idle speed correctly adjusted, recheck the throttle cable freeplay (see Section 26).

18 Nuts and bolts tightness check

1 Since vibration of the machine tends to loosen fasteners, all nuts, bolts, screws, etc. should be periodically checked for proper tightness.

2 Pay particular attention to the following:
• Spark plug
• Carburettor clamps
• Engine oil drain plug (four-stroke engines)
• Centre stand bolts
• Engine mounting bolts
• Suspension and swingarm bolts
• Handlebar lever clamp bolts
• Wheel bolts
• Brake caliper and disc mounting bolts (disc brakes)
• Brake hose banjo bolts (disc brakes)
• Exhaust system bolts/nuts

3 If a torque wrench is available, use it along with the torque specifications given in this manual.

19 Oil pump drive belt renewal – two-stroke engine

1 Refer to Chapter 2A or 2B, remove the oil pump and replace the drive belt with a new one.

20 Secondary air system clean

Two-stroke engine

1 The secondary air system is fitted to all two-stroke engines with a catalytic converter exhaust system; known as the Hi-Per2 engine on air-cooled models and Hi-Per2Pro on liquid-cooled models **(see illustration)**. If required, remove the right-hand body panel to access the system components (see Chapter 8).

2 Release the clip securing the hose to the reed valve housing, then undo the screws securing the housing and detach it **(see illustrations)**. Note the location of the reed valve inside the housing.

3 Lift off the plastic cover and the filter element **(see illustrations)**. Note the position of the cover O-ring, if fitted. If the O-ring is damaged, discard it and fit a new one on reassembly.

4 Lever the breather cap out of the drive belt cover with a small screwdriver and carefully remove the filter element from the cap **(see illustrations 1.8c and 1.8d)**.

5 Wash the filters in hot soapy water then blow them dry using compressed air. Never wring the filters dry as they may tear. If the filters are excessively dirty and cannot be cleaned properly, or are torn or damaged in any way, fit new ones.

6 Lift the reed valve out of the housing, noting which way round it fits **(see illustration)**. To check the condition of the reed valve, hold it

20.1 Location of the secondary air system

20.2a Release the clip with a small screwdriver . . .

20.2b . . . then remove the housing screws . . .

20.2c . . . and pull off the reed valve housing

20.3a Lift off the cover . . .

20.3b . . . and the filter element

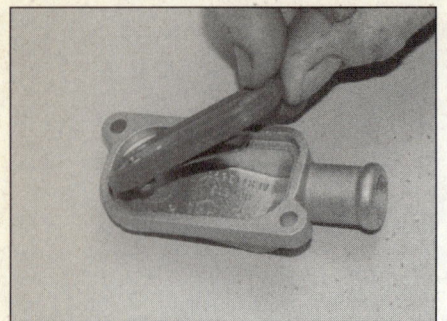

20.6a Lift out the reed valve

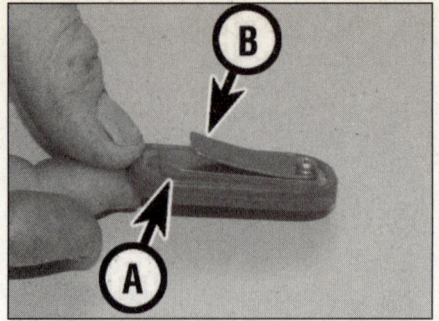

20.6b Check the position of the reed (A) and note the position of the stopper plate (B)

20.7 Secure the clip with pliers

up to the light. The valve should be closed. If light can be seen around the edge of the reed a new valve should be fitted **(see illustration)**. Clean the reed and stopper plate carefully with a suitable solvent to remove any gum.

7 Install the components in the reverse order of disassembly. If necessary, fit a new O-ring to the filter housing cover. The hose clip should be secured with pliers **(see illustration)**.

Four-stroke engine

Note: *The secondary air system is fitted to*

Runner VX125, ST125, VXR200 and ST200 models which confirm to Euro 3 regulations. The system filter should be cleaned every two years.
8 Remove the seat cowling, right-hand footrest plate and sidepanel floor panels, and the belly panel to gain access to the secondary air system (see Chapter 8). It is on the right-hand side of the engine, on top of the alternator cover **(see illustration)**.
9 Undo the screw at the front of the unit and detach the cable harness from its attachment fitting on the crankcase **(see illustration)**.

10 Remove the two bolts, and detach the metal pipe connecting the SAS valve to the cylinder head exhaust manifold noting how it fits **(see illustration)**.
11 Free the small-bore vacuum pipe from the control valve. Undo the three screws securing the SAS cover to the alternator cover and remove it complete with the SAS control valve **(see illustration)**.
12 Lift out the filter and clean it in hot soapy water, then blow it dry using compressed air **(see illustration)**. Never wring the filter out

20.8 The secondary air system is located on the right-hand side of the engine, on top of the alternator cover (arrowed)

20.9 Undo the screw at the front of the unit and detach the cable harness from the crankcase

20.10 Remove the two bolts, and detach the metal pipe from the cylinder head exhaust manifold (arrowed)

20.11 Undo the three screws securing the SAS cover to the manifold, noting how it fits

20.12 Lift out the filter

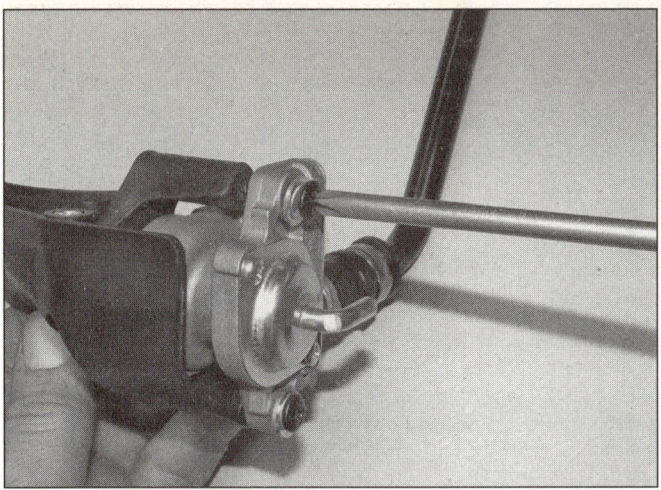

20.13 Unscrew the two screws on the SAS control valve and separate it from the cover (arrowed)

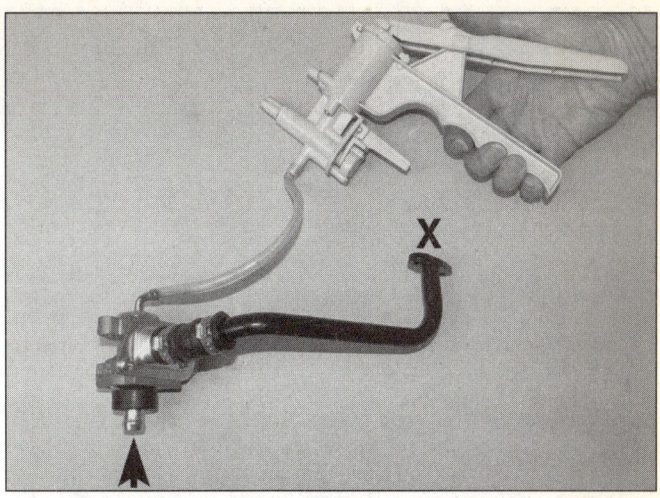

20.14a With the vacuum applied no air should flow out of the metal pipe when blown into the air inlet union (arrowed)

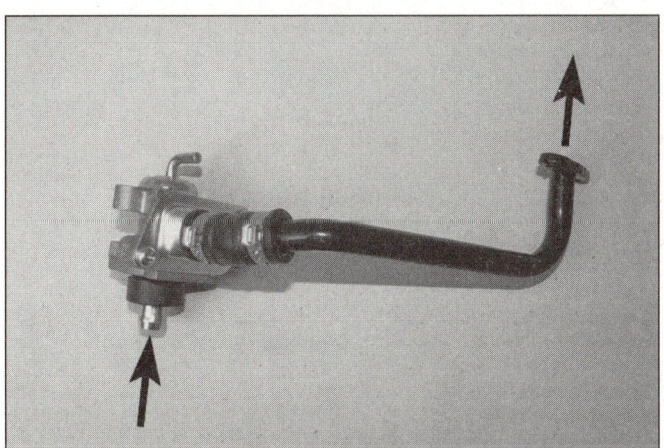

20.14b Without no vacuum applied air should flow freely through the valve

20.15 Manoeuvre the pipe and SAS unit back into place

as it may tear. If the filter is excessively dirty and cannot be cleaned properly, or is torn or damaged in any way, replace it. Insert the filter back into its housing.

13 Unscrew the two screws on the SAS control valve **(see illustration)** and separate it from the cover.

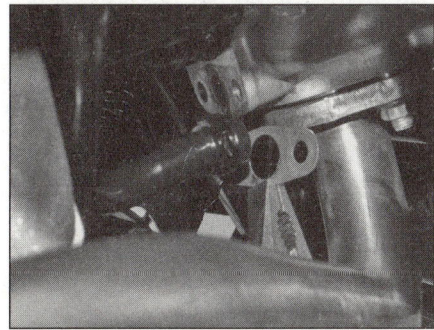

20.16 Attach the metal tube to the cylinder head using a new gasket

14 To test the control valve you will need a vacuum pump. With the vacuum pump connected to the valve and a vacuum applied, no air should flow out of the metal pipe when blown into the air inlet union **(see illustration)**. Without the vacuum pump in place, air should flow freely through the valve **(see illustration)**. If the valve fails either test, it is faulty and must be renewed.

15 Manoeuvre the pipe and SAS unit back into place behind the coolant hoses **(see illustration)**.

16 Attach the metal tube to the cylinder head using a new gasket and retain it with the two bolt. Threading the bolts into place is difficult due to the limited access **(see illustration)**.

17 Secure the SAS unit back onto the alternator cover and tighten the three screws to secure it. Now tighten the inner control valve-to-cover screw which passes through the cast lug on the engine. Reconnect the vacuum hose and secure it with the spring clip.

18 Reconnect the wiring to the control valve.

19 Refit the body panels. Screw the control valve to the cover, noting that the inner (as fitted) should be left loose.

21 Spark plug gap check and adjustment

⚠️ **Warning: Access to the spark plug is extremely restricted on some models. Ensure the engine and exhaust system are cool before attempting to remove the spark plug.**

1 Make sure your spark plug socket is the correct size before attempting to remove the plug – a suitable plug socket is supplied in the scooter's toolkit. Where appropriate, remove the engine access panels or side cover (see Chapter 8).

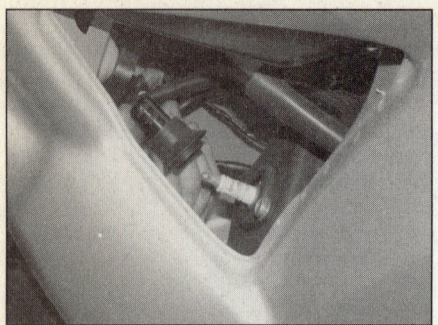

21.2a Remove the spark plug cap . . .

21.2b . . . then unscrew the spark plug

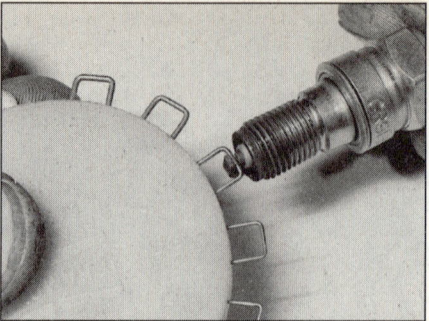

21.6a Using a wire type gauge to measure the spark plug electrode gap

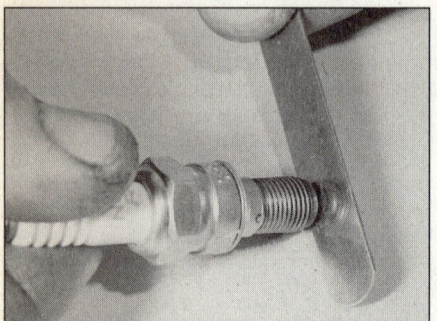

21.6b Using a feeler gauge to measure the spark plug electrode gap

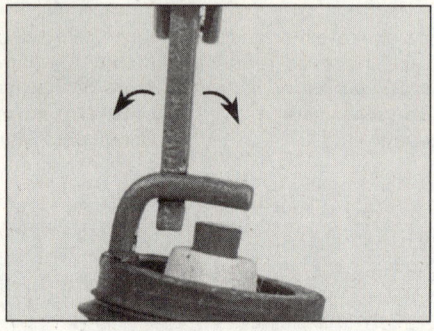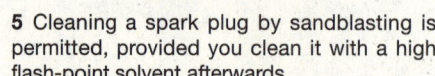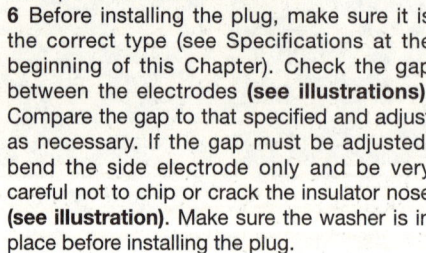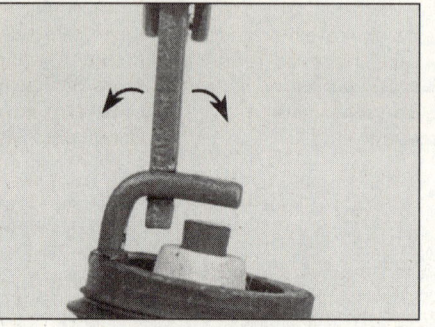

21.6c Adjust the electrode gap by bending the side electrode only

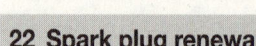

HAYNES HiNT *A stripped plug thread in the cylinder head can be repaired with a thread insert.*

2 Pull the spark plug cap off the spark plug, then unscrew the plug from the cylinder head **(see illustrations)**.

3 Inspect the electrodes for wear. Both the centre and side electrode should have square edges and the side electrode should be of uniform thickness. Look for excessive carbon deposits and evidence of a cracked or chipped insulator around the centre electrode. Compare your spark plug to the colour spark plug reading chart at the end of this manual. Check the threads, the washer and the ceramic insulator body for cracks and other damage.

4 If the electrodes are not excessively worn, and if the deposits can be easily removed with a wire brush, the plug can be re-gapped and re-used. If in doubt concerning the condition of the plug, replace it with a new one, as the expense is minimal.

5 Cleaning a spark plug by sandblasting is permitted, provided you clean it with a high flash-point solvent afterwards.

6 Before installing the plug, make sure it is the correct type (see Specifications at the beginning of this Chapter). Check the gap between the electrodes **(see illustrations)**. Compare the gap to that specified and adjust as necessary. If the gap must be adjusted, bend the side electrode only and be very careful not to chip or crack the insulator nose **(see illustration)**. Make sure the washer is in place before installing the plug.

7 Since the cylinder head is made of aluminium, which is soft and easily damaged, thread the plug into the head by hand. Once the plug is finger-tight, the job can be finished with the plug socket. Take care not to over-tighten the plug.

8 Reconnect the spark plug cap.

22 Spark plug renewal

1 Remove the old spark plug as described in Section 21 and install a new one. Ensure the new plug is the correct type (see Specifications at the beginning of this Chapter). Check the gap between the electrodes and adjust it if necessary.

23 Speedometer cable and drive gear lubrication

Note: *DNA and Ice models are fitted with an electronically operated speedometer – the 'cable' is an electrical wire connecting the sensor on the wheel hub to the speedometer. This set-up does not require lubrication – do not try to disconnect the wire from the sensor.*

1 On Runner and SKP/Stalker models, disconnect the speedometer cable from the back of the speedometer and from the drive housing (see Chapter 9).

2 Withdraw the inner cable from the outer cable, noting which way round it fits, and lubricate it with motor oil or cable lubricant. Do not lubricate the upper few inches of the cable as the lubricant may travel up into the instrument head.

3 Installation is the reverse of removal. Raise the wheel clear of the ground and rotate it by hand to ensure the inner cable is correctly located.

4 To lubricate the drive gear, remove the cap from the grease point on the underside of the drive housing and press some lithium soap-based grease up into it, then refit the cap **(see illustrations)**.

5 To remove the speedometer drive housing, first remove the front wheel (see Chapter 7).

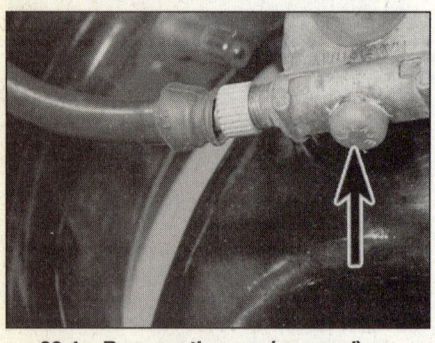

23.4a Remove the cap (arrowed) . . .

23.4b . . . and press some grease into the housing

23.5 Lift off the speedometer drive housing, noting how it fits

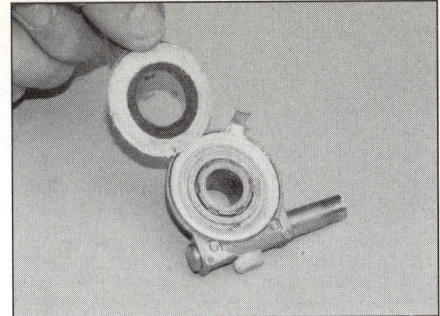

23.6 Lubricate the speedometer drive gear with clean grease

23.7 Note the location of the external drive tab (arrowed)

Lift the housing off the wheel hub, noting how it fits **(see illustration)**.

6 Lift off the seal and clean all the old grease from inside the housing, then lubricate the drive gear with clean grease **(see illustration)**. Fit a new seal if the old one is damaged.

7 Fit the housing onto the wheel hub, ensuring the drive is correctly located **(see illustration)**. Install the front wheel (see Chapter 7).

24 Steering head bearings check and adjustment

1 All models are equipped with either caged ball or taper roller steering head bearings which can become loose, rough or dented during normal use. In extreme cases, loose or worn steering head bearings can cause steering wobble – a condition that is potentially dangerous.

Check

2 Place the scooter on its centre stand. Raise the front wheel off the ground either by having an assistant push down on the rear or by placing a support under the frame.
3 Point the front wheel straight-ahead and

slowly move the handlebars from side-to-side. Any dents or roughness in the bearing races will be felt and the bars will not move smoothly and freely. If the bearings are damaged they must be renewed (see Chapter 6).

4 Next, grasp the front suspension and try to move it forwards and backwards **(see illustration)**. Any freeplay in the steering head bearings will be felt as front-to-rear movement of the steering stem. If play is felt in the bearings, adjust them as follows.

Adjustment

5 On SKP/Stalker models, remove the handlebar covers (see Chapter 8). On Runner and Ice models, displace the handlebars (see Chapter 6). On DNA models, displace or remove the helmet compartment to avoid damage should a tool slip (see Chapter 8).
6 Loosen the adjuster locknut using either a C-spanner or a suitable drift located in one of the notches **(see illustration)**. On DNA models, loosen the handlebar clamp bolts and the top yoke clamp bolts, then loosen the steering stem nut **(see illustration)**.
7 Using either the C-spanner or drift, loosen the bearing adjuster nut slightly to release pressure on the bearings, then tighten the nut until all freeplay (front-to-rear movement) is

24.4 Checking for play in the steering head bearings

removed. Check that the steering still moves freely from side-to-side. The object is to set the adjuster nut so that the bearings are under a very light loading, just enough to remove any freeplay. **Note:** *Gilera specify a torque setting for the adjuster nut; however to apply this a Gilera service tool (Part No. 020055Y), or a suitable old socket fabricated into a peg spanner is required and the handlebars, or fork top yoke on DNA models, must be removed (see Chapter 6).*

Caution: Take great care not to apply excessive pressure because this will cause premature failure of the bearings.

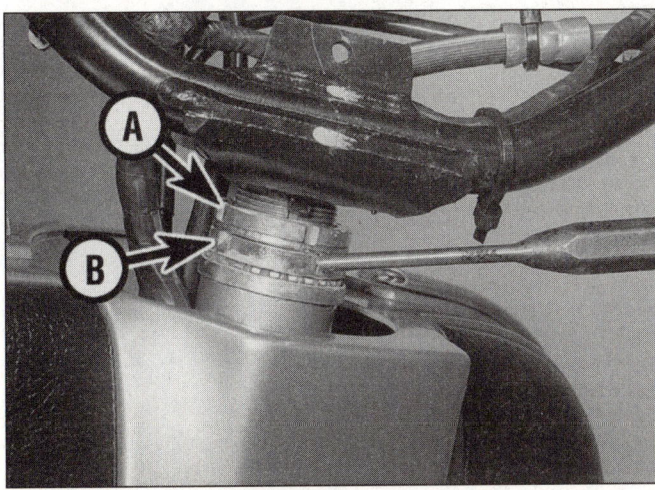

24.6a Loosen the locknut (A), then turn the adjuster (B) using a C-spanner or drift as shown

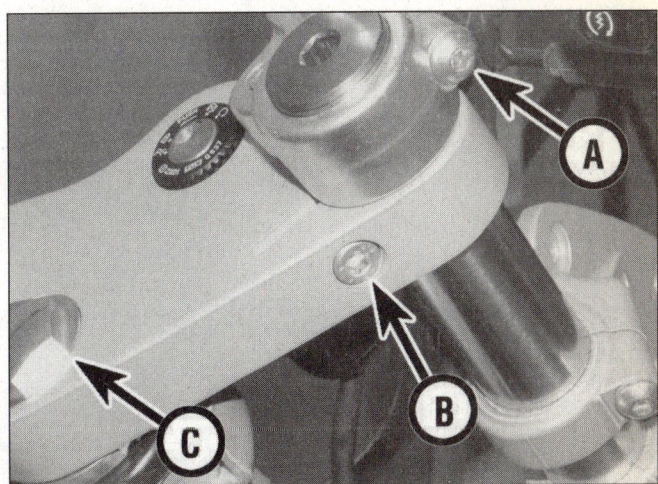

24.6b On DNA models, loosen the handlebar clamp bolts (A), top yoke clamp bolts (B) and steering stem nut (C)

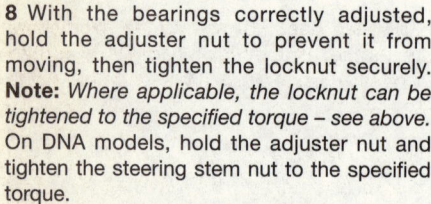

25.3a Check for signs of grease or oil leaks . . .

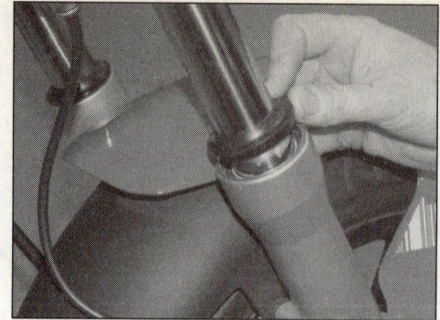

25.3b . . . then lever off the seals

25.5 Corrosion such as this wrecks seals

8 With the bearings correctly adjusted, hold the adjuster nut to prevent it from moving, then tighten the locknut securely. **Note:** *Where applicable, the locknut can be tightened to the specified torque – see above.* On DNA models, hold the adjuster nut and tighten the steering stem nut to the specified torque.

9 Check the bearing adjustment as described above and re-adjust if necessary.

10 Over a period of time the grease in the bearings will harden or may be washed out. Disassemble the steering head for re-greasing of the bearings (see Chapter 6).

25 Suspension check

1 The suspension components must be maintained in top operating condition to ensure rider safety. Loose, worn or damaged suspension parts decrease the scooter's stability and control.

Front suspension

2 While standing alongside the scooter, apply the front brake and push on the handlebars to compress the suspension several times. See if it moves up-and-down smoothly without binding. If binding is felt, the suspension should be disassembled and inspected (see Chapter 6).

3 Inspect the area around the dust seals for signs of grease or oil leaks, then carefully lever off the seals using a flat-bladed screwdriver and inspect the area behind them **(see illustrations)**. If corrosion due to the ingress of water is evident, the seals must be renewed (see Chapter 6).

4 If oil is leaking from upside-down telescopic forks, the seal in the internal damper cartridge has failed and the fork leg must be dismantled and a new cartridge fitted; if oil is leaking from conventional telescopic forks, the oil seal has failed and the fork leg must be dismantled and a new seal fitted (see Chapter 6).

5 The chromed finish on the forks is prone to corrosion and pitting, so it is advisable to keep them as clean as possible and to spray them regularly with a rust inhibitor, otherwise

the seals will not last long **(see illustration)**. If corrosion and pitting is evident, tackle it as early as possible to prevent it getting worse.

6 Check that all the suspension nuts and bolts are tight. Refer to the torque settings specified at the beginning of Chapter 6.

Rear suspension

Note: *For models fitted with twin rear shocks, both shocks must be in good condition. If either is found to be faulty, renew the shocks as a pair.*

7 Inspect the rear shock for fluid leaks and tightness of its mountings. If a leak is found, the shock should be renewed (see Chapter 6).

8 With the aid of an assistant to support the bike, compress the rear suspension several times. It should move up and down freely without binding. If any binding is felt, the worn or faulty component must be identified and renewed. The problem could be due to either the shock absorber or the pivoting swingarm between the engine unit and the frame.

9 Support the scooter so that the rear wheel is off the ground. Grab the engine at the rear and attempt to rock it from side to side – there should be no discernible freeplay between the engine and frame. If there is movement, check that the swingarm and engine mounting bolts are tight, referring to the torque settings specified at the beginning of Chapters 2 and 6, then re-check for movement. If freeplay is still felt, disconnect the rear shock(s) at its lower mounting and check again – any freeplay should be more evident. If there is freeplay, inspect the swingarm for wear (see Chapter 6).

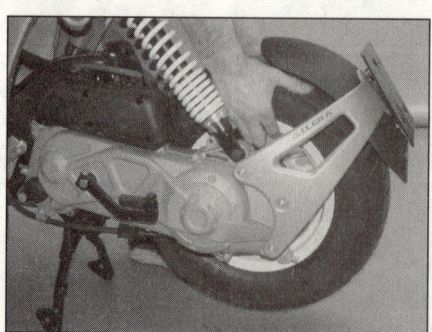

25.10 Checking for freeplay in the rear suspension mountings

10 Next, grasp the top of the rear wheel and pull it upwards – there should be no discernible freeplay before the shock absorber begins to compress **(see illustration)**. Any freeplay indicates worn shock absorber mountings. The worn components must be renewed (see Chapter 6).

26 Throttle cable and oil pump check and adjustment

Two-stroke engined models

1 With the engine stopped, make sure the throttle twistgrip rotates easily from fully closed to fully open with the front wheel turned at various angles. The twistgrip should return automatically from fully open to fully closed when released.

2 If the throttle sticks, this is probably due to a cable fault. Remove the cables (see Chapter 4) and check and lubricate them using the same method as for the brake cable (see Section 4). Install the cables, making sure they are correctly routed. If this fails to improve the operation of the throttle, the cable(s) must be renewed. Note that in very rare cases the fault could lie in the carburettor or oil pump rather than the cable (see Chapters 4 or 2A respectively).

3 With the throttle operating smoothly, check for a small amount of freeplay in the twistgrip before the throttle opens **(see illustration)**. If there is insufficient or excessive freeplay, loosen the locknut on the cable adjuster and

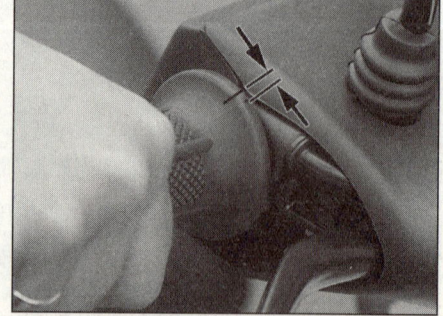

26.3a Feel for a small amount of freeplay in the throttle twistgrip

26.3b Loosen the locknut and turn the adjuster (arrowed) – Runner shown

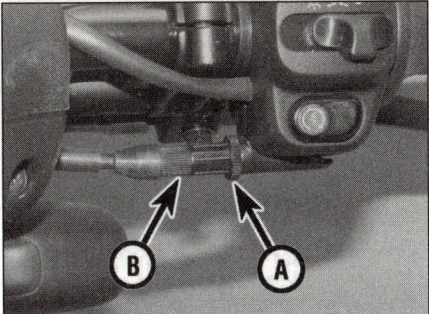

26.3c Loosen the locknut (A) and turn the adjuster (B) as required – Ice shown

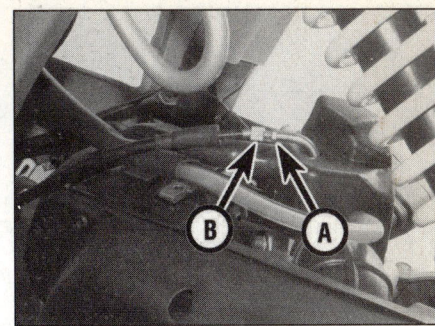

26.4 Loosen the locknut (A) and turn the adjuster (B) as required

turn the adjuster until freeplay is just evident, then retighten the locknut (see illustrations). **Note:** *It may be necessary to remove the handlebar covers to access the cable adjuster (see Chapter 8).* If the adjuster has reached its limit of adjustment, renew the cable (see Chapter 4). If the idle speed cannot be set properly, this could be due to incorrect adjustment of the cable. Turn the adjuster in – if the idle speed falls as you do, this is the case. Set the adjuster so that a small amount of freeplay is evident.

4 There should be no freeplay in the cable from the splitter to the carburettor. If any is evident, pull back the rubber boot at the carburettor end and loosen the locknut on the adjuster. Turn the adjuster out until all freeplay has just been removed, but not so far as to start to lift the throttle slide in the carburettor **(see illustration)**. Rotate the twistgrip to check the operation of the cable, then tighten the locknut and replace the boot.

5 Remove the plug from the transmission cover **(see illustration 1.8c)**. With the throttle closed, check that the cable from the splitter to the oil pump is correctly adjusted so that the scribe mark on the pump cam aligns with the mark on the pump body **(see illustration)**. If they are not aligned, loosen the cable adjuster locknut on the transmission housing, turn the adjuster in or out as required until the marks align, then retighten the locknut **(see illustration)**.

6 Start the engine and check that the idle speed does not rise as the handlebars are turned. If it does, a cable is routed incorrectly. Correct the problem before riding the scooter.

Four-stroke engined models

7 With the engine stopped, make sure the throttle twistgrip rotates easily from fully closed to fully open with the front wheel turned at various angles. The twistgrip should return automatically from fully open to fully closed when released.

8 If the throttle sticks, this is probably due to a cable fault. Remove the cable (see Chapter 4) and lubricate it using the same method as for the brake cable (see Section 4). Install the cable, making sure it is correctly routed. If this fails to improve the operation of the throttle, the cable must be renewed. Note that in very rare cases the fault could lie in the carburettor rather than the cable, necessitating the removal of the carburettor (see Chapter 4).

9 With the throttle operating smoothly, check for a small amount of freeplay in the twistgrip before the throttle opens **(see illustration 26.3a)**. If there is insufficient or excessive freeplay, loosen the locknut on the cable adjuster and turn the adjuster until freeplay is just evident, then retighten the locknut **(see illustration 26.3b)**. **Note:** *It may be necessary to remove the handlebar covers to access the cable adjuster (see Chapter 8).* If the adjuster has reached its limit of adjustment, renew the cable (see Chapter 4). If the idle speed cannot be set properly, this could be due to incorrect adjustment of the cable. Turn the adjuster in – if the idle speed falls as you do, this is the case. Set the adjuster so that a small amount of freeplay is evident.

10 Start the engine and check that the

idle speed does not rise as the handlebars are turned. If it does, the cable is routed incorrectly. Correct the problem before riding the scooter.

27 Valve clearances check and adjustment – four-stroke engine

Note: *On DNA models, access to the top of the engine is extremely restricted. If a number of areas require attention, removal of the engine is recommended, as it is easy to do so (see Chapter 2C).*

1 The engine must be completely cold for this maintenance procedure, so let the machine sit overnight before beginning. Remove any body panels necessary to gain access to the alternator and cylinder head (see Chapter 8).

2 Remove the spark plug (see Section 21).

3 Remove the valve cover (see Chapter 2C). Discard the cover gasket or O-ring as a new one must be fitted on reassembly.

4 Turn the engine in a clockwise direction until the timing mark on the camshaft sprocket aligns with the timing mark on the camshaft holder **(see illustration)**; you can do this by removing the alternator cover and rotating the crankshaft via the rotor retaining nut (see Chapter 2C). **Note:** *It is not necessary to remove the water pump or disconnect the coolant hoses in order to displace the cover.* If there are two timing marks on the camshaft sprocket, ensure you use the correct 4V mark.

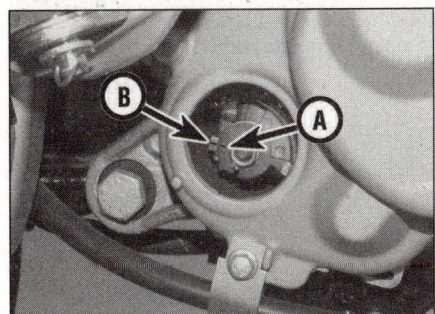

26.5a The mark on the cam (A) should align with the mark (B) on the body

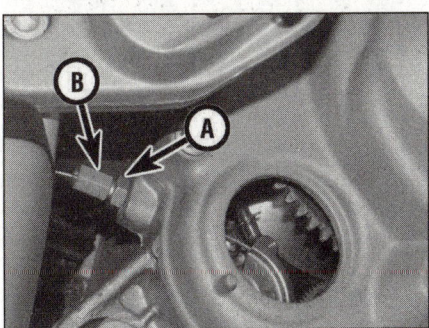

26.5b Loosen the locknut (A) and turn the adjuster (B) as required

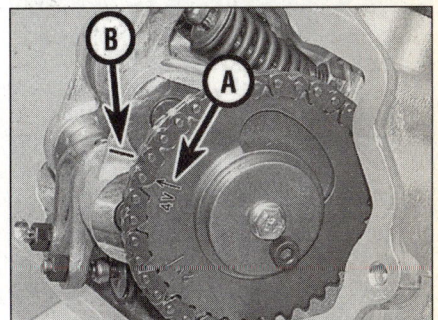

27.4 Align the mark on the sprocket (A) with the mark on the camshaft holder (B)

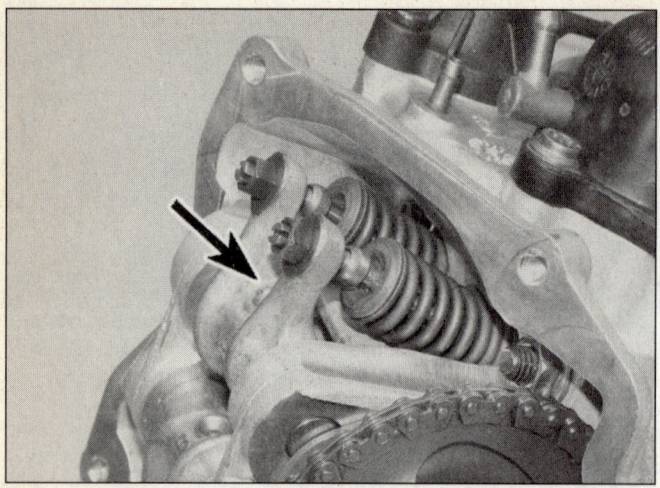

27.5 Check for clearance on the rocker arms (arrowed) with the valves closed

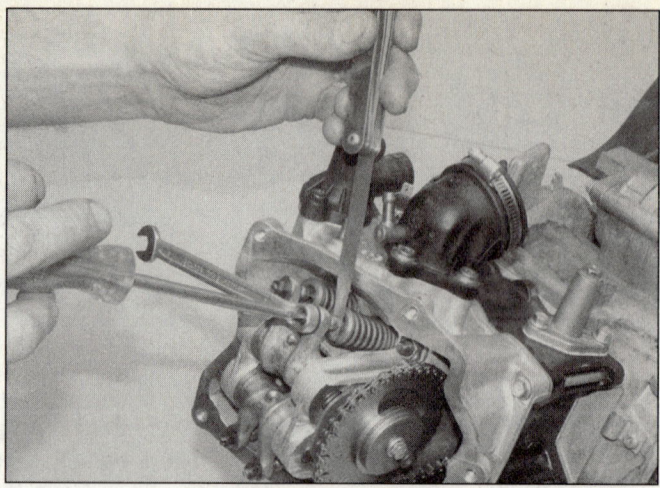

27.7 The feeler gauge should be a firm sliding fit between the adjuster and the valve stem

5 The valve clearances are checked with the engine at top dead centre (TDC) on its compression stroke; i.e. the valves are closed and a small clearance can be felt at each rocker arm **(see illustration)**. If the engine is not on its compression stroke, rotate the crankshaft clockwise one full turn (360°) so that the camshaft sprocket mark once again aligns with that on the camshaft holder.

6 Insert a feeler gauge of the same thickness as the correct valve clearance (see Specifications) between the rocker arm and stem of each valve and check that it is a firm sliding fit – you should feel a slight drag when the you pull the gauge out.

7 If the clearance is either too small or too large, loosen the locknut and turn the adjuster until a firm sliding fit is obtained, then tighten

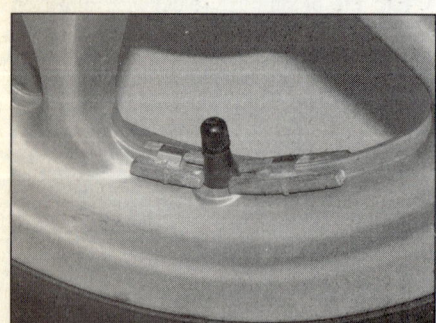

29.4 Check that the wheel weights are firmly attached

the locknut securely, making sure the adjuster does not turn as you do so **(see illustration)**. Re-check the clearances.

8 Apply some engine oil to the valve assemblies, rockers and camshaft before installing the valve cover and fit a new cover gasket or O-ring. Install the remaining components in the reverse order of removal.

28 Variator and clutch check

Variator – all models

1 Remove the drive pulley and the variator (see Chapter 2D). Disassemble the variator and check all components for wear as described. If applicable, grease the rollers and the roller tracks in the housing. **Note:** *If required, later non-greased rollers can be fitted in the earlier type variator, but the variator should be cleaned thoroughly and the rollers should not be greased.*

Clutch – two-stroke models

2 Remove the clutch and driven pulley assembly (see Chapter 2D). Disassemble the pulley assembly and check all the components as described, paying particular attention to the bearing surfaces of the inner and outer pulley halves, and the condition of the needle roller bearing.

29 Wheels and tyres check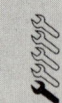

Wheels

1 Cast wheels are virtually maintenance free, but they should be kept clean and checked periodically for cracks and other damage. Never attempt to repair damaged cast wheels; they must be replaced with new ones. Avoid using a high pressure cleaner on the wheel bearing area.

2 Refer to Chapter 7 and check the wheel runout and alignment.

3 Wheel bearings will wear over a period of time and result in handling problems. Support the machine on its centre stand and check for any play in the bearings (see Chapter 7, Section 15).

4 Check the valve rubber for signs of damage or deterioration and have it renewed if necessary. Also, make sure the valve cap is in place and tight. If fitted, check that the wheel weights are firmly attached to the rim **(see illustration)**.

Tyres

5 Check the tyre condition and tread depth thoroughly – see *Daily (pre-ride) checks*. Check that the directional arrow on the tyre sidewall is pointing in the normal direction of wheel rotation.

Chapter 2 Part A:
Air-cooled two-stroke engines (SKP/Stalker, Ice)

Refer to the beginning of Chapter 1 for model identification details

Contents

Degrees of difficulty

Easy, suitable for novice with little experience		Fairly easy, suitable for beginner with some experience		Fairly difficult, suitable for competent DIY mechanic	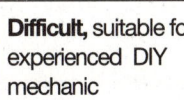	Difficult, suitable for experienced DIY mechanic		Very difficult, suitable for expert DIY or professional	

Specifications

General

Type	Single cylinder two-stroke
Capacity..	49.4 cc
Bore	40.0 mm
Stroke..	39.3 mm
Compression ratio	
SKP/Stalker	9.5:1 to 11.2:1
Ice...	9.4:1 to 10.4:1

Cylinder bore

SKP/Stalker
  Standard

Size code A..	39.990 mm
Size code B	39.995 mm
Size code C	40.000 mm
Size code D	40.005 mm
Size code E	40.010 mm
1st oversize..	40.190 to 40.210 mm
2nd oversize	40.390 to 40.410 mm

Ice
  Standard

Size code M	40.005 to 40.012mm
Size code N	40.012 to 40.019 mm
Size code O	40.019 to 40.026 mm
Size code P...	40.026 to 40.033 mm
1st oversize	
Size code M1	40.205 to 40.212 mm
Size code N1	40.212 to 40.219 mm
Size code O1	40.219 to 40.226 mm
Size code P1..	40.226 to 40.233 mm
2nd oversize	
Size code M2	40.405 to 40.412 mm
Size code N2	40.412 to 40.419 mm
Size code O2	40.419 to 40.426 mm
Size code P2..	40.426 to 40.433 mm

Connecting rod

Small-end internal diameter

Size I	17.007 to 17.011 mm
Size II	17.003 to 17.007 mm
Size III	16.999 to 17.003 mm

Piston

Piston diameter (measured 25 mm down from lower ring groove, at 90° to piston pin axis)

SKP/Stalker up to 2004

Standard

Size code A	39.940 mm
Size code B	39.945 mm
Size code C	39.050 mm
Size code D	39.955 mm
Size code E	39.960 mm
1st oversize	40.140 to 40.160 mm
2nd oversize	40.340 to 40.360 mm
Piston-to-bore clearance	0.045 to 0.055 mm
Piston pin diameter	12.001 to 12.005 mm

Ice and 2005-on Stalker

Standard

Size code M	39.943 to 39.950 mm
Size code N	39.950 to 39.957 mm
Size code O	39.957 to 39.964 mm
Size code P	39.964 to 39.971 mm

1st oversize

Size code M1	40.143 to 40.150 mm
Size code N1	40.150 to 40.157 mm
Size code O1	40.157 to 40.164 mm
Size code P1	40.164 to 40.171 mm

2nd oversize

Size code M2	40.343 to 40.350 mm
Size code N2	40.350 to 40.357 mm
Size code O2	40.357 to 40.364 mm
Size code P2	40.364 to 40.371 mm
Piston-to-bore clearance	0.055 to 0.069 mm
Piston pin diameter	12.001 to 12.005 mm

Piston rings

Ring end gap (installed)	0.10 to 0.25 mm

Crankshaft

Runout (max)

At middle and left-hand end	0.03 mm
At right-hand end	0.02 mm
Big-end side clearance	0.25 to 0.50 mm
Endfloat	0.03 to 0.09 mm

Torque settings

Alternator rotor nut	40 to 44 Nm
Crankcase bolts	12 to 13 Nm
Cylinder head nuts	10 to 11 Nm
Engine front mounting bolt	33 to 41 Nm
Rear shock absorber lower mounting bolt	33 to 41 Nm

1 General information

The engine unit is a single cylinder two-stroke, with fan assisted air cooling. The fan is mounted on the alternator rotor, which is on the right-hand end of the crankshaft. The crankshaft assembly is pressed, incorporating the connecting rod, with the big-end running on the crankpin on a needle roller bearing. The piston also runs on a needle roller bearing fitted in the small-end of the connecting rod. The crankshaft runs in caged ball main bearings. The crankcase divides vertically.

Later engines carry the 'Hi-Per2' name, denoting that the scooter is fitted with a catalytic converter and secondary air system. Some models will have a 'hi-per2' decal on the bodywork.

2 Operations possible with the engine in the frame

All components and assemblies, with the exception of the crankshaft/connecting rod assembly and its bearings, can be worked on without having to remove the engine/transmission unit from the frame. If however, a number of areas require attention at the same time, removal of the engine is recommended, as it is easy to do so.

3 Operations requiring engine removal

To access the crankshaft and connecting rod and its bearings, the engine must be removed from the frame and the crankcase halves separated.

4 Major engine repair – general note

1 It is not always easy to determine when or if an engine should be completely overhauled, as a number of factors must be considered.
2 High mileage is not necessarily an indication that an overhaul is needed, while low mileage, on the other hand, does not preclude the need for an overhaul. Frequency of servicing is probably the single most important consideration. An engine that has regular and frequent maintenance will most likely give many miles of reliable service. Conversely, a neglected engine, or one which has not been run in properly, may require an overhaul very early in its life.
3 If the engine is making obvious knocking or rumbling noises, the connecting rod and/or main bearings are probably at fault.
4 Loss of power, rough running, excessive noise and high fuel consumption rates may also point to the need for an overhaul, especially if they are all present at the same time. If a complete service as detailed in Chapter 1 does not remedy the situation, major mechanical work is the only solution.
5 An engine overhaul generally involves restoring the internal parts to the specifications of a new engine. This may require fitting new piston rings and crankcase seals, or, after a high mileage, reboring the cylinder and fitting a new piston. The end result should be a like-new engine that will give as many trouble-free miles as the original.

6 Before beginning the engine overhaul, read through the related procedures to familiarise yourself with the scope and requirements of the job. Overhauling an engine is not all that difficult, but it is time consuming. Check on the availability of parts and make sure that any necessary special tools and materials are obtained in advance.
7 Most work can be done with typical workshop hand tools, although, if required, Gilera produce a number of service tools for specific purposes such as removing the alternator rotor, disassembling the clutch and separating the crankcase halves. Precision measuring tools are required for inspecting parts to determine if they must be renewed. Alternatively, a dealer will handle the inspection of parts and offer advice concerning reconditioning and replacement. As a general rule, time is the primary cost of an overhaul so it does not pay to install worn or substandard parts.
8 As a final note, to ensure maximum life and minimum trouble from a rebuilt engine, everything must be assembled with care in a spotlessly clean environment.

5 Engine/transmission unit – removal and installation

Caution: The engine is not heavy, however engine removal and installation should be carried out with the aid of an assistant; personal injury or damage could occur if the engine falls or is dropped.

Removal

1 Support the scooter securely in an upright position. Work can be made easier by raising the machine to a suitable working height on an hydraulic ramp or a suitable platform. Make sure the scooter is secure and will not topple over.
2 Remove the bodywork as required according to model (see Chapter 8). On Ice models, remove the engine top cover.
3 If the engine is dirty, particularly around its mountings, wash it thoroughly before starting any major dismantling work. This will make work much easier and rule out the possibility of dirt falling inside.

4 Disconnect the battery negative terminal (see Chapter 9). Trace the wiring from the alternator/pulse generator coil on the right-hand side of the engine and disconnect it at the connector(s). Free the wiring from any clips on the engine. Pull the spark plug cap off the plug.
5 Either remove the carburettor, leaving the throttle cable attached if required, or just disconnect the fuel hose and vacuum hose from the unions on the carburettor and intake duct respectively, and disconnect the throttle cable (see Chapter 4). Where fitted, disconnect the automatic choke wiring connector. Disconnect the oil hose from the oil tank and clamp the hose to prevent oil leakage, and disconnect the cable from the oil pump (see Chapter 4).
6 Either remove the starter motor if required, or disconnect the starter motor leads (see Chapter 9).
7 Remove the air filter housing (see Chapter 4).
8 Remove the exhaust system (see Chapter 4).
9 If required, remove the rear wheel (see Chapter 7). **Note:** *The rear wheel and centre stand provide a convenient support for the engine unit once it is removed from the scooter. However, it is useful to loosen the rear wheel nut at this point before disconnecting the rear brake.*
10 On models with a rear drum brake, disconnect the inner brake cable from the brake arm and release the cable from the clips on the underside of the drive belt cover (see Chapter 7). On models with a disc rear brake, displace the brake caliper and release the brake hose from the clips on the underside of the drive belt cover (see Chapter 7).
11 Remove the bolt securing the rear shock absorber to the transmission casing and lower the engine unit carefully **(see illustration)**. If the rear wheel has been removed support the engine unit on a wood block to prevent damage to the casing. If required, undo the nut securing the upper end of the shock to the frame and remove the shock.
12 Check that all wiring, cables and hoses are clear of the engine/transmission unit. Undo the nut then remove the front engine mounting bolt and manoeuvre the engine back and out of the frame **(see illustrations)**.

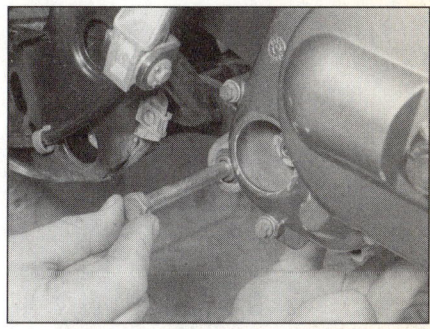

5.11 Remove the nut (A) and withdraw the shock absorber bolt (B)

5.12a Remove the nut (arrowed) . . .

5.12b . . . and withdraw the bolt

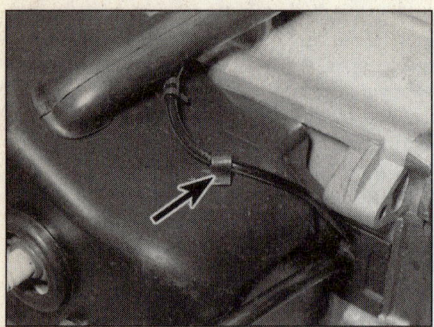

7.2a Free the oil pipe clip (arrowed) . . .

7.2b . . . then remove the screws and lift off the cowling

Installation

13 Installation is the reverse of removal, noting the following points:

• Make sure no wires, cables or hoses become trapped between the engine/transmission unit and the frame when installing the unit.

• Tighten the engine mounting bolt and shock absorber bolt to the torque settings specified at the beginning of this Chapter.

• Use new gaskets on the exhaust pipe connections, and tighten the exhaust mounting nuts securely, having applied a smear of copper-based grease to their threads to aid future removal.

• Make sure all wires, cables and hoses are correctly routed and connected, and secured by any clips or ties.

• Adjust the throttle and oil pump cable, and the rear brake cable where fitted (see Chapter 1).

6 Disassembly and reassembly – general information

Disassembly

1 Before disassembling the engine, the external surfaces of the unit should be thoroughly cleaned and degreased. This will prevent contamination of the engine internals, and will also make working a lot easier and cleaner. A high flash-point solvent, such as paraffin can be used, or better still,

a proprietary engine degreaser such as Gunk. Use old paintbrushes and toothbrushes to work the solvent into the various recesses of the engine casings. Take care to exclude solvent or water from the electrical components and inlet and exhaust ports.

⚠ **Warning: The use of petrol (gasoline) as a cleaning agent should be avoided because of the risk of fire.**

2 When clean and dry, arrange the unit on the workbench, leaving suitable clear area for working. Gather a selection of small containers and plastic bags so that parts can be grouped together in an easily identifiable manner. Some paper and a pen should be on hand to permit notes to be made and labels attached where necessary. A supply of clean rag is also required.

3 Before commencing work, read through the appropriate section so that some idea of the necessary procedure can be gained. When removing components it should be noted that great force is seldom required, unless specified. In many cases, a component's reluctance to be removed is indicative of an incorrect approach or removal method – if in any doubt, re-check with the text.

4 When disassembling the engine, keep 'mated' parts that have been in contact with each other during engine operation together. These 'mated' parts must be reused or renewed as an assembly.

5 Complete engine disassembly should be done in the following general order with reference to the appropriate Sections. Refer

to Chapter 2D for details of transmission components disassembly.

• Remove the cylinder head
• Remove the cylinder
• Remove the piston
• Remove the alternator
• Remove the variator (see Chapter 2D)
• Remove the starter motor (see Chapter 9)
• Remove the oil pump and drive belt
• Remove the reed valve (see Chapter 4)
• Separate the crankcase halves
• Remove the crankshaft

Reassembly

6 Reassemble the engine in the reverse order of disassembly.

7 Cylinder head

Note: *This procedure can be carried out with the engine in the frame. If the engine has been removed, ignore the steps which don't apply.*
Caution: The engine must be completely cool before beginning this procedure or the cylinder head may become warped.

Removal

1 Remove the engine access panels and, if required, the side panels; on Ice models, undo the three screws securing the engine top cover and remove the cover (see Chapter 8).

2 Pull out the clip securing the oil hose to the engine cowling **(see illustration)**. Undo the two screws securing the cowling and remove it, noting how it fits **(see illustration)**. Where fitted, detach the carburettor air duct from the cowling.

3 Remove the cooling fan cowling (see Section 11).

4 Note the position of the two cylinder head nuts which are threaded in the top to accept the cowling screws, then unscrew all four head nuts evenly and a little at a time in a criss-cross sequence until they are all loose and remove them **(see illustration)**.

5 Draw the head off the cylinder studs **(see illustration)**. If the head is stuck, tap around the joint face between the head and the cylinder with a soft-faced mallet to free it. Do not attempt to free the head by inserting a screwdriver between the head and cylinder – you'll damage the sealing surfaces. No cylinder head gasket is fitted as standard, the machined face of the cylinder head fits directly against the machined face of the cylinder. It may be found, however, that a gasket is fitted on aftermarket top-end kits.

Inspection

6 Remove all accumulated carbon from the cylinder head carefully using a blunt scraper.
Caution: The cylinder head and piston are made of aluminium which is relatively soft. Take great care not to gouge or score the surface when scraping.

7.4 Unscrew the cylinder head nuts

7.5 Draw the head off the cylinder studs

7 Rotate the cooling fan until the piston is at the very top of its stroke. Smear grease around the edge of the piston to trap any particles of carbon, then scrape the piston crown clean, taking care not to score or gouge it or the cylinder bore.

8 Clean out the carbon, then lower the piston and wipe away the grease and any remaining particles. Also scrape clean the intake and exhaust ports in the cylinder. If the exhaust port is heavily coked, the exhaust system will probably also require cleaning (see Chapter 4).

 **HAYNES HINT** *Finish the piston crown and the inside of the cylinder head off using a metal polish. A shiny surface is more resistant to the build-up of carbon deposits.*

9 Inspect the head very carefully for cracks and other damage. If cracks are found, a new head will be required.

10 Check the mating surfaces on the cylinder head and cylinder for signs of leakage, which could indicate that the head is warped. Using a precision straight-edge, check the head mating surface for warpage. Check vertically, horizontally and diagonally across the head, making four checks in all.

Installation

11 Lubricate the cylinder bore with the recommended two-stroke oil.

12 Ensure both cylinder head and cylinder mating surfaces are clean, then carefully fit the cylinder head onto the cylinder **(see illustration 7.5)**.

13 Install the four nuts, making sure the special nuts are positioned to accept the cowling screws, and tighten them all finger-tight **(see illustration)**. Now tighten them evenly and a little at a time in a criss-cross pattern to the torque setting specified at the beginning of this Chapter **(see illustration)**.

14 Install the remaining components in the reverse order of removal, ensuring the engine and cooling fan cowling are correctly aligned.

8 Cylinder

Note: *This procedure can be carried out with the engine in the frame.*

Removal

1 Remove the exhaust system (see Chapter 4) and the cylinder head (see Section 7).

2 Lift the cylinder up off the studs, supporting the piston as it becomes accessible to prevent it hitting the crankcase **(see illustration)**. If the cylinder is stuck, tap around the joint face between the cylinder and the crankcase with a soft-faced mallet to free it. Don't attempt

7.13a Fit the nuts in the correct positions . . .

to free the cylinder by inserting a screwdriver between it and the crankcase – you'll damage the sealing surfaces. When the cylinder is removed, stuff a clean rag into the crankcase opening to prevent anything falling inside.

3 Remove the gasket and discard it as a new one must be used on reassembly **(see illustration)**.

4 Scrape off any carbon deposits that may have formed in the exhaust port, then wash the cylinder with a suitable solvent and dry it thoroughly. Compressed air will speed the drying process and ensure that all holes and recesses are clean.

Inspection

5 Check the cylinder bore carefully for scratches and score marks. A rebore will be necessary to remove any deep scores (see Step 8).

6 Using a telescoping gauge and a micrometer, check the dimensions of the cylinder to assess the amount of wear, taper and ovality. Measure near the top (but below the level of the top piston ring at TDC), centre and bottom (but above the level of the bottom ring at BDC) of the bore both parallel to and across the crankshaft axis **(see illustration)**. Calculate any differences between the measurements to determine any taper or ovality in the bore. Compare the results to the cylinder bore specifications at the beginning of this Chapter.

7 Calculate the piston-to-bore clearance by subtracting the piston diameter (see Section 9) from the bore diameter. On SKP/Stalker models, measure the bore 20 mm from the top across the crankshaft axis; on Ice models,

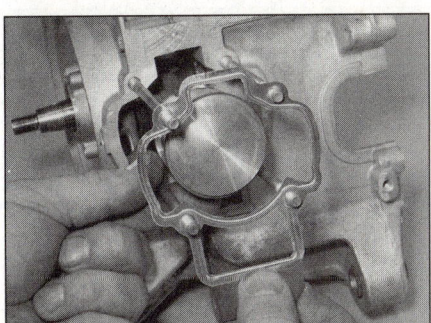
8.3 Remove the gasket and discard it

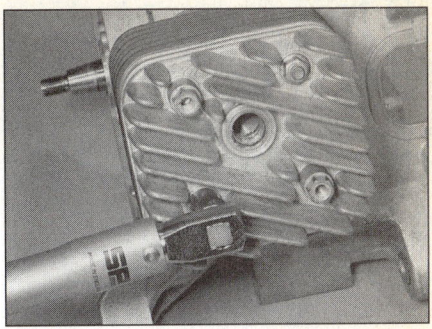
7.13b . . . then tighten them as described to the specified torque

measure the bore 15 mm from the top across the crankshaft axis. If the cylinder is in good condition and the piston-to-bore clearance is within specifications, the cylinder can be re-used.

8 If the bore is tapered, oval, or worn, badly scratched, scuffed or scored, have it rebored by a Gilera dealer or motorcycle engineer. If the cylinder is rebored, it will require an oversize piston and rings. If the cylinder has already been rebored to the maximum oversize and is worn or damaged, the cylinder must be renewed. **Note:** *Cylinders and pistons are size coded during manufacture and it is important that they are of the same size code. Gilera list five size codes (A to E) for the SKP/Stalker engine and four (M, N, O and P) for the Ice; see the specifications at the beginning of this Chapter. The size code is stamped in the gasket surface at the top or base of the cylinder, and in the piston crown.*

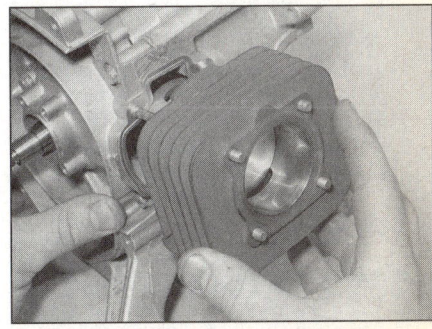
8.2 Draw the cylinder up off the studs

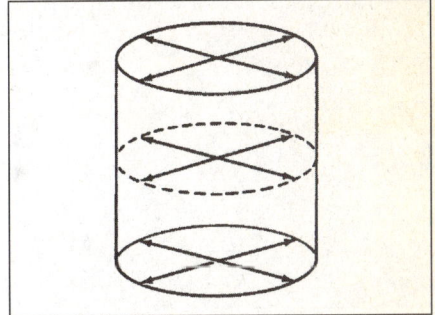
8.6 Measure the cylinder bore in the directions shown

8.11 Fit the cylinder onto the studs

When purchasing a new cylinder or piston, always supply the size code.

9 Check that the cylinder head studs are tight in the crankcase halves. If any are loose, remove them and clean their threads. Apply a suitable permanent thread locking compound and tighten them securely.

Installation

10 Remove any rag from the crankcase mouth. Lay the new base gasket in place on the crankcase making sure it is the correct way round **(see illustration 8.3)**. Never re-use the old gasket – it will have become compressed.

11 Check that the piston rings are correctly positioned so that the locating pin in each piston ring groove is between the open ends of the ring **(see illustration 10.6)**. Lubricate the cylinder bore, piston and piston rings, and the connecting rod big and small ends, with

two-stroke oil, then fit the cylinder down over the studs until the piston crown fits into the bore **(see illustration)**.

12 Gently push down on the cylinder, making sure the piston enters the bore squarely and does not get cocked sideways. Carefully compress and feed each ring into the bore as the cylinder is lowered, taking care that they do not rotate out of position. Do not use force if the cylinder appears to be stuck as the piston and/or rings will be damaged.

13 When the piston is correctly installed in the cylinder, press the cylinder down onto the base gasket.

14 Install the remaining components in the reverse order of removal.

9 Piston

Note: This procedure can be carried out with the engine in the frame.

Removal

1 Remove the cylinder and stuff a clean rag into the crankcase opening around the piston to prevent anything falling inside (see Section 8).

2 The piston top should be marked with an arrow which faces towards the exhaust. If this is not visible, mark the piston accordingly so that it can be installed the correct way round. Note that the arrow may not be visible until the carbon deposits have been scraped off and the piston cleaned.

3 Carefully prise the circlip out from one side of the piston using needle-nose pliers or a small flat-bladed screwdriver inserted into the notch **(see illustration)**. Check for burring around the circlip groove and remove any with a very fine file or penknife blade, then push the piston pin out from the other side and remove the piston from the connecting rod **(see illustration)**. Use a socket extension to push the piston pin out if required. Remove the other circlip and discard them both as new ones must be used on reassembly.

> **HAYNES HiNT**
> *To prevent the circlip from flying away or from dropping into the crankcase, pass a rod or screwdriver with a greater diameter than the gap between the circlip ends, through the piston pin. This will trap the circlip if it springs out.*

> **HAYNES HiNT**
> *If a piston pin is a tight fit in the piston bosses, heat the piston gently with a hot air gun – this will expand the alloy piston sufficiently to release its grip on the pin.*

4 The connecting rod small-end bearing is a loose fit in the rod; remove it for safekeeping, noting which way round it fits **(see illustration)**.

5 Before the inspection process can be carried out, the piston rings must be removed and the piston must be cleaned. **Note:** *If the cylinder is being renewed or rebored, piston inspection can be overlooked as a new one will be fitted.* The piston rings can be removed by hand or with an old feeler gauge blade **(see illustrations)**. Take care not to expand the rings any more than is necessary and do not nick or gouge the piston in the process.

6 Note which way up each ring fits and in which groove as they must be installed in their original positions if being re-used. The upper surface of each ring should be marked at one end (see Section 10). **Note:** *It is good practice to renew the piston rings when an engine is being overhauled. Ensure that the piston and bore are serviceable before purchasing new rings.*

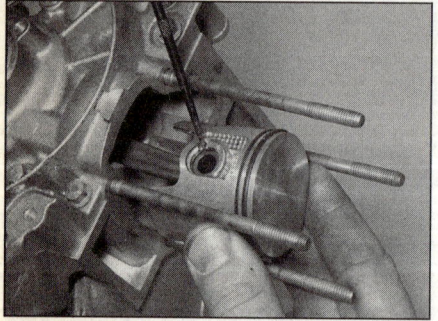

9.3a Remove the circlip . . .

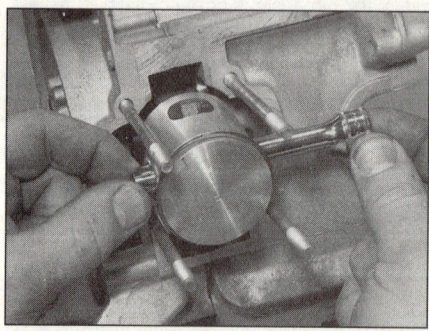

9.3b . . . and push out the piston pin, using a socket extension if required

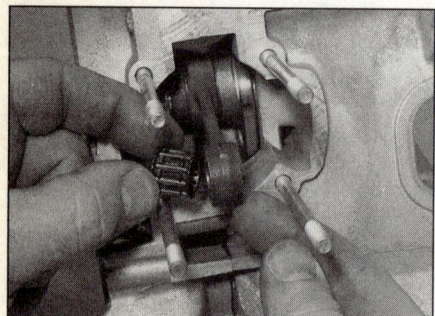

9.4 Remove the needle roller bearing, noting which way round it fits

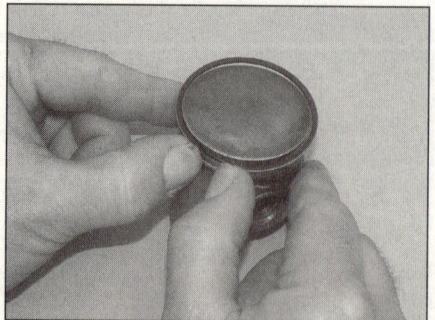

9.5a Remove the piston rings carefully using your thumbs . . .

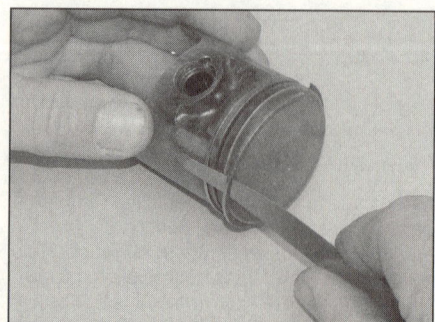

9.5b . . . or a thin blade

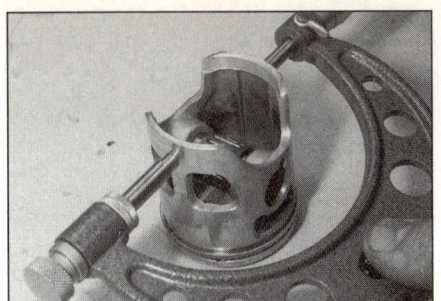

9.12 Measuring the piston diameter at the specified distance from the lower ring groove

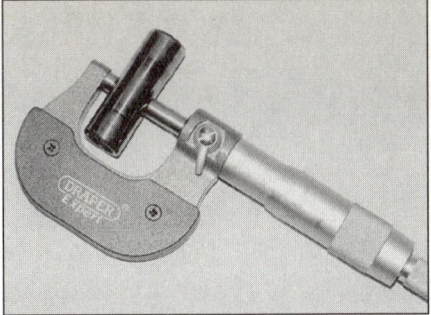

9.14 Measuring the external diameter of the piston pin

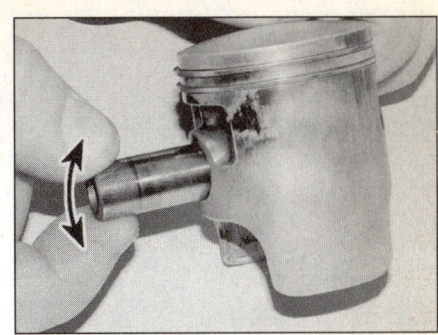

9.15 Checking for freeplay between the piston and the piston pin

7 Clean all traces of carbon from the top of the piston. A hand-held wire brush or a piece of fine emery cloth can be used once most of the deposits have been scraped away. Do not, under any circumstances, use a wire brush mounted in a drill motor; the piston material is soft and is easily damaged.

8 Use a piston ring groove cleaning tool to remove any carbon deposits from the ring grooves. If a tool is not available, a piece broken off an old ring will do the job. Be very careful to remove only the carbon deposits. Do not remove any metal and do not nick or gouge the sides of the ring grooves.

9 Once the carbon has been removed, clean the piston with a suitable solvent and dry it thoroughly. If the identification previously marked on the piston is cleaned off, be sure to re-mark it correctly.

Inspection

10 Inspect the piston for cracks around the skirt, at the pin bosses and at the ring lands. Check that the circlip grooves are not damaged. Normal piston wear appears as even, vertical wear on the thrust surfaces of the piston and slight looseness of the top ring in its groove. If the skirt is scored or scuffed, the engine may have been suffering from overheating and/or abnormal combustion, which caused excessively high operating temperatures.

11 A hole in the top of the piston, in one extreme, or burned areas around the edge of the piston crown, indicate that pre-ignition

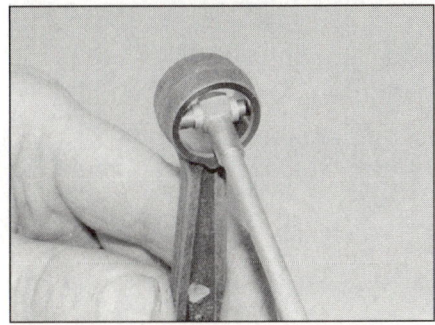

9.16 Measuring the internal diameter of the connecting rod small-end

or knocking under load have occurred. If you find evidence of any problems the cause must be corrected or the damage will occur again. Refer to Chapter 4 for carburation checks and Chapter 5 for ignition checks.

12 Check the piston-to-bore clearance by measuring the bore (see Section 8) and the piston diameter. Using a micrometer, measure the piston 25 mm down from the bottom of the lower piston ring groove and at 90° to the piston pin axis **(see illustration)**. Subtract the piston diameter from the bore diameter to obtain the clearance. If it is greater than the specified figure, check whether it is the bore or piston that is worn the most. If the bore is good, install a new piston and rings.

13 If a new piston is to be fitted, ensure the correct size of piston is ordered. Compare the piston size with the specifications at the beginning of this Chapter to determine if the piston is standard, or oversize, indicating a rebored cylinder. Note the piston size code. The size code is stamped in the piston crown, and the same size code is stamped in the gasket surface at the top or base of the cylinder. When purchasing a new piston, always supply the size code.

14 Use a micrometer to measure the piston pin in the middle, where it runs in the small-end bearing, and at each end where it runs in the piston **(see illustration)**. Compare the results with the Specifications; if the pin is worn it must be renewed.

15 If the piston pin is good, lubricate it with clean two-stroke oil, then insert it into the piston and check for any freeplay between the two **(see illustration)**. There should be no freeplay.

16 Check the condition of the connecting rod small-end bearing. A worn small-end bearing will produce a metallic rattle, most audible when the engine is under load, and increasing as engine speed rises. This should not be confused with big-end bearing wear, which produces a pronounced knocking noise. Inspect the bearing rollers and ensure there are no flat spots or pitting. Assemble the bearing and the piston pin on the connecting rod; there should be no discernible freeplay between the piston pin,

the bearing and the connecting rod. If the piston pin is good (see Step 14), measure the internal diameter of the small-end with a telescoping gauge and compare the result to the Specifications **(see illustration)**. If the small-end is worn, the connecting rod and crankshaft assembly must be renewed (see Section 15). If the small-end is good, fit a new bearing.

17 Ensure that the correct bearing is fitted. A mark on the connecting rod, either a I, II or III indicates the small-end size, and this mark must be matched with a similar mark on the new bearing, or by a colour code.

Connecting rod marked I:
   bearing colour copper
Connecting rod marked II:
   bearing colour blue
Connecting rod marked III:
   bearing colour white

Installation

18 Inspect and install the piston rings (see Section 10).

19 Lubricate the piston pin, the piston pin bore in the piston and the small-end bearing with two-stroke oil. Install the bearing in the connecting rod.

20 Install a new circlip in one side of the piston (do not re-use old circlips). Line up the piston on the connecting rod, making sure the arrow on the piston crown faces towards the exhaust, and insert the piston pin from the other side **(see illustrations)**. Secure the pin

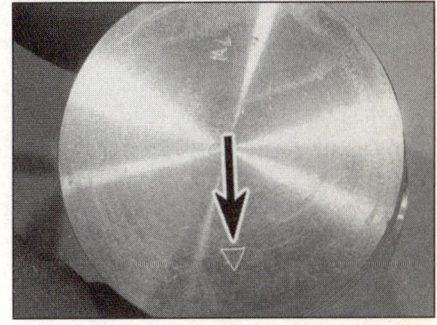

9.20a Make sure the arrow on the piston faces the exhaust port

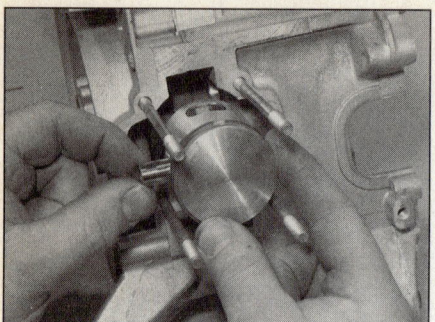

9.20b Line up the piston and insert the pin . . .

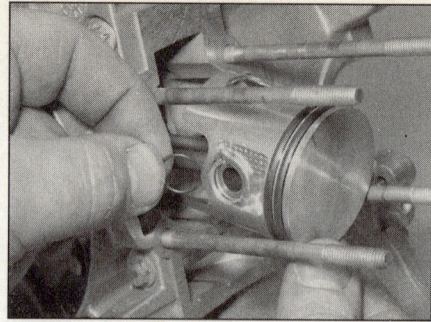

9.20c . . . and secure it with the circlip

7 The upper surface of each ring should be marked at one end. Install the lower ring first. Make sure that the identification letter near the end gap is facing up. Fit the ring into the lower groove in the piston. Do not expand the ring any more than is necessary to slide it into place **(see illustrations 9.5a and 9.5b)**.

8 Now install the top ring into the top groove in the piston. Make sure the identification letter near the end gap is facing up.

9 Once the rings are correctly installed check that their open ends are positioned each side of the pin.

10.2 Measuring piston ring installed end gap

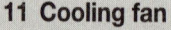

10.6 Make sure the pin in each groove is between the ends of the ring (arrowed)

11 Cooling fan

Note: *This procedure can be carried out with the engine in the frame.*

Removal

1 Remove the engine access panels and, if required, the side panels; on Ice models, undo the three screws securing the engine top cover and remove the cover (see Chapter 8).

2 Pull out the clip securing the oil hose to the engine cowling **(see illustration 7.2a)**. Undo the two screws securing the cowling and remove it, noting how it fits **(see illustration 7.2b)**. Where fitted, detach the carburettor air duct from the cowling.

3 If a secondary air system is fitted, release the clip on the lower flexible hose union and detach the hose from the exhaust pipe **(see illustration)**. Unclip the system assembly from the fan cowling and displace it.

4 Undo the three screws securing the fan cowling to the crankcase and remove it **(see illustration)**.

5 Undo the three screws securing the cooling fan to the alternator rotor and remove the fan **(see illustration)**.

Installation

6 Installation is the reverse of removal. If the secondary air system has been displaced, ensure the hose clip is secure.

with the other new circlip **(see illustration)**. When installing the circlips, compress them only just enough to fit them in the piston, and make sure they are properly seated in their grooves with the open end away from the removal notch.

21 Install the cylinder (see Section 8).

10 Piston rings

1 New piston rings should be fitted whenever an engine is being overhauled. Before installing the new rings, the end gaps must be checked.

2 Insert the top ring into the bottom of the cylinder and square it up with the cylinder walls by pushing it in with the top of the

piston. The ring should be about 20 mm from the bottom edge of the cylinder. To measure the end gap, slip a feeler gauge between the ends of the ring and compare the measurement to the specifications at the beginning of the Chapter **(see illustration)**.

3 If the gap is larger or smaller than specified, double check to make sure that you have the correct rings before proceeding.

4 Never install a piston ring with a gap smaller than specified. If the gap is larger than specified, check that the bore is not worn (see Section 8).

5 Repeat the procedure for the other ring.

6 Once the ring end gaps have been checked, the rings can be installed on the piston. First identify the ring locating pin in each piston ring groove – the rings must be positioned so that the pin is in between the open ends of the ring **(see illustration)**.

11.3 Detach the secondary air system hose from the exhaust pipe. Note the supporting clip (arrowed)

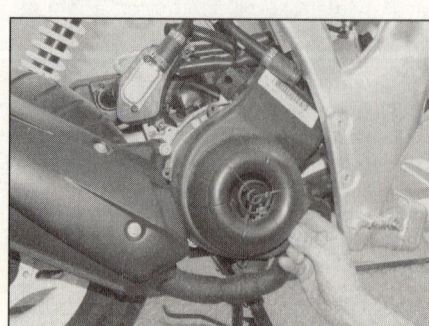

11.4 Remove the fan cowling

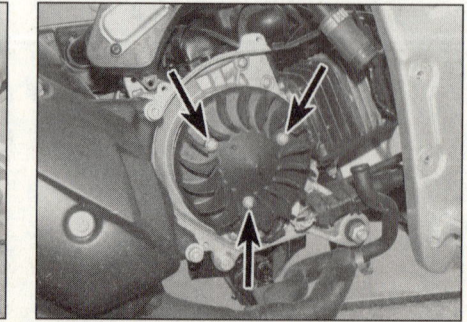

11.5 The fan is secured by three screws (arrowed)

12.3 With the rotor held securely, undo the rotor nut (arrowed)

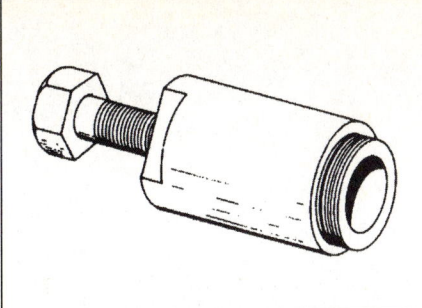

12.4a The Gilera rotor removal tool

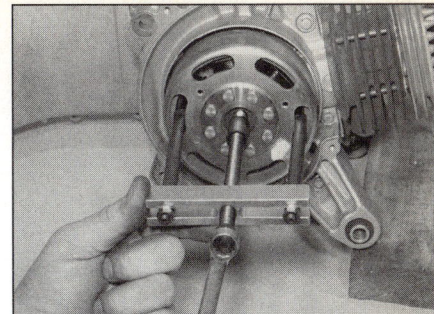

12.4b Using a two-legged puller to remove the rotor

12.4c Remove the Woodruff key for safekeeping

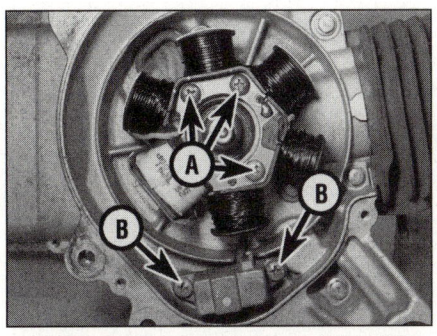

12.5a Undo the stator screws (A) and the pulse generator coil screws (B) . . .

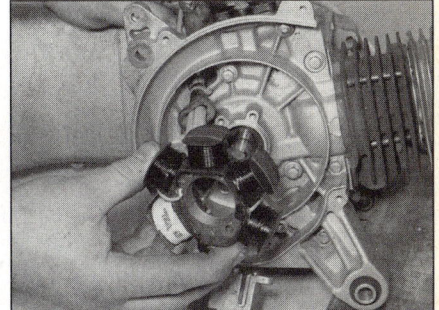

12.5b . . . and remove the assembly, feeding the wiring through the casing

12 Alternator rotor and stator

Note: *This procedure can be carried out with the engine in the frame.*

Removal

1 Remove the cooling fan (see Section 11).
2 Trace the wiring back from the alternator and pulse generator coil and disconnect it at the connectors. Free the wiring from any clips or guides and feed it through to the alternator.
3 To remove the rotor nut it is necessary to stop the rotor from turning. Gilera provide a service tool (Part No. 020565Y) to do this. Alternatively, you can make up a tool (see *Tool Tip*) which engages the slots in the rotor face **(see illustration)**. With the rotor held securely, undo the nut and discard it as a new one must be fitted on reassembly.

 *A rotor holding tool can easily be made using two strips of steel bolted together in the middle, with a bolt through each end which locates into the slots in the rotor (see Chapter 2D, Section 4). Do not allow the bolts to extend too far through the rotor slots otherwise the coils could be damaged.*

4 To remove the rotor from the shaft it is necessary to use the Gilera service tool (Part No. 020162Y) **(see illustration)** or a

two-legged puller. To use the service tool, first screw the body of the tool all the way into the threads provided in the rotor. Hold the tool with a spanner on its flats and tighten the centre bolt, exerting steady pressure to draw the rotor off the crankshaft. To use a puller, engage the puller legs in the slots in the rotor, then tighten the centre bolt exerting steady pressure to draw the rotor off the crankshaft **(see illustration)**. Remove the Woodruff key from the shaft for safekeeping, noting how it fits **(see illustration)**.
5 To remove the stator from the crankcase, it is also necessary to remove the pulse generator coil as they are a linked assembly. Unscrew the three screws securing the stator and the two screws securing the coil and remove them together **(see illustration)**. Draw the wiring seal out of the crankcase and carefully pull the wiring through the hole, taking care not to snag it **(see illustration)**.

Installation

6 Feed the wiring through the hole in the crankcase and press the seal into place, then install the stator and pulse generator coil onto the crankcase **(see illustration)**. Apply a suitable non-permanent thread locking compound to the screw threads, then install the screws and tighten them securely **(see illustration)**.
7 Clean the tapered end of the crankshaft and the corresponding mating surface on the inside of the rotor with a suitable solvent. Make sure that no metal objects have attached themselves to the magnets on the inside of the rotor. Fit the Woodruff key into its slot in the shaft, then install the rotor onto the shaft, aligning the slot in the rotor with the key **(see illustrations)**.
8 Install the new rotor nut and tighten it to the torque setting specified at the beginning

12.6a Feed the wiring through the hole . . .

12.6b . . . then install the stator and coil

12.7a Fit the Woodruff key (arrowed) . . .

12.7b . . . then align the slot in the rotor (arrowed) with the key and install the rotor

12.8a Fit the new nut . . .

12.8b . . . and tighten it to the specified torque, using the tool to hold the rotor

of the Chapter, using the method employed on removal to prevent the rotor from turning **(see illustrations)**. **Note:** *On Ice models, Gilera recommend the use of thread locking compound on the rotor nut.*

9 Reconnect the wiring at the connectors and secure it with any clips or ties.

10 Install the remaining components in the reverse order of removal.

13.2 Remove the starter pinion assembly, noting how it fits

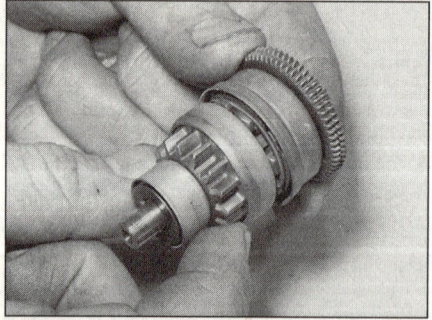

13.4 Check the outer pinion as described

14.2 Inlet hose (A), outlet hose (B). Pump is secured by the two screws (C)

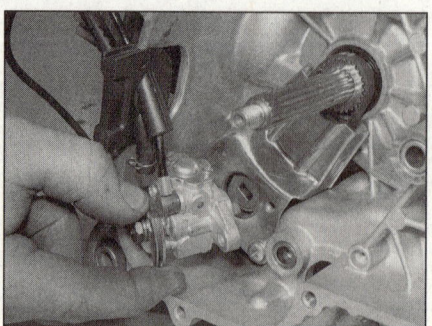

14.3 Remove the pump, with the hoses and seal if still attached

13 Starter pinion assembly

Note: *This procedure can be carried out with the engine in the frame.*

Removal

1 Remove the drive belt cover (see Chapter 2D).
2 Remove the starter pinion assembly, noting how it fits **(see illustration)**.

Inspection

3 Check the starter pinion assembly for any signs of damage or wear, particularly for chipped or broken teeth on either of the pinions.
4 Rotate the outer pinion and check that it moves smoothly up and down the shaft, and that it returns easily to its rest position **(see illustration)**.
5 The starter pinion assembly is supplied as a complete unit; if any of the component parts are worn or damaged, the unit will have to be replaced with a new one.
6 The starter pinion mechanism should not be lubricated; apply a smear of grease to both ends of the pinion shaft before installation.

Installation

7 Installation is the reverse of removal. Ensure the inner pinion engages with the starter motor shaft

14 Oil pump and belt

Note: *This procedure can be carried out with the engine in the frame.*

Removal

1 Remove the drive belt cover; to access the pump drive belt, also remove the variator (see Chapter 2D). Remove the starter pinion assembly (see Section 13).
2 If the pump is being removed rather than just being displaced for belt renewal, detach the oil inlet and outlet hoses from either the pump itself **(see illustration)**, noting which fits where, or from the oil tank and carburettor respectively. Clamp the hoses to prevent oil leakage – use any of the methods shown in *Tool Tips* at the end of Chapter 4. **Note:** *Only disconnect the hose if it is secured by a spring clip; if the hose is crimped onto the pump, disconnect it at the other end. Also disconnect the cable from the pump (see Chapter 4).*
3 Remove the two screws securing the oil pump, then remove the pump **(see illustration 14.2)**. If the hoses are still attached, slide the crankcase seal out at the same time **(see illustration)**. Note how the drive tab on the back of the pump locates in the slot in the driven pulley.

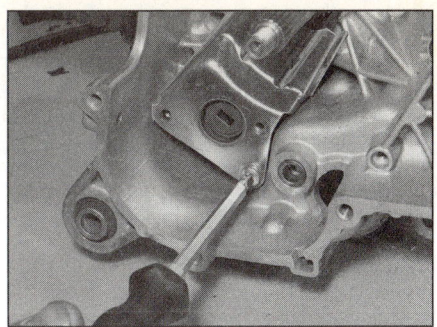

14.4a Remove the screw securing the guard plate . . .

14.4b . . . and remove the inner plate (arrowed)

14.4c Remove the belt, the driven pulley (A) and its washer, and the drive pulley (B)

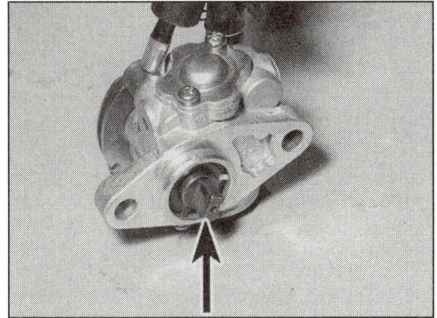

14.5a Rotate the pump drive tab (arrowed) . . .

14.5b . . . and the cable cam (arrowed) by hand

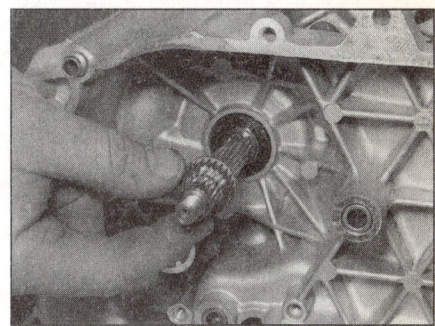

14.8a Fit the drive pulley . . .

4 Remove the screw securing the guard plate and remove the plate and the inner plate behind it **(see illustrations)**. Slide the spacer off the crankshaft and pull the drive belt off the pulleys. Remove the driven pulley and the thrust washer behind it, and slide the drive pulley off the crankshaft **(see illustration)**.

Inspection

5 Check the pump for obvious signs of damage. Turn the drive tab by hand and ensure that it rotates smoothly and freely **(see illustration)**. Also check that the cable cam turns smoothly and returns to rest under pressure of the return spring **(see illustration)**.
6 If the operation of the pump is suspect, or for internal cleaning, remove the screws securing both cover plates and remove the plates. Clean the pump using a suitable solvent, and inspect the internal components for wear and damage. No individual components are available, so if the pump is faulty or any parts are worn, fit a new pump.
7 Check along the length of the drive belt for splits, cracks or broken teeth and renew the belt if necessary. The belt should be renewed regardless of its condition at the specified service interval (see Chapter 1).

Installation

8 Slide the drive pulley, with its shouldered side innermost, onto the crankshaft, then fit the thrust washer and the driven pulley, with its slot for the pump drive tab outermost **(see illustrations)**. Fit the belt onto the pulleys,

making sure the teeth mesh correctly **(see illustration)**.
9 Fit the inner plate, locating the raised sections on the inside in the recesses in the screw holes **(see illustration)**. Fit the

14.8b . . . the thrust washer . . .

14.8d . . . and the pump drive belt

guard plate and secure it with the screw **(see illustration)**. Slide the spacer onto the crankshaft **(see illustration)**.
10 Install the pump, locating the drive tab in the slot in the driven pulley, and secure it with

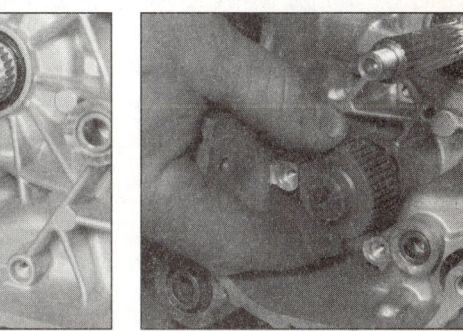

14.8c . . . the driven pulley . . .

14.9a Fit the inner plate . . .

14.9b . . . and the guard plate

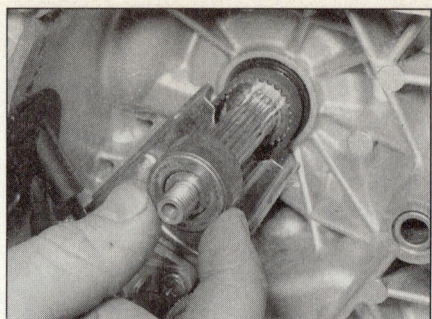

14.9c Slide the spacer onto the shaft

14.10 Install the pump and secure it with its screws

its screws **(see illustration)**. If the hoses are attached to the pump, ensure the crankcase seal is correctly located **(see illustration 14.3)**.

11 As applicable, connect the oil hoses to the pump, oil tank or carburettor, making sure they are secured by their clips. If any clips are distorted or corroded, replace them with new ones. Connect the cable to the pump cam (see Chapter 4). Bleed the pump as described below, then adjust the cable (see Chapter 1, Section 26).

Caution: Note that cable adjustment is important to ensure that the oil pump delivers the correct amount of oil to the engine and is correctly synchronised with the throttle.

12 Install the remaining components in the reverse order of removal.

Bleeding

13 Bleeding the pump is the process of

15.3 The crankcase halves are secured by eight bolts (arrowed)

14.13 Remove the bleed screw (arrowed) and allow the air to bleed out

removing the air from it and allowing it to be filled with oil. Simply remove the bleed screw, and wait until oil, without any air mixed with it, starts to flow out of the hole, then refit the screw **(see illustration)**.

14 It is important that the oil hoses are bled of air as well as the pump. Ensure the ignition switch is OFF. Disconnect the oil outlet hose from the carburettor and crank the engine with the kickstarter until oil, without any air mixed with it, flows out the hose, then reconnect the hose and secure it with the clip.

15 Crankcase halves and main bearings

Note: To separate the crankcase halves, the engine must be removed from the frame.

15.4 Drawing the right-hand crankcase half off the crankshaft

Separation

1 To access the crankshaft assembly and engine main bearings, the crankcase halves must be separated.

2 Remove the engine from the frame (see Section 5). Before the crankcases can be separated the following components must be removed:

- Cylinder head (see Section 7)
- Cylinder (see Section 8)
- Alternator rotor and stator (see Section 12)
- Reed valve (see Chapter 4)
- Starter motor (see Chapter 9)
- Oil pump and drive belt (see Section 14)
- Centre stand (see Chapter 6)

3 Tape some rag around the connecting rod to prevent it knocking against the cases. Unscrew the eight crankcase bolts evenly, a little at a time and in a criss-cross sequence until they are all finger-tight, then remove them **(see illustration)**. **Note:** *Ensure that all the crankcase bolts have been removed before attempting to separate the cases.*

4 Carefully remove the right-hand crankcase half from the left-hand half. If necessary, Gilera produce a service tool (Part No. 020163Y) to aid separation of the crankcase halves. Alternatively, heat the crankcase around the outside of the bearing housing with a hot air gun, and use the set-up shown to draw the right-hand half of the crankshaft assembly **(see illustration)**. **Note:** *Do not try and separate the halves by levering against the crankcase mating surfaces as they are easily damaged and will not seal correctly afterwards.*

5 Now press the crankshaft out of the left-hand crankcase half **(see illustration)**. Take care to apply even force and plenty of heat and have an assistant support the crankshaft assembly to prevent it from dropping if it suddenly comes free. **Note:** *The crankshaft is a pressed-together assembly – any undue shock or force could knock it out of alignment.*

6 Remove the dowels from either crankcase half for safekeeping if they are loose.

7 Note the position of the crankshaft oil seals and measure any inset before removing them **(see illustration)**. Note which way round the seals are fitted, then drive them out carefully from the inside of each case with a punch

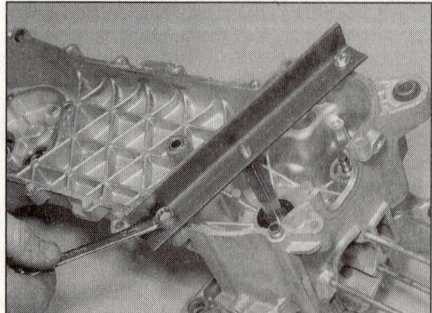

15.5 Pressing the crankshaft out of the left-hand crankcase half

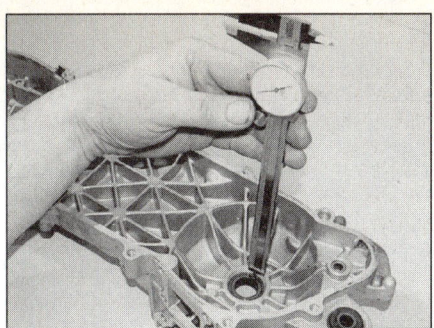

15.7a Measuring crankshaft oil seal inset

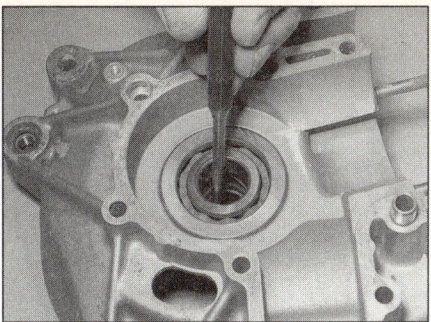

15.7b Driving out the oil seals

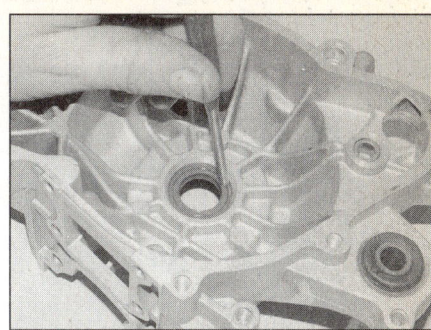

15.7c Tap the seals with a punch to displace them

(see illustration). Discard the seals as new ones must be fitted on reassembly. If the main bearings have remained in the crankcases, tap the seals gently on one side with a punch to displace them and then pull them out with pliers (see illustration).

8 If required, remove the transmission assembly from the left-hand crankcase half (see Chapter 2D).

Inspection

9 The main bearings should remain on the crankshaft during disassembly, but they may stick in the crankcase halves. If the main bearings have failed, excessive rumbling and vibration will be felt when the engine is running. Sometimes this may cause the oil seals to fail, resulting in a loss of compression and poor running. Check the condition of the bearings – they should spin freely and smoothly without any rough spots or excessive noise – and only remove them if they are unserviceable. Renew the bearings if there is any doubt about their condition and always renew both main bearings at the same time, never individually.

10 To remove the bearings from the cases, heat the bearing housings with a hot air gun and tap them out using a bearing driver or suitable socket (see illustration). Note which way round the bearings are fitted. If the bearings have remained in place on the crankshaft, they must be removed with an external bearing puller to avoid damaging the crankshaft assembly (see illustration). **Note:** *The main bearings should be fitted on the crankshaft prior to assembly.*

11 Remove all traces of old gasket from the crankcase mating surfaces, taking care not to nick or gouge the soft aluminium if a scraper is used. Wash all the components in a suitable solvent and dry them with compressed air.

Caution: Be very careful not to damage the crankcase mating surfaces which may result in loss of crankcase pressure causing poor engine performance. Check both crankcase halves very carefully for cracks and damaged threads.

12 Small cracks or holes in aluminium castings may be repaired with an epoxy resin adhesive as a temporary measure. Permanent repairs can only be effected by welding, and

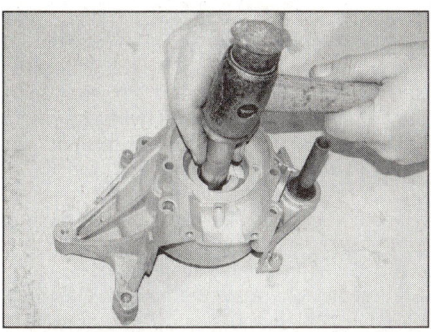

15.10a Driving a main bearing out of the crankcase

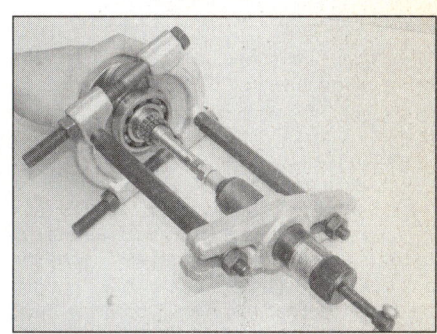

15.10b Removing a bearing from the crankshaft with an external puller

only a specialist in this process is in a position to advise on the economy or practical aspect of such a repair. Low temperature repair kits are available for repair of aluminium castings. If any damage is found that can't be repaired, renew both crankcase halves as a set.

13 Damaged threads can be reclaimed by using a thread insert of the Heli-Coil type, which is fitted after drilling and re-tapping the affected thread. Most scooter dealers and small engineering firms offer a service of this kind. Sheared screws and studs can usually be removed with screw extractors which consist of a tapered, left thread screw of very hard steel. These are inserted into a pre-drilled hole in the broken fixing, and usually succeed in dislodging the most stubborn stud or screw (see illustrations). If you are in any doubt about removing a sheared screw, consult a scooter dealer or automotive engineer.

14 Always wash the crankcases thoroughly after any repair work to ensure no dirt or metal swarf is trapped inside when the engine is rebuilt.

15 Inspect the engine mounting bushes. If they show signs of deterioration renew them all at the same time. To remove a bush, first note its position in the casing. Heat the casing with a hot air gun, then support the casing and drive the bush out with a hammer and a suitably sized socket. Alternatively, use two suitably sized sockets to press the bush out in the jaws of a vice. Clean the bush housing with steel wool to remove any corrosion, then reheat the casing and fit the new bush. **Note:** *Always support the casing when removing or fitting bushes to avoid breaking the casing.*

16 Inspect the crankshaft assembly and bearings (see Section 16).

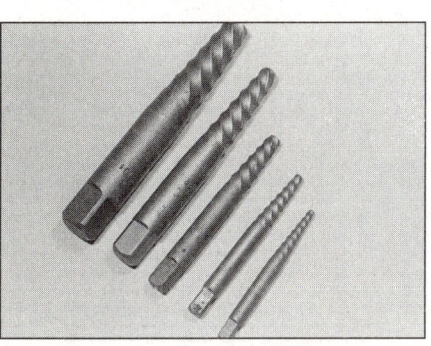

15.13a A set of screw extractors is a useful addition to the workshop

15.13b The extractor is screwed anticlockwise into the broken-off fastener

15.17a Fit the new oil seals . . .

15.17b . . . and drive them in to the correct depth

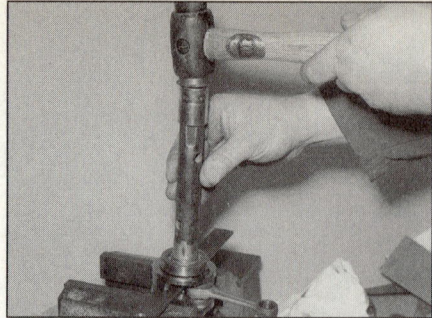

15.18 Tap the bearing onto the crankshaft – do not use excessive force

Reassembly

17 Fit the new crankshaft oil seals into the crankcase halves and drive them to the previously measured inset using a seal driver or socket (see Step 7). Ensure the seals are fitted the right way round and that they enter the cases squarely **(see illustrations)**.

18 If new main bearings are to be fitted onto the crankshaft, heat them first in an oil bath to around 100°C, then press them onto the shaft using a suitable length of tube that just fits over the shaft and bears onto the inner race only **(see illustration)**. If the bearings are difficult to fit they are not hot enough.

 Warning: This must be done very carefully to avoid the risk of personal injury.

19 Fit the crankshaft assembly into the left-hand crankcase half first, ensuring that the connecting rod is aligned with the

crankcase mouth. Lubricate the shaft, seal and bearing with the specified two-stroke oil and tape some rag around the connecting rod to prevent it knocking against the cases. Heat the bearing housing in the crankcase with a hot air gun before fitting the crankshaft **(see illustrations)**. **Note:** *Avoid applying direct heat onto the crankshaft oil seal.* If required, a freeze spray can be used on the bearing itself to aid installation. Ensure the bearing is pressed fully into its housing.

20 If applicable, allow the case to cool, then wipe the mating surfaces of both crankcase halves with a rag soaked in a suitable solvent and fit the dowels. Apply a small amount of suitable sealant to the mating surface of the left-hand case **(see illustration)**.

Caution: Do not apply an excessive amount of sealant as it will ooze out when the case halves are assembled.

21 Now fit the right-hand crankcase half.

Lubricate the shaft, seal and bearing with the specified two-stroke oil. Heat the bearing housing with a hot air gun before fitting the crankcase half and, if required, use a freeze spay on the bearing. **Note:** *Avoid applying direct heat onto the crankshaft oil seal.*

22 Check that the crankcase halves are seated all the way round and that the main bearings are pressed fully into their housings. If the casings are not correctly seated, heat the bearing housings while applying firm pressure. **Note:** *Do not attempt to pull the crankcase halves together using the crankcase bolts as the casing will crack and be ruined.*

23 Clean the threads of the crankcase bolts and install them finger-tight, then tighten them evenly a little at a time in a criss-cross sequence to the torque setting specified at the beginning of this Chapter **(see illustration)**.

24 Check the amount of crankshaft endfloat using a dial gauge and compare the result to the amount specified at the beginning of this Chapter. The dial gauge should be supported so that its tip rests against the end of the crankshaft – push and pull the crankshaft to obtain a reading on the gauge. If the amount recorded is less than the amount specified, lightly tap the end of the crankshaft with a soft-faced mallet until the specified amount is achieved **(see illustration)**. Rotate the crankshaft by hand – if there are any signs of undue stiffness, tight or rough spots, or of any other problem, the fault must be rectified before proceeding further.

25 Install the remaining components in the reverse order of removal.

15.19a Heat the crankcase . . .

15.19b . . . and install the crankshaft

15.20 Apply sealant to the crankcase mating surface

15.23 Tighten the crankcase bolts as described to the specified torque

15.24 Tap the end of the crankshaft until the endfloat is correct and the shaft turns freely

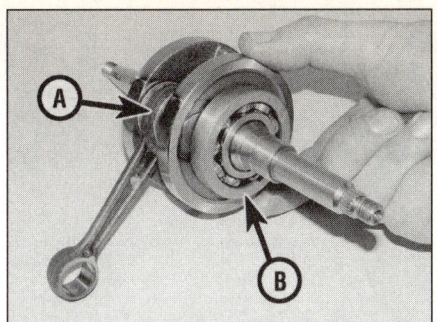

16.2 The crankshaft assembly big-end (A) and main bearings (B)

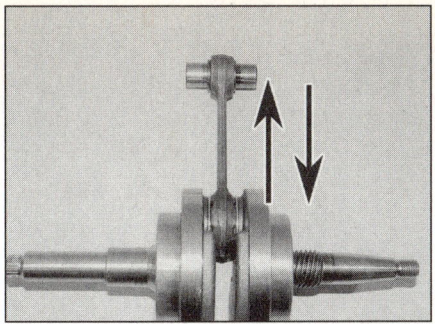

16.3 Any freeplay indicates a worn big-end bearing

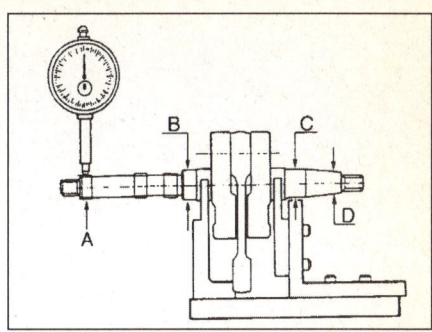

16.5 Check crankshaft runout at points A, B, C and D

16 Crankshaft assembly and big-end bearing

1 To access the crankshaft and the big-end bearing, the crankcase halves must be separated (see Section 15).

2 The crankshaft assembly should give many thousands of miles of service. The most likely problems to occur will be a worn small or big-end bearing due to poor lubrication **(see illustration)**. A worn big-end bearing will produce a pronounced knocking noise, most audible when the engine is under load, and increasing as engine speed rises. This should not be confused with small-end bearing wear, which produces a lighter, metallic rattle (see Section 9).

Inspection

3 To assess the condition of the big-end bearing, hold the crankshaft assembly firmly and push and pull on the connecting rod, checking for any up-and-down freeplay between the two **(see illustration)**. If any freeplay is noted, the bearing is worn and the crankshaft assembly will have to be replaced with a new one. **Note:** *A small amount of big-end side clearance (side-to-side movement) is acceptable on the connecting rod – see Specifications at the beginning of this Chapter.*

4 Inspect the crankshaft where it passes through the main bearings for wear and scoring. The shaft should be a press fit in the bearings; if it is worn or damaged a new assembly will have to be fitted. Evidence of extreme heat, such as discoloration or blueing, indicates that lubrication failure has occurred. Be sure to check the oil pump and bearing oilways before reassembling the engine.

5 If available, place the crankshaft assembly on V-blocks and check the runout at the main bearing journals (B and C) and at either end (A and D) using a dial gauge **(see illustration)**. **Note:** *The main bearings must be removed from the crankshaft for this check.* If the crankshaft is out-of-true it will cause excessive engine vibration. If there is any doubt about the condition of the crankshaft have it checked by a scooter dealer or automotive engineer. **Note:** *The crankshaft assembly is pressed together and is easily damaged if it is dropped.*

6 Inspect the threads on each end of the crankshaft and ensure that the retaining nuts for the alternator rotor and the variator are a good fit. Inspect the splines for the variator pulley on the left-hand end of the shaft. Inspect the taper and the slot in the right-hand end of the shaft for the alternator Woodruff key. Damage or wear that prevents the rotor from being fitted securely will require a new crankshaft assembly.

Reassembly

7 Follow the procedure in Section 15 to install the crankshaft assembly.

17 Initial start-up after overhaul

1 Make sure the oil tank is at least partly full and the pump is correctly adjusted (see Chapter 1, Section 26) and bled of air (see Section 14).

2 Make sure there is fuel in the tank.

3 With the ignition OFF, operate the kickstart a couple of times to check that the engine turns over easily.

4 Turn the ignition ON, start the engine and allow it to run at a slow idle until it reaches operating temperature. Do not be alarmed if there is a little smoke from the exhaust – this will be due to the oil used to lubricate the piston and bore during assembly and should subside after a while.

5 If the engine proves reluctant to start, remove the spark plug and check that it has not become wet and oily. If it has, clean it and try again. If the engine refuses to start, go through the fault finding charts at the end of this manual to identify the problem.

6 Check carefully that there are no fuel or oil leaks and make sure the controls, especially the brakes, function properly before road testing the machine.

7 Refer to Section 18 for the recommended running-in procedure.

18 Recommended running-in procedure

1 Treat the engine gently for the first few miles to allow any new parts to bed in.

2 If a new piston, cylinder or crankshaft assembly has been fitted, the engine will have to be run-in as when new. This means a restraining hand on the throttle until at least 300 miles (500 km) have been covered. There's no point in keeping to any set speed limit – the main idea is to keep from labouring the engine and to gradually increase performance up to the 600 mile (1000 km) mark. Make sure that the throttle position is varied to vary engine speed, and use full throttle only for short bursts. Experience is the best guide, since it's easy to tell when an engine is running freely.

3 Pay particular attention to the *Daily (pre-ride) checks* at the beginning of this manual. Check the tightness of all relevant nuts and bolts.

Chapter 2 Part B:
Liquid-cooled two-stroke engines (Runner 50, 50 DD, 50 SP and Purejet 50, DNA 50 GP, Runner FX125 and FXR180)

Refer to the beginning of Chapter 1 for model identification details

Contents

Degrees of difficulty

Easy, suitable for novice with little experience 	**Fairly easy,** suitable for beginner with some experience	**Fairly difficult,** suitable for competent DIY mechanic	**Difficult,** suitable for experienced DIY mechanic 	**Very difficult,** suitable for expert DIY or professional 

Specifications –
Runner 50, 50 DD, 50 SP and Purejet 50, DNA 50 GP

General
Type	Single cylinder two-stroke
Capacity.	49.3 cc
Bore	40.0 mm
Stroke.	39.3 mm

Compression ratio
Runner 50, 50 DD and SP	11.3:1 to 12.7:1
Purejet 50	10.6:1 to 12.4:1
DNA 50 GP	11.4:1 to 12.8:1

Cylinder bore
Runner 50, 50 DD and SP
  Standard
Size code A.	39.985 mm
Size code B.	39.990 mm
Size code C	39.995 mm
Size code D.	40.000 mm
Size code E.	40.005 mm
1st oversize.	40.185 to 40.205 mm
2nd oversize	40.205 to 40.385 mm

Cylinder bore (continued)

Runner 50 SP RST, DNA 50 RST, Purejet 50
  Standard
    Size code M .... 39.997 to 40.004 mm
    Size code N .... 40.004 to 40.011 mm
    Size code O .... 40.011 to 40.018 mm
    Size code P... 40.018 to 40.025 mm
  1st oversize
    Size code M1 .... 40.197 to 40.204 mm
    Size code N1 .... 40.204 to 40.211 mm
    Size code O1 .... 40.211 to 40.218 mm
    Size code P1 .... 40.218 to 40.225 mm
  2nd oversize
    Size code M2 .... 40.397 to 40.404 mm
    Size code N2 .... 40.404 to 40.411 mm
    Size code O2 .... 40.411 to 40.418 mm
    Size code P2 .... 40.418 to 40.425 mm
DNA 50 GP
  Standard
    Size code M .... 39.990 to 39.997 mm
    Size code N .... 39.997 to 40.004 mm
    Size code O .... 40.004 to 40.011 mm
    Size code P... 40.011 to 40.018 mm
  1st oversize
    Size code M1 .... 40.190 to 40.197 mm
    Size code N1 .... 40.197 to 40.204 mm
    Size code O1 .... 40.204 to 40.211 mm
    Size code P1 .... 40.211 to 40.218 mm
  2nd oversize
    Size code M2 .... 40.390 to 40.397 mm
    Size code N2 .... 40.397 to 40.404 mm
    Size code O2 .... 40.404 to 40.411 mm
    Size code P2 .... 40.411 to 40.418 mm

Connecting rod

Small-end internal diameter
  Size I... 17.007 to 17.011 mm
  Size II .... 17.003 to 17.007 mm
  Size III .... 16.999 to 17.003 mm

Piston

Piston diameter (measured 25 mm down from lower ring groove, at 90° to piston pin axis)
Runner 50, 50 DD and SP
  Standard
    Size code A.. 39.940 mm
    Size code B.. 39.945 mm
    Size code C .... 39.950 mm
    Size code D.. 39.955 mm
    Size code E .... 39.960 mm
  1st oversize... 40.140 to 40.160 mm
  2nd oversize.. 40.340 to 40.360 mm
  Piston-to-bore clearance .... 0.040 to 0.050 mm
  Piston pin diameter..................................... 12.001 to 12.005 mm
Runner Purejet 50, DNA 50 GP
  Standard
    Size code M .... 39.943 to 39.950 mm
    Size code N .... 39.950 to 39.957 mm
    Size code O .... 39.957 to 39.964 mm
    Size code P... 39.964 to 39.971 mm
  1st oversize
    Size code M1 .... 40.143 to 40.150 mm
    Size code N1 .... 40.150 to 40.157 mm
    Size code O1 .... 40.157 to 40.164 mm
    Size code P1 .... 40.164 to 40.171 mm
  2nd oversize
    Size code M2 .... 40.343 to 40.350 mm
    Size code N2 .... 40.350 to 40.357 mm
    Size code O2 .... 40.357 to 40.364 mm
    Size code P2 .... 40.364 to 40.371 mm
  Piston-to-bore clearance
    Purejet 50 .... 0.047 to 0.061 mm
    DNA 50 GP... 0.040 to 0.054 mm
  Piston pin diameter..................................... 12.001 to 12.005 mm

Piston rings
Ring end gap (installed) . . . .   0.10 to 0.25 mm

Crankshaft
Runout (max)
    At middle and left-hand end. . . . .   0.03 mm
    At right-hand end . . . .   0.02 mm
Big-end side clearance. . . . .   0.25 to 0.50 mm
Endfloat . . . .   0.03 to 0.09 mm

Cylinder base gasket selection

Cylinder top gasket surface to piston crown measurement	Gasket thickness
Runner 50, 50 DD and SP, DNA 50 GP	
3.25 to 3.45 mm	0.75 mm
3.10 to 3.25 mm	0.5 mm
2.85 to 3.10 mm	0.4 mm
Runner 50 SP RST, DNA 50 RST, all Runner Purejet 50	
3.24 to 3.48 mm	0.8 mm
3.04 to 3.24 mm	0.6 mm
2.80 to 3.04 mm	0.4 mm

Torque settings
Alternator rotor nut. . . . .   40 to 44 Nm
Crankcase bolts . . . .   12 to 13 Nm
Cylinder head nuts . . . .   10 to 11 Nm
Engine front mounting bolt. . . . .   33 to 41 Nm
Rear shock absorber lower mounting bolt. . . . .   33 to 41 Nm

Specifications – Runner FX125

General
Type . . . .   Single cylinder two-stroke
Capacity . . . .   123.5 cc
Bore . . . .   55.0 mm
Stroke. . . . .   52.0 mm
Compression ratio 9.9:1

Cylinder bore
Standard
    Size code A. . . . .   54.990 to 54.995 mm
    Size code B . . . .   54.995 to 55.000 mm
    Size code C . . . .   55.000 to 55.005 mm
    Size code D . . . .   55.005 to 55.010 mm
    Size code E. . . . .   55.010 to 55.015 mm
    Size code F . . . .   55.015 to 55.020 mm
    Size code G . . . .   55.020 to 55.025 mm
    Size code H . . . .   55.025 to 55.030 mm
    Size code I . . . .   55.030 to 55.035 mm
1st oversize
    Size code A. . . . .   55.190 to 55.195 mm
    Size code B . . . .   55.195 to 55.200 mm
    Size code C . . . .   55.200 to 55.205 mm
    Size code D . . . .   55.205 to 55.210 mm
    Size code E. . . . .   55.210 to 55.215 mm
    Size code F . . . .   55.215 to 55.220 mm
    Size code G . . . .   55.220 to 55.225 mm
    Size code H . . . .   55.225 to 55.230 mm
    Size code I . . . .   55.230 to 55.235 mm
2nd oversize
    Size code A. . . . .   55.390 to 55.395 mm
    Size code B . . . .   55.395 to 55.400 mm
    Size code C . . . .   55.400 to 55.405 mm
    Size code D . . . .   55.405 to 55.410 mm
    Size code E. . . . .   55.410 to 55.415 mm
    Size code F . . . .   55.415 to 55.420 mm
    Size code G . . . .   55.420 to 55.425 mm
    Size code H . . . .   55.425 to 55.430 mm
    Size code I . . . .   55.430 to 55.435 mm

Cylinder bore (continued)
3rd oversize
    Size code A... 55.590 to 55.595 mm
    Size code B... 55.595 to 55.600 mm
    Size code C... 55.600 to 55.605 mm
    Size code D... 55.605 to 55.610 mm
    Size code E... 55.610 to 55.615 mm
    Size code F... 55.615 to 55.620 mm
    Size code G... 55.620 to 55.625 mm
    Size code H... 55.625 to 55.630 mm
    Size code I... 55.630 to 55.635 mm

Connecting rod
Small-end internal diameter
    Size I... 20.009 to 20.013 mm
    Size II.. 20.005 to 20.010 mm
    Size III... 20.001 to 20.006 mm
    Size IIII.. 19.997 to 20.002 mm

Piston
Piston diameter (measured 25 mm down from lower ring groove, at 90° to piston pin axis)
  Standard
    Size code A... 54.935 to 54.940 mm
    Size code B... 54.940 to 54.945 mm
    Size code C... 54.945 to 54.950 mm
    Size code D... 54.950 to 54.955 mm
    Size code E... 54.955 to 54.960 mm
    Size code F... 54.960 to 54.965 mm
    Size code G... 54.965 to 55.970 mm
    Size code H... 54.970 to 54.975 mm
    Size code I... 54.975 to 54.980 mm
  1st oversize
    Size code A... 55.135 to 55.140 mm
    Size code B... 55.140 to 55.145 mm
    Size code C... 55.145 to 55.150 mm
    Size code D... 55.150 to 55.155 mm
    Size code E... 55.155 to 55.160 mm
    Size code F... 55.160 to 55.165 mm
    Size code G... 55.165 to 55.170 mm
    Size code H... 55.170 to 55.175 mm
    Size code I... 55.175 to 55.180 mm
  2nd oversize
    Size code A... 55.335 to 55.340 mm
    Size code B... 55.340 to 55.345 mm
    Size code C... 55.345 to 55.350 mm
    Size code D... 55.350 to 55.355 mm
    Size code E... 55.355 to 55.360 mm
    Size code F... 55.360 to 55.365 mm
    Size code G... 55.365 to 55.370 mm
    Size code H... 55.370 to 55.375 mm
    Size code I... 55.375 to 55.380 mm
  3rd oversize
    Size code A... 55.535 to 55.540 mm
    Size code B... 55.540 to 55.545 mm
    Size code C... 55.545 to 55.550 mm
    Size code D... 55.550 to 55.555 mm
    Size code E... 55.555 to 55.560 mm
    Size code F... 55.560 to 55.565 mm
    Size code G... 55.565 to 55.570 mm
    Size code H... 55.570 to 55.575 mm
    Size code I... 55.575 to 55.580 mm
Piston-to-bore clearance .... 0.050 to 0.060 mm
Piston pin diameter .... 16.001 to 16.005 mm

Piston rings
Ring end gap (installed) .... 0.20 to 0.35 mm

Crankshaft

Runout (max)	
At middle and left-hand end..	0.03 mm
At right-hand end..	0.02 mm
Big-end side clearance..	not available
Endfloat...	0.03 to 0.09 mm

Cylinder base gasket selection

Final cylinder top gasket surface to piston crown measurement......	2.74 to 2.84 mm
Gasket sizes available	0.2, 0.3, 0.4, 0.5, 0.6, 0.7 and 0.8 mm

Torque settings

Alternator rotor nut..	52 to 56 Nm
Crankcase bolts..	12 to 13 Nm
Cylinder head nuts...	10 to 11 Nm
Engine front mounting bolt...	33 to 41 Nm
Rear shock absorber lower mounting bolt...........................	33 to 41 Nm

Specifications – Runner FXR180

General

Type	Single cylinder two-stroke
Capacity..	175.8 cc
Bore..	65.6 mm
Stroke..	52.0 mm
Compression ratio	9.8:1

Cylinder bore

Standard	
Size code A...	65.590 to 65.595 mm
Size code B...	64.595 to 65.600 mm
Size code C...	65.600 to 65.605 mm
Size code D...	65.605 to 65.610 mm
Size code E...	65.610 to 65.615 mm
Size code F...	65.615 to 65.620 mm
Size code G...	65.620 to 65.625 mm
Size code H...	65.625 to 65.630 mm
Size code I..	65.630 to 65.635 mm

Connecting rod

Small-end internal diameter	
Size I...	20.009 to 20.013 mm
Size II..	20.005 to 20.010 mm
Size III...	20.001 to 20.006 mm
Size IIII..	19.997 to 20.002 mm

Piston

Piston diameter (measured 25 mm down from lower ring groove, at 90° to piston pin axis)	
Standard	
Size code A...	65.545 to 65.550 mm
Size code B...	65.550 to 65.555 mm
Size code C...	65.555 to 65.560 mm
Size code D...	65.560 to 65.565 mm
Size code E...	65.565 to 65.570 mm
Size code F...	65.570 to 65.575 mm
Size code G...	65.575 to 65.580 mm
Size code H...	65.580 to 65.585 mm
Size code I..	65.585 to 65.590 mm
Piston-to-bore clearance...	0.040 to 0.050 mm
Piston pin diameter..	16.001 to 16.005 mm

Piston rings

Ring end gap (installed)	0.20 to 0.35 mm

Crankshaft

Runout (max)	
At middle and left-hand end..	0.03 mm
At right-hand end..	0.02 mm
Big-end side clearance..	not available
Endfloat...	0.03 to 0.09 mm

Cylinder base gasket selection

Final cylinder top gasket surface to piston crown measurement . . . . . . 2.30 to 2.50 mm
Gasket sizes available . . . . 0.2, 0.4, 0.6 and 0.8 mm

Torque settings

Alternator rotor nut . . . . 52 to 56 Nm
Crankcase bolts . . . . 12 to 13 Nm
Cylinder head nuts . . . . 10 to 11 Nm
Engine front mounting bolt . . . . 33 to 41 Nm
Rear shock absorber lower mounting bolt . . . . 33 to 41 Nm

1 General information

The engine unit is a single cylinder two-stroke, with liquid cooling. The alternator rotor is on the right-hand end of the crankshaft. The crankshaft assembly is pressed, incorporating the connecting rod, with the big-end running on the crankpin on a needle roller bearing. The piston also runs on a needle roller bearing fitted in the small-end of the connecting rod. The crankshaft runs in caged ball main bearings. The crankcase divides vertically.

Later engines carry the 'Hi-Per2Pro' name, denoting that the scooter is fitted with a catalytic converter and secondary air system. Some models will have a 'hi-per2pro' decal on the bodywork.

2 Operations possible with the engine in the frame

All components and assemblies, with the exception of the crankshaft/connecting rod assembly and its bearings, and the water pump impeller, can be worked on without having to remove the engine/transmission unit from the frame. If however, a number of areas require attention at the same time, removal of the engine is recommended, as it is easy to do so.

3 Operations requiring engine removal

To access the crankshaft and connecting rod assembly and its bearings, and the water pump impeller, the engine must be removed from the frame and the crankcase halves must be separated.

4 Major engine repair – general note

1 It is not always easy to determine when or if an engine should be completely overhauled, as a number of factors must be considered.
2 High mileage is not necessarily an indication that an overhaul is needed, while

low mileage, on the other hand, does not preclude the need for an overhaul. Frequency of servicing is probably the single most important consideration. An engine that has regular and frequent maintenance will most likely give many miles of reliable service. Conversely, a neglected engine, or one which has not been run in properly, may require an overhaul very early in its life.
3 If the engine is making obvious knocking or rumbling noises, the connecting rod and/or main bearings are probably at fault.
4 Loss of power, rough running, excessive noise and high fuel consumption rates may also point to the need for an overhaul, especially if they are all present at the same time. If a complete service as detailed in Chapter 1 does not remedy the situation, major mechanical work is the only solution.
5 An engine overhaul generally involves restoring the internal parts to the specifications of a new engine. This may require fitting new piston rings and crankcase seals, or, after a high mileage, reboring the cylinder and fitting a new piston; on FXR180 models the cylinder bore is plated and cannot be rebored. The end result should be a like-new engine that will give as many trouble-free miles as the original.
6 Before beginning the engine overhaul, read through the related procedures to familiarise yourself with the scope and requirements of the job. Overhauling an engine is not all that difficult, but it is time consuming. Check on the availability of parts and make sure that any necessary special tools and materials are obtained in advance.
7 Most work can be done with typical workshop hand tools, although, if required, Gilera produce a number of service tools

for specific purposes such as removing the alternator rotor, disassembling the clutch and separating the crankcase halves. Precision measuring tools are required for inspecting parts to determine if they must be renewed. Alternatively, a dealer will handle the inspection of parts and offer advice concerning reconditioning and replacement. As a general rule, time is the primary cost of an overhaul so it does not pay to install worn or substandard parts.
8 As a final note, to ensure maximum life and minimum trouble from a rebuilt engine, everything must be assembled with care in a spotlessly clean environment.

5 Engine/transmission unit – removal and installation

Caution: The engine is not heavy, however engine removal and installation should be carried out with the aid of an assistant; personal injury or damage could occur if the engine falls or is dropped.

Removal

1 The procedure for removing the engine is the same as for air-cooled models, with the following additions.
2 Drain the cooling system (see Chapter 1). Loosen the clips securing the cooling system hoses to the cylinder head and to the coolant pipe on the right-hand side of the engine, and detach the hoses from their unions, noting which fits where **(see illustrations)**.
3 Pull back the boot on the coolant temperature sensor wiring terminal and disconnect the connector **(see illustration 5.2a)**.

5.2a Detach the hoses (A) from their unions on the cylinder head. Note the wiring connector (B)

5.2b Detach the hose (arrowed) from its union on the engine

4 On Purejet 50 models, refer to Chapter 4, Section 10, and disconnect the throttle position sensor wiring connector from the throttle body and release the wiring from any clips or ties. Disconnect the wiring connectors from the fuel and air injectors. Disconnect the throttle cable from the throttle body. Disconnect the fuel hoses from the injector manifold – press the hose union down and hold it down, then lift the release ring on the union and disconnect the hose. **Note:** *The fuel system is pressurised – cover the union with a clean rag to prevent fuel spraying over yourself or the machine.*

5 Refer to Chapter 2A, Section 5 for the rest of the procedure.

Installation

6 Installation is the reverse of the procedure in Chapter 2A, noting the additional points:

• Make sure the cooling system hoses are properly connected and secured by their clips **(see illustration 5.2a and 2b)**.

• Don't forget to replace the temperature sensor wiring boot.

• Fill the cooling system (see Chapter 1, Section 10).

• On Purejet 50 models, ensure the fuel hose unions are securely clipped in position.

6 Disassembly and reassembly –
general information

Disassembly

1 Before disassembling the engine, the external surfaces of the unit should be thoroughly cleaned and degreased. This will prevent contamination of the engine internals, and will also make working a lot easier and cleaner. A high flash-point solvent, such as paraffin can be used, or better still, a proprietary engine degreaser such as Gunk. Use old paintbrushes and toothbrushes to work the solvent into the various recesses of the engine casings. Take care to exclude solvent or water from the electrical components and intake and exhaust ports.

 Warning: The use of petrol (gasoline) as a cleaning agent should be avoided because of the risk of fire.

2 When clean and dry, arrange the unit on the workbench, leaving suitable clear area for working. Gather a selection of small containers and plastic bags so that parts can be grouped together in an easily identifiable manner. Some paper and a pen should be on hand to permit notes to be made and labels attached where necessary. A supply of clean rag is also required.

3 Before commencing work, read through the appropriate section so that some idea of the necessary procedure can be gained. When removing components it should be noted that great force is seldom required, unless specified. In many cases, a component's

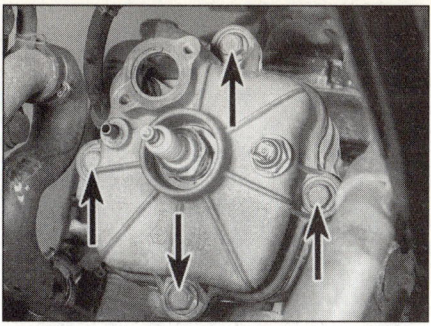

7.4a Unscrew the bolts (arrowed) and remove the cover

reluctance to be removed is indicative of an incorrect approach or removal method – if in any doubt, re-check with the text.

4 When disassembling the engine, keep 'mated' parts that have been in contact with each other during engine operation together. These 'mated' parts must be reused or renewed as an assembly.

5 A complete engine disassembly should be done in the following general order with reference to the appropriate Sections and Chapters.

• Remove the cylinder head
• Remove the cylinder
• Remove the piston
• Remove the alternator
• Remove the variator (see Chapter 2D)
• Remove the starter motor (see Chapter 9)
• Remove the oil pump and drive belt
• Remove the reed valve (see Chapter 4)
• Remove the water pump (see Chapter 3)
• Separate the crankcase halves
• Remove the crankshaft

Reassembly

6 Reassembly is accomplished by reversing the general disassembly sequence.

7 Cylinder head

Note: *This procedure can be carried out with the engine in the frame. If the engine has been removed, ignore the steps which don't apply.*
Caution: The engine must be completely

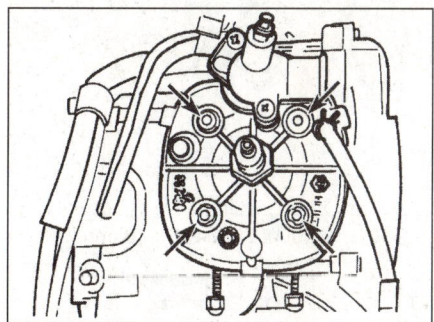

7.6a Cylinder head nuts (arrowed) – all 50 cc engines

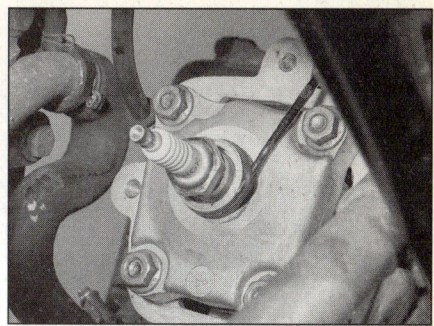

7.4b Remove the O-ring and discard it

cool before beginning this procedure or the cylinder head may become warped.

Removal

1 Remove the engine access panel and, if required, the side panels (see Chapter 8).

2 Drain the cooling system (see Chapter 1, Section 10). Release the clamps securing the cooling system hoses to the cylinder head, and detach the hoses from their unions, noting which fits where **(see illustration 5.2a)**.

3 Pull back the boot on the coolant temperature sensor wiring terminal and disconnect the connector.

4 On Runner FX125 and FXR180 models, remove the four bolts securing the cylinder head cover and remove the cover and seal **(see illustration)**. Remove the O-ring from the spark plug housing and discard it as a new one must be used on reassembly **(see illustration)**.

5 On Purejet 50 models, refer to Chapter 4, Section 10, and disconnect the wiring connectors from the fuel and air injectors. Disconnect the fuel hoses from the injector manifold – press the hose union down and hold it down, then lift the release ring on the union and disconnect the hose. Remove the Torx screw securing the air hose union to the injector manifold and lift off the union. **Note:** *It is not necessary to disconnect the air hose from the union. If the hose is disconnected, Gilera recommend fitting a new hose.*

6 Unscrew the four cylinder head nuts evenly and a little at a time in a criss-cross sequence until they are all loose and remove them **(see illustrations)**.

7.6b Cylinder head nuts (arrowed) – Runner FX125 and FXR180 engines

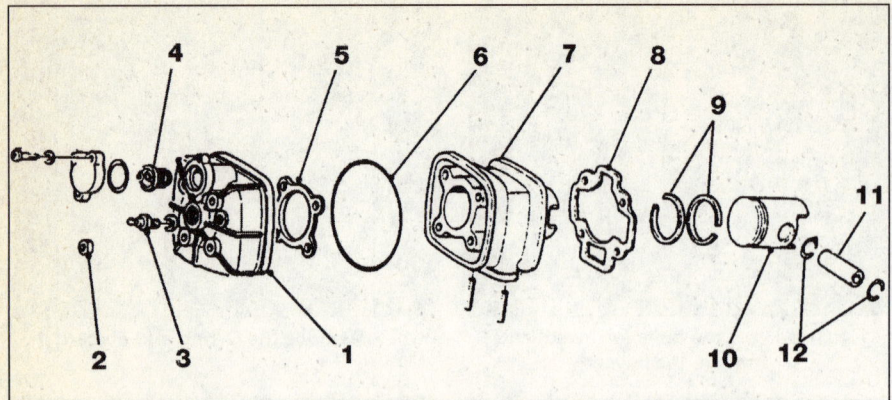

7.16a Cylinder head and cylinder components – all 50 cc engines

1 Cylinder head	4 Thermostat	8 Base gasket
2 Cylinder head nut – 4 off	5 Cylinder head gasket	9 Piston rings
3 Temperature sender	6 O-ring	10 Piston
	7 Cylinder	11 Piston pin
		12 Circlips

7 Draw the head off the cylinder studs. If the head is stuck, tap around the joint face between the head and the cylinder with a soft-faced mallet to free it. Do not attempt to free the head by inserting a screwdriver between the head and cylinder – you'll damage the sealing surfaces. Discard the cylinder head O-ring and gasket (where fitted) as new ones must be used. Where no gasket is fitted, the machined face of the cylinder head fits directly against the machined face of the cylinder.

8 If required, remove the thermostat and housing (see Chapter 3).

9 On Purejet 50 models, if required, remove the injector assembly (see Chapter 4).

10 Remove the alternator cover (see Section 11).

Inspection

11 Follow the procedure in Chapter 2A,

Section 7, and clean the carbon off the cylinder head and piston, then inspect the head for damage and warpage.

12 If the thermostat has been removed, ensure the recess in the head is clean and free from corrosion.

Installation

13 If removed, install the thermostat and housing (see Chapter 3).

14 On Purejet 50 models, if removed, install the injector assembly (see Chapter 4).

15 Lubricate the cylinder bore with the recommended two-stroke oil.

16 Ensure both cylinder head and cylinder mating surfaces are clean, then carefully fit the cylinder head onto the cylinder using a new gasket (where fitted) and O-ring **(see illustrations)**.

17 Install the four nuts and tighten them all finger-tight **(see illustration 7.6a or 6b)**. Now

tighten them evenly and a little at a time in a criss-cross pattern to the torque setting specified at the beginning of this Chapter.

18 On Purejet 50 models, refer to Chapter 4, Section 10, and install the air hose union on the injector manifold and secure it with the Torx screw. Connect the fuel hoses to the injector manifold – press the hose union down and ensure the release ring clicks into position. Ensure the hose unions are secure. Connect the wiring connectors from the fuel and air injectors.

19 On Runner FX125 and FXR180 models, check the condition of the head cover gasket and fit a new one if necessary **(see illustration)**. Also fit a new O-ring around the plug housing **(see illustration 7.4b)**.

20 Install the remaining components in the reverse order of removal, then refill the cooling system (see Chapter 1, Section 10).

8 Cylinder

Note: *This procedure can be carried out with the engine in the frame.*

Removal and inspection

1 Remove the exhaust system (see Chapter 4) and the cylinder head (see Section 7). The procedure for removal and inspection of the cylinder is the same as for air-cooled models (see Chapter 2A, Section 8) with the following additions.

2 When calculating the piston-to-bore clearance on DNA 50 GP models, measure the bore 15 mm from the top across the crankshaft axis. On all other models, measure the bore 20 mm from the top across the crankshaft axis.

3 Cylinder bore specifications are given at the beginning of this Chapter. Gilera list five size codes (A to E) for the Runner 50, 50 DD and SP engines, four (M, N, O and P) for the Purejet 50 and DNA 50 GP, and nine (A to I) for the FX125 and FXR180. **Note:** *The FXR180 engine has a Nicasil plated bore. The Nicasil plating has a high resistance to wear and should last the life of the engine unless serious damage, such as a seizure,*

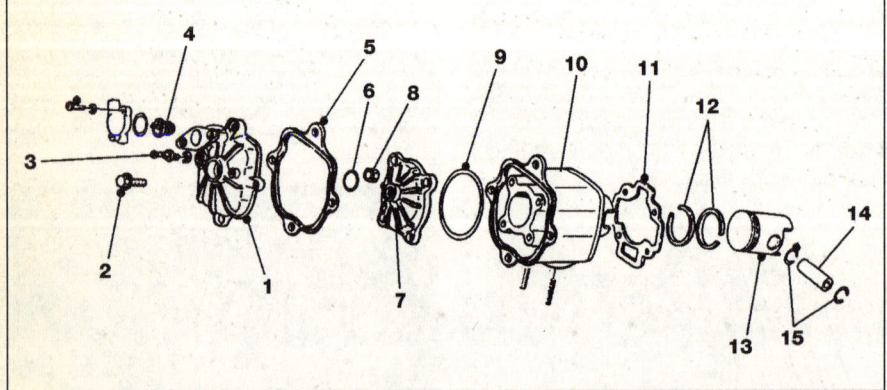

7.16b Cylinder head and cylinder components – Runner FX125 and FXR180 engines

1 Cylinder head cover	6 O-ring	11 Base gasket
2 Cover bolt – 4 off	7 Cylinder head	12 Piston rings
3 Temperature sender	8 Cylinder head nut – 4 off	13 Piston
4 Thermostat	9 O-ring	14 Piston pin
5 Cover seal	10 Cylinder	15 Circlips

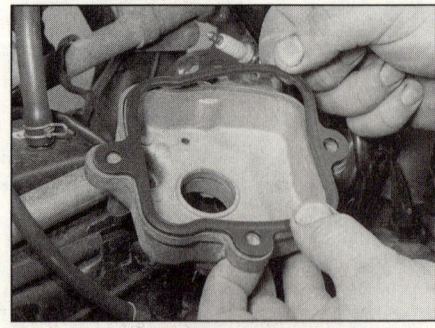

7.19 Check the cover gasket and renew if necessary

has occurred; in this event, a new cylinder, piston and rings should be fitted – the cylinder cannot be rebored.

Installation

4 Different thickness cylinder base gaskets are available (see Specifications at the beginning of this Chapter). To determine which thickness of gasket to use, assemble the cylinder on the crankcase and piston without a base gasket and measure the height of the piston at TDC in relation to the cylinder top gasket surface with a dial gauge as follows. Gilera provide a gauge mounting bracket (Part No. 020268Y) for this purpose **(see illustration)**.

5 Check that the mating surfaces of the cylinder and crankcase are clean and remove any rag from the crankcase mouth, then follow the procedure in Steps 11 and 12 and install the cylinder. Press the cylinder down onto the crankcase.

6 Set the dial gauge in the mounting bracket, and with the bracket and the gauge tip resting against the cylinder top gasket surface, zero the gauge.

7 Rotate the crankshaft via the alternator rotor nut so that the piston is partway down the bore, then clamp the mounting bracket diagonally across two of the cylinder studs and secure it by tightening the stud nuts to the specified torque setting. Rotate the crankshaft so that the piston rises to the top of its stroke (TDC) and the gauge tip rests on the centre of the piston crown. At this point read off the dial gauge **(see illustration)**.

8 On Runner 50, 50 DD, SP and Purejet 50 models and DNA 50 GP models, compare the reading with the specifications at the beginning of this Chapter to determine the gasket thickness.

9 On Runner FX125 models, subtract 2.74 to 2.84 mm from the reading to obtain the gasket thickness. On FXR180 models, subtract 2.30 to 2.50 mm from the reading to obtain the gasket thickness. Ensure the selected gasket thickness maintains the specified measurement between the piston crown and the cylinder top gasket surface (see Specifications at the beginning of this Chapter).

10 Having established the correct gasket thickness, lift off the cylinder and fit the new gasket to the crankcase making sure it is the correct way round.

11 Check that the piston rings are correctly positioned so that the locating pin in each piston ring groove is between the open ends of the ring **(see illustration 10.6, Chapter 2A)**. Lubricate the cylinder bore, piston and piston rings, and the connecting rod big- and small-ends, with two-stroke oil, then fit the cylinder down over the studs until the piston crown fits into the bore **(see illustration 8.11, Chapter 2A)**.

12 Gently push down on the cylinder, making sure the piston enters the bore squarely and does not get cocked sideways. Carefully

compress and feed each ring into the bore as the cylinder is lowered, taking care that they do not rotate out of position. Do not use force if the cylinder appears to be stuck as the piston and/or rings will be damaged.

13 When the piston is correctly installed in the cylinder, press the cylinder down onto the base gasket.

14 Install the remaining components in the reverse order of removal.

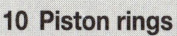

9 Piston

Note: *This procedure can be carried out with the engine in the frame.*

1 The procedure for removal, inspection and installation of the piston is the same as for air-cooled engines (see Chapter 2A, Section 9) with the following addition.

2 On FX125 and FXR180 models, four sizes of connecting rod small-end bearing are available. A mark on the connecting rod, either a I, II, III or IIII indicates the small-end size, and this mark must be matched with a similar mark on the new bearing, or by a colour code.
Connecting rod marked I:
   bearing colour copper
Connecting rod marked II:
   bearing colour blue
Connecting rod marked III:
   bearing colour white
Connecting rod marked IIII:
   bearing colour green

10 Piston rings

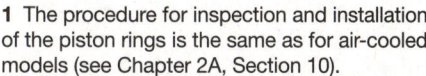

1 The procedure for inspection and installation of the piston rings is the same as for air-cooled models (see Chapter 2A, Section 10).

11 Alternator rotor and stator

Note: *This procedure can be carried out with the engine in the frame.*

1 Remove the engine access panels and, if required, the side panels (see Chapter 8).

2 If a secondary air system is fitted, release the clip on the lower flexible hose union and detach the hose from the exhaust pipe **(see illustration 11.3**, Chapter 2A). Unclip the system assembly from the alternator cover and displace it.

3 Remove the screws securing the alternator cover and remove the cover, noting how it fits.

4 The procedure for removal and installation of the alternator rotor and stator is the same as for air-cooled models (see Chapter 2A, Section 12). **Note:** *Liquid-cooled models*

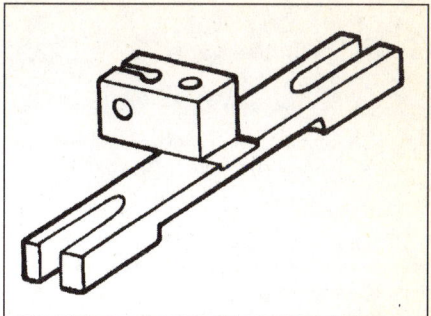

8.4 Dial gauge mounting bracket

have no cooling fan mounted on the rotor. If the secondary air system has been displaced, ensure the hose clip is secure on installation.

12 Starter pinion assembly

Note: *This procedure can be carried out with the engine in the frame.*

1 The procedure for removal, inspection and installation of the starter pinion assembly is the same as for air-cooled models (see Chapter 2A, Section 13).

13 Oil pump and drive belt

Note: *This procedure can be carried out with the engine in the frame.*

1 The procedure for removal, inspection and installation of the oil pump and drive belt, and for bleeding the oil pump, is the same as for air-cooled models (see Chapter 2A, Section 14).

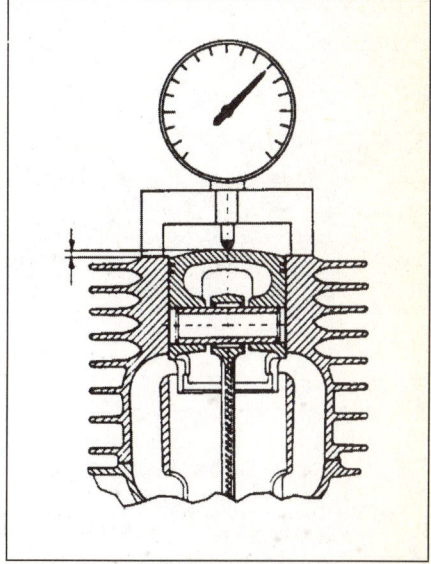

8.7 Set-up for measuring the piston height at TDC

14 Crankcase halves and main bearings

Note: *To separate the crankcase halves, the engine must be removed from the frame.*

Separation

1 To access the crankshaft assembly and engine main bearings, the crankcase halves must be separated.

2 Remove the engine from the frame (see Section 5). Before the crankcases can be separated the following components must be removed:

- Cylinder head (Section 7)
- Cylinder (Section 8)
- Alternator rotor and stator (Section 11)
- Reed valve (Chapter 4)
- Starter motor (Chapter 9)
- Oil pump and drive belt (Section 13)
- Centre stand (see Chapter 6)

3 The remainder of the procedure for separation and joining of the crankcase halves and for removal of the crankshaft assembly is the same as for air-cooled models (see Chapter 2A, Section 15), with the following additions.

4 The water pump shaft and its bearings are housed in the left-hand crankcase half and the pump impeller is located between the crankcase halves. Access to the impeller and its seal can only be achieved after the crankcases have been separated (see Chapter 3).

5 On Purejet 50 models, the fuel injection system air compressor is located on the rear of the crankcase. Follow the procedure in Chapter 4 to remove the compressor before separating the crankcase halves.

Reassembly

6 Do not forget to install the water pump impeller and seal before joining the crankcase halves. If required, the pump drive shaft and bearings can be installed after joining the halves (see Chapter 3).

15 Crankshaft assembly and big-end bearing

1 The procedure for inspection of the crankshaft and the big-end bearing is the same as for air-cooled models (see Chapter 2A, Section 16).

16 Initial start-up after overhaul

1 Make sure the oil tank is at least partly full and the pump is correctly adjusted (see Chapter 1, Section 26) and bled of air (see Section 13).

2 Fill the coolant reservoir with fresh coolant (see Chapter 1, Section 10).

3 Make sure there is fuel in the tank.

4 With the ignition OFF, operate the kickstart a couple of times to check that the engine turns over easily.

5 Turn the ignition ON, start the engine and allow it to run at a slow idle until it reaches operating temperature. Do not be alarmed if there is a little smoke from the exhaust – this will be due to the oil used to lubricate the piston and bore during assembly and should subside after a while.

6 If the engine proves reluctant to start, remove the spark plug and check that it has not become wet and oily. If it has, clean it and try again. If the engine refuses to start, go through the fault finding charts at the end of this manual to identify the problem.

7 Check carefully that there are no fuel or oil leaks and make sure the controls, especially the brakes, function properly before road testing the machine.

8 Check the coolant level (see *Daily (pre-ride) checks*) after the engine has cooled down and bleed the cooling system of air as described in Chapter 1, Section 10.

9 Refer to Section 17 for the recommended running-in procedure.

17 Recommended running-in procedure

1 Treat the engine gently for the first few miles to allow any new parts to bed in.

2 If a new piston, cylinder or crankshaft assembly has been fitted, the engine will have to be run-in as when new. This means a restraining hand on the throttle until at least 300 miles (500 km) have been covered. There's no point in keeping to any set speed limit – the main idea is to keep from labouring the engine and to gradually increase performance up to the 600 mile (1000 km) mark. Make sure that the throttle position is varied to vary engine speed, and use full throttle only for short bursts. Experience is the best guide, since it's easy to tell when an engine is running freely.

3 Pay particular attention to the *Daily (pre-ride) checks* at the beginning of this manual. Check the tightness of all relevant nuts and bolts.

Chapter 2 Part C:
Liquid cooled four-stroke engine (Runner VX125, VXR180 and VXR200, ST125 and ST200, DNA 125 and DNA 180)

Refer to the beginning of Chapter 1 for model identification details

Contents

Degrees of difficulty

Easy, suitable for novice with little experience 	**Fairly easy,** suitable for beginner with some experience	**Fairly difficult,** suitable for competent DIY mechanic 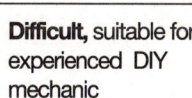	**Difficult,** suitable for experienced DIY mechanic 	**Very difficult,** suitable for expert DIY or professional 

Specifications

General

Type	Single cylinder four-stroke
Capacity	
VX125, ST125 and DNA 125	124.2 cc
VXR180 and DNA 180	181.7 cc
VXR200 and ST200	197.7 cc
Bore	
VX125, ST125 and DNA 125	57.0 mm
VXR180 and DNA 180	69.0 mm
VXR200 and ST200	72.0 mm
Stroke.	48.6 mm
Compression ratio	
VX125, ST125 and DNA 125	11.5:1 to 13.0:1
VXR180 and DNA 180	11.5:1 to 12.5:1
VXR200 and ST200	11.0:1 to 12.0:1

Camshaft

Intake lobe height	30.285 mm
Exhaust lobe height	29.209 mm
Left-hand journal diameter	
Standard	36.950 to 36.975 mm
Service limit (min)	36.940 mm
Right-hand journal diameter	
Standard	19.959 to 19.980 mm
Service limit (min)	19.950 mm
Camshaft end-float	
Standard	0.11 to 0.41 mm
Service limit	0.42 mm

Cylinder head

Warpage (max)	0.05 mm
Left-hand camshaft bearing housing diameter	37.000 to 37.025 mm
Right-hand camshaft journal housing diameter	20.000 to 20.021 mm
Rocker arm shaft housing	12.000 to 12.018 mm
Rocker arm shaft diameter	11.977 to 11.985 mm
Rocker arm internal diameter	12.000 to 12.011 mm
Valve seat width (max)	1.6 mm

Valves, guides and springs

Valve clearances	see Chapter 1
Intake valve	
Overall standard length	94.6 mm
Stem diameter	
Standard	4.972 to 4.987 mm
Service limit (min)	4.960 mm
Guide bore diameter	
Standard	5.000 to 5.012 mm
Service limit (max)	5.022 mm
Stem/valve guide clearance	
Standard	0.013 to 0.040 mm
Service limit	0.062 mm
Face width	
Standard	0.99 to 1.27 mm
Service limit (max)	1.6 mm
Exhaust valve	
Overall standard length	94.4 mm
Stem diameter	
Standard	4.960 to 4.975 mm
Service limit (min)	4.950 mm
Guide bore diameter	
Standard	5.000 to 5.012 mm
Service limit (max)	5.022 mm
Stem/valve guide clearance	
Standard	0.025 to 0.052 mm
Service limit	0.072 mm
Face width	
Standard	0.99 to 1.27 mm
Service limit (max)	1.6 mm

Cylinder bore

125 cc engine bore diameter (measured 41 mm down from top edge of the cylinder, at 90° to piston pin axis)

Standard	
Size code A	56.997 to 57.004 mm
Size code B	57.004 to 57.011 mm
Size code C	57.011 to 57.018 mm
Size code D	57.018 to 57.025 mm
1st oversize	
Size code A1	57.197 to 57.204 mm
Size code B1	57.204 to 57.211 mm
Size code C1	57.211 to 57.218 mm
Size code D1	57.218 to 57.225 mm

Cylinder bore (continued)

125 cc engine bore diameter (continued)
  2nd oversize
    Size code A2.. 57.397 to 57.404 mm
    Size code B2.. 57.404 to 57.411 mm
    Size code C2.. 57.411 to 57.418 mm
    Size code D2.. 57.418 to 57.425 mm
  3rd oversize
    Size code A3.. 57.597 to 57.604 mm
    Size code B3.. 57.604 to 57.611 mm
    Size code C3.. 57.611 to 57.618 mm
    Size code D3.. 57.618 to 57.625 mm
180 cc engine bore diameter (measured 41 mm down from top edge of the cylinder, at 90° to piston pin axis)
  Standard
    Size code A.. 68.990 to 68.997 mm
    Size code B.. 68.997 to 69.004 mm
    Size code C.. 69.004 to 69.011 mm
    Size code D.. 69.011 to 69.018 mm
200 cc engine bore diameter (measured 33 mm down from top edge of the cylinder, at 90° to piston pin axis)
  Standard
    Size code A.. 71.990 to 71.997 mm
    Size code B.. 71.997 to 72.004 mm
    Size code C.. 72.004 to 72.011 mm
    Size code D.. 72.011 to 72.018 mm

Piston

125 cc engine piston diameter (measured 41.1 mm down from top edge of the piston, at 90° to piston pin axis)
  Standard
    Size code A.. 56.945 to 56.952 mm
    Size code B.. 56.952 to 56.959 mm
    Size code C.. 56.959 to 56.966 mm
    Size code D.. 56.966 to 56.973 mm
  1st oversize
    Size code A1.. 57.145 to 57.152 mm
    Size code B1.. 57.152 to 57.159 mm
    Size code C1.. 57.159 to 57.166 mm
    Size code D1.. 57.166 to 57.173 mm
  2nd oversize
    Size code A2.. 57.345 to 57.352 mm
    Size code B2.. 57.352 to 57.359 mm
    Size code C2.. 57.359 to 57.366 mm
    Size code D2.. 57.366 to 57.373 mm
  3rd oversize
    Size code A3.. 57.545 to 57.552 mm
    Size code B3.. 57.552 to 57.559 mm
    Size code C3.. 57.559 to 57.566 mm
    Size code D3.. 57.566 to 57.573 mm
  Piston-to-bore clearance (when new)........................ 0.045 to 0.059 mm
180 cc engine piston diameter (measured 33 mm down from top edge of the piston, at 90° to piston pin axis)
  Standard
    Size code A.. 68.953 to 68.960 mm
    Size code B.. 68.960 to 68.967 mm
    Size code C.. 68.967 to 68.974 mm
    Size code D.. 68.974 to 68.981 mm
  Piston-to-bore clearance (when new)........................ 0.030 to 0.044 mm
200 cc engine piston diameter (measured 33 mm down from top edge of the piston, at 90° to piston pin axis)
  Standard
    Size code A.. 71.953 to 71.960 mm
    Size code B.. 71.960 to 71.967 mm
    Size code C.. 71.967 to 71.974 mm
    Size code D.. 71.974 to 71.981 mm
  Piston-to-bore clearance (when new)........................ 0.030 to 0.044 mm
Piston pin diameter .... 14.996 to 15.000 mm
Piston pin bore diameter in piston .... 15.001 to 15.006 mm

Piston rings

Ring end gap (installed) – 125/180 cc engine
    Top ring
        Standard . . . . 0.20 to 0.40 mm
        Service limit (max) . . . . 1.0 mm
    2nd ring
        Standard . . . . 0.10 to 0.30 mm
        Service limit (max) . . . . 1.0 mm
    Oil control ring
        Standard . . . . 0.15 to 0.35 mm
        Service limit (max) . . . . 1.0 mm
Ring end gap (installed) – 200 cc engine
    Top ring
        Standard . . . . 0.15 to 0.30 mm
    2nd ring and oil control ring
        Standard . . . . 0.20 to 0.40 mm
Ring-to-groove clearance
    Top ring
        Standard . . . . 0.025 to 0.070 mm
        Service limit (max) . . . . 0.080 mm
    2nd ring and oil control ring
        Standard . . . . 0.015 to 0.060 mm
        Service limit (max) . . . . 0.070 mm

Lubrication system

Engine oil pressure (at 90°C) . . . . 0.5 to 1.2 Bars @ 1650 rpm / 3.2 to 4.2 Bars @ 6000 rpm
Oil pump
    Inner rotor tip-to-outer rotor clearance (max) . . . . 0.12 mm
    Outer rotor-to-body clearance (max) . . . . 0.20 mm
    Rotor end-float (max) . . . . 0.09 mm
Relief valve spring length . . . . 54.2 mm

Connecting rod

Small-end internal diameter
    Standard . . . . 15.015 to 15.025 mm
    Service limit (max) . . . . 15.030 mm
Big-end side clearance . . . . 0.20 to 0.50 mm
Big-end radial play . . . . 0.036 to 0.054 mm

Crankshaft

Combined width of flywheels and big-end
    Runner VX125, ST125 and DNA 125 . . . . 55.75 to 55.90 mm
    Runner VXR180/200, ST200 and DNA 180 . . . . 51.40 to 51.45 mm
Runout A (max) . . . . 0.15 mm
Runout B (max) . . . . 0.01 mm
Runout C (max) . . . . 0.10 mm
End-float . . . . 0.15 to 0.40 mm

Torque settings

Alternator rotor nut . . . . 54 to 60 Nm
Alternator stator/pulse generator coil screws . . . . 3 to 4 Nm
Cam chain tensionor blade bolt . . . . 10 to 14 Nm
Cam chain tensioner bolts . . . . 11 to 13 Nm
Cam chain tensioner spring cap bolt . . . . 5 to 6 Nm
Camshaft retaining plate bolts . . . . 4 to 6 Nm
Camshaft sprocket bolt . . . . 11 to 15 Nm
Crankcase bolts . . . . 11 to 13 Nm
Cylinder head bolts (outside) . . . . 11 to 13 Nm
Cylinder head nuts . . . . 28 to 30 Nm
Decompressor mechanism bolt . . . . 7 to 8.5 Nm
Engine front mounting bolt . . . . 33 to 41 Nm
Oil pressure switch . . . . 12 to 14 Nm
Oil pump drive chain cover screws . . . . 0.7 to 0.9 Nm
Oil pump driven sprocket bolt . . . . 10 to 14 Nm
Oil pump mounting screws . . . . 5 to 6 Nm
Sump cover bolts . . . . 10 to 14 Nm
Valve cover bolts . . . . 11 to 13 Nm

1 General information

The engine unit is a liquid-cooled, single cylinder four-stroke. The water pump is mounted on the alternator rotor, which is on the right-hand end of the crankshaft. The crankshaft assembly is pressed together, incorporating the connecting rod, with the big-end running on the crankpin on a bronze bearing. The crankshaft runs in plain main bearings. The crankcase divides vertically.

The camshaft is chain-driven off the left-hand end of the crankshaft, and operates four valves via rocker arms.

2 Operations possible with the engine in the frame

All components and assemblies, with the exception of the crankshaft/connecting rod assembly and its bearings, can be worked on without having to remove the engine/transmission unit from the frame. However, access is extremely limited and if a number of areas require attention at the same time, removal of the engine is recommended, as it is easy to do so.

3 Operations requiring engine removal

To access the crankshaft and connecting rod assembly and its bearings, the engine must be removed from the frame and the crankcase halves must be separated.

4 Major engine repair – general note

1 It is not always easy to determine when or if an engine should be completely overhauled, as a number of factors must be considered.
2 High mileage is not necessarily an indication that an overhaul is needed, while low mileage, on the other hand, does not preclude the need for an overhaul. Frequency of servicing is probably the single most important consideration. An engine that has regular and frequent oil and filter changes, as well as other required maintenance, will most likely give many miles of reliable service. Conversely, a neglected engine, or one which has not been run in properly, may require an overhaul very early in its life.
3 Exhaust smoke and excessive oil consumption are both indications that piston rings and/or valve guides are in need of attention, although make sure that the fault is not due to oil leakage.

5.6a Disconnect the multi-pin wiring connector

4 If the engine is making obvious knocking or rumbling noises, the connecting rod and/or main bearings are probably at fault.
5 Loss of power, rough running, excessive valve train noise and high fuel consumption rates may also point to the need for an overhaul, especially if they are all present at the same time. If a complete service as detailed in Chapter 1 does not remedy the situation, major mechanical work is the only solution.
6 A full engine overhaul generally involves restoring the internal parts to the specifications of a new engine. The piston and piston rings are renewed and the cylinder is rebored (125 cc) or renewed (180/200 cc). The valve seats are re-ground and new valve springs are fitted. If the connecting rod bearings are worn a new crankshaft assembly is fitted. The end result should be a like new engine that will give as many trouble-free miles as the original.
7 Before beginning the engine overhaul, read through the related procedures to familiarise yourself with the scope and requirements of the job. Overhauling an engine is not all that difficult, but it is time consuming. Plan on the scooter being tied up for a minimum of two weeks. Check on the availability of parts and make sure that any necessary special tools and materials are obtained in advance.
8 Most work can be done with typical workshop hand tools, although, if required, Gilera produce a number of service tools for specific purposes such as removing the alternator rotor, disassembling the clutch

5.6b Disconnect the lead from the starter motor terminal (arrowed)

and separating the crankcase halves. Precision measuring tools are required for inspecting parts to determine if they must be renewed. Alternatively, a dealer will handle the inspection of parts and offer advice concerning reconditioning and replacement. As a general rule, time is the primary cost of an overhaul so it does not pay to install worn or substandard parts.
9 As a final note, to ensure maximum life and minimum trouble from a rebuilt engine, everything must be assembled with care in a spotlessly clean environment.

5 Engine/transmission unit – removal and installation

Caution: The engine is not heavy, however engine removal and installation should be carried out with the aid of an assistant; personal injury or damage could occur if the engine falls or is dropped.

Removal

1 Support the scooter securely in an upright position. Work can be made easier by raising the machine to a suitable working height on an hydraulic ramp or a suitable platform. Make sure the scooter is secure and will not topple over. If the sump cover is going to be removed, or the crankcase halves separated, drain the engine oil (see Chapter 1).
2 Remove the bodywork as required according to model; on DNA models, remove the engine top cover (see Chapter 8).
3 Drain the cooling system (see Chapter 1, Section 10), then disconnect the coolant hoses from the water pump and the thermostat housing (see Chapter 3). Disconnect the coolant temperature sensor wiring connector.
4 Remove the air filter housing (see Chapter 4).
5 If the engine is dirty, particularly around its mountings, wash it thoroughly before starting any major dismantling work. This will make work much easier and avoid the possibility of dirt falling inside.
6 Disconnect the battery negative (-ve) terminal (see Chapter 9). Trace the wiring from the alternator/pulse generator coil on the right-hand side of the engine and disconnect it at the multi-pin connector **(see illustration)**. Free the wiring from any clips and secure it clear of the engine. Pull the spark plug cap off the plug. Undo the nut securing the starter motor lead to the starter motor terminal **(see illustration)**.
7 Either remove the carburettor, or disconnect the fuel hose and the throttle cable from the carburettor (see Chapter 4). Disconnect the vacuum hose either from the union on the intake manifold or from the T-piece union in the line between the engine and the fuel tap. If the carburettor is left in place, disconnect the automatic choke wiring connector **(see illustration)**.

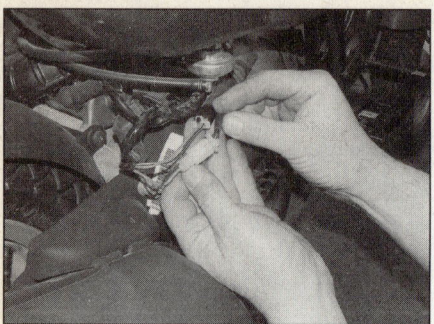

5.7 Disconnect the choke wiring connector

5.8a Free the throttle cable clip (arrowed) . . .

5.8b . . . and the engine earth wire (arrowed)

8 Temporarily undo the bolt on the drive belt cover that secures the throttle cable clip and free the clip and cable **(see illustration)**. Where fitted, cut the cable tie that secures the drive belt air duct to the front of the belt cover and detach the duct, then undo the bolt that secures the engine unit earth wire to the drive belt cover **(see illustration)**.

9 Remove the right-hand rear shock absorber (see Chapter 6).

10 Remove the rear wheel (see Chapter 7). Displace the rear disc brake caliper and secure the caliper clear of the engine unit; ensure the brake hose is free from any clips on the underside of the drive belt cover. If required, pull the disc and hub off the driveshaft and support the rear of the engine unit on a wood block to prevent damage to the casing. Alternatively, temporarily reinstall the wheel. **Note:** *The rear wheel and centre stand provide a convenient support for the engine unit once it is removed from the scooter.*

11 Remove the bolt securing the lower end of the left-hand shock absorber to the transmission casing **(see illustration)**. Note the spacers in the lower shock mounting and remove them for safekeeping.

12 Check that all wiring, cables and hoses are well clear of the engine unit.

13 Have an assistant steady the rear of the scooter. Undo the nut securing the front engine mounting bolt and remove the bolt, then lift the frame off the engine unit **(see illustration)**.

Installation

14 Installation is the reverse of removal, noting the following:

• Make sure no wires, cables or hoses become trapped between the engine and the frame when installing the engine.

• Tighten the engine mounting bolt and shock absorber bolts to the specified torque settings.

• Make sure all wires, cables and hoses are correctly routed and connected, and secured by any clips or ties.

• Adjust the throttle cable (see Chapter 1).

• Fill the cooling system with the specified coolant mixture (see Chapter 1, Section 10).

• If required, fill the engine with the specified quantity of oil (see Chapter 1, Section 12) and check the oil level as described in Daily (pre-ride) checks.

6 Disassembly and reassembly – general information

Disassembly

1 Before disassembling the engine, the external surfaces of the unit should be thoroughly cleaned and degreased to avoid the possibility of dirt falling inside. A high flash-point solvent, such as paraffin can be used, or better still, a proprietary engine degreaser such as Gunk. Use old

paintbrushes and toothbrushes to work the solvent into the various recesses of the engine casings. Take care to exclude solvent or water from the electrical components and inlet and exhaust ports.

⚠ *Warning: The use of petrol (gasoline) as a cleaning agent should be avoided because of the risk of fire.*

2 When clean and dry, arrange the unit on the workbench, leaving suitable clear area for working. Gather a selection of small containers and plastic bags so that parts can be grouped together in an easily identifiable manner. Some paper and a pen should be on hand to permit notes to be made and labels attached where necessary. A supply of clean rag is also required.

3 Before commencing work, read through the appropriate section so that some idea of the necessary procedure can be gained. When removing components it should be noted that great force is seldom required, unless specified. In many cases, a component's reluctance to be removed is indicative of an incorrect approach or removal method – if in any doubt, re-check with the text.

4 When disassembling the engine, keep 'mated' parts that have been in contact with each other during engine operation together. These 'mated' parts must be reused or renewed as an assembly.

5 Complete engine disassembly should be done in the following general order with reference to the appropriate Sections. Refer to Chapter 2D for details of transmission components disassembly.

• Remove the valve cover
• Remove the camshaft and rockers
• Remove the cylinder head
• Remove the cylinder
• Remove the piston
• Remove the alternator
• Remove the starter motor (see Chapter 9)
• Remove the sump cover
• Remove the oil pump
• Separate the crankcase halves
• Remove the crankshaft

Reassembly

6 Reassembly is the reverse of the general disassembly sequence.

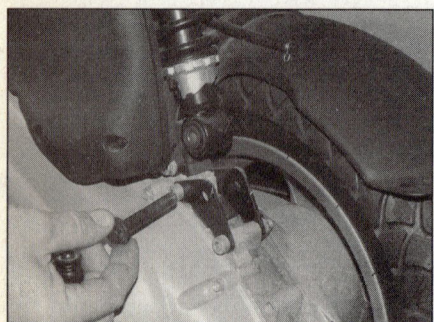

5.11 Undo the lower shock mounting bolt

5.13 Undo the nut (arrowed) on the front mounting bolt

7 Valve cover

Note 1: *This procedure can be carried out with the engine in the frame. If the engine has been removed, ignore the steps which do not apply.*

Note 2: *On DNA models, access to the top of the engine is extremely restricted. If a number of areas require attention, removal of the engine is recommended, as it is easy to do so (see Section 5).*

Removal

1 Remove the bodywork as required by your model to access the engine (see Chapter 8).

2 Undo the bolts securing the breather unit to the valve cover and lift it off; discard the O-ring as a new one must be fitted **(see illustrations)**.

3 Unscrew the bolts securing the valve cover, then lift the cover off the cylinder head **(see illustration)**. If it is stuck, do not try to lever it off with a screwdriver. Tap it gently with a rubber hammer or block of wood to dislodge it. Remove the gasket and discard it as a new one must be used.

4 If required, release the clip that secures the breather unit to the hose and disconnect the hose. Discard the clip as a new one must be fitted on reassembly.

Installation

5 Clean the mating surfaces of the cylinder head and the valve cover with a suitable solvent.

6 Lay the new gasket into the groove in the valve cover, making sure it fits correctly **(see illustration)**.

7 Position the valve cover on the cylinder head, making sure the gasket stays in place, then install the cover bolts. Tighten the bolts evenly and in a criss-cross sequence to the torque setting specified at the beginning of the Chapter.

7.2a Remove the breather unit . . .

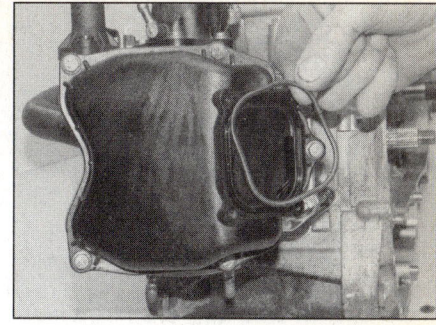

7.2b . . . and lift out the O-ring

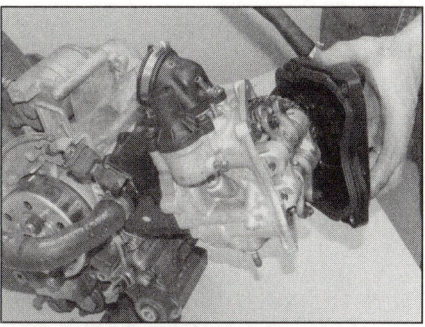

7.3 Lift off the valve cover

8 Install the remaining components in the reverse order of removal.

8 Cam chain tensioner

Note: *This procedure can be carried out with the engine in the frame. If the engine has been removed, ignore the steps which do not apply.*

Removal

1 Remove the bodywork as required by your model to access the engine (see Chapter 8).

2 Remove the silencer (see Chapter 4).

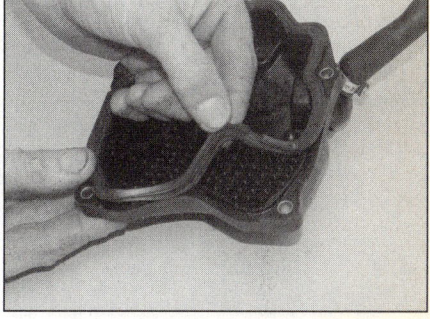

7.6 Ensure the new gasket is fitted correctly

Displace the alternator cover and water pump (see Section 17).

3 Remove the valve cover (see Section 7).

4 Turn the engine in a clockwise direction using the alternator rotor nut, until the timing mark on the rotor aligns with the index mark on the crankcase, and the timing mark (4V) on the camshaft sprocket aligns with the index mark on the camshaft holder **(see illustrations)**. At this point the engine is at TDC (top dead centre) on the compression stroke (all valves closed). **Note:** *On some engines there is no timing mark on the alternator rotor. To ensure correct reassembly, paint a mark on the rotor aligned with the index mark on the crankcase.*

8.4a Align rotor timing mark (A) with index mark (B)

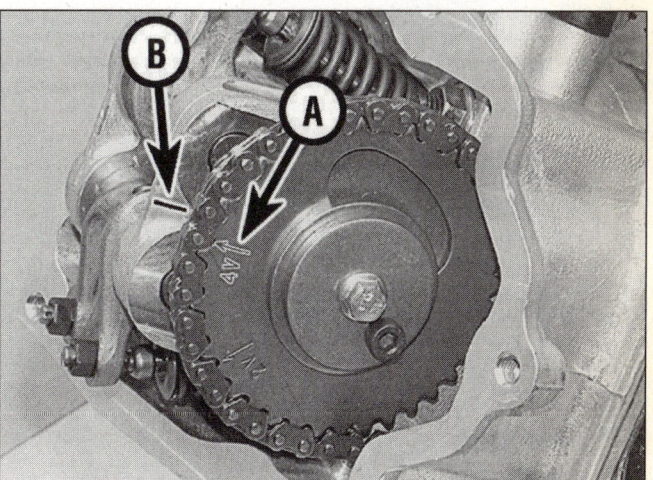

8.4b Align 4V timing mark (A) with index mark (B)

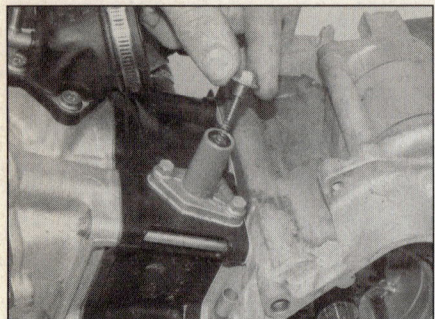

8.5 Remove the cap bolt and spring

8.6 Undo the bolts and remove the cam chain tensioner

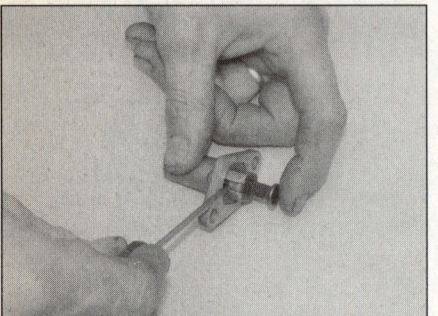

8.9 Check the operation of the ratchet and plunger

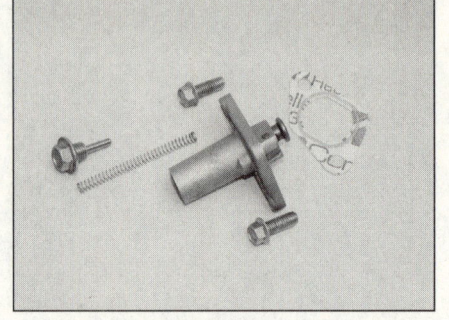

8.10 If necessary, renew the tensioner as an assembly

5 Unscrew the chain tensioner spring cap bolt and withdraw the spring from the tensioner body **(see illustration)**. Discard the sealing washer as a new one must be fitted on reassembly.

6 Unscrew the two tensioner mounting bolts and withdraw the tensioner from the back of the cylinder **(see illustration)**.

7 Remove the gasket from the base of the tensioner or from the cylinder and discard it as a new one must be used.

Inspection

8 Examine the tensioner components for signs of wear or damage.

9 Use a small screwdriver to release the ratchet mechanism on the tensioner plunger and check that the plunger moves freely in and out of the tensioner body **(see illustration)**.

10 If the tensioner mechanism or the spring

are worn or damaged, or if the plunger is seized in the body, the tensioner must be renewed as an assembly **(see illustration)**. Individual components are not available.

Installation

11 Turn the engine in a clockwise direction using the alternator rotor nut. This removes all the slack in the front run of the cam chain between the crankshaft and the camshaft and transfers it to the back run where it will be taken up by the tensioner.

12 Release the ratchet mechanism and press the tensioner plunger all the way into the tensioner body **(see illustration 8.9)**.

13 Place a new gasket on the tensioner body, then install it in the cylinder and tighten the bolts to the torque specified at the beginning of the Chapter **(see illustration 8.6)**.

14 Install a new sealing washer on the spring cap bolt. Install the spring and cap bolt and

tighten the bolt to the specified torque **(see illustration 8.5)**. As the cap bolt is tightened, the plunger should release and take up chain slack.

15 Check that the cam chain is tensioned as it passes over the camshaft sprocket. If it is slack, the tensioner plunger did not release when the cap bolt was tightened. Remove the tensioner and check the operation of the plunger again.

16 Install the alternator cover (see Section 17) and the valve cover (see Section 7). Install the remaining components in the reverse order of removal.

9 Cam chain, blades and sprockets

Note 1: *This procedure can be carried out with the engine in the frame although access to the top of the engine is extremely restricted. If the engine has been removed, ignore the steps which do not apply.*

Note 2: *Early model four-stroke engines were fitted with an automatic decompressor mechanism. This feature was discontinued during the production run of the engine. Follow the appropriate procedure when removing and installing the camshaft sprocket.*

Removal

1 Remove the valve cover (see Section 7).

2 If the cam chain and crankshaft sprocket are to be removed, remove the oil pump driven sprocket, drive chain and drive sprocket (see Section 19).

3 Displace or remove the alternator cover and water pump as required (see Section 17). Turn the engine in a clockwise direction using the alternator rotor nut, until the timing mark on the rotor aligns with the index mark on the crankcase **(see illustration 8.4a)**.

Note: *On some engines there is no timing mark on the alternator rotor. To ensure correct reassembly, paint a mark on the rotor aligned with the index mark on the crankcase. Ensure the timing mark (4V) on the camshaft sprocket aligns with the index mark on the camshaft holder **(see illustration 8.4b)**. At this point the engine is at TDC (top dead centre) on the compression stroke (all valves closed). If the 4V mark is not in alignment, rotate the engine 360° and re-align the timing marks.*

Engine fitted with decompressor mechanism

4 Undo the camshaft sprocket centre bolt and lift off the decompressor mechanism cover **(see illustrations)**. Hold the alternator to prevent the sprocket from turning.

5 Undo the decompressor mechanism bolt, then hold the bob weight return spring and withdraw the bolt and static weight **(see illustrations)**.

6 Lift off the bob weight – note the nylon bush on the back of the weight and how it

9.4a Undo the centre bolt . . .

9.4b . . . and remove the decompressor mechanism cover

9.5a Undo the decompressor mechanism bolt . . .

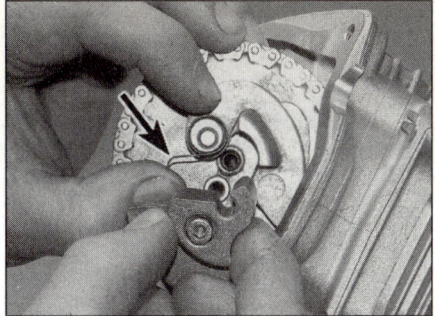

9.5b . . . and remove the static weight. Note the return spring (arrowed)

9.6 Remove the bob weight. Note the position of the bush (arrowed)

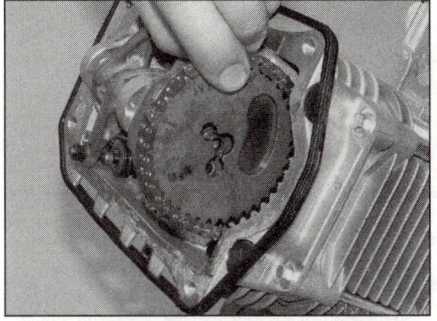

9.8a Lift off the sprocket and backing plate . . .

9.8b . . . and disengage it from the chain

9.9a Remove the thrust washer . . .

locates in the slot in the cam chain sprocket **(see illustration)**. Remove the bush for safekeeping.

7 Remove the cam chain tensioner (see Section 8).

8 Lift the sprocket and its backing plate off the end of the camshaft, then disengage it from the cam chain **(see illustrations)**.

9 If required, secure the chain with a cable tie to prevent it falling into the engine. If the chain is to be removed, mark it with paint so that if it is re-used it can be fitted the same way round. Remove the thrust washer from the end of the crankshaft, then lower the chain down its tunnel and slip it off the sprocket on the crankshaft **(see illustrations)**. Draw the sprocket off the crankshaft, noting how it locates on the pin on the shaft **(see illustration)**.

10 If required, follow the procedure in Step 16 and remove the cam chain blades.

Engine not fitted with decompressor mechanism

11 Loosen the camshaft sprocket centre bolt and the offset bolt **(see illustration 19.14a)**. Hold the alternator to prevent the sprocket from turning.

12 Remove the cam chain tensioner (see Section 8).

13 Lift the chain off the camshaft sprocket **(see illustration)**. If required, secure the chain with a cable tie to prevent it falling into the engine. If the chain is to be removed, mark it with paint so that if it is re-used it can be fitted the same way round. Remove the thrust washer from the end of the crankshaft,

then lower the chain down its tunnel and slip it off the sprocket on the crankshaft **(see illustrations 9.9a and 9b)**. Draw the sprocket off the crankshaft, noting how it locates on the pin on the shaft **(see illustration 9.9c)**.

9.9b . . . then lift out the cam chain

9.13 Lift the cam chain off the sprocket

14 Undo the camshaft sprocket centre bolt and the offset bolt, then lift off the two spacers, noting how they fit **(see illustrations)**.

15 Lift the sprocket and its backing plate off

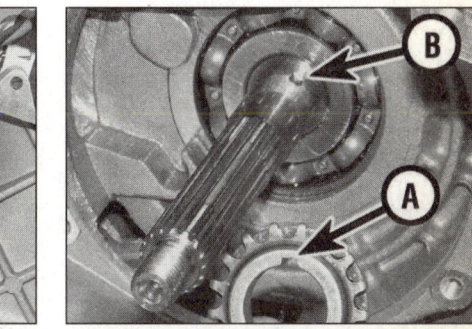

9.9c Notch in sprocket (A) locates on pin (B)

9.14a Undo the centre bolt (A) and the offset bolt (B) . . .

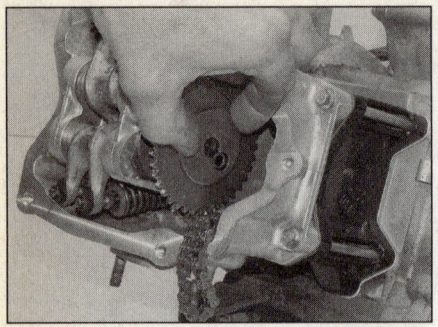

9.14b . . . then remove the spacers

9.15a Lift off the camshaft sprocket . . .

9.15b . . . and the backing plate

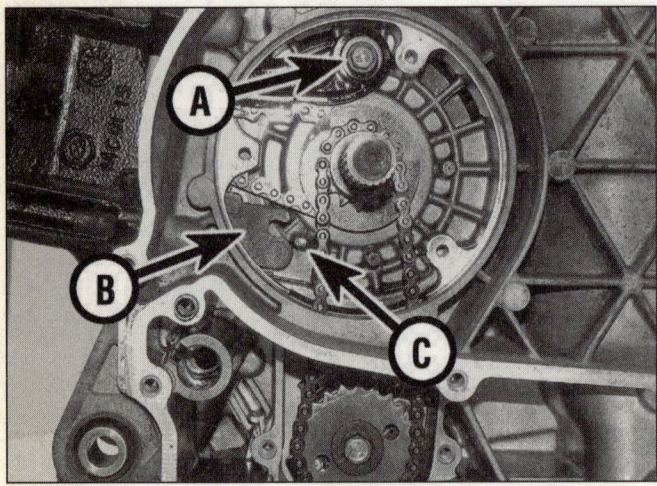

9.16 Cam chain tensioner blade is secured by bolt (A). Lower blade (B) locates on peg (C)

9.23a Install the backing plate . . .

the end of the camshaft, noting how they fit **(see illustrations)**.

16 If required, remove the bolt securing the cam chain tensioner blade to the crankcase and withdraw the blade, noting which way round it fits, and the spacer. The cam chain lower blade locates in a groove in the front edge of the cam chain tunnel in the cylinder. To remove the blade, first remove the cylinder head (see Section 11), then lift out the blade, noting how the lower end locates on the peg in the crankcase **(see illustration)**.

Inspection

17 Check the sprockets for wear and damaged teeth, renewing them if necessary. If the sprocket teeth are worn, the chain will also be worn and should be renewed.

18 Check the chain tensioner blade and guide blade for wear or damage and renew them if necessary. Damaged or severely worn blades are an indication of a worn or improperly tensioned chain. Check the operation of the cam chain tensioner (see Section 8).

19 Where fitted, inspect the components of the decompressor mechanism. Check the nylon bush for wear and flat spots and renew it if necessary. Temporarily assemble the

mechanism on the camshaft (see below) and check its operation – check the spring tension and ensure the bob weight does not bind on the cover.

Installation

20 If removed, install the cam chain lower blade (see Step 16). If removed, install the tensioner blade and spacer, then tighten the retaining bolt to the torque setting specified at the beginning of this Chapter. Ensure both blades are fitted the correct way round.

21 Install the sprocket on the crankshaft, aligning the notch in the sprocket with the

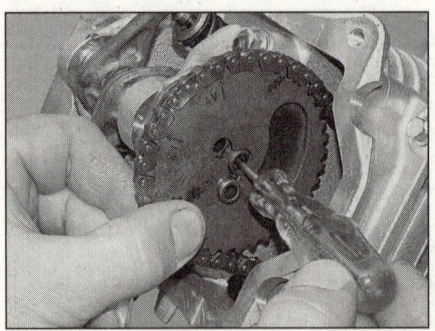

9.23b . . . and the camshaft sprocket as described

pin on the shaft **(see illustration 9.9c)**. Lower the cam chain down through the tunnel and fit it onto the sprocket. If the chain is being re-used, ensure it is fitted the right way round.

22 Check that the timing mark on the alternator rotor still aligns with the index mark on the crankcase and that the engine is at TDC on the compression stroke (see Step 3).

Engine fitted with decompressor mechanism

23 Install the camshaft sprocket backing plate on the end of the camshaft **(see illustration)**. Slip the camshaft sprocket into the top of the chain, then take up the slack in the lower run of the chain and fit the sprocket onto the camshaft, aligning the timing mark (4V) on the sprocket with the index mark on the camshaft holder **(see illustration)**. Note: *To prevent the backing plate falling off the end of the camshaft while the sprocket is being installed, pass the blade of a small screwdriver through the centre of the sprocket, the backing plate and the camshaft.*

Caution: If the marks are not aligned exactly as described, the valve timing will be incorrect and the valves may strike the piston, causing extensive damage to the engine.

24 Apply some grease to the nylon bush

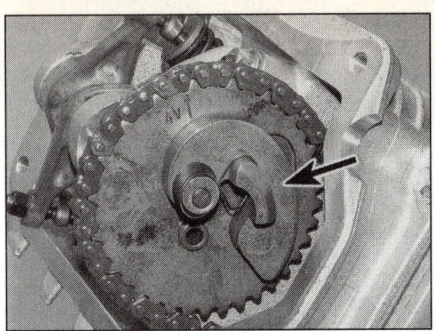

9.24 Install the bob weight (arrowed)

and fit it onto the back of the cam timing bob weight, then install the bob weight – ensure the bush locates in the slot in the cam chain sprocket **(see illustration)**.

25 Lift the bob weight return spring and install the static weight, ensuring that the spring is located over the top of the static weight **(see illustration 9.5b)**. Tighten the decompressor mechanism bolt finger-tight. Check the operation of the decompressor mechanism – the bob weight should move freely on its spindle and return to the rest position under the tension of the spring.

26 Install the decompressor mechanism cover, aligning the small hole in the cover with the head of the decompressor mechanism bolt. Fit the camshaft sprocket centre bolt and tighten it finger-tight **(see illustration)**.

27 Install the cam chain tensioner (see Section 8).

28 Tighten the camshaft sprocket bolt and the decompressor mechanism bolt to the specified torque settings. Hold the alternator to prevent the sprocket from turning.

29 Follow the procedure in Steps 34 and 35 and install the remaining components.

Engine not fitted with decompressor mechanism

30 Install the camshaft sprocket backing plate on the end of the camshaft, then install the sprocket **(see illustrations 9.15b and a)**. Ensure the timing mark (4V) on the sprocket is aligned with the index mark on the camshaft holder.

31 Fit the two spacers onto the sprocket, then install the centre bolt and the offset bolt finger-tight **(see illustrations 9.14b and a)**.

32 Take up the slack in the lower run of the cam chain and slip it onto the camshaft sprocket. Ensure the timing mark (4V) on the sprocket is still aligned with the index mark on the camshaft holder, then install the cam chain tensioner (see Section 8). After installation, rotate the engine and check again that all the timing marks align (see Step 3). If not, remove the tensioner and chain and align the marks correctly.

Caution: If the marks are not aligned exactly as described, the valve timing will be incorrect and the valves may strike the piston, causing extensive damage to the engine.

33 Hold the alternator to prevent the camshaft sprocket from turning and tighten the centre bolt to the specified torque setting. Tighten the offset bolt securely.

34 Fit the thrust washer onto the end of the crankshaft, then install the oil pump drive sprocket, chain and driven sprocket (see Section 19).

35 Install the remaining components in the reverse order of removal.

10 Camshaft and rockers

Note: *This procedure can be carried out with the engine in the frame although access to the top of the engine is extremely restricted. If the engine has been removed, ignore the steps which do not apply.*

Removal

1 Remove the valve cover (see Section 7).

2 Displace or remove the alternator cover and water pump as required (see Section 17). Turn the engine in a clockwise direction using the alternator rotor nut, until the timing mark on the rotor aligns with the index mark on the crankcase, and the timing mark (4V) on the camshaft sprocket aligns with the index mark on the camshaft holder **(see illustration 8.4a and b)**. At this point the engine is at TDC (top dead centre) on the compression stroke (all valves closed). If the 4V mark is not in alignment, rotate the engine 360° and re-align the timing marks.

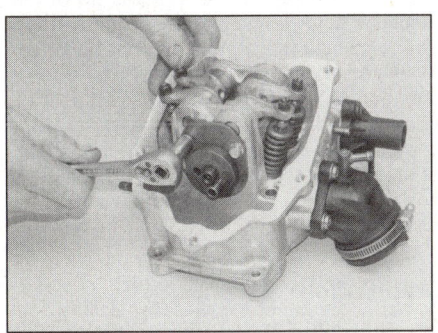

10.5a Undo the bolts . . .

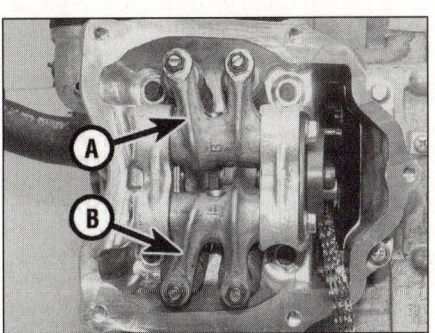

10.6 Layout of the intake (A) and exhaust (B) rocker arms

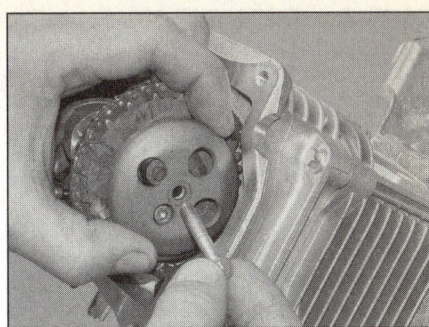

9.26 Install the cover and centre bolt

3 Where fitted, remove the decompressor mechanism (see Section 9).

4 Remove the camshaft sprocket (see Section 9), then secure the cam chain with a cable tie or length of wire to prevent it dropping into the engine. Stuff a clean rag into the cam chain tunnel to prevent anything falling into the engine.

5 Undo the two bolts securing the camshaft retaining plate and lift out the plate **(see illustrations)**.

6 The rocker arms are fitted on two separate shafts **(see illustration)**. The intake rocker arm is on the intake (carburettor) side of the cylinder head, and the exhaust arm is on the exhaust side of the head. Mark the ends of the shafts and the rocker arms so that they can be installed in their original positions.

7 Support each rocker arm in turn and withdraw its shaft **(see illustration)**. Do not mix the rocker arms and shafts up – they

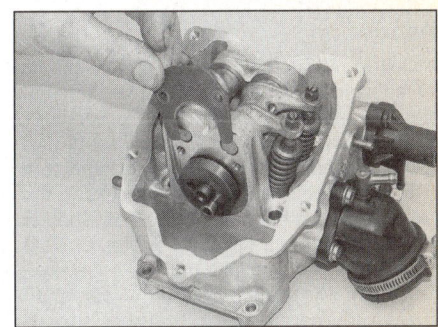

10.5b . . . and lift out the plate

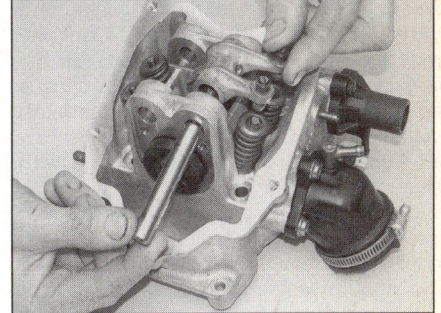

10.7a Withdraw the rocker shafts

10.7b Keep each rocker arm and its shaft together

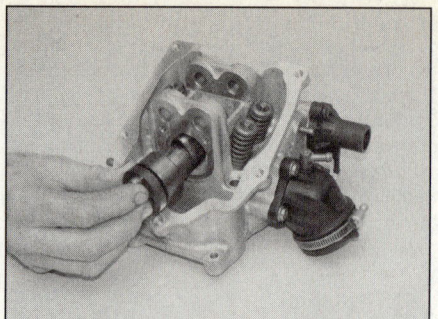

10.8 Withdraw the camshaft

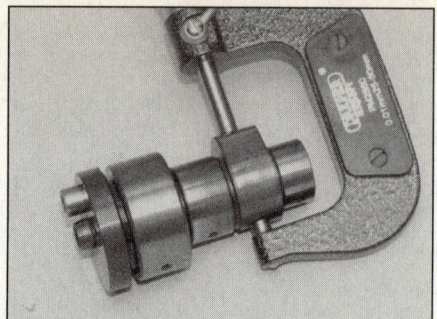

10.9 Measuring the camshaft lobe height

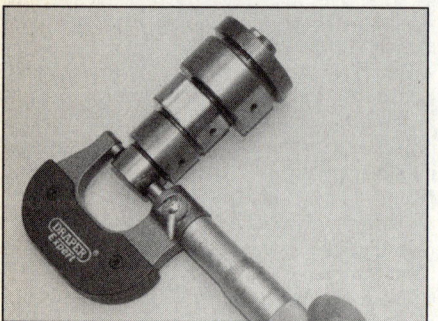

10.10a Measuring the camshaft journals

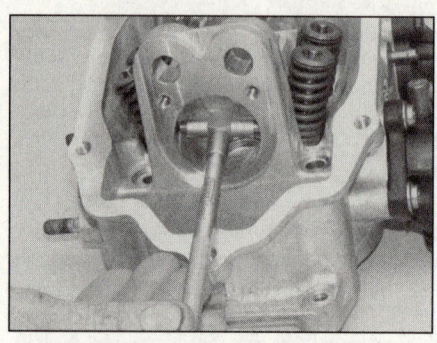

10.10b Measuring the internal diameter of the camshaft housing journals

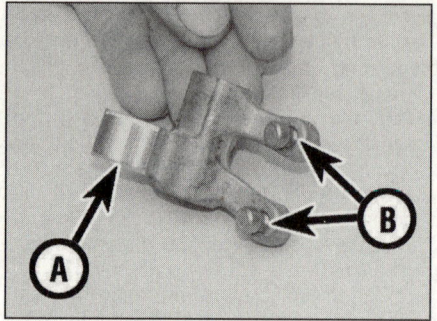

10.12 Inspect the rocker arm face (A) and adjuster screw tips (B)

must be installed in their original positions (see illustration).

8 Mark the end of the camshaft so that it can be refitted in the same position (TDC, both valves closed), then withdraw the camshaft from its housing (see illustration).

Inspection

9 Clean all the components with a suitable solvent and dry them. Inspect the camshaft lobes for heat discoloration (blue appearance), score marks, chipped areas, flat spots and spalling. Measure the height of both lobes with a micrometer and compare the results to the specifications at the beginning of this Chapter (see illustration). If damage is noted or wear is excessive, the camshaft must be renewed.

10 Check the condition of the camshaft bearing journals and the housing journals in the cylinder head. Measure the camshaft journals with a micrometer and, if available, measure the internal diameter of the housing journals with a telescoping gauge and micrometer (see illustrations). Compare the results to the specifications at the beginning of this Chapter and, if damage is noted or wear is excessive, renew the faulty component.

11 Lubricate the camshaft journals with clean engine oil, install the camshaft in the cylinder head and secure it with the retaining plate. The camshaft should rotate freely with no discernible up-and-down movement. If available, measure the camshaft end-float with a dial gauge and compare the result to the specifications at the beginning of this Chapter. If the end-float is excessive, inspect

the retaining plate and the slot in the camshaft for wear and renew the worn component.

12 Blow through the oil passages in the rocker arms with compressed air, if available. Inspect each rocker arm face for pits and spalling and check the articulated tip of the adjusting screws for wear (see illustration). The tip should move freely but not be loose. Measure the internal diameter of each rocker arm, the internal diameters of the rocker shaft housings and the diameter of the rocker shaft and compare the results to the specifications at the beginning of this Chapter. If damage is noted or wear is excessive, renew the faulty component.

Installation

13 Lubricate the camshaft journals with clean engine oil, then install the camshaft in the cylinder head. Ensure the cam lobes are facing the same way as on disassembly (see Step 8).

14 Lubricate the rocker shafts with engine oil. Hold the intake rocker arm in position, then slide the intake shaft through its housing and the arm (see illustration 10.7a). Press the shaft fully into place. Follow the same procedure and install the exhaust rocker arm. With the camshaft in the correct position there should be no pressure on the rocker arms. Align the camshaft retaining plate with the slot in the camshaft, slide the plate into position and secure it with the bolts. Tighten the bolts to the specified torque setting.

15 Follow the procedure in Section 9 to install the camshaft sprocket, decompressor

mechanism and cam chain tensioner as applicable, then check the valve timing.

Caution: If the marks are not aligned exactly as described, the valve timing will be incorrect and the valves may strike the piston, causing extensive damage to the engine.

16 Check the valve clearances and adjust them if necessary (see Chapter 1).

17 Install the remaining components in the reverse order of removal.

11 Cylinder head

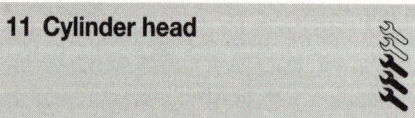

Note: *This procedure can be carried out with the engine in the frame although access to the top of the engine is extremely restricted. If the engine has been removed, ignore the steps which do not apply.*

Caution: The engine must be completely cool before beginning this procedure or the cylinder head may become warped.

Removal

1 Remove the carburettor and exhaust system (see Chapter 4). On models fitted with a secondary air system, disconnect its pipe from the cylinder head (see Chapter 1, Section 20).

2 Drain the cooling system (see Chapter 1, Section 10).

3 Release the clips securing the cooling system hoses to the cylinder head and detach the hoses form their unions, noting where they fit.

4 Disconnect the coolant temperature sensor wiring connector. Pull the spark plug cap off the plug.

5 Remove the valve cover (see Section 7).

6 If applicable, remove the decompressor mechanism (see Section 9).

7 Remove the camshaft sprocket, then secure the cam chain with a cable tie or length of wire to prevent it dropping into the engine (see Section 9).

8 Undo the two cylinder head bolts on the left-hand side of the engine **(see illustration)**. Undo the four cylinder head nuts evenly, a little at a time, in a criss-cross pattern and remove them **(see illustration)**.

9 Lift the cylinder head off carefully, feeding the cam chain down through the tunnel in the head **(see illustration)**. If the head is stuck, tap around the joint face with a soft-faced mallet to free it. Do not attempt to free the head by inserting a screwdriver between the head and cylinder – you'll damage the sealing surfaces. **Note:** *Avoid lifting the cylinder off the crankcase when the head is removed, otherwise a new cylinder base gasket will have to be fitted (see Section 14).*

10 Remove the old cylinder head gasket and discard it as a new one must be fitted on reassembly **(see illustration)**. Note the two dowels on the cylinder studs and remove them for safekeeping if they are loose **(see illustration)**.

11 Inspect the cylinder head gasket and the mating surfaces on the head and cylinder for signs of leakage, which could indicate that

the head is warped. Refer to Section 13 and check the head gasket mating surface for warpage.

12 Clean all traces of old gasket material from the cylinder head and cylinder with a suitable solvent. Take care not to scratch or gouge the soft aluminium. Be careful not to let any dirt fall into the crankcase, the cylinder bore or the oil passage.

Installation

13 Ensure both cylinder head and cylinder mating surfaces are clean. Ensure both the dowels are in place in the cylinder **(see illustration 11.10b)**. Lay the new gasket in place on the cylinder, making sure the oil and coolant passage holes are correctly aligned **(see illustration)**. Never re-use the old gasket.

14 Carefully lower the head onto the cylinder, feeding the cam chain up through the tunnel. Make sure the dowels are correctly aligned with the gasket and the cylinder head.

15 Install the internal cylinder head nuts finger-tight, then tighten them in a criss-cross pattern, in two or three stages to the torque setting specified at the beginning of this Chapter.

16 Install the two cylinder head bolts on the left-hand side of the engine and tighten them to the specified torque setting.

17 Install the camshaft sprocket and the remaining components in the reverse order of removal, referring to the relevant Sections or Chapters.

12 Valves, valve seats and valve guides – general note

1 If a valve spring compressor is available, the home mechanic can remove the valves from the cylinder head, grind in the valves and renew the valve stem seal. If the necessary measuring tools are available, you can assess the amount of wear on the valves and guides and measure the valve-to-seat contact areas (see Section 13).

2 If the valve guides or the valve seats in the cylinder head are worn beyond their service limits a new head will have to be fitted.

3 After any servicing or repair work, be sure to clean the head very thoroughly to remove any metal particles or abrasive grit that may still be present. Use compressed air, if available, to blow out all the holes and passages.

13 Cylinder head and valves

1 Disassembly, cleaning and inspection of the valves and related components can be done by the home mechanic if the necessary special tools are available. If there is any doubt about the condition of any components, have them checked by a Gilera dealer.

11.8a Undo the two external cylinder head bolts . . .

11.8b . . . then the four internal cylinder head nuts

11.9 Lift off the cylinder head

11.10a Remove the head gasket

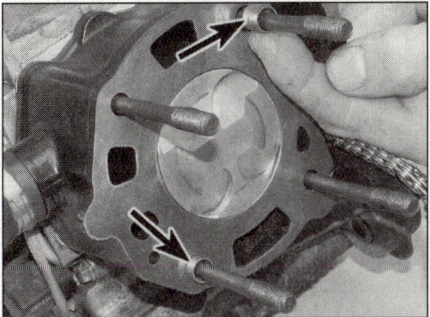

11.10b Note the dowels (arrowed) on the cylinder studs

11.13 Ensure the holes in the gasket are aligned correctly

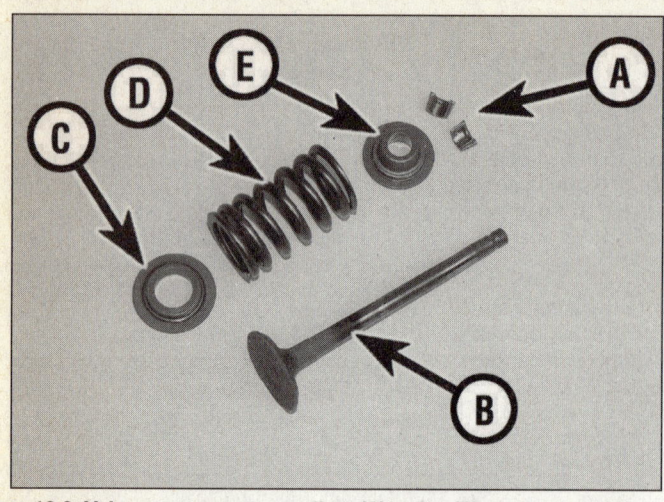

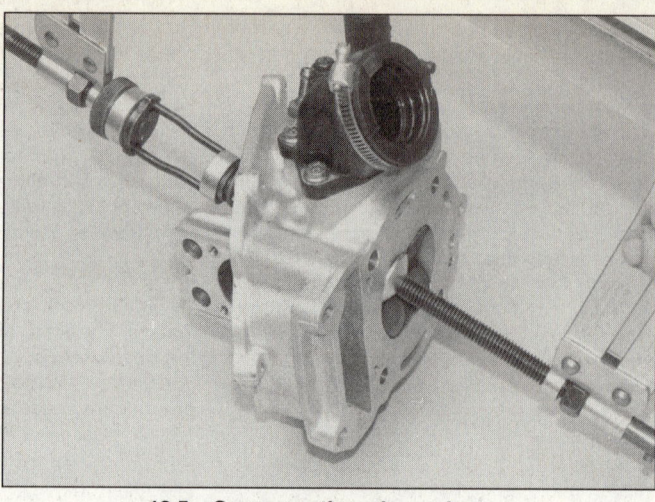

13.3 Valve components – collets (A), valve (B), spring seat (C), spring (D) and spring retainer (E)

13.5a Compress the valve spring . . .

2 To disassemble the valve components without the risk of damaging them, a valve spring compressor suitable for motorcycle engines is absolutely necessary.

Disassembly

3 Before proceeding, arrange to label and store the valves and their related components so that they can be returned to their original location without getting mixed up **(see illustration)**.

4 If not already done, remove the camshaft and rockers (see Section 10), then undo the bolts securing the thermostat housing to the head and remove the housing and thermostat

(see Chapter 3). Clean the sealing surfaces of the cylinder head and thermostat housing with a suitable solvent. Take care not to scratch or gouge the soft aluminium.

5 Compress the valve spring on the first valve with a spring compressor, making sure it is correctly located onto each end of the valve assembly **(see illustration)**. On the underside of the head, make sure the plate on the compressor only contacts the valve and not the soft aluminium of the head – if the plate is too big for the valve, use a spacer between them. Do not compress the spring any more than is absolutely necessary to release the collets. Remove the collets, using

either needle-nose pliers, tweezers, a magnet or a screwdriver with a dab of grease on it **(see illustration)**. Carefully release the valve spring compressor and remove the spring retainer, noting which way up it fits, and the spring, and lift the valve from the head **(see illustrations)**. If the valve binds in the guide (won't pull through), push it back into the head and deburr the area around the collet groove with a very fine file **(see illustration)**. Once the valve has been removed, pull the valve stem oil seal off the top of the valve guide with pliers and discard it (the old seal should never be reused) and remove the spring seat **(see illustration)**.

6 Repeat the procedure for the remaining valves. Remember to keep the parts for each valve together and labelled so they can be reinstalled in the correct location.

7 Carefully scrape away the carbon deposits from the inside of the cylinder head and the exhaust port, then clean the cylinder head with solvent and dry it thoroughly. Compressed air will speed the drying process and ensure that all holes and recessed areas are clean.

8 Clean the valve springs, collets, retainers, and spring seats with solvent and dry them thoroughly. Work on the parts from one valve at a time so as not to mix them up.

13.5b . . . and remove the collets

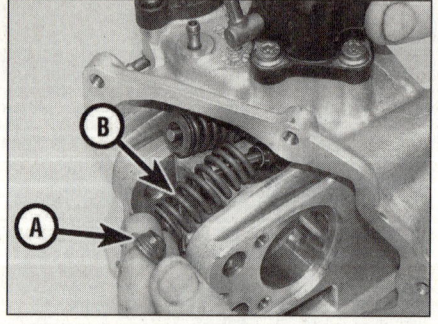

13.5c Remove the spring retainer (A) and spring (B) . . .

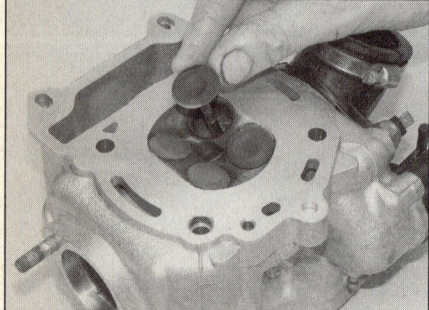

13.5d . . . then lift out the valve

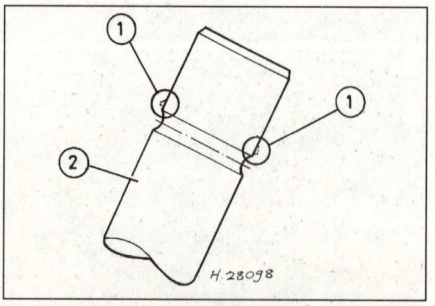

13.5e If the valve stem (2) won't pull through the guide, deburr the area (1) above the collet groove

13.5f Pull the stem seal off with pliers

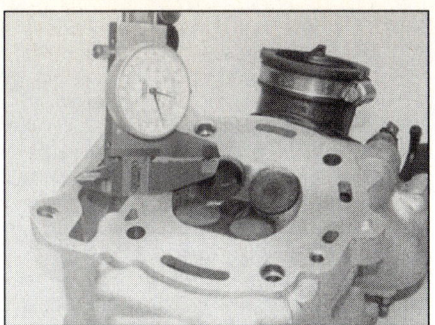

13.12 Measuring the valve seat width with a Vernier caliper

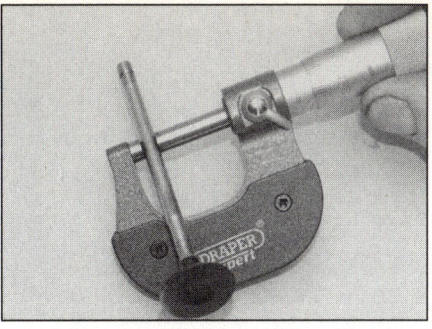

13.13 Measuring the valve stem diameter with a micrometer

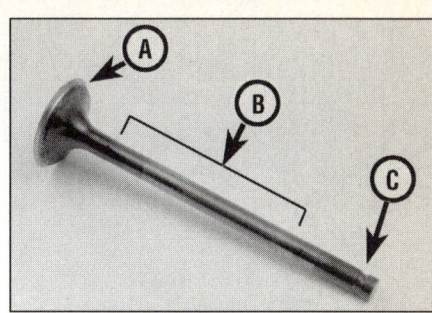

13.14 Check the valve face (A), stem (B) and collet groove (C) for signs of wear and damage

9 Scrape off any heavy carbon deposits that may have formed on the valves, then use a motorised wire brush to remove deposits from the valve heads. Again, make sure the valves do not get mixed up.

Inspection

10 Inspect the head very carefully for cracks and other damage. If cracks are found, a new head will be required.

11 Using a precision straight-edge and a feeler gauge, check the head gasket mating surface for warping. Lay the straight-edge across the head lengthways and diagonally, intersecting the stud holes, and try to slip the feeler gauge under it on either side of the combustion chamber. If the feeler gauge can be inserted between the straight-edge and the cylinder head, the head is warped and should be machined. Consult a Gilera dealer or specialist engineer. If warpage has reached the limit listed in the specifications at the beginning of the Chapter, a new head will have to be fitted.

12 Examine the valve seats in the combustion chamber. If they are deeply pitted, cracked or burned, it may be possible to have them repaired by a specialist engineer, otherwise a new head will be required. Measure the valve seat width and compare it to this Chapter's Specifications **(see illustration)**.

13 Measure the valve stem diameter **(see illustration)**. If the stem is worn beyond its service limit a new valve must be fitted. Clean the valve guides to remove any carbon build-up, then measure the inside diameters

of the guides (at both ends and the centre of the guide) with a small hole gauge and micrometer. The guides are measured at the ends and at the centre to determine if they are worn unevenly. Gilera do not list replacement valve guides, so if any guide is worn unevenly, or if the valve stem/guide clearance is more than the service limit, have the head checked by a specialist engineer. It may be possible to bore out the guide and fit a sleeve in it, otherwise a new cylinder head will have to be fitted.

14 Inspect each valve face for cracks, pits and burned spots; measure the valve face and compare the result with the specifications. Check the valve stem and the collet groove area for cracks **(see illustration)**. Rotate the valve and check for any obvious indication that it is bent. Check the end of the stem for pitting and excessive wear. Worn valve faces, or the presence of any of the above conditions indicates the need for new valves. If the stem end is pitted or worn, also check the contact area of the valve clearance adjuster in the rocker arm

15 Inspect the end of each valve spring for wear and pitting. Check the spring for bend by placing a set square against it **(see illustration)**. If the bend in a spring is excessive, it must be renewed. Gilera do not specify a service limit for the valve springs, but it is good practice to fit new springs when the head has been disassembled for valve servicing.

16 Check the spring retainers and collets for obvious wear and cracks. Any questionable parts should not be reused, as extensive

damage will occur in the event of failure during engine operation.

17 If the inspection indicates that no overhaul work is required, the valve components can be reinstalled in the head.

Reassembly

18 Unless a valve overhaul has been performed, before installing the valves in the head they should be ground in (lapped) to ensure a positive seal between the valves and seats. This procedure requires coarse and fine valve grinding compound and a valve grinding tool. If a grinding tool is not available, a piece of rubber or plastic hose can be slipped over the valve stem (after the valve has been installed in the guide) and used to turn the valve.

19 Apply a small amount of coarse grinding compound to the valve face, then slip the valve into the guide **(see illustration)**. **Note:** *Make sure each valve is installed in its correct guide and be careful not to get any grinding compound on the valve stem.*

20 Attach the grinding tool (or hose) to the valve and rotate the tool between the palms of your hands. Use a back-and-forth motion (as though rubbing your hands together) rather than a circular motion (i.e. so that the valve rotates alternately clockwise and anti-clockwise rather than in one direction only) **(see illustration)**. Lift the valve off the seat and turn it at regular intervals to distribute the grinding compound properly. Continue the grinding procedure until the valve face and seat contact areas are of uniform width

13.15 Check the valve springs for squareness

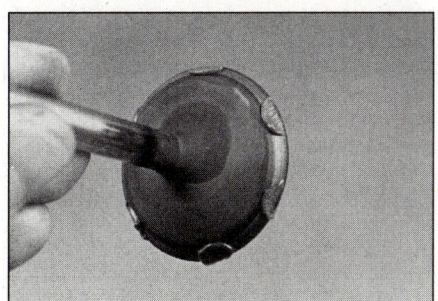

13.19 Apply the grinding compound very sparingly, in small dabs, to the valve face only

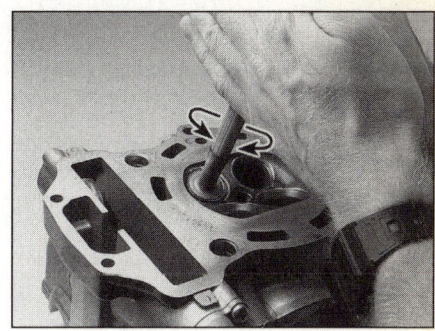

13.20a Rotate the tool back and forth between the palms of your hands

13.20b The valve face (arrowed) . . .

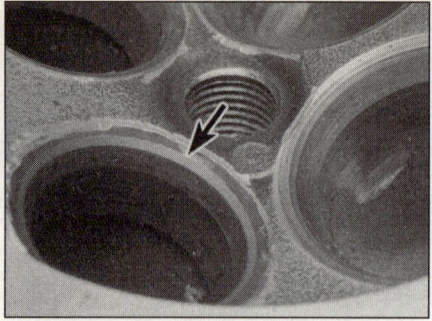

13.20c . . . and seat (arrowed) should show as a uniform unbroken ring

and unbroken around the circumference **(see illustrations)**.

21 Carefully remove the valve from the guide and wipe off all traces of grinding compound. Use solvent to clean the valve and wipe the seat area thoroughly with a solvent soaked cloth.

22 Repeat the procedure with fine valve grinding compound, then repeat the entire procedure for the other valve.

Check for proper sealing of each valve by pouring a small amount of solvent into the valve port while holding the valve shut. If the solvent leaks past the valve into the combustion chamber the valve grinding operation should be repeated.

23 Lay the spring seat for the intake valve in place in the cylinder head, then install a

new valve stem seal onto the guide. Use an appropriate size deep socket to push the seal over the end of the valve guide until it is felt to clip into place. Don't twist or cock it, or it will not seal properly against the valve stem. Also, don't remove it again or it will be damaged.

24 Lubricate the intake valve stem with molybdenum disulphide grease, then install it into its guide, rotating it slowly to avoid damaging the seal. Check that the valve moves up and down freely in the guide. Next, install the spring, with its closer-wound coils facing down into the cylinder head, followed by the spring retainer, with its shouldered side facing down so that it fits into the top of the spring **(see illustration 13.5c)**.

25 Apply a small amount of grease to the collets to help hold them in place as the pressure is released from the spring. Compress the spring with the valve spring compressor and install the collets **(see illustration 13.5b)**.

When compressing the spring, depress it only as far as is necessary to slip the collets into place. Make certain that the collets are securely locked in their retaining grooves.

26 Repeat the procedure for the exhaust valve.

27 Support the cylinder head on blocks so the valves can't contact the workbench top, then very gently tap each of the valve stems with a soft-faced hammer. This will help seat the collets in their grooves.

28 Install the thermostat housing (see Chapter 3). Install the camshaft and rockers (see Section 10).

14 Cylinder

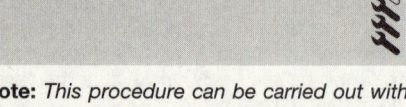

Note: *This procedure can be carried out with the engine in the frame although access to the top of the engine is extremely restricted.*

Removal

1 Remove the cylinder head (see Section 11).

2 Note how the cam chain lower blade locates in a groove in the front edge of the cam chain tunnel in the cylinder, then lift out the blade, noting which way round it fits **(see illustration)**.

3 If required, release the clip securing the cooling system hose to the cylinder and detach the hose from its union.

4 Lift the cylinder up off the studs, carefully feeding the cam chain down through the tunnel; support the piston as it becomes accessible to prevent it hitting the crankcase **(see illustrations)**. If the cylinder is stuck, tap around its joint face with a soft-faced mallet to free it from the crankcase. Don't attempt to free the cylinder by inserting a screwdriver between it and the crankcase – you'll damage the sealing surfaces. When the cylinder is removed, stuff a clean rag around the piston to prevent anything falling into the crankcase.

5 Note the two dowels in the cylinder and remove them for safekeeping if they are loose.

6 Remove the gasket carefully and make a note of the thickness (0.4, 0.6 or 0.8) stamped into the material. If the original cylinder and piston are used on reassembly, a new gasket of the same thickness should be used. Discard the old gasket.

Inspection

7 Inspect the cylinder bore carefully for scratches and score marks. A rebore (125 cc engine) or new cylinder (180/200 cc engines) will be necessary if the cylinder is deeply scored. **Note:** *The VXR180/200, ST200 and DNA 180 engines have Nicasil plated bores. The Nicasil plating has a high resistance to wear and should last the life of the engine unless serious damage, such as a seizure, has occurred; in this event, a new cylinder, piston and rings should be fitted – the cylinder cannot be rebored.*

8 Using a telescoping gauge and micro-meter, check the dimensions of the cylinder to assess the amount of wear,

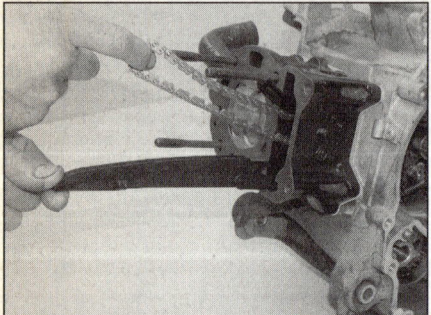

14.2 Lift out the cam chain lower blade

14.4a Lower the cam chain (arrowed) through the cylinder . . .

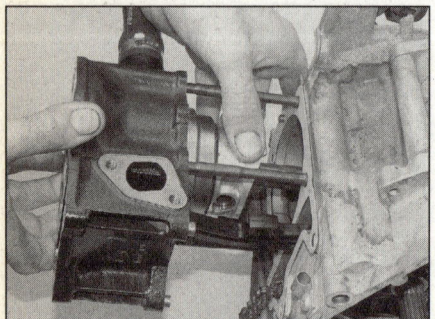

14.4b . . . then support the piston to prevent damage

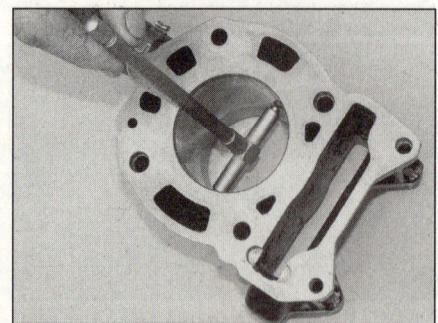

14.8a Measure the cylinder bore with a telescoping gauge as described

14.8b Cylinder size code (arrowed) stamped into the lower edge

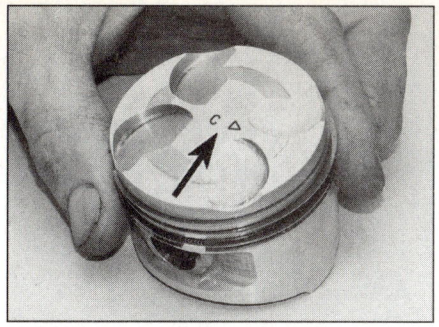

14.8c Piston size code (arrowed) stamped into the crown

14.14 Zero the dial gauge on the cylinder top gasket face

taper and ovality. Gilera recommend the bore is measured at 6 mm, 41 mm and 78 mm stages down from the top edge, both parallel to and across the crankshaft axis **(see illustration)**. Compare the results to the cylinder bore specifications at the beginning of this Chapter. **Note**: *Cylinders and pistons are size coded during manufacture and it is important that they are of the same size code. Gilera list four standard size codes (A to D) for the 125, 180 and 200 cc engines, but first, second and third oversizes (rebored cylinders) are only listed for the 125 cc engine.* The size code is stamped into the lower edge of the cylinder, and in the piston crown **(see illustrations)**. When purchasing a new cylinder or piston, always supply the size code.

9 Calculate any differences between the measurements to determine any taper or ovality in the bore. Gilera specify a wear limit of 0.05 mm between any of the measurements. If the cylinder is worn beyond this service limit, badly scratched, scuffed or scored, have it rebored by a Gilera dealer or motorcycle engineer or fit a new cylinder. If the cylinder is rebored (125 cc engine), it will require an oversize piston and rings. If the cylinder has already been rebored to the maximum oversize and is worn or damaged, the cylinder must be renewed.

10 Measure the cylinder bore diameter at the specified distance down from the top edge, then calculate the piston-to-bore clearance by subtracting the piston diameter (see Section 15) from the bore diameter. If the cylinder is in good condition and the piston-to-bore clearance is within specifications, the cylinder can be re-used.

11 Check that all the cylinder head studs are tight in the crankcase halves. If any are loose, remove them and clean their threads. Apply a suitable permanent thread locking compound and tighten them securely.

Installation

12 Check that the mating surfaces of the cylinder and crankcase are clean.

13 Three different thicknesses of cylinder base gasket are available from Gilera. If the original cylinder and piston are being re-used, fit a gasket the same thickness as the original

(see Step 6). If new components are being used, the cylinder must be assembled on the crankcase and piston (see Steps 21 and 22) without a base gasket, and a dial gauge mounted against the crown of the piston to establish which thickness is required.

14 Set the dial gauge in the mounting plate, and with its gauge tip resting against the cylinder top gasket face, zero the gauge dial **(see illustration)**. Rotate the crankshaft so that the piston is partway down the bore.

15 Clamp the mounting plate diagonally across two of the cylinder studs, and secure it by tightening the stud nuts to 28 – 30 Nm.

16 Rotate the crankshaft via the alternator rotor nut so the piston rises to the top of its stroke (TDC) and the gauge tip rests on the centre of the piston crown. At this point read off the dial gauge **(see illustration)**.

17 On 125 cc engines, with the piston at TDC, the dial gauge reading will show the distance the centre of the piston crown is above the top of the cylinder bore. The further the piston crown is above the top of the bore, the thicker the base gasket should be. If the dial gauge reading is between 2.25 and 2.35 mm a 0.4 mm gasket is required, between 2.35 and 2.55 mm a 0.6 mm gasket is required, and between 2.55 and 2.65 mm a 0.8 mm gasket is required.

18 On 180 cc engines, with the piston at TDC, the dial gauge reading will be distance the centre of the piston crown is below the top of the cylinder bore. The further the piston crown is below the top of the cylinder bore, the thinner the base gasket should be. If the reading is between 0.9 to 1.0 mm a 0.8 mm gasket is required, between 1.0 to 1.2 mm a

0.6 mm gasket is required, and between 1.2 to 1.3 mm a 0.4 mm gasket is required.

19 On 200 cc engines, with the piston at TDC, the dial gauge reading will be distance the centre of the piston crown is below the top of the cylinder bore. The further the piston crown is below the top of the cylinder bore, the thinner the base gasket should be. If the reading is between 1.3 to 1.4 mm a 0.8 mm gasket is required, between 1.4 to 1.6 mm a 0.6 mm gasket is required, and between 1.6 to 1.7 mm a 0.4 mm gasket is required.

20 Having established the correct gasket thickness, fit the new gasket to the crankcase **(see illustration)**. Never re-use the old gasket.

21 Lubricate the cylinder bore, piston and piston rings, and the connecting rod bearings with clean engine oil, then check that the piston ring end gaps are positioned as described in Section 16. If required, use a piston ring clamp to compress the piston rings while the cylinder is fitted.

22 Lower the cylinder down over the studs until the piston crown fits into the bore, then gently push down on the cylinder, making sure the piston enters the bore squarely and does not get cocked sideways. If a piston ring clamp is not being used, carefully compress and feed each ring into the bore as the cylinder is lowered. If possible, have an assistant to support the cylinder while this is done. If necessary, use a soft mallet to gently tap the cylinder down, but do not use force if it appears to be stuck as the piston and/or rings will be damaged. If a clamp is used, remove it once the piston is in the cylinder.

23 When the piston is correctly installed in

14.16 Take the reading off the piston crown at TDC

14.20 Fit a new cylinder base gasket onto the crankcase

15.1 Mark the piston before removal

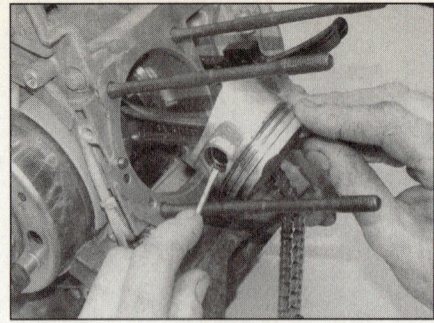

15.2a Remove the circlip . . .

15.2b . . . and push out the piston pin

the cylinder, press the cylinder down onto the base gasket.

24 Fit the cam chain lower guide into the cam chain tunnel; ensure the lower end locates on the peg in the crankcase (see Section 9) and the upper end is fitted into the groove in the cam chain tunnel (see Step 2).

25 Install the cylinder head (see Section 11). **Note:** *If removed, fit the coolant hose to the cylinder and secure it with the clip after the cylinder head has been installed to avoid damaging the seating of the cylinder base gasket.*

15 Piston

Note: *This procedure can be carried out with the engine in the frame although access to the top of the engine is extremely restricted.*

Removal

1 Remove the cylinder (see Section 14). Before removing the piston from the connecting rod, stuff a clean rag into the hole around the rod to prevent the circlips or anything else from falling into the crankcase. The piston should have an arrow marked on its crown which should face towards the exhaust valves (front of engine). If this is not visible, mark the piston accordingly so that it can be installed the correct way round **(see illustration)**. Note that the arrow may not be visible until the carbon deposits have been scraped off and the piston cleaned.

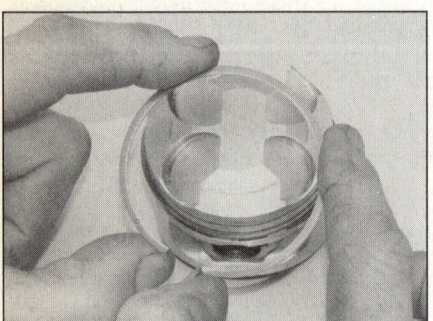

15.3 Removing the piston rings

2 Carefully prise out the circlip on one side of the piston using a pointed instrument or a small flat-bladed screwdriver inserted into the notch **(see illustration)**. Push the piston pin out from the other side to free the piston from the connecting rod **(see illustration)**. Remove the other circlip and discard them both as new ones must be used. Use a socket extension to push the piston pin out if required.

> **HAYNES HiNT** *To prevent the circlip from flying away or from dropping into the crankcase, pass a rod or screwdriver with a greater diameter than the gap between the circlip ends, through the piston pin. This will trap the circlip if it springs out.*

> **HAYNES HiNT** *If a piston pin is a tight fit in the piston bosses, heat the piston gently with a hot air gun – this will expand the alloy piston sufficiently to release its grip on the pin.*

Inspection

3 Before the inspection process can be carried out, the piston rings must be removed and the piston must be cleaned. Note that if the cylinder is being rebored (125 cc engine only), piston inspection can be overlooked as a new one will be fitted. All three piston rings can be removed by hand; a ring removal and installation tool can be used on the two

15.8 Measure the piston diameter as described

compression rings, but do not use it on the oil control ring **(see illustration)**. Carefully note which way up each ring fits and in which groove as they must be installed in their original positions if being re-used. The upper surface of each ring should be marked at one end. Do not nick or gouge the piston in the process.

4 Scrape all traces of carbon from the top of the piston. A hand-held wire brush or a piece of fine emery cloth can be used once most of the deposits have been scraped away. Do not, under any circumstances, use a wire brush mounted in a drill motor to remove deposits from the piston; the piston material is soft and will be eroded away.

5 Use a piston ring groove cleaning tool to remove any carbon deposits from the ring grooves. If a tool is not available, a piece broken off an old ring will do the job. Be very careful to remove only the carbon deposits. Do not remove any metal and do not nick or gouge the sides of the ring grooves. Once the deposits have been removed, clean the piston with solvent and dry it thoroughly.

6 Inspect the piston for cracks around the skirt, at the pin bosses and at the ring lands. Normal piston wear appears as even, vertical wear on the thrust surfaces of the piston and slight looseness of the top ring in its groove. If the skirt is scored or scuffed, the engine may have been suffering from overheating and/or abnormal combustion, which caused excessively high operating temperatures. Also check that the circlip grooves are not damaged.

7 A hole in the piston crown is an extreme example that abnormal combustion (pre-ignition) was occurring. Burned areas at the edge of the piston crown are usually evidence of spark knock (detonation). If any of the above problems exist, the causes must be corrected or the damage will occur again.

8 Check the piston-to-bore clearance by measuring the bore (see Section 14) and the piston diameter. Measure the piston the specified distance (see Specifications) down from the top edge and at 90° to the piston pin axis **(see illustration)**. Subtract the piston diameter from the bore diameter to obtain the clearance. If it is greater than the specified figure, the piston must be renewed (assuming

15.9a Measure both ends of the piston pin . . .

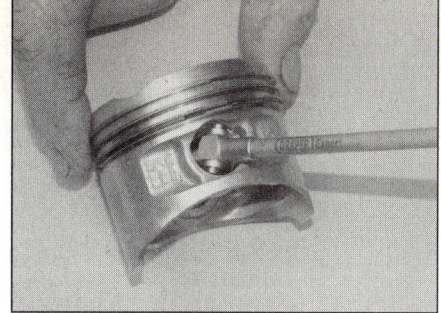

15.9b . . . and the internal diameter of the piston pin boss

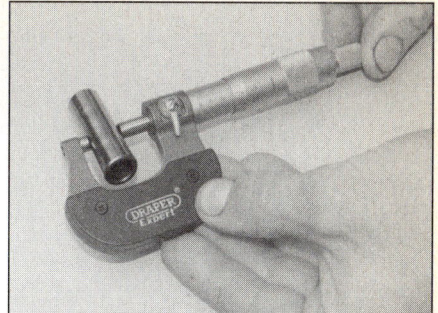

15.10a Measure the centre of the piston pin . . .

15.10b . . . and the internal diameter of the small-end

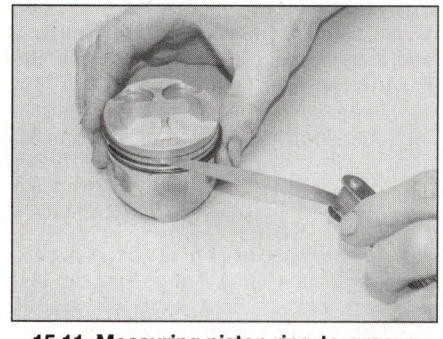

15.11 Measuring piston ring-to-groove clearance

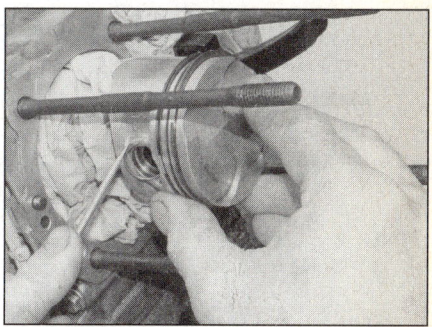

15.13a Secure the piston pin with new circlips

the bore itself is within limits, otherwise a rebore (125 cc engine only) or new piston and cylinder (180/200 cc engines) is necessary. Remember that the pistons and cylinders are size-coded – make sure you have matched components.

9 Use a micrometer and a telescoping gauge to check for wear between the piston pin and piston. Measure the piston pin diameter at both ends and the internal diameter of each pin boss in the piston and compare the results with the Specifications **(see illustrations)**.

10 To check for wear between the piston pin and connecting rod small-end, measure the piston pin diameter at its centre and the internal diameter of the rod small-end **(see illustrations)**. The piston pin should not be worn below its specified diameter and the small-end measurement should not be greater then the specified service limit. Renew any worn components; if the small-end is worn a

new connecting rod and crankshaft assembly will have to be fitted (see Section 20).

11 Piston ring-to-groove clearance can be measured to determine whether the ring grooves in the piston are worn. Install the rings on the piston (see Section 16), then use a feeler gauge to measure the clearance between the ring and groove and compare the result with the specifications **(see illustration)**. If the clearance is greater than the service limit, repeat the check using new rings, if the clearance is still too great, the piston should be renewed.

Installation

12 Inspect and install the piston rings (see Section 16).

13 Lubricate the piston pin, the piston pin bore and the connecting rod small-end bore with clean engine oil. Install a new circlip in one side of the piston (do not re-use old

circlips). Line up the piston on the connecting rod, making sure the arrow on the piston crown faces down towards the exhaust, and insert the piston pin. Secure the pin with the other new circlip **(see illustration)**. When installing the circlips, compress them only just enough to fit them in the piston, and make sure they are properly seated in their grooves with the open end away from the removal notch **(see illustration)**.

14 Install the cylinder (see Section 14).

16 Piston rings

1 New piston rings should be fitted whenever an engine is being overhauled. Before fitting the new rings, their end gaps must be checked with the rings installed in an unworn part of the bore.

2 To measure the installed ring end gap, insert the top ring into the bottom of the bore and square it up with the bore walls by pushing it in with the top of the piston. The ring should be about 15 mm from the bottom of the bore. To measure the end gap, slip a feeler gauge between the ends of the ring and compare the measurement to the specifications at the beginning of the Chapter **(see illustration)**.

3 If the gap is larger or smaller than specified, double check to make sure that you have the correct rings before proceeding. If the gap is too small the ends may come in contact with

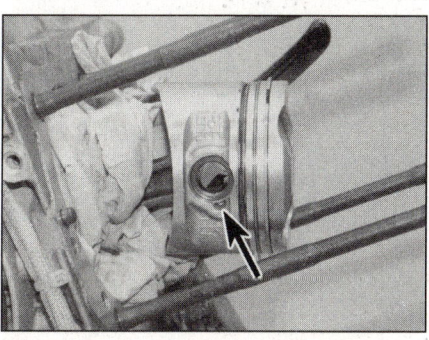

15.13b Ensure the circlip ends are clear of the notch (arrowed)

16.2 Measuring piston ring installed end gap

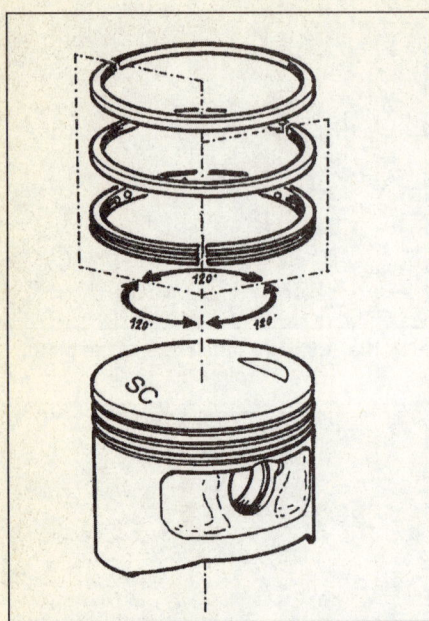

16.8 Ensure that the ring end gaps are positioned at 120° intervals

each other during engine operation, which can cause serious damage. Check the piston and bore diameters with the specifications to confirm whether they are standard or oversize.

4 Excess end gap is not critical unless it exceeds the service limit. Again, double-check to make sure you have the correct rings for your engine and check that the bore is not worn.

5 Repeat the procedure for the other two rings.

6 Once the ring end gaps have been checked, the rings can be installed on the piston.

7 The oil control ring (lowest on the piston) is installed first. Always install this ring by hand and do not expand the ring any more than is necessary to slide it into place. Next install the 2nd compression ring, noting that there is usually a marking or letter near one end to denote the upper surface of the ring. Finally install the top ring into its groove. A ring installation tool can be used on the two compression rings if desired.

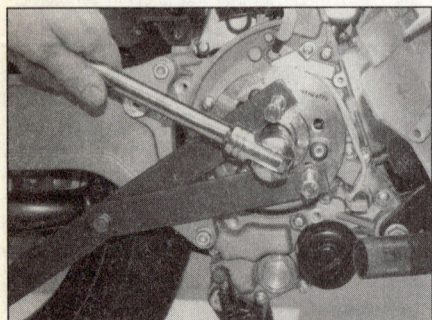

17.6 With the rotor held securely, unscrew the rotor nut

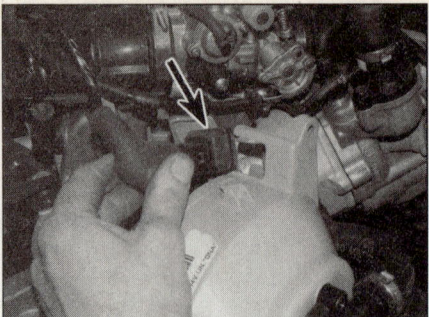

17.5a Unclip the connector (arrowed) from the alternator cover

8 Once the rings are correctly installed, check they move freely without snagging and stagger their end gaps as shown **(see illustration)**.

17 Alternator rotor and stator

Note: *This procedure can be carried out with the engine in the frame. If the engine has been removed, ignore the steps which do not apply.*

Removal

1 Remove the bodywork as required by your model to access the alternator cover and water pump on the right-hand side of the engine (see Chapter 8).

2 If the alternator cover is being displaced in

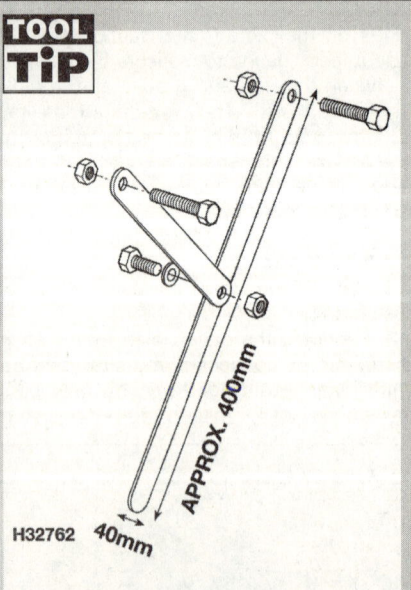

A rotor holding tool can easily be made using two strips of steel bolted together in the middle, with a bolt through each end which locates into the holes in the rotor. Do not allow the bolts to extend too far through the rotor holes otherwise the coils could be damaged.

H32762 40mm APPROX. 400mm

17.5b Lift off the cover, noting how the water pump drive engages

order to turn the engine using the alternator rotor nut, follow Steps 4 and 5 only. Follow Step 15 to install the cover.

3 If the alternator cover is being fully removed, drain the cooling system and disconnect the coolant hoses from the water pump (see Chapter 1).

4 Remove the silencer (see Chapter 4).

5 Undo the bolts securing the alternator cover and lift it away from the crankcase, then detach the alternator multi-pin connector from the cover **(see illustration)**. Displace or remove the cover as required. Note how the dampers on the alternator rotor locate in the water pump drive **(see illustration)**. **Note:** *It is not necessary to remove the water pump from the alternator cover.*

6 To undo the alternator rotor nut it is necessary to stop the rotor from turning. Gilera produce a service tool (Part. No. 020656Y) which locates in the holes in the rotor. A similar tool can be made **(see illustration and Tool Tip)**. With the rotor held securely, unscrew the nut.

7 To remove the rotor from the crankshaft it is necessary to use the Gilera service tool (Part No. 020162Y) or a two-legged puller. If using the service tool, ensure that its centre bolt is backed-out sufficiently to allow the body of the tool to be screwed all the way into the threads provided in the rotor **(see illustration)**. With the tool in place, hold the body of the tool using a spanner on its flats while tightening the centre bolt (turn it clockwise) to draw the rotor off the end of the shaft **(see illustration)**. If using a two-legged puller, temporarily install the rotor nut to

17.7a Ensure the service tool is correctly installed . . .

17.7b . . . then draw the rotor off the shaft as described

17.7c Removing the rotor with a two-legged puller

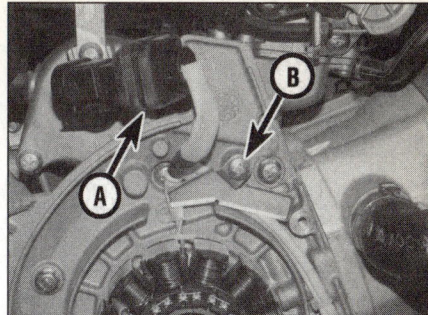

17.8 Alternator multi-pin connector (A) and wiring guide screw (B)

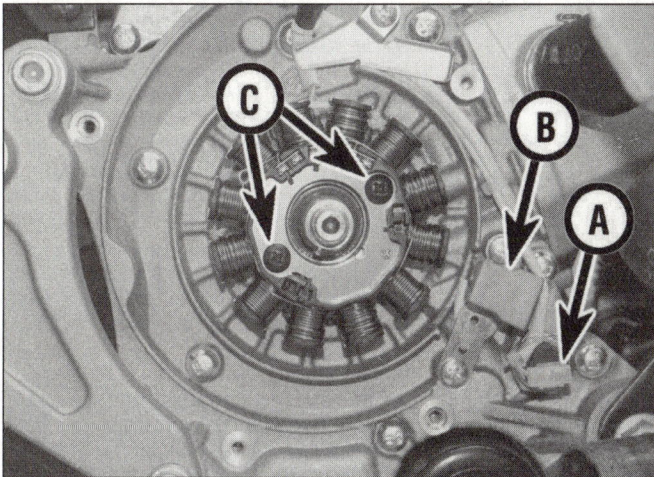

17.9 Oil pressure switch wiring connector (A), pulse generator coil (B) and stator screws (C)

17.12 Align the slot (arrowed) with the Woodruff key

protect the end of the shaft, then assemble the puller legs through the holes in the rotor on 125 cc engines or behind the outer edge of the rotor on 180/200 cc engines. Tighten the centre bolt down onto the crankshaft end until the rotor is drawn off **(see illustration)**. If it is loose, remove the Woodruff key from the shaft, noting how it fits.

8 To remove the stator, it is also necessary to remove the pulse generator coil as they come as a linked assembly. Disconnect the alternator wiring multi-pin connector and undo the screw that secures the alternator wiring guide to free the wiring from the crankcase **(see illustration)**.

9 Disconnect the oil pressure switch wiring connector, then undo the screws that secure the pulse generator coil and the stator and remove the two units together **(see illustration)**.

Installation

10 Install the stator and pulse generator coil onto the crankcase; ensure that the wiring for the generator coil and the oil pressure switch is correctly positioned. Install the stator and generator coil screws and tighten them to the specified torque.

11 Connect the oil pressure switch wiring connector, the alternator wiring multi-pin

connector, and install the alternator wiring guide.

12 Clean the tapered end of the crankshaft and the corresponding mating surface on the inside of the rotor with a suitable solvent. Make sure that no metal objects have attached themselves to the magnets on the inside of the rotor. If removed, fit the Woodruff key into its slot in the shaft, then install the rotor onto the shaft, aligning the slot in the rotor with the key **(see illustration)**.

13 Install the rotor nut and tighten it to the torque setting specified at the beginning of the Chapter, using the method employed on removal to prevent the rotor from turning.

14 Position the rotor so that the raised section aligns with the pulse generator coil, then measure the air gap between the rotor and the coil with a feeler gauge **(see illustration)**. The air gap should be between 0.34 to 0.76 mm. If the gap is outside the specified limits inspect the coil mounting for distortion. If the gap is too small the rotor may strike to coil and damage it; if the gap is too large the performance of the ignition system will be reduced.

15 Align the dampers on the alternator rotor with the pump drive and install the alternator cover **(see illustration 17.5b)**. Ensure the alternator multi-pin connector is positioned in

the recess in the top of the cover and tighten the cover bolts securely.

16 Connect the coolant hoses to the unions on the water pump and refill the cooling system (see Chapter 1).

17 Install the remaining components in the reverse order of removal.

18 Starter pinion assembly

Note: *This procedure can be carried out with the engine in the frame.*

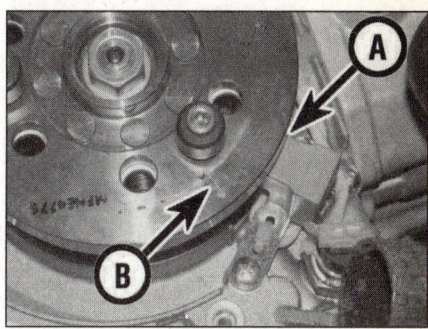

17.14 Measure the air gap at (A) as described. Note the rotor timing mark (B)

18.3 Lift the starter pinion out from behind the starter driven gear

1 Remove the drive belt cover (see Chapter 2D).

2 Follow the procedure in Chapter 2D, Section 3, and remove the drive pulley nut. Hold the inner pulley half in position on the crankshaft to prevent the variator rollers being displaced, then ease the starter driven gear away from the variator inner pulley half.

3 When there is sufficient clearance between the starter driven gear and the starter pinion, lift out the starter pinion assembly, noting how it fits **(see illustration)**.

Inspection

4 Check the starter pinion assembly for any signs of damage or wear, particularly for chipped or broken teeth on either of the pinions. Check the corresponding teeth on the starter motor pinion and the starter driven gear.

5 Rotate the outer pinion and check that it moves smoothly up and down the shaft, and that it returns easily to its rest position **(see illustration)**.

6 The starter pinion assembly is supplied as a complete unit; if any of the component parts are worn or damaged, the unit will have to be replaced with a new one.

Installation

7 Installation is the reverse of removal, noting the following. Ensure the inner pinion engages with the starter motor shaft. Follow the procedure in Chapter 2D to install the drive pulley nut and belt cover.

19.13a Undo the sump cover bolts . . .

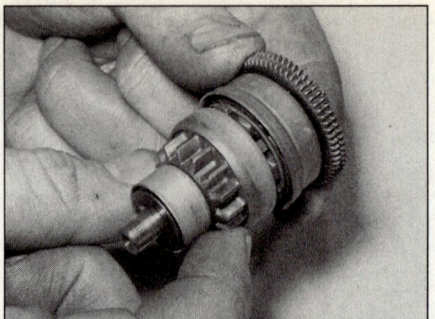

18.5 Check the pinion as described

19 Oil pump and relief valve

Pressure check

1 This engine is fitted with an oil pressure switch and warning light. The function of the circuit is described in Chapter 9.

2 If there is any doubt about the performance of the engine lubrication system, the oil pressure should be checked. The check provides useful information about the condition of the lubrication system. If you do not have the facilities to check the oil pressure yourself, have it done by a Gilera dealer.

3 To check the oil pressure, a suitable pressure gauge (which screws into the crankcase) will be needed. Gilera produce a gauge (Part No. 020193Y) and gauge adapter (Part No. 020434Y) for this purpose.

4 Check the engine oil level (see *Daily (pre-ride) checks*), then warm the engine up to normal operating temperature and stop it.

⚠ **Warning: To prevent accidents caused by the rear wheel contacting the ground, ensure that the scooter is on its centre stand and if necessary place a support under the scooter to prevent the rear wheel contacting the ground. Increasing engine speed will engage the transmission. It is vital that the rear wheel is off the ground and does not contact surrounding objects.**

5 Displace the alternator cover (see Section 17). Disconnect the oil pressure switch wiring

19.13b . . . and remove the cover

connector **(see illustration 17.9)**, then unscrew the oil pressure switch from the crankcase and swiftly screw in the gauge adapter. Connect the pressure gauge to the adapter. Discard the pressure switch sealing washer as a new one must be fitted on reassembly. **Note: *The alternator cover cannot be installed with the gauge in place. The water pump drive is therefore disconnected during the test and care should be taken so as not to overheat the engine. Also ensure that the pump drive dampers on the alternator rotor do not foul the alternator cover when the engine is running.***

⚠ **Warning: Take great care not to burn your hand on the hot engine unit, exhaust pipe or with engine oil when connecting the gauge adapter to the crankcase. Do not allow exhaust gases to build up in the work area; either perform the check outside or use an exhaust gas extraction system.**

6 Start the engine and increase the engine speed to 6000 rpm whilst watching the pressure gauge reading. The oil pressure should be similar to that given in the Specifications at the beginning of this Chapter.

7 If the pressure is significantly lower than the standard, either the oil strainer or filter is blocked, the pressure relief valve is stuck open, the oil pump is faulty, the piston oil jet in the crankcases has become dislodged, or there is considerable engine main bearing wear. Begin diagnosis by checking the oil filter and strainer (see Chapter 1), then the relief valve and oil pump (see Steps 11 to 38). If those items are good, the crankcases will have to be split to check the oil jet and the main bearings (see Section 20).

8 If the pressure is too high, either an oil passage is clogged, the relief valve is stuck closed or the wrong grade of oil is being used.

9 Stop the engine and unscrew the gauge and adapter from the crankcase.

10 Fit a new sealing washer to the oil pressure switch and install the switch. Tighten the switch to the specified torque setting, then check the oil level (see *Daily (pre-ride) checks*). **Note: *Rectify any problems before running the engine again.***

Oil pump and relief valve

Note: *This procedure can be carried out with the engine in the frame.*

Removal

11 Drain the engine oil (see Chapter 1).

12 Remove the drive pulley and variator (see Chapter 2D).

13 Undo the bolts securing the sump cover and remove the cover **(see illustrations)**. Discard the gasket as a new one must be used. Note how the relief valve spring locates on the lug on the inside of the cover and remove it carefully. If necessary, withdraw the relief valve from its location in the sump. Note the location of the cover dowels and remove them for safekeeping if they are loose.

14 Remove the screws and washers securing

19.14a Undo the cover screws (arrowed) . . .

19.14b . . . and pull out the cover . . .

19.14c . . . noting the location of the chain guide (arrowed)

19.15 Remove the pump sprocket plate (arrowed)

19.16 Undo the pump sprocket bolt (arrowed)

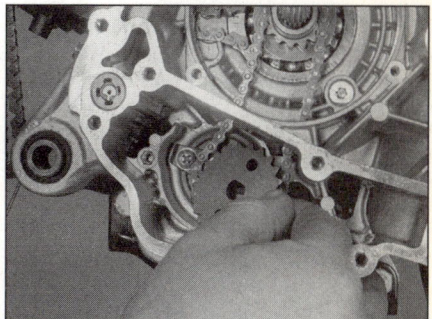

19.17a Remove the pump sprocket . . .

the pump drive chain cover and remove the cover **(see illustrations)**. **Note:** *The cover is a tight fit in the casing; pull it out carefully by the cast projections.* Discard the cover O-ring as a new one must be fitted on reassembly. Note the chain guide on the back of the cover **(see illustration)**

15 Remove the screws securing the pump sprocket plate and remove the plate, noting how it fits **(see illustration)**.

16 Insert a pin punch or screwdriver through one of the holes in the pump sprocket and locate it against the pump body to stop the sprocket turning, then unscrew the sprocket bolt **(see illustration)**. Note the Belleville washer on the bolt.

17 Draw the sprocket off the pump and slip it out of the chain; if required, draw the chain up into the transmission housing and remove it from the drive sprocket **(see illustrations)**. **Note:** *Before the chain is removed, mark it so that it can be fitted the same way round.* Slide the drive sprocket off the end of the crankshaft **(see illustration)**.

18 Remove the pump drive pinion and discard the O-ring as a new one must be fitted. Undo the two screws securing the oil pump and remove the pump, noting how it fits **(see illustration)**. Also remove the gasket from behind the pump and discard it as a new one must be fitted.

Inspection

19 Clean the relief valve and spring in solvent. Inspect the surface of the valve for wear and scoring. Measure the free length of the spring and compare the result with

the specifications at the beginning of this Chapter. If the valve is worn or the spring has shortened, renew them. Inspect the valve housing in the casing; any dirt lodged in the housing will prevent the valve from seating

properly and must be cleaned out carefully to avoid scratching the surface of the housing.

20 Remove the two screws securing the cover to the pump body, then remove cover **(see illustration)**.

19.17b . . . and the chain

19.17c Slide the drive sprocket off the shaft

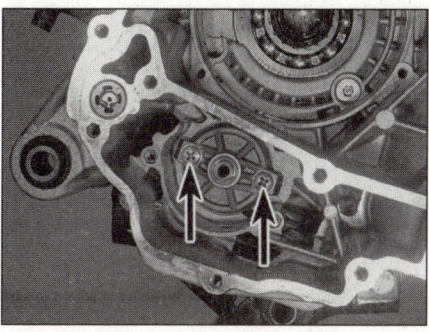

19.18 The pump is secured by two screws (arrowed)

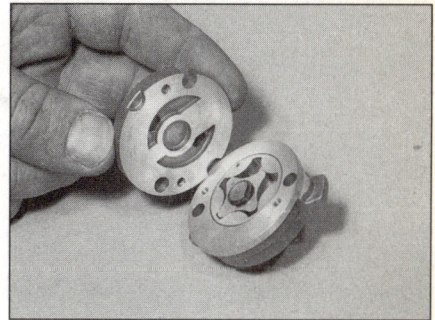

19.20 Remove the pump cover

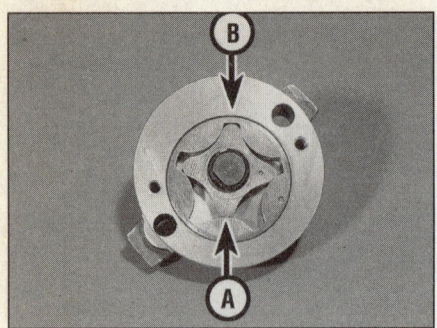

19.22 Measure inner-to-outer rotor clearance (A) and outer rotor-to-body clearance (B)

21 Note the position of the reference marks on the pump rotors. It is not necessary to disassemble the pump (individual components are not available) but, if required, remove the central circlip with circlip pliers, then lift out the rotors. Clean the pump body and rotors in solvent and dry them with compressed air, if available. Inspect the body and rotors for scoring and wear. If any damage, scoring, uneven or excessive wear is evident, renew the pump. If the pump has been disassembled, fit the rotors back into the body, ensuring that the reference marks are visible, and install the circlip.

22 Measure the clearance between the inner rotor tip and the outer rotor with a feeler gauge as shown, and compare the result to the specifications at the beginning of this Chapter **(see illustration)**.

23 Measure the clearance between the outer rotor and the pump body and compare the result to the specifications at the beginning of this Chapter **(see illustration 19.22)**. If either clearance measured is greater than the maximum listed, fit a new pump.

24 Lay a straight-edge across the rotors and the pump body and, using a feeler gauge, measure the rotor end-float (the gap between the rotors and the straight-edge). If the clearance measured is greater than the maximum listed, fit a new pump.

25 Check the pump drive chain and sprockets for wear or damage, and renew them as a set if necessary.

26 If the pump is good, make sure all the

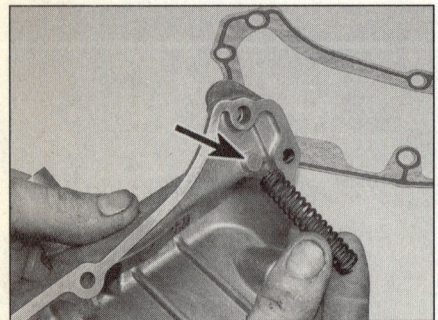

19.35 Relief valve spring locates on lug (arrowed) inside cover

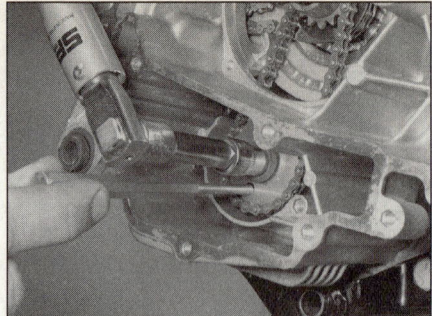

19.32 Hold the sprocket and tighten the bolt to the specified torque

components are clean, then lubricate them with clean engine oil.

27 Fit the cover, noting that it can only be fitted one way, and tighten the screws securely.

28 Rotate the pump shaft by hand and check that the rotors turn smoothly.

Installation

29 Lay a new pump gasket onto the crankcase, making sure the holes in the gasket align correctly with the oil holes.

30 Install the pump, noting that it can only be fitted one way, and tighten the screws to the torque setting specified at the beginning of this Chapter. Fit a new O-ring to the drive pinion and install the pinion.

31 Slide the drive sprocket, with its shouldered end facing out, onto the crankshaft, then fit the drive chain around the sprocket and slip it down into the sump (see Step 17).

32 Fit the pump sprocket into the chain, then fit the sprocket onto the pump, aligning the flat with that on the pump shaft. Fit the Belleville washer onto the sprocket bolt so that the raised outer edge of the washer faces the pump sprocket, then install the bolt. Use the method employed on removal to stop the sprocket turning and tighten the bolt to the specified torque **(see illustration)**.

33 Install the pump sprocket plate and tighten its screws securely.

34 Remove any traces of old gasket from the sump cover and crankcase mating surfaces with solvent. Take care not to scratch or gouge the soft aluminium.

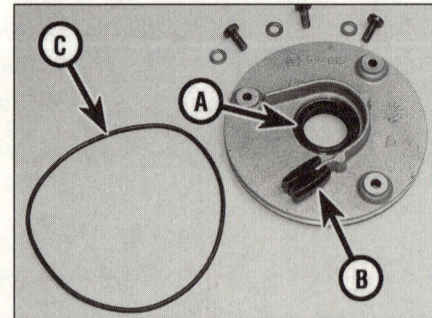

19.36 Pump drive chain cover oil seal (A), chain guide (B) and O-ring (C)

35 Lubricate the relief valve with clean engine oil, then install the valve into the casing. Fit the spring onto the lug on the inside of the sump cover **(see illustration)**. Ensure the dowels for the sump cover are in place and install the cover using a new gasket. Install the cover bolts and tighten them to the specified torque.

36 Check the condition of the centre oil seal in the pump drive chain cover **(see illustration)**. If there are any signs of oil leaking inside the drive belt casing, renew the seal. If the chain guide is worn, unclip it and fit it the other way round, or fit a new guide. Fit a new O-ring onto the cover and smear it with grease. Slide the cover carefully over the crankshaft to avoid damaging the centre seal, align the holes for the fixing screws and install the screws and washers finger-tight. Tighten the screws a little at a time, in turn, to draw the cover into the casing, then ensure the screws are tightened to the specified torque.

37 Install the drive pulley and variator (see Chapter 2D).

38 Fill the engine with the correct type and quantity of oil (see Chapter 1). Start the engine and check that there are no leaks around the sump. Check the engine oil level (see *Daily (pre-ride) checks*).

20 Crankcase halves, main bearings and crankshaft assembly

Note: *To separate the crankcase halves, the engine must be removed from the frame.*

Separation

1 To access the main bearings and crankshaft assembly, the crankcase halves must be separated.

2 Remove the engine from the frame (see Section 5). Before the crankcases can be separated the following components must be removed:

• Cam chain, blades and sprockets (see Section 9)
• Cylinder head (see Section 11)
• Cylinder (see Section 14)
• Alternator rotor and stator (see Section 17)
• Variator (see Chapter 2D)
• Starter motor (see Chapter 9)
• Oil pump (see Section 19)
• Centre stand (see Chapter 6)

3 Before separating the crankcases, measure the crankshaft end-float with a dial gauge and compare the result with the specifications at the beginning of this Chapter. Excessive end-float is an indication of wear on the crankshaft or the crankcases and should be investigated when the cases have been separated.

4 Unscrew the eleven crankcase bolts evenly, a little at a time and in a criss-cross sequence until they are all finger-tight, then remove them **(see illustration)**. Support the engine unit on the work surface, left-hand (transmission) side down. Carefully lift the right-hand crankcase

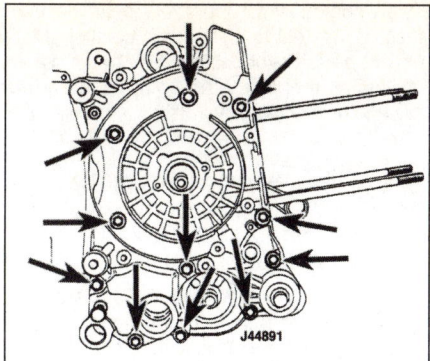

20.4 Crankcase bolt locations (arrowed)

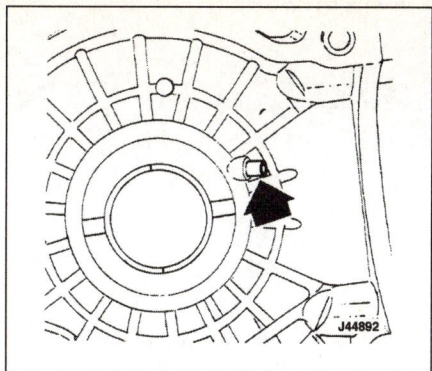

20.13 Left-hand crankcase half oil jet (arrowed)

half off the left-hand half, taking care not to score the surface of the right-hand main bearing on the crankshaft. If the halves do not separate easily, tap around the joint with a soft-faced mallet. **Note:** *Do not try and separate the halves by levering against the crankcase mating surfaces as they are easily scored and will not seal correctly afterwards.* Note the position of the two crankcase dowels and remove them for safekeeping if they are loose.

5 Lift the crankshaft assembly out of the left-hand crankcase, again taking care not to mark the bearing surface. Discard the gasket as a new one must be fitted on reassembly. On 180 and 200 cc engines, two thrust washers are fitted to the crankshaft – note the position of the washers so that they can be correctly installed on assembly.

6 Clean the crankcases thoroughly with solvent and dry them with compressed air. Clean the crankshaft assembly with solvent. **Note:** *Gilera warn against blowing compressed air through the connecting rod oil passage to avoid the danger of compacting dirt and blocking the passage to the big-end bearing.*

7 Remove all traces of old gasket from the mating surfaces with solvent. Take care not to scratch or gouge the soft aluminium.

Caution: Be very careful not to nick or gouge the crankcase mating surfaces, or oil leaks will result. Check both crankcase halves very carefully for cracks and other damage.

8 Note the position of the crankshaft oil seal in the right-hand crankcase half, then drive the seal out with a bearing driver or suitable sized socket. Take care not to damage the surface of the main bearing.

Inspection

Crankcases

9 Small cracks or holes in aluminium castings can be repaired with an epoxy resin adhesive as a temporary measure. Permanent repairs can only be effected by argon-arc welding, and only a specialist in this process is in a position to advise on the economy or practical aspect of such a repair. Low temperature

repair kits are available for repair of aluminium castings. If any damage is found that can't be repaired, renew the crankcase halves as a set.

10 Damaged threads can be economically reclaimed by using a diamond section wire insert, of the Heli-Coil type, which is easily fitted after drilling and re-tapping the affected thread. Sheared studs or screws can usually be removed with stud or screw extractors; if you are in any doubt consult a Gilera dealer or specialist motorcycle engineer.

11 Always wash the crankcases thoroughly after any repair work to ensure no dirt or metal swarf is trapped inside when the engine is rebuilt.

12 Inspect the engine mounting bushes. If they show signs of deterioration renew them both at the same time. To remove a bush, first note its position in the casing. Heat the casing with a hot air gun, then support the casing and drive the bush out with a hammer and a suitably sized socket. Clean the bush housing with steel wool to remove any corrosion, then reheat the casing and fit the new bush. **Note:** *Always support the casing when removing or fitting bushes to avoid breaking the casing.*

Main bearings

13 Blow out the oil passages for the oil pump, relief valve, main bearing and piston oil jet in the left-hand crankcase half with compressed air **(see illustration)**. Blow out the oil passages for the main bearing, the cylinder head oil supply and the oil

seal drain in the right-hand crankcase half.

14 Check the condition of the main bearings. There are two bearings in each crankcase half; the surface of the inner bearing is plain and the outside bearing has an oilway in it. The surface of each bearing should be smooth with no scoring or scuff marks. The condition of the bearings and the corresponding crankshaft journals is vital to the performance of the lubrication system. If the bearings are damaged or worn, oil pressure will drop and the oil feed to the connecting rod big-end and the cylinder head will be insufficient to prevent rapid wear and possible seizure.

15 Use a telescoping gauge and a micrometer to measure the internal diameter or each bearing in three directions as shown **(see illustration)**. Ensure that the measurements are taken in the centre of each bearing surface. The bearings are colour-coded red, blue or yellow; ensure all three measurements for each bearing are within the specifications in the table below. Gilera do not supply new bearings; if any of the bearings are worn beyond the specifications new crankcase halves will have to be fitted. If there is any doubt about the condition of the bearings consult a Gilera dealer.

Crankshaft assembly

16 Check the condition of the crankshaft journals. The surface of each journal should be smooth with no scoring, pitting or scuff marks. Use a micrometer to measure the diameter of each journal in two positions (A and B), to correspond with the two main bearings, and in two directions as shown **(see illustration)**. There are two size categories for the crankshaft journals, Class 1 and Class 2, which match the colour coding of the crankcase bearings. Compare the results with the table and ensure that the journal size is within the specifications for the appropriate bearing. If the crankshaft journals are damaged or worn beyond the specifications a new crankshaft will have to be fitted.

17 Measure the connecting rod big-end side clearance with a feeler gauge and compare it with the specifications at the beginning of

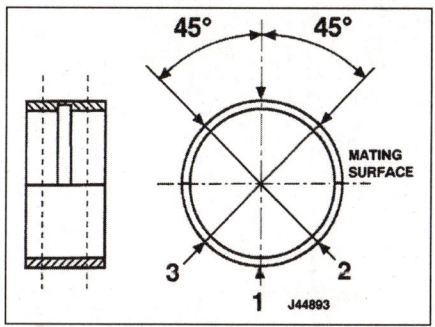

20.15 Measure the main bearings as described

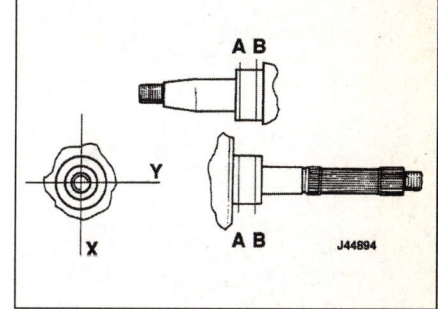

20.16 Measure the crankshaft journals as described

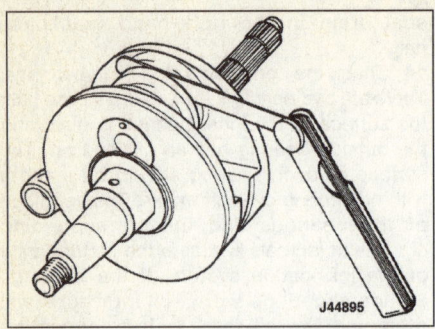

20.17a Checking the connecting rod big-end bearing side clearance

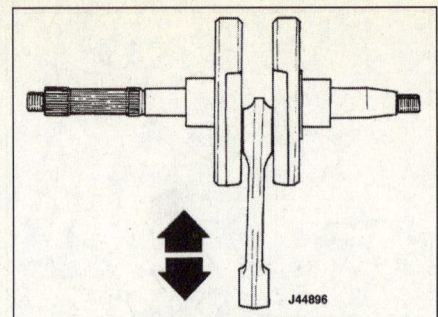

20.17b Measure the radial play on the connecting rod

this Chapter **(see illustration)**. Measure the up-and-down (radial) play on the rod with a dial gauge and measure the width of the flywheels at several points to ensure they are not out of alignment **(see illustrations)**. Compare the results with the specifications at the beginning of this Chapter.

18 Place the crankshaft assembly on V-blocks and check the runout at the main bearing journals and at the ends of the shafts **(see illustration)**. If the runout exceeds the specified limit, or if either of the connecting rod measurements exceed the limit, the crankshaft assembly must be renewed.

Reassembly

19 Ensure that the crankcase mating surfaces are clean. Support the left-hand crankcase half on the work surface, transmission side down, and check that the crankcase dowels are in place, then install a new gasket.

20 Lubricate the main bearings and crank-shaft journals with clean engine oil. On 180 and 200 cc engines, ensure that the

thrust washers are correctly positioned on the crankshaft. Insert the crankshaft all the way into the left-hand crankcase half, positioning the connecting rod in-line with the crankcase mouth. Guide the crankcase right-hand half over the crankshaft end and press it down until the two halves meet. Use a soft-faced mallet to help the casing seat, but don't apply too much pressure. **Note:** *If the crankcases do not meet, remove the right-hand half and investigate the problem – do not be tempted to pull the crankcases together using the bolts.*

21 Clean the threads of the crankcase bolts and install them finger-tight. Tighten the bolts evenly, in a criss-cross sequence, to the specified torque setting. Hold the connecting rod to prevent it hitting the crankcase mouth, then rotate the crankshaft to check that it is moves freely. If necessary, trim any excess crankcase gasket off the cylinder mating surface with a sharp knife.

22 Lubricate the new crankshaft oil seal with clean engine oil, then install it in the right-hand crankcase half in the same position as noted on removal. Use a bearing driver or a suitably-

sized socket which contacts only the outer face of the seal to drive it into position. **Note:** *Do not press the oil seal too far into the casing.*

23 Install the remaining components in the reverse order of removal.

21 Initial start-up after overhaul

1 Make sure the engine oil and coolant levels are correct (see *Daily (pre-ride) checks*).

2 Make sure there is fuel in the tank.

3 Turn the ignition ON, start the engine and allow it to run at a slow idle until it reaches operating temperature. Do not be alarmed if there is a little smoke from the exhaust – this will be due to the oil used to lubricate the piston and bore during assembly and should subside after a while.

4 If the engine proves reluctant to start, remove the spark plug and check that it has not become wet and oily. If it has, clean it and try again. If the engine refuses to start, go through the fault finding charts at the end of this manual to identify the problem.

5 Check carefully that there are no oil leaks and make sure the controls, especially the brakes, function properly before road testing the machine. Refer to Section 22 for the recommended running-in procedure.

6 Upon completion of the road test, and after the engine has cooled down completely, recheck the valve clearances (see Chapter 1) and check the engine oil and coolant levels (see *Daily (pre-ride) checks*).

22 Recommended running-in procedure

1 Treat the machine gently for the first few miles to make sure oil has circulated throughout the engine and any new parts installed have started to seat.

2 Even greater care is necessary if the engine has been rebored (125 cc engine) or has a new piston and cylinder, or if a new crankshaft assembly has been installed. In these circumstances, the scooter will have to be run in as when new. This means a restraining hand on the throttle until at least 600 miles (1000 km) have been covered. There's no point in keeping to any set speed limit – the main idea is to keep from labouring the engine and not to maintain any one speed for too long. Experience is the best guide, since it's easy to tell when an engine is running freely. Once past the 600 mile (1000 km) mark, gradually increase performance, using full throttle for short bursts to begin with.

3 If a lubrication failure is suspected, stop the engine immediately and try to find the cause. If an engine is run without oil, even for a short period of time, severe damage will occur.

Main bearing size table

Crankcase main bearing		Crankshaft journal diameter	
Class	Size	Class	Size
A (red)	29.025 to 29.040 mm	1	28.998 to 29.004 mm
B (blue)	29.019 to 29.034 mm		
B (blue)	29.028 to 29.043 mm	2	29.004 to 29.010 mm
C (yellow)	29.022 to 29.037 mm		

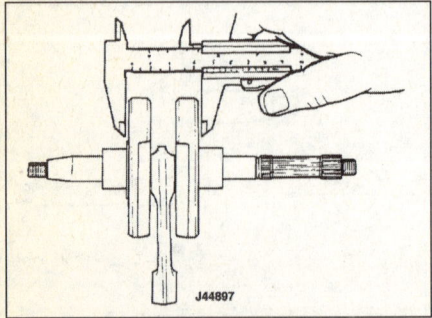

20.17c Measure the width of the flywheels as described

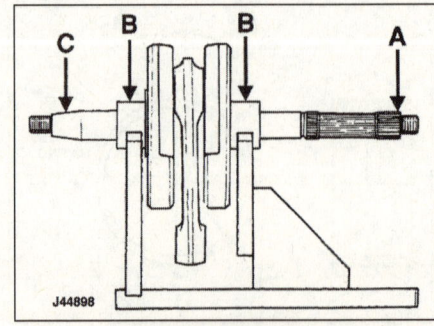

20.18 Check the crankshaft runout as described

Chapter 2 Part D:
Transmission

Refer to the beginning of Chapter 1 for model identification details

Contents

Degrees of difficulty

Easy, suitable for novice with little experience	**Fairly easy,** suitable for beginner with some experience	**Fairly difficult,** suitable for competent DIY mechanic	**Difficult,** suitable for experienced DIY mechanic	**Very difficult,** suitable for expert DIY or professional 

Specifications

Variator

Roller diameter (min)
All 50 cc and 125 cc models . . . . 18.5 mm
Runner FXR180 . . . . 19.5 mm
Runner VXR180/200, ST200, DNA 180 . . . . 20.0 mm
Collar diameter (min)
All 50 cc models. . . . . 19.95 mm
Runner FX125, FXR180 . . . . 25.93 mm
Runner VX125, ST125, VXR180/200, ST200, DNA 125/180 . . . . 25.95 mm
Bush diameter (max)
All 50 cc models. . . . . 20.12 mm
Runner FX125, FXR180 . . . . 26.10 mm
Runner VX125, ST125, VXR180/200, ST200, DNA 125/180 . . . . 26.12 mm

Clutch and driven pulley

Clutch drum diameter (max)
All 50 cc models. . . . . 107.5 mm
All other models . . . . 134.5 mm
Clutch drum out-of-round (max) – all models . . . . 0.2 mm
Inner pulley shaft diameter (min)
All 50 cc models. . . . . 33.96 mm
All other models . . . . 40.96 mm
Outer pulley bore diameter (max)
All 50 cc models. . . . . 34.08 mm
All other models . . . . 41.08 mm
Spring free length (min)
All 50 cc models. . . . . 110 mm (113mm 2005-on Stalker)
Runner FX125, FXR180 . . . . 136 mm
Runner VX125, ST125, VXR180/200, ST200, DNA 125/180 . . . . 106 mm
Clutch shoe lining material thickness (min) – all models . . . . 1 mm

Drive belt

Minimum width of outer run
All 50 cc models. . . . . 17.5 mm
Runner FX125. . . . . 20.5 mm
Runner FXR180 . . . . 21.0 mm
Runner VX125, ST125, DNA 125 . . . . 21.5 mm
Runner VXR180/200, ST200, DNA 180 . . . . 19.5 mm

Torque settings

Belt support roller bolt . . . . 11 to 13 Nm
Clutch assembly nut
  All 50 cc models . . . . 40 to 44 Nm (55 to 60 Nm 2005-on Stalker)
  All 125, 180 and 200 cc models . . . . 55 to 60 Nm
Clutch drum nut
  All 50 cc models . . . . 40 to 44 Nm
  Runner FX125, FXR180 . . . . 52 to 56 Nm
Drive pulley nut
  All 50 cc models . . . . 40 to 44 Nm
  Runner FX125, FXR180 . . . . 75 to 80 Nm
  Runner VX125, ST125, VXR180/200, ST200, DNA 125/180 . . . . 75 to 83 Nm
Gearbox cover bolts
  All 50 cc models . . . . 12 to 13 Nm
  Runner FX125, FXR180 . . . . 13 to 15 Nm
  Runner VX125, ST125, VXR180/200, ST200, DNA 125/180 . . . . 24 to 27 Nm
Gearbox input shaft nut
  Runner VX125, ST125, VXR180/200, ST200, DNA 125/180 . . . . 54 to 60 Nm
Kickstart lever pinch bolt . . . . 12 to 13 Nm

1 General information

The transmission on all models is fully automatic in operation. Power is transmitted from the engine to the rear wheel by belt, via a variator on the drive pulley (which automatically varies the gearing with engine speed), an automatic clutch on the driven pulley, and a reduction gearbox. Both the variator and the automatic clutch work on the principal of centrifugal force.

Note: *On some models the internal components of the transmission may differ slightly to those components described or shown. When dismantling always note the fitted position, order and way round of each component as it is removed.*

2 Drive belt cover and kickstart

Removal

1 If the engine is still in the frame, remove any bodywork as required to access the drive belt cover on the left-hand side of the engine (see Chapter 7).

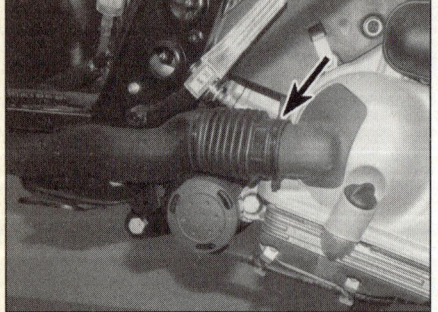

2.3 Cut the cable tie (arrowed) and detach the air duct

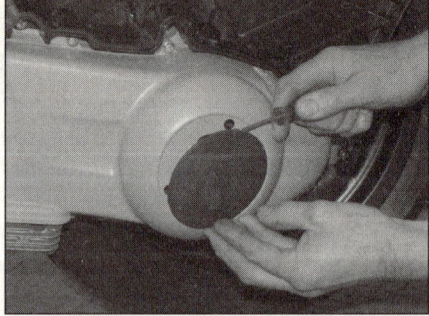

2.4a Remove the plastic cap

2 Displace or remove the air filter housing (see Chapter 4).
3 Where fitted, detach the air cooling duct from the front of the cover **(see illustration)**.
4 On some models, the gearbox input shaft passes through the drive belt cover and is supported by a bearing in the cover. To undo the nut on the outer end of the shaft, first unclip the plastic cap on the clutch bearing housing **(see illustration)**. The clutch drum must be locked against the belt cover to prevent the shaft turning while the nut is undone; Gilera produce a service tool (Part No. 020423Y) to do this. Alternatively, insert two large screwdrivers through the holes in the belt cover to engage the holes in the clutch drum and have an assistant hold the screwdrivers while the nut is undone, then remove the nut and washer **(see illustrations)**. On Runner VX125, ST125, VXR180/200, ST200 and DNA 125/180 models, remove the oil filler cap **(see illustration)**.
5 Unscrew the bolts securing the drive belt over, noting the position of the cable and rear brake hose clips on the bolts **(see illustration)**. Remove the cover, noting how it fits **(see illustration)**. On models where the gearbox shaft passes through the drive belt cover, note the spacer on the shaft **(see illustration)**.

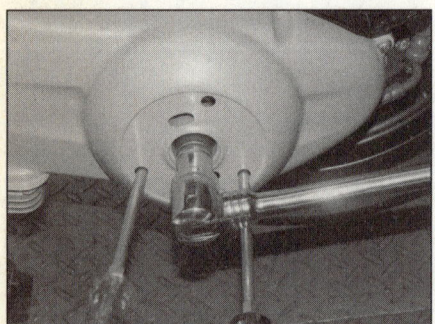

2.4b Lock the clutch drum as described . . .

2.4c . . . and remove the nut and washer

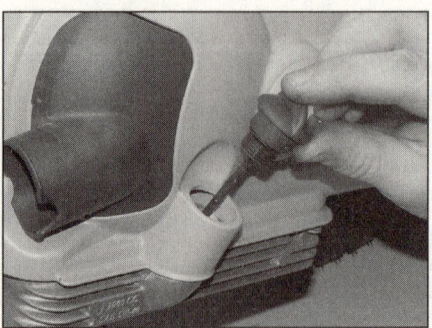

2.4d Remove the oil filler cap

Inspection – kickstart mechanism (where fitted)

Note: *It is not advisable to disassemble the kickstart mechanism unless a component needs to be renewed – the return spring can be very difficult to fit.*

6 Where fitted, remove the kickstart mechanism cover on the inside of the belt cover (**see illustration**). Remove any old and hardened grease.

7 Manually operate the kickstart lever and check that the mechanism operates smoothly and returns to its rest position under pressure of the spring. Check for any signs of wear or damage on the pinion teeth, and check for rounded dogs on the engaging pinion and its corresponding plate on the drive pulley (**see illustration**).

8 If the kickstart action is suspect or if any components are damaged, first remove the kickstart lever pinch bolt and draw the lever off the shaft (**see illustration**). Where fitted, remove the circlip securing the shaft in the cover (**see illustration**). Lift the engaging pinion out of the cover, noting how it is located by its spring clip (**see illustration**). Note how the shaft pinion return spring ends are located on the pinion and the casing, and note how the pinion butts up against the rubber pad under spring pressure. Pull the shaft out of the cover carefully; the spring will release its tension and uncoil as the end detaches from the pinion (**see illustration**). Remove the spring.

9 Clean all components in solvent. Check the spring for cracks and distortion and the shafts

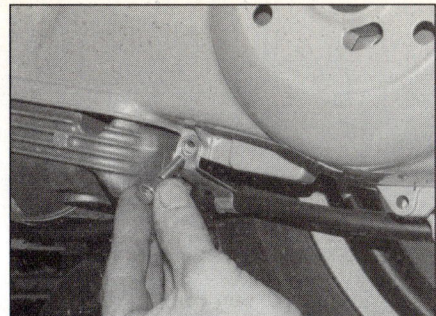

2.5a Note the position of any clips retained by the cover bolts

2.5c Note the spacer on the gearbox input shaft

and their bushes in the cover for wear. Check the condition of the rubber pad. Renew any components that are worn or damaged.

10 To reassemble the mechanism, first install the pinion return spring, locating its

2.5b Remove the drive belt cover – DNA 180 shown

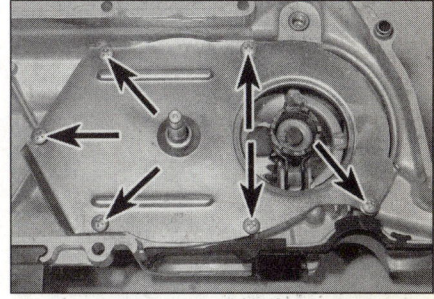

2.6 Where fitted, remove the screws (arrowed) securing the kickstart mechanism cover

hooked end against the raised section in the cover (**see illustration**). Apply some grease to the kickstart shaft and its bore. Fitting the shaft pinion and tensioning the return spring can be difficult. Gilera produce a service

2.7 Check the engaging pinion dogs and their mating plate for wear and damage

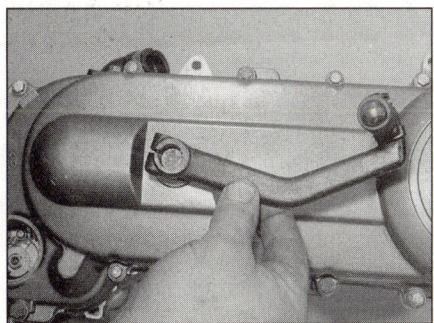

2.8a Unscrew the bolt and remove the kickstart lever

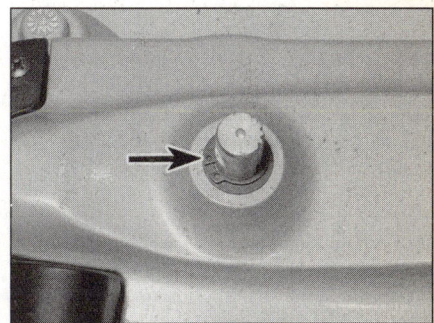

2.8b Remove the circlip (arrowed) securing the shaft

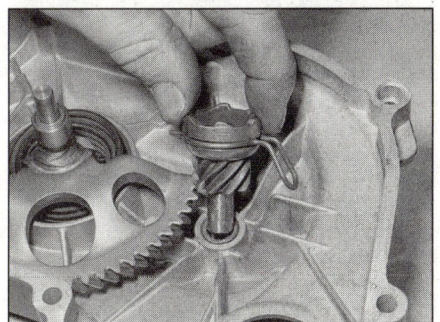

2.8c Remove the engaging pinion, noting how it fits

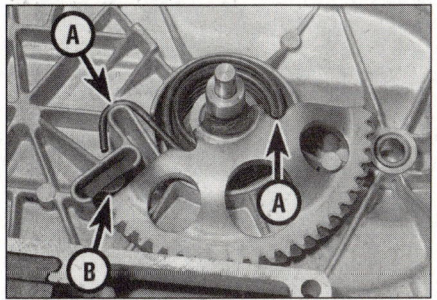

2.8d Note how the spring ends (A) locate, and how the pinion butts against the rubber pad (B)

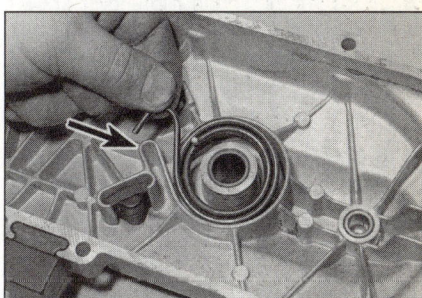

2.10a Fit the return spring, locating its hooked end against the raised section (arrowed)

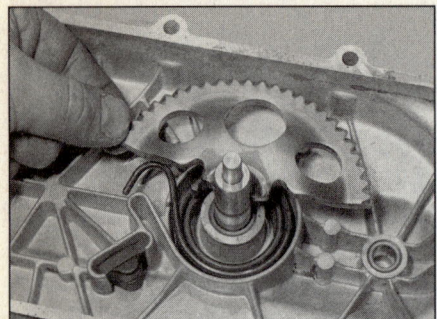

2.10b Install the pinion as shown . . .

2.10c . . . then locate the steel rod onto the spring end and against the pinion . . .

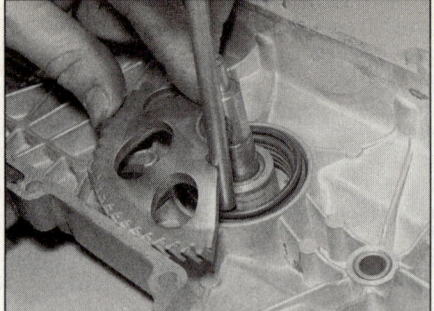

2.10d . . . and move the pinion around, bringing the spring with it . . .

2.10e . . . until the pinion end clears the rubber pad and can be tapped down against it

2.11 The installed assembly should be as shown, though on some models the engaging spring end locating section is positioned differently

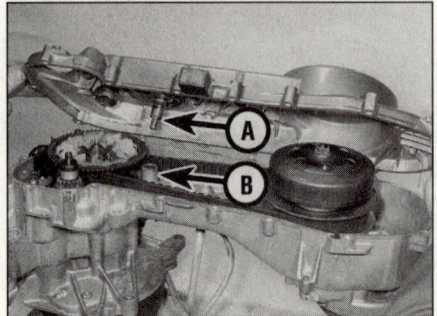

2.14 Where applicable, make sure the shaft (A) locates in its bore (B)

tool (Part No. 020261Y) for this purpose. Alternatively, obtain a length of steel rod and drill a hole up one end deep enough to accommodate the upturned end of the return spring. Locate the pinion in its bore, with the cutout in the pinion adjacent to the end of the spring, then fit the drilled rod over the end of the spring **(see illustrations)**. Hold the rod against the pinion and use the rod to turn the pinion anti-clockwise so that the spring is tensioned. When the pinion clears the rubber pad, press or tap it down into its installed position, so that it butts against the pad **(see illustrations)**. Pull the rod off the spring end, which will automatically locate itself in the cutout in the pinion.

11 Apply some grease to the engaging pinion shaft and fit it into its bore **(see illustration 2.8c)**, locating the spring clip end as shown **(see illustration)**. Secure the kickstart shaft with the circlip, where fitted **(see illustration 2.8b)**. Fit the kickstart lever and tighten the bolt to the specified torque **(see illustration 2.8a)**. Check the operation of the mechanism. Where fitted, install the mechanism cover **(see illustration 2.6)**.

Inspection – drive belt cover

12 Where fitted, check the condition of the bearing in the cover. The bearing should turn smoothly and freely without excessive play between the inner and outer races. If there is any doubt about the condition of the bearing, replace it with a new one. On models where

the gearbox shaft passes through the cover, remove the retaining circlip on the inside of the cover, then press the bearing out from the outside with a driver or suitably sized socket. If necessary, heat the cover on the inside around the bearing housing with a hot air gun to aid removal. Note which way round the bearing is fitted. Press the new bearing in with a socket that contacts the outer race only and secure it with the circlip.

13 On some models, the bearing locates in a blind hole in the cover and must be removed with an expanding bearing puller and slide-hammer attachment. Alternatively, heat the cover around the bearing housing, then tap it face down on the work surface to dislodge the bearing. Take care to avoid damaging the surface of the cover's edge.

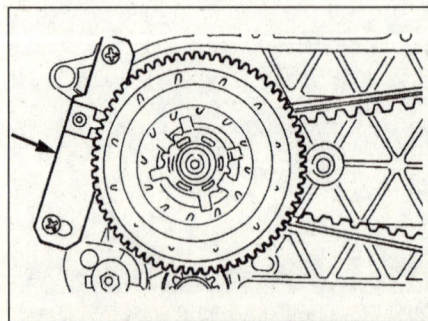

3.3 Gilera tool (arrowed) used to lock drive pulley

Installation

14 Installation is the reverse of removal. Ensure the kickstart shaft end locates correctly in its bore next to the drive pulley where applicable **(see illustration)**. On models where the gearbox input shaft passes through the belt cover, ensure the spacer is in place on the shaft before fitting the cover **(see illustration 2.5c)**.

3 Drive pulley and variator

Removal

1 Remove the drive belt cover (see Section 2).
2 To remove the drive pulley nut, the pulley must be locked to prevent it turning. Gilera produce a range of service tools for this purpose.
3 On all 50 cc models (service tool Part No. 020165Y) and Runner FX125/FXR180 models (service tool Part No. 020264Y) the tool bolts onto the engine case and has a toothed section which locates into the drive pulley **(see illustration)**. A similar home-made tool can be made.
4 On Runner VX125, ST125 and DNA 125 models (service tool Part No. 020368Y) and Runner VXR180/200, ST200 and DNA 180 models (service tool Part No. 020442Y) the tool locates in the outer face of the starter driven gear **(see illustration)**.

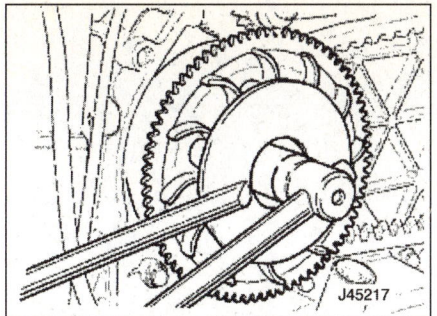

3.4 Gilera tool used to lock starter driven gear

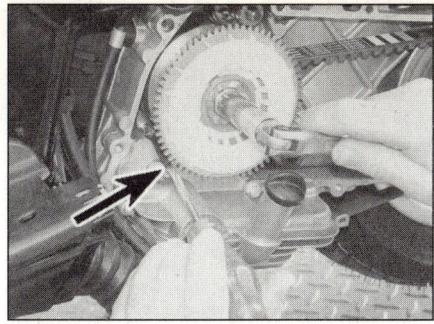

3.5 Lock the starter driven gear with a screwdriver (arrowed)

3.6a Remove the mating plate . . .

3.6b . . . the finned plate . . .

3.6c . . . and the starter driven gear

3.7a Remove the two washers . . .

5 Alternatively, locate a large flat-bladed screwdriver between the teeth of the starter driven gear and have an assistant hold it firmly against the engine casing **(see illustration)**.

With the pulley locked, unscrew the nut exerting steady pressure to avoid damaging the components. Note that on Runner VXR180/200 and DNA 180 models, a combined nut and

washer is used. Piaggio recommend that a new nut is used on assembly on all models.
6 Where fitted, remove the kickstart engaging pinion mating plate, the plastic finned plate and the starter driven gear **(see illustrations)**.
7 On Runner VX125, ST125 and DNA 125 models, remove the two washers and the starter driven gear **(see illustrations)**.
8 On Runner VXR180/200, ST200 and DNA 180 models, first note the alignment of the index marks on the starter driven gear and the outer half of the drive pulley, then slide them off the shaft **(see illustrations)**.
9 Move the drive belt aside, and remove the washer from the end of the shaft **(see illustration). Note:** *It is not necessary to remove the drive belt from the machine. If the belt is removed, note any directional arrows or mark the belt so that it can be installed the right way round.*

3.7b . . . and the starter driven gear as described

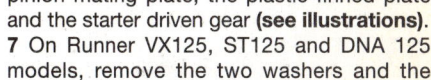

3.8a Note the index mark on the driven gear (A) and the drive pulley (B)

3.8b Slide off the driven gear . . .

3.8c . . . and the drive pulley outer half

3.9 Remove the washer

3.10a Draw out the collar . . .

3.10b . . . and slide the variator off the shaft

3.11a On early models remove the screws (arrowed) . . .

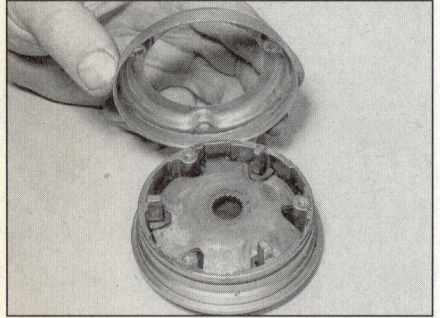

3.11b . . . and lift off the cover

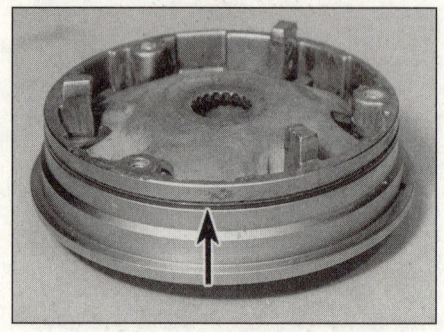

3.11c Discard the O-ring (arrowed)

3.11d Lift out the ramp plate . . .

10 Grip the variator so that the ramp plate at the back is held into the housing; draw out the collar from the centre of the variator, then slide the variator off the shaft (see illustrations).

11 Note: *Two types of variator are fitted; on early models the variator rollers are greased and the variator has a cover, on later models the rollers are not greased and no cover is fitted.* To disassemble the early-type variator, first remove the three screws and lift off the cover, then remove the O-ring and discard it as a new one must be used (see illustrations). On all models, lift out the ramp plate, then remove the rollers, noting which fits where as, unless new ones are used, they should be installed in their original locations (see illustrations). Clean and, where applicable, de-grease all the components.

Inspection

12 Check the rollers and the corresponding ramps in the variator housing and ramp plate for damage, wear and flat spots, and renew the rollers, the housing and the plate if necessary (see illustration). Measure the diameter of the rollers and compare the result to the specifications at the beginning of the Chapter. Renew the rollers as a set if any are worn below the minimum diameter (see illustration). Note: *Always specify the model*

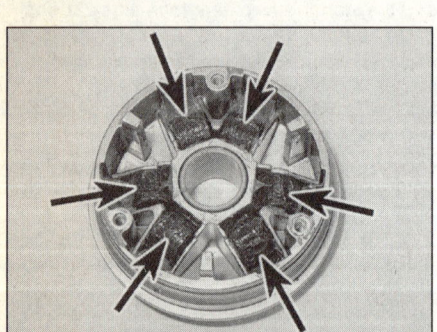

3.11e . . . and remove the rollers (arrowed)

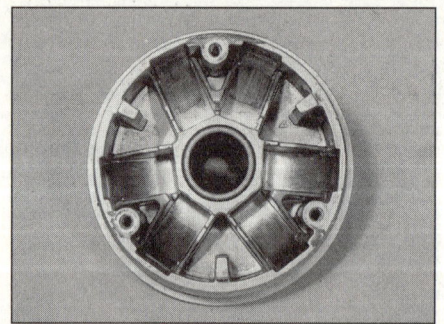

3.12a Check the ramps for wear

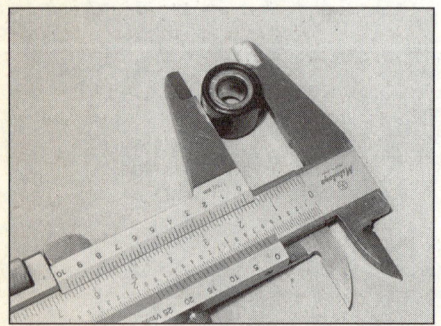

3.12b Measure the diameter of the rollers

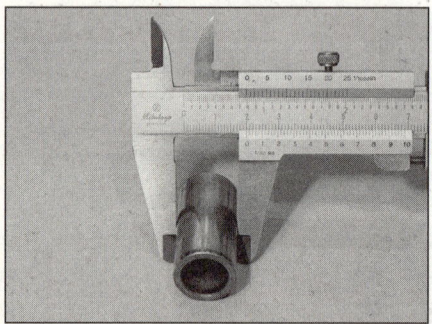

3.13a Measure the collar external diameter . . .

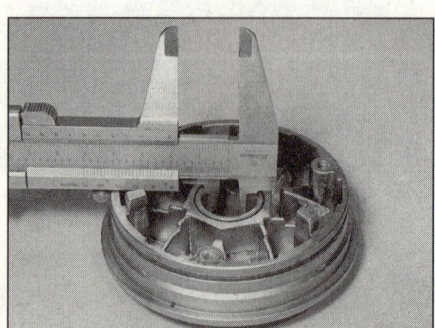

3.13b . . . and the bush internal diameter

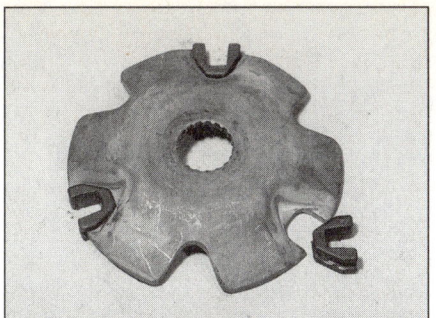

3.14 Check the guide shoes and renew them if necessary

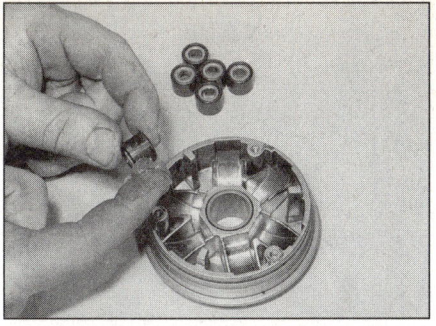

3.15a On early models, grease the rollers and fit them into the housing

3.15b Fit the ramp plate, locating the guide shoes as shown

3.16 Hold the variator assembly together to keep the rollers in place

3.17 Locate the belt over the shaft

3.18 Make sure the tabs (arrowed) are correctly located

and year of your scooter when buying new variator rollers. If supplied, later non-greased rollers can be fitted in the earlier type variator, but the variator should be cleaned thoroughly and the rollers should not be greased.

13 Check the collar and its bush in the housing for wear and damage and renew them if necessary. Measure the external diameter of the collar and the internal diameter of the bush and compare the results to the specifications at the beginning of the Chapter. Renew either or both if they are worn beyond their limit **(see illustrations)**.

14 Check the condition of the guide shoes on the ramp plate and renew them if they are worn or damaged **(see illustration)**. Also check the splines on the plate and renew the plate if they are worn.

Installation

15 On early models fitted with the original rollers, grease the rollers and the ramps with lithium soap-based grease (NLGI 3). On all models, fit the rollers into the housing, making sure they are fitted in their original positions (unless new ones are used) **(see illustration)**. Check that the guide shoes are correctly fitted on the ramp plate, then install the plate **(see illustration)**. On early models, if the original greased rollers are fitted, fit a new O-ring around the housing, then install the cover and tighten its screws securely **(see illustrations 3.11c, b and a)**.

16 Grip the variator so that the ramp plate is held into the housing and slide the variator onto the crankshaft **(see illustration)**. Install the collar, then fit the washer **(see illustration 3.9)**.

Note: *If the ramp plate moves and the rollers are dislodged, disassemble the variator and reposition the rollers correctly.*

17 Position the drive belt around the shaft **(see illustration)**. Ensure there is sufficient slack in the belt to avoid it being trapped when the starter driven gear is installed.

18 On all 50 cc models and Runner FX125/FXR180 models, where fitted, install the starter driven gear, the finned plate and the mating plate **(see illustrations 3.6c, b, and a)**, making sure the mating plate is correctly located **(see illustration)**. Apply a suitable non-permanent thread locking compound to the threads of a new drive pulley nut. Use the method employed on removal to prevent the pulley turning and tighten the nut to the torque setting specified at the beginning of this Chapter. **Note:** *It is important that the nut tightens against the mating plate, and does not bottom on the shouldered end of the crankshaft.*

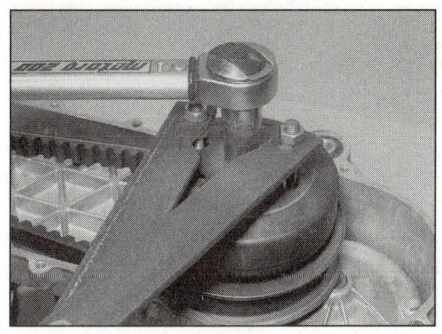

4.2 Undo the clutch drum nut as described

19 On Runner VX125, ST125 and DNA 125 models, fit the starter driven gear and the two washers **(see illustration 3.7a)**.

20 On Runner VXR180/200, ST200 and DNA 180 models, fit the outer half of the drive pulley, then align the index mark on the starter driven gear with the mark on the pulley and install the driven gear **(see illustration 3.8a)**.

21 On Runner VX125, ST125, VXR180/200, ST200 and DNA 125/180 models, apply a suitable non-permanent thread locking compound to the threads of a new drive pulley nut. Use the method employed on removal to prevent the pulley turning and tighten the nut to the torque setting specified at the beginning of this Chapter.

22 Install the drive belt cover (see Section 2).

4 Clutch and driven pulley

Removal

1 Remove the drive belt cover (see Section 2). Where fitted, remove the spacer on the end of the gearbox input shaft **(see illustration 2.5c)**.

2 On all 50 cc models and Runner FX125/FXR180 models the clutch drum is held by a nut. To remove the nut it is necessary to hold the clutch and stop it from turning. Gilera produce a service tool (Part No 020565Y) for this purpose, or alternatively a home-made equivalent can be made (see **Tool Tip**). With the drum securely held, unscrew the nut **(see illustration)**. Gilera

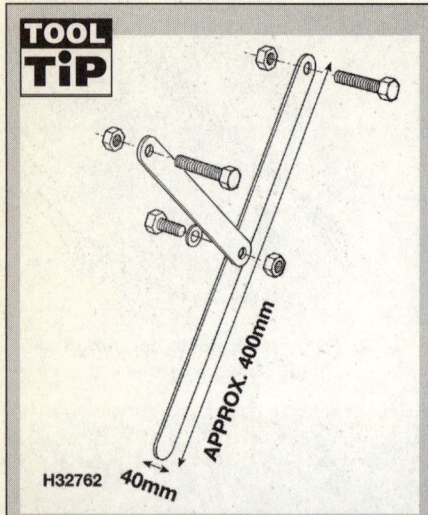

TOOL TiP

H32762

APPROX. 400mm

40mm

A holding tool can easily be made using two strips of steel bolted together in the middle, and with a bolt through each end which locates in the slots in the drum.

recommend that a new nut is used on assembly.

3 Remove the clutch drum, then draw the clutch and driven pulley assembly off the shaft and disengage the drive belt from it **(see illustrations)**. **Note:** *If the belt is removed from the machine, note any directional arrows or mark the belt so that it can be installed the right way round.*

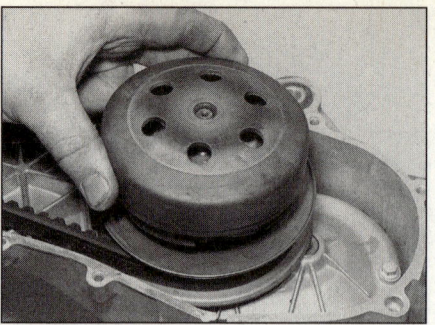

4.3a Remove the clutch drum . . .

4 To disassemble the clutch and driven pulley assembly, it is necessary to hold the clutch spring compressed while the clutch assembly nut is undone. Gilera produce a service tool (Part No. 020444Y) to do this. Alternatively, use the set-up shown, ensuring no pressure is applied to the rim of the pulley and that there is adequate room to undo the nut **(see illustrations)**.

5 Fit a strap wrench around the clutch shoes to hold the assembly while the nut is undone, then release the spring pressure slowly by undoing the clamp **(see illustration)**.

6 Remove the clutch, then remove the spring seat, the spring and the centre sleeve **(see illustrations)**.

7 Withdraw the guide pins and separate the pulley halves **(see illustrations)**.

8 Remove the two seals and the O-rings from the pulley outer half and discard them

4.3b . . . then draw the assembly off the shaft and disengage the belt

as new ones must be used on assembly **(see illustration)**.

9 Clean all the components with a suitable solvent.

Inspection

10 Check the inner surface of the clutch drum for damage and scoring and inspect the splines in its centre; renew it if necessary. Measure the internal diameter of the drum at several points to determine if it is worn or out-of-round. If it is worn or out-of-round beyond the service limit, renew it **(see illustration)**.

11 Check the amount of friction material remaining on the clutch shoes and renew the clutch if any shoe is worn to its service limit **(see illustration)**.

12 Inspect the shoe springs for wear and stretching. Ensure that the shoes are not seized on their pivot pins and that the

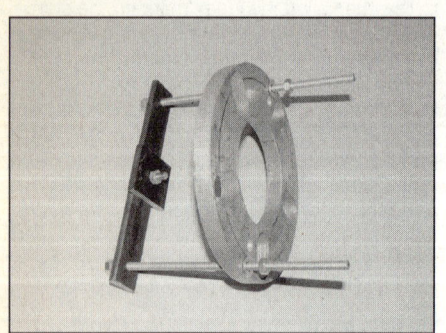

4.4a A home-made clamp for disassembling the clutch

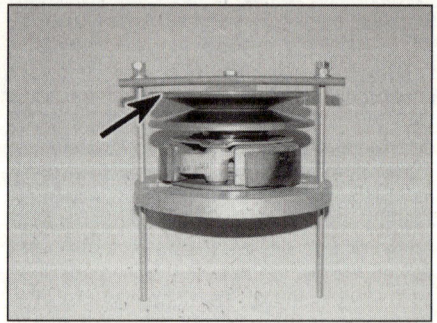

4.4b Ensure the clamp does not rest on the rim (arrowed) of the pulley

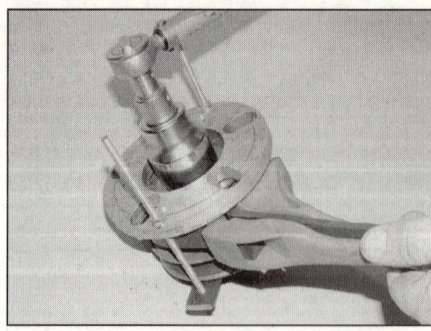

4.5 Hold the clutch with a strap wrench and unscrew the nut

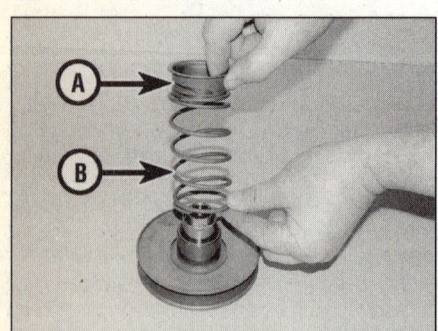

4.6a Lift off the spring seat (A) and spring (B) . . .

4.6b . . . then remove the centre sleeve

4.7a Withdraw the guide pins . . .

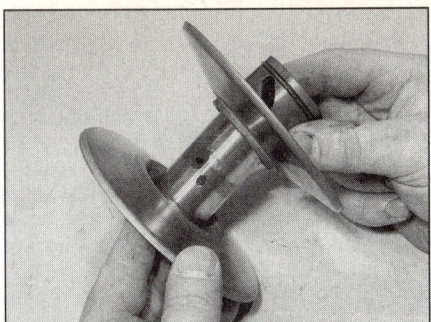

4.7b ... and separate the pulley halves

4.8 Lever out the internal seals (A) and remove the O-rings (B)

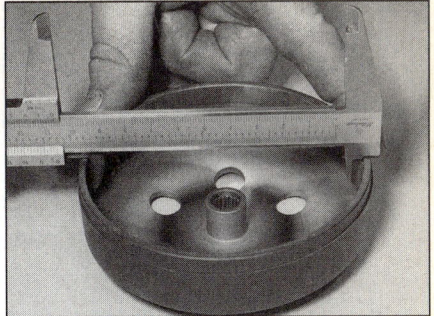

4.10 Measure the drum diameter as described

4.11 Check the friction material on the shoes

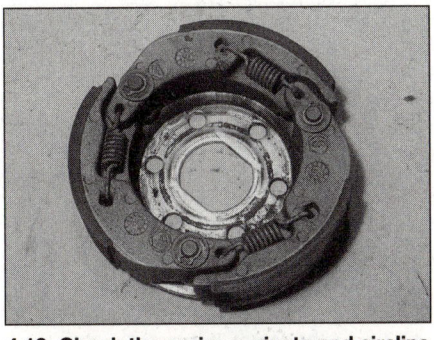

4.12 Check the springs, pivots and circlips

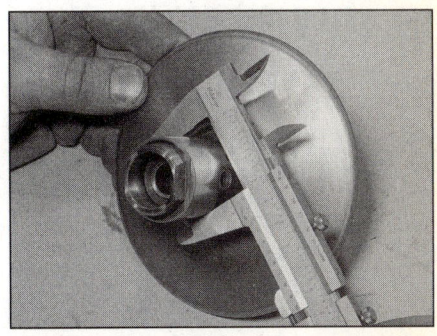

4.13a Measure the diameter of the inner pulley shaft . . .

retaining circlips are secure on the ends of the pins **(see illustration)**. Clutch components are not available as individual items; if any parts are worn or damaged, fit a new clutch.

13 Inspect the inner faces of the clutch pulley for signs of overheating or blueing, caused by the pulley running out of alignment and renew them if necessary. Measure the external diameter of the inner pulley shaft and the internal diameter of the outer pulley bore and compare the results to the specifications at the beginning of the Chapter. Renew either or both if they are worn beyond their limits **(see illustrations)**.

14 A needle roller bearing is fitted in the hub of the pulley inner half; inspect the bearing rollers for flat spots and pitting. On some models, a sealed ball bearing is also fitted inside the pulley inner half – check that it turns smoothly **(see illustrations)**. If either bearing is worn or damaged, drive it out from the opposite end of the pulley half with a hammer and suitable drift. Use a drawbolt to install the new bearings – using a drift on a new needle bearing will damage the bearing.

15 Check the condition of the spring. If it is bent or appears weak, renew it. Measure the free length of the spring and compare it with the figure in the Specifications **(see illustration)**. Renew the spring if it has sagged to less than the limit.

Installation

16 Fit new seals and O-rings to the pulley outer half **(see illustration 4.8)**. Lubricate the inner pulley shaft with molybdenum disulphide grease, then fit it into the outer

pulley bore and install the guide pins **(see illustrations 4.7b and a)**. Apply grease to the guide pin slots and around the O-rings **(see illustration)**, then fit the centre sleeve **(see illustration 4.6b)**.

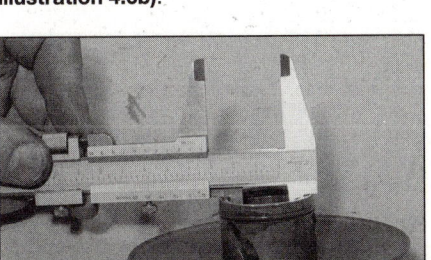

4.13b ... and of the outer pulley bore

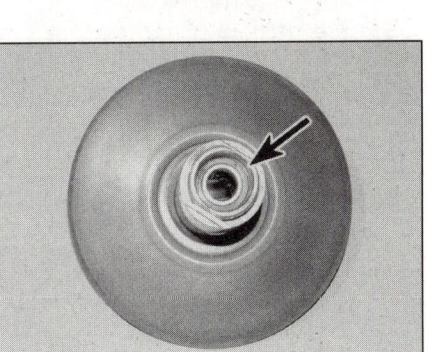

4.14b ... and the sealed bearing, where fitted

17 Install the spring and the spring seat **(see illustration 4.6a)**.

18 Position the clutch on the spring seat and compress the assembly using the same method as for disassembly **(see Step 4)**.

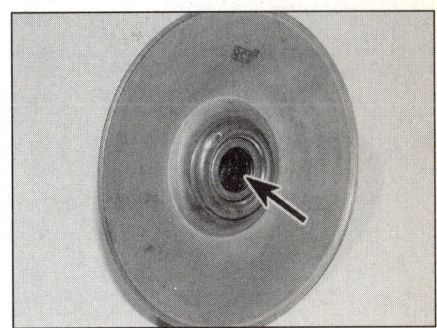

4.14a Check the needle bearing (arrowed) . . .

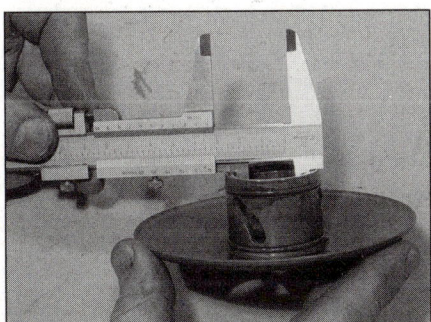

4.15 Measure the spring free length

4.16 Apply grease to the slots and around the O-rings

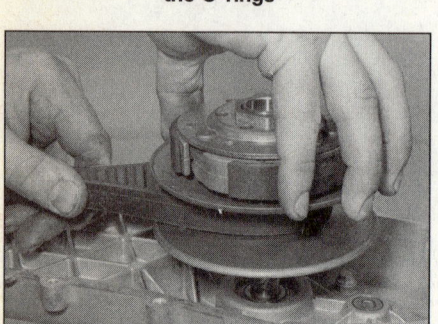

4.21b ... and fit the clutch assembly onto the shaft

Ensure the flats on the clutch backplate are aligned with the pulley hub and install the assembly nut finger-tight. Hold the assembly around the clutch shoes with a strap wrench and tighten the nut to the specified torque

5.2 Measure the width of the belt to determine wear

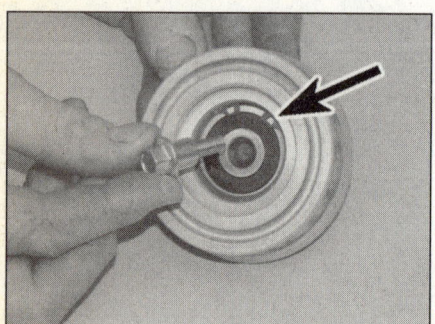

5.4b Roller is retained by centre bolt. Note the circlip (arrowed)

4.21a Squeeze the belt to part the pulley halves if slack is needed ...

4.23 As applicable, fit the clutch drum nut

setting, then release the clamp slowly **(see illustration 4.5)**.
19 Lubricate the needle bearing in the hub of the pulley inner half with molybdenum disulphide grease.

5.4a Location of the belt support roller (arrowed)

5.6 Manoeuvre the belt out of the clutch pulley

20 Clean both inner faces of the clutch pulley and the inside surface of the clutch drum with a suitable solvent.
21 Engage the driven pulley with the drive belt, then, if the drive pulley has not been removed, squeeze the belt to force the driven pulley halves apart, thereby providing some slack in the belt, and slide the assembly onto the gearbox shaft **(see illustrations)**.
22 Install the clutch drum, ensuring the splines align with the shaft.
23 On all 50 cc models and Runner FX125/ FXR180 models, apply a suitable non-permanent thread locking compound to the drum nut and install it on the shaft **(see illustration)**. Using the method employed on removal to prevent the clutch turning, tighten the nut to the specified torque setting **(see illustration 4.2)**.
24 If applicable, install the spacer on the end of the shaft **(see illustration 2.5c)**.
25 Install the drive belt cover (see Section 2).

5 Drive belt and support roller

Inspection

1 Remove the drive belt cover (see Section 2). Check along the entire length of the belt for cracks, splits, frays and damaged teeth and renew the belt if any damage is found.
2 Measure the width of the belt and compare the measurement to the minimum width specified **(see illustration)**. If the belt has worn below the limit, renew it.
3 The belt should be inspected and renewed according the service interval (see Chapter 1). **Note:** *Oil or grease inside the casing will contaminate the belt and prevent it gripping the pulleys. Any evidence of oil inside the casing suggests a worn seal on either the crankshaft or the gearbox input shaft; evidence of grease suggests worn seals in the clutch centre.*
4 On Runner VXR180 / 200 and DNA 180 models, a belt support roller is fitted midway between the variator and the clutch pulley **(see illustration)**. Check that the roller turns smoothly and freely. If the roller centre bearing is worn or damaged, undo the centre bolt and remove the roller **(see illustration)**. Remove the retaining circlip and press the bearing out from the back of the roller with a driver or suitably sized socket. Note which way round the bearing is fitted. Press the new bearing in with a socket that contacts the outer race only and secure it with the circlip.

Renewal

5 Follow the procedure in Section 3 and remove the starter driven gear. **Note:** *Hold the variator in position on the crankshaft when the gear is removed to avoid dislodging the rollers. If the ramp plate moves and the rollers are dislodged, disassemble the variator and reposition the rollers correctly.*

6 Lift the belt off the crankshaft and ease it out of the clutch pulley. If necessary, pull the outer clutch pulley half back against the spring tension and manoeuvre the belt out **(see illustration)**.

7 Fit the new belt, making sure any directional arrows point in the direction of normal rotation **(see illustration)**. Ensure there is sufficient slack in the belt to avoid it being trapped when the starter driven gear is installed.

8 Install the starter driven gear (see Section 3) and the belt cover (see Section 2).

6 Gearbox

Removal

1 Remove the clutch and driven pulley (see Section 4) and the rear wheel (see Chapter 7).
2 Drain the gearbox oil (see Chapter 1).

Models with gearbox cover behind the clutch

3 Unscrew the bolts securing the gearbox cover and remove the cover – the input shaft will come away with it **(see illustration)**.

4 Remove the outer thrust washer from the reduction gear shaft, then lift out the output shaft, followed by the reduction gear, and remove the inner thrust washer **(see illustrations)**.

5 If required, drive the input shaft from the gearbox cover using a soft-faced hammer on the shaft end, but note that the bearing

5.7 Arrows should point in the normal direction of rotation

and oil seal will have to be renewed if you do so. If there are no signs of oil leakage on the outside of the cover (behind the clutch), and if the shaft turns smoothly and freely with no sign of freeplay in the bearing or between the shaft and the bearing, it is better not to remove it, unless it is worn or damaged.

Models with gearbox cover behind the rear wheel

6 Displace the disc brake caliper and remove the rear hub (see Chapter 7).

7 Unscrew the bolts securing the gearbox cover and remove the cover **(see illustration)**. Note the location of the bolts – the three bolts on the right-hand side of the cover are shorter than the others. Note the location of the guides for the gearbox breather hose. Discard the gasket as a new one must be fitted on reassembly.

8 Lift out the output shaft and the reduction

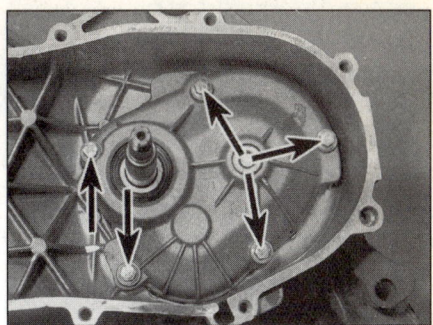
6.3a Undo the bolts (arrowed) . . .

gear. If required, press the input shaft out of its bearing in the transmission casing, but note that the shaft oil seal will have to be renewed if you do so (see Step 5).

Inspection

9 Remove all traces of old sealant or gasket from the gearbox and cover mating surfaces, taking care not to nick or gouge the soft aluminium if a scraper is used. Wash all of the components in clean solvent and dry them off.

10 Check the gear teeth for cracking, chipping, pitting and other obvious wear or damage. Any pinion that is damaged must be renewed. Check the splines on the shafts for wear and damage.

11 Check for signs of scoring or blueing on the pinions and shaft. This could be caused by overheating due to inadequate lubrication. Renew any damaged pinions. On early

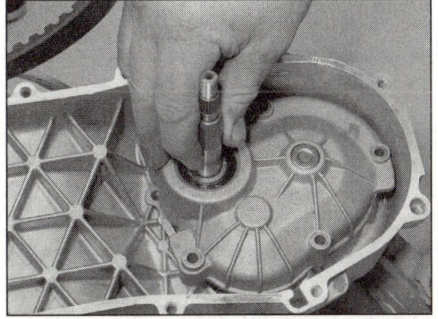
6.3b . . . and remove the gearbox cover with the input shaft

6.4a Remove the outer thrust washer . . .

6.4b . . . the output shaft . . .

6.4c . . . the reduction gear . . .

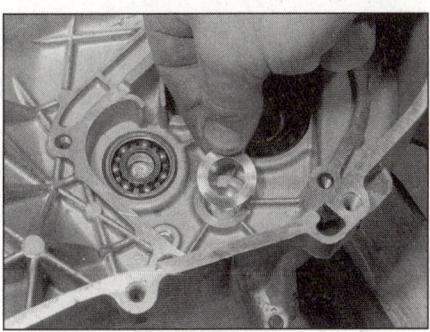
6.4d . . . and the inner thrust washer

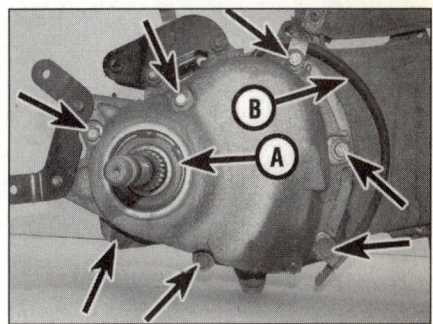
6.7 Undo the bolts (arrowed). Note the bearing circlip (A) and breather (B)

6.11 Remove the circlip (arrowed) and slide the pinion off the output shaft

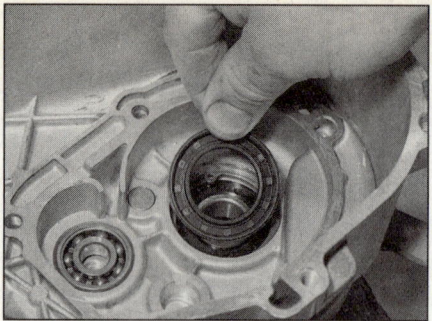

6.13a Lever out the seal . . .

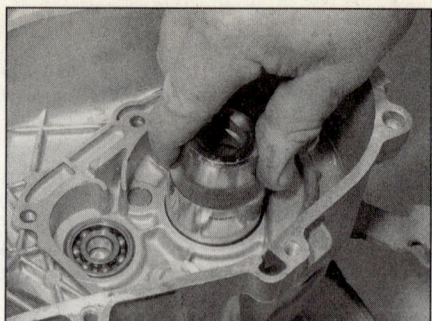

6.13b . . . and drive a new one in using a socket

6.15 The output shaft bearing is secured by a circlip (arrowed)

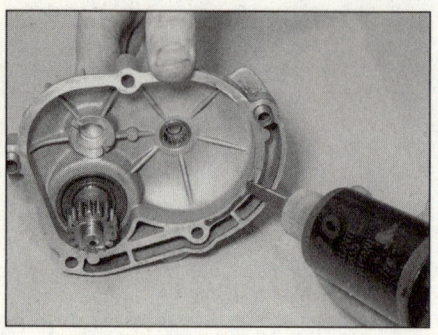

6.18a Apply a suitable sealant . . .

6.18b . . . and tighten the cover bolts to the specified torque

models, remove the circlip securing the pinion on the output shaft and check the splines on both the shaft and the pinion for wear and damage **(see illustration)**.

12 Check the thrust washers where fitted and renew them if they are bent or appear weakened or worn. Use new ones if in any doubt.

13 Note which way round the output shaft oil seal is fitted, then lever it out and discard it as a new one must be used **(see illustration)**. After checking the bearing (Step 14), fit the new seal and drive it in using a seal driver or suitable socket, making sure it enters squarely **(see illustration)**.

14 Check that all the bearings turn smoothly and freely without excessive play between the inner and outer races. The bearings should be a tight fit in the casing; if a bearing is loose, and the casing is not damaged, use a suitable bearing locking compound to hold it in place. On some models the inner end of the output shaft runs in a needle bearing. Inspect the surface of the rollers for wear and pitting. Renew any bearing that is worn.

15 To renew a bearing, first lever out the oil seal where fitted **(see illustration 6.13a)**. If the bearing is secured by a circlip, remove the circlip **(see illustration)**. Note the position of the bearing, then heat the cover using a hot-air gun and drive the bearing out with a bearing driver or suitably sized socket. Install the new bearing with a bearing driver or socket large enough to contact the outer race of the bearing. Install the circlip and new oil seal as required.

16 Bearings fitted in blind holes require an internal bearing puller to extract them without damaging the case; consult a Piaggio dealer or specialist motorcycle engineer if they need removing.

Installation

Models with gearbox cover behind the clutch

17 Fit the inner thrust washer, followed by the reduction gear, then the output shaft, and fit the outer thrust washer onto the reduction gear **(see illustrations 6.4d, c, b and a)**. If removed, fit the input shaft into the cover.

18 Apply a suitable sealant, such as Loctite 501, to the cover mating surface, then fit the cover, making sure the dowels locate correctly **(see illustration)**. Tighten the cover bolts evenly and in a criss-cross pattern to the torque setting specified at the beginning of this Chapter **(see illustration)**. Ensure that the input and output shafts turn freely.

19 Install the clutch and driven pulley (see Section 4) and the rear wheel (see Chapter 7).

20 Fill the gearbox with the specified amount and type of oil (see Chapter 1).

Models with gearbox cover behind the rear wheel

21 If removed, press the input shaft into its bearing, then install the reduction gear and the output shaft.

22 Fit a new gasket over the dowels on the transmission casing, then fit the cover. Install the cover bolts with the guides for the breather hose (see Step 7). Tighten the cover bolts evenly and in a criss-cross pattern to the torque setting specified at the beginning of this Chapter. Ensure that the input and output shafts turn freely, then follow Steps 19 and 20.

Chapter 3
Cooling system (liquid-cooled engines)

Refer to the beginning of Chapter 1 for model identification details

Contents

Degrees of difficulty

Easy, suitable for novice with little experience 	**Fairly easy,** suitable for beginner with some experience	**Fairly difficult,** suitable for competent DIY mechanic	**Difficult,** suitable for experienced DIY mechanic	**Very difficult,** suitable for expert DIY or professional

Specifications

Coolant
Type . . . .   50% distilled water and 50% ethylene glycol anti-freeze
System capacity
   Runner 50 (inc. Purejet), Runner VX125, ST125,
      VXR180/200 and ST200, all DNA models. . . . .   0.9 litre
   Runner FX125, FXR180 . . . .   1.7 litre

Thermostat
Opening temperature . . . .   69.5 to 72.5°C
Valve lift . . . .   3.5 mm at 80°C

Torque settings
Temperature gauge sender. . . . .   6 to 8 Nm
Thermostat housing screws . . . .   3 to 4 Nm
Water pump mounting screws – Runner VX125, ST125,
   VXR180/200 and ST200, DNA 125/180 models. . . . .   3 to 4 Nm

1 General information

The cooling system uses a water/antifreeze coolant to carry excess energy away from the engine in the form of heat. The cylinder is surrounded by a water jacket through which the coolant is circulated by thermo-syphonic action in conjunction with a water pump.

On Runner 50 (inc. Purejet), DNA 50 GP, Runner FX125 and FXR180 models, the pump is mounted inside the crankcases and is driven by a shaft running off the oil pump. On Runner VX125, VXR180/200, ST125, ST200 and DNA 125/180 models, the water pump is mounted externally on the alternator cover.

The heated coolant passes upwards to the thermostat and through to the radiator. The coolant then flows across the radiator core, where it is cooled by the passing air, to the water pump and back to the engine where the cycle is repeated.

A thermostat is fitted in the system to prevent the coolant flowing through the radiator when the engine is cold, therefore accelerating the speed at which the engine reaches normal operating temperature. A coolant temperature sender mounted in the cylinder head transmits information to the temperature gauge or warning light in the instrument panel. On Runner FX125, FXR180, VX125, VXR180/200, ST125, ST200 and DNA 125/180 models, a thermostatically-controlled cooling fan is fitted behind the radiator to aid cooling in extreme conditions. A coolant circuit from the thermostat housing supplies the heater mounted on the side of the carburettor on Runner VX125, VXR180/200, ST125, ST200 and DNA 125/180 models to prevent carburettor icing (see Chapter 4).

⚠ *Warning: Do not remove the reservoir cap when the engine is hot. Scalding hot coolant and steam may be blown out under pressure, which could cause serious injury.*

⚠ *Warning: Do not allow antifreeze to come in contact with your skin or painted or plastic surfaces of the scooter. Rinse off any spills immediately with plenty of water. Antifreeze is highly toxic if ingested. Never leave antifreeze lying around in an open container or in puddles on the floor; children and pets are attracted by its sweet smell and may drink it. Check with the local authorities about disposing of used antifreeze. Many communities have collection centres which will see that antifreeze is disposed of safely.*

Caution: At all times use the specified type of antifreeze, and always mix it with distilled water in the correct proportion.

2.2 Detach the hoses (arrowed) and drain the reservoir

The antifreeze contains corrosion inhibitors which are essential to avoid damage to the cooling system. A lack of these inhibitors could lead to a build-up of corrosion which would block the coolant passages, resulting in overheating and severe engine damage. Distilled water must be used as opposed to tap water to avoid a build-up of scale which would also block the passages.

2 Coolant reservoir

Removal

⚠ *Warning: Ensure that the engine is cold before working on the coolant reservoir.*

1 The coolant reservoir on all models except the DNA is located at the front of the scooter and is housed within the front bodywork panels. Remove the panels for access (see Chapter 8). On DNA models, the reservoir is located underneath the helmet compartment – displace the helmet compartment to gain access (see Chapter 8).

2 Release the clip securing the hose to the top of the reservoir and detach the hose **(see illustration)**.

3 Place a suitable container underneath the reservoir, then release the clip securing the hose to the base of the reservoir. Detach the hose and allow the coolant to drain into the container **(see illustration 2.2)**.

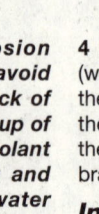

2.4a Remove the seal from the reservoir neck

4 Unscrew the reservoir mounting screw (where fitted). If not already done, unscrew the reservoir cap and remove the seal around the reservoir neck **(see illustration)**. Lift out the reservoir, noting how the lugs locate in the bracket **(see illustration)**.

Installation

5 Installation is the reverse of removal. Make sure the hoses are correctly installed and secured with their clips. On completion, refill the reservoir as described in Chapter 1.

3 Cooling fan, motor and switch

Note: *The cooling fan is fitted to 125, 180 and 200 cc engines only.*

Cooling fan and motor

Check

1 If the engine is overheating and the cooling fan isn't coming on, first check the fuse which feeds the fan circuit (see Chapter 9) and then the fan switch as described in Step 9 below.

2 If the fan does not come on, (and the fan switch is good), the fault lies in either the cooling fan motor or the relevant wiring. Test all the wiring and connections as described in Chapter 9.

3 To test the cooling fan motor, on Runner models remove the right-hand side access panel and on DNA models remove the right-hand side panel (see Chapter 8). Disconnect the fan wiring connector **(see**

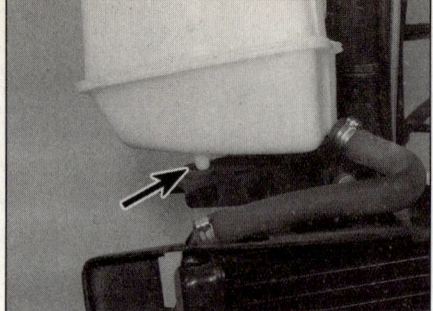

2.4b Note how the lugs locate in the grommets (arrowed)

illustration). Using a 12 volt battery and two jumper wires, connect the battery positive (+ve) lead to the red/black wire terminal and the battery negative (-ve) lead to the green wire terminal on the fan motor side of the connector. Once connected the fan should operate. If it does not, and the wiring is all good, then the fan motor is faulty. Individual components are not available for the fan assembly.

Renewal

⚠ *Warning: The engine must be completely cool before carrying out this procedure.*

4 Disconnect the battery negative (-ve) lead.

5 Remove the radiator (see Section 6). Remove the screws securing the fan assembly to the radiator and separate them, noting how they fit. Slacken the clamp securing the fan shroud to the motor and draw the shroud off.

6 Installation is the reverse of removal.

7 Install the radiator (see Section 6). Reconnect the battery (-ve) lead.

Cooling fan switch

Check

8 If the engine is overheating and the cooling fan isn't coming on, first check the fuse which feeds the fan circuit (see Chapter 9). If the fuse is blown, check the fan circuit for a short to earth (see *Wiring diagrams*).

9 If the fuse is good, remove the appropriate bodywork panels (see Chapter 8), and disconnect the wiring connectors from the fan switch on the side of the radiator **(see illustrations)**. Note that on Runner VX125/

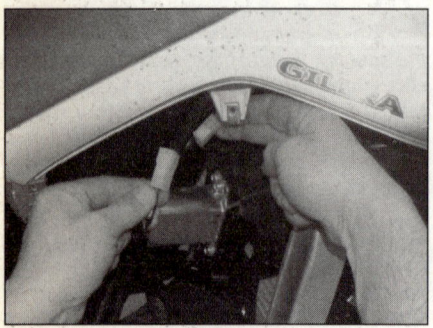

3.3 Disconnect the fan wiring connector – Runner shown

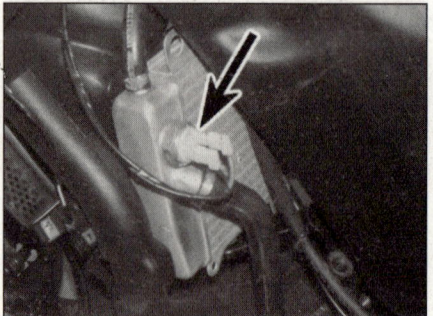

3.9a Radiator fan switch (arrowed) – Runner shown

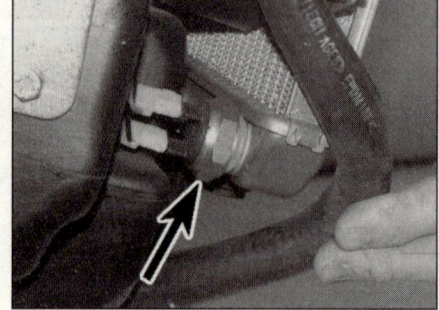

3.9b Radiator fan switch (arrowed) – DNA shown

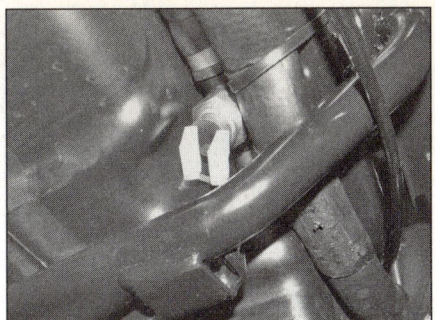

3.9c Radiator fan switch (arrowed) – Runner VX125/VXR200 RST

VXR200 RST and ST125/200 models, the fan switch is situated in the coolant hose running under the right-hand side of the frame **(see illustration)**; remove the floorpanels and belly panel for access (see Chapter 8). Using a jumper wire, connect the wiring terminals together. The fan should come on when the ignition is turned ON. If it does, the fan switch is confirmed faulty and must be renewed. If it does not come on, the fan should be tested (see Step 3).

10 If the fan is on the whole time, even when the engine is cold, disconnect the switch wiring connectors and keep them apart. The fan should stop. If it does, the switch is defective and must be renewed. If it keeps running, check the wiring between the switch and the fan motor for a short to earth.

Renewal

 Warning: The engine must be completely cool before carrying out this procedure.

11 Disconnect the battery negative (-ve) lead. Drain the cooling system (see Chapter 1).

12 Remove the appropriate bodywork panels to access the switch (see Chapter 8), and disconnect the wiring connectors from the fan switch on the radiator **(see illustration 3.9a or b)**. Unscrew the switch and withdraw it from the radiator. Discard the seal as a new one must be used.

13 Apply a suitable sealant to the switch threads, then install the switch using a new seal and tighten it securely. Take care not to overtighten the switch as the radiator could be damaged.

14 Reconnect the switch wiring and refill the cooling system (see Chapter 1). Reconnect the battery (-ve) lead.

---

4 Coolant temperature gauge, warning light and sender

Check

1 The circuit consists of the sender mounted on the cylinder head and the gauge assembly or coolant warning light (as applicable) mounted in the instrument cluster. If the system malfunctions check first that the battery is fully charged and that the fuses are all good. In the case of models with a warning light check that the bulb has not blown (see Chapter 9).

2 If the gauge is not working, or to test the warning light circuit, remove the access panel for the engine (see Chapter 8). Pull the cover off the terminal and disconnect the wire from the sender, then turn the ignition switch ON **(see illustrations)**. The temperature gauge needle should be on the (C) on the gauge, or the bulb should be extinguished. Now earth the sender wire on the engine. The needle should swing immediately over to the (H) on the gauge or the bulb should illuminate. If the gauge or warning light operate as described above, the sender is proven defective and must be renewed.

Caution: Do not earth the wire for any longer than is necessary to take the reading, or the gauge may be damaged.

3 If the needle movement is still faulty, or if it does not move at all, the fault lies in the wiring or the gauge itself. Check all the relevant wiring and wiring connectors (see Chapter 9). If all appears to be well, the gauge is defective and must be replaced. If the bulb does not illuminate and has not blown, check the bulb wiring and wiring connectors.

Renewal

4 The temperature gauge is integral with the instrument cluster, for which individual instruments are not available. If the gauge is faulty, the entire cluster must be renewed (See Chapter 9). For warning light bulb renewal refer to Chapter 9.

5 To renew the sender, first drain the cooling system (see Chapter 1). Disconnect the battery negative (-ve) lead.

 Warning: The engine must be completely cool before carrying out this procedure.

6 Disconnect the sender wiring connector **(see illustrations 4.2b)**. Unscrew the sender from the cylinder head.

7 Apply a smear of sealant to the threads of the new sender, then install it into the cylinder head and tighten it to the specified torque. Connect the sender wiring.

8 Refill the cooling system (see Chapter 1). Reconnect the battery negative (-ve) lead.

---

5 Thermostat

Removal

 Warning: The engine must be completely cool before carrying out this procedure.

1 The thermostat is automatic in operation and should give many years service without requiring attention. In the event of a failure, the valve will probably jam open, in which case the engine will take much longer than normal to warm up. Conversely, if the valve jams shut, the coolant will be unable to circulate and the engine will overheat. Neither condition is acceptable, and the fault must be investigated promptly.

2 Remove the access panel to the engine (See Chapter 8) and drain the cooling system (See Chapter 1).

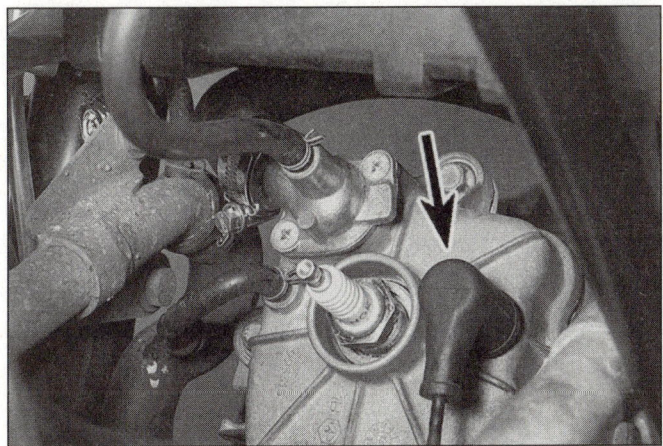

4.2a Lift off the cover (arrowed) . . .

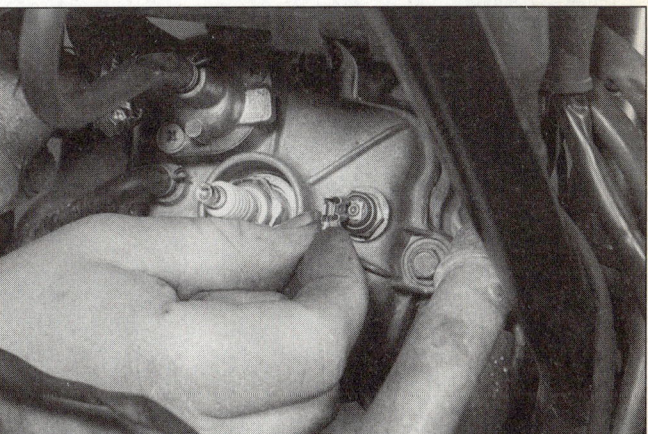

4.2b . . . and disconnect the wiring connector from the sender

5.3a On two-stroke engines remove the screws (arrowed)

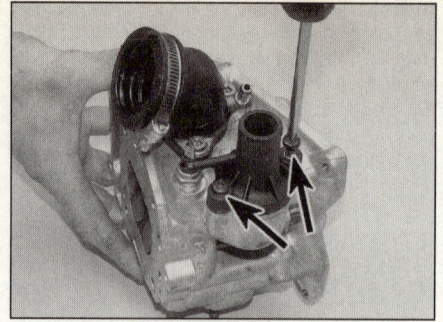

5.3b On four-stroke engines remove the screws (arrowed)

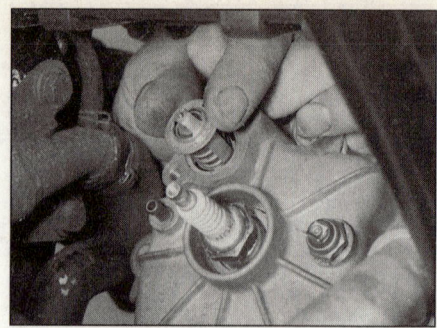

5.3c Removing the thermostat on two-stroke engines

3 The thermostat is located in the cylinder head. Detach the hose(s) from the thermostat housing if required, though it is not absolutely necessary. Remove the two screws securing the housing and remove it **(see illustrations)**. Lift out the thermostat, noting how it fits **(see illustrations)**. Discard the cover O-ring, if fitted, as a new one must be used.

Check

4 Examine the thermostat before carrying out the test. If it remains in the open position at room temperature, it should be renewed.
5 Suspend the thermostat in a container of cold water. Place a thermometer capable of reading temperatures up to 100°C in the water so that the bulb is close to the thermostat **(see illustration)**. Heat the water, noting the temperature when the thermostat opens, and compare the result with the specifications given at the beginning of this Chapter. Also check the amount the valve opens after it has been heated at 80°C for a few minutes and compare the measurement to the specifications. If the readings obtained differ from those given, the thermostat is faulty and must be replaced with a new one.

6 In the event of the thermostat jamming closed, *as an emergency measure only*, it can be removed and the machine used without it. **Note:** *Take care when starting the engine from cold, as it will take much longer than usual to warm up.* Ensure that a new unit is installed as soon as possible.

Installation

7 Fit the thermostat into the cylinder head. If applicable, locate the cut-out around the lug, making sure that the thermostat seats correctly **(see illustration)**.

8 If applicable, fit a new O-ring onto the housing, using a dab of grease to keep it in place if required **(see illustration)**.
9 Fit the housing, then install the two screws and tighten them to the specified torque **(see illustrations 5.3a or b)**.
10 Refill the cooling system (see Chapter 1).

6 Radiator

Removal

> ⚠️ *Warning: The engine must be completely cool before carrying out this procedure.*

1 Disconnect the battery negative (-ve) lead. Remove the bodywork panels necessary to access the radiator (see Chapter 8). Note that on Runner models the radiator surround can be displaced without removing the steering stem in order to access the radiator mounting screws. Drain the cooling system (see Chapter 1).
2 Disconnect the fan motor wiring connector **(see illustration 3.3)**. Also disconnect the wiring connectors from the fan switch in the radiator **(see illustration 3.9a or 3.9b)**.
3 Loosen or release the clips securing the radiator hoses to the radiator and detach them from the radiator **(see illustration)**.

Caution: The radiator unions are fragile. Do not use excessive force when attempting to remove the hoses.

5.3d Removing the thermostat on four-stroke engines

5.5 Set-up for testing the thermostat

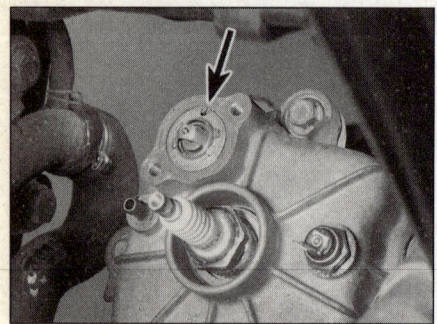

5.7 On two-stroke engines, locate the cut-out over the lug (arrowed) . . .

5.8 . . . and fit a new O-ring into the groove in the housing

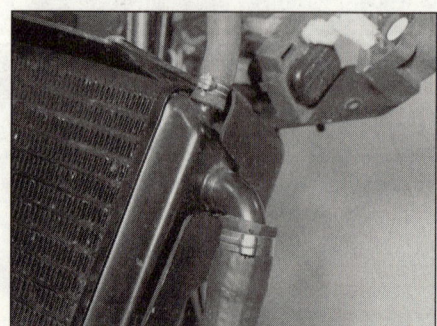

6.3 Release the clips and detach the hoses

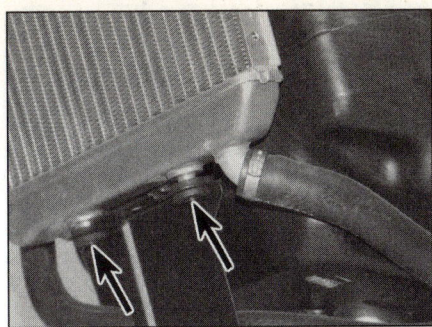

6.4 Radiator is supported in grommets (arrowed) on the lower edge – DNA shown

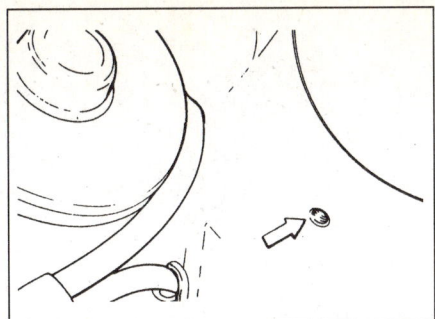

7.2 Water pump seal drainage hole (arrowed) in crankcase left-hand half

7.4 Remove the screws (arrowed) and pull the coolant pipe out of its bore

HAYNES HINT *If a radiator hose is corroded in place on its union, slit it with a sharp knife and peel it off the union. A new hose will obviously be needed.*

4 Remove the screws securing the radiator and fan assembly to the frame, then lift the assembly until the lugs on the bottom of the shroud or radiator body are clear of their grommets **(see illustration)**.

5 If necessary, separate the cooling fan (see Section 3) from the radiator.

6 Check the radiator for signs of damage and clear any dirt or debris that might obstruct air flow and inhibit cooling (see Chapter 1, Section 9). If the radiator fins are badly damaged or broken the radiator must be renewed. Also check the rubber mounting grommets, and renew them if necessary.

Installation

7 Installation is the reverse of removal, noting the following:
• Make sure the locating lugs fit correctly into the rubber grommets.
• Make sure that the fan wiring is correctly connected.
• Ensure the coolant hoses are in good condition (see Chapter 1, Section 9), and are

securely retained by their clips; fit new clips if necessary.
• On completion refill the cooling system as described in Chapter 1.
• Reconnect the battery negative (-ve) lead.

---

7 Water pump

All 50 cc models, Runner FX125 and FXR180 models

Check

1 The water pump is located within the crankcase. The pump is driven by a shaft off the oil pump.

2 A seal prevents coolant leaking from the pump housing into the crankcase. A drainage hole on the left-hand crankcase half allows coolant to escape should the seal fail. If the drainage hole shows signs of leakage, the pump shaft must be removed and the seal renewed **(see illustration)**.

Removal

Note: *If the crankcase halves are being separated, the water pump assembly can be removed afterwards (see Chapter 2B).*

3 Drain the coolant (see Chapter 1) and remove the alternator cover (see Chapter 2B).

4 Remove the screw or screws securing the coolant pipe bracket and pull the pipe out of its bore in the right-hand crankcase half, below the alternator **(see illustration)**. Discard the pipe O-ring as a new one must be used.

5 Remove the oil pump and its drive belt and driven pulley (see Chapter 2B).

6 Remove the water pump drive shaft star clip and discard it as a new one must be used, then remove the washer from behind the star clip **(see illustration 7.9)**.

7 Locate an 8 mm socket wrench through the water pipe bore in the right-hand crankcase half onto the hexagon in the centre of the pump impeller. Hold the left-hand end of the pump shaft to prevent it turning, then unscrew the impeller, noting that it has a left-hand thread and must therefore be unscrewed in a clockwise direction **(see illustration)**. Draw the shaft, complete with its bearings, out of the crankcase. Check the condition of the bearings on the shaft. If they do not run smoothly and freely the shaft must be renewed as the bearings are not available individually. The new shaft with be supplied with the bearings already in place **(see illustration)**.

8 Using an expanding bearing/seal puller and slide-hammer attachment, remove the water pump seal and discard it **(see illustration)**.

9 To remove the water pump impeller, the crankcase halves must be separated (see

7.7a Water pump shaft must be unscrewed clockwise

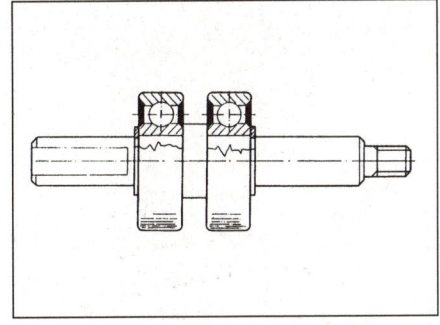

7.7b Cross-section of water pump shaft complete with bearings

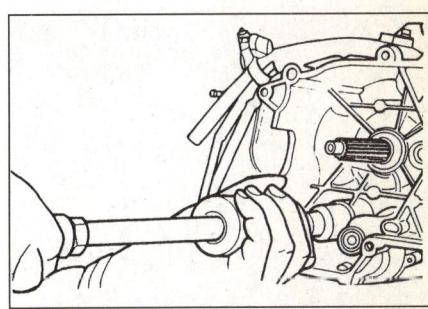

7.8 Use a slide-hammer with internally-expanding attachment to extract the water pump seal

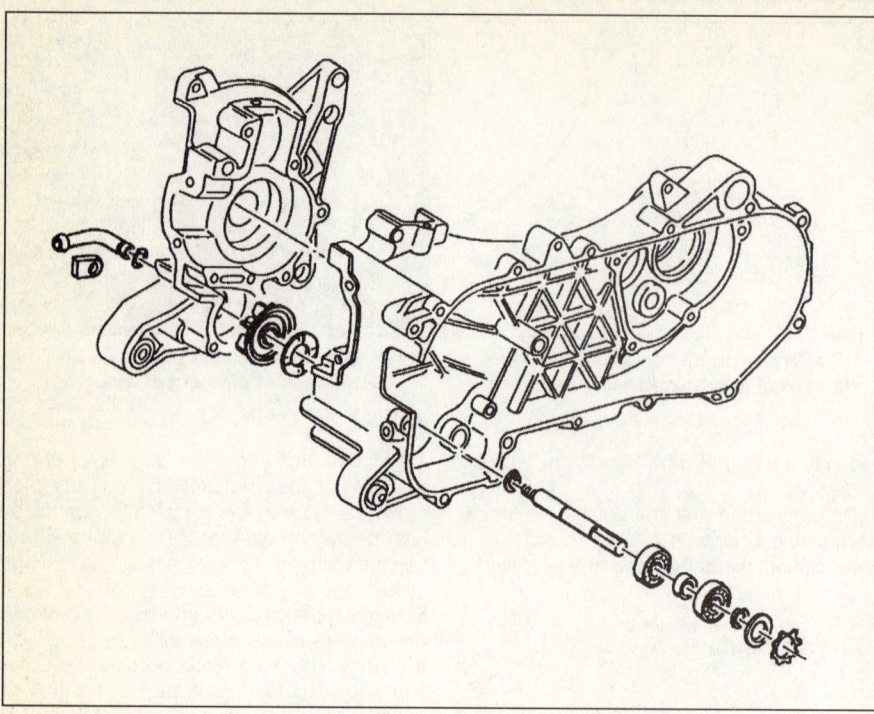

7.9 Water pump assembly for liquid-cooled two-stroke engines

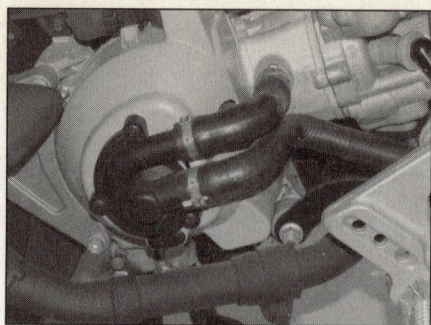

7.17 Location of the water pump on four-stroke engines

Chapter 2B). The impeller can then be lifted out of its housing (see illustration).

Installation

10 If the crankcases have been split, install the water pump assembly before joining the crankcase halves (see Chapter 2B).
11 If the crankcases have not been disassembled, first ensure the seal housing is clean, then oil the seal and fit it into the housing, making sure it fits squarely. Use a drift which bears on the outer edge of the seal to drive it into the crankcase; ensure that the drainage hole in the crankcase remains uncovered.
12 Press the pump shaft and bearings into the crankcase. Support the impeller with the 8 mm socket as on removal and locate the impeller onto the end of the shaft. Hold the shaft to prevent it turning and thread on the impeller, not forgetting that it has a left-hand

thread and must therefore be tightened anti-clockwise.
13 Fit the washer onto the end of the shaft, then fit a new star clip.
14 Install the oil pump and its drive belt and gear (see Chapter 2B).
15 Fit a new O-ring onto the water pipe and fit it into its bore, then fit the bracket screw(s) (see illustration 7.4).
16 Fit the alternator cover and refill the cooling system (see Chapter 1).

Runner VX125, ST125, VXR180/200, ST200 and DNA 125/180 models

Check

17 The water pump is located on the alternator cover (see illustration). The pump is driven via dampers on the alternator rotor (see illustration 7.29).

18 The pump body to alternator cover joint is sealed by an O-ring. A ceramic seal and rubber gasket in the alternator cover prevents coolant leaking down the pump impeller shaft into the cover. A hole in the bottom of the cover drains any coolant should the seal fail. If the drainage hole shows signs of leakage, the pump impeller must be removed and the seal renewed.

Removal

19 Drain the cooling system and disconnect the coolant hoses from the water pump (see Chapter 1). Undo the screws securing the pump body and lift it off (see illustration). Discard the O-ring as a new one must be used.
20 Remove the alternator cover (see Chapter 2F).
21 The impeller is a press fit in the pump bearings (see illustration). To remove the impeller, support the alternator cover upside down on the work surface with sufficient clearance below it to allow the impeller to be driven out (see illustration). **Note:** *Take great care not to damage the sealing surface of the alternator cover. Use a soft drift (preferably aluminium or brass) to carefully drive the impeller out.*
22 Turn the cover over and carefully lever out

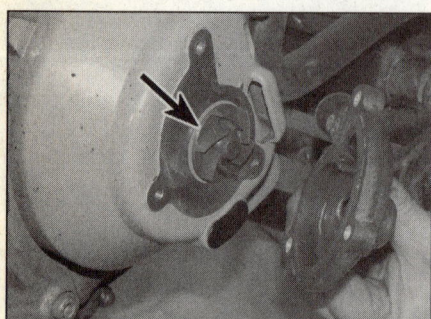

7.19 Remove the pump body. The impeller (arrowed) is located in the alternator cover

7.21a Location of the pump impeller shaft (arrowed)

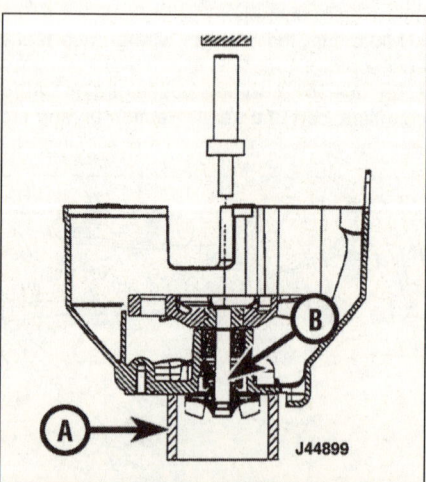

7.21b Place a suitable support (A) under the cover to drive out the impeller (B)

the seal **(see illustration)**. Take care not to damage the edge of the seal housing. Lift out the rubber gasket. **Note:** *Once the seal and gasket are removed new ones must be fitted; do not re-use the old seal and gasket.*

23 Check the condition of the two bearings in the alternator cover. If they do not run smoothly they must be renewed. Note the position of the bearings; the innermost bearing is fitted flush with the inside lip of the bearing housing in the cover. Support the cover so that it is level, then use a suitable drift to drive the bearings out **(see illustration)**. If the bearings are a tight fit, heat the housing inside the cover with a hot air gun. **Note:** *Heat the cover gently to avoid damaging the paint finish.*

24 Ensure the bearing housing is clean and free from corrosion, then heat the housing again to aid fitting the new bearings. Install the bearings from the inside of the cover and ensure that the first (outermost) bearing fits against its seat before driving in the second bearing with a suitable socket or bearing driver.

25 Check the impeller for wear and damage. If the shaft is corroded, fit a new impeller.

Installation

26 Lubricate the new gasket and ceramic seal with anti-freeze and press them carefully into place with a suitably sized socket.

27 To prevent the bearings being displaced when the impeller is fitted, support them from the inside of the cover, leaving sufficient space for the impeller shaft when it is installed. Carefully press the impeller shaft into the bearings from the outside. Ensure the impeller turns freely once fitted.

28 Fit a new O-ring into the groove in the pump body, then install the pump body and tighten the screws to the specified torque setting.

29 Align the dampers on the alternator rotor

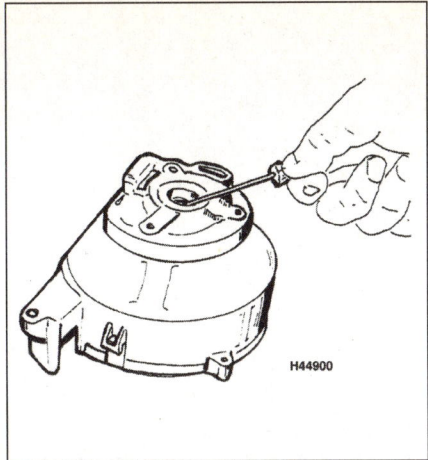

7.22 Lever out the impeller seal

with the pump drive and install the alternator cover **(see illustration)**.

30 Refill the cooling system (see Chapter 1).

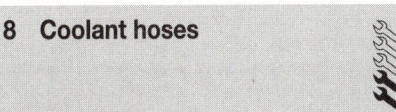

8 Coolant hoses

Removal

1 Before removing a hose, drain the coolant (see Chapter 1).

2 Release or loosen the hose clips, either with a screwdriver or pliers depending upon the design of the clip, then slide them back along the hose and clear of the union spigot **(see illustrations)**. **Note:** *Some clips cannot be re-used – check before removing a coolant hose and be prepared to fit new clips of the correct size.*

3 Pull the hose off its union. If a hose proves stubborn, release it by rotating it on its union

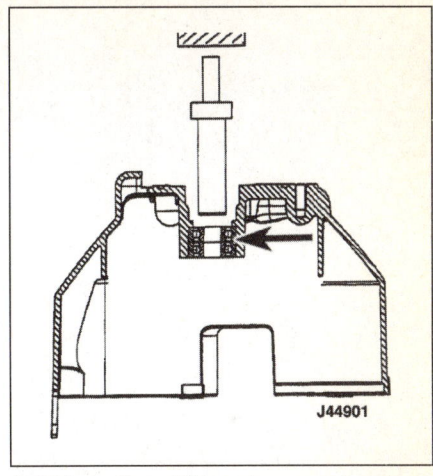

7.23 Location of the water pump bearings (arrowed)

before working it off. If all else fails, slit the hose with a sharp knife at each union (see *Haynes Hint* in Section 6).

Caution: The radiator unions are fragile. Do not use excessive force when attempting to remove the hoses.

Installation

4 Slide the clips onto the hose and then work it on to its respective unions.

5 Rotate the hose on its unions to settle it in position before sliding the clips into place and tightening them securely.

HAYNES HINT *If the hose is difficult to push on its union, it can be softened by soaking it in very hot water, or alternatively a little soapy water can be used as a lubricant.*

7.29 Align the dampers with the pump drive inside the cover

8.2a Release the clip with a screwdriver . . .

8.2b . . . or with pliers as required

Chapter 4
Fuel and exhaust systems

Refer to the beginning of Chapter 1 for model identification details

Contents

Degrees of difficulty

Easy, suitable for novice with little experience	**Fairly easy,** suitable for beginner with some experience	**Fairly difficult,** suitable for competent DIY mechanic	**Difficult,** suitable for experienced DIY mechanic	**Very difficult,** suitable for expert DIY or professional 

Specifications

Fuel
Fuel type . . . . Unleaded petrol (gasoline) min 95 octane
Fuel tank capacity . . . . see Chapter 1

Automatic choke
Resistance @ 20°C
  Walbro carburettor . . . . 30 ohms (approx)
  Keihin carburettor . . . . 20 ohms
  All other carburettors . . . . 30 to 40 ohms
Plunger protrusion
  Walbro carburettor
    Initial @ 20°C . . . . 12.5 to 13.0 mm
    Final (after 5 minutes constant power) . . . . 18.5 to 19.0 mm
  Keihin carburettor . . . . Not available
  All other carburettors
    Initial @ 22°C . . . . 10.9 to 11.5 mm
    Final (after 5 minutes constant power) . . . . 14.0 to 15.0 mm

SKP/Stalker with Weber slide carburettor
Type/ID no . . . . Weber 12 OM
Pilot screw setting . . . . 2 3/4 turns out
Fuel level . . . . 3.5 mm
Idle speed . . . . 1800 to 2000 rpm
Starter jet 50
Pilot jet 34
Main jet 72
Jet needle (clip position) . . . . V (3rd notch from top)

Ice with Weber slide carburettor
Type/ID no . . . . Weber 18 OM
Pilot screw setting . . . . 2 1/2 turns out
Fuel level . . . . 3.5 mm
Idle speed . . . . 1700 to 1900 rpm
Starter jet 50
Pilot jet 30
Main jet 60
Jet needle (clip position) . . . . AK (3rd notch from top)

Ice, Stalker, DNA 50 GP and Runner 50 SP RST with Dell'Orto slide carburettor

Type/ID no.	Dell'Orto PHVA 17.5 RD
Pilot screw setting	1 1/2 turns out
Fuel level	5 mm
Idle speed	1700 to 1900 rpm
Starter jet	50
Pilot jet	32
Main jet	56 (53 – Runner 50 SP RST and Stalker)
Jet needle (clip position)	A22 (1st notch from top)

Runner 50 (all models) with Weber slide carburettor

Type/ID no.	Weber 12 OM
Pilot screw setting	2 1/4 to 3 turns out
Fuel level	3.5 mm
Idle speed	1800 to 2000 rpm
Starter jet	68
Pilot jet	34 L
Main jet	60
Jet needle (clip position)	U (2nd notch from top)

Runner FX125 with Mikuni slide carburettor

Type/ID no.	Mikuni VM 20
Pilot screw setting	1 1/4 turns out
Fuel level	6.5 ± 0.5 mm
Idle speed	1400 to 1600 rpm
Starter jet	gs 40
Pilot jet	35
Main jet	85
Jet needle (clip position)	3CK01 (3rd notch from top)

Runner FXR180 with Mikuni slide carburettor

Type/ID no.	Mikuni VM 20
Pilot screw setting (turns out)	1 1/4 turns out
Fuel level	6.5 ± 0.5 mm
Idle speed	1400 to 1600 rpm
Starter jet	gs 40
Pilot jet	27.5
Main jet	97.5
Jet needle (clip position)	3DJ8 (3rd notch from top)

Runner VX125 and DNA 125 with Walbro constant vacuum (CV) carburettor

Type/ID no.	Walbro WVF-7C
Float height	see Section 9
Idle speed	1600 to 1700 rpm
Starter jet	50
Pilot jet	36
Main jet	108
Jet needle (clip position)	51c (2nd notch from top)
Cut-off valve spring free length (service limit)	24 mm

Runner VX125 RST and ST125 with Keihin constant vacuum (CV) carburettor

Type/ID no	CVEK-30 (CVK306D)
Pilot screw setting	2 turns out
Float height	see Section 9
Idle speed	1550 to 1750
Starter jet	42
Pilot jet	35
Main jet	98
Jet needle	NDYA

Runner VXR180 and DNA 180 with Walbro constant vacuum (CV) carburettor

Type/ID no.	Walbro WVF-7D
Float height	see Section 9
Idle speed	1600 to 1700 rpm
Starter jet	50
Pilot jet	34
Main jet	118
Jet needle (clip position)	465 (3rd notch from top)
Cut-off valve spring free length (service limit)	24 mm

Runner VXR200 with Walbro constant vacuum (CV) carburettor

Type/ID no.	Walbro WVF-7H
Float height.	see Section 9
Idle speed.	1600 to 1700 rpm
Starter jet	50
Pilot jet	34
Main jet.	118
Jet needle (clip position).	465 (2nd notch from top)
Cut-off valve spring free length (service limit)	24 mm

Runner VXR200 RST and ST200 with Keihin constant vacuum (CV) carburettor

Type/ID no .	CVEK-30 (CVK309C)
Pilot screw setting	2 ± ½ turns out
Float height	see Section 9
Idle speed.	1550 to 1750
Starter jet	42
Pilot jet	35
Main jet	90
Jet needle.	NDYC

1 General information and precautions

The fuel system on all models except the Runner Purejet consists of the fuel tank, fuel tap, filter, carburettor, fuel hoses and control cables. Due to the position of the fuel tank, Runner and DNA models have a fuel pump. The Runner Purejet has a fuel injection system controlled by the engine control module (see Section 10); the fuel system components consist of the tank, filter, pump and throttle body, air and fuel injectors and hoses.

The fuel tap is automatic in operation and is opened by engine vacuum. The fuel filter is either fitted inside the fuel tank as part of the tap, or is a separate in-line filter.

In addition to the main fuel tank, Runner models have a small header tank which ensures an immediate supply of fuel to the carburettor when the machine has been standing unused. On these models the fuel tap is fitted to the header tank. DNA models have a non-return valve in the fuel line between the tank and the filter.

For cold starting, an electrically-operated automatic choke is fitted in the carburettor. On some models a carburettor heater is linked to the cooling system to prevent carburettor icing.

Air is drawn into the carburettors via an air filter which is housed above the transmission casing.

The exhaust system on most models is a two-piece design with a separate pipe and silencer. On later 50 cc models the exhaust system is a one-piece design incorporating a resonator tube and catalytic converter.

Many of the fuel system service procedures are considered routine maintenance items and for that reason are included in Chapter 1.

Precautions

⚠️ **Warning: Petrol (gasoline) is extremely flammable, so take extra pre-cautions when you work on** *any part of the fuel system. Don't smoke or allow open flames or bare light bulbs near the work area, and don't work in a garage where a natural gas-type appliance is present. If you spill any fuel on your skin, rinse it off immediately with soap and water. When you perform any kind of work on the fuel system, wear safety glasses and have a fire extinguisher suitable for a class B type fire (flammable liquids) on hand.*

Always perform service procedures in a well-ventilated area to prevent a build-up of fumes.

Never work in a building containing a gas appliance with a pilot light, or any other form of naked flame. Ensure that there are no naked light bulbs or any sources of flame or sparks nearby.

Do not smoke (or allow anyone else to smoke) while in the vicinity of petrol or of components containing it. Remember the possible presence of vapour from these sources and move well clear before smoking.

Check all electrical equipment belonging to the house, garage or workshop where work is being undertaken (see the Safety first! section of this manual). Remember that certain electrical appliances such as drills, cutters etc. create sparks in the normal course of operation and must not be used near petrol or any component containing it. Again,

remember the possible presence of fumes before using electrical equipment.

Always mop up any spilt fuel and safely dispose of the rag used.

Any stored fuel that is drained off during servicing work must be kept in sealed containers that are suitable for holding petrol, and clearly marked as such; the containers themselves should be kept in a safe place.

Read the Safety first! section of this manual carefully before starting work.

2 Fuel tap and filter

⚠️ *Warning: Refer to the precautions given in Section 1 before starting work.*

Fuel tap and filter

Check

1 The fuel tap is located on the underside of the fuel tank or, on all Runner models except the Purejet 50, on the underside of the fuel header tank **(see illustrations)**. Remove any body panels as required by your model for access (see Chapter 8). The tap is automatic, operated by a vacuum created when the engine is running which opens a diaphragm

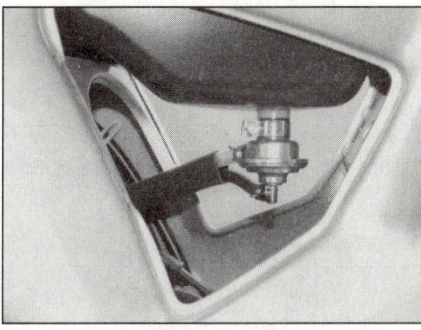

**2.1a Location of the fuel tap –
Ice shown**

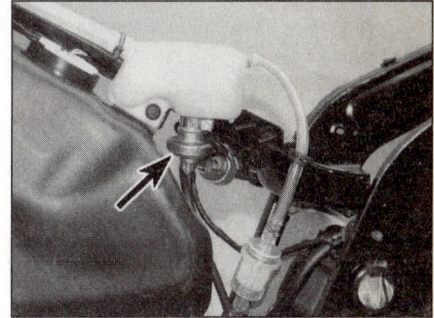

**2.1b Location of the fuel tap –
Runner shown**

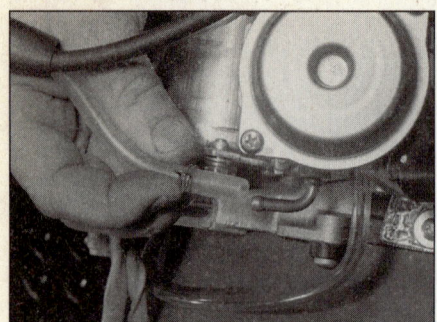

2.2a Detach the fuel hose from the carburettor

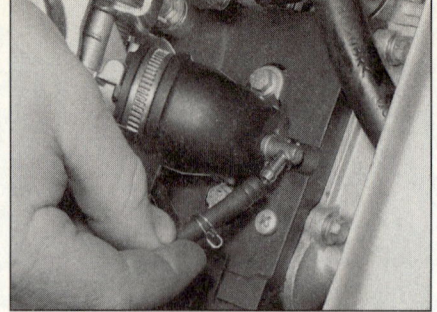

2.2b Detach the vacuum hose from the intake manifold . . .

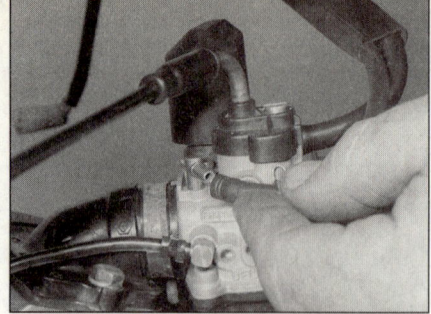

2.2c . . . or from the carburettor, as applicable

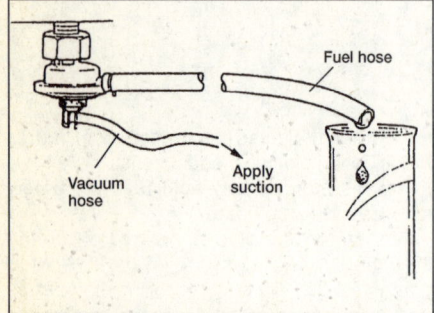

2.2d Place the fuel hose in a container and apply suction to the vacuum hose

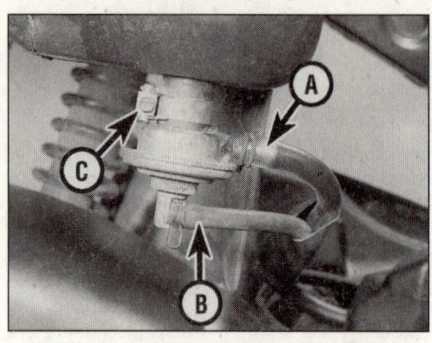

2.5 Fuel hose (A), vacuum hose (B), tap retaining clamp (C)

2.6 Withdraw the fuel tap and filter from the tank

inside the tap. If the tap is faulty, it must be renewed – it is a sealed unit for which no individual components are available. The most likely problem is a hole or split in the tap diaphragm.

2 To check the tap, detach the fuel hose from the carburettor and place the open end in a small container **(see illustration)**. Detach the vacuum hose from the intake manifold or carburettor, according to model **(see illustrations)**, and apply a vacuum to it (suck on the pipe end) – if you are not sure which hose is which on your model, trace the hoses from the tap **(see illustration 2.5)**. Fuel should flow from the tap and into the container – if it doesn't, the diaphragm is probably split **(see illustration)**.

3 Before renewing the tap, check that the vacuum hose is securely attached, and that there are no splits or cracks in the hose. If in doubt, attach a spare hose to the vacuum union on the tap and again apply a vacuum. If fuel still does not flow, remove the tap and fit a new one.

Removal

4 The tap should not be removed unnecessarily from the tank otherwise the O-ring or filter may be damaged.

5 Before removing the tap, connect a drain hose to the fuel hose union and insert its end in a container suitable and large enough for storing the petrol **(see illustration)**. Detach the vacuum hose from the inlet manifold and apply a vacuum to it, and allow the tank to drain.

6 Loosen the clamp securing the tap and withdraw the tap assembly **(see illustration)**.

Check the condition of the O-ring; it is advisable to use a new one. If it is in any way deteriorated or damaged it must be renewed.
7 Clean the gauze filter to remove all traces of dirt and fuel sediment. Check the gauze for holes. If any are found, a new tap should be fitted as the filter is not available individually.

Installation

8 Install the fuel tap into the tank, using a new O-ring, and tighten the clamp securely.
9 Fit the fuel and vacuum hoses onto their respective unions and secure them with their clips.

In-line fuel filter

10 Runner Purejet 50, FX125, FXR180, VX125, ST125, VXR180/200, ST200 models, and DNA 125/180 models, have an in-line fuel filter which must be renewed at the specified service interval (see Chapter 1, Section 13).

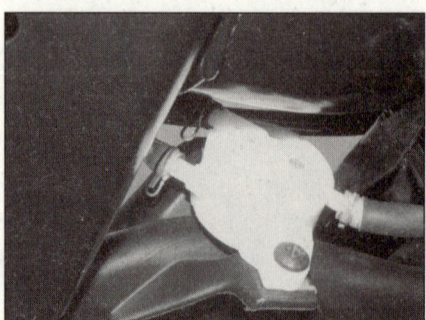

3.2a Location of the fuel pump on Runner models

11 Periodically check the filter for signs of sediment or a clogged element – remove any body panels as required by your model and trace the fuel hose from the carburettor to the filter (see Chapter 8)
12 The filter is a sealed unit. If it is dirty or clogged, fit a new one (see Chapter 1).

---

3 Fuel pump

> ⚠ *Warning: Refer to the precautions given in Section 1 before pro-ceeding.*

Runner (except Purejet 50) and DNA models

Check

1 The fuel pump is operated by the alternating vacuum and pressure in the crankcase when the engine is running, which opens and closes a diaphragm in the pump. On Runner models, the pump supplies fuel to a header tank which ensures a supply of fuel to the carburettor when the scooter has been standing unused. On DNA models, the pump supplies fuel direct to the carburettor via a non-return valve. The most likely cause of pump failure will be a split in the diaphragm.
2 On Runner models, remove the left-hand side panel (see Chapter 8); the fuel pump is mounted on the lower, left-hand side of the frame **(see illustration)**. On DNA models,

3.2b Location of the fuel pump (arrowed) on DNA models

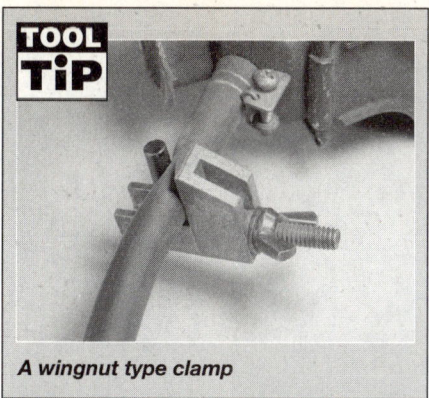

A wingnut type clamp

Two sockets and self-locking grips

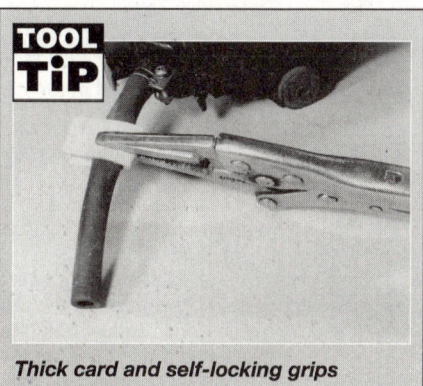

Thick card and self-locking grips

remove the belly panel (see Chapter 8); the fuel pump is mounted on the underside of the fuel tank **(see illustration)**.

3 To check whether the pump is operating, release the clip securing the fuel supply hose to the carburettor or header tank as applicable, and detach the hose. Place the open end in a container suitable for storing petrol. Turn the engine over on the starter motor and check whether fuel flows from the hose into the container. If fuel flows, the pump is working correctly.

4 If no fuel flows from the pump hose, first check that this is not due to a blocked filter or fuel hose, or due to a split in the vacuum hose from the crankcase, before renewing the pump. Check all the hoses for splits, cracks and kinks, and check that they are securely connected on each end by a good clip. On DNA models, check that fuel is passing through the non-return valve. If all the components are good, renew the pump.

Renewal

5 Remove the bodywork as required by your model to access the fuel pump (see Step 2).

6 Release the clips securing the fuel and vacuum hoses and detach them from the pump, noting which fits where. Be prepared to catch any residual fuel in a suitable container. The fuel hoses should be clamped to prevent fuel leakage using any of the methods shown (*see* **Tool Tips**). **Note:** *On Runner models, there is no fuel tap on the main tank – the fuel hose from the tank to the pump must be clamped before it is disconnected from the pump.*

7 On Runner models, undo the screws securing the pump to the frame. On DNA models, undo the screws securing the pump to the tank **(see illustrations 3.2a or b)**. Remove the pump, noting which way round it fits.

8 Install the new pump, making sure the hoses are correctly attached and secured with the clips. If the old clips are corroded or deformed, fit new ones.

Runner Purejet 50

Check

9 The fuel pump is operated electronically and draws fuel from the tank via the fuel filter,

then pumps it up to the injector. The pump is activated initially for 4 to 5 seconds when the ignition is first switched ON, then continues to deliver fuel once the engine is running.

10 To access the pump, remove the right-hand side panel (see Chapter 8); the fuel pump is mounted on the frame in front of the fuel tank **(see illustration)**.

11 To check whether the pump is operating correctly, disconnect the fuel supply hose from the injector – press the hose union down and hold it down, then lift the release ring on the union and disconnect the hose. **Note:** *The fuel system is pressurised – cover the union with a clean rag to prevent fuel spraying over yourself or the machine.* Place the open end in a container suitable for storing petrol. Turn the ignition (main) switch ON. Fuel should flow for 4 to 5 seconds and then stop; if this is the case, the pump is working correctly.

12 If no fuel flows from the supply hose, first check that this is not due to a blocked filter or blocked or kinked fuel hose. It should be possible to hear the pump run – if you can't hear anything, refer to the *Wiring diagram* in Chapter 9 and check the fuel system fuses and wiring. Check the operation of the ignition (main) switch (see Chapter 9). If the pump still will not run, fit a new one.

Renewal

13 Remove the right-hand side panel (see Chapter 8).

14 Disconnect the battery negative (-ve)

lead, then disconnect the fuel pump wiring connectors.

15 Release the clip securing the fuel union from the pump and disconnect the fuel supply hose from the pump. Be prepared to catch any residual fuel in a suitable container. **Note:** *There is no fuel tap on the main tank – the fuel hose from the tank to the pump must be clamped before it is disconnected from the pump.*

16 Undo the screws securing the pump bracket to the frame, then remove the pump from the bracket, noting which way round it fits.

17 Install the new pump, making sure the hoses are correctly attached and secured with the clips. If the old clips are corroded or deformed, fit new ones.

18 Connect the pump wiring connectors.

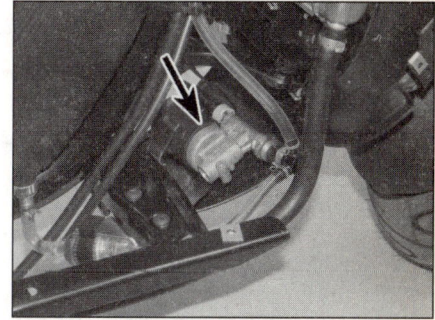

3.10 Location of the fuel pump on Runner Purejet 50 models

An automotive brake hose clamp

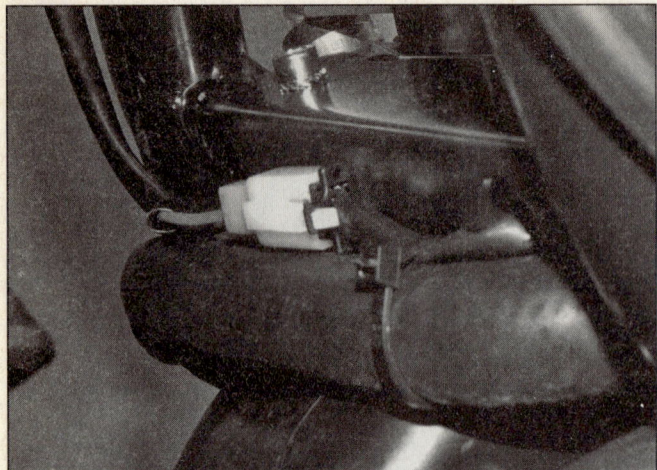

3.21 The fuel pump wiring connector

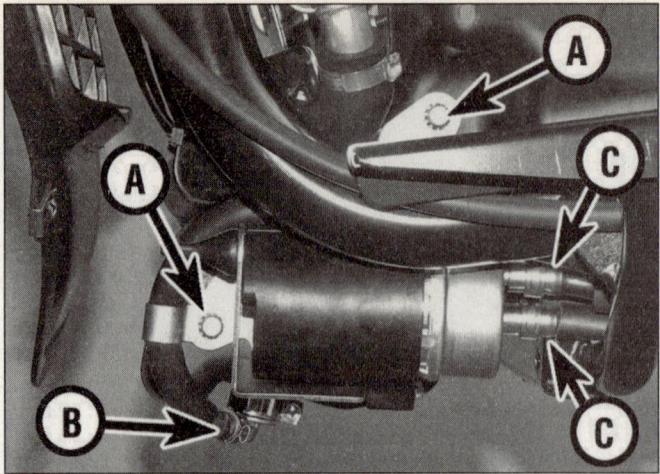

3.22 Fuel pump mounting bolts (A), outlet elbow (B) and delivery pipes (C)

Check the operation of the pump (see Step 11). **Note:** *Do not operate the pump without fuel in the tank – damage to the pump may occur.*

Runner VX/VXR RST and ST

19 The fuel pump is situated on the lower left side of the fuel tank, with its wiring connector located on the frame rail between the radiator and the grille. The wires are red/white and black.

20 To gain access to the fuel pump remove the side panels, floor panels and the belly panel (see Chapter 8),

21 Locate the wiring connector at the front of the pump and disconnect it **(see illustration)**.

22 Undo the two bolts securing the pump to the tank and manoeuvre the pump out to access the pipes **(see illustration)**.

23 Place a container suitable for storing petrol under the fuel tank outlet, then slacken the clip on the outlet elbow and drain all fuel from the tank. Cap the container and store the fuel safely. Place a rag under the unions to catch fuel spills, then slacken the pipe clips and pull off the pipes.

24 Installation is the reverse of removal. Use new clips on the fuel pipes and outlet elbow. Fill the tank with fuel and check that there are no leaks before refitting the bodywork.

4 Air filter housing

Removal

1 Where applicable, remove the bodywork to access the filter housing, which is located above the drive belt cover on the left-hand side of the scooter. Release the clips or cut the plastic ties securing the air inlet and outlet ducts and, where fitted the breather hose, and detach them from the housing **(see illustrations)**.

2 Remove the bolts securing the air filter housing to the engine and manoeuvre the housing away, noting how it fits **(see illustrations)**.

Installation

3 Installation is the reverse of removal. Use new plastic cable ties to secure the air inlet and outlet ducts where the originals were cut free.

5 Idle fuel/air mixture adjustment

⚠️ *Warning: Adjustment of the pilot screw is made with the engine running. To prevent accidents caused by the rear wheel contacting the ground, ensure that the scooter is on its centre stand and if necessary place a support under the scooter to prevent the rear wheel contacting the ground.*

1 On all scooters fitted with carburettors, the idle fuel/air mixture is set using the pilot screw **(see illustration 8.1 or 9.1)**. Adjustment of the pilot screw is not normally necessary and should only be performed if the engine is running roughly, stalls continually, or if a new pilot screw has been fitted.

2 If the pilot screw is removed during a carburettor overhaul, record its current setting by turning the screw it in until it seats lightly,

4.2a Unscrew the bolts (arrowed) . . .

4.1a Release the ties securing the air ducts (arrowed) . . .

4.1b . . . and the clamp securing the breather hose (arrowed), where fitted

4.2b . . . and remove the housing

counting the number of turns necessary to achieve this, then unscrew it fully. On installation, turn the screw in until it seats lightly, then back it out the number of turns you've previously recorded. If fitting a new pilot screw, turn the screw in until it seats, then back it out the number of turns specified at the beginning of the Chapter. **Note:** *A base setting for the pilot screw is not available for four-stroke engined models (VX125, ST125, VXR180/200, ST200, DNA125/180). If fitting a new pilot screw install to the number of turns out recorded when removing the old screw, then carry out adjustment as described below. Fine tuning of the pilot screw setting requires the use of an exhaust gas analyser to ensure that the exhaust gas CO content does not exceed 3.8 ± 0.7%.*

3 Pilot screw adjustment must be made with the engine running and at normal working temperature. Run the engine then stop it and screw the pilot screw in until it seats lightly, then back it out the number of turns specified at the beginning of this Chapter (two-stroke models) or as previously recorded (four-stroke models). Start the engine and set the idle speed to the specified amount (see Specifications).

4 Now try turning the pilot screw inwards by no more than a 1/4 turn, noting its effect on the idle speed, then repeat the process, this time turning the screw outwards.

5 The pilot screw should be set in the position which gives the most consistent even idle speed, without the automatic transmission engaging, and so that the engine does not stall when the twistgrip is opened. **Note:** *It will not be possible to achieve an even idle speed if the spark plug needs adjustment or if the air filter element is dirty. On four-stroke engined models, ensure the valve clearances are correctly set (see Chapter 1). Also on four-stroke engined models, check that the carburettor cut-off valve, where fitted, is in good condition (see Section 9).*

6 Once a satisfactory pilot screw setting has been achieved, further adjustments to the idle speed can be made with the idle speed adjuster screw (see Chapter 1).

7 If it is not possible to achieve a satisfactory idle speed after adjusting the pilot screw, take the scooter to a Gilera dealer and have the fuel/air mixture adjusted with the aid of an exhaust gas analyser.

6 Carburettor overhaul – general information

1 Poor engine performance, difficult starting, stalling, flooding and backfiring are all signs that carburettor maintenance may be required.

2 Keep in mind that many so-called carburettor problems can often be traced to mechanical faults within the engine or ignition system malfunctions. Try to establish for certain that the carburettor is in need of main-tenance before beginning a major overhaul.

3 Check the air filter, fuel tap and filter, the fuel and vacuum hoses, the fuel pump (where fitted), the intake manifold joint clamps, and the ignition system and spark plug before assuming that a carburettor overhaul is required.

4 Most carburettor problems are caused by dirt particles, varnish and other deposits which build up in and eventually block the fuel jets and air passages inside the carburettor. Also, in time, gaskets and O-rings deteriorate and cause fuel and air leaks which lead to poor performance.

5 When overhauling the carburettor, disassemble it completely and clean the parts thoroughly with a carburettor cleaning solvent. If available, blow through the fuel jets and air passages with compressed air to ensure they are clear. Once the cleaning process is complete, reassemble the carburettor using new gaskets and O-rings.

6 Before disassembling the carburettor, make sure you have the correct carburettor gasket set, some carburettor cleaner, a supply of clean rags, some means of blowing out the car-burettor passages and a clean place to work.

7 Carburettor – removal and installation

⚠ *Warning: Refer to the precautions given in Section 1 before starting work.*

Removal

1 Remove the bodywork as required **(see illustration)** by your model to access the carburettor (see Chapter 8). On Ice and DNA models, remove the engine top cover, and on Ice and SKP/Stalker models remove the carburettor cover, noting how it fits **(see illustration)**.

2 Trace the wiring from the automatic choke unit and disconnect it at the connector **(see illustration)**. Note that on the Keihin CV carburettor there is no connector – pull off the rubber cover from the choke unit, then remove its screw and retaining plate so that the choke unit can be withdrawn from the carburettor body **(see illustration)**. On all CV carburettors, either undo the bolt securing the heater union to the side of the carburettor, or clamp the two coolant pipes **(see illustration)**

7.1a Removal of the access plate in the base of the storage unit enables full access to the carburettor

7.1b Remove the cover (arrowed) – Ice shown

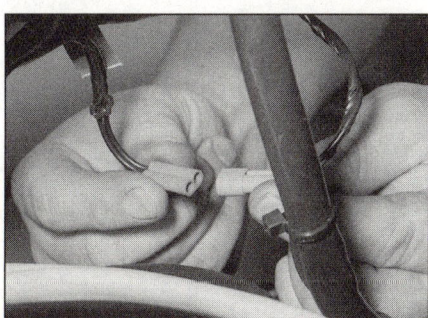

7.2a Disconnect the choke wiring at the connector

7.2b Automatic choke unit must be detached from Keihin type CV carburettor

7.2c Clamp each coolant pipe as shown (arrowed)

7.4a Release the clip or tie (arrowed) . . .

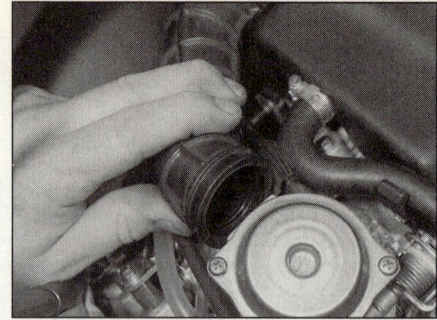

7.4b . . . and detach the air duct from the carburettor

7.6 Carburettor drain screw (arrowed)

which connect to the unions on the front of the carburettor before disconnecting the pipes – be prepared for a little coolant loss.

3 To detach the throttle cable from a slide-type carburettor, first remove the screw securing the top cover, noting that the cover is under spring pressure, then lift the cover and withdraw the throttle slide **(see illustrations 12.7a and b)**. To detach the throttle cable on a CV carburettor, first unscrew the nut securing the outer cable in its bracket and lift the cable out of the bracket, then detach the cable end from the cam on the carburettor **(see illustrations 12.13a and b)**.

4 Release the clip or cut the tie securing the air intake duct and detach it from the carburettor **(see illustrations)**.

5 Release the clips securing the fuel hose and vacuum hose, and oil hose on two-stroke

engines, noting which fits where **(see illustrations 2.2a, b and c)**. Be prepared to catch any residual fuel in a suitable container. The fuel and oil hoses should be clamped to prevent leakage using any of the methods shown (see Section 3 **Tool Tips**). The breather and drain hoses can usually be left attached and withdrawn with the carburettor as their lower ends are not secured. Note their routing as they are withdrawn. **Note:** *The vacuum hose can be left attached to the manifold if the carburettor is being removed without it (see Step 7).*

6 Loosen the drain screw and drain all the fuel from the carburettor into a suitable container **(see illustration)**. Discard the drain screw O-ring as a new one must be used. On installation, fit the new O-ring and tighten the drain screw securely. **Note:** *If a cleaning*

solvent is going to be used, fit the new O-ring after the cleaning process.

7 Either loosen the clamp securing the carburettor to the intake manifold on the engine and remove the carburettor, or undo the bolts securing the manifold to the engine and remove it and the carburettor together **(see illustrations)**.

Caution: Stuff clean rag into the intake after removing the carburettor to prevent anything from falling inside.

Installation

8 Installation is the reverse of removal, noting the following:

• Make sure the carburettor is fully engaged with the intake manifold and the clamp is securely tightened. On the Keihin carburettor, align the tabs to ensure the carburettor is positioned upright **(see illustration)**.

• Make sure all hoses and pipes are correctly routed, not trapped or kinked, and secured with their clamps or clips. Where crimp type clamps are used, always renew them and ensure they are properly secured. Check that there is no sign of fuel leakage (or coolant leakage, where applicable).

• Refer to Section 12 for installation of the throttle cable. Check the operation of the cable and adjust it as necessary (see Chapter 1).

• On liquid-cooled models, top-up the cooling system if necessary (see *Daily (pre-ride) checks*).

• Check the idle speed and adjust as necessary (see Chapter 1).

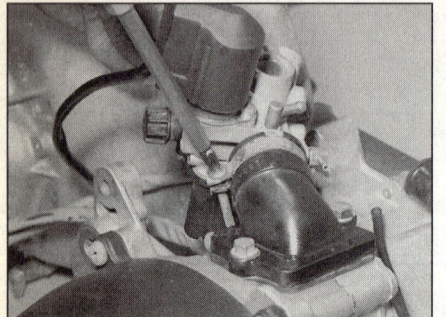

7.7a Either slacken the clamp . . .

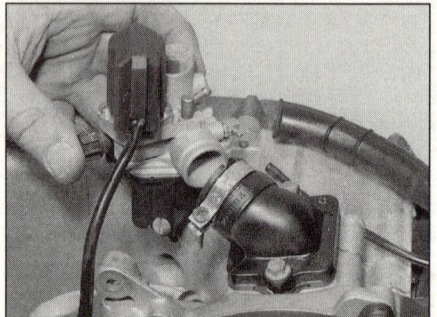

7.7b . . . and detach the carburettor from the manifold . . .

7.7c . . . or remove the manifold bolts (arrowed) . . .

7.7d . . . and remove the carburettor with it attached

7.8 Align the tabs (arrowed) to ensure carburettor is upright

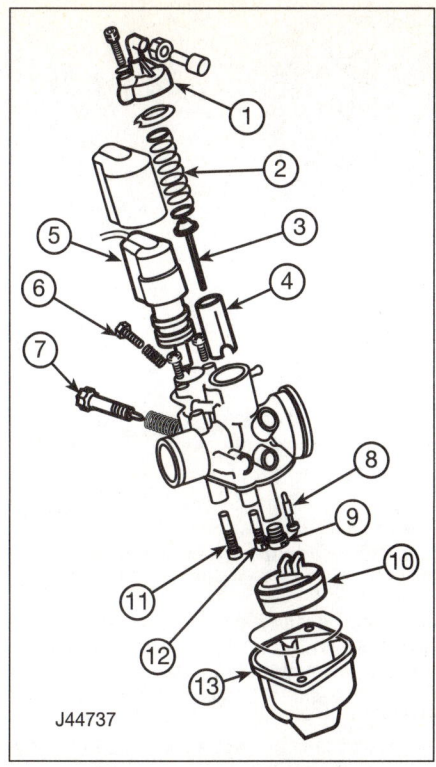

8.1 Slide type carburettor components

1 Top cover	7 Idle speed
2 Slide spring	adjuster screw
3 Needle	8 Float needle valve
4 Slide	9 Main jet
5 Automatic choke	10 Float
unit	11 Starter jet
6 Pilot screw	12 Pilot jet
	13 Float chamber

8 Carburettor – slide type

Note: *The slide-type carburettor is fitted to SKP/Stalker, Ice, all Runner 50 models (inc. Purejet), Runner FX125/FXR180 and DNA 50 GP models.*

⚠️ **Warning: Refer to the precautions given in Section 1 before starting work.**

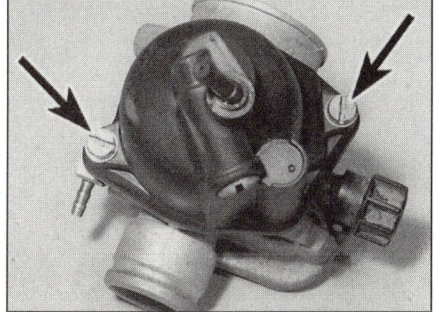

8.4a Undo the screws (arrowed) . . .

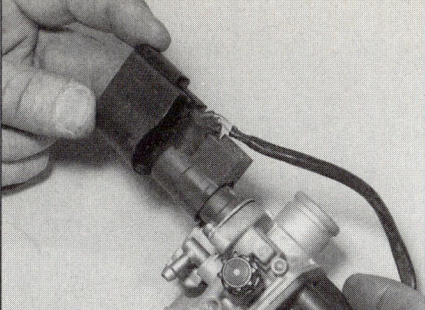

8.2a Remove the choke cover . . .

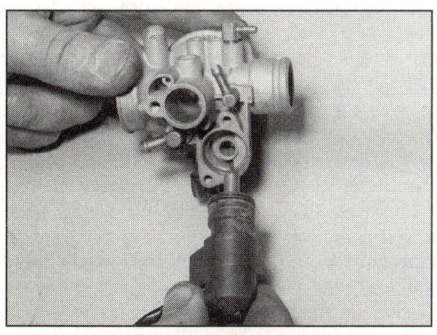

8.2c . . . and withdraw the choke unit

Disassembly

1 Remove the carburettor (see Section 7). Take care when removing components to note their exact locations and any springs or O-rings that may be fitted **(see illustration)**.
2 Where fitted, remove the cover on the automatic choke unit, then remove the clamp securing the choke in the carburettor **(see**

> **HAYNES HiNT** *To record the pilot screw's current setting, turn the screw in until it seats lightly, counting the number of turns necessary to achieve this, then unscrew it fully. On installation, turn the screw in until it seats, then back it out the number of turns you've recorded.*

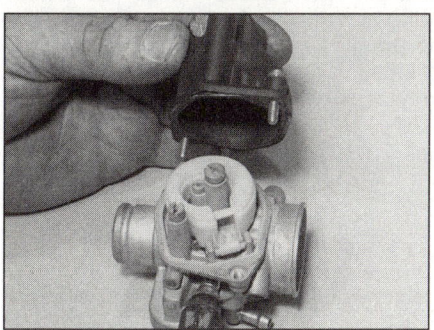

8.4b . . . and lift off the chamber

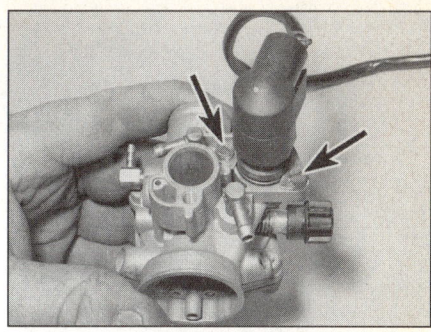

8.2b . . . then remove the clamp screws (arrowed) . . .

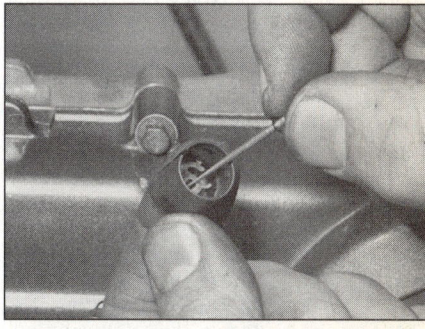

8.3 Remove the needle from the throttle slide if required

illustrations). Withdraw the choke, noting how it fits **(see illustration)**.
3 The carburettor top cover and throttle slide assembly will have already been removed to detach the throttle cable from the carburettor. Disconnect the cable from the slide, then remove the spring seat, spring and cover from the cable (see Section 12). Lift the needle out of the throttle slide **(see illustration)**.
4 Undo the screws securing the float chamber to the base of the carburettor and remove it **(see illustrations)**. Discard the gasket as a new one must be used.
5 Using a pair of thin-nose pliers, carefully withdraw the float pin **(see illustration)**. If necessary, displace the pin using a small punch or a nail. Remove the float and unhook the float needle valve, noting how it fits onto the tab on the float.

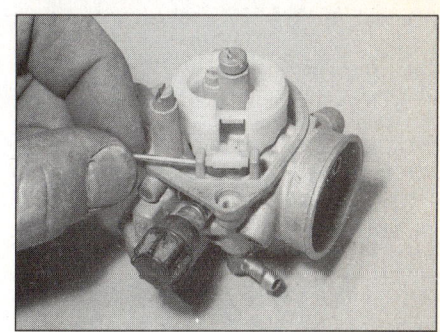

8.5 Withdraw the float pin

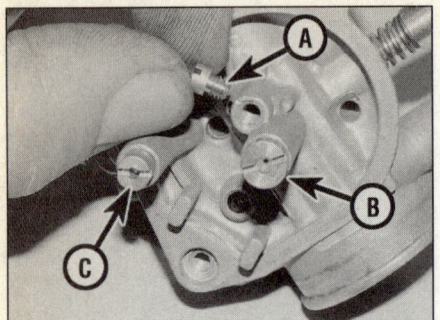

8.6 Pilot jet (A), main jet (B) and starter jet (C)

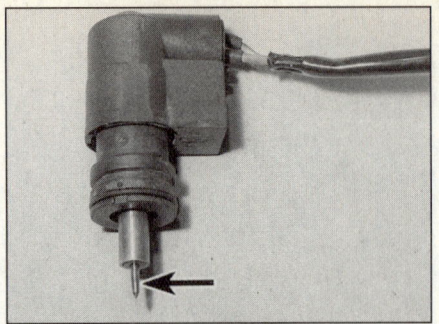

8.18a Check the automatic choke unit plunger and needle condition

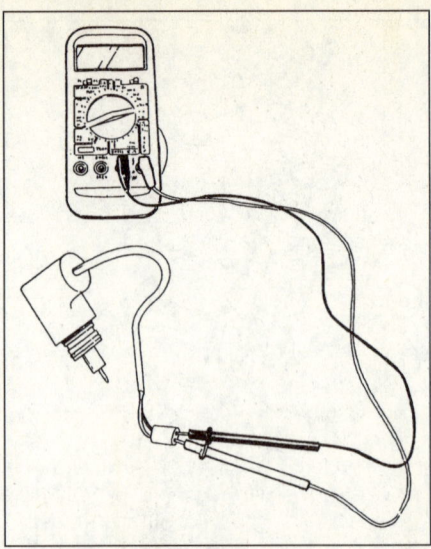

8.18b Automatic choke unit operation check

6 Unscrew and remove the pilot jet and the starter jet, then unscrew the main jet from the base of the needle jet **(see illustration)**.

7 The needle jet is a press fit in the carburettor body; if required, displace the jet, noting how it fits.

8 The pilot screw can be removed if required, but note that its setting will be disturbed (see *Haynes Hint*). Unscrew and remove the pilot screw along with its spring and O-ring, where fitted.

Cleaning

Caution: Use only a petroleum-based solvent for carburettor cleaning. Don't use caustic cleaners.

9 Submerge the metal components in carburettor cleaning solvent for approximately thirty minutes (or longer, if the directions recommend it).

10 After the carburettor has soaked long enough for the cleaner to loosen and dissolve most of the varnish and other deposits, use a nylon-bristled brush to remove the stubborn deposits. Rinse it again, then dry it with compressed air.

11 If available, use compressed air to blow out all the fuel jets and the air passages in the carburettor body, not forgetting the passages in the carburettor intake.

Caution: Never clean the jets or passages with a piece of wire or a drill bit, as they will be enlarged, causing the fuel and air metering rates to be upset.

Inspection

12 If removed, check the tapered portion of the pilot screw and the spring for wear or damage. Fit a new O-ring and renew the screw or spring if necessary.

13 Check the carburettor body, float chamber and top cover for cracks, distorted sealing surfaces and other damage. If any defects are found, renew the faulty component, although a new carburettor will probably be necessary (check with a Gilera dealer on the availability of separate components).

14 Insert the throttle slide in the carburettor body and check that it moves up-and-down smoothly. Check the surface of the slide for wear. If it's worn excessively or doesn't

move smoothly, renew the components as necessary.

15 Check the needle for straightness by rolling it on a flat surface such as a piece of glass. Fit a new needle if it's bent or if the tip is worn. Check the position of the clip on the needle (see Specifications at the beginning of this Chapter).

16 Inspect the tip of the float needle valve and the valve seat. If either has grooves or scratches in it, or is in any way worn, they must be renewed as a set. **Note:** *A worn or incorrectly sized carburettor float needle valve seat will not be able to shut off the fuel supply sufficiently to prevent carburettor flooding and excessive use of fuel.*

17 Check the float for damage. This will usually be apparent by the presence of fuel inside the float. If the float is damaged, it must be renewed.

18 Inspect the automatic choke unit plunger and needle for signs of wear and renew the unit if necessary **(see illustration)**. The resistance of the choke unit should be checked with a multi-meter after the engine has been warmed to normal operating temperature and then allowed to cool for ten minutes. With an ambient (air) temperature of 20°C, disconnect the choke unit wiring connector and measure the resistance between the terminals on the choke unit side of the connector **(see illustration)**. If the result is not as specified at the beginning of the Chapter, renew the choke unit. To check that the plunger is not seized in the choke body, first measure the protrusion of the plunger from the body. Next, use jumper wires to connect a fully-charged 12V battery to the choke unit terminals and measure the protrusion again after 5 minutes. If the measurements are not as specified the unit is faulty and should be renewed.

Reassembly and fuel level check

Note: *When reassembling the carburettor, be sure to use new O-rings and gaskets. Do not overtighten the carburettor jets and screws as they are easily damaged.*

19 If removed, install the pilot screw, spring and O-ring; adjust the screw to the setting as noted on removal (see Step 8).

20 If removed, install the needle jet. Where

applicable, ensure the flat in the bottom of the jet aligns with the pin in the carburettor. Screw the main jet into the end of the needle jet.

21 Install the pilot jet and the starter jet **(see illustration 8.6)**.

22 Hook the float needle valve onto the float tab, then position the float assembly in the carburettor, making sure the needle valve enters its seat. Install the float pin, making sure it is secure **(see illustration 8.5)**.

23 Fit a new gasket onto the float chamber, making sure it is seated properly in its groove, then install the chamber onto the carburettor and tighten the screws securely **(see illustrations 8.4b and a)**.

24 The carburettor fuel level should be checked at this point to ensure that the float and needle valve are working correctly. Support the carburettor upright in a vice and connect a length of clear fuel hose to the drain union on the base of the float chamber. Use tape to secure the hose up against the side of the carburettor and mark it level with the float chamber joint **(see illustration)**. Using a small funnel to avoid spills, carefully pour a small amount of fuel into the carburettor via the fuel hose union, then undo the drain screw

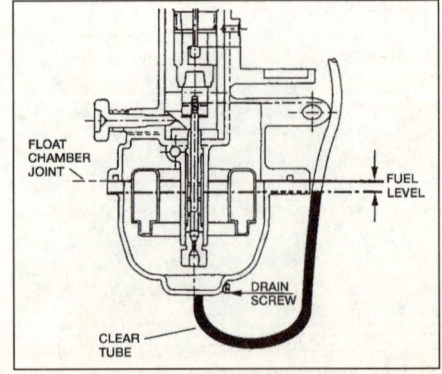

8.24 Set-up for measuring the fuel level

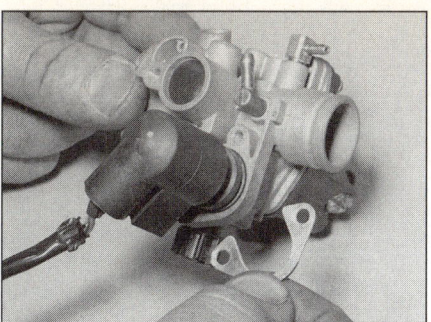

8.25 Secure the choke unit with the clamp

in the bottom of the float chamber enough to allow fuel to flow into the clear hose. Continue pouring fuel into the fuel hose until the float needle valve shuts off the supply, at which point the level in the clear hose should be the specified distance below the mark (see Specifications at the beginning of this Chapter). If the fuel level is incorrect, and the float needle valve and the valve seat are good, check the float tab for wear or damage. If the float tab is metal it can be adjusted carefully to correct the fuel height, otherwise a new float will have to be fitted.

25 Install the choke unit and secure it with the clamp and screws **(see illustration)**. Install the choke unit cover, if fitted.

26 Install the carburettor (see Section 7). Install the jet needle in the throttle slide, then follow the procedure in Section 12 to install the throttle slide assembly onto the cable and fit the carburettor top cover.

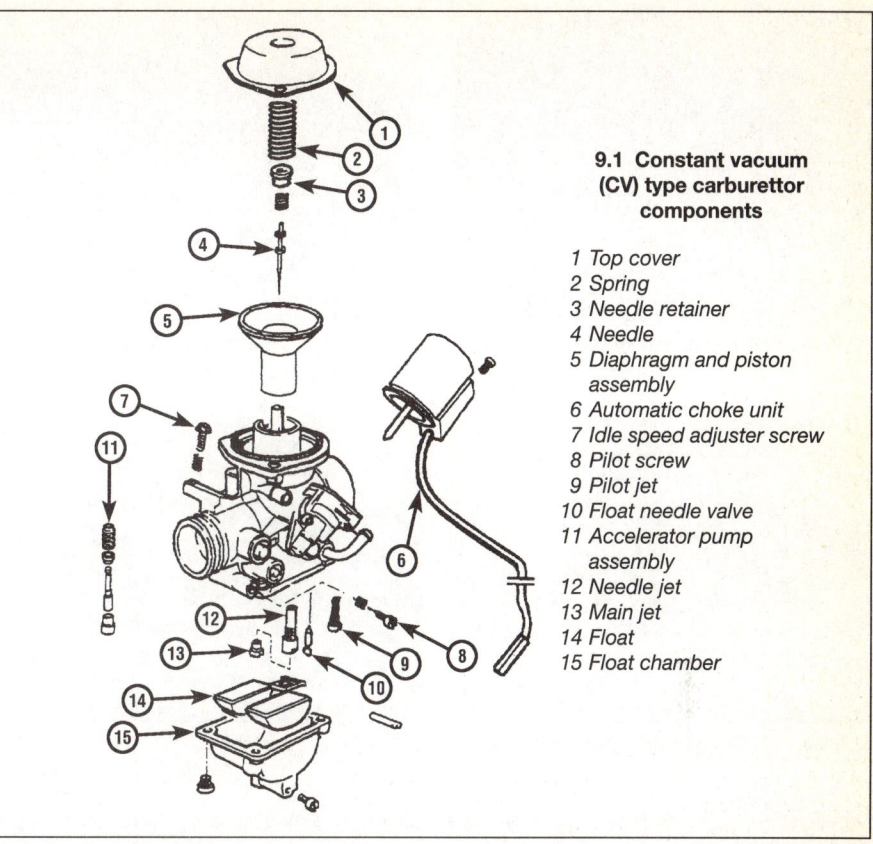

9.1 Constant vacuum (CV) type carburettor components

1 Top cover
2 Spring
3 Needle retainer
4 Needle
5 Diaphragm and piston assembly
6 Automatic choke unit
7 Idle speed adjuster screw
8 Pilot screw
9 Pilot jet
10 Float needle valve
11 Accelerator pump assembly
12 Needle jet
13 Main jet
14 Float
15 Float chamber

---

9 Carburettor – constant vacuum (CV) type

Note: *The constant vacuum (CV) carburettor is fitted to Runner VX125, ST125, VXR180/200, ST200 and DNA 125/180 models.*

⚠ **Warning: Refer to the precautions given in Section 1 before proceeding.**

Disassembly

1 Remove the carburettor (see Section 7). Take care when removing components to note their exact locations and any springs or O-rings that may be fitted **(see illustration)**.

2 Unless detached during the carburettor removal procedure, remove the cover on the automatic choke unit, then remove the clamp securing the choke unit in the carburettor **(see illustrations 8.2a and b)**. Withdraw the choke, noting how it fits **(see illustration)**. If required, undo the screws securing the choke unit mounting and remove it. Discard the gasket as a new one must be fitted. If required, undo the screw securing the accelerator pump lever and remove the lever and return spring.

3 Some CV carburettors have a cut-off valve

and filter on the right-hand side of the body **(see illustration)**. Undo the screws securing the valve cover and lift it off carefully – a

spring inside the cover holds the valve in position **(see illustration)**. Lift out the valve, noting how it fits **(see illustration)**. Remove

9.2 Remove the choke unit. Screws (arrowed) secure the mounting

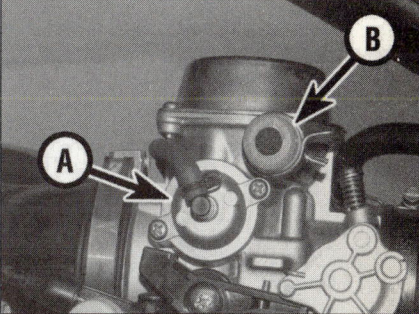

9.3a Cut-off valve (A) and filter (B)

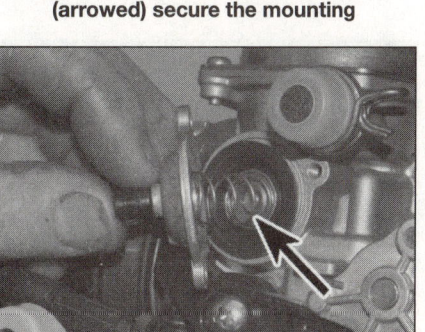

9.3b Remove the cover, noting the spring (arrowed)

9.3c Lift out the valve

9.3d Remove the clip . . .

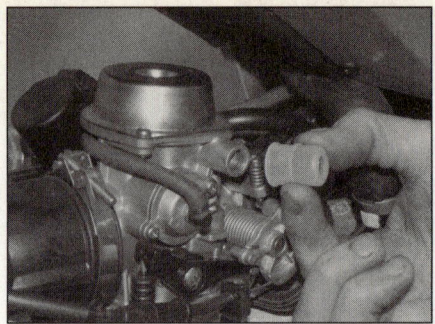

9.3e . . . and pull off the filter

9.4a Remove the screws and the cover . . .

9.4b . . . then withdraw the spring . . .

9.4c . . . and the diaphragm/piston assembly

9.5a Remove the retainer (arrowed)

the clip securing the filter and pull it off **(see illustrations)**.

4 Unscrew and remove the top cover retaining screws (either 2 or 4 screws), then lift off the cover and remove the spring from inside the piston **(see illustrations)**. Carefully peel the diaphragm away from its sealing groove in the carburettor and withdraw the diaphragm and piston assembly **(see illustration)**. Note how the tab on the diaphragm fits in the recess in the carburettor body on Walbro carburettors.

Caution: Do not use a sharp instrument to displace the diaphragm as it is easily damaged.

5 On Walbro carburettors, unscrew the jet needle retainer, then remove the retainer, the spring and spring seat (where fitted) **(see illustration)**. Push the needle up from the bottom of the piston and withdraw it from the top **(see illustration)**. On Keihin carburettors, withdraw the spring seat and needle **(see illustrations)**.

6 Undo the screws securing the float chamber to the base of the carburettor and remove it **(see illustration)**. Discard the gasket as a new one must be used.

7 Unscrew the accelerator pump assembly from the float chamber **(see illustration)**. Discard the O-ring as a new one must be fitted.

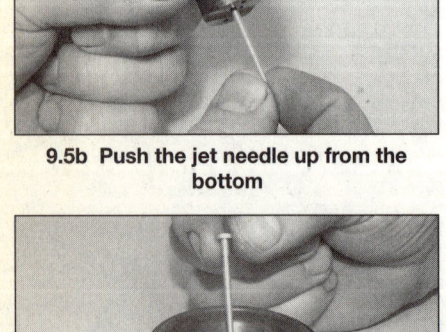

9.5b Push the jet needle up from the bottom

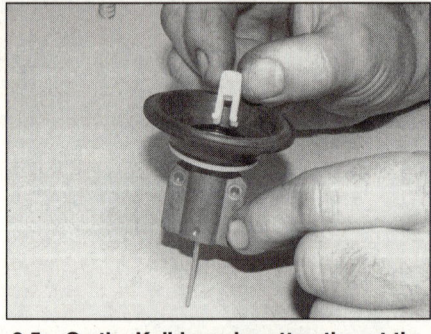

9.5c On the Keihin carburettor, tip out the needle retainer . . .

9.5d . . . and the needle

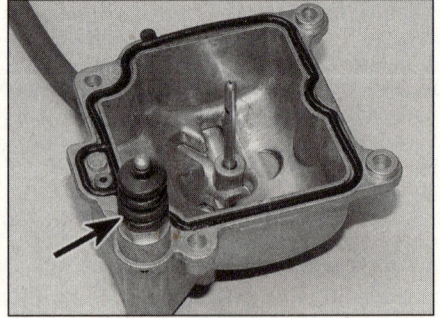

9.6 Float chamber screws (arrowed)

9.7 Unscrew the accelerator pump assembly (arrowed)

9.8 Remove the float pin (arrowed)

9.9a Remove the clamp screw (arrowed) . . .

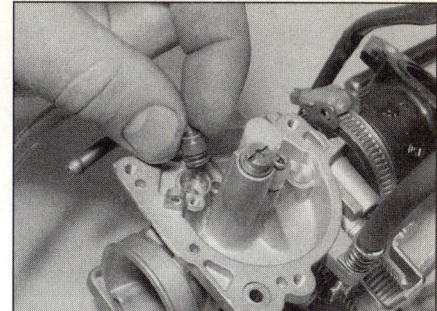

9.9b . . . and withdraw the float needle valve seat

9.10a Remove the plastic jet cover

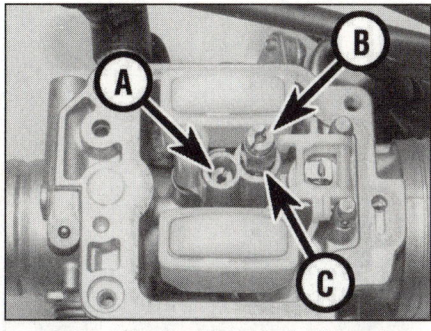

9.10b Pilot jet (A), main jet (B) and needle jet (C)

9.11 Pilot screw (arrowed)

8 Using a pair of thin-nose pliers or a punch, carefully withdraw the float pin; if necessary, displace the pin using a small punch or a nail **(see illustration)**. Remove the float and unhook the float needle valve, noting how it fits onto the tab on the float.

9 Where fitted, undo the screw securing the float needle valve seat clamp, then withdraw the valve seat **(see illustrations)**. Discard the O-ring as a new one should be used. The float valve seat is a press fit on the Keihin carburettor.

10 Where fitted, remove the plastic jet cover from the starter jet **(see illustration)**. **Note:** *The starter jet is a press fit in the carburettor body and should not be removed.* Unscrew the pilot jet, the main jet and the needle jet **(see illustration)**. The fuel atomiser is retained by the needle jet; if the atomiser is loose, remove it for safekeeping.

11 The pilot screw can be removed if required, but note that its setting will be disturbed (see **Haynes Hint**). Unscrew and remove the pilot screw along with its spring and O-ring, where fitted **(see illustration)**.

> **HAYNES HINT** *To record the pilot screw's current setting, turn the screw in until it seats lightly, counting the number of turns necessary to achieve this, then unscrew it fully. On installation, turn the screw in until it seats, then back it out the number of turns you've recorded.*

Cleaning
Caution: Use only a petroleum-based

solvent for carburettor cleaning. Don't use caustic cleaners.

12 Follow Steps 9 to 11 in Section 8 to clean the carburettor body and internal components. Also unscrew the float chamber drain screw and clean the float chamber, paying particular attention to the fuel passage for the accelerator pump. The accelerator fuel passage is fitted with a one-way valve; blow through the fuel passage with compressed air from the bottom of the pump piston housing.
Caution: Never clean the jets or passages with a piece of wire or a drill bit, as they will be enlarged, causing the fuel and air metering rates to be upset.

Inspection
13 If removed, check the tapered portion of the pilot screw and the spring for wear or damage. Fit a new O-ring and renew the screw or spring if necessary.

14 Check the carburettor body, float chamber and top cover for cracks, distorted sealing surfaces and other damage. If any defects are found, renew the faulty component, although fitting a new carburettor will probably be necessary (check with a Gilera dealer on the availability of separate components).

15 Inspect the piston diaphragm for splits, holes and general deterioration. Holding it up to a light will help to reveal problems of this nature. Insert the piston in the carburettor body and check that the piston moves up-and-down smoothly. Check the surface of the piston for wear. If it's worn excessively or doesn't move smoothly, renew the components as necessary.

16 Check the jet needle for straightness by rolling it on a flat surface such as a piece of glass. Fit a new needle if it's bent or if the tip is worn.

17 Inspect the tip of the float needle valve and the valve seat. If either has grooves or scratches in it, or is in any way worn, they must be renewed as a set. **Note:** *A worn or incorrectly sized carburettor float needle valve seat will not be able to shut off the fuel supply sufficiently to prevent carburettor flooding and excessive use of fuel.*

18 Operate the throttle shaft to make sure the throttle butterfly valve opens and closes smoothly. If it doesn't, cleaning the throttle linkage may help. Otherwise, renew the carburettor. **Note:** *Do not remove the screws securing the throttle butterfly to the throttle shaft.*

19 Check the float for damage. This will usually be apparent by the presence of fuel inside the float. If the float is damaged, it must be renewed.

20 Follow the procedure in Section 8, Step 18 to check the automatic choke unit.

21 Inspect the accelerator pump piston and its seat in the float chamber for signs of wear. Ensure that the spring and the rubber boot are not damaged or deformed and renew them if necessary.

22 Where fitted, inspect the cut-off valve diaphragm for splits and hardening and renew it if necessary. Measure the length of the spring; if it is shorter than the service limit, renew it. Wash the filter in hot soapy water and dry it thoroughly. If the filter is excessively dirty and cannot be cleaned properly, fit a new one.

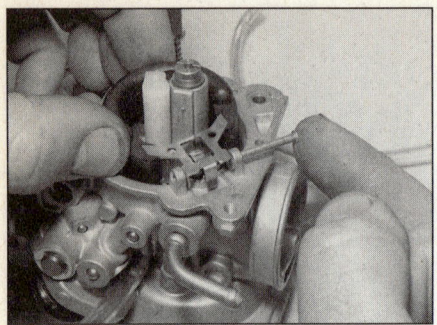

9.27 Install the float pin

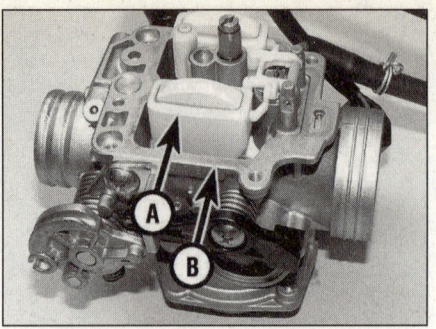

9.28 Straight-edge of float (A) should be parallel with gasket face (B)

9.29 Ensure the float chamber gasket is correctly located

Reassembly and float height check

Note: *When reassembling the carburettor, be sure to use new O-rings and seals. Do not overtighten the carburettor jets and screws as they are easily damaged.*

23 If removed, install the pilot screw, spring and O-ring; adjust the screw to the setting as noted on removal (see Step 11).

24 If removed, install the fuel atomiser, then install the needle jet.

25 Install the main jet and the pilot jet and fit the plastic cover (where fitted) on the starter jet **(see illustrations 9.10b and a)**.

26 If applicable, install the float needle valve seat using a new O-ring, then fit the clamp and tighten the screw **(see illustrations 9.9a and b)**.

27 Hook the float needle valve onto the float tab, then position the float assembly in the carburettor, making sure the needle valve enters its seat. Install the pin, making sure it is secure **(see illustration)**.

28 The carburettor float height should be checked at this point. Turn the carburettor upside-down and check the alignment of the float chamber gasket face and the bottom straight edge of the float – they should be parallel **(see illustration)**. If the float height is incorrect, it can be adjusted by carefully bending the metal float tab a little at a time until the correct height is obtained.

29 Fit a new O-ring to the accelerator pump assembly, then screw the assembly into the float chamber **(see illustration 9.7)**. Fit a new gasket onto the float chamber, making sure it is seated properly in its groove **(see illustration)**. Install the chamber onto the carburettor and tighten the screws securely

30 On Walbro carburettors, check that the clip is correctly positioned on the jet needle (see Specifications at the beginning of this Chapter) then insert the jet needle into the piston **(see illustration)**. Install the spring and spring seat (where fitted) and the jet needle retainer **(see illustrations)**. Insert the piston assembly into the carburettor body and push it down lightly, ensuring the needle is correctly aligned with the needle jet **(see illustration 9.4c)**. Align the tab on the diaphragm with the recess in the carburettor body, then press the diaphragm outer edge into its groove, making sure it is correctly seated **(see illustration)**. Check the diaphragm is not creased, and that the piston moves smoothly up and down in its bore.

31 On Keihin carburettors, insert the needle in the piston (clip position is fixed). Install the needle retainer, then install the piston and diaphragm unit into the carburettor so that the needle passes into the needle jet **(see illustrations)**. Note that the piston will only fit one way. Seat the edge of the diaphragm in its groove and check that the piston moves smoothly up and down in its bore.

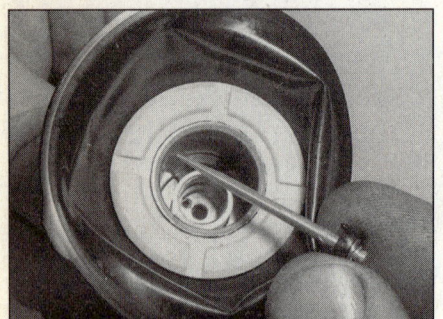

9.30a Install the jet needle . . .

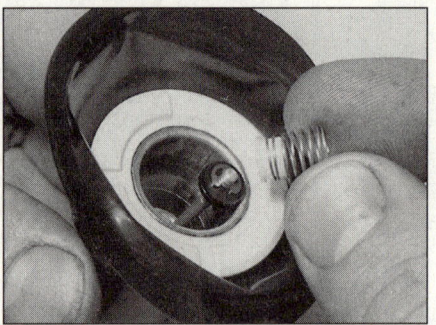

9.30b . . . the spring and spring seat . . .

9.30c . . . and the retainer

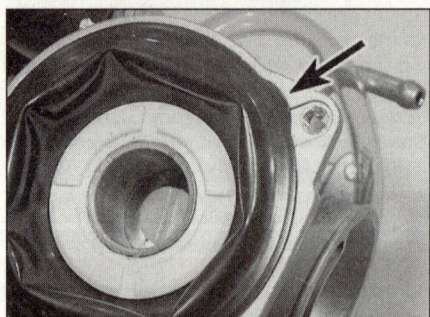

9.30d Make sure the diaphragm and its tab (arrowed) are correctly seated

9.31a When installing the piston/ diaphragm on the Keihin carburettor . . .

9.31b . . . ensure the needle locates in the needle jet (arrowed)

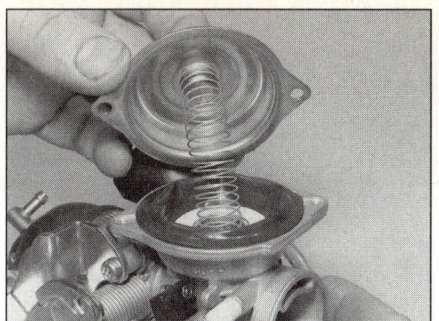

9.32 Locate the cover onto the spring and fit it onto the carburettor

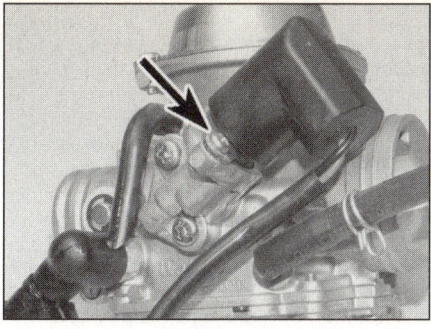

9.34 Secure the choke unit with the clamp (arrowed)

9.35 Accelerator pump lever is retained by screw (arrowed)

32 On all models install the spring into the piston and fit the top cover to the carburettor, making sure the spring locates over the raised section on the inside of the cover, then tighten the cover screws securely **(see illustration)**.

33 If removed, install the choke unit mounting with a new gasket.

34 Install the automatic choke unit and secure it with its clamp **(see illustration)**. If fitted, install the choke unit cover.

35 If removed, install the accelerator pump lever and return spring and secure them with the screw **(see illustration)**.

36 If applicable, install the cut-off valve, making sure that the pin is located in its seat **(see illustration 9.3c)**. Fit the spring and the valve cover and secure them with the screws, ensuring that the vacuum inlet points upwards. Install the filter and secure it with the clip.

37 Install the carburettor (see Section 7).

10 Fuel injection system – Runner Purejet 50

General information

1 The fuel injection system consists of two integrated component groups, the fuel supply system and the electronic control system.

2 The fuel system consists of the tank, filter, pump and fuel injector. Fuel is pumped under pressure from the tank to the fuel injector where it is atomised and mixed with air from the air injector before entering the cylinder. The air injector is supplied by a mechanical pump (air compressor) located externally on the back of the crankcase which draws air from inside the crankcase. Air is supplied directly into the crankcase via the throttle body, which is connected by cable to the throttle twistgrip, and the reed valve

3 The electronic control system consists of the engine control module (ECM), which operates and co-ordinates the injection and ignition systems, and the various sensors and components which provide the ECM with information on engine operating conditions **(see illustration)**.

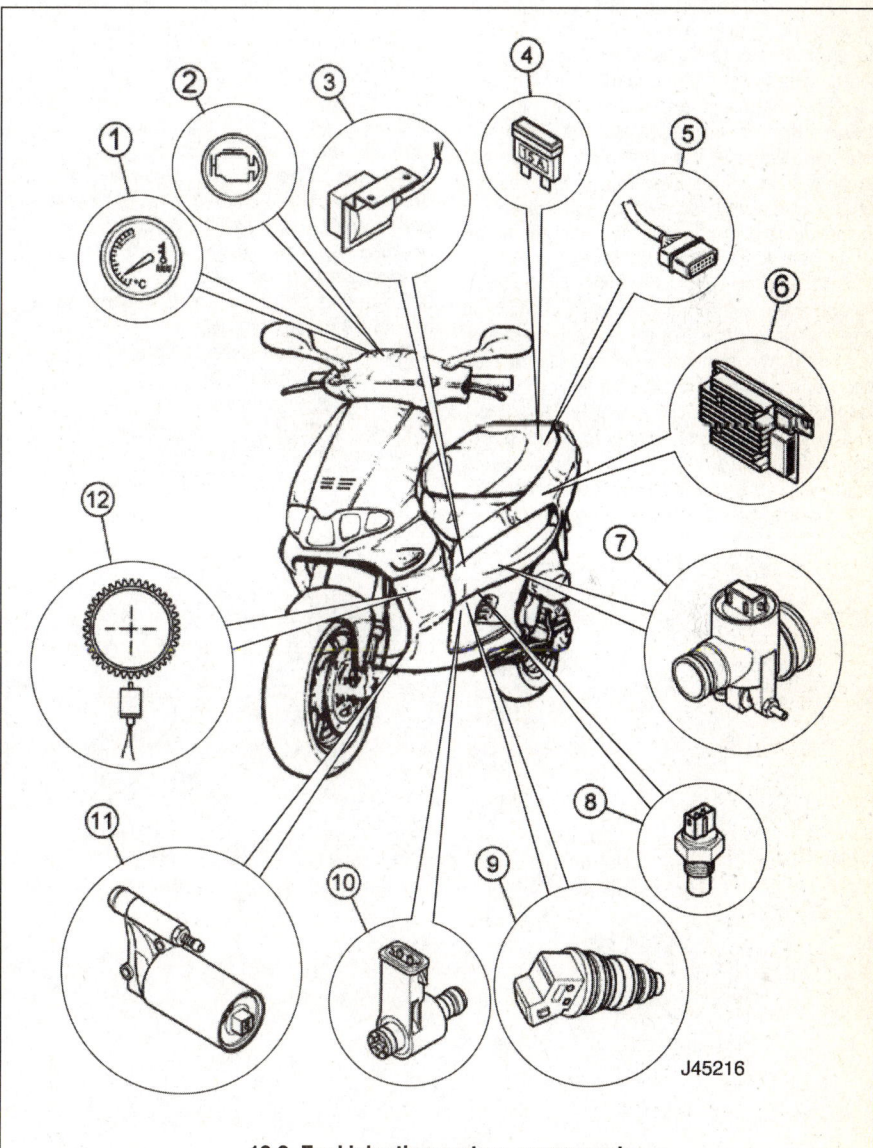

J45216

10.3 Fuel injection system components

1 *Temperature gauge*	5 *Diagnostic socket*
2 *Injection fault warning light*	6 *ECM*
3 *HT coil*	7 *Throttle body*
4 *15 A fuses*	8 *Coolant temperature sensor*
9 *Fuel injector*	
10 *Air injector*	
11 *Fuel pump*	
12 *Crankshaft sensor*	

4 The ECM monitors signals from the following sensors and components:
• Throttle position sensor
• Crankshaft position sensor
• Coolant temperature sensor
• Fuel injector
• Air injector
• HT coil primary circuit
• Fuel pump

5 Based on the information it receives, the ECM calculates the appropriate ignition and fuel requirements for the engine. By varying the length of the electronic pulse it sends to the injector, the ECM controls the length of time the injector is held open and thereby the amount of fuel/air mix that is supplied to the engine. Fuel supply varies according to the engine's needs for starting, warming-up, idling, cruising and acceleration.

6 In the event of an abnormality in any of the information received, the ECM will determine whether the engine can still be run safely. If it can, a back-up mode replaces the sensor signal with a fixed signal, restricting performance but allowing the scooter to be ridden home or to a dealer. When this occurs, the fault warning light in the instrument cluster will come on. If the unit decides that the fault is too serious, the appropriate system will be shut down and the engine will not run. When this occurs, the warning light will flash. **Note:** *Although the fuel pump is part of the electronic control system, pump failure is not indicated by the fault warning light since the engine will not run with the pump inoperable.*

7 If a component failure is suspected, or if the fault warning light illuminates, there are a number of system checks that can be undertaken (see Step 8). If the fault cannot be identified, have the system checked by a Gilera dealer with the appropriate diagnostic equipment. **Note:** *The system incorporates a self-diagnostic function whereby any faults are stored in the ECM's memory. If the warning light illuminates, DO NOT disconnect the scooter's battery until the fault has been verified by the Gilera diagnostic equipment.*

System checks

8 First check the wiring and connectors between the system components and the ECM (see *Wiring diagram* at the end of Chapter 9). A continuity test of all wires will locate a break or short in any circuit. Inspect the terminals inside the wiring connectors and ensure they are not loose or corroded. Spray the inside of the connectors with a proprietary electrical terminal cleaner before reconnection.
Caution: The ECM should not be disconnected while the battery is connected, and the battery should not be disconnected if the Gilera diagnostic equipment is to be used.
9 Check the following, referring to the relevant Sections or Chapters:
• Battery condition (see Chapter 9)
• Fuses (see Chapter 9)
• Spark plug and plug cap (see Chapter 1)
• HT coil primary circuit (see Chapter 5)
• Air supply – air filter element (see Chapter 1)
• Air supply – air compressor (see Steps 33 to 41 of this Section)

10.10 Location of the fuel injector assembly (arrowed)

• Fuel supply (see Section 3)

Fuel injector

10 Remove the bodywork as required to access the injector assembly (see Chapter 8). The injector assembly is mounted on the top of the cylinder head **(see illustration)**.
11 Disconnect the wiring connectors from the fuel and air injectors **(see illustration)**.
12 Disconnect the fuel hoses from the injector manifold – press the hose union down and hold it down, then lift the release ring on the union and disconnect the hose **(see illustration)**.
13 Remove the Torx screw securing the air hose union to the injector manifold and lift off the union. **Note:** *It is not necessary to disconnect the air hose from the union. If the hose is disconnected, Gilera recommend fitting a new hose.*
14 Undo the two screws securing the injector manifold to the cylinder head, then carefully pull the injector assembly out of the head. The air injector should come out with the manifold; if not, pull it out of the head.
15 If required, pull the air injector out of the injector manifold.
16 Undo the two screws securing the fuel injector to the injector manifold and pull the injector out.
17 Remove the O-rings from the air and fuel injectors and discard them as new ones must be fitted. Ease the carbon seal off the

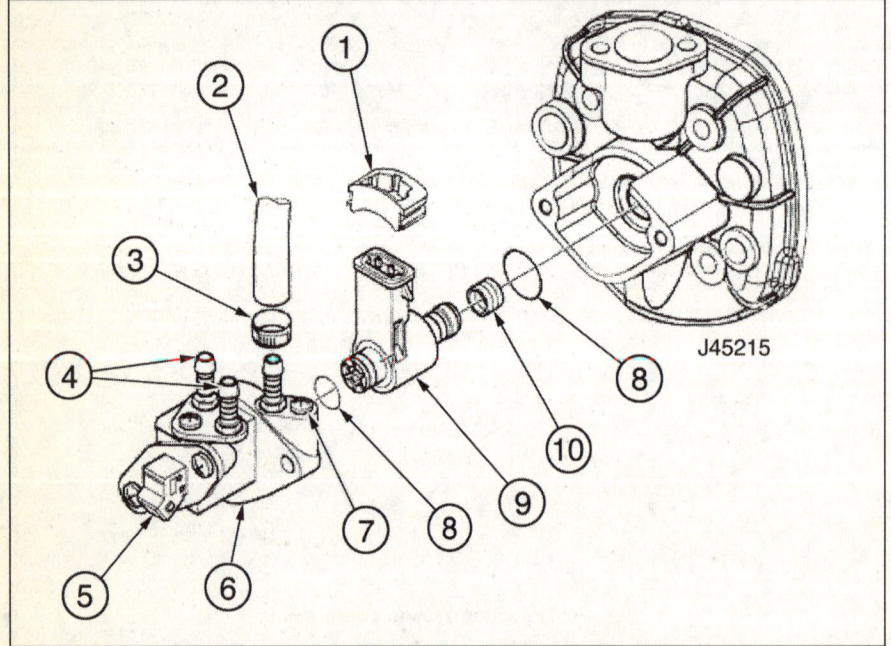

10.11 Fuel injector components

1 *Seal*	4 *Fuel unions*	8 *O-ring*
2 *Air hose from compressor*	5 *Fuel injector*	9 *Air injector*
3 *Hose clip*	6 *Injector manifold*	10 *Carbon seal*
	7 *Air hose union Torx screw*	

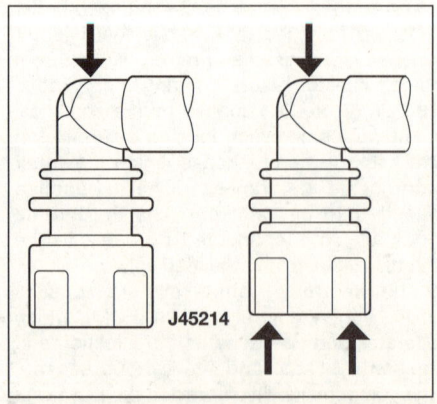

10.12 Press and hold the union down, then lift the release ring as described

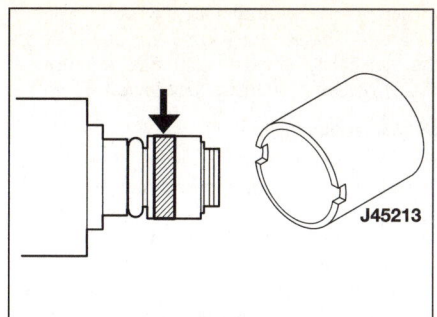

10.20 Gilera tool for installing the carbon seal (arrowed)

air injector as a new one must be fitted. **Note:** *The seal will break when it is removed.*

18 Clean the air injector with a suitable solvent to remove any carbon deposits.

19 Clean the seat of the air injector in the cylinder head.

20 Installation is the reverse of removal. Fit new O-rings to the injectors and lubricate them with a smear of clean engine oil to aid installation. Gilera provide a special tool for installing the carbon seal; the seal must be pressed over the end of the air injector carefully to avoid damaging it **(see illustration)**.

21 Insert the air injector into the cylinder head and press it fully in, then press the injector manifold over the air injector. Ensure the components are correctly aligned with the head, then secure them with the screws.

22 Install the air hose union on the injector manifold and secure it with the Torx screw. Connect the fuel hoses to the injector manifold – press the hose union down and ensure the release ring clicks into position. Ensure the hose unions are secure. Connect the wiring connectors from the fuel and air injectors.

Throttle body

23 Remove the bodywork as required to access the throttle body (see Chapter 8). The throttle body is mounted on the top of the crankcase **(see illustration)**.

24 Disconnect the throttle position sensor

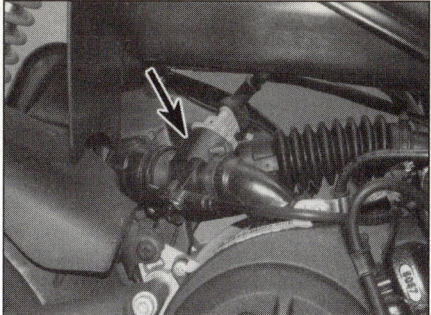

10.23 Location of the throttle body (arrowed)

wiring connector from the throttle body and release the wiring from any clips or ties.

25 Disconnect the throttle cable from the throttle body (see Section 12).

26 Loosen the clip securing the air intake from the air filter housing to the throttle body, and the clip securing the throttle body to the intake manifold, then ease the throttle body off. Note the alignment of the throttle body with the manifold **(see illustration)**.

27 Undo the two Torx screws securing the manifold to the crankcase, then lift of the manifold, the diaphragm and the gasket. Discard the gasket as a new one must be fitted.

28 Check the operation of the throttle body valve. If the valve is loose or sticks, or if the return spring has lost its tension, fit a new throttle body.

29 Clean the diaphragm and inspect the sealing surface; if it is damaged, renew it.

30 If required, remove the reed valve (see Section 11).

31 Installation is the reverse of removal. Fit the gasket and the diaphragm with the printed sides face down, then fit the manifold and secure it with the screws. Ensure the square peg on throttle body is correctly aligned with the cut-out in the manifold before tightening the clip.

32 Ensure the throttle position sensor wiring connector is secure and reconnect the throttle cable (see Section 12).

Air compressor

33 Remove the alternator cover (see Chap-ter 2B).

34 Remove the throttle body (see above). Cover the crankcase opening with a clean rag to prevent anything falling inside.

35 Remove the bodywork as required to access the injector assembly (see Chapter 8). Disconnect the air hose union from the injector manifold (see Step 13).

36 Undo the bolt securing the air hose bracket to the crankcase.

37 Undo the four screws securing the air compressor to the crankcase and lift it out **(see illustration)**. Discard the O-ring as a new one must be fitted.

38 Inspect the surface of the compressor roller for wear, pitting and signs of overheating **(see illustration)**. If the roller is worn or damaged, does not turn freely or move up and down in the compressor body, replace the compressor with a new one.

39 Check the condition of the air hose; if it is cracked or perished, fit a new one.

40 Rotate the crankshaft via the alternator rotor nut and inspect the surface of the roller track on the crankshaft. If the surface of the track is damaged, a new crankshaft assembly will have to be fitted (see Chapter 2B).

41 Installation is the reverse of removal. Fit a new O-ring to the air compressor, then rotate the crankshaft so that the roller track is at its lowest point and install the compressor. Tighten the compressor screws securely.

11 Reed valve

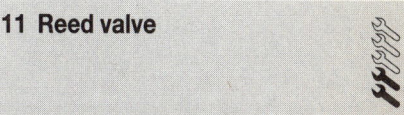

Note: *The reed valve is fitted to SKP/Stalker, Ice, all Runner 50 models (inc. Purejet 50), Runner FX125/FXR180 and DNA 50 GP models.*

Removal

1 On all models except the Runner Purejet 50, remove the carburettor along with the intake manifold (see Section 7).

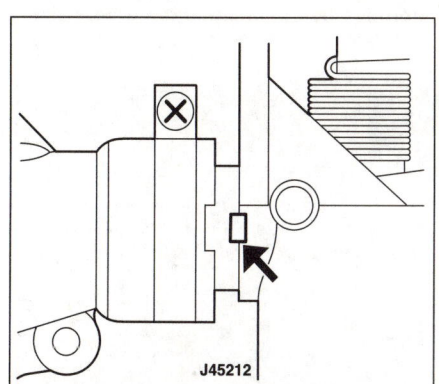

10.26 Note the alignment of the throttle body (arrowed) with the manifold

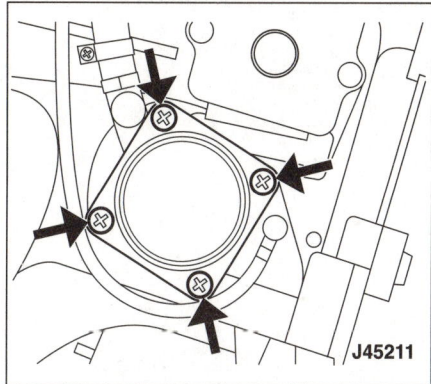

10.37 Air compressor is secured by four screws (arrowed)

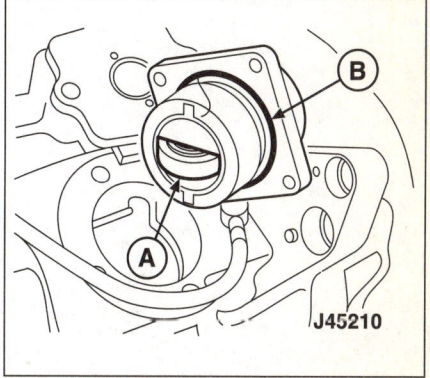

10.38 Check the condition of the compressor roller (A). Note the O-ring (B)

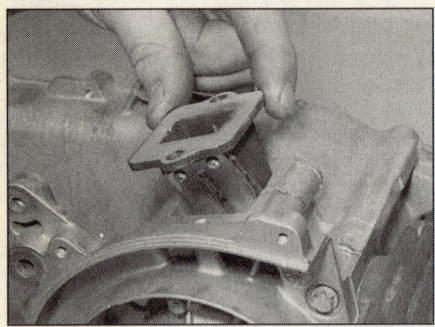

11.3 Withdraw the reed valve from the crankcase

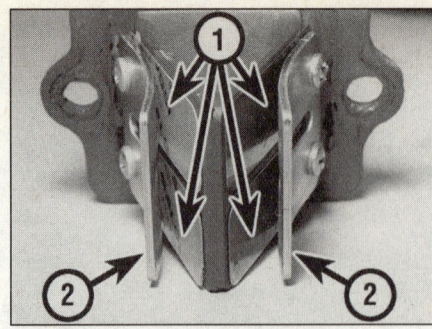

11.5 Check that the reeds (1) sit flat against the valve body when the valve is closed. Stopper plates (2)

2 On the Purejet 50, remove the throttle body and intake manifold (see Section 10). Lift off the diaphragm and the gasket; discard the gasket as a new one must be fitted.
3 Withdraw the reed valve from the crankcase, noting which way round it fits **(see illustration)**.

Inspection

4 Check the reed valve body closely for cracks, distortion and any other damage, particularly around the mating surfaces between the crankcase and the intake manifold – a good seal must be maintained between the components, otherwise

crankcase pressure and therefore engine performance will be affected.
5 Check the reeds themselves for cracks, distortion and any other damage. Check also that there are no dirt particles trapped between the reeds and their seats. The reeds should sit flat against the valve body so that a good seal is obtained when the crankcase is under pressure **(see illustration)**. After prolonged use, the reeds become bent and will not therefore seal properly, in which case they should be renewed. A good way to check is to hold the valve up to the light – if light is visible between the reeds and the body they are not sealing properly. If the engine is difficult

to start or idles erratically, this could be the problem. Check with your Gilera dealer as to the availability of individual reeds – otherwise the complete valve must be renewed.

Installation

6 Installation is the reverse of removal. Ensure that the mating surfaces between the reed valve and crankcase and between the reed valve and intake manifold are clean and perfectly smooth. Check that the stopper plate retaining screws are tight **(see illustration 11.5)**; severe engine damage could result from a screw falling into the engine.

12 Throttle cable

⚠️ *Warning: Refer to the precautions given in Section 1 before proceeding.*

SKP/Stalker, Ice, all Runner 50 models (inc. Purejet 50), Runner FX125/FXR180 and DNA 50 GP models

Removal

1 Three separate cables are fitted – the main cable from the throttle twistgrip goes into a splitter located behind the kickpanel or floor panel, with separate cables going from the splitter to the carburettor (throttle body on Purejet models) and oil pump **(see illustration)**. If a cable problem is diagnosed, first check which cable is faulty. Gilera list all three cables and the splitter individually; in the case of models with carburettors, specify which type of carburettor is fitted because the cables from the splitter to the carburettor differ between different carburettor types.
2 To access the cable at the throttle twistgrip on SKP/Stalker and Runner models, first remove the handlebar front cover (see Chapter 8). To access the cable at the carburettor or throttle body, remove the storage compartment, engine top cover and any bodywork as required according to model (see Chapter 8). To access the cable at the oil pump, remove the plug in the transmission cover **(see illustration)**. To access the cable

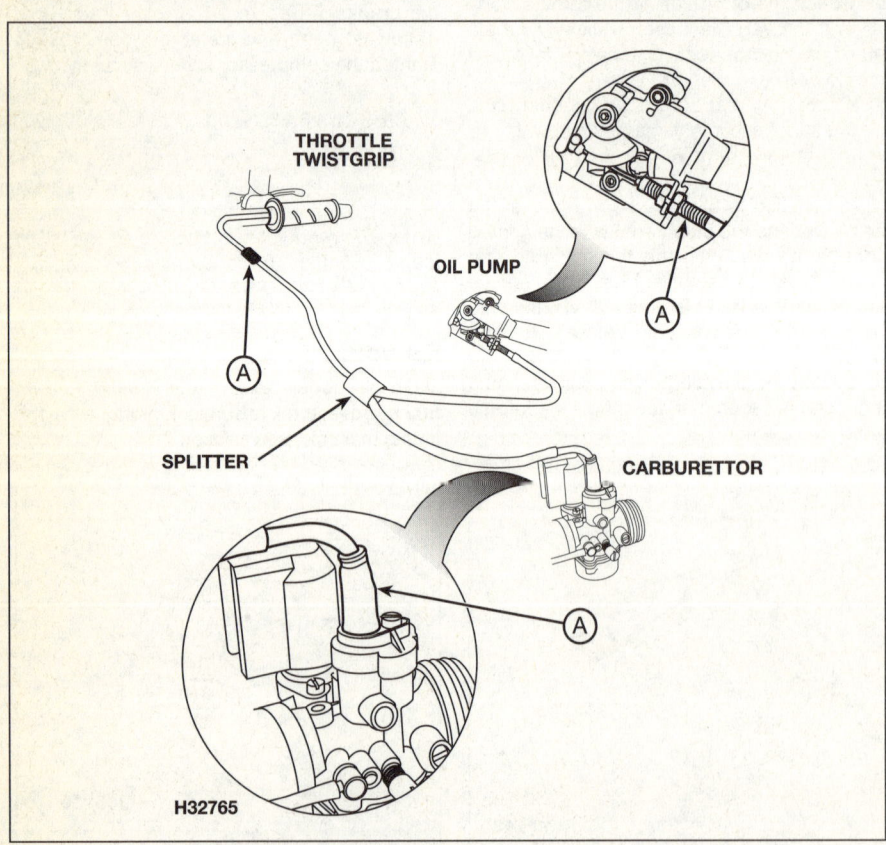

12.1 Throttle cable arrangement for two-stroke engines

Location of cable adjusters (A)

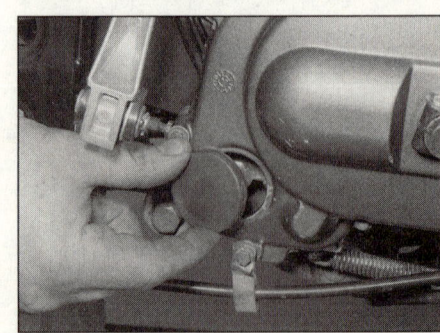

12.2 Remove the rubber plug to access the oil pump cable

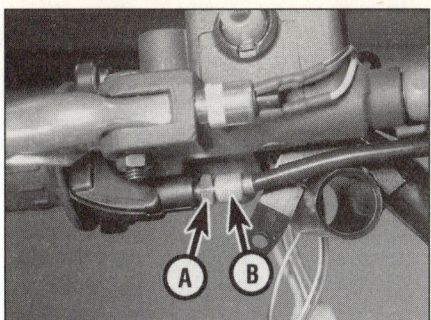

12.4 Loosen the locknut (A) and thread the adjuster (B) fully in

12.5a Undo the cover screws . . .

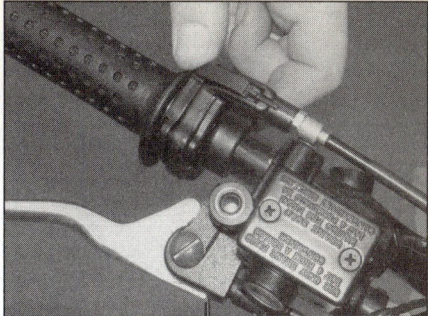

12.5b . . . and displace the cover as described

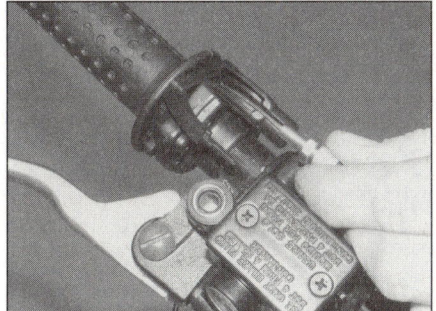

12.5c Pull the cable out of the elbow . . .

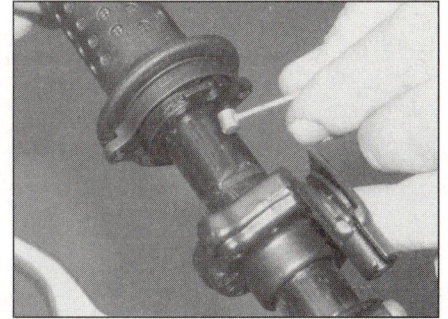

12.5d . . . and detach it from the twistgrip

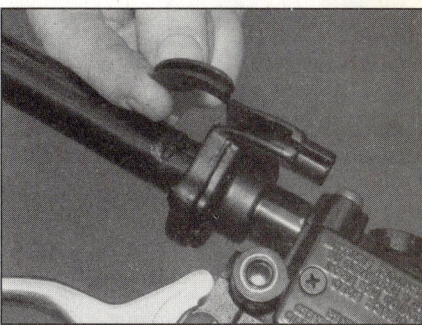

12.5e Note the location of the cable guide

12.6a Note the location of the throttle cable

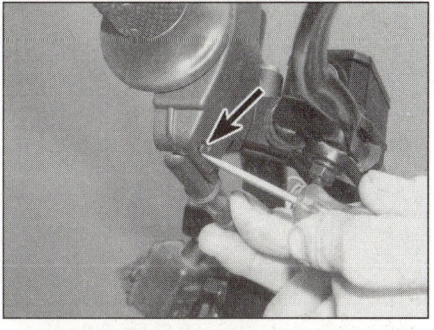

12.6b Release the clip (arrowed) . . .

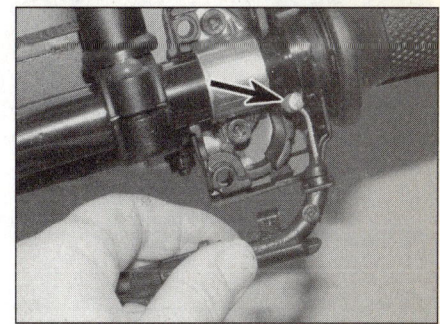

12.6c . . . and detach the cable end (arrowed) from the twistgrip

splitter, remove the kickpanel or floor panel (see Chapter 8).

3 Before removing a cable, make a careful note of its routing to ensure correct installation.

4 To detach the cable from the throttle twistgrip, first loosen the cable adjuster locknut and thread the adjuster fully into the elbow on the twistgrip housing **(see illustration)**.

5 On SKP/Stalker and Runner models, pull back the twistgrip rubber, then undo the screws securing the cover and displace it, noting how it fits over the slot in the elbow **(see illustrations)**. Pull the cable out of the elbow and withdraw the twistgrip from the housing, then detach the inner cable end from the twistgrip **(see illustrations)**. If required, remove the cable guide from the elbow, noting which way round it fits **(see illustration)**.

6 On Ice and DNA models, undo the screws

on the front of the twistgrip housing and lift off the back half of the housing. Note how the cable elbow locates in the housing **(see illustration)**. Release the clip to detach the elbow and detach the inner cable end from the twistgrip **(see illustrations)**.

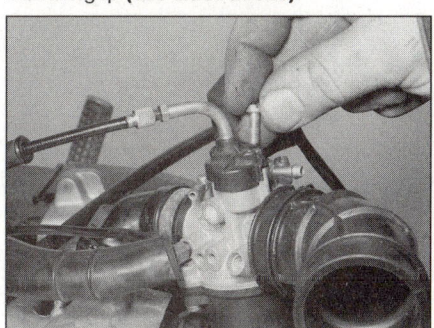

12.7a Remove the screw . . .

7 To detach the cable from the carburettor, remove the screw securing the carburettor top cover, noting that the cover is under spring pressure, then lift the cover and withdraw the throttle slide **(see illustrations)**. Holding the cover, push the slide to compress the spring,

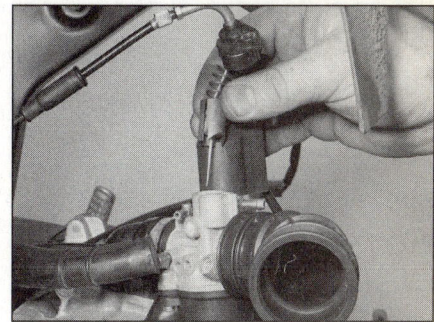

12.7b . . . and lift off the cover and throttle slide

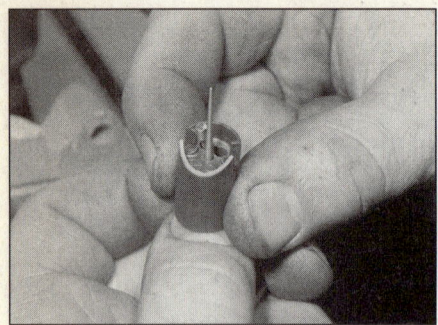

12.7c Free the cable end from its slot . . .

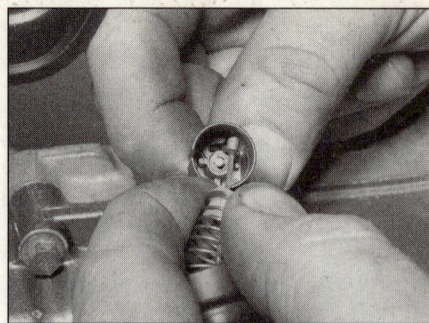

12.7d . . . and draw it out of the slide

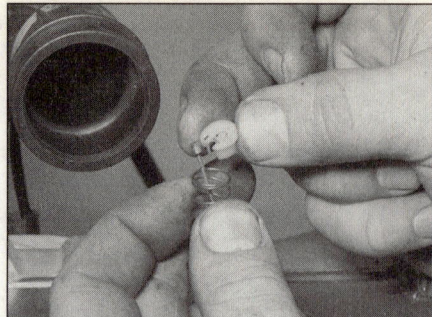

12.7e Remove the spring seat . . .

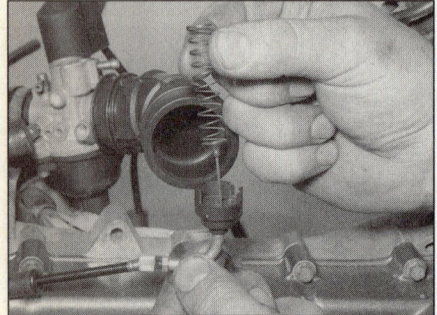

12.7f . . . and the spring . . .

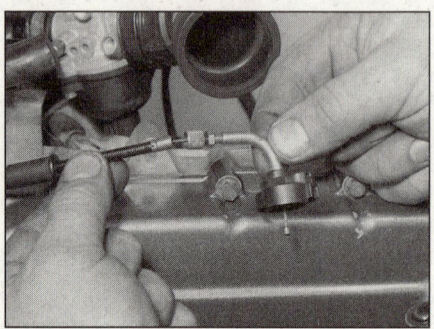

12.7g . . . and draw the cable out of the top cover

12.7h Detach the outer cable (arrowed) from the bracket on the throttle body – Purejet

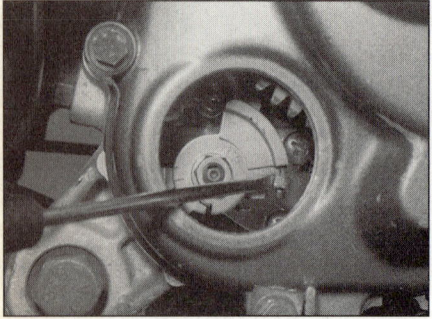

12.8a Lever up the tab securing the cable end . . .

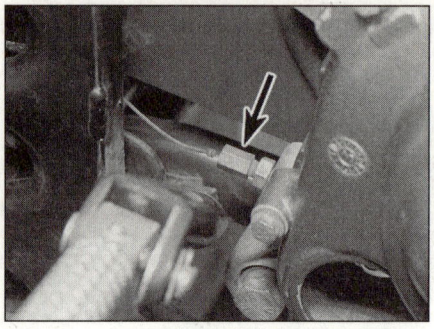

12.8b . . . and draw the cable out of the adjuster

inner cable end from the cam, noting how it fits **(see illustration)**.

8 To detach the cable from the oil pump, lever up the tab securing the cable end, then release the cable from the pump cam and draw it out of the front of the transmission housing **(see illustrations)**. Manually move the cam round to provide some slack in the cable if required (doing this will certainly help installation of the cable). If required, loosen the locknut on the cable adjuster, then unscrew the adjuster from the transmission housing.

9 To detach the cables from splitter, first detach them from the carburettor and the oil pump as described above. Detach the splitter from the frame and draw off the covers **(see illustrations)**. Remove the cap from the splitter and draw the slider out of the housing using the main cable from the twistgrip **(see illustrations)**. Detach the cable(s) from the

thereby creating freeplay in the cable. Free the cable end from its slot in the bottom of the slide and align it with the larger adjacent hole so that the slide can be drawn off the cable **(see illustrations)**. Remove the spring seat, noting how it fits, then remove the spring and

draw the cable out of the elbow on the top of the cover **(see illustrations)**. To detach the cable from the throttle body on the Runner Purejet, pull back the boot and undo the nut securing the outer cable in its bracket and lift the cable out of the bracket, then detach the

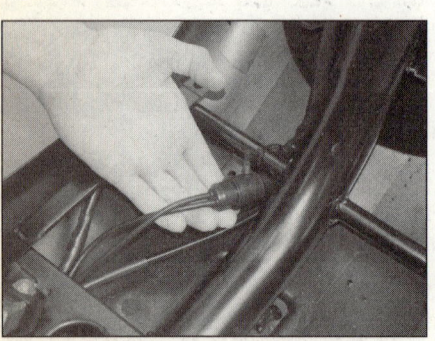

12.9a Detach the splitter from the frame . . .

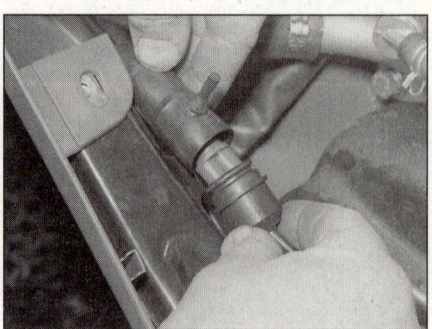

12.9b . . . and draw off the covers

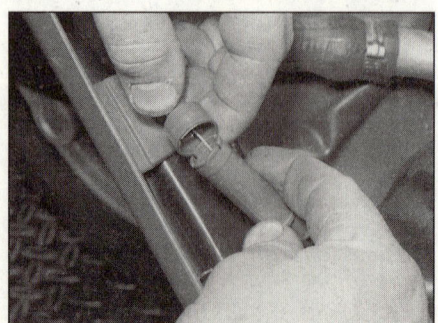

12.9c Remove the cap . . .

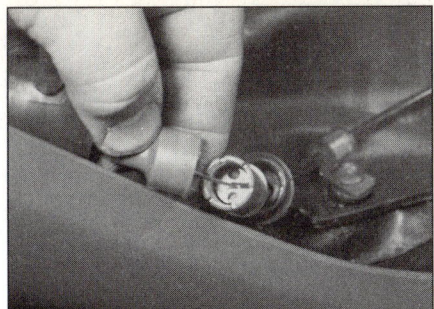

12.9d . . . and draw out the slider

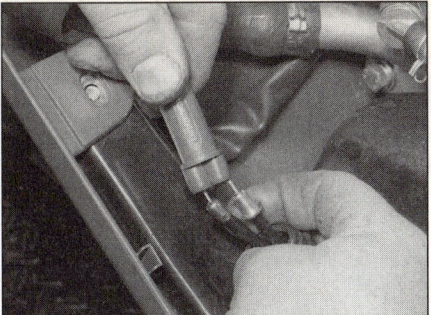

12.9e Note how the outer cables locate in the splitter

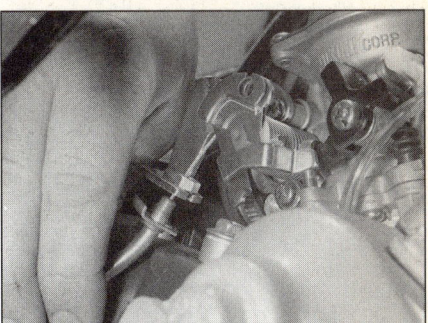

12.13a Detach the cable from the bracket . . .

12.13b . . . then detach the inner cable end from the cam

splitter as required, noting their relative positions **(see illustration)**.

Installation

10 Installation is the reverse of removal, noting the following points:
• Lubricate the inner cable ends with multi-purpose grease.
• Make sure the cables are correctly routed. They must not interfere with any other component and should not be kinked or bent sharply. Turn the handlebars back and forth to make sure the cable doesn't cause the steering to bind.
• Operate the throttle to check that it opens and closes smoothly and freely.
• Check and adjust the cable freeplay and the oil pump setting (see Chapter 1). This is vital to ensure that the engine receives the correct lubrication supply.
• Start the engine and check that the idle speed does not rise as the handlebars are turned. If it does, a cable is routed incorrectly. Correct the problem before riding the scooter.

Runner VX125, ST125, VXR180/200, ST200 and DNA 125/180 models

Removal

11 To access the cable at the throttle twistgrip on Runner models, first remove the handlebar front cover (see Chapter 8). To access the cable at the carburettor, remove the storage compartment on Runner models and the engine top cover on DNA models (see Chapter 8).
12 To detach the cable from the throttle twistgrip, follow the appropriate procedure in

Steps 3 to 6, according to your model.
13 To detach the cable from the carburettor, undo the nut securing the outer cable in its bracket and lift the cable out of the bracket, then detach the inner cable end from the cam, noting how it fits **(see illustrations)**. Withdraw the cable from the scooter noting the correct routing.

> **HAYNES HiNT** *When fitting a new cable, tape the lower end of the new cable to the upper end of the old cable before removing it from the machine. Slowly pull the lower end of the old cable out, guiding the new cable down into position. Using this method will ensure the cable is routed correctly.*

Installation

14 Installation is the reverse of removal, noting the following points:
• Lubricate the inner cable ends with multi-purpose grease.
• Make sure the cable is correctly routed. It must not interfere with any other component and should not be kinked or bent sharply. Turn the handlebars back and forth to make sure the cable doesn't cause the steering to bind.
• Operate the throttle to check that it opens and closes smoothly and freely.
• Check and adjust the cable freeplay (see Chapter 1).
• Start the engine and check that the idle speed does not rise as the handlebars are turned. If it does, the cable is routed incorrectly. Correct the problem before riding the scooter.

13 Exhaust system

> ⚠ *Warning: If the engine has been running the exhaust system will be very hot. Allow the system to cool before carrying out any work.*

Note: *Some models are fitted with a one-piece exhaust system. Follow the procedure for removing the complete system.*

Downpipe removal

1 Remove the engine access panel and, if required by your model, the right-hand side panel (see Chapter 8).
2 Unscrew the two nuts securing the downpipe to the cylinder (two-stroke engine) or cylinder head exhaust port (four-stroke engine) and the two bolts or clamp securing the downpipe to the silencer and remove the downpipe **(see illustrations)**. Remove

13.2a Unscrew the two nuts (arrowed) at the exhaust port . . .

13.2b . . . and the two bolts (arrowed) . . .

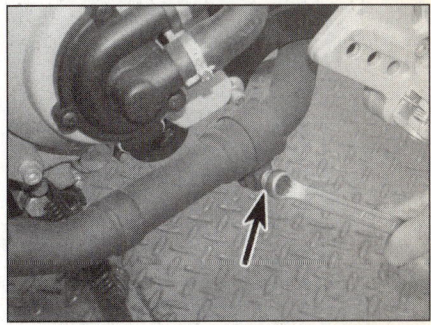

13.2c . . . or clamp (arrowed) at the silencer

13.3a Remove the mounting bolts (arrowed) . . .

13.3b . . . and lift off the silencer

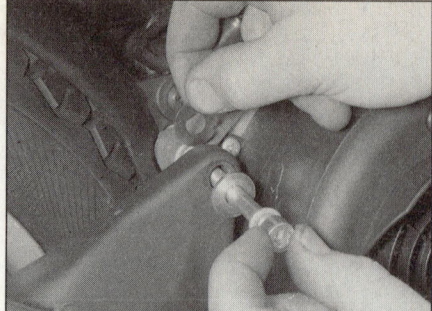

13.3c Note the location of the washer behind the silencer bracket

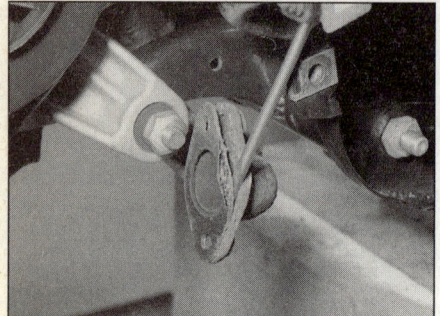

13.3d Remove the gasket and discard it

13.6 Remove the gasket from the exhaust port

the gasket from the exhaust port and from the downpipe to silencer joint, where fitted. Discard the gaskets as new ones must be used on reassembly.

> **HAYNES HiNT** *Exhaust system clamp bolts tend to become corroded and seized. It is advisable to spray them with penetrating oil several hours before attempting to loosen them.*

Silencer removal

3 Unscrew the two bolts or clamp securing the silencer to the downpipe **(see illustrations 13.2b and 2c)** and the bolts securing the silencer to the engine or the rear subframe and remove the silencer **(see illustrations)**. Where fitted, note the spring washer between the silencer bracket and the engine casing **(see illustration)**. If fitted, remove the gasket from the silencer to downpipe joint **(see illustration)**. Discard it as a new one must be used.

Complete system removal

4 Remove the engine access panel and, if required by your model, the right-hand side panel (see Chapter 8).

5 On models fitted with a secondary air system (see Chapter 1, Section 20), loosen the clip securing the air hose to the extension on the exhaust downpipe and disconnect the hose.
6 Unscrew the two nuts securing the downpipe to the cylinder or cylinder head exhaust port. Support the silencer, then undo the bolts securing the silencer to the engine or the rear subframe and remove the exhaust system **(see illustrations 13.2a, 13.3a and 3b)**. Remove the gasket from the exhaust port and discard it as a new one must be used on reassembly **(see illustration)**.

Installation

7 Installation is the reverse of removal, noting the following:
• When installing the silencer or the complete system, install the silencer-to-engine bolts first to take the weight – do not allow the other mountings to take the weight by themselves. Don't forget to fit the spring washers between the silencer bracket and the engine if applicable.
• Leave all fasteners loose until the entire system has been installed, making alignment of the various sections easier. Tighten the silencer mountings last. Note that on some models the top silencer mounting bolt threads into a nut which sits captive, but not fixed, in

a slot in the crankcase – make sure the nut is correctly positioned.
• Use a new gasket in the exhaust port and between the downpipe and the silencer, where fitted.
• Run the engine to check that there are no exhaust gas leaks from the system joints.

14 Catalytic converter

1 To minimise the amount of engine exhaust pollutants escaping into the atmosphere, later models are fitted with an exhaust system incorporating a simple, open-loop catalytic converter. Two-stroke engines are designated Hi-Per2 for air-cooled and Hi-Per2Pro for liquid-cooled types. Four-stroke engines with a catalytic converter are the VX125, ST125, VXR200 and ST200 which meet Euro 3 standard.
2 The catalytic converter has no link with the fuel and ignition systems, and requires no routine maintenance. However the following points should be noted:
• *Always use unleaded fuel – the use of leaded fuel will destroy the converter.*
• *Do not use any fuel or oil additives.*
• *Keep the fuel and ignition systems in good order – if the fuel/air mixture is suspected of being incorrect, have it checked by a Gilera dealer equipped with an exhaust gas analyser.*
• *When the exhaust system is removed from the scooter handle it with care to avoid damaging the catalytic converter.*
3 The catalytic converter works in conjunction with the secondary air system which promotes the burning of any excess fuel present in the exhaust gasses. Ensure the secondary air system and system filters are checked at the specified service interval (see Chapter 1, Section 20).

Chapter 5
Ignition system

Refer to the beginning of Chapter 1 for model identification details

Contents

Degrees of difficulty

| **Easy,** suitable for novice with little experience | | **Fairly easy,** suitable for beginner with some experience |  | **Fairly difficult,** suitable for competent DIY mechanic | 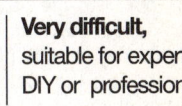 | **Difficult,** suitable for experienced DIY mechanic | | **Very difficult,** suitable for expert DIY or professional |  |

Specifications

Spark plug
Type and gap	see Chapter 1
Cap resistance	5 K-ohms

Ignition timing
Ignition full advance
SKP/Stalker, Ice, DNA 50 GP, Runner 50, 50 DD and 50 SP	16 to 18° BTDC @ 4000 rpm
DNA 50 RST	19 to 21° BTDC @ 4000 rpm
Runner FX125 and FXR180	22° BTDC @ 7500 rpm
Runner VX125, ST125 and DNA 125	33 to 35° BTDC @ 6000 rpm
Runner VXR180/200, ST200 and DNA 180	29 to 31° BTDC @ 6000 rpm

Ignition source coil
Coil resistance
SKP/Stalker, Ice, Runner 50, 50 DD and 50 SP	800 to 1100 ohms
DNA 50 GP	930 to 1030 ohms
DNA 50 RST, Runner 50 SP RST	1 ohm
Runner FX125 and FXR180	122 to 132 ohms
Runner VX125, ST125, VXR180/200, ST200, DNA 125/180	0.7 to 0.9 ohm

Ignition pulse generator coil
Coil resistance
SKP/Stalker, Ice, Runner 50, 50 DD and 50 SP	90 to 140 ohms
DNA 50 GP	83 to 93 ohms
DNA 50 RST, Runner 50 SP RST	170 ohms
Runner FX125 and FXR180	102 to 112 ohms
Runner VX125, ST125, VXR180/200, ST200, DNA 125/180	105 to 124 ohms
Coil output voltage – Runner VX125, ST125, VXR180/200, ST200, DNA 125/180	less than 2V

Ignition HT coil
Primary circuit resistance
Runner FX125 and FXR180	0.48 to 0.52 ohm
Runner VX125, ST125, VXR180/200, ST200, DNA 125/180	0.4 to 0.5 ohms
Secondary circuit resistance
Runner FX125 and FXR180	4.55 to 5.05 K-ohms
Runner VX125, ST125, VXR180/200, ST200, DNA 125/180	2.7 to 3.3 K-ohms

Immobiliser
Transponder aerial resistance	7 to 9 ohms

1 General information

All models covered in this manual are fitted with a fully transistorised electronic ignition system, which due to its lack of mechanical parts is totally maintenance-free.

On all models except the Runner Purejet, the system comprises a source coil, rotor, pulse generator coil, ignition control unit and ignition HT coil (refer to the *Wiring diagrams* at the end of Chapter 9 for details).

The ignition trigger, which is on the alternator rotor on the right-hand end of the crankshaft, magnetically operates the pulse generator coil as the crankshaft rotates. The pulse generator coil sends a signal to the ignition control unit which then supplies the ignition HT coil with the power necessary to produce a spark at the plug.

The ignition control unit (ICU) incorporates an electronic advance system controlled by signals generated by the ignition trigger and the pulse generator coil. There is no provision for adjusting the ignition timing on these scooters.

On the Runner Purejet, the functions of the ignition and fuel injection systems are fully integrated and are controlled by the engine control module (ECM). In the event of a component failure, the fault warning light in the instrument cluster will come on and the system may be shut down (see Chapter 4, Section 10). If the fault cannot be traced using the list in Chapter 4, have the system checked by a Gilera dealer with the appropriate diagnostic equipment.

The ignition system incorporates a safety circuit which prevents the engine from being started unless one of the brake levers is pulled in (see *Wiring diagrams,* Chapter 9).

Runner VX125, ST125, VXR180/200 and ST200 models covered in this manual are fitted

A simple spark gap testing tool can be made from a block of wood, a large alligator clip and two nails, one of which is fashioned so that a spark plug cap or bare HT lead end can be connected to its end. Make sure the gap between the two nail ends is the same as specified.

with an ignition immobiliser. On DNA 125 and 180 models, provision is made in the wiring loom for fitting an immobiliser if required.

Because of their nature, the individual ignition system components can be checked but not repaired. If ignition system troubles occur, and the faulty component can be isolated, the only cure for the problem is to replace the part with a new one.

Note: *Keep in mind that most electrical parts, once purchased, cannot be returned. To avoid unnecessary expense, make very sure the faulty component has been positively identified before buying a replacement part.*

2 Ignition system fault finding

⚠️ *Warning: The energy levels in electronic systems can be very high. On no account should the ignition be switched on whilst the plug or plug cap is being held – shocks from the HT circuit can be most unpleasant. Secondly, it is vital that the engine is not turned over with the plug cap removed, and that the plug is soundly earthed when the system is checked for sparking. The ignition system components can be seriously damaged if the HT circuit becomes isolated.*

1 As no means of adjustment is available, any failure of the system can be traced to failure of a system component or a simple wiring fault. Of the two possibilities, the latter is by far the most likely. In the event of failure, check the system in a logical fashion, as described below. On the Runner Purejet, because of the inter-relationship between the ignition and fuel injection systems, fuel system components and their wiring should be checked as a possible cause of ignition failure (see Chapter 4).

2 Disconnect the HT lead from the spark plug. Connect the lead to a spare spark plug and lay the plug on the engine with its threads contacting the engine. If necessary, hold the spark plug with an insulated tool.

⚠️ *Warning: Do not remove the spark plug from the engine to perform this check – atomised fuel being pumped out of the open spark plug hole could ignite, causing severe injury!*

3 Having observed the above precautions, turn the ignition switch ON and turn the engine over on the starter motor. If the system is in good condition a regular, fat blue spark should be evident at the plug electrodes. If the spark appears thin or yellowish, or is non-existent, further investigation will be necessary. Before proceeding further, turn the ignition OFF.

4 The ignition system must be able to produce a spark which is capable of jumping a particular size gap. Gilera do not provide a specification, but a healthy system should produce a spark capable of jumping at least 6 mm. A simple testing

tool can be made to test the minimum gap across which the spark will jump (see **Tool Tip**). Alternatively, spark gap testers can be purchased and many are adjustable to set the spark gap.

5 Connect the spark plug HT lead to the protruding electrode on the test tool, and clip the tool to a good earth on the engine. Turn the ignition switch ON and turn the engine over on the starter motor. If the system is in good condition a regular, fat blue spark should be seen to jump the gap between the nail ends. If the test results are good the entire ignition system can be considered good. If the spark appears thin or yellowish, or is non-existent, further investigation will be necessary.

6 Ignition faults can be divided into two categories, namely those where the ignition system has failed completely, and those which are due to a partial failure. The likely faults are listed below, starting with the most probable source of failure. Work through the list systematically, referring to the subsequent sections for full details of the necessary checks and tests. **Note:** *Before checking the following items ensure that the battery is fully charged and that all fuses are in good condition.*

• Loose, corroded or damaged wiring connections, broken or shorted wiring between any of the component parts of the ignition system (see Chapter 9).

• Faulty HT lead or spark plug cap, faulty spark plug with dirty, worn or corroded plug electrodes, or incorrect gap between electrodes.

• Faulty ignition (main) switch (see Chapter 9).

• Faulty pulse generator coil or damaged trigger on rotor.

• Faulty ignition HT coil/ignition control unit (50 cc models).

• Faulty ignition HT coil or ignition control unit (125/180/200 cc models).

• Faulty fuel injection system (Runner Purejet – see Chapter 4).

7 If the above checks don't reveal the cause of the problem, have the ignition system tested by a Gilera dealer.

3 Ignition control unit (ICU) and HT coil

Check – 50 cc models

1 On all 50 cc models except the Runner Purejet 50, the ICU and HT coil are integrated in one unit (see illustration). Gilera provide no test specifications for this unit. In order to determine conclusively that the unit is defective, it should be substituted with a known good one. If the fault is rectified, the original unit is thus confirmed faulty. **Note:** *Always disconnect the battery negative (-ve) lead before disconnecting the ICU wiring connector.*

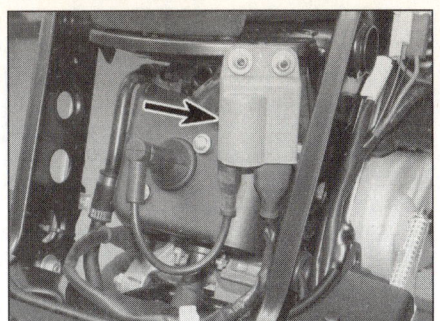

3.1 Combined ignition control unit and HT coil – SKP/Stalker shown

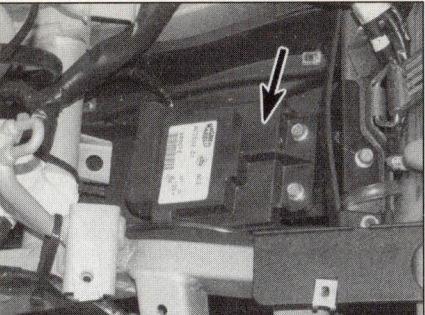

3.3a Ignition control unit – DNA 180 shown

3.3b Ignition control unit – Runner VX125 shown

2 On the Runner Purejet, the engine control module (ECM) controls the functions of both the ignition and fuel injection systems. If a component failure is suspected, or if the injection fault warning light illuminates on the instrument cluster, have the system checked by a Gilera dealer with the appropriate diagnostic equipment. **Note:** *If the injection fault warning light illuminates, DO NOT disconnect the scooter's battery until the fault has been verified by the Gilera diagnostic equipment.*

Check – 125/180/200 cc models

3 On these models, the ICU and HT coil are separate **(see illustrations)**. Gilera provide no test specifications for the ICU. In order to determine conclusively that the unit is defective, it should be substituted with a known good one. If the fault is rectified, the original unit is faulty. To access the ICU on Runner models remove the front panel, and on DNA models remove the seat (see Chapter 8). **Note:** *Always disconnect the battery negative (-ve) lead before disconnecting the ICU wiring connector.*
Caution: If a new ignition control unit with an integral immobiliser has been fitted, refer to Section 6 for details of how to programme it.
4 The HT coil should be checked visually for cracks and other damage, then the primary and secondary coil resistance should be measured with a multi-meter. To test the HT coil, first remove the engine access panel or bodywork as required according to model

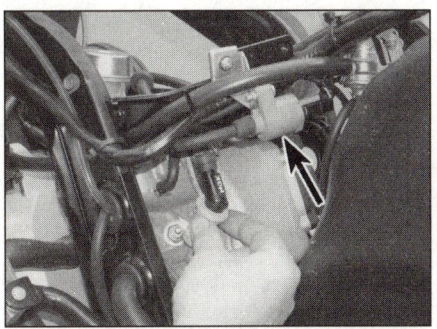

3.3c HT coil – Runner VXR180 shown

(see Chapter 8). Disconnect the battery negative (-ve) lead.

Runner FX125 and FXR180 models

5 Disconnect the primary circuit electrical connector and the HT lead from the coil.
6 To check the condition of the primary windings, set the meter to the ohms x 1 scale and measure the resistance between the primary circuit terminal on the coil and the coil mounting which goes to earth **(see illustration)**. If the reading obtained is not within the range shown in the Specifications at the beginning of this Chapter, it is likely that the coil is defective and must be renewed.
7 To check the condition of the secondary windings, set the meter to the K-ohms scale, then measure the resistance between the HT lead socket on the coil and the coil mounting which goes to earth **(see illustration)**. If the reading obtained is not within the range

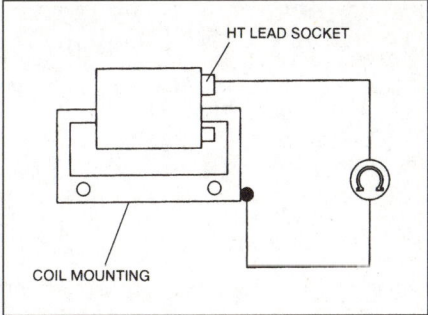

3.3d HT coil – Runner VX125 shown

shown in the Specifications, it is likely that the coil is defective and must be renewed.

Runner VX125, ST125, VXR180/200, ST200, DNA 125/180 models

8 Disconnect the primary circuit electrical connectors from the coil, noting where they fit, and the spark plug cap from the plug. Unscrew the plug cap from the HT lead
9 To check the condition of the primary windings, set the meter to the ohms x 1 scale and measure the resistance between the primary circuit terminals on the coil **(see illustration)**. If the reading obtained is not within the range shown in the Specifications at the beginning of this Chapter, it is likely that the coil is defective and must be renewed.
10 To check the condition of the secondary windings, set the meter to the K ohms scale, then measure the resistance between the core of the HT lead and the black wire terminal

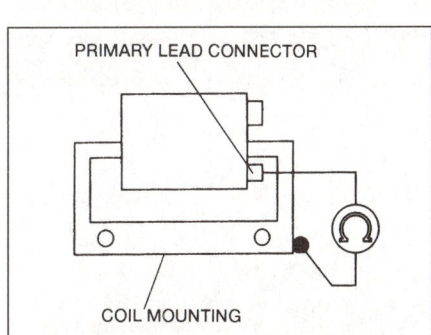

3.6 HT coil primary winding check – Runner FX125/FXR180

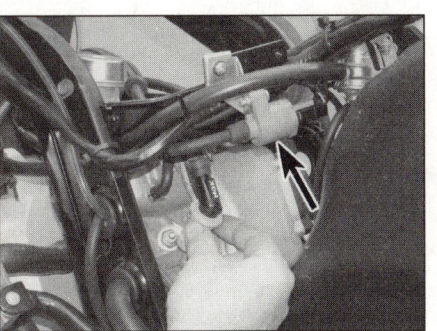

3.7 HT coil secondary winding check – Runner FX125/FXR180

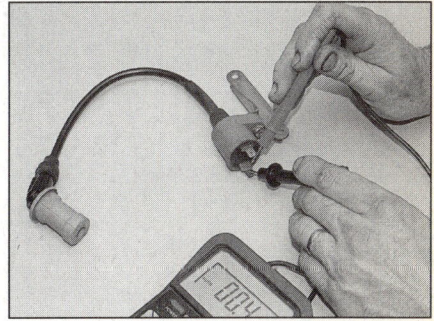

3.9 HT coil primary winding check – Runner VX, VXR, ST and DNA 125/180

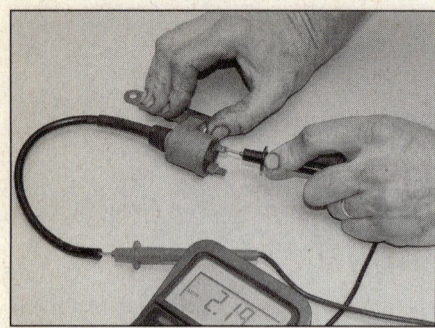

3.10 HT coil secondary winding check – Runner VX, VXR, ST and DNA 125/180, plug cap removed

on the coil **(see illustration)**. If the reading obtained is not within the range shown in the Specifications, it is likely that the coil is defective and must be renewed.

11 If the secondary windings resistance is good, measure the spark plug cap resistance and fit a new cap if the reading obtained is outside the specification.

Removal

12 Remove the engine access panel or bodywork as required according to model (see Chapter 8). Disconnect the battery negative (-ve) lead.

13 Disconnect the electrical connectors from the unit and, if applicable, disconnect the HT lead from the spark plug. **Note:** *Mark the locations of all wires before disconnecting them.*

14 Unscrew the bolts securing the unit and remove it. Note the routing of the wiring.

Installation

15 Installation is the reverse of removal. Make sure the wiring connectors and HT lead are securely connected.

4 Source coil and pulse generator coil

Check

1 Remove the engine access panel or bodywork as required according to model (see Chapter 8) and disconnect the battery negative (-ve) lead.

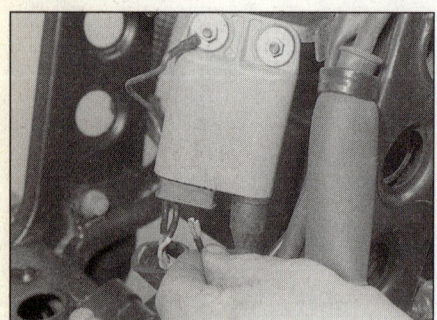

4.2 Disconnecting the wiring on a combined ICU/HT coil

All 50 cc models and Runner FX125/FXR180

Note: *These tests do not apply to the Runner Purejet 50.*

2 Trace the source coil and pulse generator coil wiring from the back of the alternator housing and disconnect it at the connector on the ICU **(see illustration)**. Using a multi-meter set to the ohms x 100 scale, measure the source coil resistance by connecting the meter probes between the green and white terminals in the connector (between the green wire terminal and earth on RST models). Also measure the pulse generator coil resistance by connecting the meter probes between the red and white wire terminals in the connector on 50 cc models (between the red wire terminal and earth on RST models). Measure the pulse generator coil resistance on Runner FX125 and FXR180 models between the red and brown wire terminals.

3 Compare the readings obtained with those given in the Specifications at the beginning of this Chapter. If the readings obtained differ greatly from those given, particularly if the meter indicates a short circuit (no measurable resistance) or an open circuit (infinite, or very high resistance), the entire alternator stator assembly must be renewed as no individual components are available. However, first check that the fault is not due to a damaged or broken wire from the coil to the connector; pinched or broken wires can usually be repaired.

Runner VX125, ST125, VXR180/200, ST200, DNA 125/180

4 To check the source coil, first disconnect the alternator wiring multi-pin connector **(see illustration)**. Using a multi-meter set to the ohms scale, measure the coil resistance by connecting the meter probes between the yellow wire terminals on the alternator side of the connector. Compare the result with the Specifications at the beginning of this Chapter. Also check for continuity between each terminal and earth – there should be no continuity. If the results are good, reconnect the connector and trace the wiring to the regulator. Disconnect the regulator wiring connector and repeat the test between the wire terminals on the wiring side of the

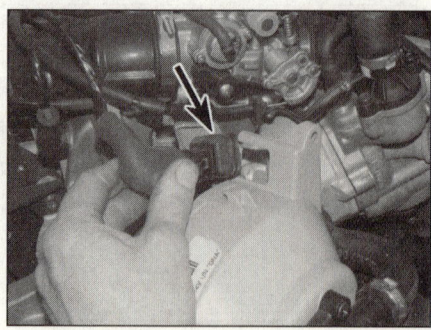

4.4a Disconnecting the alternator wiring connector (arrowed)

connector **(see illustration)**. If the readings differ from those given, there is a fault in the wiring between the alternator connector and the regulator connector.

5 To check the pulse generator coil resistance, connect the meter probes between the green wire terminal in the alternator multi-pin connector and earth (ground). Compare the result with the Specifications at the beginning of this Chapter. If the result is good, reconnect the connector and trace the wiring to the ICU. Disconnect the ICU wiring connector and repeat the test between the green wire terminal in the connector and the black (earth/ground) wire terminal. If the reading differs from that given, there is a fault in the wiring between the alternator connector and the ICU connector. Now set the multi-meter to the Volts (DC) scale, connect the positive (+ve) meter probe to the green wire terminal and the negative (-ve) probe to the black wire terminal. Use the starter motor to turn the engine over and measure the pulse generator coil output voltage, then compare the result to the Specifications.

6 If any of the readings obtained differ greatly from those given, particularly if the meter indicates a short circuit (no measurable resistance) or an open circuit (infinite, or very high resistance), the entire alternator stator/pulse generator coil assembly must be renewed as no individual components are available. However, first check that the fault is not due to a damaged or broken wire from the coil to the connector; pinched or broken wires can usually be repaired.

Renewal

7 The source coil and pulse generator coil are integral with the alternator stator. Refer to the relevant Section of Chapter 2A, 2B or 2C for the removal and installation procedure.

5 Ignition timing

General information

Note: *On the Runner Purejet, the ignition timing can only be checked by a Gilera dealer with the appropriate diagnostic equipment.*

4.4b Disconnect the regulator wiring connector (arrowed)

5.4a The timing mark on the rotor (arrowed)

5.4b Static timing mark on the alternator cover (arrowed)

1 Since no provision exists for adjusting the ignition timing and since no component is subject to mechanical wear, there is no need for regular checks; only if investigating a fault such as a loss of power or a misfire, should the ignition timing be checked.

2 The ignition timing is checked dynamically (engine running) using a stroboscopic lamp. The inexpensive neon lamps should be adequate in theory, but in practice may produce a pulse of such low intensity that the timing mark remains indistinct. If possible, one of the more precise xenon tube lamps should be used, powered by an external source of the appropriate voltage. **Note:** *Do not use the machine's own battery as an incorrect reading may result from stray impulses within the machine's electrical system.*

⚠️ *Warning: The ignition timing check is made with the engine running. To prevent accidents caused by the rear wheel contacting the ground, ensure that the scooter is on its centre stand and if necessary place a support under the scooter to prevent the rear wheel contacting the ground.*

Check

3 Warm the engine up to normal operating temperature then turn it OFF.

4 On all 50 cc models and Runner FX125/FXR180 models, remove the alternator cover (see Chapter 2A or 2B). Locate the timing mark on the cooling fan or alternator rotor, then refit the alternator cover **(see illustration)**. On SKP/Stalker and Ice models, locate the static timing mark on the alternator cover **(see illustration)**. On Runner models, remove the inspection cap from the alternator cover and identify the static timing mark inside the hole **(see illustration 5.5)**.

5 On Runner VX125, ST125, VXR180/200, ST200 and DNA 125/180 models, remove the inspection cap from the alternator cover and locate the timing mark on the water pump drive. The static timing mark is inside the hole **(see illustration)**.

HAYNES HiNT *The timing marks can be highlighted with white paint to make them more visible under the stroboscope light.*

6 On all models connect the timing light to the spark plug HT lead as described in the manufacturer's instructions.

7 Start the engine and aim the light at the static timing mark. With the machine idling at the specified speed, the timing mark on the rotor should align with the idle timing mark.

8 Slowly increase the engine speed whilst observing the timing mark on the rotor. The timing mark should be seen to move anti-clockwise as the timing advances.

⚠️ *Warning: Increasing engine speed will engage the transmission. It is vital that the rear wheel is off the ground and does not contact surrounding objects.*

9 As already stated, there is no means of adjustment of the ignition timing on these machines. If the ignition timing is incorrect, or suspected of being incorrect, one of the ignition system components is at fault, and the system must be tested as described in the preceding Sections of this Chapter.

| 6 | Immobiliser system – Runner VX125, ST125, VXR180/200 and ST200 |

General information

1 Two coded keys and a code card are supplied with the vehicle from new, and the system will already have been programmed with your code. The red or brown-tagged key is the master key and should be kept in a safe place along with the code card – if the master key is lost you will need a new immobiliser system! The blue or black-tagged keys are the service keys for everyday use – additional service keys can be programmed (to a maximum of seven).

5.5 Remove the inspection cap

2 Whenever the key is inserted, the immobiliser is disarmed (assuming the code is accepted). When the key is removed, with the ignition in either the OFF or LOCK positions, the system is automatically activated.

3 If the machine does not start when the service key is inserted in the lock and the ignition is switched ON, turn the switch back to the OFF position and try again. If the machine still does not start, use the master key. If the machine still does not start, contact your Gilera dealer. They have a special electronic analyser which can locate the fault in the system. If the engine starts but will not rev above 2000 rpm (slightly more than idle speed) the immobiliser needs reprogramming (see Steps 7 to 9).

4 The immobiliser LED flashes for 48 hours and then goes out to minimise battery discharge, although the immobiliser system remains active.

5 The LED should flash once when the ignition is first switched ON. If the LED stays off, use a multi-meter to check for battery voltage at the ICU. Remove the right-hand side panel to access the ICU (see Chapter 8). Ensure the ignition is OFF, then disconnect the ICU wiring connector and check for battery voltage between the red/black wire terminal in the connector and earth (ground), and then between the red/black wire terminal

and the black wire terminal. If there is no voltage, inspect the wiring between the ICU and the battery and check the ICU 15 amp fuse (see *Wiring diagrams* at the end of Chapter 9).

6 Ensure that the engine kill switch on the handlebar is in the RUN position. Turn the ignition ON and check for battery voltage between the light blue wire terminal in the ICU connector and the black wire terminal. If there is no voltage, refer to Chapter 9 and check the individual components in the starting system. If there is battery voltage, the ICU is probably faulty and should be checked by a Gilera dealer.

Programming

7 With the ignition switch in the OFF position, insert the master key. Turn the switch on for 1 to 3 seconds, then turn it OFF again. Remove the key.

8 Within 10 seconds of removing the master key, insert the service key. Immediately turn the switch on for 1 to 3 seconds, then turn it OFF again. Remove the key. If required, repeat this procedure for any additional service keys.

9 Within 10 seconds of removing the service key, insert the master key again. Immediately turn the switch on for 1 to 3 seconds, then turn it OFF again. Remove the key. The immobiliser system is now programmed.

Caution: The use of the correct, resistor type, spark plug and suppresser cap is essential to prevent interference with the immobiliser system and possible loss of key programming.

Malfunction codes

10 The LED should flash once when the ignition is switched ON. If the LED then flashes twice and then stays on permanently to indicate an ignition fault, try using the master key to turn the ignition ON. If this works, the service key has lost its programme. If the fault persists, remove the kickpanel to access the immobiliser transponder aerial located behind the ignition switch (see Chapter 8). Trace the transponder wiring and disconnect it at the connector. Use a multi-meter set to the ohms scale to check the resistance of the aerial. If the result is not as specified, fit a new aerial. If the result is good, the ICU is probably faulty and should be checked by a Gilera dealer.

11 If the LED flashes three times and then stays on permanently to indicate an ignition fault, try using the master key to turn the ignition ON. If this works, the service key has lost its programme. If the fault persists, the ICU is probably faulty and should be checked by a Gilera dealer.

Chapter 6
Frame, steering and suspension

Refer to the beginning of Chapter 1 for model identification details

Contents

Degrees of difficulty

Easy, suitable for novice with little experience 	**Fairly easy,** suitable for beginner with some experience 	**Fairly difficult,** suitable for competent DIY mechanic 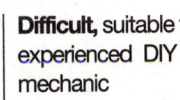	**Difficult,** suitable for experienced DIY mechanic 	**Very difficult,** suitable for expert DIY or professional

Specifications

Front forks

Upside-down forks
  Grease type . . . . Esso Beacon ET2 or Tradal Complex 2
Telescopic forks
  Fork oil type
    Ice, all DNA models . . . . 10W fork oil
    Runner VX125, ST125, VXR180/200, ST200 . . . . 20W fork oil
  Fork oil capacity
    Ice . . . . 90 cc each leg
    all DNA models . . . . 280 cc each leg
    Runner VX125, ST125, VXR180/200, ST200 . . . . 80 cc each leg
  Front fork spring free length – all DNA models . . . . 430 mm

Torque settings

Handlebar bracket pinch bolts – all DNA models . . . . 20 to 22 Nm
Handlebar bracket locating bolts – all DNA models . . . . 20 to 22 Nm
Handlebar stem/clamp bolt
  SKP/Stalker (up to 2004), all Runner 50 models . . . . 19.6 to 21.5 Nm
  Ice, Stalker (2005-on), Runner VX125, ST125, VXR180/200
    and ST200 . . . . 45 to 50 Nm
  Runner FX125 and FXR180 . . . . 65 to 70 Nm

Torque settings (continued)

Steering head bearing adjuster nut
  Initial setting for SKP/Stalker (up to 2004), all Runner 50 models,
    FX125 and FXR180 .... 50 to 60 Nm (then slacken by 90°)
  Ice, Stalker (2005-on), Runner VX125 and VXR180/200 .... 8 to 10 Nm
  VX125/VXR200 RST, ST125 and ST200..................... 10 to 13 Nm (then slacken by 90°)
  DNA 50 GP, DNA 125/180
    Initial setting .... 20 to 25 Nm (then slacken off)
    Final setting .... 10 to 13 Nm (then slacken by 90°)
  DNA 50 RST .... 8 to 10 Nm
Steering head bearing locknut
  SKP/Stalker, Ice, all Runner 50 models .... 30 to 40 Nm
  Runner FX125, FXR180, VX125, ST125, VXR180/200 and ST200... 30 to 40 Nm
Steering stem nut – all DNA models......................... 30 to 36 Nm (RST model – 35 to 40 Nm)
Upside-down telescopic forks
  Upper fork damper rod nuts..................... 20 to 25 Nm
  Axle bracket bolts............................. 20 to 25 Nm
Conventional telescopic forks
  Front fork leg clamp bolts
    Ice, Runner VX125, ST125, VXR180/200 and ST200.......... 20 to 25 Nm
    DNA 50 GP (upper and lower bolts) .... 30 to 35 Nm
  Front fork leg top bolt – Ice (where fitted), DNA 50 GP ...... 20 to 25 Nm
  Front fork leg damper bolt – Ice, DNA 50 GP .... 15 to 20 Nm
Rear shock absorber upper mounting
  SKP/Stalker, Ice, all Runner 50 models .... 20 to 25 Nm
  DNA 50 GP, DNA 125/180.............................. 33 to 41 Nm
  Runner FX125, FXR180, VX125 and VXR180/200 .... 20 to 25 Nm
  Runner VX125/VXR200 RST and ST125/200................. 33 to 41 Nm
Rear shock absorber lower mounting – all models .... 33 to 41 Nm
Rear shock absorber lower mounting bracket bolt .... 20 to 25 Nm
Swingarm pivot bolt-to-engine........................... 33 to 41 Nm
Swingarm pivot bolt-to-frame
  SKP/Stalker, all Runner 50 models, Runner FX125 and FXR180.... 33 to 41 Nm
  Ice and DNA 50 GP, Runner VX125, ST125, VXR180/200, ST200
    and DNA 125/180................................ 64 to 72 Nm
Swingarm central pivot bolt (see text) .... 64 to 72 Nm
Centre stand mounting bracket bolt nuts
  SKP/Stalker, all Runner 50 models....................... 19 Nm
  Ice... 25 Nm
  DNA 50 GP .... 20 Nm
Centre stand pivot bolt nut
  Runner VX125, ST125, VXR180/200 and ST200 .... 30 Nm
  DNA 125/180 .... 20 Nm

1 General information

All scooters covered by this manual are fitted with a tubular and pressed steel one-piece frame.

The engine and transmission unit is linked to the frame by a pivoting swingarm assembly at the front and by the rear shock absorber(s), making the unit an integral part of the rear suspension. Models with twin rear shock absorbers have a subframe bolted to the engine on the right-hand side which supports the transmission driveshaft and the lower end of the right-hand shock.

Front suspension is by conventional or upside-down telescopic forks.

Ancillary items such as stands and handlebars are covered in this Chapter.

2 Frame

1 The frame should not require attention unless accident damage has occurred. In most cases, frame renewal is the only satisfactory remedy for such damage. A few frame specialists have the jigs and other equipment necessary for straightening the frame to the required standard of accuracy, but even then there is no simple way of assessing to what extent the frame may have been over-stressed.

2 After a high mileage, the frame should be examined closely for signs of cracking or splitting at the welded joints. Loose engine mounting and suspension bolts can cause ovaling or fracturing of the mounting points. Minor damage can often be repaired by specialist welding, depending on the extent and nature of the damage.

3 Remember that a frame which is out of alignment will cause handling problems. If misalignment is suspected as the result of an accident, it will be necessary to strip the machine completely so the frame can be thoroughly checked.

3 Stands

Check

1 Since the stand pivots are exposed to the elements, they should be lubricated periodically to ensure safe and trouble-free operation (see illustration).

2 In order for the lubricant to be applied

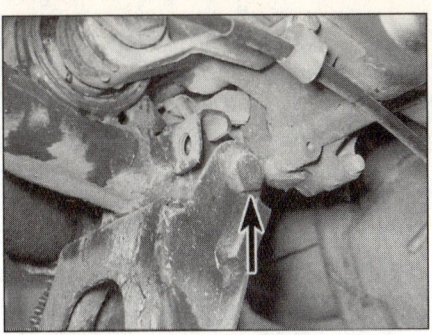

3.1 Centre stand pivot bolt (arrowed)

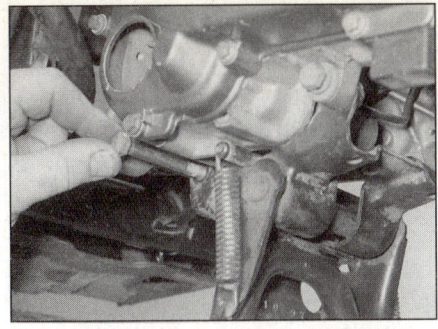

3.6a Withdraw the stand bracket bolts . . .

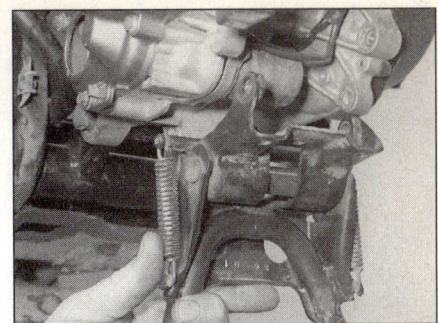

3.6b . . . and remove the stand assembly

where it will do the most good, first clean the stand pivot points thoroughly. On Runner VX125, ST125, VXR180/200 and ST200, and DNA 125/180 models, the centre stand pivot bolt can be removed for lubrication. However, if chain or cable lubricant is being used, it can be applied to the pivot points and will usually work its way into the areas where friction occurs. If motor oil or light grease is being used, apply it sparingly as it may attract dirt (which could cause the pivots to bind or wear at an accelerated rate).

3 The return springs must be capable of retracting the stand fully and holding the stand retracted when the scooter is in use. If any spring has sagged or broken it must be renewed (see below).

Removal and installation

Centre stand

4 Support the scooter securely in an upright position using an auxiliary stand. **Note:** *Do not rest the weight of the machine on the bodywork; if applicable, remove the belly panels to expose the frame (see Chapter 8). Alternatively, have an assistant support the machine.*

5 On Runner VX125, ST125, VXR180/200 and ST200, and DNA 125/180 models, unhook the stand spring, noting how it fits. Unscrew the pivot bolt nut and remove the washer, then withdraw the pivot bolt and remove the stand **(see illustration 3.1)**.

6 On all other models with a stand bracket bolted to the underside of the engine, unscrew the nuts and withdraw the bolts securing the

bracket, then remove the stand and bracket as an assembly **(see illustrations)**. To remove the stand from the bracket, the head of the pivot pin must first be drilled out. A new pin must be used on assembly and its end peened over to secure the pin.

7 Thoroughly clean the stand and remove all road dirt and old grease. Inspect the pivot bolt or pin and the pivot holes in the bracket for wear and renew any components as necessary. Inspect the spring; if it is sagged or is cracked a new spring must be fitted. Inspect the rubber stop on the stand and renew it if it is worn or perished.

8 Installation is the reverse of removal, noting the following:

• Apply grease to the pivot bolt and all pivot points.

• Tighten the nuts to the specified torque settings, where available.

• Ensure that the spring holds the stand up securely when it is not in use – an accident is almost certain to occur if the stand extends while the machine is being ridden. If necessary, fit a new spring.

Side stand

9 Some models are supplied with an optional side stand which bolts to the underside of the frame. To remove the stand, first support the scooter on its centre stand.

10 Undo the stand bracket bolts and remove the stand and bracket as an assembly.

11 Clean and inspect the stand components (see Step 7).

12 Installation is the reverse of removal, noting the following:

• Lubricate the pivot points.

• Check the spring tension – it must hold the stand up when it is not in use. If necessary, fit a new spring.

| 4 | Handlebars and levers |

Handlebars

Removal – SKP/Stalker, Ice and all Runner models

1 Remove the handlebar covers (see Chapter 8).

2 On Ice and Runner models, the handlebars can be displaced from the steering head for access to the bearings without having to detach any cables or remove the brake lever brackets, or where applicable, the front and rear brake master cylinders. If this is the case, ignore the Steps which do not apply.

3 Where fitted, undo the centre screws for the bar end weights and remove the weights **(see illustration)**.

4 Disconnect the wiring from each brake light switch **(see illustration)**.

5 Detach the throttle cable from the twistgrip and slide the twistgrip off the end of the handlebar (see Chapter 4). If required, undo the bolts securing the front half of the twistgrip housing to the handlebar and lift it off **(see illustration)**. Alternatively, undo the housing

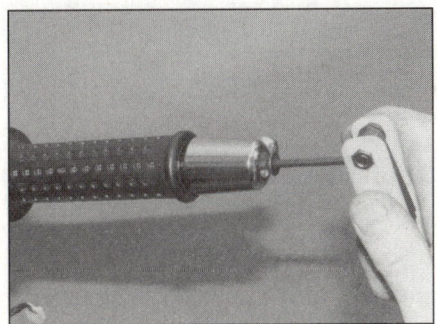

4.3 Remove the bar end weights

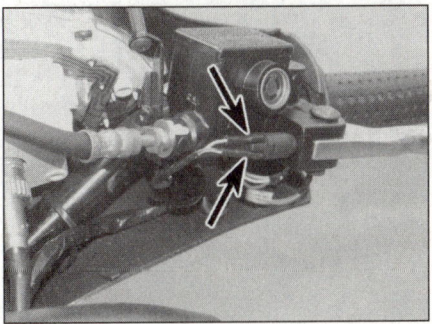

4.4 Disconnect the wiring connectors (arrowed) from each brake light switch

4.5a Front half of the housing is secured by two bolts (arrowed)

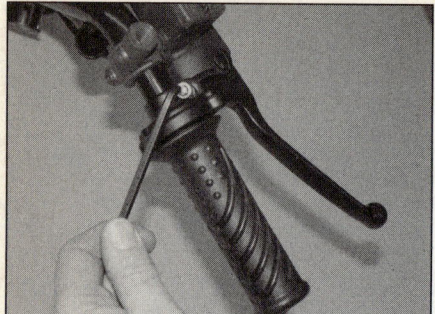

4.5b Undo the pinch bolt . . .

4.5c . . . and lift out the spacer

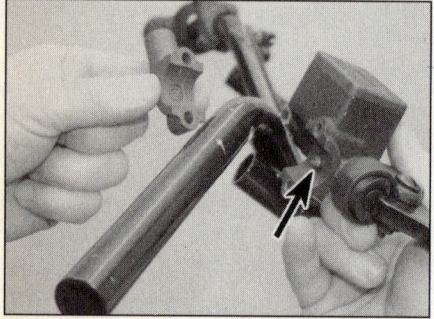

4.7 Note how the pin (arrowed) locates in the hole in the handlebar

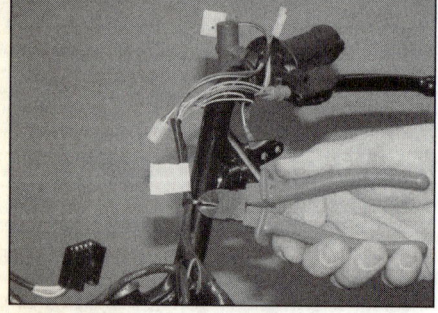

4.8 Brake lever bracket bolts

is placed on the hydraulic hose. Keep the hydraulic reservoir upright to prevent fluid loss and air entering the system.

8 On models with a cable-operated rear brake, first detach the cable from the lever if required (see Chapter 7). Note the type of lever bracket fitted to your machine. On some models, the bracket is secured with two bolts **(see illustration)**. Undo the bolts and lift off the top and bottom halves of the bracket. On some models, the bracket is secured by a single clamp bolt. First remove the left-hand grip (peel the grip off the bar end, or if necessary cut it off). Undo the clamp bolt and slide the bracket off the end of the handlebar.

9 On SKP/Stalker models, cut the cable ties securing the wiring to the handlebars **(see illustration)**. Loosen the bolt that passes down through the handlebar stem, then strike the bolt with a soft-faced mallet to free the cone inside the steering stem **(see illustration)**. Lift off the handlebars, noting how the peg in the centre of the bar assembly locates in the slot in the top of the steering stem **(see illustration)**. Note the cone in the end of the handlebar tube **(see illustration)**.

10 On models with the handlebars secured by a clamp and pinch bolt, remove the nut and withdraw the bolt, then lift the handlebars off the stem **(see illustrations)**.

11 If the handlebar components have been left attached, position the handlebars so that no strain is placed on any of the cables, hoses or wiring. If you are removing the handlebars completely, make note of how the wiring is taped to the handlebar before freeing it.

pinch bolt, then lift out the spacer and slide the housing off the handlebar **(see illustrations)**.

6 On Ice models, detach the left-hand handlebar switch unit from the handlebar (see Chapter 9).

7 Unscrew the front and, where fitted, rear disc brake master cylinder assembly clamp bolts and lift off the assembly, noting how it fits **(see illustration)**. Position the assembly clear of the handlebar, making sure no strain

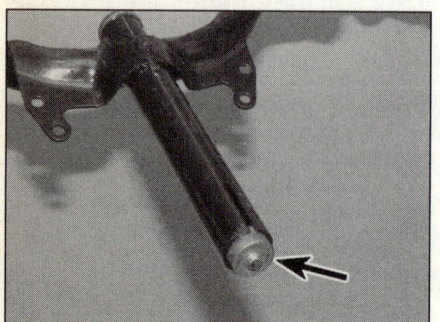

4.9a Cut the ties securing the wiring

4.9b Strike the bolt (arrowed) to free it – SKP/Stalker

4.9c Note how the peg (arrowed) locates in the slot

4.9d Note the location of the cone (arrowed)

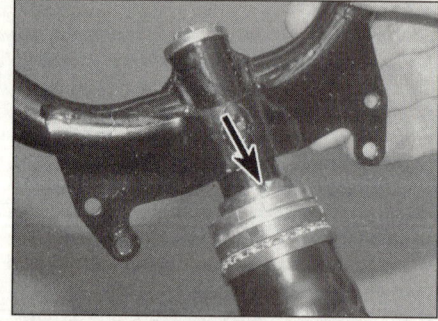

4.10a Remove the pinch bolt (arrowed)

4.10b Note the slot for the bolt (arrowed)

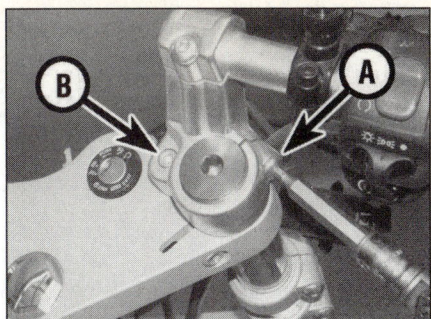

4.14a Handlebar bracket pinch bolt (A) and locating bolt (B)

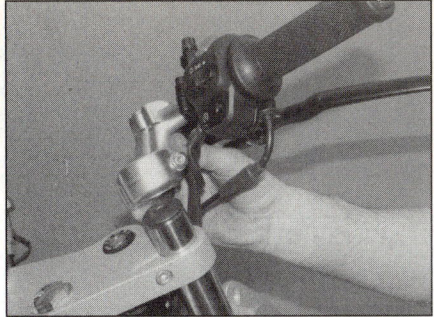

4.14b Lift off the handlebar assembly

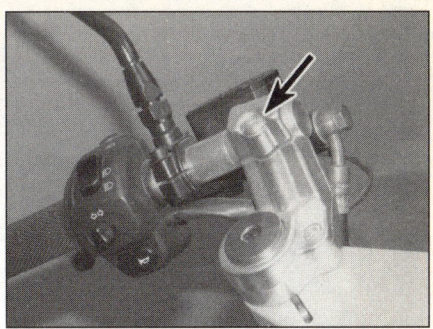

4.14c Handlebar pinch bolt (arrowed)

Removal – DNA models

12 If required, the handlebars can be displaced from the front forks without having to detach any wiring or cables or remove the front and rear brake master cylinders. If this is the case, ignore the Steps which do not apply.

13 Follow the procedures in Steps 4 to 7 and remove the switches, throttle twistgrip and brake master cylinders as required.

14 Loosen the handlebar bracket pinch bolt, then undo the bracket locating bolt and lift the handlebar assembly off the fork tube **(see illustrations)**. Alternatively, undo the handlebar pinch bolt and remove it from the bracket, then pull the bar out of the bracket **(see illustration)**. Note the slot in the bar which should align with the pinch bolt on reassembly. If the handlebar components have been left attached, position the

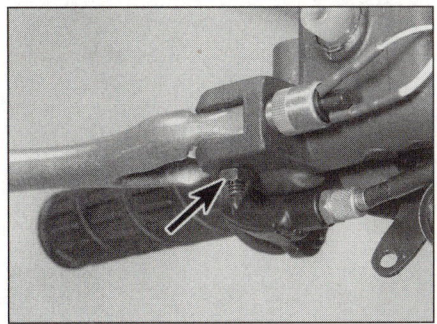

4.16a Unscrew the locknut (arrowed) . . .

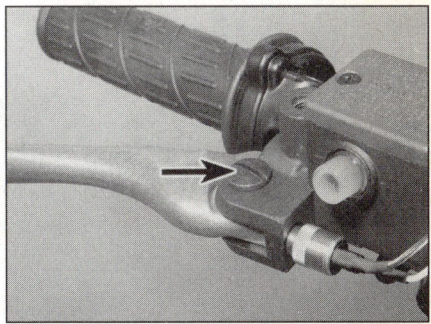

4.16b . . . and remove the pivot bolt (arrowed)

handlebars so that no strain is placed on any of the cables, hoses or wiring.

Installation

15 Installation is the reverse of removal, noting the following:
• Refer to the Specifications at the beginning of this Chapter and tighten the nut on the handlebar clamp bolt, the stem bolt SKP/Stalker models and the handlebar bracket bolts on DNA models to the specified torque settings.
• Don't forget to reconnect the brake light switch wiring connectors.
• Use a suitable adhesive between the left-hand grip and the handlebar.

Brake levers

Removal

16 Unscrew the lever pivot bolt locknut, then withdraw the pivot bolt and remove the lever

(see illustrations). If applicable, detach the brake cable from the lever as you remove it.

Installation

17 Installation is the reverse of removal. Apply grease to the pivot bolt shank and the contact areas between the lever and its bracket, and to the inner cable end where applicable.

5 Steering stem

Removal

1 Remove the front wheel (see Chapter 7). Secure the brake caliper clear of the front forks with a cable tie to avoid straining the hydraulic hose – note that there is no need to disconnect the hose. Release the hose from any clips securing it to the steering stem assembly **(see illustration)**. Displace or remove the handlebars (see Section 4). Although not essential, it is advisable to remove any front body panels or, where fitted, the front mudguard to avoid the possibility of damaging the paintwork (see Chapter 8).

2 Where fitted, displace the plastic collar from the top of the steering stem, noting how it fits **(see illustrations)**.

3 On DNA models, if required, remove the front fork legs (see Section 7). Alternatively, if the legs are being left in place, loosen the upper front fork leg clamp bolts **(see**

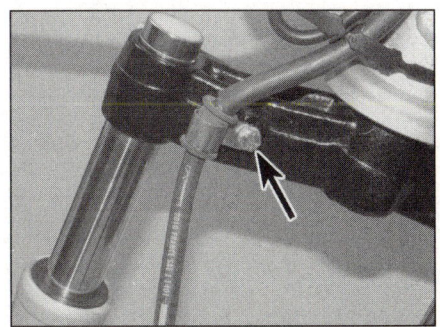

5.1 Detach the brake hose clip from the steering stem

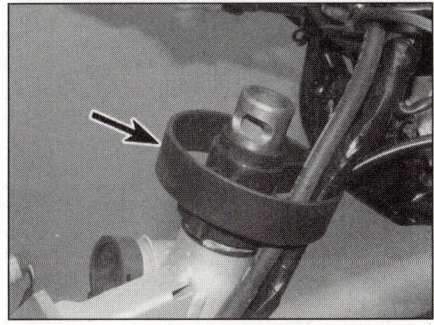

5.2a Hoses and wiring are routed through a plastic collar

5.2b Pull the collar up to displace it

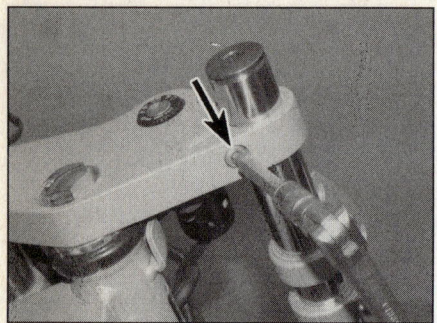

5.3a Loosen the upper fork leg clamp bolts

5.3b Release the speedometer wire and brake hose guides

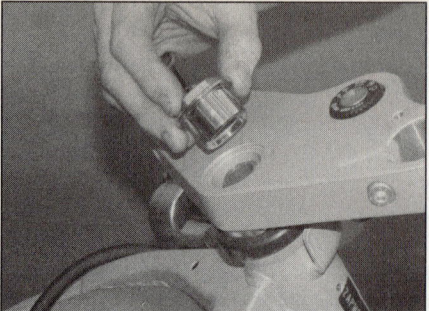

5.3c Remove the steering stem nut . . .

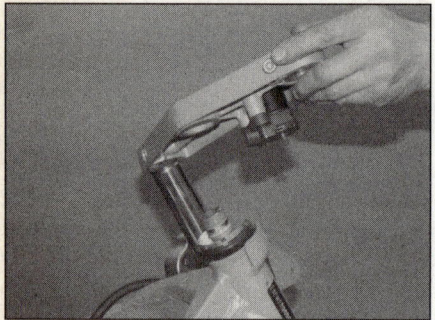

5.3d . . . and lift off the top yoke

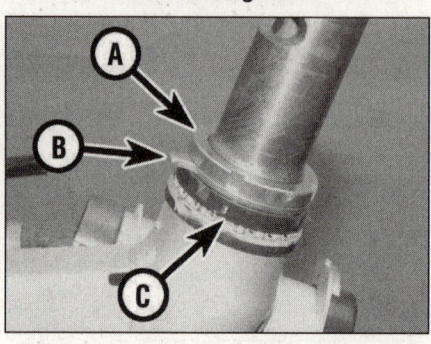

5.4a Locknut (A), washer (B) and bearing adjuster nut (C)

5.4b Undoing the locknut with a C-spanner

illustration). Undo the screw securing the ignition (main) switch wiring connector and disconnect it, noting how it fits (see Chapter 9). Undo the bolts securing the speedometer wire and the front brake hose guides to the underside of the fork bottom yoke (see illustration). Undo the steering stem nut, then lift off the top yoke (see illustrations).

4 On all models except the DNA, undo the bearing adjuster locknut using either a suitable C-spanner, a peg-spanner or a drift located in one of the notches (see illustrations). Remove the washer, noting how it fits.

5 Support the steering stem. Undo the bearing adjuster nut using either a C-spanner, a peg-spanner or a drift located in one of the notches, then remove the nut, the dust cover on DNA models, and the spacer where fitted (see illustrations).

6 Carefully lower the steering stem out of the frame (see illustration).

7 As applicable, remove the upper bearing balls from the top of the steering head – the lower bearing balls and inner race will be on the steering stem. **Note:** *On some later models, the lower bearing is a taper roller bearing.* Remove all traces of old grease from the bearings and races and check them for wear or damage as described in Section 6. **Note:** *Do not attempt to remove the outer races from the frame or the lower bearing inner race from the steering stem unless they are to be renewed.*

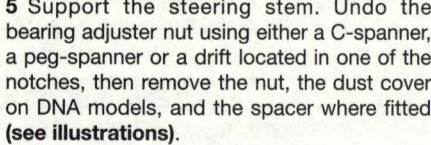

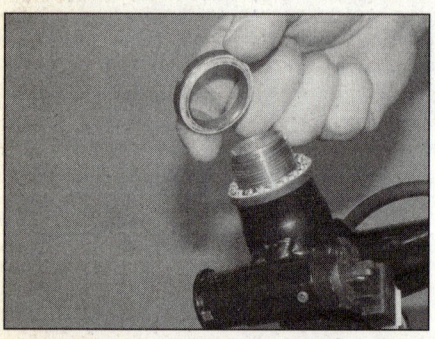

5.5a Remove the bearing adjuster nut – SKP/Stalker shown

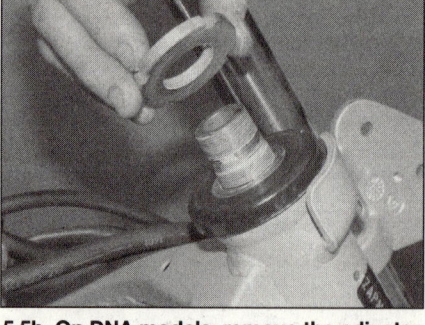

5.5b On DNA models, remove the adjuster nut . . .

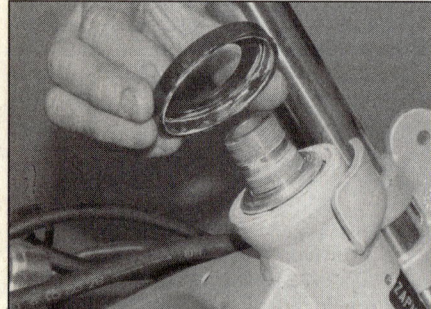

5.5c . . . the dust cover . . .

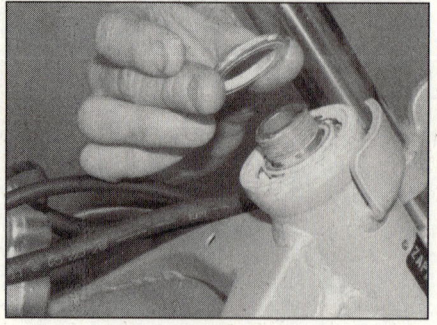

5.5d . . . and the spacer

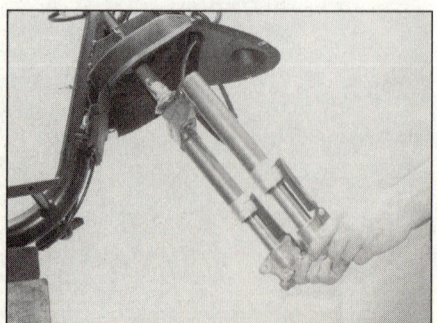

5.6 Lower the steering stem out of the frame

Installation

8 Smear a liberal quantity of grease on the bearing outer races in the frame. Also grease both the upper and lower bearing assemblies. If removed, install the lower bearing assembly over its inner race.

9 Carefully lift the steering stem up through the frame. If removed, install the upper bearing assembly. As applicable, install the spacer, the bearing cover on DNA models, then thread the bearing adjuster nut onto the steering stem.

10 Tighten the adjuster nut to the specified torque setting (see Specifications) if you have the Gilera service tool (Part No. 020055Y) or a home-made alternative **(see illustrations)**. If it is not possible to apply a torque wrench to the adjuster nut, tighten the nut and adjust the bearings as described in Chapter 1.

11 On all models, check the adjustment as described in Chapter 1 **(see illustration)**.

Caution: Take great care not to apply excessive pressure because this will cause premature failure of the bearings.

12 On DNA models, install the top yoke and secure it with the steering stem nut; tighten the nut finger-tight. If the fork legs have been removed, install them and secure them with the lower clamp bolts; do not tighten the upper clamp bolts (see Section 7). Hold the adjuster nut to prevent it from moving and tighten the stem nut to the torque setting specified, then tighten the upper clamp bolts to the specified torque. Check the bearing adjustment then install the remaining components in the reverse order of removal.

13 On all other models, install the washer, making sure the inner tab locates in the slot on the steering stem **(see illustration)**. Install the locknut, then hold the adjuster nut to prevent it from moving and tighten the locknut to the specified torque setting. Check the bearing adjustment then install the remaining components in the reverse order of removal.

6 Steering head bearings

Inspection

1 Remove the steering stem (see Section 5).

2 Remove all traces of old grease from the bearings and races and check them for wear or damage **(see illustrations)**.

3 The outer races in the steering head should be polished and free from indentations **(see illustration)**. Inspect the ball or roller bearings for signs of wear, damage or discoloration, and examine the bearing retainer cage for signs of cracks or splits. Spin the bearing by hand. It should spin freely and smoothly. If there are any signs of wear on any of the above components both upper and lower bearing assemblies must be replaced as a

5.10a Tightening the adjuster nut with a home-made peg spanner

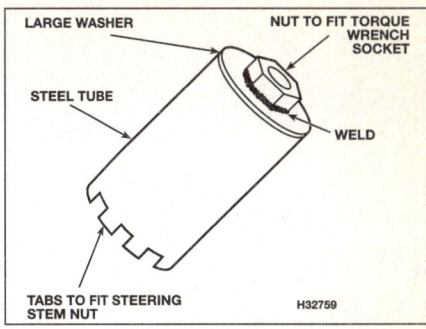
5.10b Details of a home-made peg spanner

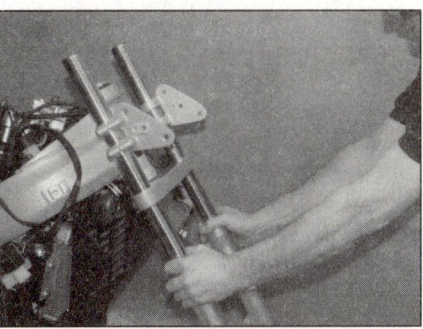
5.11 Checking the bearings for freeplay

5.13 Note the tab (arrowed) on the inside of the washer

6.2a Upper bearing caged ball race

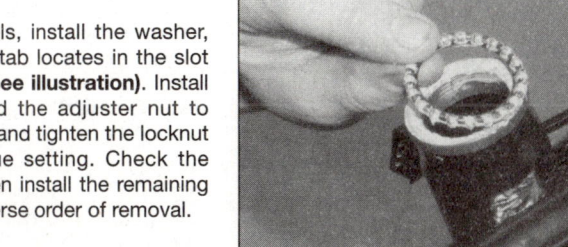
6.2b Upper bearing radial ball race

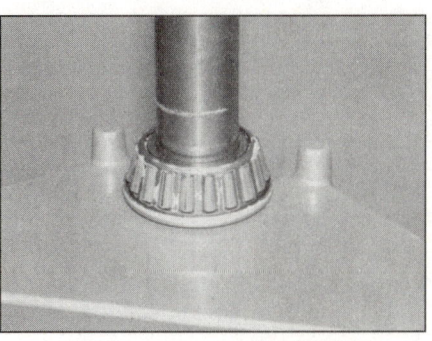
6.2c Lower taper roller bearing

6.3 Check the outer races in the steering head

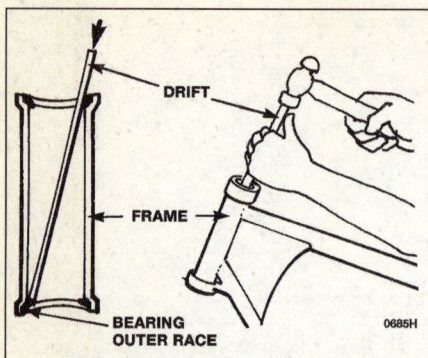

6.4 Drive the bearing outer races from the frame as shown

set. Only remove the races if they need to be renewed – do not re-use them once they have been removed.

Renewal

4 The outer races are an interference fit in the frame and can be tapped from position with a suitable drift **(see illustration)**. Tap firmly and evenly around each race to ensure that it is driven out squarely. It may prove advantageous to curve the end of the drift slightly to improve access.

5 Alternatively, the races can be pulled out using a slide-hammer with internal expanding extractor.

6 The new outer races can be pressed into the frame using a drawbolt arrangement **(see illustration)**, or by using a large diameter tubular drift which bears only on the outer

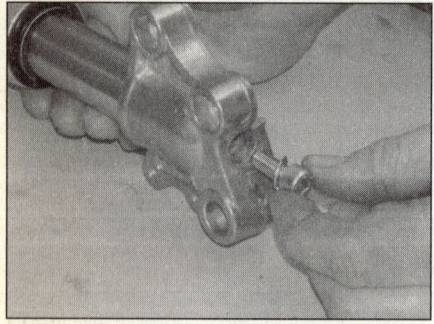

7.2a Remove the Allen bolt . . .

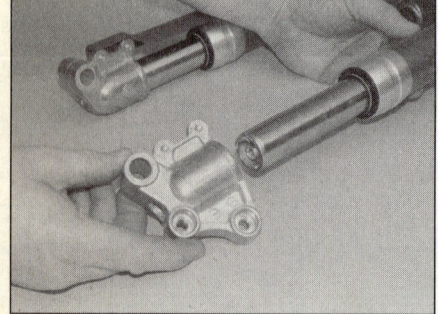

7.2b . . . and pull off the axle/brake caliper bracket

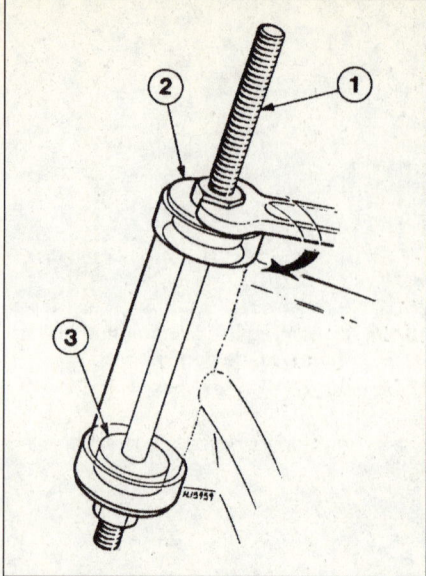

6.6 Drawbolt arrangement for fitting steering head bearing outer races

1   Long bolt or threaded bar
2   Thick washer
3   Guide for lower outer race

edge of the race. Ensure that the drawbolt washer or drift (as applicable) bears only on the outer edge of the race and does not contact the working surface. Alternatively, have the races installed by a Gilera dealer equipped with the bearing race installing tools.

> **HAYNES HINT**
> *Installation of new bearing outer races is made much easier if the races are left overnight in the freezer. This causes them to contract slightly making them a looser fit.*

7 To remove the lower bearing inner race from the steering stem, use two screwdrivers placed on opposite sides of the race to work it free **(see illustration)**. If the bearing is firmly in place it will be necessary to use a bearing puller, or drive a chisel between the underside of the race and the bearing seat. Take the steering stem to a Gilera dealer if required. Check the condition of the dust seal that fits

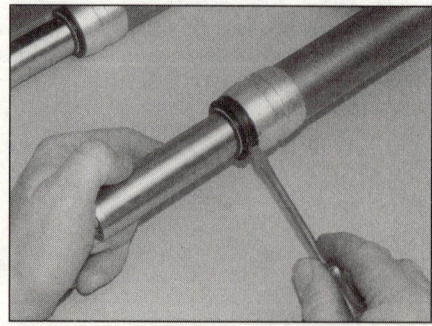

7.2c Lever out the seal

6.7 Lever the lower race off the steering stem

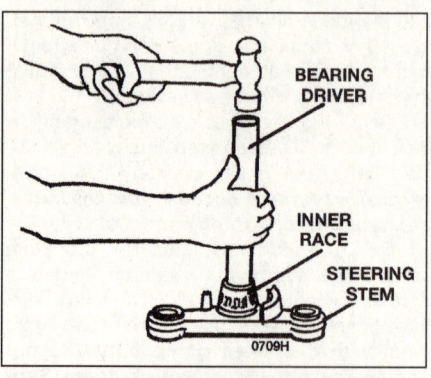

6.8 Drive the new lower race on with a suitable driver or length of pipe

under the race and replace it if it is worn, damaged or deteriorated.

8 Fit the new lower inner race onto the steering stem. A length of tubing with an internal diameter slightly larger than the steering stem will be needed to tap the new bearing into position **(see illustration)**. Ensure that the drift bears only on the inner edge of the race and does not contact its working surface.

9 Install the steering stem (see Section 5).

7   Front suspension

SKP/Stalker, all Runner 50 models and Runner FX125/FXR180

Note: *These models are fitted with upside-down telescopic forks.*

Seal renewal

1 Remove the front wheel and displace the brake caliper (see Chapter 7). Secure the caliper with a cable tie to avoid straining the hydraulic hose – note that there is no need to disconnect the hose

2 Remove the Allen bolt from the base of the fork slider and pull the axle/brake caliper bracket off the bottom **(see illustrations)**. If necessary, heat the bracket with a hot air gun to aid removal. Lever the seal out of the bottom of the fork tube and remove it from the slider **(see illustration)**.

7.4a Slide on the new seal . . .

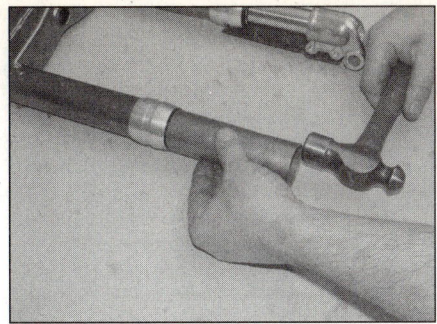

7.4b . . . and press it into position

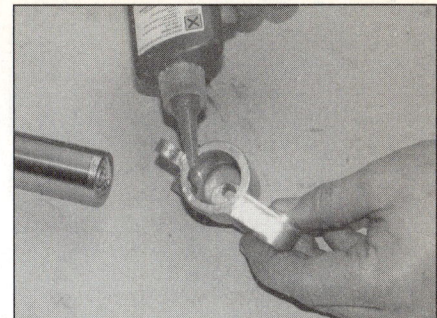

7.5a Apply locking compound to the inside of the bracket . . .

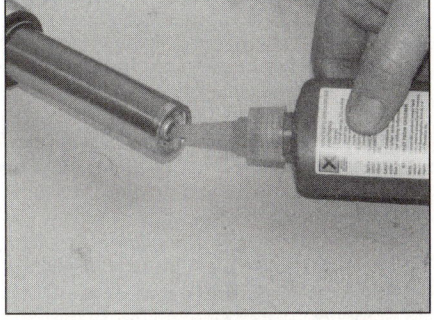

7.5b . . . and to the bolt threads

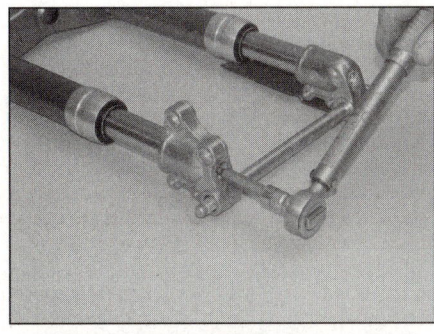

7.5c Use the axle as shown to prevent the slider rotating

3 Clean the bottom of the slider and the inside of the axle/brake caliper bracket and remove any traces of corrosion.

4 Apply grease to the inside and outside of the new seal, then fit it over the slider and press it into position in the bottom of the tube **(see illustrations)**.

5 Apply Loctite 242E or a similar locking compound to the inside of the axle/brake caliper bracket, then fit the bracket and tighten the bolt to the torque setting specified at the beginning of this Chapter **(see illustrations)**. If necessary, insert the axle through the bracket to prevent the slider rotating **(see illustration)**.

6 Install the front brake caliper and the front wheel (see Chapter 7). Check the operation of the front forks.

Disassembly

Note 1: *The internal components of these forks are retained by circlips which makes them difficult to disassemble. Also, some models have had undocumented changes to the internal components and may differ to those described. A certain amount of reader input may be required if the forks are to be dismantled completely.*

Note 2: *Always dismantle the fork legs separately and store all components in separate, clearly marked containers to avoid interchanging parts. Check the availability of new parts with a Gilera dealer before disassembling the forks.*

7 Follow the procedure in Steps 1 and 2, then remove the circlip from inside the bottom of the fork tube using a pair of internal circlip pliers **(see illustrations)**.

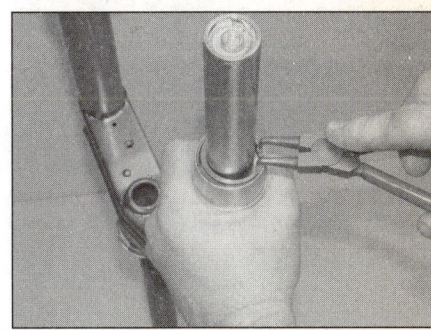

7.7b Removing the circlip

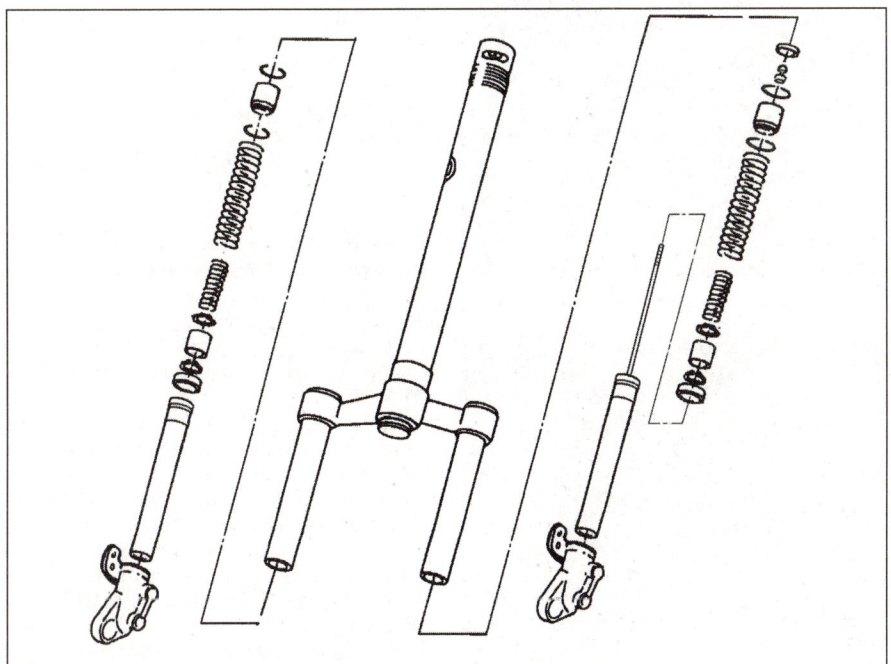

7.7a Upside-down front fork components

7.8 Remove the damper rod nut and cup washer

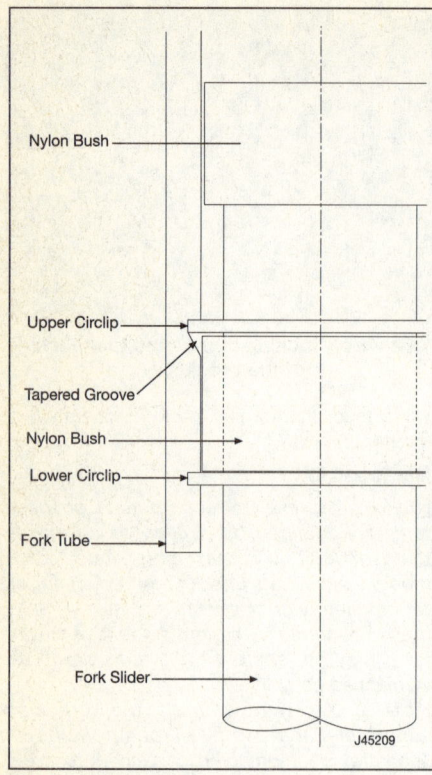

7.9 Arrangement of circlips inside the fork tube

Nylon Bush

Upper Circlip

Tapered Groove

Nylon Bush

Lower Circlip

Fork Tube

Fork Slider

J45209

8 If disassembling the left-hand fork leg, undo the damper rod nut on the top of the fork tube and remove the cup washer **(see illustration)**.

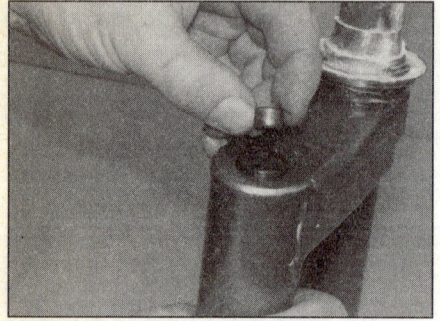

7.17a Remove the insert . . .

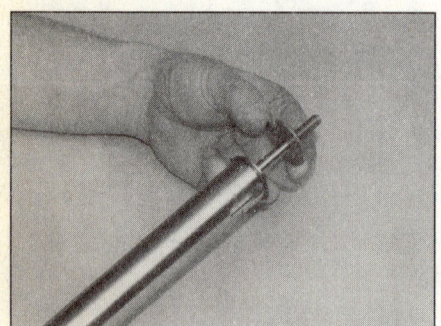

7.19 Install the spring seat

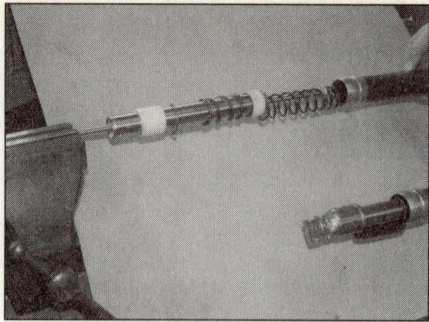

7.10 Pull the slider out of the fork tube

9 The slider assembly is retained by a circlip that fits in a tapered groove inside of the fork tube **(see illustration)**. Dislodge the circlip by pulling the slider down sharply. If necessary, screw a suitable bolt into the thread in the bottom of the slider, then tighten the bolt in a vice. Strike the underside of the steering stem with a heavy mallet to dislodge the circlip. If water has penetrated the seal, it is likely that the circlip will be very difficult to remove.

10 Pull the slider out of the fork tube together with the lower bush, retaining circlip, rebound spring, upper bush, spring seat and compression spring. Note the order of the fork components for reassembly **(see illustration)**. Remove the upper bush lower circlip, the bush and the upper circlip from the slider. Discard the circlips if they are corroded and fit new ones on reassembly. **Note:** *The damper is an integral part of the left-hand slider and cannot be removed from it.*

7.17b . . . and check the condition of the seal

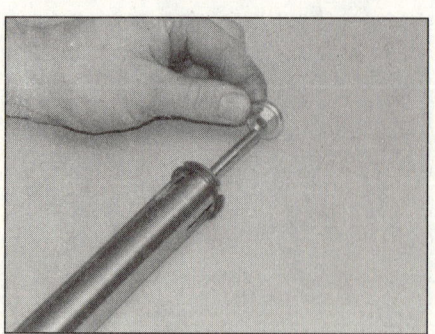

7.20 Thread the inner damper rod nut all the way on

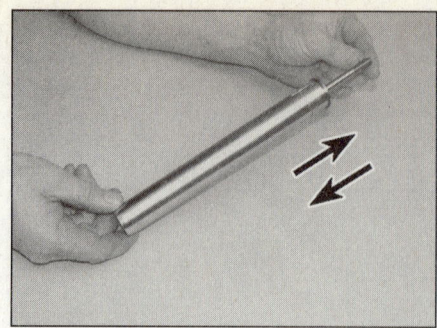

7.14 Check the action of the damper

Inspection

11 Clean all parts with a suitable solvent and dry them with compressed air, if available.
12 Examine the sliders for score marks, pitting or flaking of the chrome finish and excessive or abnormal wear. If available, check the sliders for runout using V-blocks and a dial gauge. If the runout is excessive, the sliders should be renewed.

⚠ *Warning: If the slider is bent, it should not be straightened; replace it with a new one.*

13 Look for dents in the fork tubes and fit a new steering stem assembly if any are found (see Section 5).
14 Check the action of the damper; it should operated smoothly and with resistance. If the rod slides freely in and out of the cartridge without any resistance, or if the rod binds in the cartridge, fit a new damper/slider assembly **(see illustration)**.
15 Examine the springs for cracks, sagging and other damage. If any defects are found, renew the springs in pairs, never renew only one spring.
16 Examine the working surfaces of each bush; if they are worn or scuffed, renew the bushes as a set.
17 Remove the insert from the seal in the top of the left-hand fork tube and check the condition of the seal **(see illustrations)**. If it is distorted or perished, fit a new seal.

Reassembly

18 Install the various components in the reverse order of removal, coating them with grease as you install them.
19 Ensure the spring seat is pressed firmly into the top of the slider **(see illustration)**.
20 If removed, thread the inner damper rod nut and cup washer all the way down the thread on the damper rod **(see illustration)**.
21 Install the upper circlip onto the slider, then slide on the upper bush and secure it with the lower circlip **(see illustrations)**. Ensure the circlips are securely located in their grooves and position the open ends of the circlips away from the slots in the top of the slider.
22 On the left-hand fork leg, pull the damper rod all the way out of the cartridge, then install the compression spring over the damper rod

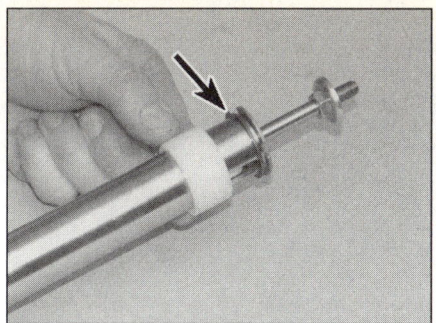

7.21a Install the upper circlip (arrowed) then slide on the upper bush . . .

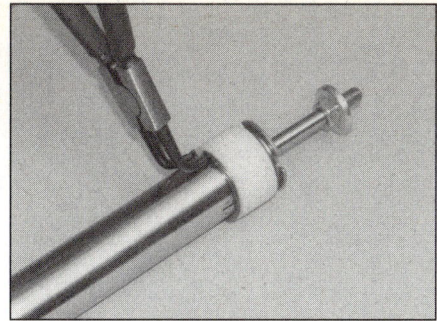

7.21b . . . and secure it with the lower circlip

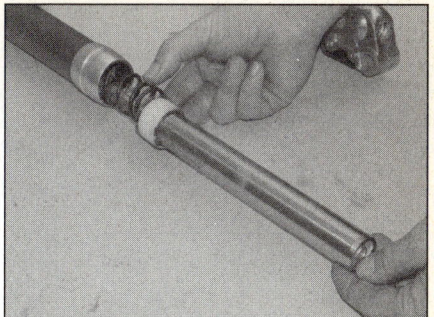

7.22a Install the spring and left-hand fork leg assembly

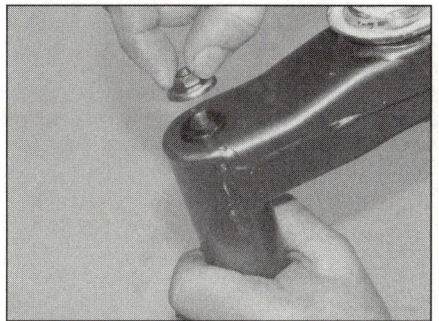

7.22b Fit the cup washer and nut . . .

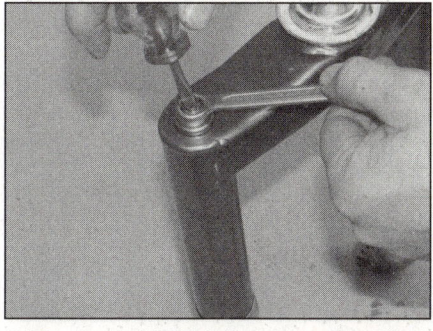

7.22c . . . and tighten the nut as described

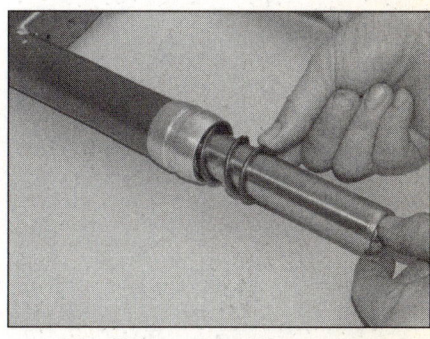

7.24 Slide on the rebound spring

and install the assembly into the fork tube **(see illustration)**. Locate the damper rod through the top seal. Apply a suitable non-permanent thread locking compound to the rod and secure it with the cup washer and nut, then hold the rod with a screwdriver to prevent it turning and tighten the nut securely **(see illustrations)**.

23 On the right-hand fork leg, install the compression spring and the slider into the fork tube.

24 Slide on the rebound spring and push it up inside the fork tube **(see illustration)**.

25 Using internal circlip pliers, locate the retaining circlip inside the fork tube above the groove for the lower circlip **(see illustration)**. Use a suitable length of tubing to push the circlip squarely into the tube until it locates in its groove.

26 Slide on the lower bush and tap it into position using the tubing **(see illustrations)**. Secure the bush with the lower circlip **(see illustration 7.7b)**.

27 Follow the procedure in Steps 4 and 5, then install the front brake caliper and the front wheel (see Chapter 7). Check the operation of the front forks.

Ice, Runner VX125, ST125, VXR180/200 and ST200, all DNA models

Note: *These models are fitted with conventional telescopic forks.*

Removal – Ice, Runner VX125, ST125, VXR180/200 and ST200

28 Remove the front wheel and displace the brake caliper (see Chapter 7).

29 Remove the front mudguard (see Chapter 8).

30 Where fitted, prise the circlip out of the groove in the top of the fork tube **(see illustration)**.

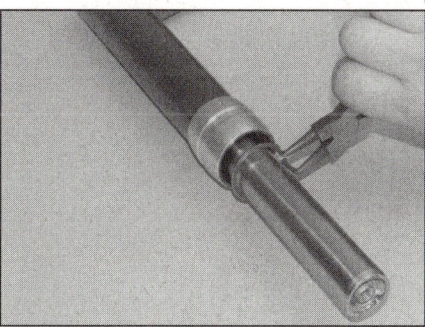

7.25 Install the retaining circlip as described

7.26b . . . and press it into position

31 Undo the fork leg clamp bolts then remove the fork leg by twisting it and pulling it downwards **(see illustrations)**. Note 1: *On Runner models, access to the clamp bolts is extremely restricted. If necessary, remove the*

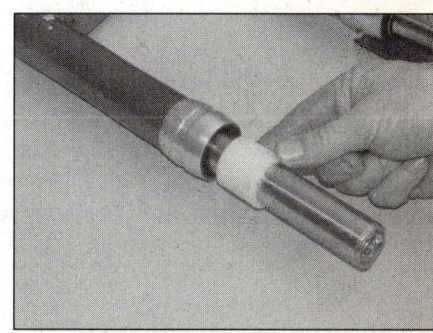

7.26a Slide on the lower bush . . .

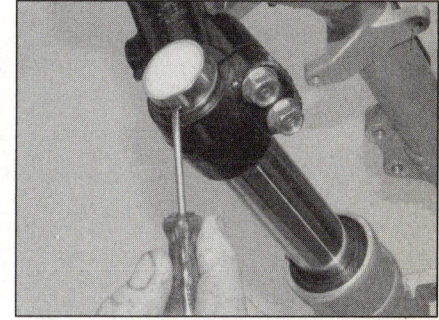

7.30 Remove the circlip from the top of the fork tube

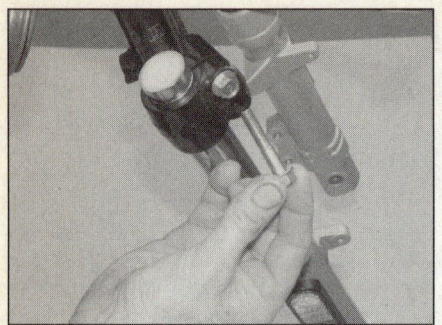

7.31a Undo the clamp bolts . . .

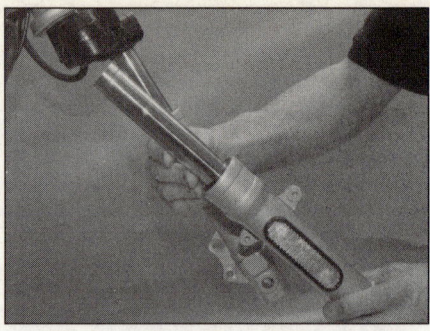

7.31b . . . and pull the fork leg out of the yoke

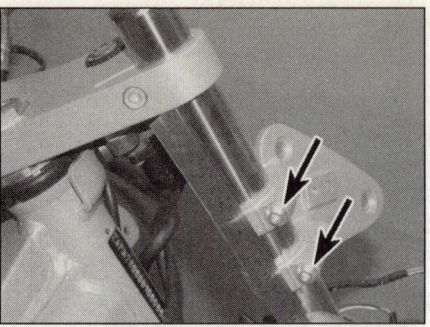

7.38 Note the position of the headlight bracket, then loosen the bolts (arrowed)

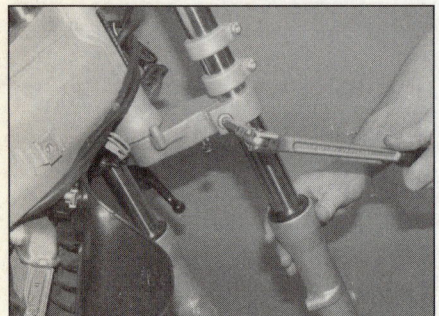

7.39a Loosen the lower clamp bolt . . .

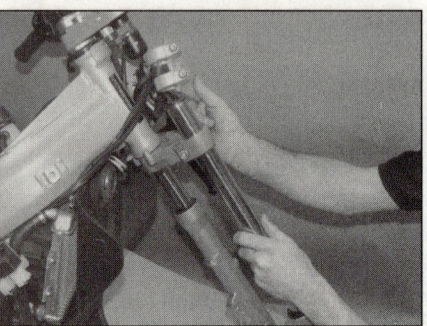

7.39b . . . then pull the leg out of the yoke and lift off the headlight bracket

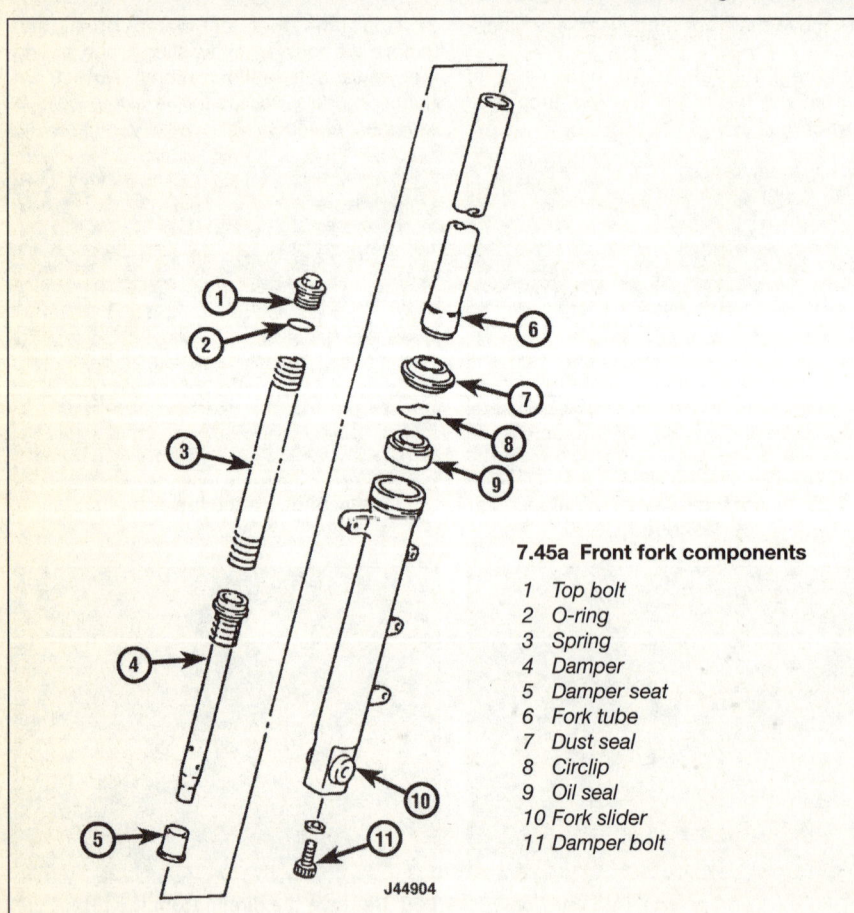

7.45a Front fork components

1 *Top bolt*
2 *O-ring*
3 *Spring*
4 *Damper*
5 *Damper seat*
6 *Fork tube*
7 *Dust seal*
8 *Circlip*
9 *Oil seal*
10 *Fork slider*
11 *Damper bolt*

J44904

steering stem (see Section 5). **Note 2:** *If the fork leg is going to be dismantled, loosen the clamp bolts, then push the leg up through the yoke a short distance and temporarily tighten the clamp bolts. Loosen the fork top nut, then loosen the clamp bolts and remove the fork leg.*

> **HAYNES HiNT**
> *If the fork legs are seized in the yoke, spray the area with penetrating oil and allow time for it to soak in before trying again.*

Installation – Ice, Runner VX125, ST125, VXR180/200 and ST200

32 Remove all traces of corrosion from the fork tubes and the fork yoke.

33 Slide the leg up through the yoke until the top edge of the fork tube is level with the top edge of the yoke. If applicable, align the circlip groove with the edge of the yoke and fit the circlip.

34 Tighten the clamp bolts to the torque setting specified at the beginning of this Chapter.

35 Install the remaining components in the reverse order of removal. Check the operation of the front forks.

Removal – DNA models

36 Follow Steps 28 and 29, then displace the handlebars (see Section 4). Measure the height of the fork tube above the top yoke.

37 Remove the headlight assembly (see Chapter 9). Note the routing of the various cables, hoses and wiring around the forks.

38 Note the position of the headlight bracket on the fork tube, then loosen the bracket clamp bolts **(see illustration)**.

39 Loosen the upper fork leg clamp bolt **(see illustration 5.3a)**. Support the leg and loosen the lower clamp bolt, then remove the fork leg by twisting it and pulling it downwards and lift off the headlight bracket **(see illustrations)**. **Note:** *If the fork leg is going to be dismantled, loosen the fork top bolt after loosening the upper clamp bolt and while the leg is still held in the bottom yoke.*

Installation – DNA models

40 Romovo all traces of corrosion from tho fork tubes and the yokes.

41 Slide the leg up through the bottom yoke and fit the headlight bracket onto the tube, ensuring it is the right way round. Ensure the cables, hoses and wiring are on the correct side of the leg as noted on removal, then slide the leg through the top yoke until it protrudes the measured distance above the yoke. Tighten the lower and then the upper clamp bolts to the torque setting specified at the beginning of this Chapter.

42 Position the headlight bracket as noted on removal and tighten the clamp bolts.

43 Install the remaining components in the reverse order of removal. Check the operation of the front forks.

Disassembly

Note: *Always dismantle the fork legs separately and store all components in separate, clearly marked containers to avoid interchanging parts. Check the availability of new parts with a Gilera dealer before disassembling the forks.*

44 Remove the fork leg (see the appropriate procedure above).

45 The damper bolt should be loosened at this stage. Invert the fork leg and compress the fork tube in the slider so that the spring exerts maximum pressure on the damper, then loosen the bolt in the base of the fork slider **(see illustrations)**.

46 If not already done, loosen the fork top bolt. Clamp the fork tube in a vice equipped with soft jaws, taking care not to overtighten or score the tube's surface, and loosen the top bolt. Some Ice models have a plastic plug fitted instead of a top bolt. Prise the plug out with a screwdriver and discard it as a new one must be fitted on reassembly.

47 Unscrew the top bolt and remove it. Note the O-ring fitted to the top bolt; if it is damaged, fit a new one on reassembly **(see illustration)**. On Ice models fitted with a plastic plug, once the plug has been removed, press down on the spring spacer inside the top of the fork tube and remove the circlip. Release the pressure on the compression spring spacer carefully.

⚠️ **Warning: The compression spring is pressing on the fork top bolt with considerable pressure. Unscrew the bolt very carefully, keeping**

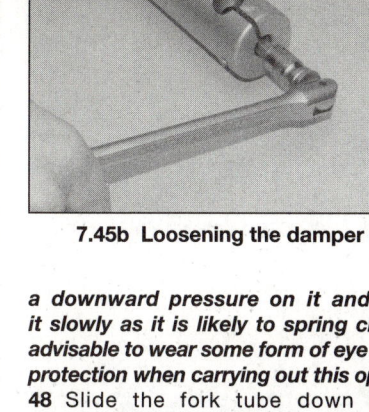
7.45b Loosening the damper bolt

a downward pressure on it and release it slowly as it is likely to spring clear. It is advisable to wear some form of eye and face protection when carrying out this operation.

48 Slide the fork tube down into the slider and withdraw the spring spacer and compression spring **(see illustrations)**. Note which way up the spring is fitted.

49 Invert the fork leg over a suitable container and pump the fork vigorously to expel as much fork oil as possible.

50 Remove the previously loosened damper bolt and its sealing washer from the bottom of the slider. Discard the sealing washer as a new one must be used on reassembly.

51 Pull the fork tube out of the slider, then withdraw the damper and rebound spring from inside the tube, noting how they fit **(see illustration)**. A bush is fitted in the lower end of the tube; remove it for safekeeping if it is loose.

52 Carefully prise out the dust seal from the top of the slider.

53 Where fitted, prise out the oil seal retaining clip, then carefully prise the oil seal out of the slider. Discard the oil and dust seals as a new ones must be used on reassembly.

Inspection

54 Clean all parts with a suitable solvent and dry them with compressed air, if available.

55 Examine the fork tubes for score marks, pitting or flaking of the chrome finish and excessive or abnormal wear. If available, check the tubes for runout using V-blocks and a dial gauge. If the amount of runout is excessive, the tubes should be renewed.

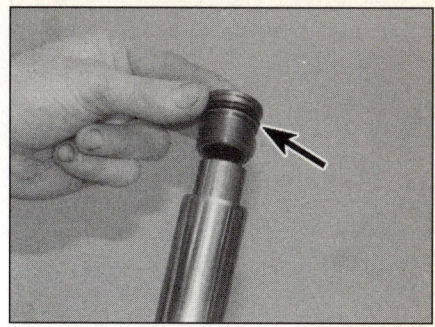
7.47 Remove the top bolt – note the O-ring (arrowed)

⚠️ *Warning: If the tube is bent, it should not be straightened; replace it with a new one.*

56 Examine the internal surface of each fork slider; if they are scored or scuffed, renew the sliders.

57 Examine the springs for cracks, sagging and other damage. If any defects are found, renew the springs in pairs, never renew only one spring. Gilera specify a spring free length for DNA models; measure the springs and if either one has sagged, renew them both.

Reassembly

58 If removed, press the bush into the bottom of the fork tube, then insert the rebound spring and damper. Insert the tube all the way into the slider, then insert the compression spring.

59 Fit a new sealing washer to the damper bolt and apply a few drops of a suitable, non-permanent thread-locking compound. Invert the fork leg, holding the damper in position with the compression spring, then install the bolt into the bottom of the slider and tighten it securely, or to the torque setting where specified. If the damper rotates inside the slider, hold the damper with spring pressure. Remove the compression spring once the damper bolt has been tightened.

60 Slide the tube all the way into the slider. Lubricate the new oil seal with the specified fork oil, then press it into place in the slider with its markings facing up **(see illustration)**. If necessary, use a suitable piece of tubing to tap the seal carefully into position; the tubing must be slightly smaller in diameter than the

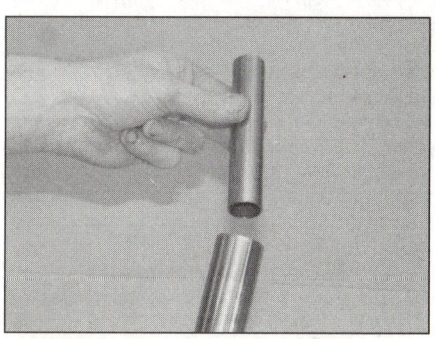
7.48a Withdraw the spring spacer . . .

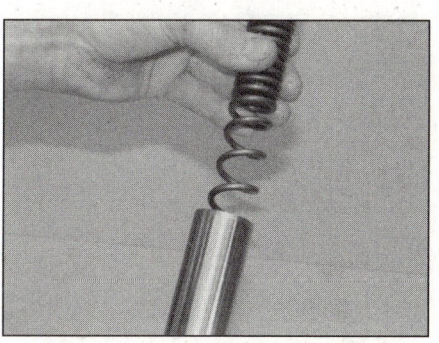
7.48b . . . and the compression spring

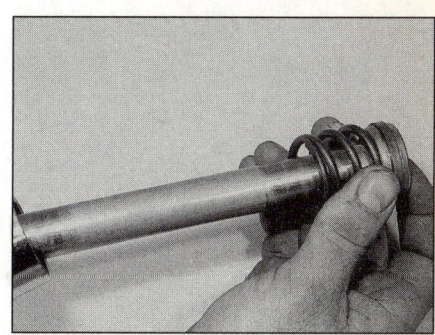
7.51 Withdraw the damper and rebound spring

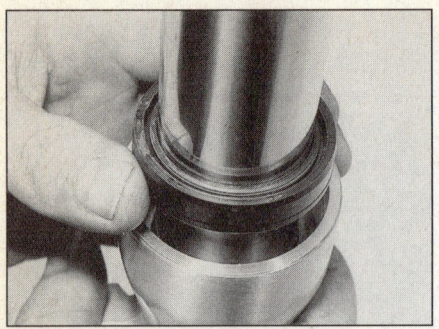

7.60a Install the oil seal with markings facing up

7.60b Install the oil seal retaining clip

7.61 Install the dust seal

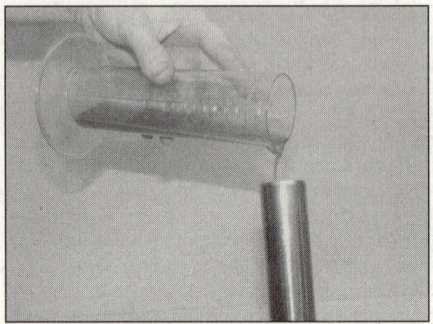

7.62 Pour the oil into the top of the tube

seal recess in the slider. If applicable, install the retaining clip, making sure it is correctly located in its groove **(see illustration)**.
61 Lubricate the new dust seal and press it into place in the top of the slider **(see illustration)**.

62 Slowly pour in the correct quantity of the specified grade of fork oil and carefully pump the fork to distribute the oil evenly **(see illustration)**.
63 Pull the fork tube out of the slider to its full

extension and install the compression spring with the wider-spaced coils facing down **(see illustration 7.48b)**. Install the spring spacer.
64 If necessary, fit a new O-ring to the fork top bolt. Keep the fork leg fully extended and press down on the spring spacer whilst threading the top bolt into the top of the fork tube. Turn the bolt carefully to ensure it is not cross-threaded. Hold the fork leg and tighten the top bolt securely or to the torque setting where specified. On Ice models fitted with a plastic plug, press down on the spring spacer and install the circlip. Ensure the circlip is securely located in its groove, then release the pressure on the spring spacer carefully. Press the plastic plug into the top of the fork tube.

⚠ **Warning: It will be necessary to compress the spring by pressing it down with the top bolt in order to engage the threads of the top bolt with the fork tube. This is a potentially dangerous operation and should be performed with care, using an assistant if necessary. Wipe off any excess oil before starting to prevent the possibility of slipping.**

65 Install the fork leg (see the appropriate procedure above).

---

8 Rear shock absorber

Preload adjustment

Note: *The shock absorbers fitted to some SKP/Stalker models have no provision for adjustment.*
1 Preload adjustment is made by turning the spring seat on one end of the shock absorber **(see illustration)**.
2 To alter the preload, turn the spring seat using a suitable C-spanner (one is provided in the toolkit). Align the setting required with the adjustment stopper **(see illustration)**.
3 On models with twin rear shocks, the preload setting should be the same for both units.

Removal

4 Support the scooter on its centre stand, then position a support under the rear wheel so that the engine does not drop when the shock absorber is removed. Check that the weight of the machine is off the rear suspension so that the shock is not compressed.
5 The lower end of the shock absorber is secured to the gearbox casing and, on twin shock models, to a stud on the right-hand subframe. Unscrew the nut and, where fitted, remove the bolt securing the bottom of the shock absorber and pull the shock away from its mounting **(see illustrations)**. **Note:** *On twin shock models, it may be necessary to displace the air filter housing and remove the silencer to access the lower fixing (see Chapter 4).*

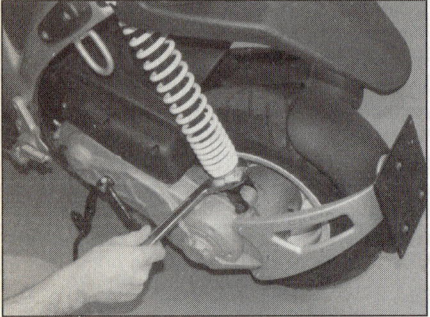

8.1 Adjusting the spring preload – Ice shown

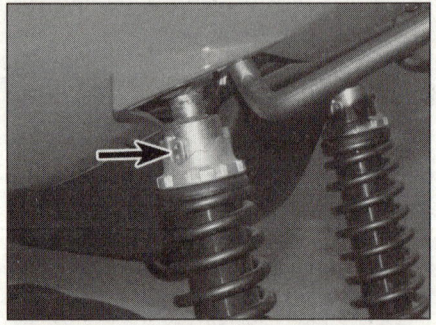

8.2 Align the setting with the stopper (arrowed)

8.5a Unscrew the nut (arrowed) and withdraw the bolt . . .

8.5b . . . or remove the nut and washer – twin shock model shown

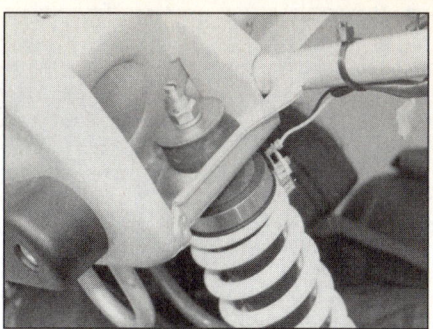

**8.6a Upper shock absorber mounting –
Ice shown**

**8.6b Upper shock absorber mounting –
DNA shown**

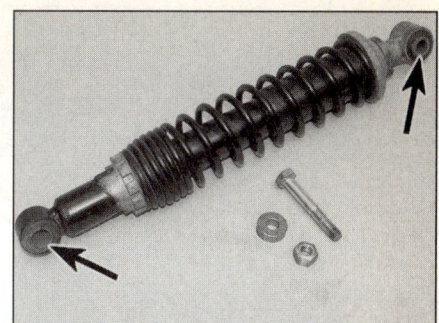

**8.10 Check the mounting bolts and bushes
(arrowed) for wear**

6 The upper end of the shock absorber is secured to the frame either by a nut and washer assembly, or by a nut and bolt **(see illustrations)**. Lift up or remove the seat, or remove the body panels as necessary according to model to access the upper shock mounting(s) (see Chapter 7).

7 As required, position a ring spanner on the nut and hold the centre of the damper rod with a screwdriver to prevent it turning, then undo the nut. Note the location of the washers and rubber bush, then manoeuvre the shock

away from the machine. Alternatively, undo the upper mounting nut, then support the shock and withdraw the bolt, noting the position of any spacers.

Inspection

8 Inspect the shock absorber for obvious physical damage and the coil spring for looseness, cracks or signs of fatigue.

9 Inspect the damper rod for signs of bending, pitting and oil leaks.

10 Inspect the pivot hardware at the top and bottom of the shock for wear or damage **(see illustration)**.

11 Individual parts can be obtained for the shock absorber on certain models – check availability with a Gilera dealer before dismantling the unit. Carefully note the relative positions of all components and how and which way up they fit **(see illustration)**. Compress the spring using a coil spring compressor by just enough to remove the pressure on the spring seat at the top. Unscrew the top nut and remove the various components according to model, noting their order, then carefully release the compressor until the spring is relaxed. Remove the spring, noting which way up it fits. Install the new components and rebuild the shock in a reverse of the disassembly procedure.

Installation

12 Installation is the reverse of removal. Tighten the shock absorber mountings to the torque settings specified at the beginning of this Chapter.

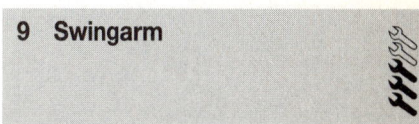

9 Swingarm

Removal

1 Remove the engine and support the frame on an auxiliary stand (see Chapter 2A, 2B or 2C). Where fitted, remove the bodywork to access the front mounting for the swingarm (see Chapter 8).

2 The swingarm is secured to the frame by a pivot bolt. Undo the nut on the end of the bolt, then withdraw the bolt and remove the swingarm, noting how it fits **(see illustrations)**. On Runner FX125, FXR180, VX125, VXR180/200, ST125, ST200 and DNA 125/180 models, the swingarm assembly incorporates a balance spring. Unhook the spring before removing the swingarm mounting bolt **(see illustration)**.

Inspection

3 Thoroughly clean the swingarm components, removing all traces of dirt, corrosion and grease.

4 Inspect the swingarm closely, looking for obvious signs of wear to the pivot bolt holes, and cracks or distortion due to accident damage. A damaged or worn component must be renewed.

5 On Runner FX125, FXR180, VX125, VXR180/200, ST125, ST200 and DNA 125/180 models, the swingarm is a two-piece assembly

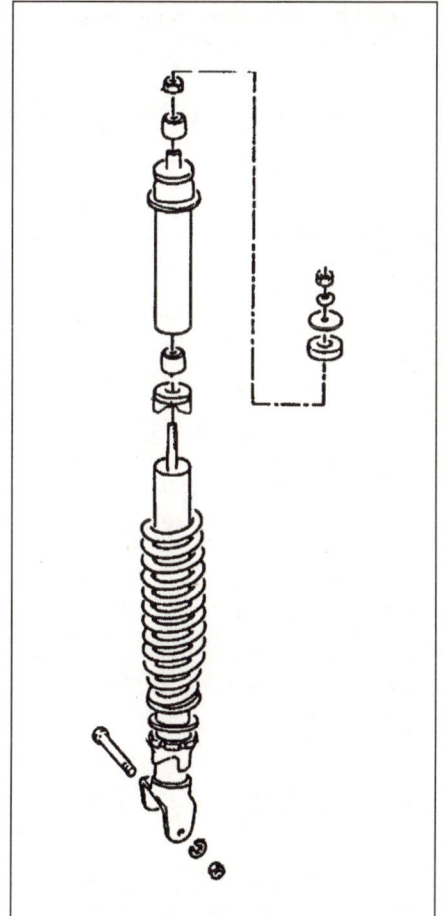

8.11 Rear shock absorber components

9.2a Withdraw the pivot bolt . . .

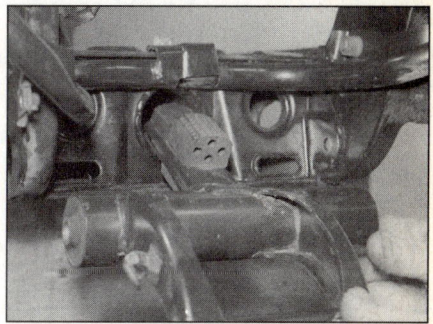

9.2b . . . and remove the swingarm

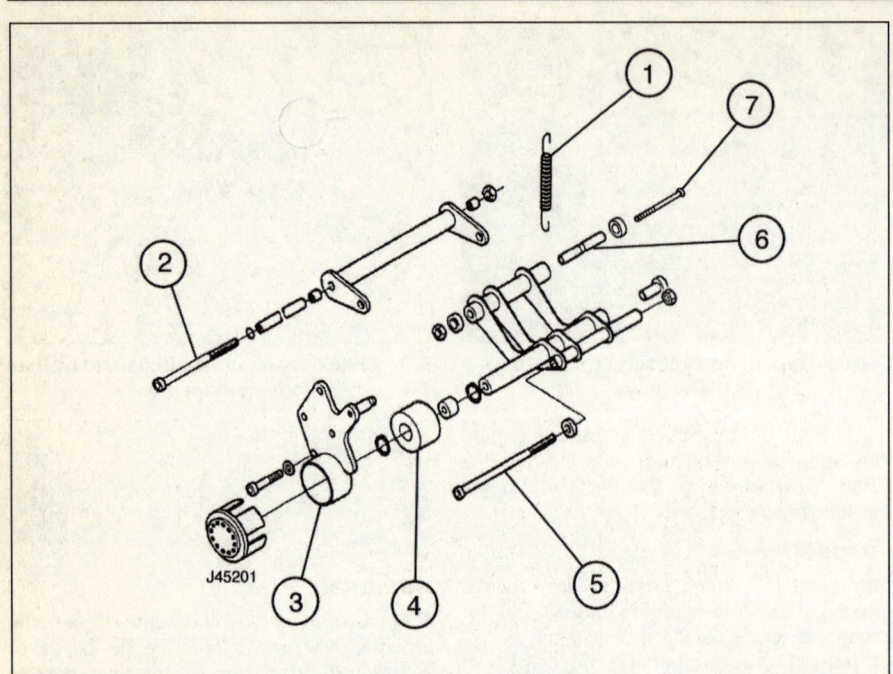

9.2c Swingarm components –
Runner FX125, FXR180, VX125, VXR180/200, ST125, ST200 and DNA 125/180 models

1 Balance spring   3 Support flange   5 Engine mounting   6 Pivot bolt bush
2 Pivot bolt   4 Silentbloc bush   bolt   7 Central pivot bolt

9.7 Check the condition of the bushes

9.8 Where fitted, check the damping rubbers

(see illustration 9.2c). If required, undo the nut on the end of the central pivot bolt, then withdraw the bolt and separate the assembly, noting the position of the pivot bushes and spacers.

6 Check the swingarm pivot bolt and mounting bolt(s) for straightness by rolling them on a flat surface such as a piece of plate glass (first wipe off all old grease and remove any corrosion using steel wool).

7 Check the various bushes for wear, cracks and deterioration **(see illustration)**. On some models, the Silentbloc bushes can be renewed although they are a very tight fit and the job is best done by a Gilera dealer or specialist engineer. On other models a new swingarm will have to be fitted.

8 Check the condition of the swingarm damping rubbers, where fitted, and renew them if necessary **(see illustration)**.

Installation

9 Installation is the reverse of removal. Smear some grease onto the pivot bolt(s) and metal bushes before assembly and tighten the nut(s) to the torque setting specified at the beginning of this Chapter. On Runner FX125, FXR180, VX125, VXR180/200, ST125, ST200 and DNA 125/180 models, install the balance spring.

10 Install the engine.

11 Check the operation of the rear suspension before taking the machine on the road.

Chapter 7
Brakes, wheels and tyres

Refer to the beginning of Chapter 1 for model identification details

Contents

Degrees of difficulty

Easy, suitable for novice with little experience	**Fairly easy,** suitable for beginner with some experience	**Fairly difficult,** suitable for competent DIY mechanic 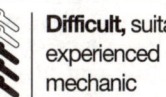	**Difficult,** suitable for experienced DIY mechanic	**Very difficult,** suitable for expert DIY or professional 

Specifications

Disc brake

Fluid type	DOT 4
Pad minimum thickness.	1.5 mm
Disc maximum runout	0.1 mm
Front disc minimum thickness – Ice.	3.5 mm

Drum brake

Lining minimum thickness	1.5 mm
Brake lever freeplay	10 to 15 mm

Wheels

Maximum wheel runout (front and rear)	
Axial (side-to-side)	2.0 mm
Radial (out-of-round)	2.0 mm
Maximum axle runout (front and rear)	0.2 mm

Tyres

Tyre pressures and sizes	see Chapter 1

Torque settings

Brake caliper mounting bolts	20 to 25 Nm
Brake caliper joining bolts	20 to 25 Nm
Brake disc mounting bolts	
SKP/Stalker up to 2004, all Runner 50 models, Runner FX125/FXR180 .	7 Nm
Stalker 2005-on	8 to 12 Nm
DNA 50	11 to 13 Nm (RST model – 8 to 12 Nm)
Ice.	5 to 6.5 Nm
Runner VX125, ST125, VXR180/200, ST200 (front)	11 to 13 Nm (RST and ST models – 5 to 6.5 Nm)
Runner VX125, ST125, VXR180/200, ST200 (rear).	14 to 17 Nm (RST and ST models – 5 to 6.5 Nm)
DNA 125/180 (front)	5 to 6.5 Nm
DNA 125/180 (rear).	14 to 17 Nm
Brake hose banjo bolts	
SKP/Stalker up to 2004, all Runner 50 models	8 to 12 Nm
Stalker 2005-on, Runner FX125, FXR180, VX125, VXR180/200,	
ST125, ST200	20 to 25 Nm
Brake hose-to-caliper banjo bolt – Ice, all DNA models	20 to 25 Nm
Brake hose-to-master cylinder banjo bolt – Ice, all DNA models	16 to 20 Nm
Front axle nut	
SKP/Stalker up to 2004, all Runner 50 models, Runner FX125	
and FXR180	40 to 50 Nm
Ice, Stalker 2005-on, Runner VX125, VXR180/200, ST125, ST200 . .	45 to 50 Nm
Front axle – all DNA models.	45 to 50 Nm
Front axle pinch bolt – all DNA models	20 to 22 Nm (RST model – 6 to 7 Nm)
Rear wheel hub nut	
SKP/Stalker up to 2004, all Runner 50 models	90 to 110 Nm
Ice, Stalker 2005-on, DNA (all models), Runner VX125,	
VXR180/200, ST125, ST200	104 to 126 Nm
Runner FX125, FXR180 (nut may be marked 8.8)*	150 to 170 Nm
*If the nut is marked 6S, tighten it to 110 – 130 Nm	
Rear wheel bolts	
SKP/Stalker, all Runner 50 models, Runner VX125,	
VXR180/200, ST125, ST200, all DNA models	20 to 25 Nm
Rear subframe mounting bolts.	20 to 25 Nm

1 General information

The front brake is a single, hydraulically operated disc with either an opposed-piston (one piston on each side of the caliper), or twin piston sliding caliper (two pistons on the same side of the caliper). The brake master cylinder is integral with the fluid reservoir on the right handlebar.

The rear brake is either a cable-operated single leading shoe drum or an hydraulically operated disc. The brake master cylinder is integral with the fluid reservoir on the left handlebar.

All models covered in this manual are fitted with cast alloy wheels designed for tubeless tyres only.

Caution: Disc brake components rarely require disassembly. Do not disassemble components unless absolutely necessary. If an hydraulic brake hose is loosened, the entire system must be disassembled, drained, cleaned and then properly filled and bled upon reassembly. Do not use solvents on internal brake components. Solvents will cause the seals to swell and distort. Use only clean brake fluid or denatured alcohol for cleaning. Use care when working with brake fluid as it can injure your eyes and it will damage painted surfaces and plastic parts.

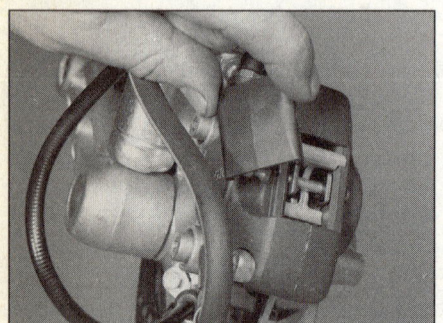

2.1 Remove the cover from the caliper

2.2a Remove the retaining clip . . .

2 Brake pads

⚠ *Warning: The dust created by the brake may contain asbestos which is harmful to your health. Never blow it out with compressed air and don't inhale any of it. An approved filtering mask should be worn when working on the brakes.*

Removal

Opposed piston caliper

Note: *On some models, due to a lack of clearance, it may be necessary to displace the brake caliper to remove the pads (see Section 3).*

1 Where fitted, remove the pad cover from the caliper **(see illustration)**.

2 Remove the retaining clip from the end of the pad pin, then draw the pad pin out using pliers **(see illustrations)**. Note how the pin keeps the pad spring pressed onto the pads, then remove the spring, noting which way round it fits **(see illustration)**.

3 Lift the pads out of the caliper **(see illustration)**.

Twin piston sliding caliper

4 Displace the brake caliper (see Section 3).

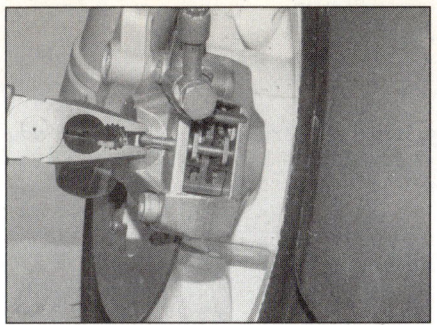

2.2b . . . then draw out the pad pin

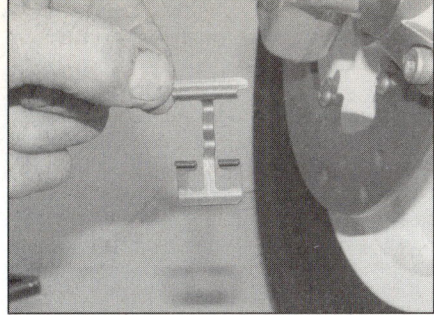

2.2c Note which way round the spring fits

2.3 Lift out the pads

5 Unscrew the pad pins and withdraw them from the caliper, then lift out the pads noting how they fit **(see illustrations)**.

6 The pad spring is a press fit in the back of the caliper; note its location and remove it if it is loose or damaged **(see illustration)**.

Note: *Do not operate the brake lever while the pads are out of the caliper.*

Inspection

7 Inspect the surface of each pad for contamination and check that the friction material has not worn to or beyond the specified minimum thickness **(see illustration)**. If either pad is worn down to, or beyond, the service limit, fouled with oil or grease, or heavily scored or damaged, both pads must be renewed as a set. **Note:** *It is not possible to degrease the friction material; if the pads are contaminated in any way they must be renewed.*

8 If the pads are in good condition, clean them carefully, using a fine wire brush which is completely free of oil and grease to remove all traces of road dirt and corrosion. Any areas of glazing may be removed using emery cloth, bearing in mind the *Warning* above.

9 Check the condition of the brake disc (see Section 4).

10 Remove all traces of corrosion from the pad pin(s) and pad spring. Inspect the pin and spring for signs of wear and renew them if necessary. Inspect the retaining clip, where fitted, and renew it if it is sprained or badly corroded.

Installation

11 If new pads are being fitted, push the pistons as far back into the caliper as possible using hand pressure or a piece of wood as leverage. Due to the increased friction material thickness of new pads, it may be necessary

to remove the master cylinder reservoir cover and diaphragm and siphon out some fluid.

12 Smear the backs of the pads and the shank of the pad pin with copper-based grease, making sure that none gets on the front or sides of the pads.

13 On the twin piston sliding caliper, ensure the pad spring is a firm fit in the caliper and install the pads in the correct order **(see illustrations)**.

14 Insert the pads into the caliper so that the friction material faces the disc.

15 On the opposed piston caliper, install the pad spring, then press the pin into position through the caliper and the pads, ensuring the spring is correctly located under the pin **(see illustration 2.2b)**. Fit the retaining clip. If applicable, fit the pad cover.

16 On the twin piston sliding caliper, install the pad pins and tighten them securely. Install the caliper (see Section 3).

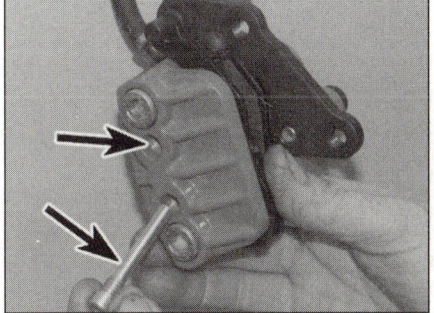

2.5a Remove the pad pins (arrowed) . . .

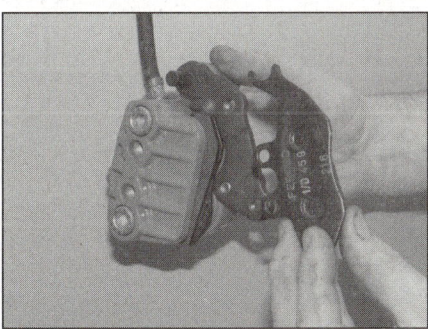

2.5b . . . then lift out the pads

2.6 Location of the pad spring

2.7 Check the amount of friction material remaining on each pad

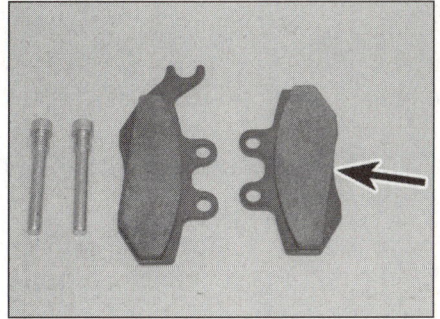

2.13a On twin piston calipers, the smaller pad (arrowed) . . .

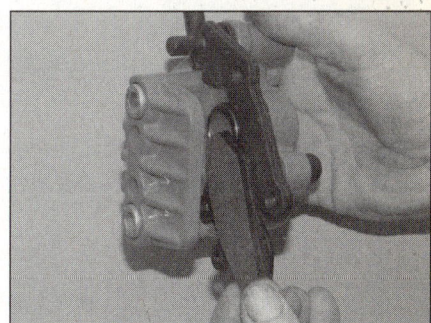

2.13b . . . fits against the pistons

17 If necessary, top-up the master cylinder reservoir (see *Daily (pre-ride) checks*).
18 Operate the brake lever several times to bring the pads into contact with the disc. Check the operation of the brake before riding the scooter.

3 Brake caliper

⚠ *Warning: If a caliper indicates the need for an overhaul (usually due to leaking fluid or sticky operation), all old brake fluid should be flushed from the system. Also, the dust created by the brakes may contain asbestos, which is harmful to your health. Never blow it out with compressed air and don't inhale any of it. An approved filtering mask should be worn when working on the brakes. Do not, under any circumstances, use petroleum-based solvents to clean brake parts. Use clean brake fluid, brake cleaner or denatured alcohol only.*

Note 1: *Before overhauling the caliper, check with a Gilera dealer as to the availability of a seal kit and pistons for your model.*

Removal

1 If the caliper is being overhauled, remove the brake pads (see Section 2), then loosen and lightly retighten the bolts which join the caliper halves **(see illustrations)**. If the caliper is just being displaced, the pads can be left in place and the caliper half joining bolts should not be disturbed.

2 If the caliper is just being displaced, do not disconnect the brake hose. If the caliper is being overhauled, note the alignment of the banjo union on the caliper, then undo the banjo bolt and separate the hose from the caliper **(see illustration)**. Wrap a plastic bag tightly around the banjo union to minimise fluid loss and prevent dirt entering the system. Discard the sealing washers as new ones must be used on installation. **Note:** *If you are planning to overhaul the caliper and don't have a source of compressed air to blow out the pistons, just loosen the banjo bolt at this stage and retighten it lightly. The bike's hydraulic system can then be used to force the pistons out of the body once the pads have been removed. Disconnect the hose once the pistons have been sufficiently displaced.*

3 Unscrew the caliper mounting bolts, and slide the caliper off the disc **(see illustrations)**. On some models, there is very little clearance between the caliper and the wheel; ease the pistons back into the caliper by pressing on the brake pads to gain clearance between the pads and the disc, but do not lever directly against the disc. If the caliper is just being displaced, secure it to a convenient part of the machine with a cable tie to prevent straining the brake hose. **Note:** *Do not operate the brake lever while the caliper is off the disc.*

Overhaul

4 On the twin piston sliding caliper, pull off the caliper bracket, noting how it fits **(see illustration)**.
5 Clean the exterior of the caliper with denatured alcohol or brake system cleaner.
6 On the opposed piston caliper, displace the pistons as far as possible from the caliper body, either pumping them out by operating the brake lever, or forcing them out with compressed air. If compressed air is used, place a wad of rag between the pistons to act as a cushion, then direct the air into the fluid inlet. Use only low pressure to ease the pistons out – if the air pressure is too high and the pistons are forced out, the caliper and/or pistons may be damaged. Make sure both pistons are displaced at the same time. Unscrew the joining bolts and separate the caliper halves, then lift out the pistons. Mark each piston and the caliper body with a felt marker to ensure that the pistons can be matched to their original bores on reassembly. Remove the O-ring from one half of the caliper body and discard it as a new one must be used.

⚠ *Warning: Never place your fingers in front of the pistons in an attempt to catch or protect them when applying compressed air, as serious injury could result.*

7 On the twin piston sliding caliper, unscrew the joining bolts and separate the caliper halves. The pistons can be displaced either by pumping them out by operating the brake

3.1a Caliper half joining bolts (arrowed) – Ice shown

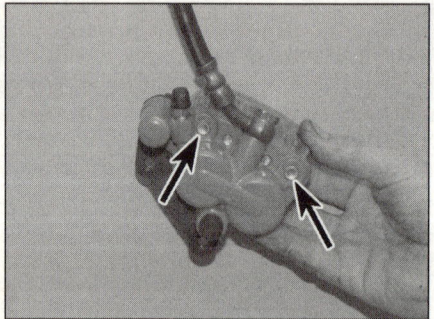

3.1b Caliper half joining bolts (arrowed) – DNA shown

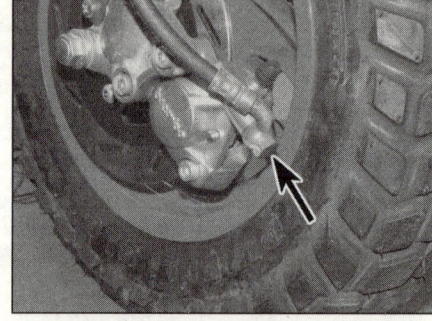

3.2 Note the alignment of the union, then undo the banjo bolt (arrowed)

3.3a Remove the caliper mounting bolts (arrowed) . . .

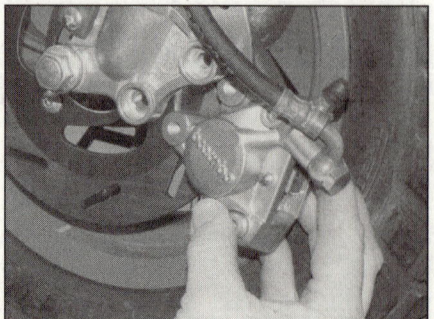

3.3b . . . and slide the caliper off the disc

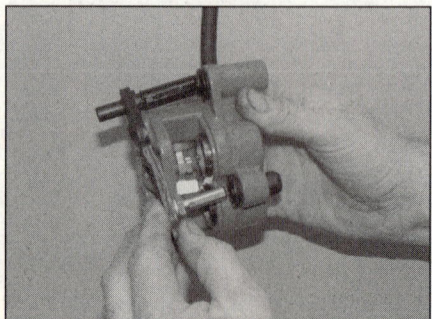

3.4 Separate the mounting bracket from the caliper

lever, or forcing them out with compressed air. If compressed air is used, use only low pressure to ease the pistons out – if the air pressure is too high and the pistons are forced out, the caliper and/or pistons may be damaged. Make sure both pistons are displaced at the same time. Mark each piston and the caliper body with a felt marker to ensure that the pistons can be matched to their original bores on reassembly.

8 Using a wooden or plastic tool to avoid damaging the caliper bores, remove the dust seals and the piston seals from the bores **(see illustration)**. Discard them as new ones must be used on installation.

9 Clean the pistons and bores with denatured alcohol, clean brake fluid or brake system cleaner. If compressed air is available, use it to dry the parts thoroughly (make sure it's filtered and unlubricated).

Caution: Do not, under any circumstances, use a petroleum-based solvent to clean brake parts.

10 Inspect the caliper bores and pistons for signs of corrosion, nicks and burrs and loss of plating. If surface defects are present, the pistons or the caliper assembly must be renewed as required. If the caliper is in bad shape the master cylinder should also be checked.

11 Lubricate the new piston seals with clean brake fluid and install them in their grooves in the caliper bores.

12 Lubricate the new dust seals with clean brake fluid and install them in their grooves in the caliper bores.

13 Lubricate the pistons with clean brake fluid and install them closed-end first into the caliper bores. Using your thumbs, push the pistons all the way in, making sure they enter the bores squarely.

14 On the opposed piston caliper, fit a new O-ring into one half of the caliper body, then join the halves together and tighten the bolts. On the twin piston sliding caliper, assemble the caliper halves and tighten the joining bolts. If required, to provide support, the bolts can be tightened to the specified torque after the calipers have been installed.

15 On the twin piston sliding caliper, clean all old grease from the caliper bracket slider pins and the rubber boots in the caliper body. Check that the boots are in good condition and not split or perished, then smear silicone grease over the slider pins and insert the bracket in the caliper **(see illustration 3.4)**.

Installation

16 If removed, install the brake pads (see Section 2).

17 Install the caliper on the brake disc making sure the pads sit squarely each side of the disc.

18 Install the caliper mounting bolts and tighten them to the torque setting specified at the beginning of this Chapter.

19 If the caliper was just displaced, operate the brake lever several times to bring the pads into contact with the disc.

3.8 Removing the dust seal – a pencil works well

20 If the caliper was overhauled and the joining bolts were not fully tightened earlier, tighten them to the specified torque setting.

21 If removed, connect the brake hose to the caliper, using new sealing washers on each side of the banjo union. Align the union as noted on removal. Tighten the banjo bolt to the torque setting specified at the beginning of this Chapter.

22 If the caliper was overhauled, top-up the master cylinder reservoir (see *Daily (pre-ride) checks*) and bleed the hydraulic system (see Section 8).

23 Check that there are no fluid leaks.

24 Check the operation of the brake before riding the scooter.

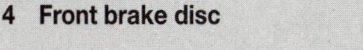

4	Front brake disc

Inspection

1 Inspect the surface of the disc for score marks and other damage. Light scratches are normal after use and won't affect brake operation, but deep grooves and heavy score marks will reduce braking efficiency and accelerate pad wear. If a disc is badly grooved it must be machined or renewed.

2 To check disc runout, support the scooter on its centre stand with the front wheel raised off the ground. Attach a dial gauge to the front fork with the gauge pointer touching the surface of the disc about 13 mm (1/2 in)

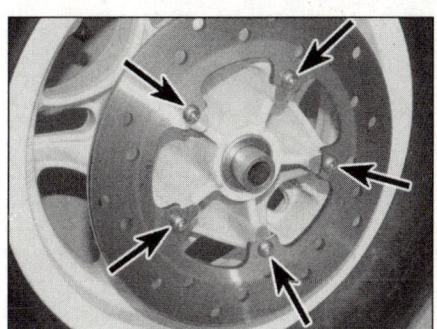

4.5 Brake disc mounting bolts

4.2 Set-up for checking brake disc runout

from the outer edge **(see illustration)**. Rotate the wheel and watch the gauge needle, comparing the reading with the limit listed in the Specifications at the beginning of this Chapter. If the runout is greater than the service limit, check the wheel bearings for play (see Section 15). If the bearings are worn, renew them, then repeat this check. If the disc runout is still excessive, the disc will have to be renewed.

3 The disc must not be allowed to wear or be machined too thin. Gilera only provide a minimum thickness specification for the front disc on the Ice model, however if the disc is obviously worn where the pads are in contact, and a substantial ridge can be felt between the rim and the contact area, it must be renewed.

Removal

4 Remove the front wheel (see Section 13).

5 Mark the relationship of the disc to the wheel, so it can be installed in the same position if required. Unscrew the disc retaining bolts, loosening them a little at a time in a criss-cross pattern to avoid distorting the disc, then remove the disc **(see illustration)**. If necessary, clean the threads of the bolts with a wire brush.

Installation

6 Ensure the mating surface of the wheel is clean, then install the disc, making sure the directional arrow points in the direction of normal wheel rotation **(see illustration)**. If applicable, align the previously applied reference marks.

4.6 Disc directional arrow

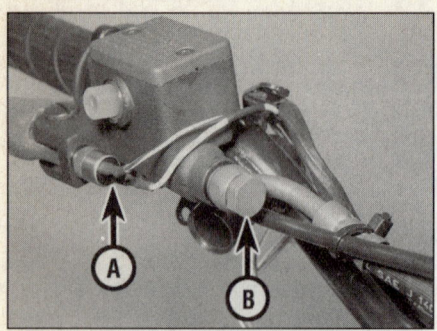

5.4a Brake switch electrical connectors (A), brake hose banjo bolt (B)

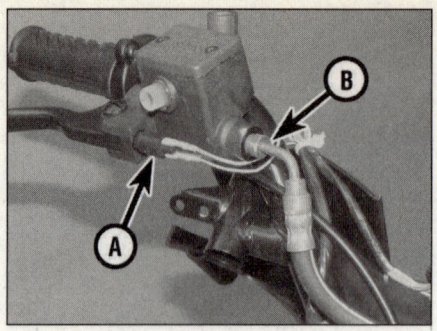

5.4b Brake switch electrical connectors (A), brake pipe gland nut (B)

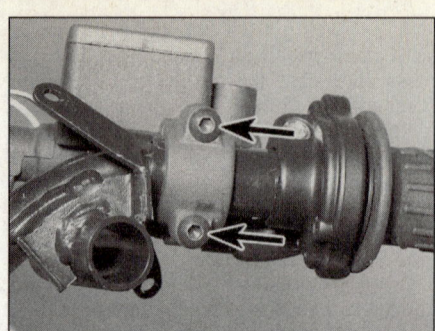

5.6 Master cylinder clamp bolts (arrowed)

7 Apply a suitable non-permanent thread locking compound to the disc retaining bolts, then install the bolts and tighten them in a criss-cross pattern evenly and progressively to the torque setting specified at the beginning of this Chapter. Clean the disc using acetone or brake system cleaner. If a new disc has been installed, remove any protective coating from its working surfaces.
8 Install the wheel (see Section 13).
9 Operate the front brake lever several times to bring the brake pads into contact with the disc. Check the operation of the brake before riding the scooter.

5 Brake master cylinder

Note 1: *Before dismantling the master cylinder, check with a Gilera dealer as to the availability of a cylinder rebuild kit for your model.*
Note 2: *If the master cylinder is just being displaced and not completely removed from the scooter, do not remove the brake lever or disconnect the brake hose. Support the master cylinder in an upright position to prevent air entering the system.*

1 If the master cylinder is leaking fluid, or if the lever does not produce a firm feel when the brake is applied and bleeding the brakes does not help (see Section 8), and the hydraulic hoses are in good condition, then the master cylinder must be overhauled or renewed.

Removal

2 The front brake master cylinder is mounted on the right handlebar. The master cylinder has an integral fluid reservoir and is activated directly by pressure from the brake lever. If applicable, remove the handlebar covers for access (see Chapter 8).
3 Remove the front brake lever (see Chapter 6, Section 4).
4 Disconnect the electrical connectors from the brake light switch **(see illustrations)**. If required, remove the switch.
5 Note the alignment of the brake pipe union on the master cylinder, then undo the banjo bolt or gland nut and separate the hose from the master cylinder **(see illustrations 5.4a and b)**. Wrap a plastic bag tightly around the banjo union to minimise fluid loss and prevent dirt entering the system, and secure the hose in an upright position. Discard the sealing washers as new ones must be used on installation.
6 Unscrew the master cylinder clamp bolts, then lift the master cylinder off the handlebar **(see illustration)**.
7 Remove the reservoir cover retaining screws and lift off the cover, the diaphragm plate and the diaphragm. Drain the brake fluid from the reservoir into a suitable container. Wipe any remaining fluid out of the reservoir with a clean rag.
Caution: Disassembly, overhaul and reassembly of the brake master cylinder must be done in a spotlessly clean work area to avoid contamination and possible failure of the brake hydraulic system components. To prevent damage from spilled brake fluid, always cover the surrounding bodywork when working on the master cylinder.

Overhaul

8 Before disassembling the master cylinder, read through the entire procedure and make sure that you have obtained all the new parts required including some new DOT 4 brake fluid and some clean rags **(see illustration)**.

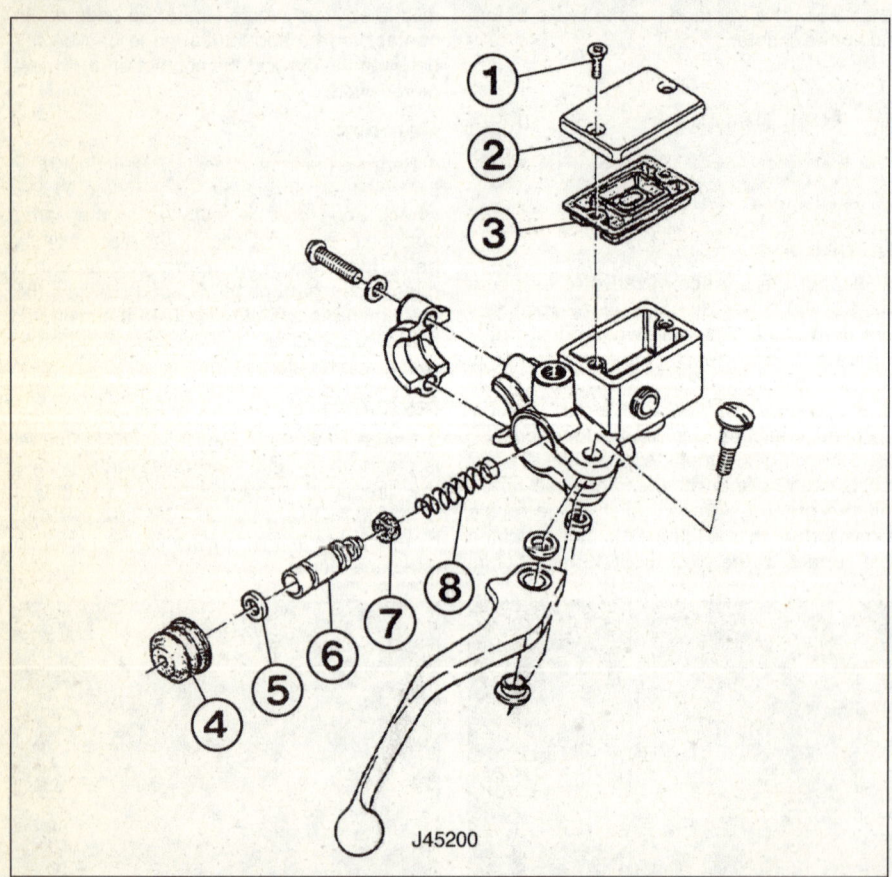

5.8 Front brake master cylinder components

1 Cover screw	3 Diaphragm	5 Retaining ring	7 Seal
2 Reservoir cover	4 Dust boot	6 Piston	8 Spring

6.2a Note the location of the pad spring (arrowed) . . .

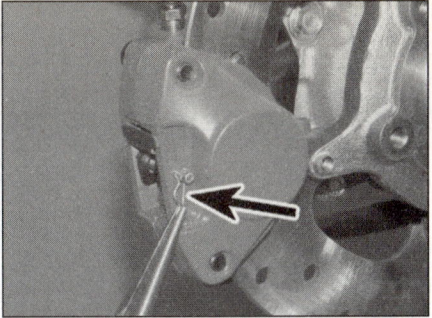

6.2b . . . then remove the retaining clip . . .

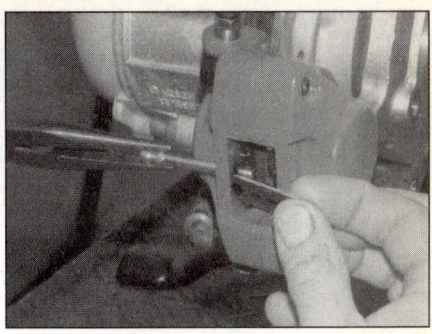

6.2c . . . and pad pin

9 Remove the dust boot. Using a small screwdriver, prise the retaining ring out from the recess in the end of the master cylinder, then withdraw the piston, seal and spring, noting how they fit **(see illustration 5.8)**. If they are difficult to remove, apply low pressure compressed air to the fluid outlet inside the reservoir.

10 If required, clean the inside of the reservoir and the master cylinder with clean brake fluid or denatured alcohol. Ensure the fluid inlet and outlet ports in the master cylinder are clear.

Caution: Do not, under any circumstances, use a petroleum based solvent to clean brake parts.

11 Check the master cylinder bore for corrosion, scratches and score marks. If damage or wear is evident, the master cylinder must be renewed. If the master cylinder is in poor condition, then the brake caliper should be checked as well.

12 The dust boot, retaining ring, piston assembly, seal and spring are all included in the rebuild kit. Use all of the new parts, regardless of the apparent condition of the old ones.

13 Install the new spring in the master cylinder, wide end first.

14 Lubricate the new piston and seal with clean brake fluid, then install them in the master cylinder, making sure the piston is the correct way round. Install the new retaining ring over the end of the piston, then depress the piston and press the ring firmly into its recess with a suitably sized small socket or tube.

15 Install the dust boot.

Installation

16 Position the master cylinder on the handlebar and fit the clamp, then tighten the bolts securely **(see illustration 5.6)**.

17 Connect the brake hose to the master cylinder, using new sealing washers on each side of the banjo union, if applicable. Align the union as noted on removal **(see illustration 5.4a)**. Tighten the banjo bolt to the torque setting specified at the beginning of this Chapter.

18 If removed, install the brake light switch and connect the wiring connectors.

19 Install the brake lever (see Chapter 6).

20 Fill the reservoir with new DOT 4 brake fluid and bleed the hydraulic system (see Section 8).

21 Check for leaks and test the operation of the front brake before riding the scooter.

6 Rear disc brake

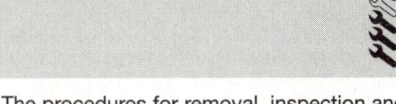

1 The procedures for removal, inspection and renewal of the rear disc brake pads, caliper, disc and master cylinder are the same as for the front brake, with the following additions.

2 Remove the rear wheel (see Section 14). Remove the retaining clip and pad pin, noting the location of the pad spring, before displacing the caliper from the caliper bracket **(see illustrations)**.

3 Undo the caliper mounting bolts and draw the caliper off the disc, then withdraw the pads from the caliper **(see illustrations)**. Follow the procedure in Section 2 for inspection and installation of the pads. **Note:** *The rear brake caliper fitted to all models is of the opposed piston type.*

4 Note the routing of the rear brake hose and the position of the hose clips. If the caliper is just being displaced and not removed from the scooter, release the hose from the clips. Secure the caliper to a convenient part of the machine with a cable tie to prevent straining the brake hose. **Note:** *Do not operate the rear brake lever while the caliper is off the disc.*

5 To remove the disc and hub assembly, first displace the caliper, then pull the hub off the driveshaft, noting which way round it fits **(see illustration)**. Note the directional arrow on the disc **(see illustration)**. Follow the procedure in Section 4 for inspection, removal and installation of the disc.

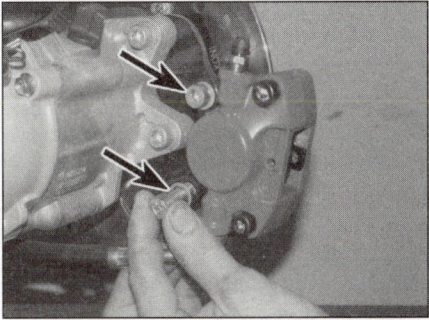

6.3a Remove the caliper mounting bolts (arrowed)

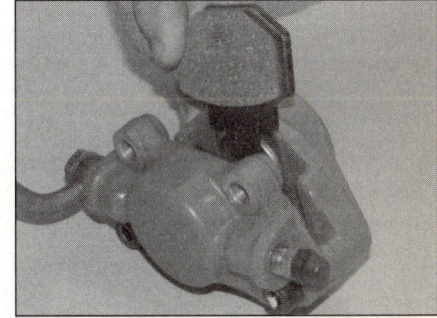

6.3b Withdraw the pads from the caliper

6.5a Pull the hub off the driveshaft

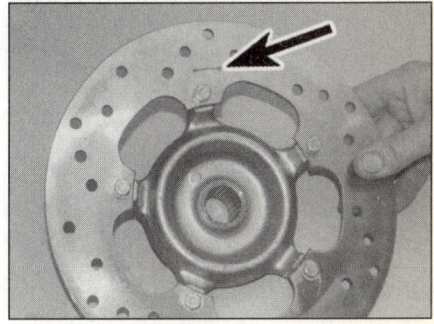

6.5b Note the directional arrow on the disc

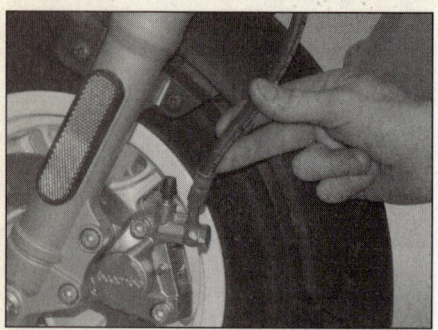

7.2a Check the condition of the brake hose . . .

7.2b . . . and check where the hose joins the banjo union

6 The rear brake master cylinder has an integral fluid reservoir and is mounted on the left handlebar.

7 After working on any component in the brake system, always check the operation of the brake before riding the scooter.

7 Brake hoses, pipes and unions

Inspection

Note: *On models fitted with a rear disc brake it will be necessary to remove the floor panel or belly panel to inspect the rear brake pipe (see Chapter 8).*

1 Brake hose and pipe condition should be checked regularly and the hoses renewed at the specified interval (see Chapter 1).

2 Twist and flex the hose while looking for cracks, bulges and seeping fluid **(see illustration)**. Check extra carefully around the areas where the hose connects with the master cylinder and caliper banjo unions, as these are common areas for hose failure.

3 Inspect the banjo unions connected to the brake hose. If the unions are rusted, scratched or cracked, renew them.

Renewal

4 Cover the surrounding area with plenty of rags, then unscrew the banjo bolt at each end of the hose, noting the alignment of the banjo union. Discard the sealing washers as new ones must be used. Free the hose from any

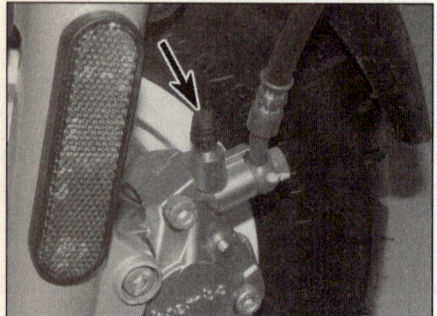

8.6a Remove the bleed valve dust cap

clips or guides and remove it.

5 Position the new hose, making sure it isn't twisted or otherwise strained. Align the banjo union as noted on removal, then install the banjo bolts using new sealing washers on both sides of the unions. Tighten the banjo bolts to the torque setting specified at the beginning of this Chapter.

6 Make sure the hose is correctly aligned and routed clear of all moving components. Secure the hose with any clips or guides.

7 Top-up the appropriate fluid reservoir (see *Daily (pre-ride) checks*) and bleed the brake system (see Section 8). Check that there are no fluid leaks and test the operation of the brake before riding the scooter.

8 Brake system bleeding

Caution: Support the scooter in a upright position and ensure that the fluid reservoir is level while carrying-out these procedures.

1 Bleeding the brakes is simply the process of removing all the air bubbles from the fluid reservoir, master cylinder, the hose and the brake caliper. Bleeding is necessary whenever a brake system connection is loosened, when a component or hose is renewed, or when the master cylinder or caliper is overhauled. Leaks in the system may also allow air to enter, but leaking brake fluid will reveal their presence and warn you of the need for repair.

2 To bleed the brake, you will need some

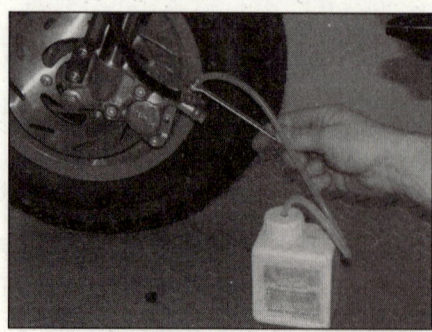

8.6b Set-up for bleeding the brakes

new DOT 4 brake fluid, a length of clear vinyl or plastic tubing, a small container partially filled with clean brake fluid, some rags and a spanner to fit the brake caliper bleed valve.

3 If applicable, remove the handlebar covers for access to the fluid reservoir (see Chapter 8).

4 Cover any bodywork or painted components to prevent damage in the event that brake fluid is spilled.

5 Remove the reservoir cover, diaphragm plate and diaphragm and slowly pump the brake lever a few times, until no air bubbles can be seen floating up from the holes in the bottom of the reservoir. Doing this bleeds the air from the master cylinder end of the system. Temporarily refit the reservoir cover.

6 Pull the dust cap off the caliper bleed valve **(see illustration)**. Attach one end of the clear vinyl or plastic tubing to the bleed valve and submerge the other end in the brake fluid in the container **(see illustration)**. **Note:** *To avoid damaging the bleed valve during the procedure, loosen it and then tighten it temporarily with a ring spanner before attaching the hose. With the hose attached, the valve can then be opened and closed with an open-ended spanner.*

7 Check the fluid level in the reservoir. Do not allow the fluid level to drop below the lower mark during the procedure.

8 Carefully pump the brake lever three or four times and hold it in while opening the caliper bleed valve. When the valve is opened, brake fluid will flow out of the caliper into the clear tubing and the lever will move toward the handlebar.

9 Tighten the bleed valve, then release the brake lever gradually. Repeat the process until no air bubbles are visible in the brake fluid leaving the caliper and the lever is firm when applied. On completion, disconnect the hose, ensure the bleed valve is tightened securely and fit the dust cap.

10 Top-up the reservoir, install the diaphragm, diaphragm plate and cover, and wipe up any spilled brake fluid. Check that there are no fluid leaks and test the operation of the brake before riding the scooter.

> **HAYNES HiNT** *If it's not possible to produce a firm feel to the lever the fluid may be aerated. Let the brake fluid in the system stabilise for a few hours and then repeat the procedure when the tiny bubbles in the system have settled out. To speed this process up, tie the brake lever to the handlebar so that the system is pressurised.*

> **HAYNES HiNT** *Old brake fluid is invariably much darker in colour than new fluid, making it easy to see when all old fluid has been expelled from the system.*

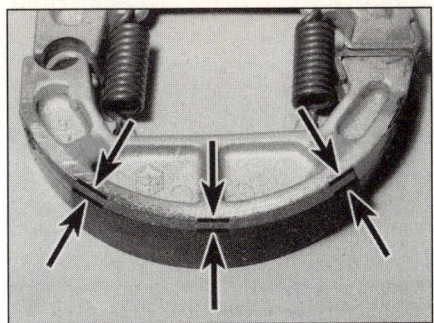

9.2 Check the amount of friction material remaining on each shoe

9.5 Check the surface of the drum for scoring and wear

9.7 Removing the brake shoes

9 Rear drum brake

 Warning: The dust created by the brake may contain asbestos which is harmful to your health. Never blow it out with compressed air and don't inhale any of it. An approved filtering mask should be worn when working on the brakes.

Check

1 Remove the rear wheel (see Section 14).

2 Inspect the surface of each brake shoe for contamination and check that the friction material has not worn to or beyond the specified minimum thickness **(see illustration)**. If either shoe is worn down to, or beyond, the service limit, fouled with oil or grease, or heavily scored or damaged, both shoes must be renewed as a set. **Note:** *It is not possible to degrease the friction material; if the shoes are contaminated in any way they must be renewed.*

3 If the shoes are in good condition, clean them carefully, using a fine wire brush which is completely free of oil and grease to remove all traces of dirt and corrosion. Any areas of glazing may be removed using emery cloth, bearing in mind the **Warning** above.

4 Check the condition of the brake shoe springs; if they appear weak or are obviously deformed or damaged, remove the shoes and fit new springs (see Step 7).

5 Clean the surface of the brake drum with brake cleaner or a rag soaked in solvent. Examine the surface for scoring and excessive wear **(see illustration)**. While light scratches are expected, any heavy scoring will impair braking. Check for a ridge between the rim of the drum and the shoe contact area. If the drum is badly scored or worn, it might be possible to have the surface skimmed by a specialist engineer, otherwise the wheel should be renewed.

6 Check that the brake cam operates smoothly and to its full limits of travel by operating the lever arm. Clean off all traces of old and hardened grease from the cam. If the bearing surfaces of the cam are worn or damaged it should be renewed.

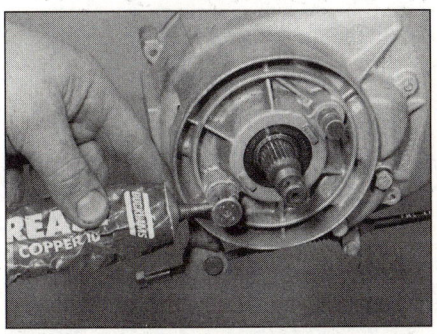

9.9 Apply some copper grease to the cam

Shoe removal and installation

7 With the wheel removed, grasp the outer edge of each shoe and fold them upwards to form a 'V' **(see illustration)**, noting that they are under pressure from the springs. Lift the shoes away, noting how they locate around the cam and the pivot. Remove the springs from the shoes.

8 Check the shoes, drum and cam as outlined above.

9 Apply some copper grease to the bearing surfaces on the cam, taking care not to apply too much as it could find its way onto the shoes **(see illustration)**.

10 Install the brake shoes in a reverse of the removal procedure – fit the springs onto the shoes, then position the shoes so that the flat ends fit on the cam and the rounded ends fit on the pivot **(see illustration)**. Make sure the shoes sit correctly on each side of the cam

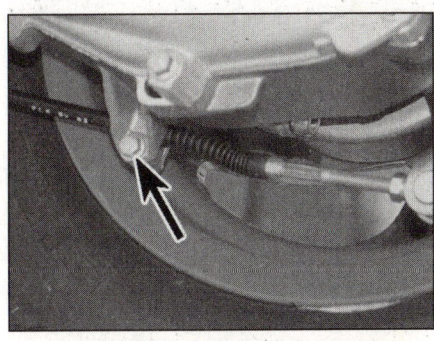

10.1 Free the cable from the holder

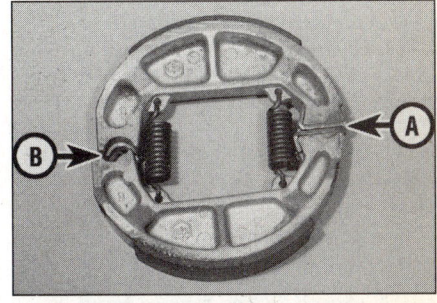

9.10 Fit the springs and locate the flat ends (A) against the cam and the rounded ends (B) against the pivot

and the pivot as you fold them into position. Operate the lever arm to check that the cam and shoes work correctly.

11 Install the rear wheel. Check the operation of the brake before riding the scooter.

10 Rear drum brake cable

Removal and installation

Note: *For details of cable adjustment and lubrication see Chapter 1.*

1 Remove the outer cable clamp bolt at the lower end of the cable and free the cable from its holder **(see illustration)**.

2 Fully unscrew the adjuster nut on the lower end of the cable, then draw the cable out of the brake lever arm **(see illustration)**.

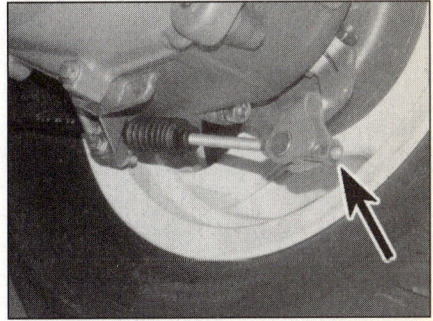

10.2 Unscrew and remove the adjuster nut (arrowed)

10.4a Pull the outer cable from the bracket . . .

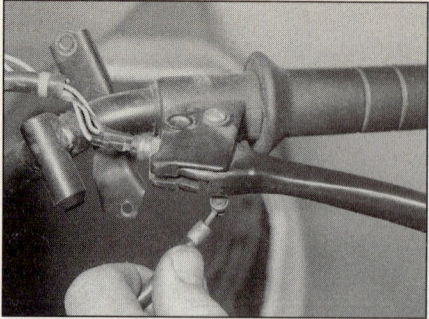

10.4b . . . and release the inner cable end from the lever

3 If applicable, remove the handlebar front cover (see Chapter 8).

4 Pull the outer cable out of the brake lever bracket and free the inner cable end from its socket in the underside of the lever **(see illustrations)**.

5 As applicable, remove the front panel, floor panel or belly panel to gain access to the cable run. Free the cable from any clips or ties, then withdraw it carefully, noting its routing and any guides it passes through.

6 Install the new cable in a reverse of the removal procedure (see **Haynes Hint**). Apply some grease to the upper and lower ends of the inner cable before fitting them into the handlebar lever and brake arm respectively.

7 Adjust the cable freeplay (see Chapter 1). Check the operation of the brake before riding the scooter.

 When fitting a new cable, tape the lower end of the new cable to the upper end of the old cable before removing it from the machine. Slowly pull the lower end of the old cable out, guiding the new cable down into position. Using this method will ensure the cable is routed correctly.

11 Wheel inspection and repair

Note: *If, when checked in place on the*

scooter, wheel runout is excessive, check the wheel bearings for wear before renewing the wheel (see Section 15).

1 In order to carry out a proper inspection of the wheels, support the scooter upright on its centre stand with the wheel being checked raised off the ground. Clean the wheels thoroughly to remove mud and dirt that may interfere with the inspection procedure or mask defects. Make a general check of the wheels (see Chapter 1) and tyres (see *Daily (pre-ride) checks*).

2 To check wheel runout, attach a dial gauge to either the front fork or the transmission casing, with the gauge pointer touching the side of the rim **(see illustration)**. Rotate the wheel slowly and check the axial (side-to-side) runout of the rim. In order to accurately check radial (out of round) runout with the dial gauge, the wheel should be removed from the machine, and the tyre from the wheel. With a suitable axle clamped in a vice or jig and the dial gauge positioned on the top of the rim, the wheel can be rotated to check the runout.

3 An easier, though slightly less accurate, method is to use a stiff wire pointer in place of the dial gauge. Attach the pointer as required and position the end of the pointer a fraction of an inch from the wheel rim where the wheel and tyre join. If the wheel is true, the distance from the pointer to the rim will be constant as the wheel is rotated.

4 Inspect the wheels for cracks, flat spots on the rim and other damage. Look very closely for dents in the area where the tyre bead contacts the rim. Dents in this area may prevent complete sealing of the tyre against

the rim, which leads to deflation of the tyre over a period of time. If damage is evident, or if runout in either direction is excessive, the wheel will have to be replaced with a new one. Never attempt to repair a damaged cast alloy wheel.

12 Wheel alignment check

1 Misalignment of the wheels can cause strange and potentially dangerous handling problems and will most likely be due to bent frame or suspension components as the result of an accident. If the frame or suspension is at fault, repair by a frame specialist or replacement with new parts are the only options.

2 To check wheel alignment you will need an assistant, a length of string or a perfectly straight piece of wood or metal bar, and a ruler. A plumb bob or spirit level for checking that the wheels are vertical will also be required. Support the scooter in an upright position on its centre stand.

3 If a string is used, have your assistant hold one end of it about halfway between the floor and the centre of the rear wheel, with the string touching the back edge of the rear tyre sidewall.

4 Run the other end of the string forward and pull it tight so that it is roughly parallel to the floor. Slowly bring the string into contact with the front sidewall of the rear tyre, then turn the front wheel until it is parallel with the string. Measure the distance (offset) from the front tyre sidewall to the string **(see illustration)**. **Note:** *Where the same size tyre is fitted front and rear, there should be no offset.*

5 Repeat the procedure on the other side of the machine. The distance from the front tyre sidewall to the string should be equal on both sides.

6 As mentioned, a perfectly straight length of wood or metal bar may be substituted for the string **(see illustration)**.

7 If the distance between the string and tyre is greater on one side, or if the rear wheel appears to be out of alignment, have your machine checked by a Gilera dealer.

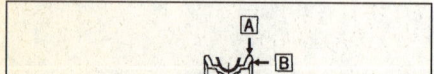
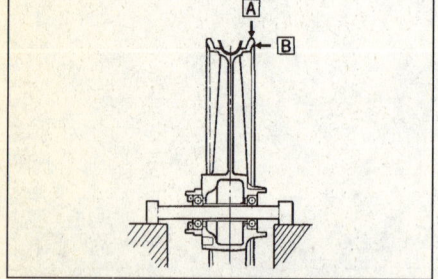

11.2 Check the wheel for radial (out-of-round) runout (A) and axial (side-to-side) runout (B)

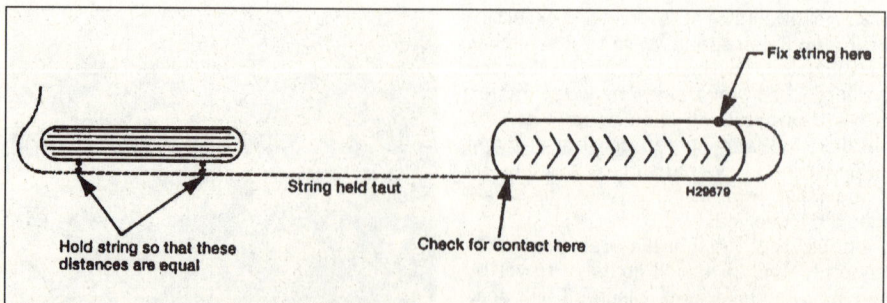

12.4 Wheel alignment check using the string method

Tyres of different widths front and rear illustrated

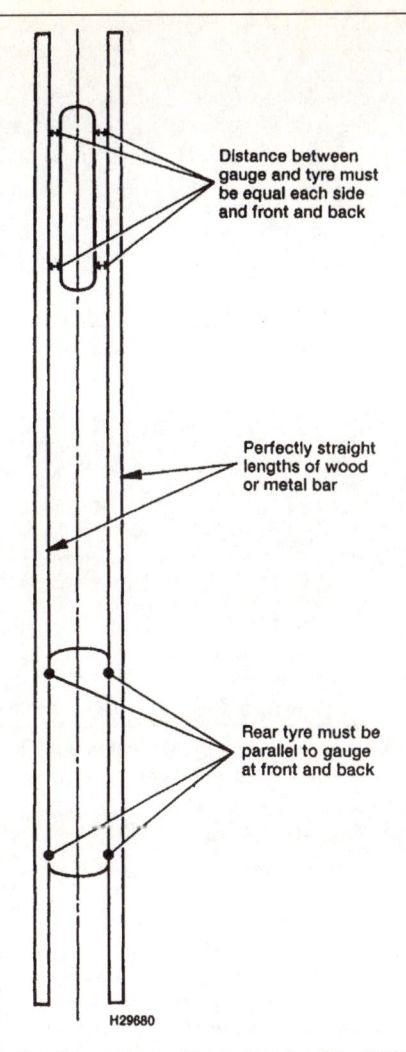

12.6 Wheel alignment check using a straight-edge

Tyres of different widths front and rear illustrated

8 If the front-to-back alignment is correct, the wheels still may be out of alignment vertically.
9 Using a plumb bob or spirit level, check the rear wheel to make sure it is vertical. To do this, hold the string of the plumb bob against the tyre upper sidewall and allow the weight

13.5b . . . then lift off the speedometer sensor . . .

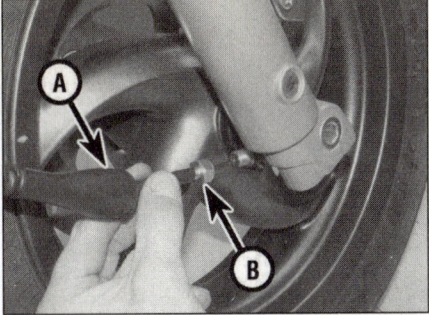

13.3 Pull back the boot (A) then undo the nut (B)

13.4b . . . and on DNA models

to settle just off the floor. If the string touches both the upper and lower tyre sidewalls and is perfectly straight, the wheel is vertical. If it is not, adjust the centre stand until it is.
10 Once the rear wheel is vertical, check the front wheel in the same manner. If both wheels are not perfectly vertical, the frame and/or major suspension components are bent.

13 Front wheel

Removal

1 Position the scooter on its centre stand and support it with front wheel off the ground.
2 Displace the front brake caliper (see Section 3). **Note:** *Do not operate the front brake lever while the caliper is off the disc.*

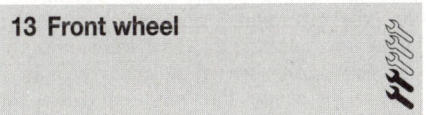

13.5c . . . and the left-hand side spacer (arrowed)

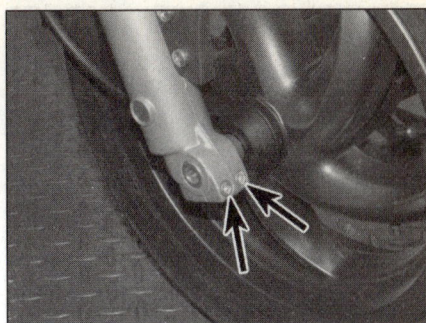

13.4a Loosen the axle pinch bolts on Runner models . . .

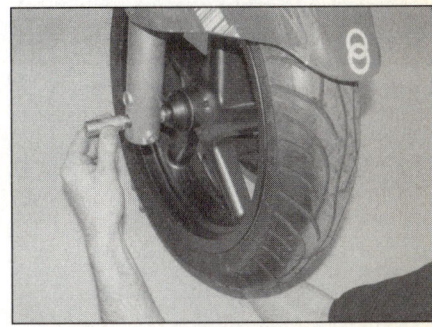

13.5a On DNA models, withdraw the axle . . .

3 On models fitted with a speedometer cable, pull back the boot on the end of the lower end of the cable, then unscrew the nut and draw the cable out of the drive housing **(see illustration)**. **Note:** *Most later models are fitted with electronically operated speedometers – do not try to disconnect the speedometer wire from the sensor (see Chapter 9).*
4 Where fitted, loosen the axle pinch bolt(s) **(see illustrations)**.
5 On DNA models, support the wheel and unscrew the axle from the left-hand fork slider, then withdraw the axle from the wheel **(see illustration)**. Lower the wheel and lift the speedometer sensor off the right-hand side of the wheel hub, noting how it fits **(see illustration)**. Remove the spacer from the left-hand side of the hub **(see illustration)**.
6 On all other models, counterhold the axle and undo the axle nut **(see illustration)**.

13.6a Counterhold the axle and undo the axle nut

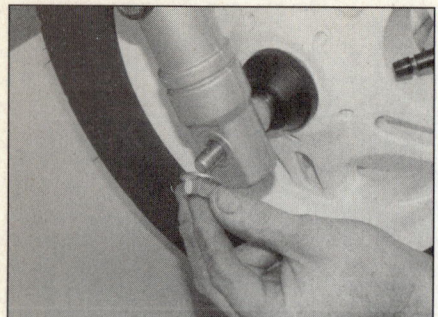

13.6b Remove the nut and washer . . .

13.6c . . . then withdraw the axle

13.6d Lift off the speedometer drive housing . . .

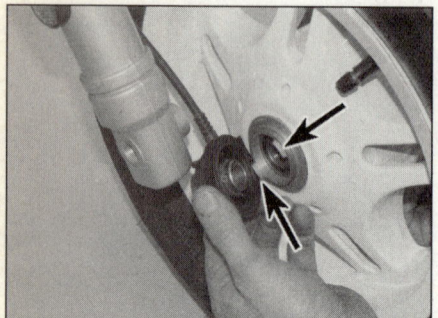

13.6e . . . or sensor – note the drive tabs (arrowed)

13.6f Remove the thrust washer where fitted

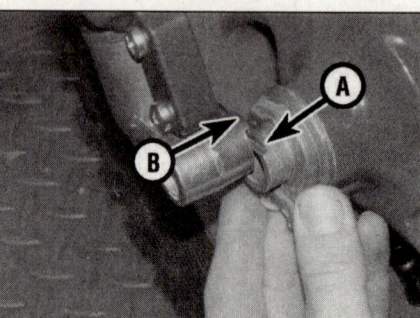

13.10a Drive housing (A) locates against fork slider (B)

Remove the nut and washer, then support the wheel and withdraw the axle (see illustrations). Lower the wheel and lift the speedometer drive housing or sensor off the right-hand side of the wheel hub, noting how it fits (see illustrations). Where fitted, remove the thrust washer (see illustration). If it is loose, remove the spacer from the left-hand side of the hub; on some models the spacer is retained by the seal.

Caution: Don't lay the wheel down and allow it to rest on the disc – the disc could become warped. Set the wheel on wood blocks so the disc doesn't support the weight of the wheel.

7 Clean the axle with a suitable solvent and remove any corrosion using steel wool. Check the axle for straightness by rolling it on a flat surface such as a piece of plate glass. If available, check the axle for runout using V-blocks and a dial gauge. If the axle is bent or the runout is excessive, renew it.

13.10b Speed sensor (A) locates against tab (B) on fork slider

8 Check the condition of the wheel bearings (see Section 15).

Installation

9 Manoeuvre the wheel into position. Where fitted, apply some grease to the inside of the speedometer drive housing. If applicable, fit the thrust washer, then install the drive housing or sensor onto the hub, making sure the drive tab locates correctly. If removed, install the spacer in the left-hand side of the hub. Apply a thin coat of grease to the axle.

10 Lift the wheel into place between the forks, making sure the stepped section on the speedometer drive housing or sensor locates correctly against the corresponding section on the bottom of the right-hand fork slider (see illustrations). Install the axle.

11 On DNA models, ensure the axle is correctly aligned with the left-hand slider, then tighten it to the torque setting specified at the beginning of this Chapter.

12 On all other models, install the axle nut and washer, then tighten the nut to the torque setting specified at the beginning of this Chapter.

13 Where fitted, tighten the axle pinch bolt(s) to the specified torque setting.

14 If applicable, connect the speedometer cable and tighten the knurled ring. Install the rubber boot.

15 Install the brake caliper (see Section 3).

16 Operate the front brake lever several times to bring the pads into contact with the disc. Check the operation of the brake before riding the scooter.

14 Rear wheel and hub assembly

Note: On some models, due to a lack of clearance, it may be necessary to remove the silencer or exhaust system before removing the wheel (see Chapter 4).

Drum brake models

Removal

1 Position the scooter on its centre stand. On Ice models, remove the lower rear mudguard assembly (see Chapter 8).

2 Lever off the wheel cover using a small flat-bladed screwdriver (see illustration). Remove the split pin from the end of the axle then remove the cage nut (see illustration). Discard the split pin as a new one must be used.

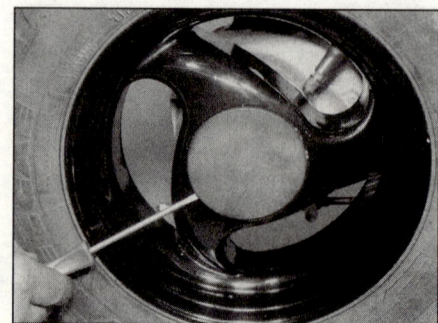

14.2a Lever off the cover . . .

14.2b . . . and remove the split pin (arrowed) and cage nut

14.3a Unscrew the nut . . .

14.3b . . . remove the washer . . .

3 Have an assistant apply the rear brake to prevent the wheel from turning, then unscrew the wheel nut **(see illustration)**. Remove the washer and draw the wheel off the driveshaft **(see illustrations)**.

4 Check the splines on the driveshaft and on the inside of the wheel for wear and damage and renew either or both components as required.

Installation

5 Apply some grease to the splines on the shaft and slide the wheel into position **(see illustration 14.3c)**.

6 Fit the washer and the wheel nut **(see illustrations 14.3b and a)**, then tighten the wheel nut to the torque setting specified at the beginning of this Chapter, applying the rear brake to prevent the wheel from turning **(see illustration)**.

7 Fit the cage nut and secure the nut using

a new split pin, bending its ends around the cage nut **(see illustration)**. Fit the wheel cover.

8 Install the remaining components in the reverse order of removal.

Disc brake models with single rear shock absorber

Removal

9 Position the scooter on its centre stand.

10 Have an assistant apply the rear brake to prevent the wheel from turning, then undo the bolts securing the wheel to the hub assembly and lift the wheel off the hub **(see illustration)**.

11 If required, refer to Section 6 to remove the rear hub assembly.

12 Check the splines on the driveshaft and on the inside of the hub for wear and damage and renew either or both components as required.

Installation

13 If removed, install the hub assembly and install the rear brake caliper (see Section 6).

14 Fit the wheel onto the hub and tighten the wheel bolts to the torque setting specified at the beginning of this Chapter, applying the rear brake to prevent the wheel from turning.

15 Install the remaining components in the reverse order of removal.

Disc brake models with twin rear shock absorbers

Removal

16 Position the scooter on its centre stand.

17 Remove the silencer (see Chapter 4).

18 Remove the split pin from the end of the driveshaft then remove the cage nut **(see illustrations)**. Discard the split pin as a new one must be used.

14.3c . . . and draw the wheel off the driveshaft

14.6 Tighten the nut to the specified torque

14.7 Fit the cage nut then fit a new split pin as described

14.10 Undo the wheel bolts

14.18a Remove the split pin (arrowed) . . .

14.18b . . . and the cage nut

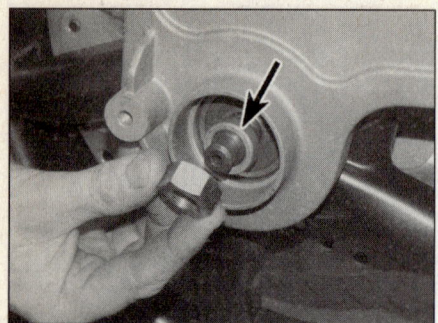

14.19 Remove the hub nut and large washer (arrowed)

14.20a Undo the lower shock fixing . . .

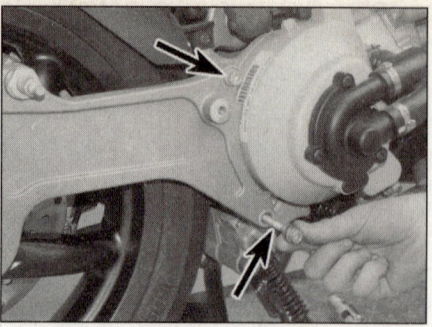

14.20b . . . and the subframe mounting bolts

19 Have an assistant apply the rear brake to prevent the wheel from turning, then unscrew the hub centre nut and remove the nut and large washer (see illustration).

20 Undo the nut and washer securing the lower end of the right-hand shock absorber to the subframe and displace the shock, then undo the bolts securing the subframe to the engine casing (see illustrations).

21 Lift off the subframe and slide the spacer off the driveshaft, noting which way round it fits (see illustrations). Check the condition of the bearing and seals in the subframe. If there is any doubt about the condition of the bearing, follow the procedure in Section 15 and replace it with a new one (see illustration).

22 Undo the bolts securing the wheel to the hub assembly and remove the wheel (see illustrations).

23 If required, refer to Section 6 to remove the rear hub assembly.

24 Check the splines on the driveshaft and on the inside of the hub for wear and damage and renew either or both components as required (see illustration).

Installation

25 If removed, install the hub assembly and install the rear brake caliper (see Section 6).

26 Fit the wheel onto the hub and tighten the wheel bolts to the torque setting specified at the beginning of this Chapter, applying the rear brake to prevent the wheel from turning.

27 Install the spacer on the driveshaft (see illustration 14.21b).

28 Install the subframe and secure it to the engine casing with the mounting bolts; tighten the bolts to the specified torque.

29 Fit the lower end of the rear shock onto the stud on the subframe and secure it with the washer and nut (see illustration 14.20a).

30 Install the large washer and hub centre

nut on the driveshaft. Tighten the nut to the specified torque setting, applying the rear brake to prevent the wheel from turning.

31 Fit the cage nut and secure the nut using a new split pin, bending its ends around the cage nut (see illustration 14.18a).

32 Install the silencer (see Chapter 4).

15 Wheel bearings

Check

1 Wheel bearings will wear over a period of time and cause handling problems.

2 Support the scooter upright on its centre stand. Check for any play in the bearings by pushing and pulling the wheel against the hub (see illustration).

14.21a Lift off the subframe . . .

14.21b . . . and slide the spacer off the driveshaft

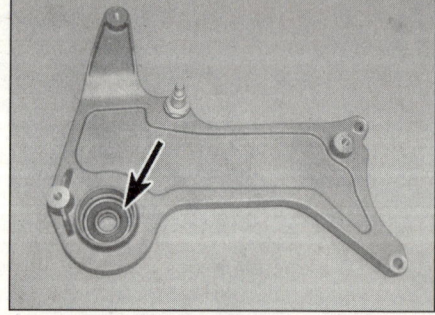

14.21c Check the condition of the subframe bearing

14.22a Undo the bolts . . .

14.22b . . . and lift off the wheel

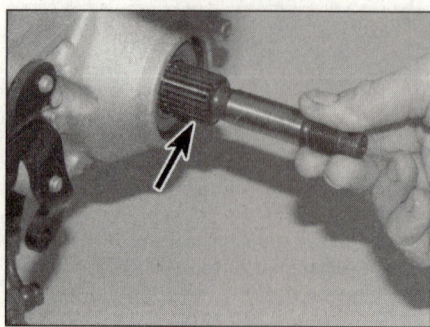

14.24 Inspect the driveshaft splines (arrowed) for wear

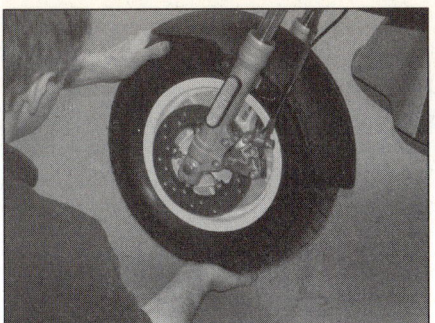
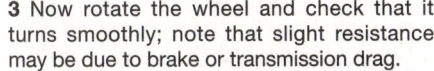

15.2 Checking for play in the wheel bearings

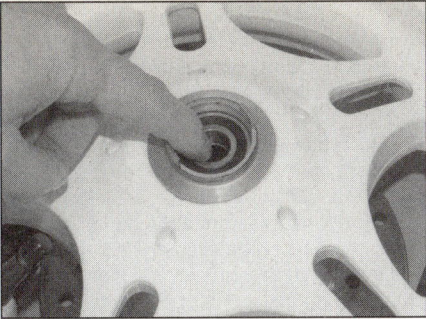

15.5 Check the bearings for freeplay and rough spots

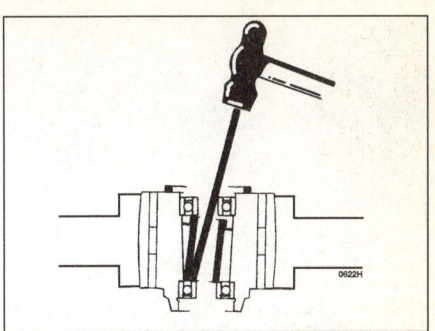

15.8 Locate the drift as shown when driving out the bearings

3 Now rotate the wheel and check that it turns smoothly; note that slight resistance may be due to brake or transmission drag.

4 The front wheel bearings are housed in the wheel hub. There are no rear wheel bearings as such; the driveshaft bearings which support the rear wheel are housed in the gearbox (see Steps 15 and 16).

5 If any play or roughness is detected, first check that the axle and wheel mountings are tight, then remove the wheel and check the bearings carefully. Rotate the inner race – if there is excessive freeplay between the inner and outer bearing races, or if the bearing doesn't turn smoothly, has rough spots or is noisy, replace it with a new one **(see illustration)**. On models with twin rear shock absorbers, check the condition of the bearing in the rear subframe (see Section 14, Step 21).

Removal and installation

Front wheel bearings

Note: *Always renew the wheel bearings in pairs. Never renew the bearings individually.*

6 Remove the wheel (see Section 13).

7 Set the wheel on wood blocks. Do not to allow the weight of the wheel to rest on the brake disc.

8 On DNA models, no separate bearing seals are fitted. To remove the bearings use either an expanding bearing puller and slide-hammer to pull them out of each side of the hub, or a suitable drift (such as a metal rod or a brass drift punch) inserted from the opposite side to the bearing being removed **(see illustration)**. Tap evenly around the inner

race of the bearing and drive it out of the hub, then remove the central spacer. Turn the wheel over and remove the other bearing.

9 On Runner and Ice models, a metal seal is fitted in the left-hand side of the hub – do not attempt to lever the seal out as it will be damaged. First remove the right-hand side bearing, either with an expanding bearing puller and slide-hammer **(see illustration)**, or a suitable drift, as described in Step 8. Lift out the central spacer. Now remove the left-hand bearing, spacer and seal. The tool used must locate on the bearing inner race to draw or drive the bearing, spacer and seal out together.

10 On SKP/Stalker models, metal seals are fitted in both sides of the hub – do not attempt to lever the seals out as they will be damaged **(see illustration)**. Use either an expanding bearing puller and slide-hammer, or a suitable drift, as described in Step 8. If a drift is being used, and it is difficult to locate

it on the outer bearing spacer or bearing inner race, locate it on the upper rim of the central bearing spacer, and drive the central spacer, bearing, outer spacer and seal out together.

11 Thoroughly clean the hub area of the wheel. First install the right-hand bearing into its recess in the hub, with the marked or sealed side facing outwards. Using a bearing driver or a socket large enough to contact the outer race of the bearing, drive it in until it is completely seated **(see illustration)**.

12 Turn the wheel over and install the central spacer. Install the left-hand bearing as described above.

13 On Runner, Ice and SKP/Stalker models, position the left-hand spacer so that the shoulder is against the bearing, then press the metal seal into the hub, using a large socket if required **(see illustrations)**. On SKP/Stalker models, repeat the procedure and fit the right-hand spacer.

15.9 Removing a bearing with a puller and slide-hammer

15.10 Metal seal (arrowed) fitted to SKP/Stalker front wheel

15.11 Using a socket to drive in the bearings

15.13a Fit the shouldered spacer . . .

15.13b . . . then the seal

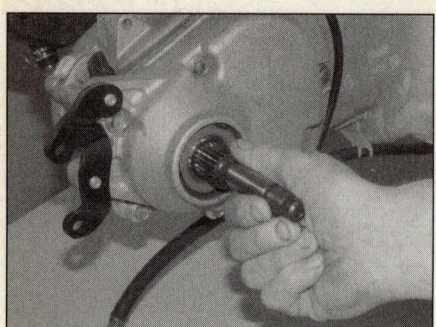

15.15 Checking for freeplay in the driveshaft

14 Clean the brake disc with acetone or brake system cleaner, then install the wheel (see Section 13).

Rear wheel bearings

15 The rear wheel itself has no bearings; the driveshaft bearings which support the wheel are fitted inside the gearbox. Follow the procedure in Section 14 and remove the rear wheel, then remove the rear hub assembly.

Grasp the driveshaft and try to move it up and down – if any freeplay is noted, the driveshaft bearings are worn **(see illustration)**. Refer to Chapter 2D for renewal of the driveshaft bearings.

16 On models with twin rear shock absorbers, support the subframe outside face down, and drive the bearing out with a bearing driver or suitably-sized socket. Ensure the bearing housing is clean and free from corrosion, then install the new bearing with a bearing driver or a socket large enough to contact the outer race of the bearing.

16 Tyres –
general information

General information

1 The wheels fitted to all models covered by this manual are designed for tubeless tyres only. Tyre sizes are given in the Specifications at the beginning of Chapter 1.

2 Refer to *Daily (pre-ride) checks* at the beginning of this manual for tyre maintenance.

Fitting new tyres

3 When selecting new tyres, refer to the tyre information label on the scooter and the tyre options listed in the owners handbook. Ensure that front and rear tyre types are compatible, the correct size and correct speed rating; if necessary seek advice from a Gilera dealer or tyre fitting specialist.

4 It is recommended that tyres are fitted by a motorcycle tyre specialist rather than attempted in the home workshop. This is particularly relevant in the case of tubeless tyres because the force required to break the seal between the wheel rim and tyre bead is substantial, and is usually beyond the capabilities of an individual working with normal tyre levers. Additionally, the specialist will be able to balance the wheels after tyre fitting.

5 Note that punctured tubeless tyres can in some cases be repaired. Gilera recommend that such repairs are carried out only by an authorised dealer.

Chapter 8
Bodywork

Contents

Degrees of difficulty

Easy, suitable for novice with little experience	Fairly easy, suitable for beginner with some experience	Fairly difficult, suitable for competent DIY mechanic 	Difficult, suitable for experienced DIY mechanic 	Very difficult, suitable for expert DIY or professional

1 General information

Almost all the functional components of the scooters covered by this manual are enclosed by body panels, making removal of relevant panels a necessary part of most servicing and maintenance procedures. Panel removal is straightforward, and as well as facilitating access to mechanical components, it avoids the risk of accidental damage to the panels.

Before attempting to remove any body panel, study it closely, noting any fasteners and associated fittings. Most panels are retained by screws and inter-locking tabs, although in some cases trim clips are used. Once the evident fasteners have been removed, try to withdraw the panel as described but DO NOT FORCE IT – if it will not release, check that all fasteners have been removed and try again. Where a panel engages another by means of tabs, be careful not to break the tab or its mating slot. Remember that a few moments of patience at this stage will save you a lot of money in replacing broken body panels! In some cases

the aid of an assistant will be required when removing panels.

When installing a body panel, check the fasteners and associated fittings removed with it, to be sure of returning everything to its correct place. Ensure all the fasteners are in good condition, including all trim clips and grommets; any of these should be renewed if faulty before the panel is reassembled. Check also that all mounting brackets are straight and repair or renew them if necessary before attempting to install the panel. Where assistance was required to remove a panel, make sure your assistant is on hand to install it.

Tighten the fasteners securely, but be careful not to overtighten any of them or the panel may break (not always immediately) due to the uneven stress. Where quick-release fasteners are fitted, turn them 90° anti-clockwise to release them, and 90° clockwise to secure them.

 **Note that a small amount of lubricant (liquid soap or similar) applied to rubber mounting grommets will assist the lugs to engage without the need for undue pressure.**

In the case of damage to the body parts, it is usually necessary to remove the broken component and replace it with a new (or used) one. There are however some shops that specialise in 'plastic welding', so it may be worthwhile seeking the advice of one of these specialists before consigning an expensive component to the bin. Additionally proprietary repair kits can be obtained for repair of small components **(see illustration)**.

1.0 A typical repair kit

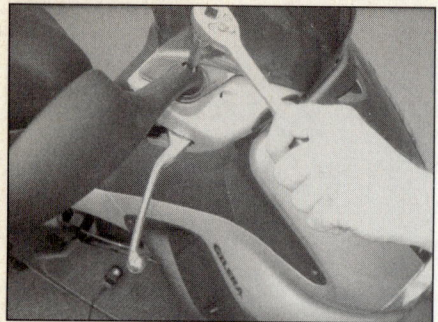

2.1 On Runner models, mirror is secured by single bolt

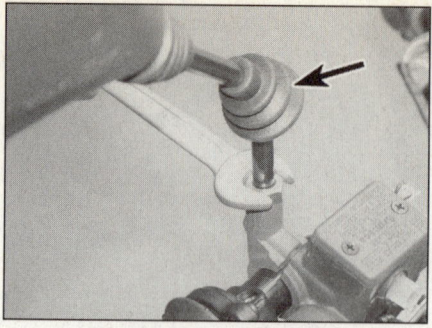

2.2a Pull back the boot (arrowed) and loosen the locknut . . .

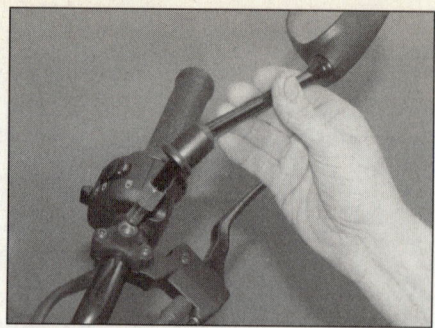

2.2b . . . then unscrew the mirror from the bracket

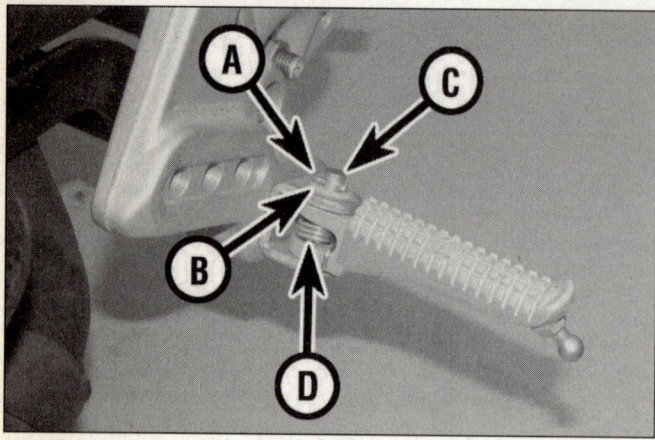

3.1 DNA footrest – note the clip (A), washer (B), pivot pin (C) and return spring (D)

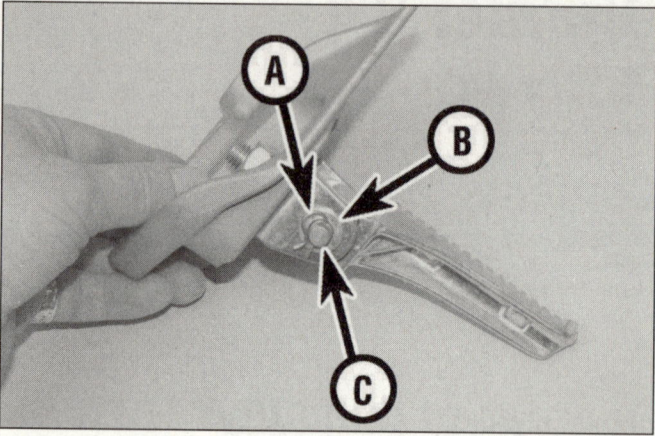

3.4a Remove the retaining clip (A), washer (B) and pivot pin (C)

2 Rear view mirrors

1 On Runner models, unscrew the bolt securing the mirror to the handlebars and lift off the mirror **(see illustration)**. Note that later models have a plastic plug inserted over the mounting bolt which must be carefully prised out with a small screwdriver **(see illustraton 5.33)**.
2 On all other models, if the mirror stem is covered by a rubber boot, pull back the lower end of the boot to expose the top of the fixing. Loosen the locknut on the mirror stem, then unscrew the mirror from the handlebar bracket **(see illustrations)**.

3 Installation is the reverse of removal. On Runner models, position the mirror as required, then hold it in place and tighten the bolt. On all other models, screw the mirror stem into the handlebar bracket, position the mirror as required, then hold it in place and tighten the locknut.
4 Install the rubber boot.

3 Footrests

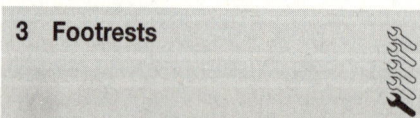

Rider's footrests – DNA models

1 DNA models are fitted with motorcycle-type footrests **(see illustration)**. To remove the footrest, remove the retaining clip and washer, then withdraw the pivot pin, noting how the return spring fits. Alternatively, undo the nut on the back of the footrest bracket and remove the footrest and pivot bracket **(see illustration 3.4c)**.
2 Installation is the reverse of removal. If removed, apply a smear of grease to the pivot pin and ensure the return spring is correctly positioned. If the retaining clip is corroded or sprained, fit a new one.

Passenger's footrests – Ice, Runner and DNA models

3 Ice, Runner and DNA models are fitted with folding passenger footrests. On Runner models, the footrests are secured directly to the frame; on Ice and DNA models the footrests are mounted on separate brackets.
4 Remove the retaining clip and washer from the footrest pivot pin, then withdraw the pivot pin **(see illustration)**. Remove the footrest carefully – it is held in position with a detent plate, ball and spring; note how they are fitted and take care that they do not spring out when removing the footrest **(see illustration)**. Alternatively, undo the nut on the back of the footrest bracket and remove the footrest and pivot bracket **(see illustration)**.

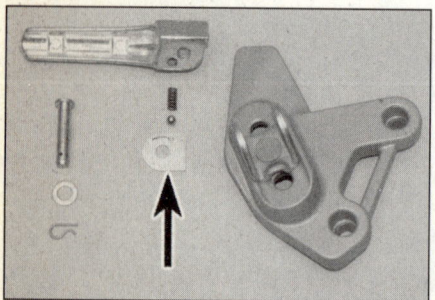

3.4b Components of the passenger footrest assembly – note the detent plate (arrowed)

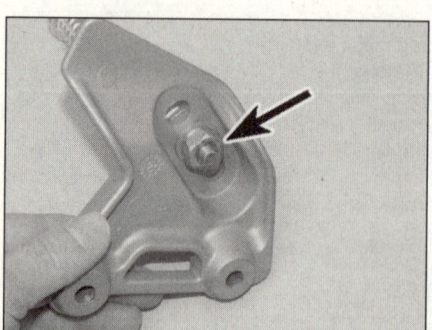

3.4c Footrest is secure to the bracket by nut (arrowed)

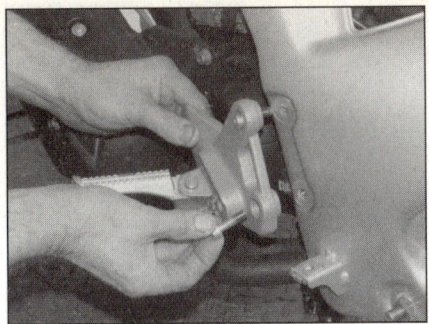

3.5a Removing the passenger footrest bracket – Ice shown

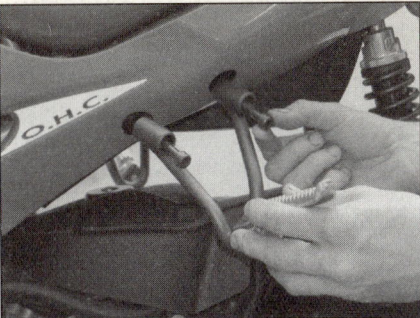

3.5b Removing the passenger footrest bracket – DNA shown

5 If required, undo the footrest bracket mounting bolts and lift off the bracket **(see illustrations)**.

6 Installation is the reverse of removal. If removed, apply a smear of grease to the pivot pin. Install the spring, ball and detent plate, then locate the footrest in its bracket and secure it with the pivot pin. Fit the washer and retaining clip; if the retaining clip is corroded or distorted, fit a new one.

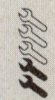

4 Runner body panels

Seat

1 Unlock the seat and swing it upright.
2 Remove the screws securing the seat hinge to the storage compartment and remove the seat **(see illustration)**.
3 Installation is the reverse of removal.

Engine access panels

4 Unlock the seat and swing it upright.
5 Remove the single screw securing the access panel in the bottom of the storage compartment and remove the panel **(see illustration)**.
6 Remove the screw securing each engine side access panel and lift off the panel, noting the tabs on the panel lower edge **(see illustration)**.
7 Installation is the reverse of removal.

Side access panels

8 Remove the two screws on the rear edge of the panel and the two screws on the front edge of the panel, then lift the panel off **(see illustrations)**.
9 Installation is the reverse of removal.

Rear carrier

10 Carefully unclip the carrier centre panel and lift it off, noting how the tabs locate in the carrier **(see illustration)**.
11 Remove the four screws securing the carrier and lift it off **(see illustrations)**.

4.2 Remove the two screws securing the seat hinge

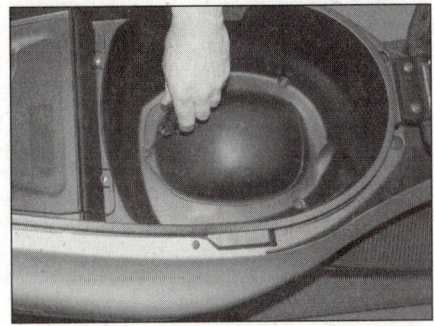

4.5 Engine access panel is secured by single screw

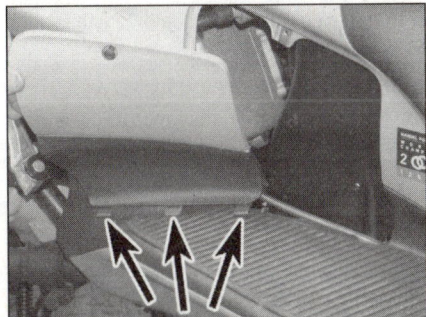

4.6 Note the tabs (arrowed) on the engine side access panels

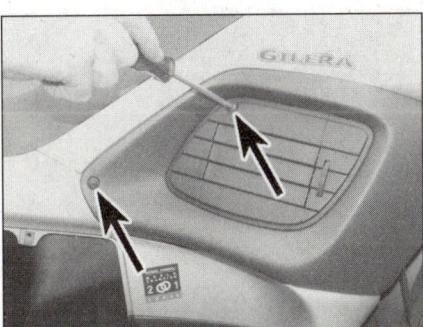

4.8a Remove the two screws on the rear edge . . .

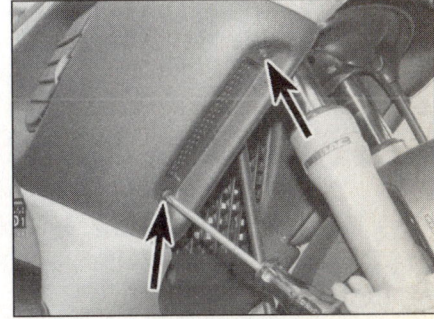

4.8b . . . and the two screws on the front edge . . .

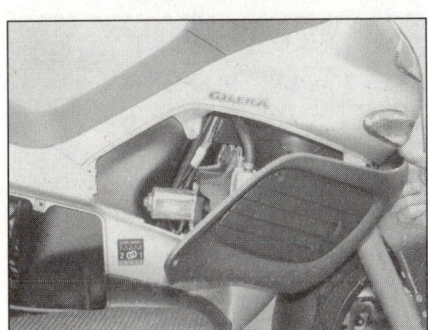

4.8c . . . then lift off the panel

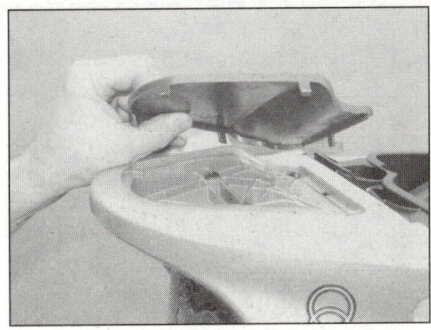

4.10 Unclip the centre panel, noting how the tabs locate

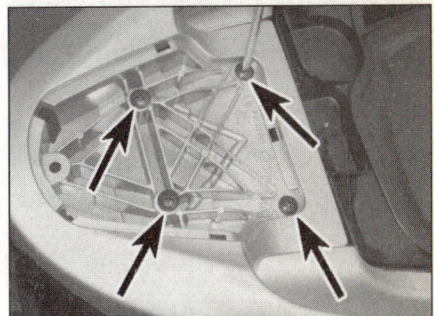

4.11a Remove the screws (arrowed) . . .

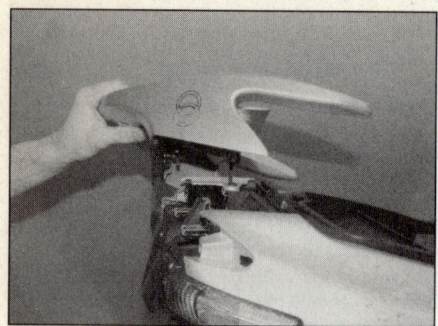

4.11b . . . and lift off the carrier

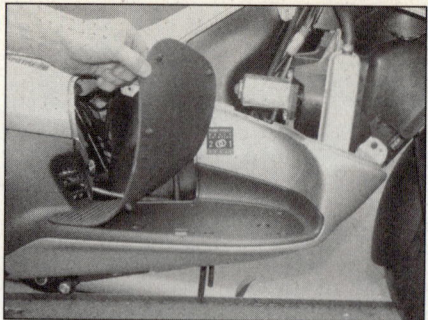

4.15a Remove the rubber mat . . .

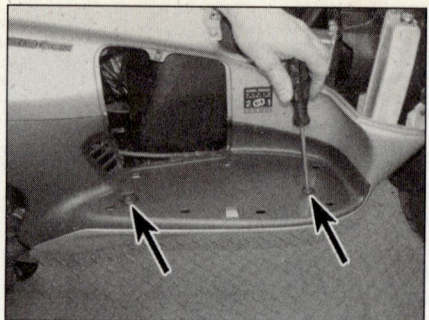

4.15b . . . and remove the two screws (arrowed)

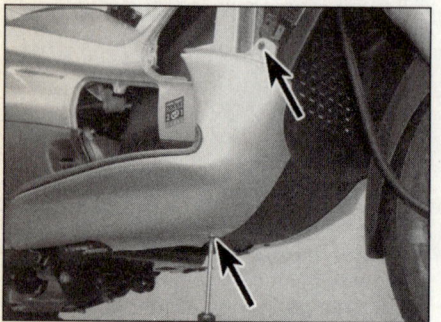

4.16 Remove the two screws (arrowed)

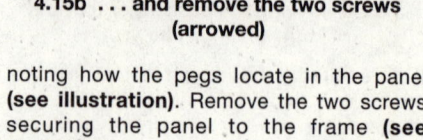

4.17 Remove the screw (arrowed)

noting how the pegs locate in the panel **(see illustration)**. Remove the two screws securing the panel to the frame **(see illustration)**.

16 Remove the screw on the underside of the panel and the screw on the front top edge of the panel **(see illustration)**.

17 Remove the screw securing the panel to the rear edge of the front side panel **(see illustration)**.

18 Remove the screws securing the upper and lower rear edges of the panel **(see illustrations)**.

19 Ease the panel off, noting how the hooked tabs on the underside of the centre panel locate in the slots along the top edge **(see illustrations)**. When removing the left-hand side panel, note how the seat latch mechanism engages with the seat lock **(see illustration)**.

20 Installation is the reverse of removal; ensure the seat lock is correctly engaged with the latch mechanism before installing the seat.

12 Installation is the reverse of removal.

Side panels

13 Each side panel incorporates the corresponding floor panel and belly panel – it

is recommended that an assistant is on hand to help remove the side panels.

14 Remove the seat, the appropriate side access panel and the rear carrier (see above).

15 Pull back the floor panel rubber mat,

Handlebar covers

21 Remove the rear view mirrors (see Section 2).

22 To remove the front cover, first remove the two screws from the rear cover **(see illustration)**. Carefully lever up the top edge of the front cover to release the pegs which locate into holes in the top edge of the rear cover **(see illustration)**.

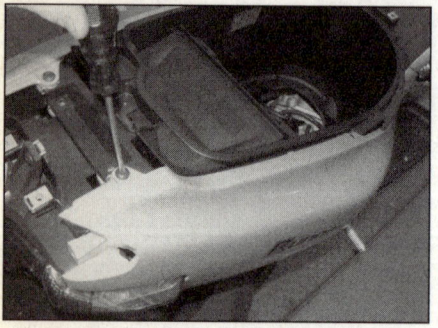

4.18a Remove the screw on the upper . . .

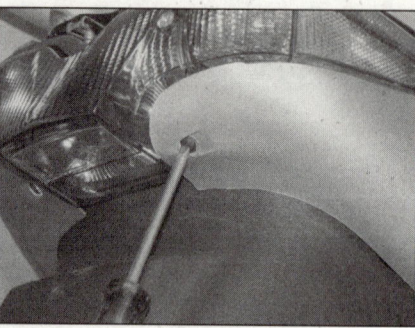

4.18b . . . and lower rear edges of the panel

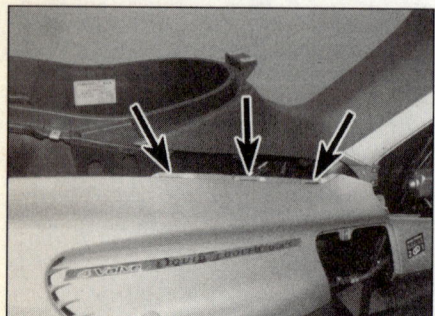

4.19a Unhook the tabs (arrowed)

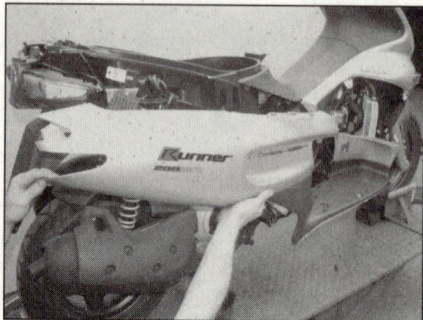

4.19b . . . and lift the side panel off

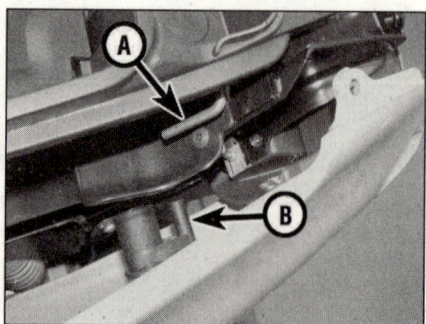

4.19c Note how the latch mechanism (A) engages with the lock (B)

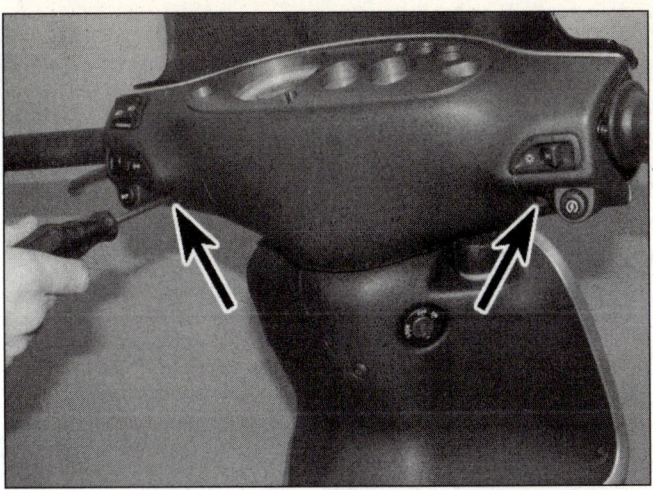

4.22a Remove the two screws (arrowed) in the rear cover

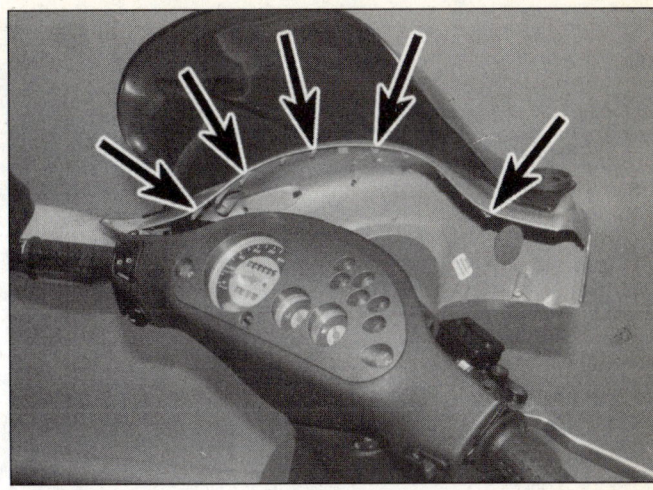

4.22b Remove the cover carefully to avoid damaging the pegs (arrowed)

23 To remove the rear cover, first unscrew the knurled ring that secures the speedometer cable and disconnect the cable **(see illustration)**.

24 Remove the three screws that secure the rear cover to the handlebars and ease the cover away from the bars **(see illustration)**. If required, unclip the instrument cluster and handlebar switch wiring connectors and lift off the cover (see Chapter 9). Mark or label the connectors so that they can be reconnected correctly on reassembly.

25 Installation is the reverse of removal. Make sure the wiring connectors are correctly and securely connected, and check the operation of all switches before riding the scooter.

Front panel

26 Remove the screw inside the upper opening in the panel **(see illustration)**. Note that on some models, the screw is behind the Gilera badge – lever the badge off carefully to access the screw.

27 Push the panel up to release the tabs along the sides from the slots in the front side panels, then lift the panel off **(see illustrations)**.

28 Installation is the reverse of removal; ensure the tabs are located in the slots before pressing the panel into position.

Front side panels

29 Remove the side panels (see Steps 13 to 19). Remove the front panel (see above) and the headlight assembly (see Chapter 9).

30 Remove the screws from the upper and lower front edges of the panel, then remove the screws from the lower side and the frame upper cover **(see illustrations)**. Note that on the left-hand panel, an extra screw is located inside the fuel filler flap **(see illustration)**.

4.23 Disconnect the speedometer cable

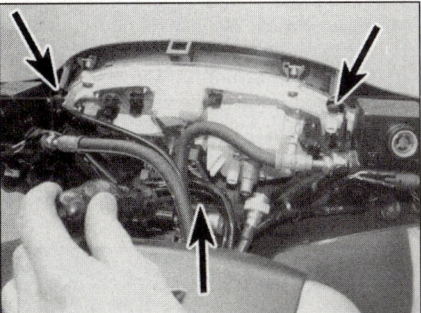

4.24 Remove the screws (arrowed) securing the cover to the handlebars

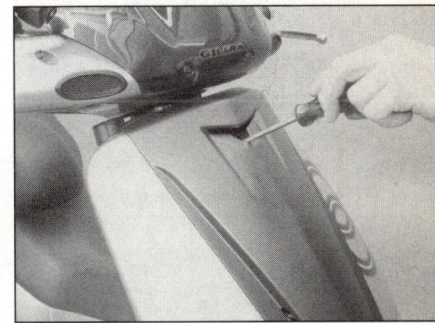

4.26 Remove the fixing screw

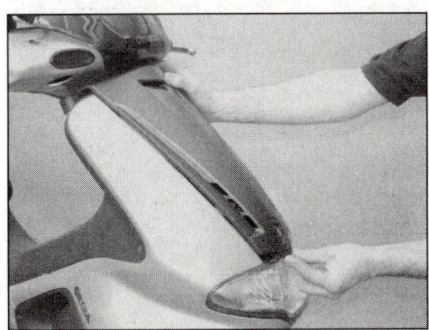

4.27a Push the panel up . . .

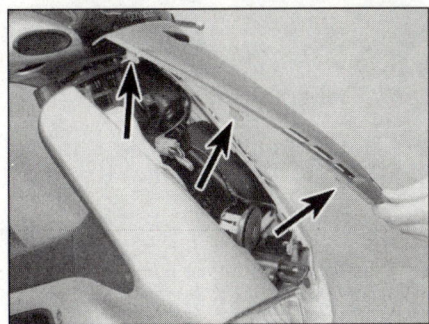

4.27b . . . then lift it off, noting the tabs (arrowed)

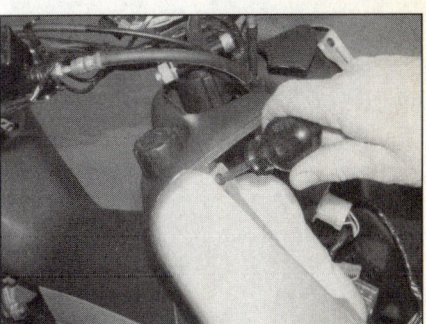

4.30a Remove the screw from the upper front edge . . .

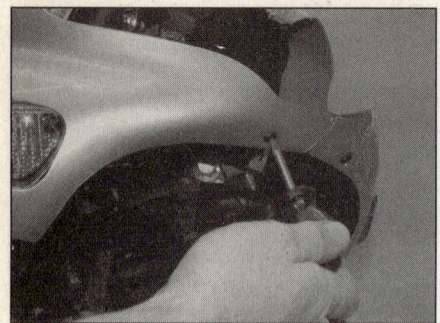

4.30b . . . and the lower front edge of the panel

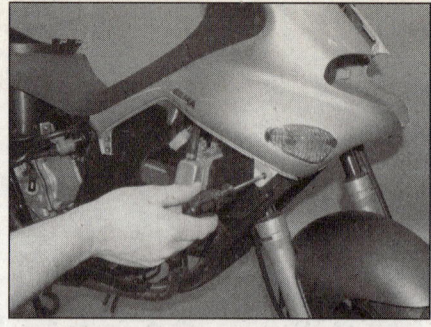

4.30c Remove the screw below the front turn signal assembly

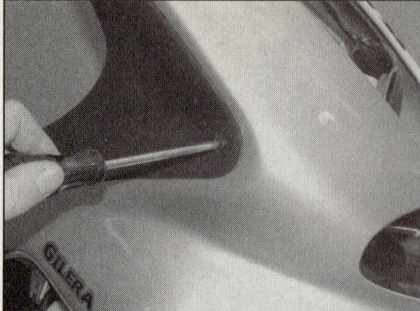

4.30d Remove the screw from the frame upper cover

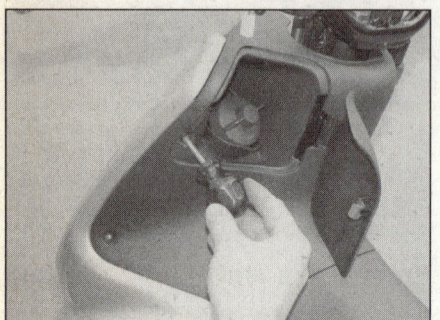

4.30e Note the screw inside the fuel filler flap on the left-hand side

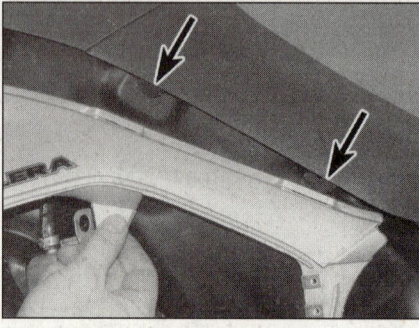

4.31a Remove the panel carefully to avoid damaging the tabs (arrowed) . . .

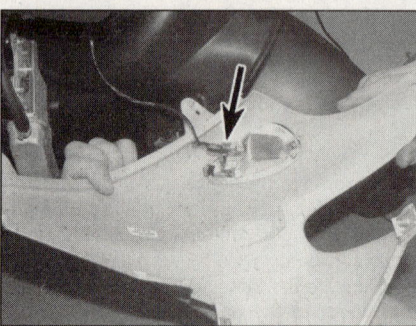

4.31b . . . and disconnect the turn signal wiring

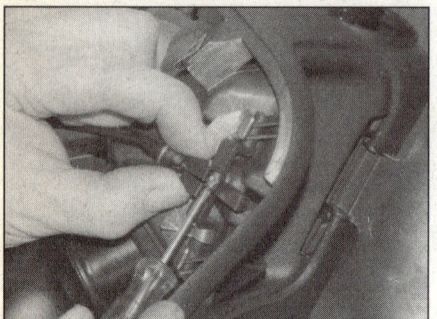

4.34a Disconnect the cable end from the latch mechanism . . .

31 Displace the panel carefully to release the tabs along the lower edge of the frame upper cover from the slots in the panel, then disconnect the turn signal wiring connectors (see illustrations).

32 Installation is the reverse of removal. Make sure the turn signal wiring connectors are correctly and securely connected, and check the operation of the signals and headlight before riding the scooter.

Frame centre panel

33 Remove the front side panels (see above).

34 Disconnect the inner cable end from the fuel filler flap latch mechanism, then squeeze the outer cable end and push it out of the cable stop (see illustrations). Note that on some models the latch mechanism is secured by a single screw – undo the screw and remove the mechanism, noting how the return spring fits (see illustration).

35 Remove the fuel filler cap and the coolant filler cap, then carefully prise the sealing collar off the coolant filler neck (see illustrations).

36 Remove the two screws next to the seat hinge fixing and the screw in the centre of the panel next to the ignition (main) switch (see illustrations).

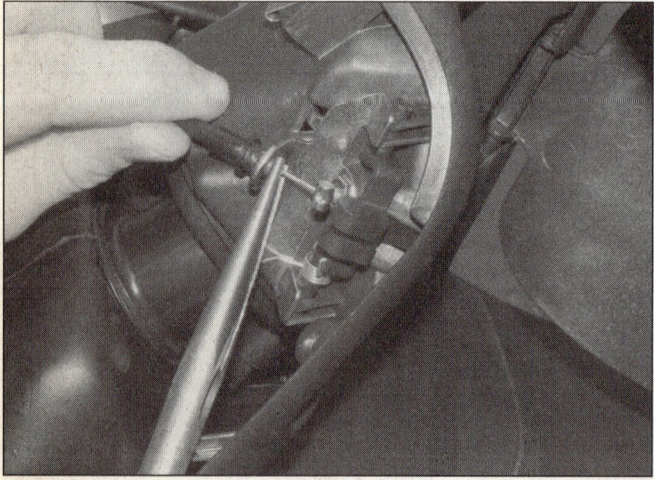

4.34b . . . then release the outer cable from the stop as described

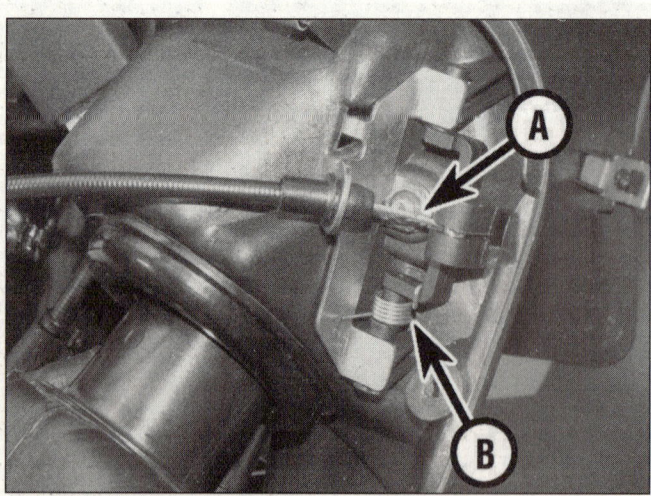

4.34c Remove the screw (A), noting how the spring (B) fits

4.35a Remove the fuel filler cap . . .

4.35b . . . and the coolant filler cap . . .

4.35c . . . and prise off the sealing collar

4.36a Remove the two screws (arrowed) . . .

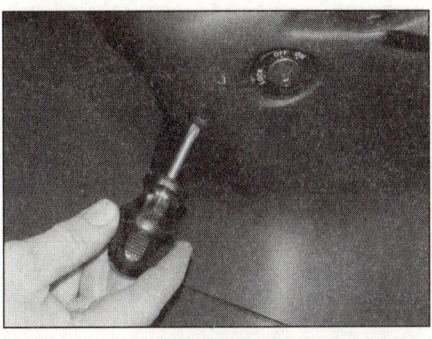

4.36b . . . and the single screw next to the main switch

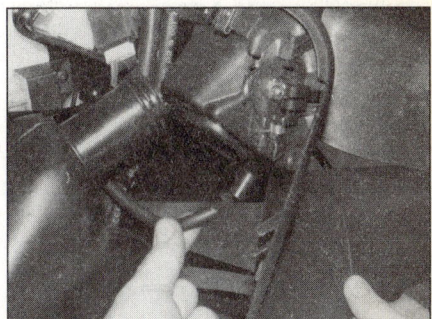

4.37 Disconnect the fuel drain hose

37 Ease the panel off the fuel and coolant filler necks and disconnect the fuel drain hose **(see illustration)**.

38 Raise the back of the panel and lift it off **(see illustration)**.

39 Installation is the reverse of removal. Don't forget to connect the fuel drain hose and make sure the fuel filler neck does not displace the collar in the panel. Check the operation of the filler flap latch mechanism before installing the left-hand front side panel.

Storage compartment

40 Remove the battery (see Chapter 9). Unclip the fuse holder from inside the battery compartment **(see illustration)**.

41 Remove the side panels (see Steps 13 to 19). Remove the frame centre panel (see Steps 33 to 38).

42 On all Runner 50 models and Runner FX125 and FXR180 models, remove the oil tank filler cap and prise the sealing collar off the filler neck.

43 Remove the two screws securing the compartment to the frame **(see illustration)**.

44 Lift the storage compartment out and feed the fuse holder and the battery cables through the hole in the side of the compartment **(see illustration)**. If removed, refit the oil filler cap.

45 Installation is the reverse of removal. Ensure no wiring is trapped between the compartment and the frame. On Runner 50 models and Runner FX125 and FXR180 models, don't forget to fit the collar to the oil filler neck.

Rear mudguard assembly

46 Remove the side panels (see Steps 13 to 19).

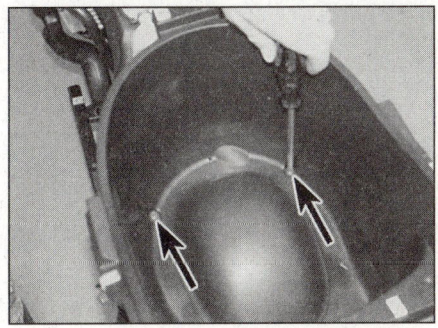

4.38 Raise the back of the panel and lift it off

4.43 Remove the two screws (arrowed) . . .

47 Remove the left and right hand screw securing the assembly to the frame **(see illustration)**.

48 Remove the three screws at the back

4.40 Unclip the fuse holder

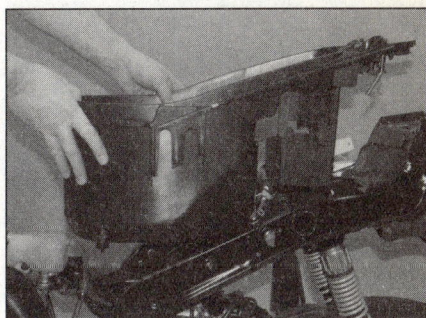

4.44 . . . and lift out the storage compartment

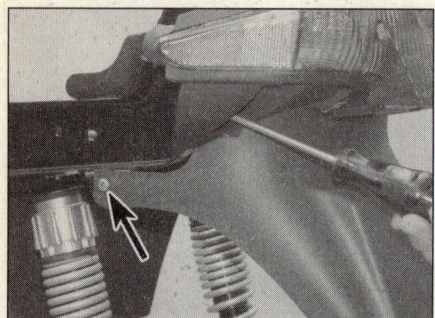

4.47 Remove the screw (arrowed) on both sides

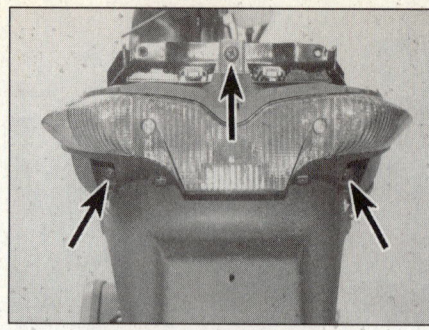

4.48a Remove the three screws (arrowed) . . .

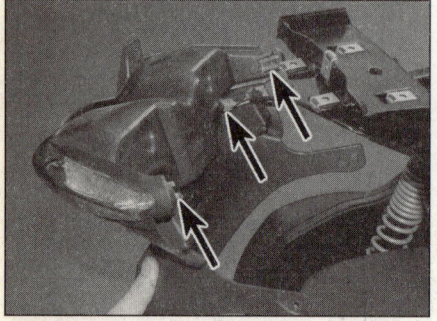

4.48b . . . and disconnect the wiring connectors (arrowed)

4.54 Left-hand screw secures the transmission cooling duct

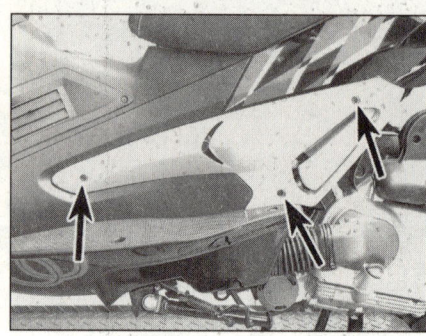

and lift the assembly away, then disconnect the tail light assembly and turn signal wiring connectors **(see illustrations)**.

49 Installation is the reverse of removal. Make sure the wiring connectors are correctly and securely connected, and check the operation of the signals, brake light and tail light before riding the scooter.

Front mudguard

50 Remove the four screws securing the mudguard to the fork sliders and lift off the mudguard.

51 Installation is the reverse of removal.

Radiator surround

52 Remove the steering stem (see Chapter 6).

53 Remove the side panels (see Steps 13 to 19).

54 Remove the two screws securing the front lower edge of the surround and the two screws securing the sides of the surround, then lift off the surround. Note that the left-hand screw also secures the transmission air cooling duct **(see illustration)**.

55 Installation is the reverse of removal.

5	Runner RST body panels

Seat

1 Press the ignition switch in to release the seat and hinge it upwards. If required, the seat can be released from its bracket by removing the two nuts.

Side panels and floor panels

2 Fold down the passenger footrest to reveal a screw, undo this along with the three other screws **(see illustrations)** and pull off the side panel. Remove the footrest plate on the other side.

3 Next remove each grab handle by undoing its two bolts **(see illustration)**.

5.2a Fold down the passenger footrest to reveal the screw (arrowed)

5.2b Remove the three screws (arrowed) . . .

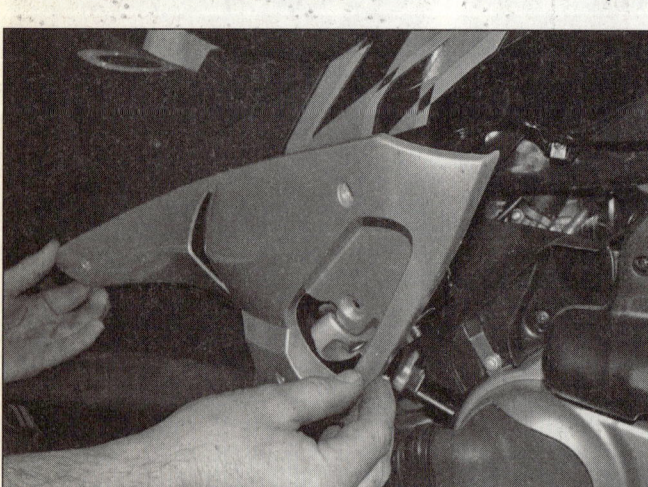

5.2c . . . and pull off the side panel

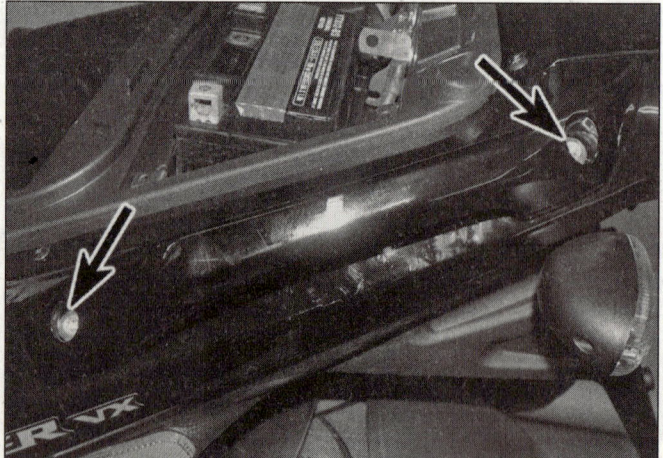

5.3 Undo the two bolts securing the grab handle (arrowed) . . .

5.4 Remove the tail panel screws

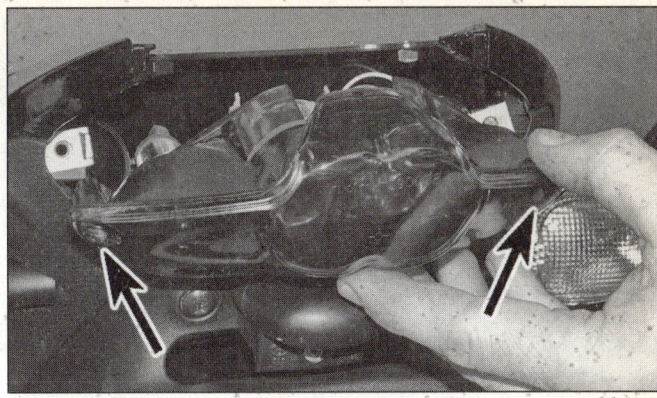

5.5 Remove the screws holding the tail light unit in place (arrowed)

4 Remove the tail panel that is held in place by two screws at its front edge and clips on the rear corners **(see illustration)**.

5 Remove the tail light unit held in place by two screws **(see illustration)**. Withdraw the light unit and disconnect the wiring.

6 Take off the licence plate holder by undoing four screws, two at the lower outer edges and two at the top end of the holder, next to the turn signals **(see illustrations)**. Gently pull out the wiring and release the wiring connector **(see illustration)**.

7 Remove each side panel by undoing the lower screw on the main part of the panel and two on the top of the panel **(see illustrations)**. **Note:** *The right-hand side panel has an extra screw on the underside.* Cut the cable-tie securing the wiring to the frame and disconnect the two turn signal wires (black wire right side,

pink wire left side) **(see illustration)**. Carefully remove the side panel from the machine.

8 Next remove each air vent panel which is

attached by a single screw **(see illustration)**. Pull the panel off noting how the six lugs are located **(see illustration)**.

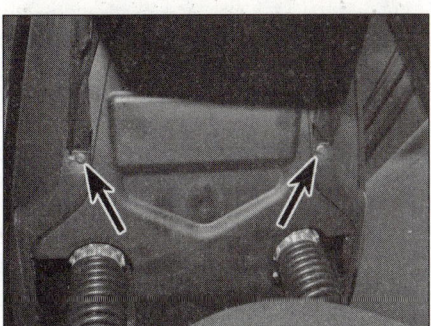

5.6a Remove the two lower screws (arrowed) . . .

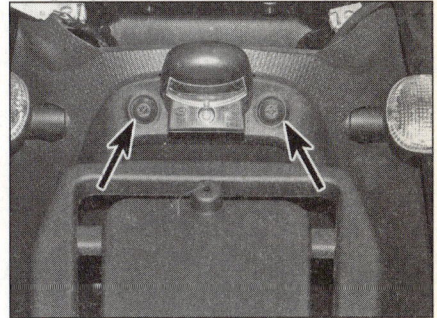

5.6b . . . the two upper screws (arrowed) . . .

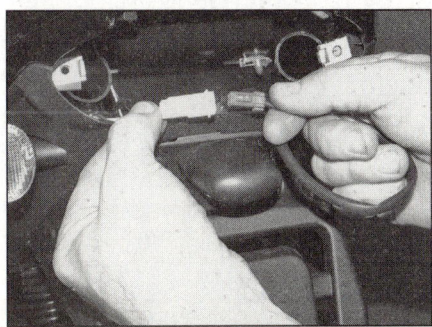

5.6c . . . then gently pull out the wiring connector and disconnect it

5.7a Undo the lower screw (arrowed) . . .

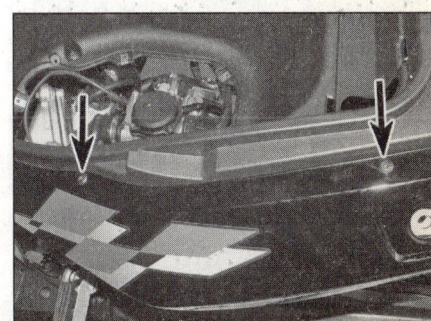

5.7b . . . and the two upper screws (arrowed) to remove the panel

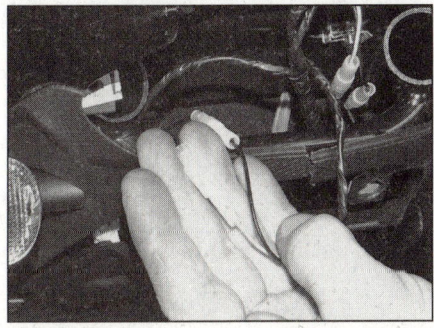

5.7c Disconnect the turn signal wiring

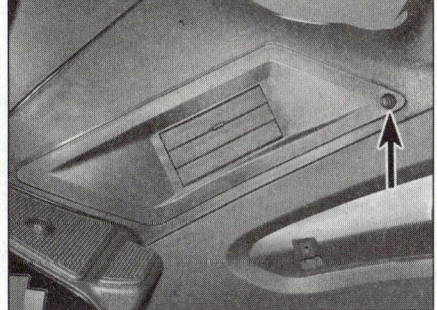

5.8a Remove the single screw from the air vent panel (arrowed) . . .

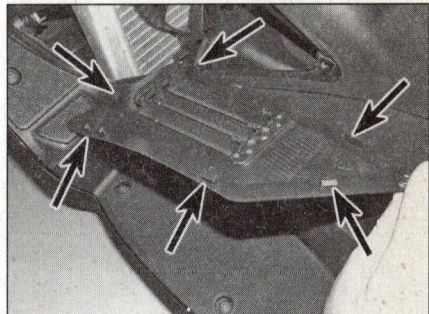

5.8b . . . pull the panel away noting the location of the six lugs (arrowed)

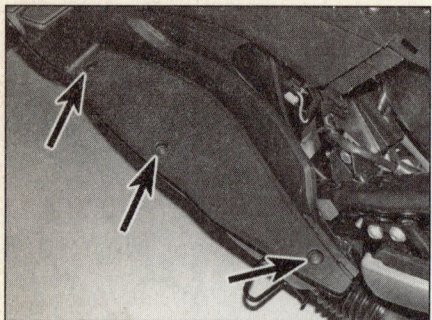

5.9a Remove three screws (arrowed) . . .

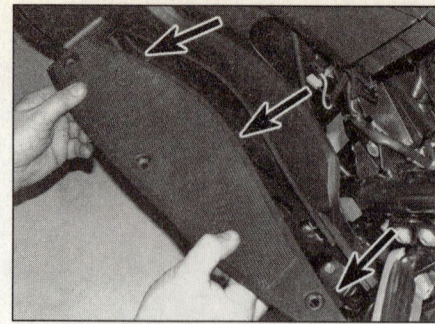

5.9b . . . noting how the lugs are slotted into place

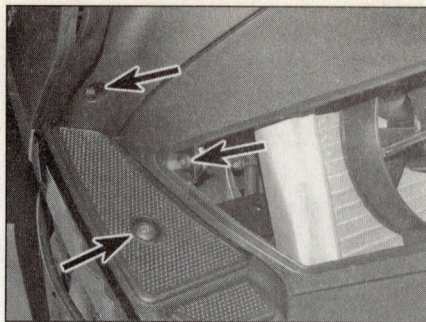

5.10 Remove the screw inside the air vent panel aperture, the middle of the footplate and at the bottom of the frame centre panel (arrowed)

9 Remove each floor panel unscrewing the three screws that secure it and pull it away noting how the lugs are slotted into place (see illustrations).

10 Remove each high level footplate by undoing the screw in the middle of the footplate, the screw at the bottom of the frame centre panel and the screw located inside the air vent panel aperture (see illustration) taking note how the lugs on the footplate are located up and under the adjoining panels.

11 Remove the remaining side panel by pulling it downwards to free it from the fuel tank cover panel, noting how it fits (see illustration).

Belly panel

12 Remove the side panels and floor panels (see Steps 2 to 11).

13 Undo the two screws at the bottom of the front grille on each side (see illustration), and the two screws which retain the belly panel to the front panel (see illustration).

14 Remove the bolts which retain the belly panel to the frame on each side. Carefully pull the side edges of the belly panel outwards to free them from the frame and withdraw the belly panel as one piece.

15 Installation is the reverse of removal. Note

how the belly panel fits over the inner panel edge and over the frame mountings.

Storage compartment

16 Unlock and remove the seat; it is held by two nuts at the front (see illustration).

17 Disconnect and remove the battery (see illustration).

18 Remove both side panels as described in Steps 2 to 7.

19 Disconnect the seat release cable from the latch and pull the cable out the side of

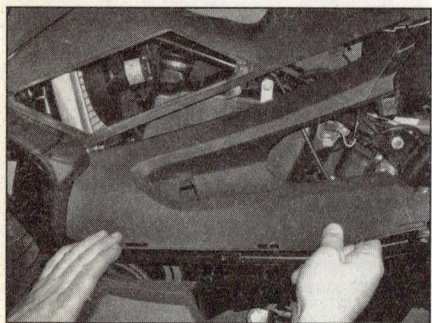

5.11 Pull the remaining panel downwards

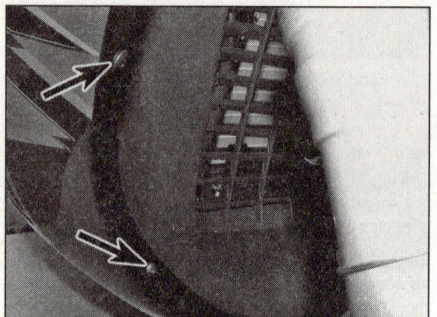

5.13a Remove the screws at the bottom of the grille (arrowed) . . .

5.13b . . . and the two screws retaining the belly panel (arrowed)

5.16 Remove the two nuts at the front (arrowed)

5.17 Disconnect and take out the battery

5.19a Disconnect the seat release cable

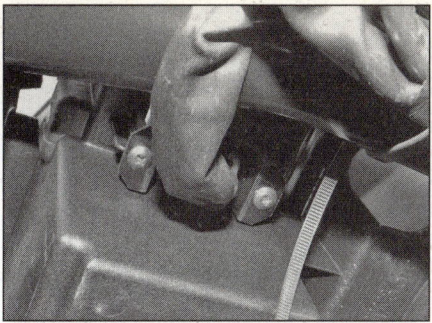

5.19b Undo the screws which retain the fusebox

5.19c Release the single screw to separate the undertray from the storage unit

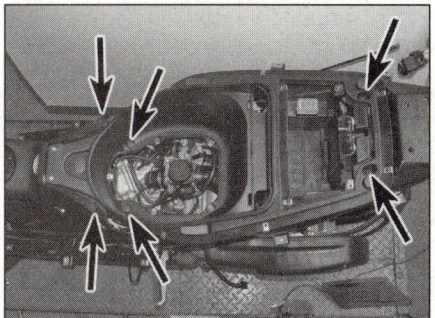

5.20 Storage unit mounting bolts

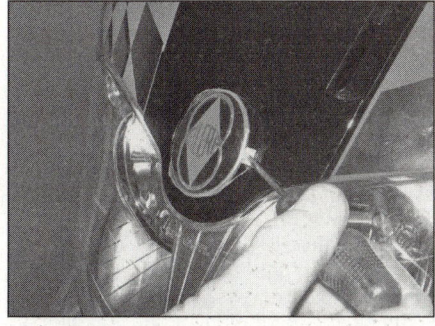

5.23a Prise the Gilera emblem off . . .

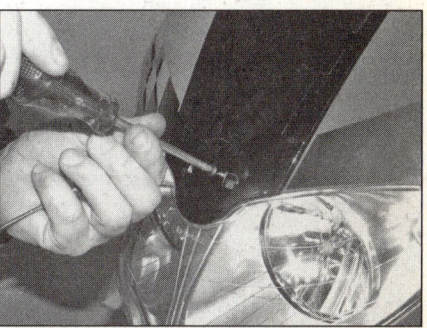

5.23b . . . remove the single screw from behind the emblem . . .

the storage unit. Also undo the screw from the underside which retains the fusebox **(see illustrations)**, and detach the undertray from the storage unit.

20 Remove its six mounting bolts and lift the storage compartment out of the frame **(see illustration)**.

21 Refit in a reverse of the removal procedure, noting that the front extension of the storage unit should fit over the seat hinge mounting lugs. Note that the storage compartment has a detachable engine access panel in its base and a rear shock top mounting access panel which simply clips into place.

Front panel

22 First remove the seat, both side panels, the floor panels and footplates before removing the front panel.

23 Prise the Gilera emblem off using a screwdriver to the right-hand side of it **(see illustration)**. Remove the single screw behind the emblem and take off the inspection panel. Push it upwards and pull outwards to disengage its clips **(see illustrations)**. With the panel removed access is now possible to the headlight bulbs and coolant reservoir.

24 Disconnect the headlight wiring connector tucked behind the fairing **(see illustration)**. Pass a screwdriver through the aperture and remove the screw from the coolant reservoir top mounting.

25 Free the frame centre panel from the front panel by removing its joining screws – note that the centre panel itself can remain in place. Remove the centre screw, plus the three screws (on each side) down the edge of the panel **(see illustration)**. Also remove the screw on each side at the top edge of the

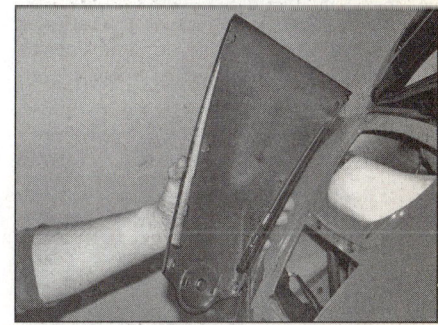

5.23c . . . push the inspection panel upwards and pull outwards

centre panel; turn the handlebars for access **(see illustration)**. Unscrew the coolant filler cap, then prise the rubber surround out

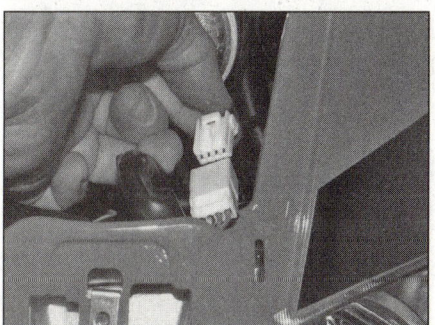

5.24 Disconnect the headlight wiring

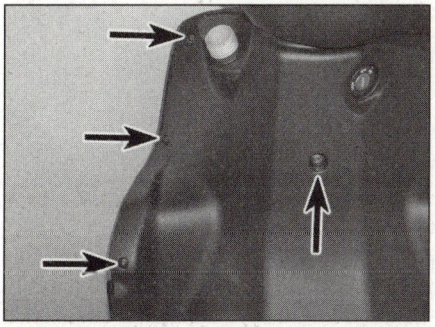

5.25a Remove the centre panel screw, plus the three screws at the edge (arrowed)

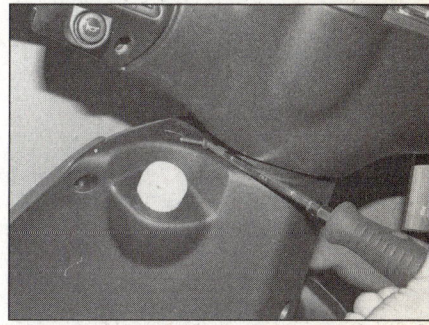

5.25b Remove the screw on each side at the top edge of the centre panel

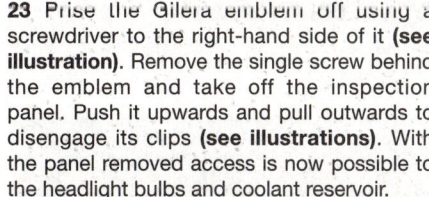

5.25c Unscrew the coolant filler cap and prise off the rubber surround

5.26a Undo the two front bolts (arrowed) . . .

5.26b . . . the two screws at the belly panel joint

from the neck of the coolant reservoir **(see illustration)** – this will allow slight movement of the front and centre panels to enable their tabs and clips to be disengaged.

26 Undo the two front bolts (arrowed), the screws on each side at the joint with the belly panel **(see illustration)** the single screw up under the headlight **(see illustration)** and single screw each side of the wheel **(see illustration)**.

27 Remove the turn signal retaining screw from each side and release the turn signal outwards through the panel. Manoeuvre the turn signals through their holes as you pull the front panel gently away **(see illustration)**.

28 Installation is a reverse of the removal procedure, noting the following:

• Make sure all spring clips which serve as captive nuts are in place on the panels before offering up the front panel – they have an

irritating habit of becoming dislodged during assembly if not a secure fit.

• Pass the turn signals through their apertures as the front panel is moved into position. Note that each turn signal has a tab which must engage the rear edge of the aperture.

• It is important that the edge of the front panel correctly engages the inner panel and the belly panel.

• Loosely fit all screws and check that everything aligns correctly before final tightening of the screws.

• Check the operation of the headlights, sidelights and front turn signals afterwards.

Frame centre panel

29 Remove the side panels and floor panels (see Steps 2 to 11).

30 Remove the front panel (see Steps 23 to 27).

31 Remove the fuel filler cap as described in Section 10, Steps 8 to 10 and then remove the screw which joins the centre panel to the fuel tank panel.

32 Installation is a reverse of the removal procedure.

Handlebar covers

33 Prise out the rubber plug at the base of each mirror stem and undo the screw to free the mirror **(see illustration)**.

34 Remove the fly screen by unscrewing the four screws **(see illustration)**. Take note of their positions – the screws are of different lengths.

35 To remove the front handlebar cover unscrew the two screws, one on each side below the switches **(see illustration)**. Pull the

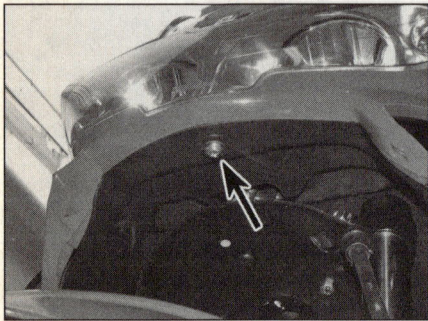

5.26c . . . a single screw under the headlight (arrowed) . . .

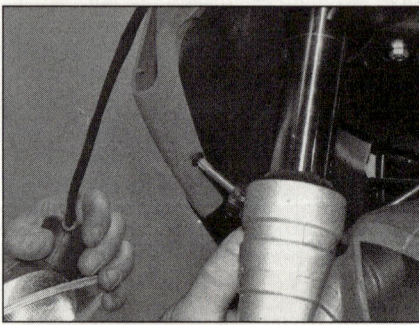

5.26d . . . and then the single screw on either side of the wheel

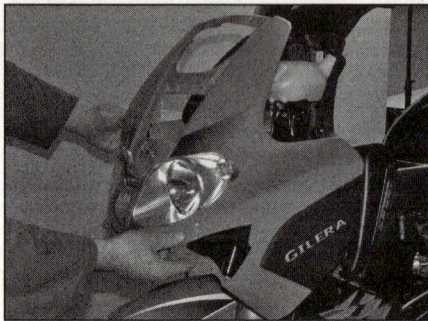

5.27 Withdraw the front panel, having already freed the turn signals

5.33 Prise out the rubber plug at the base of the mirror

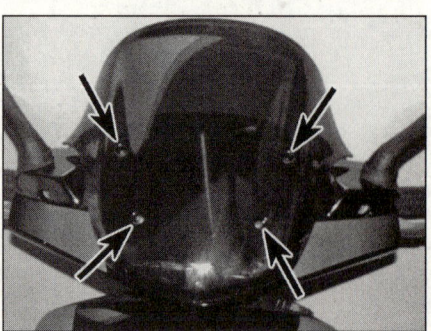

5.34 Remove the four screws (arrowed) noting their different lengths

5.35 Undo the screw on each side below the switches

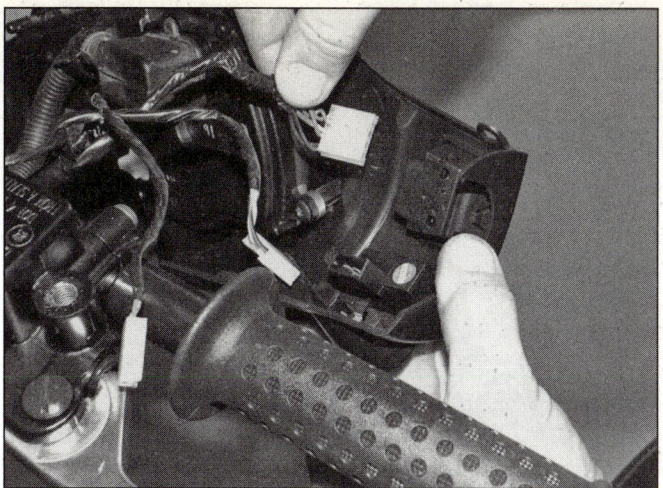

5.36a Disconnect the wiring connectors from the switches . . .

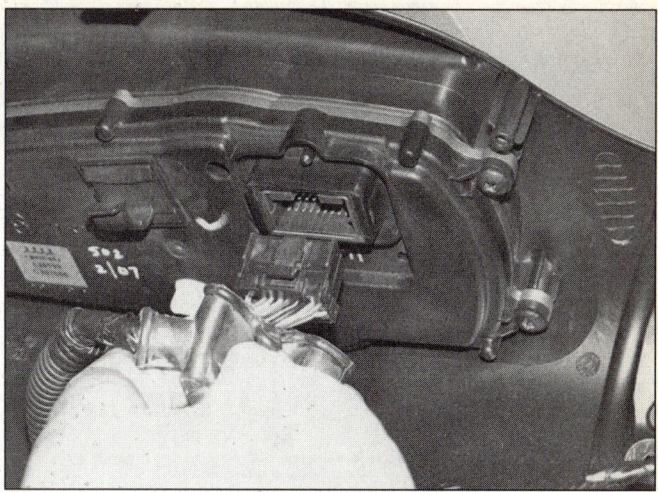

5.36b . . . and remove the rubber boot from the instrument wiring connector

cover forwards, disengaging its tabs on the top edge.

36 Disconnect the wiring connectors from the back of the switches **(see illustrations)**. Remove the rubber boot from the instrument wiring connector and disconnect it **(see illustration)**.

37 Remove the three screws and pull away the rear cover complete with the instruments **(see illustration)**.

38 Installation is the reverse of removal.

Front mudguard

39 To remove the front mudguard, refer to Section 4, Step 50.

| 6 | Runner ST body panels |

Seat

1 Press the ignition switch in to release the seat and hinge it upwards. If required, the seat bracket can be released by removing its two screws **(see illustration)**.

Footrest plates, rear carrier, sidepanels and floor panels

2 Fold down the passenger footrest to reveal a screw, undo this along with the three smaller screws **(see illustration)** and detach the footrest plate. Perform the same operation to remove the footrest plate on the other side of the scooter.

3 Remove the three screws to free the rear carrier, followed by the four bolts which retain its mounting bracket **(see illustrations)**. Two screws retain the tail light panel **(see illustration)**; note how the tabs at the rear

5.37 Remove the three screws to free the rear cover with the instruments

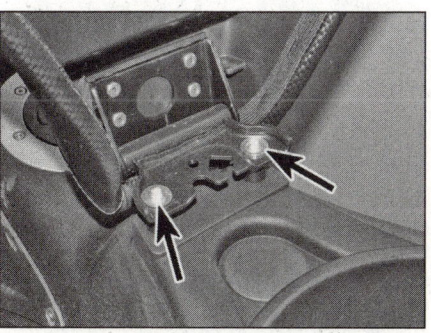

6.1 Seat bracket screws (arrowed)

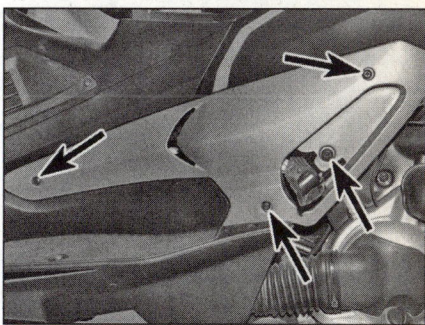

6.2 Footrest plate is held by four screws (arrowed)

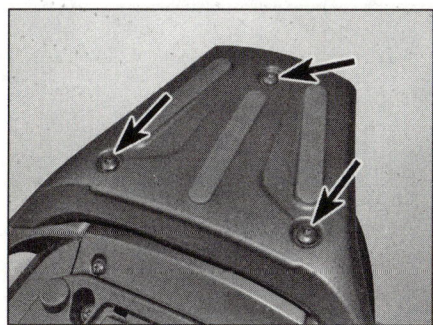

6.3a Remove the rear carrier bolts (arrowed) . . .

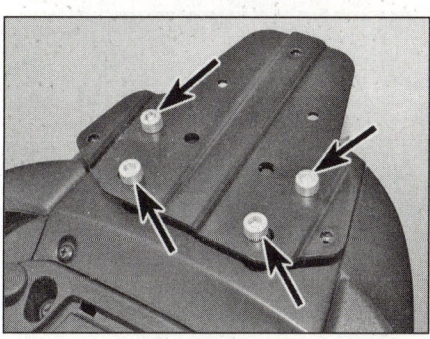

6.3b . . . followed by its mounting bracket bolts (arrowed)

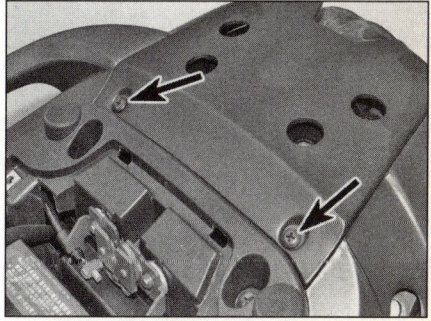

6.3c Tail light panel is retained by two screws at the front (arrowed) . . .

6.3d . . . and clips at the rear on each side

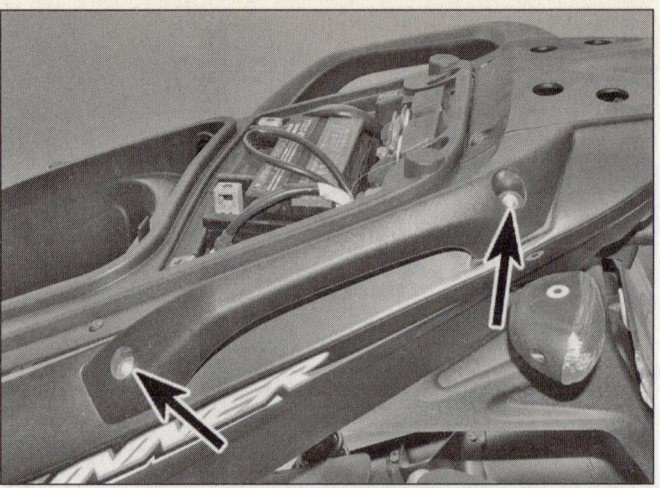

6.4 Grab handle bolts (arrowed)

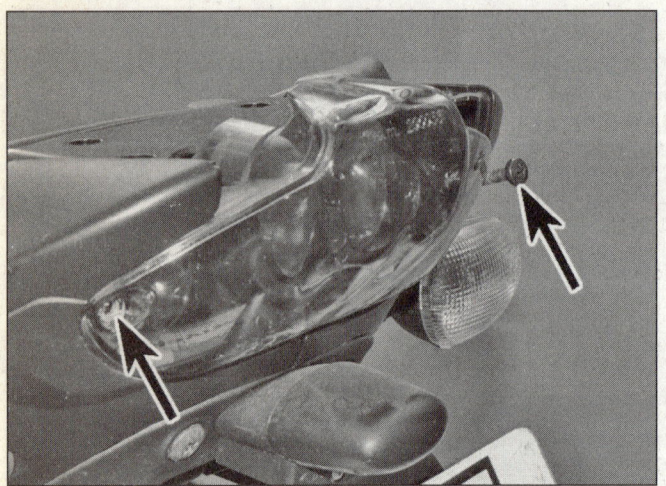

6.5a Two screws retain tail light unit (arrowed)

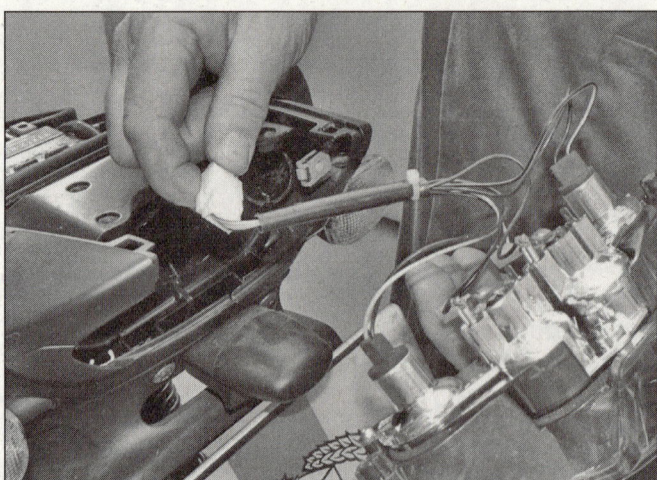

6.5b Release the wire connector to free the tail light

of the panel engage the cut-outs in each sidepanel **(see illustration)**.

4 Remove the two bolts to free each grab handle **(see illustration)**.

5 Remove the two screws to free the tail light unit, then disconnect the wiring to remove the tail light unit complete with bulbs **(see illustrations)**.

6 Remove the licence plate holder complete with licence plate. It is held by two screws on the underside (which are of different lengths) and by two screws at the rear **(see illustrations)**. Release the licence plate light wiring at the connector **(see illustration)**.

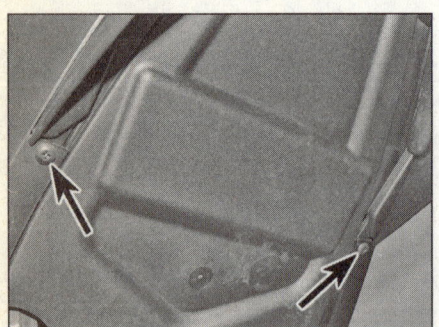

6.6a Licence plate holder screws on the underside (arrowed) . . .

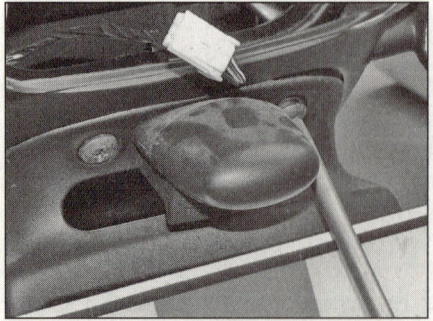

6.6b . . . and at the rear, each side of licence plate light

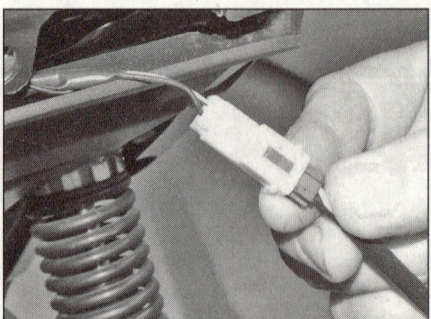

6.6c Release the licence plate light wire connector

6.7a Sidepanel screw at the front . . .

6.7b . . . along the top edge . . .

6.7c . . . and on the right side only, on the underside

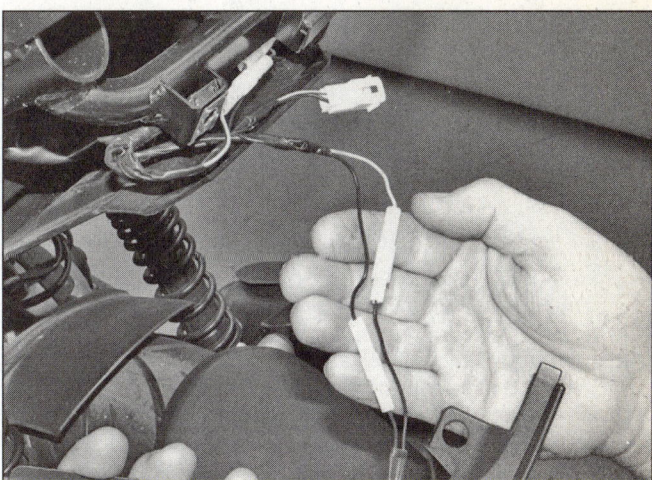

6.7d Disconnect the turn signal wiring at the connectors

7 Each sidepanel is retained by a screw at the front edge, two screws along the top and, on the right-hand side only, by a screw on the underside **(see illustrations)**. Disconnect the turn signal wiring and remove the sidepanel complete with the turn signal **(see illustration)**.

8 Remove the single screw to free the air vent panel, noting how its tabs engage the frame centre panel **(see illustrations)**.

9 Three screws retain the floor panel; note the locating tabs which engage the frame centre panel **(see illustration)**.

10 Remove the screw from the centre of the high level footplate, the screw inside

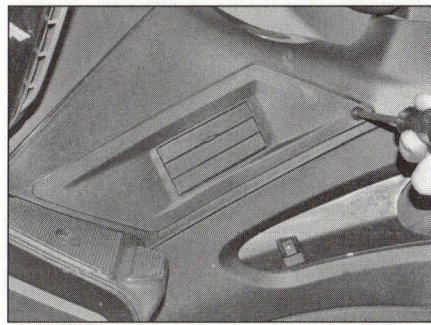

6.8a Air vent is retained by a single screw . . .

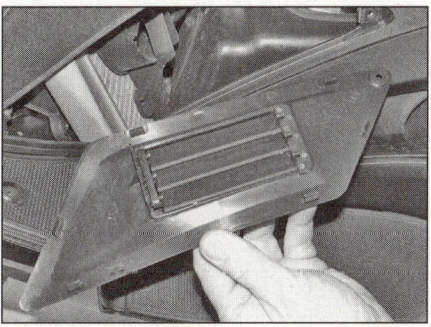

6.8b . . . and by six tabs on the inside

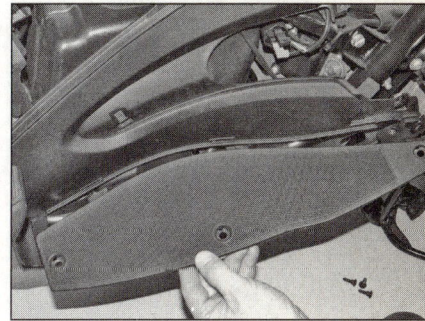

6.9 Floor panel tabs engage slots in insert panel

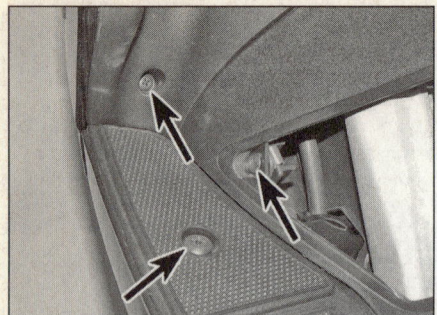

6.10a Removal of screws in footrest plate, body centre panel, inside air vent aperture . . .

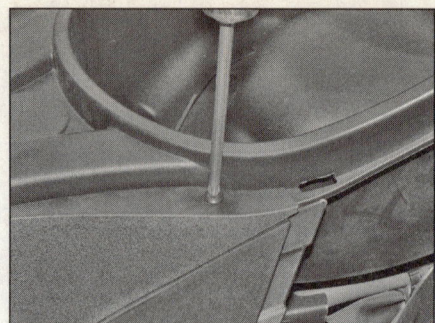

6.10b . . . and at the rear of the fuel tank panel . . .

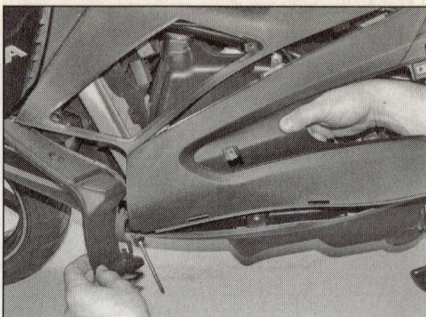

6.10c . . . will allow removal of the footrest plate and insert panel

6.11 Footrest plate and insert panel lock together on the inner side

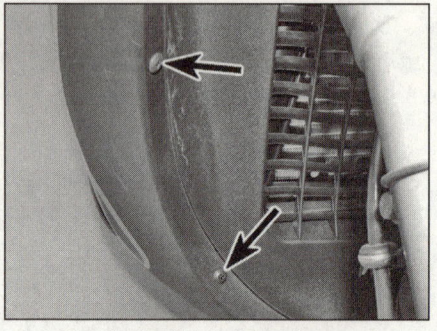

6.13a Each side of the belly panel is retained by two screws at the front . . .

6.13b . . . and two screws on the inside

the air vent panel aperture and the screw at the bottom edge of the centre panel (see illustration). Remove the screw at the rear edge of the fuel tank panel and carefully disengage the three tabs at the top of the insert panel from the frame (see illustrations). Disengage the insert panel from the footplate.

11 Installation is a reversal of removal, noting the following:

● The high level footplate and insert panel engage one another by clips on their inner edges and may be best joined together before installation (see illustration).

● When reconnecting the turn signal wiring, note that the pink wire connects to the left side and the white/blue wire to the right.

● Most of the panel screws are secured by captive nuts which are a push fit on the

panel tabs. Check that the captive nuts have not dropped free during the removal process.

● Check the operation of the seat release before closing the seat and check the operation of the tail light, licence plate light and rear turn signals.

Belly panel

12 Remove both sidepanels and both floor panels as described above.

13 Undo the two screws at the bottom of the front grille on each side (see illustration), and the two screws which retain the belly panel to the front panel on each side (see illustration).

14 Ease the belly panel edges off the frame mounting lugs and remove the panel (see illustration).

15 Installation is a reversal of removal.

Storage compartment

16 Unlock and raise the seat. Remove the two screws which retain the seat bracket and lift the seat and bracket off.

17 Remove each sidepanel as described in Steps 2 to 7, then remove the single screw on each side which retains the insert panel (see illustration 6.10b).

18 Refer to Chapter 9 to disconnect the battery, then lift the battery out.

19 Slide off the red plastic locking piece from the seat release cable latch, then disconnect the cable from the latch and withdraw the cable from the right-hand side (see illustration).

20 Withdraw the fusebox from the underside – it is retained by two screws (see illustration). Remove the single screw

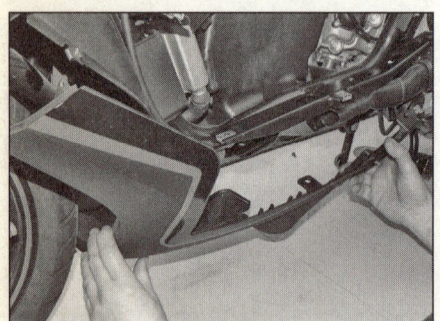

6.14 Ease the edges of the belly panel off the frame mountings

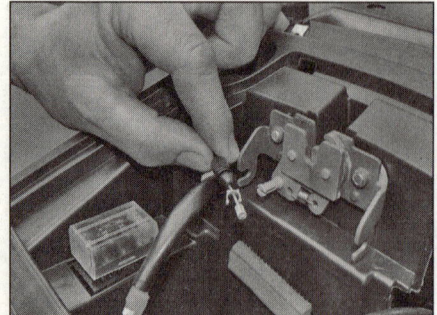

6.19 Free the seat release cable from the latch

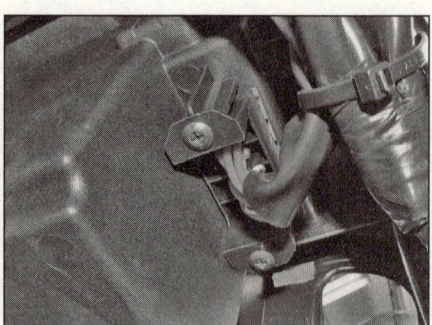

6.20a Fusebox is held to the underside of the storage compartment by two screws

6.20b Undertray retaining screw

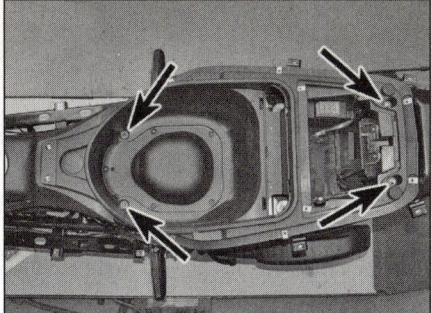

6.21 Storage compartment bolts (arrowed)

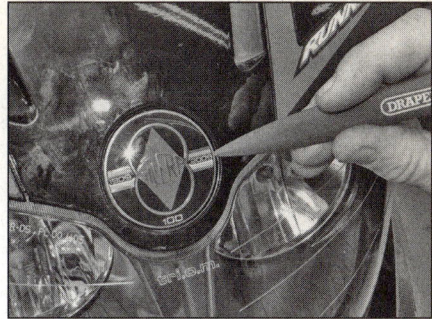

6.24a Locate a plastic pointer in the cut-out to free the badge . . .

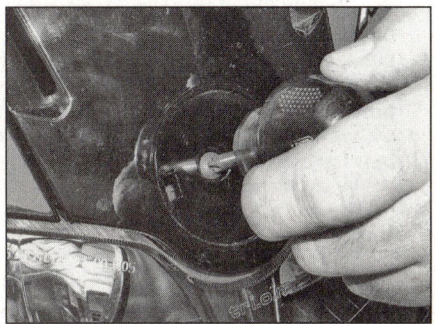

6.24b . . . release the screw underneath . . .

6.24c . . . and slide the centre panel upwards to release its six tabs

6.25 Disconnect the headlight wiring connector

to release the undertray from the storage compartment **(see illustration)**.

21 Remove the four bolts to free the storage compartment to the frame **(see illustration)**.

22 Note that the storage compartment contains an engine access panel in its base and an access panel for the rear shock mountings.

Front panel

23 First remove the footrest plates, rear carrier, sidepanels and floor panels (Steps 2 to 10), then the belly panel (Steps 13 and 14).

24 Prise the Gilera emblem off using a small screwdriver to the left-hand side of it **(see illustration)**. Remove the single screw under the emblem and slide the inspection panel upwards to disengage its tangs **(see illustrations)**.

25 Disconnect the headlight wiring connector tucked behind the front panel **(see illustration)**.

26 Remove the four screws down each side of the centre panel **(see illustration)**. Turn the handlebars for access and remove the screw at the top edge of the centre panel on each side **(see illustration)**.

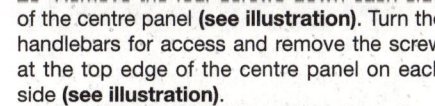

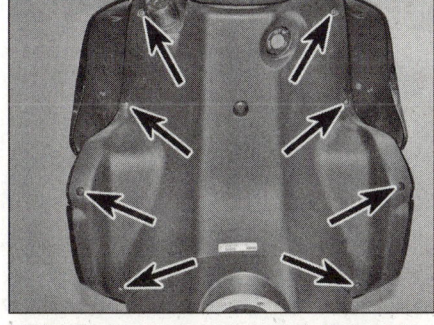

6.26a Front cover screws pass through the body centre panel . . .

27 Undo the two front bolts **(see illustration)**, the single screw up under the headlight and the single screw on each side of the wheel **(see illustrations)**.

28 Gently pull the front panel away

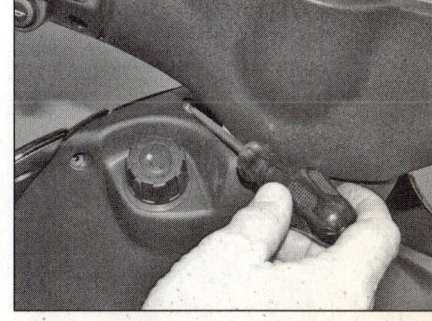

6.26b . . . and are also located each side of the steering head

6.27a Front cover mounting screws (arrowed) at the front . . .

6.27b . . . under the headlight . . .

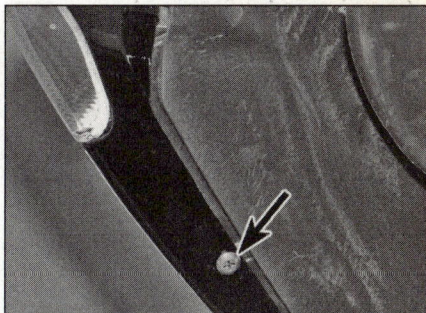

6.27c . . . and each side on the lower edge

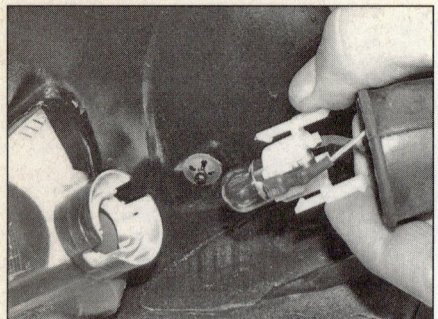

6.28 Squeeze ears of turn signal bulbholder and pull it free

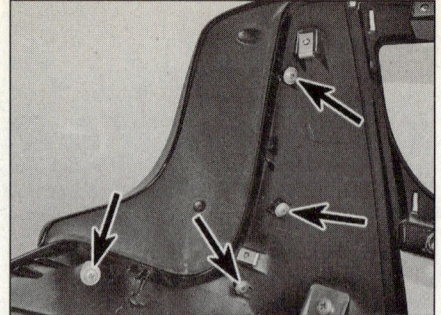

6.29 Front panel side section screws (arrowed)

6.34a Note position of shouldered spacers when removing windshield screws

and squeeze the ears of the turn signal bulbholders to allow the bulbholders and bulbs out of the front panel **(see illustration)**.
29 The front panel side sections can be detached if required – four screws retain the section **(see illustration)**.
30 Installation is a reversal of removal, noting the following:

● Most of the panel screws are secured by captive nuts which are a push fit on the panel tabs. Check that the captive nuts have not dropped free during the removal process.
● Check that the front panel engages correctly with the centre panel before tightening the screws.
● Check the operation of the headlights, sidelights and front turn signals.

Fuel tank panel

31 First remove the footrest plates, rear carrier, sidepanels and floor panels (Steps 2 to 10).
32 Remove the fuel filler cap and single screw with joins the fuel tank panel to the centre panel as described in Section 10, Steps 8 to 10.
33 Installation is a reversal of removal.

Handlebar covers

34 Remove the four windshield mounting screws, noting the shouldered spacers on the screws and remove the windshield **(see illustrations)**. Now remove the two screws at the top of the mounting brackets, noting their shouldered spacers **(see illustration)**.
35 Prise out the rubber plug at the base of each mirror stem and undo the screw to free the mirror **(see illustrations)**.
36 Remove the two screws from the rear cover, then disengage the cover tabs at the end and centre positions along the top edge **(see illustrations)**. Remove the front half of the handlebar cover.

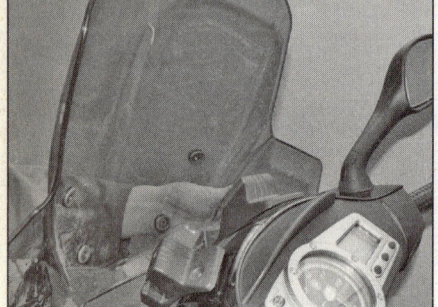

6.34b Windshield mounts to front of handlebar cover . . .

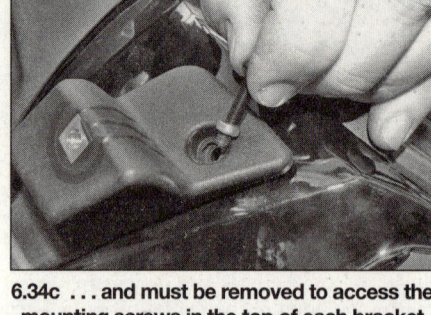

6.34c . . . and must be removed to access the mounting screws in the top of each bracket

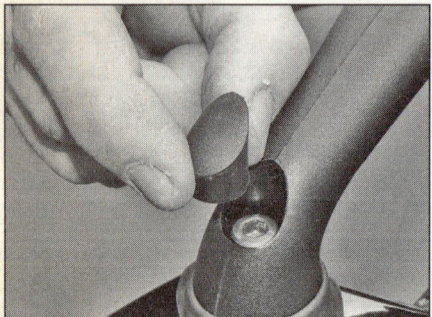

6.35a Prise out the plug, remove the Allen screw . . .

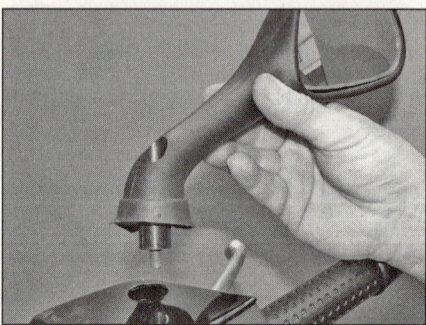

6.35b . . . and detach each mirror

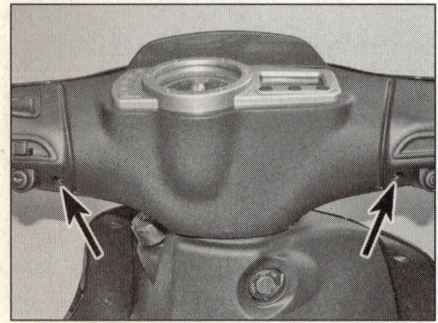

6.36a Handlebar covers and joined by screws at the lower edge (arrowed) . . .

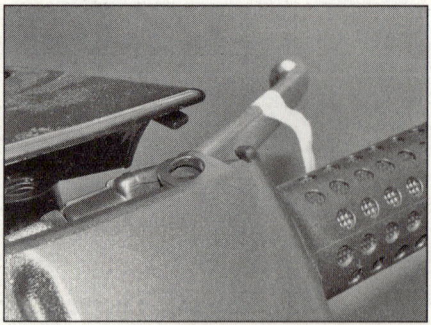

6.36b . . . tabs at the outer edge on each side . . .

6.36c . . . and a tab at the centre

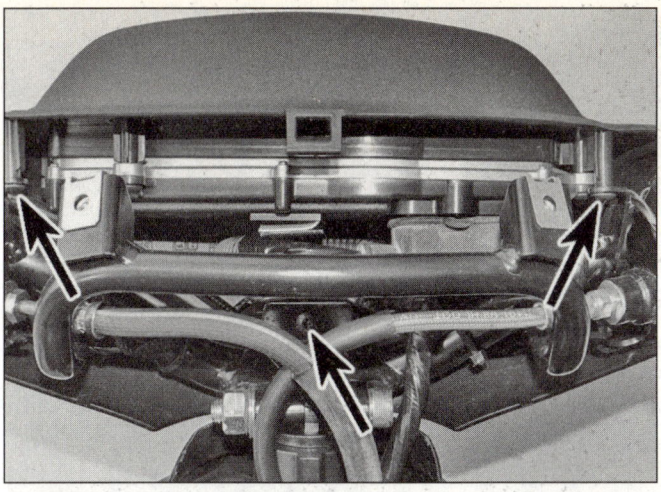

6.37a Three screws (arrowed) retain rear cover to handlebar

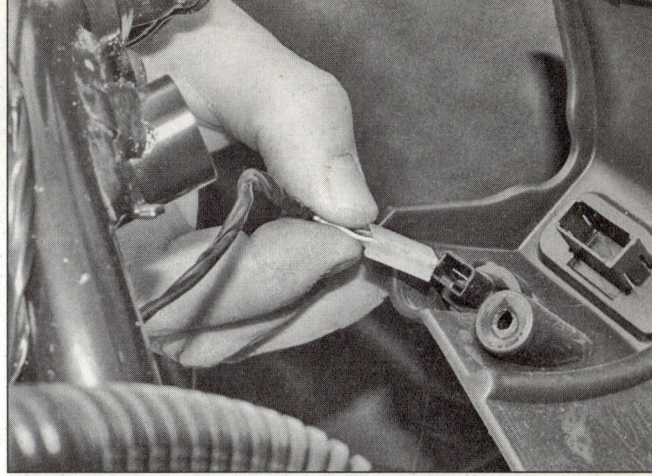

6.37b Switch wiring connectors are simply pulled off the back of the switches . . .

37 Remove the three screws which retain the rear half to the handlebars, then disconnect the wiring connections to the handlebar switches and the instruments **(see illustrations)**.

38 Installation is a reversal of removal.

7 DNA body panels

Seat

1 Unlock the seat, then lift the back of the seat and pull it backwards to disengage the fixing pegs on the frame from the underside of the seat **(see illustration)**.

2 Installation is the reverse of removal.

Engine top cover

3 The engine top cover is secured by two screws at the back, one screw on the

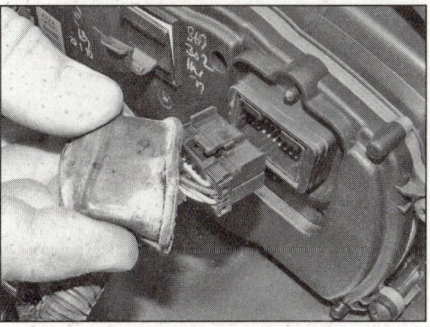

6.37c . . . and the instruments

left-hand side and a quick-release fastener on the right-hand side; undo the fixings and lift off the panel **(see illustration)**.

4 Installation is the reverse of removal.

Side panels

5 Each side panel is secured to the frame by

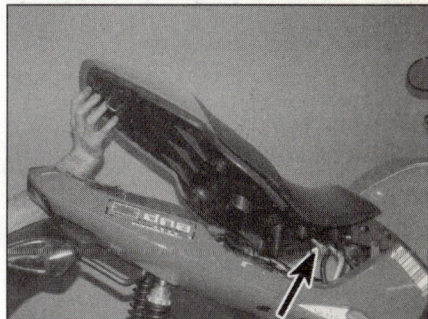

7.1 Disengage the fixing pegs (arrowed)

three screws and to the radiator/belly panel by two screws on the side and three screws on the inside front edge **(see illustration)**. Remove the screws and lift off the panel. Note the location of the screw clips and renew any that are sprained or damaged **(see illustrations)**.

7.3 Lift off the engine top cover

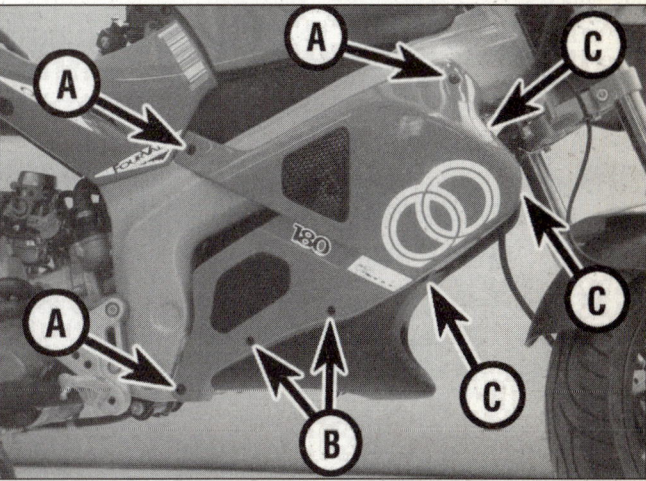

7.5a Side panel is secured to the frame by screws (A) and to the radiator/belly panel by screws (B) and (C)

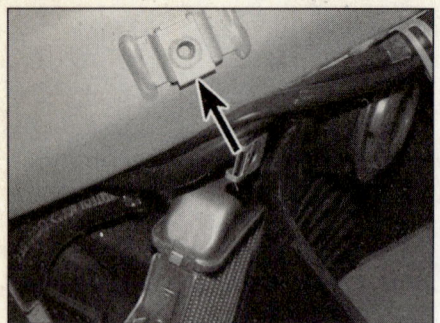

7.5b Note the location of the screw clips (arrowed) on the frame . . .

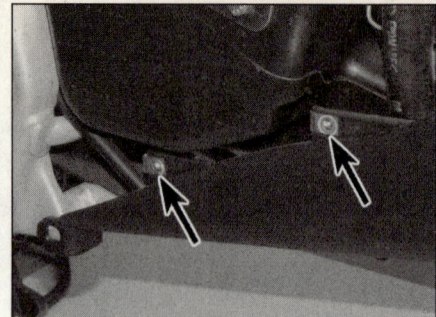

7.5c . . . and on the belly panel

7.7 Wiring and brake hose (arrowed) are routed through the panel

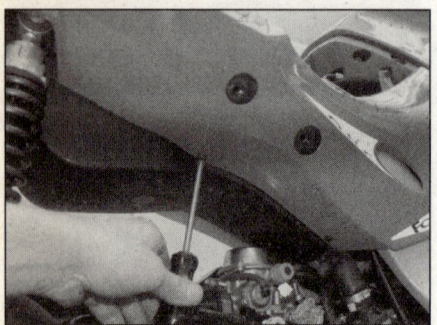

7.11a Remove the screws as described . . .

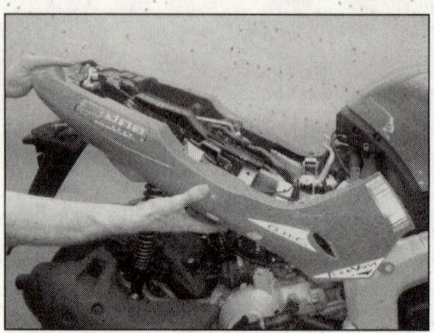

7.11b . . . then lift off the panel

7.15 Disconnect the lower cable (arrowed)

6 Installation is the reverse of removal. Ensure the screw clips are in position before installing the screws.

Radiator/belly panel

7 Remove the left and right-hand side panels (see above). To displace the panel, unclip it from the lugs on the frame and move it to the left-hand side – the panel cannot be removed from the machine without first disconnecting the main wiring loom and the rear brake hydraulic hose which are routed through the left-hand side of the panel (see illustration).

8 Installation is the reverse of removal. Ensure the upper front and lower rear screw holes are aligned with the side panel mountings before installing the side panels.

Seat cowling

9 Remove the seat (see Step 1).

10 The seat cowling is a two-piece assembly. To remove the right-hand panel, first remove the right-hand passenger footrest bracket (see Section 3), then remove the right-hand side panel (see Step 5).

11 Remove five screws on the upper edge and the five screws on the lower edge of the seat cowling panel and lift the panel off (see illustrations).

12 Follow the same procedure to remove the left-hand panel.

13 Installation is the reverse of removal. Ensure the passenger footrest bracket bolts are tightened securely

Storage compartment

14 Remove both seat cowling panels.

15 Open the storage compartment and support the lid, then prise off the latch mechanism cover. Disconnect the lower inner cable end from the mechanism arm, then disconnect the cable outer from the bracket (see illustration). Position the cable clear of the helmet compartment.

16 Remove the five small jointing screws along the back edge of the compartment (see illustration). Unscrew the coolant reservoir cap and lift off the reservoir cover. Remove the two screws securing the compartment to the frame (see illustration).

17 Unscrew the fuel filler cap (see illustration). Ease the join along the back edge of the compartment apart and lift the

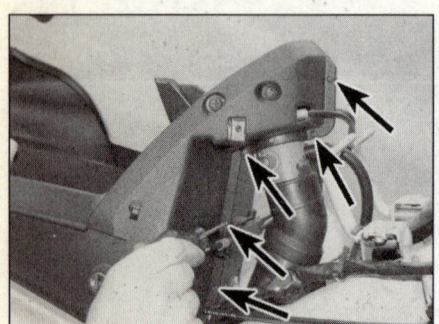

7.16a Remove the five screws (arrowed) . . .

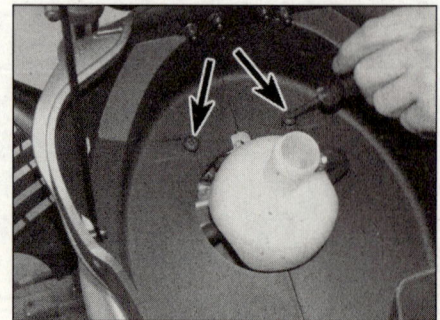

7.16b . . . and the two screws in the bottom of the compartment

7.17a Remove the fuel filler cap . . .

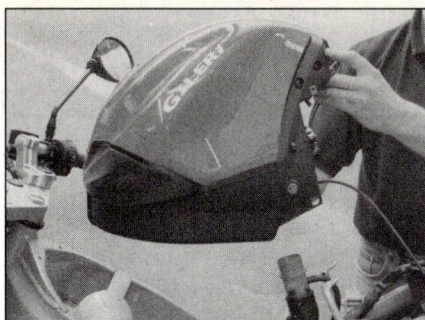

7.17b ... then lift off the storage compartment

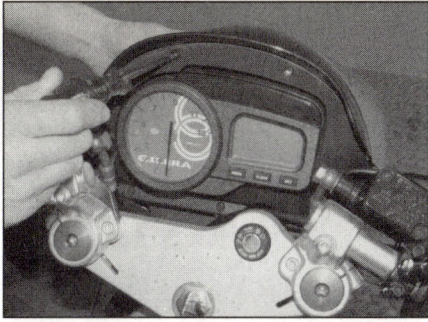

7.19a Remove the screws from around the edge of the fairing ...

7.19b ... then lift it off

7.20a Remove the screws (arrowed) ...

7.20b ... then remove the lower fairing half

7.24a Remove the screws (arrowed) ...

compartment up off the fuel filler neck **(see illustration)**. Refit the filler cap.

18 Installation is the reverse of removal. Ensure the compartment is fitted below the thread on the fuel filler neck before installing the jointing screws. Check the operation of the latch mechanism before closing the lid.

Front fairing

19 Remove the eight small screws around the edge of the fairing and lift it off **(see illustrations)**. Note it is not necessary to remove the screen and the screen should only be removed if it is being renewed.

20 To remove the lower fairing half, first remove the headlight unit, the instrument cluster and the front turn signals (see Chapter 9). Undo the

screws securing the fairing assembly and lift off the support brackets, noting how they fit **(see illustration)**. Ease the wiring through the back of the panel and lift it off **(see illustration)**.

21 Installation is the reverse of removal. Check the operation of the headlight and the turn signals before riding the scooter.

Rear mudguard assembly

22 Remove both seat cowling panels (see Steps 9 to 12).

23 Displace or remove the tail light assembly and disconnect the turn signal wiring connectors (see Chapter 9).

24 Remove the screws securing the mudguard assembly and lift it off **(see illustrations)**.

25 If required, undo the nuts securing the support bracket and lift it off, noting which way round it fits.

26 Installation is the reverse of removal. Make sure the wiring connectors are correctly and securely connected, and check the operation of the signals, brake light and tail light before riding the scooter.

Front mudguard

27 Remove the front wheel (see Chapter 7).

28 Remove the four screws securing the mudguard to the fork sliders and lift off the mudguard – note the position of the guide for the speedometer wire and ensure it is correctly positioned on installation **(see illustration)**.

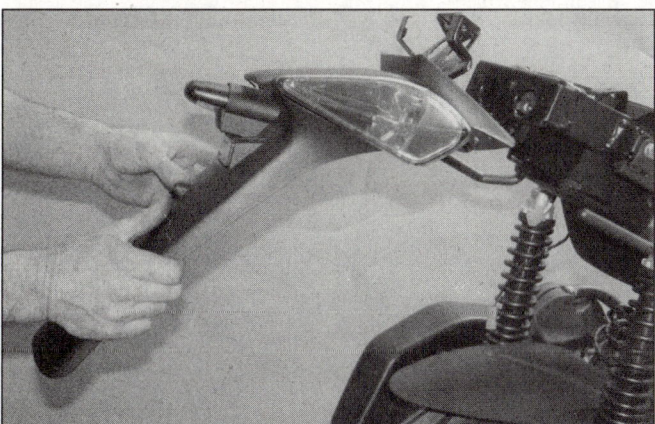

7.24b ... and lift off the mudguard assembly

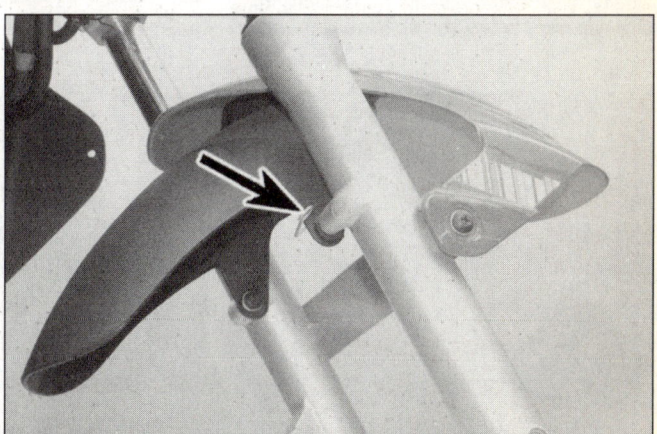

7.28 Note the guide (arrowed) for the speedometer wire

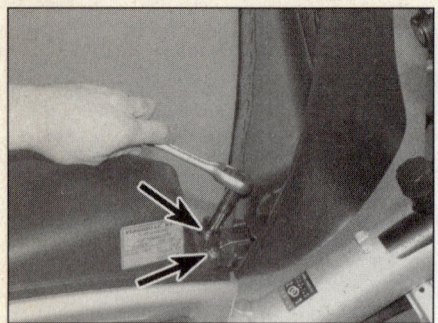

8.1a Remove the two nuts (arrowed) . . .

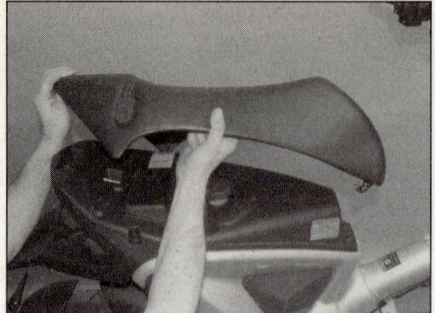

8.1b . . . and lift off the seat

8.3a Remove the screws (arrowed) . . .

8 Ice body panels

Seat

1 Unlock the seat using the ignition key and swing it upright. Remove the nuts securing the seat hinge to the frame and lift off the seat **(see illustrations)**.

2 Installation is the reverse of removal.

3 The seat latch mechanism is secured by three screws; remove the screws and lift out the mechanism **(see illustrations)**. The lock is secured by an R-clip; pull out the clip and withdraw the lock **(see illustrations)**

Engine access panels

4 The engine top cover is secured by two screws on the right-hand side and one screw on the left-hand side; remove the screws and lift off the cover **(see illustration)**.

5 The side covers clip into the frame; lever them off carefully, noting how they fit **(see illustration)**.

6 The front panel is secured by one screw on the left and right-hand side; remove the screws and pull the panel forwards, noting the location of the tabs on the top edge **(see illustrations)**.

7 Installation is the reverse of removal. Take care when installing the side covers – hook

8.3b . . . and lift out the latch mechanism

the lower clips over the frame, then press the top edge of the of the cover into place.

Frame covers

8 To remove the top cover, lift it at the back

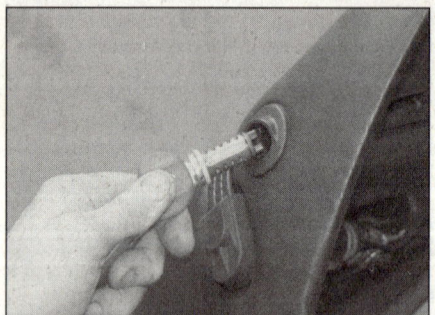

8.3d . . . and withdraw the lock

8.3c Pull out the R-clip . . .

edge and pull it back to disengage the clips at the front **(see illustrations)**.

9 To remove the lower cover, first remove the front engine access panel (see Step 6). Undo the screw, then pull the cover back

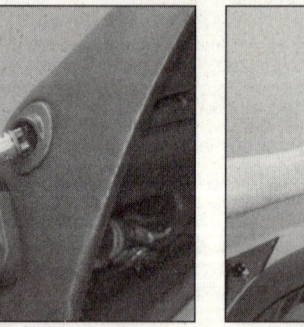

8.4 Lift off the engine top cover

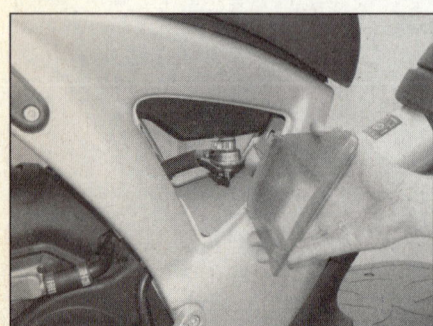

8.5 Access covers clip into the side of the frame

8.6a Remove the screws on each side . . .

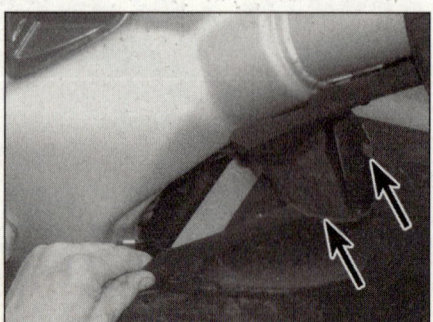

8.6b . . . then pull the panel forwards, noting the tabs (arrowed)

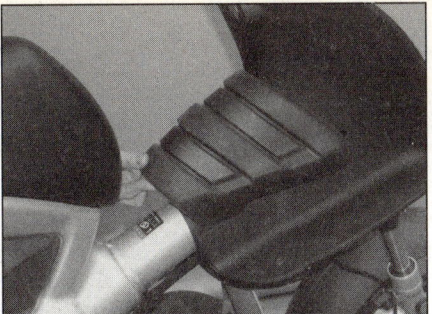

8.8a Lift the cover and pull it back . . .

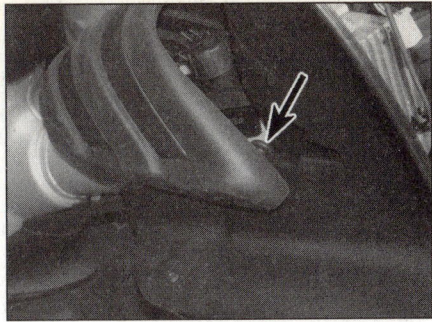

8.8b . . . to disengage the clip (arrowed)

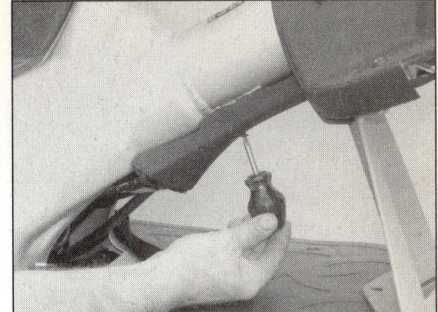

8.9a Remove the screw . . .

to disengage the tabs and lift it off **(see illustrations)**.

10 Installation is the reverse of removal.

Handlebar covers

11 To remove the front cover, first remove the two screws from the rear cover, then carefully lever up the top edge of the rear cover to release the clips along the joining edge **(see illustrations)**. Note the pairing of the turn signal wiring connectors, then disconnect the connectors and lift the cover off (see Chapter 9).

12 If required, remove the turn signals from the cover (see Chapter 9).

13 To remove the rear cover, undo the three screws securing the cover to the handlebars **(see illustration)**.

14 Ease the cover back and displace the boot on the instrument cluster wiring connector **(see illustration)**. Use a small screwdriver to unclip the wiring connector and lift the cover off **(see illustration)**.

15 If required, remove the two screws securing the instrument cluster in the cover **(see illustration)**.

16 Installation is the reverse of removal. Make sure the turn signal wiring connectors are correctly and securely connected, and check the operation of the signals before riding the scooter.

Front top panel

17 Remove the handlebar covers (see above).

18 Lever the Gilera badge off carefully to

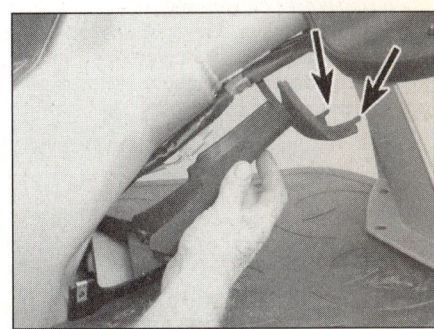

8.9b . . . then pull the panel off – note the tabs (arrowed)

8.11a Remove the two screws (arrowed) in the rear cover

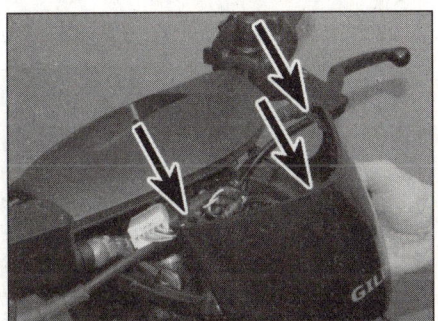

8.11b Remove the cover carefully to avoid damaging the pegs (arrowed)

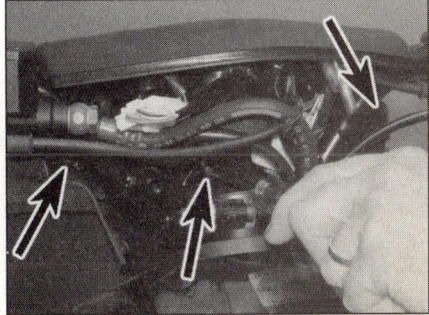

8.13 Remove the three screws (arrowed)

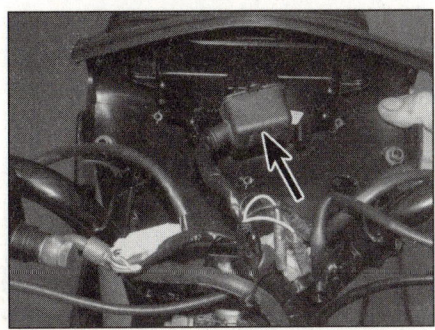

8.14a Displace the boot (arrowed) . . .

8.14b . . . then unclip the wiring connector

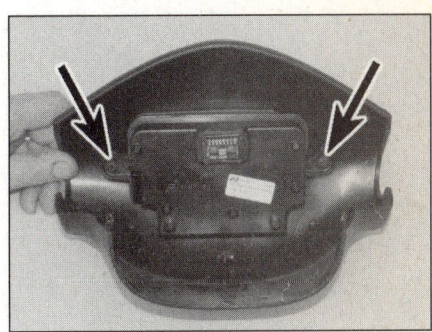

8.15 Instrument cluster is secured by two screws

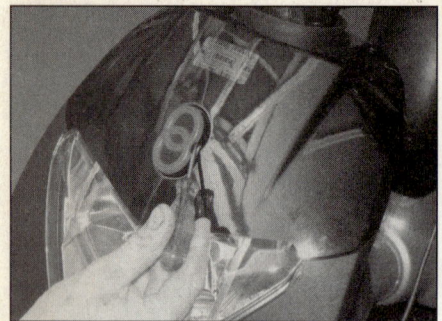

8.18a Lever off the Gilera badge . . .

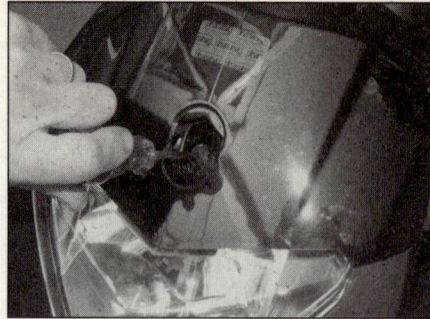

8.18b . . . then remove the screw

8.19a Remove the screws (arrowed) . . .

access the screw underneath, then remove the screw **(see illustrations)**.

19 Remove the two screws on the top of the panel, then lift the panel off **(see illustrations)**.

20 Installation is the reverse of removal.

Headlight panel

21 Remove the front top panel (see above).

22 Undo the fairing protector screws and remove the left and right-hand protectors **(see illustration)**.

23 Remove the two screws on the top edge of the panel, then loosen the two screws on the lower rear edge of the kick panel **(see illustrations)**.

24 Pull the panel forwards and disconnect the headlight unit wiring connector, then lift the panel off **(see illustrations)**.

25 Installation is the reverse of removal. Ensure the tabs on the lower rear edge fit over the frame bracket underneath the kick panel and are secured by the screws in the kick panel **(see illustration 8.23b)**. Make sure the headlight wiring connector is securely connected, and check the operation of the headlight before riding the scooter.

Kick panel

26 Remove the handlebar covers, the front top panel and the headlight panel (see above).

27 Remove the frame covers (see Steps 8 and 9).

28 Disconnect the inner cable end from the glove compartment cover latch mechanism, then detach the outer cable end from the cable stop **(see illustrations)**.

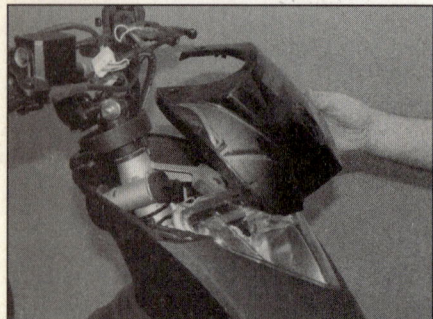

8.19b . . . then lift off the panel

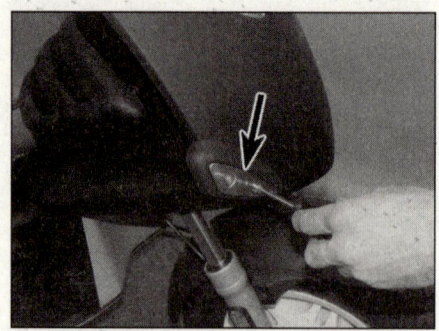

8.22 Remove the fairing protectors

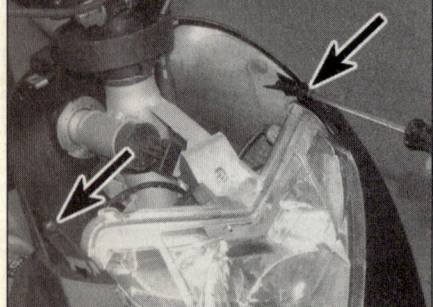

8.23a Remove the screws (arrowed) . . .

8.23b . . . then loosen the screws (arrowed) in the kick panel

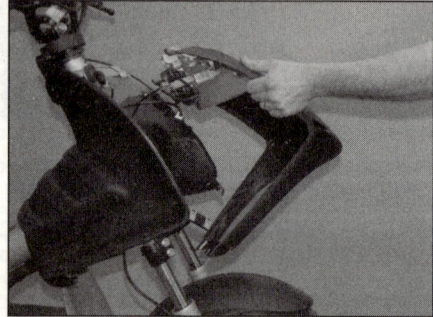

8.24a Pull the panel forwards . . .

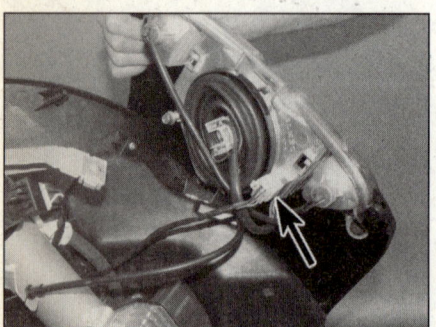

8.24b . . . and disconnect the headlight unit wiring connector (arrowed)

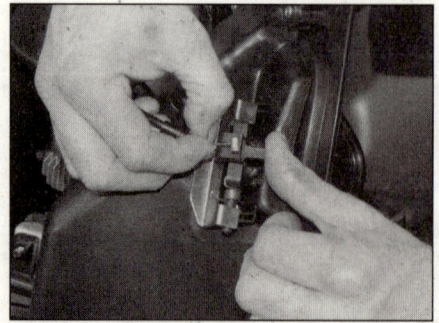

8.28a Disconnect the inner cable from the latch mechanism . . .

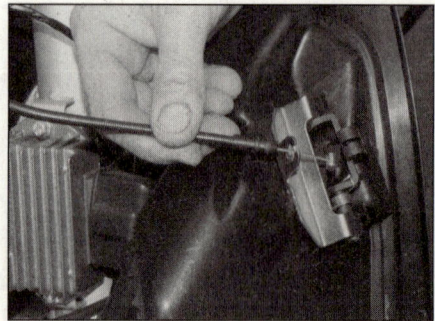

8.28b . . . and the outer cable from the stop

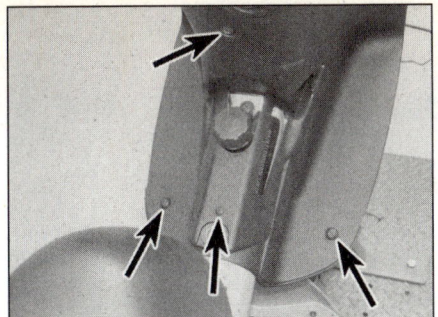

8.29 Remove the four screws (arrowed)

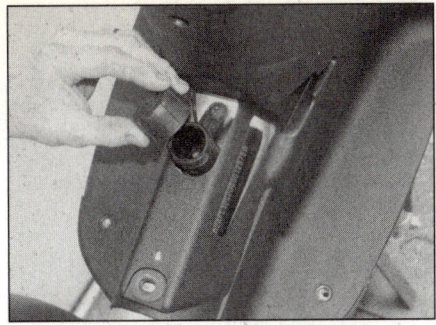

8.30a Remove the oil tank filler cap . . .

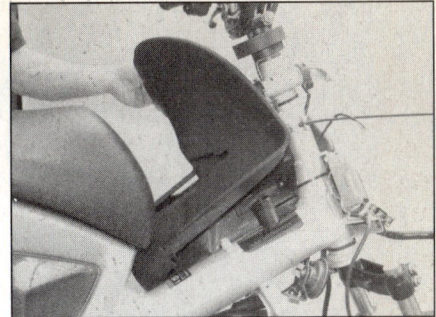

8.30b . . . then lift off the panel

29 Remove the four screws securing the panel to the frame **(see illustration)**.
30 Remove the oil tank filler cap, then lift off the panel **(see illustrations)**. Refit the filler cap.
31 Installation is the reverse of removal. Check the operation of the glove compartment latch mechanism before installing the headlight panel.

Legshield

32 Remove the kick panel (see above).
33 Remove the two screws securing the top of the legshield to the frame, then remove the three screws securing the legshield to the floor panel and lift it off **(see illustrations)**.
34 Installation is the reverse of removal.

Floor and belly panels

35 Remove the legshield (see above).
36 Remove the two screws on the front underside of the belly panel **(see illustration)**.
37 Remove the four screws securing the floor panel to the frame and lift if off **(see illustration)**.
38 The belly panel is clipped over the frame supports for the floor panel; note how it fits then lift it off carefully **(see illustration)**.
39 Installation is the reverse of removal. Ensure the belly panel is correctly positioned on the frame supports and secured by the floor panel screws.

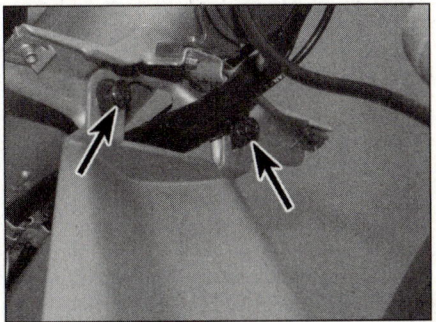

8.33a Remove the two top screws (arrowed) . . .

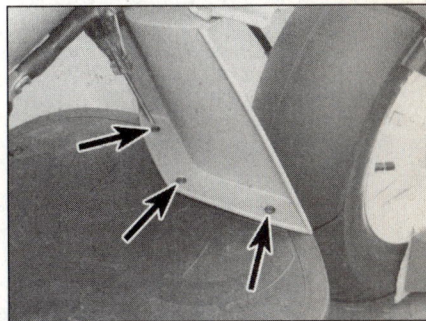

8.33b . . . and the three lower screws . . .

8.33c . . . then lift the legshield off

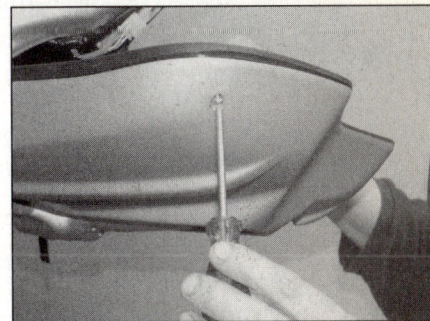

8.36 Remove the two screws on the underside of the belly panel

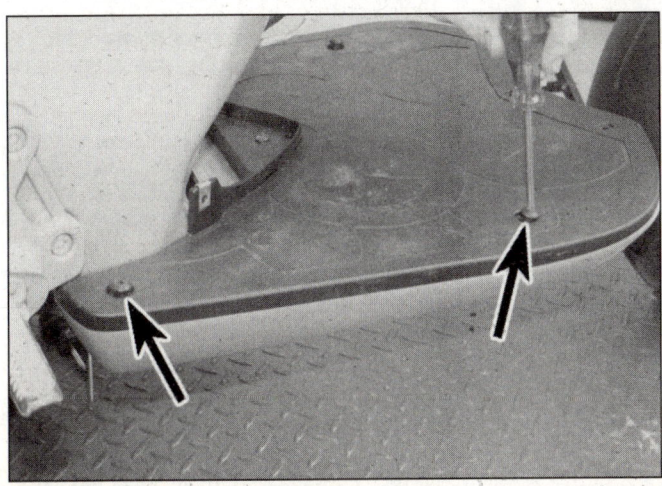

8.37 Floor panel is secured by two screws (arrowed) on each side

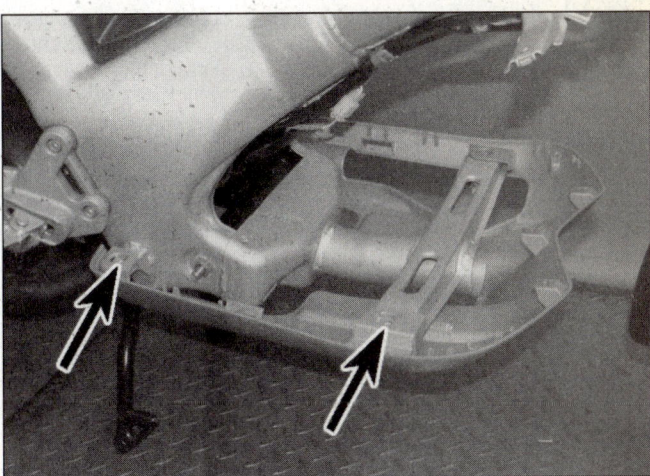

8.38 Belly panel clips over the frame supports on both sides

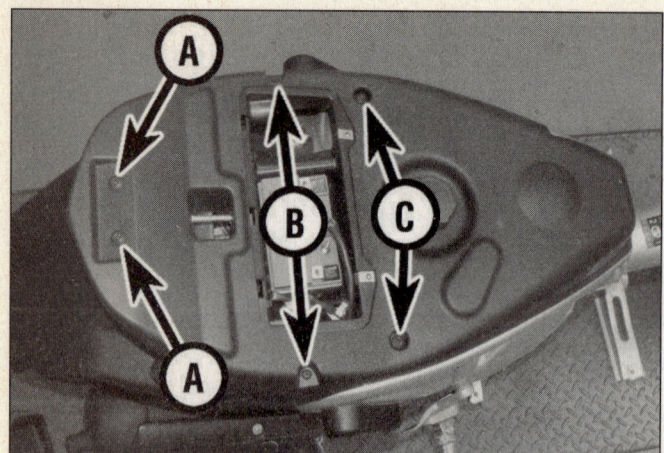

8.40 Remove screws (A) and (B). Screws (C) secure underseat panel

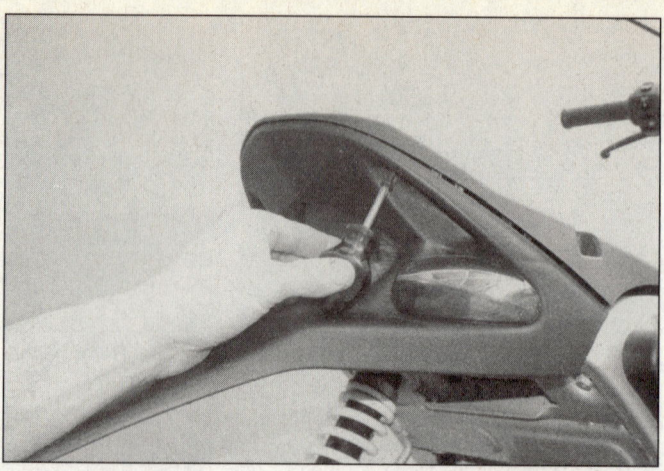

8.41 Remove the screws above the rear turn signals

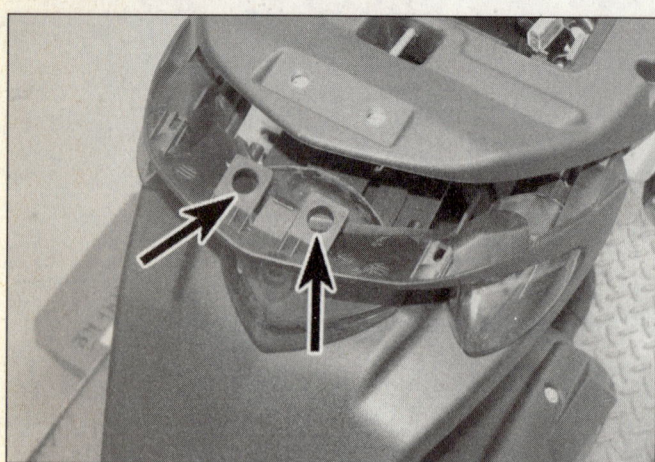

8.42a Note how the tabs (arrowed) locate on the frame

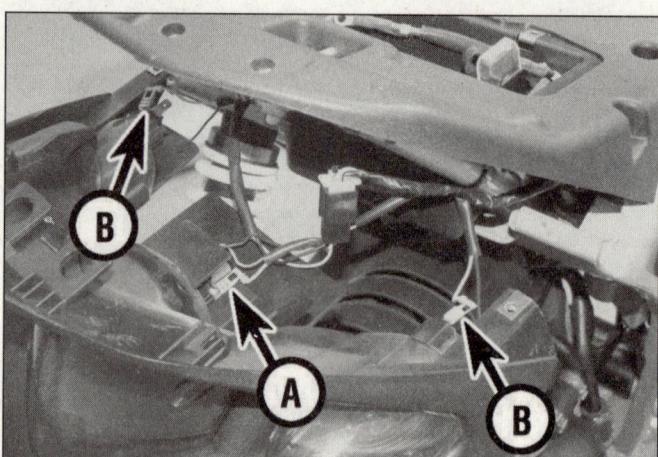

8.42b Disconnect the tail light (A) and turn signal (B) wiring connectors

Rear mudguard assembly

40 Unlock the seat and swing it upright. Remove the two screws on the back edge of the underseat panel, then remove the left and right-hand screws in the panel in line with the battery **(see illustration)**.

41 Remove the two screws above the turn signals **(see illustration)**.

42 Ease the assembly off, noting how the tabs on the top edge locate between the frame and the underseat panel **(see illustration)**. Disconnect the tail light and turn signal wiring connectors, noting where they fit, and remove the rear light panel **(see illustration)**.

43 Installation is the reverse of removal. Make sure the wiring connectors are correctly and securely connected, and check the operation of the signals, brake light and tail light before riding the scooter.

Underseat panel

44 Remove the seat (see Step 1). Remove the battery and unclip the fuse holder from inside the battery compartment (see Chapter 9).

45 Remove the rear mudguard assembly (see above).

46 Remove the two screws securing the left and right-hand sides of the panel to the frame **(see illustration 8.40)**.

47 Unscrew the fuel filler cap, then lift off the panel and feed the fuse holder and the battery cables through the hole in the side of the battery compartment **(see illustration)**. Refit the cap.

48 Installation is the reverse of removal. Ensure no wiring is trapped between the panel and the frame.

Front mudguard

49 Remove the four screws securing the mudguard to the fork sliders and lift off the mudguard – note the position of the guide for the speedometer wire and ensure it is correctly positioned on installation **(see illustration)**.

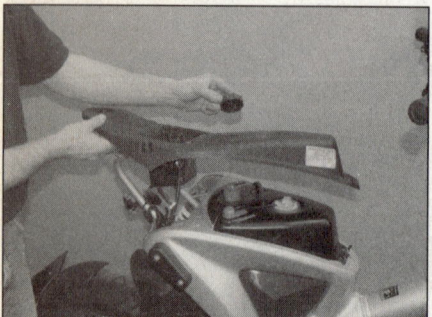

8.47 Remove the fuel filler cap and lift off the panel

8.49 Note the guide (arrowed) for the speedometer wire

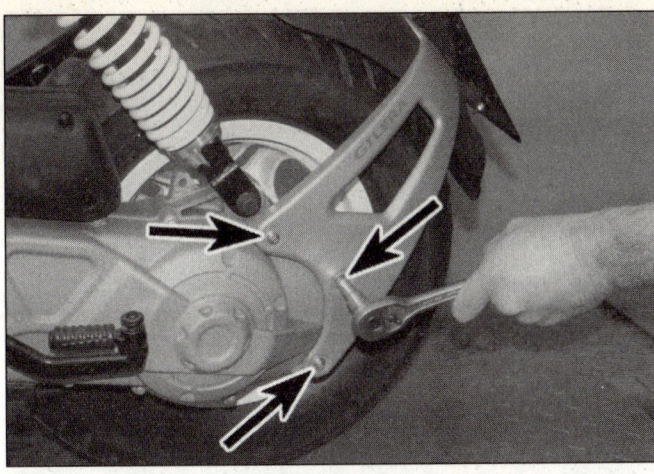

8.50a Remove the mudguard bracket screws (arrowed) . . .

8.50b . . . and lift off the mudguard assembly

Lower rear mudguard assembly

50 Remove the screws securing the mudguard bracket and lift off the mudguard assembly **(see illustrations)**.
51 If required, undo the bolts securing the mudguard to the bracket and remove it **(see illustration)**.
52 Installation is the reverse of removal.

---

9 SKP/Stalker body panels

Seat

1 Unlock the seat and swing it upright.
2 Remove the screws securing the seat hinge to the storage compartment and remove the seat **(see illustration)**.
3 Installation is the reverse of removal.
4 To remove the seat lock, first undo the fixing screw and pull off the lever, noting

how it aligns with the latch mechanism **(see illustration)**. Now remove the lock fixing screw and withdraw the lock.

Engine access panels

5 Unlock the seat and swing it upright. Remove the single screw securing the access panel in the bottom of the storage compartment and remove the panel.

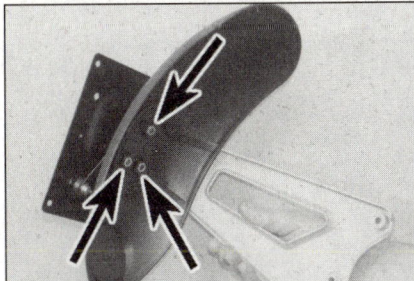

8.51 Mudguard is secured by three bolts (arrowed)

6 The front panel is secured by a single screw; remove the screw, then pull the lower edge of the panel, noting how the tabs on the top edge locate in the front underseat panel **(see illustration)**.
7 Installation is the reverse of removal.

Side panels

8 To remove either the left or right-hand side

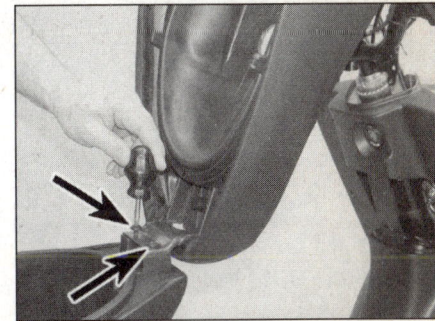

9.2 Seat is secured by two screws (arrowed)

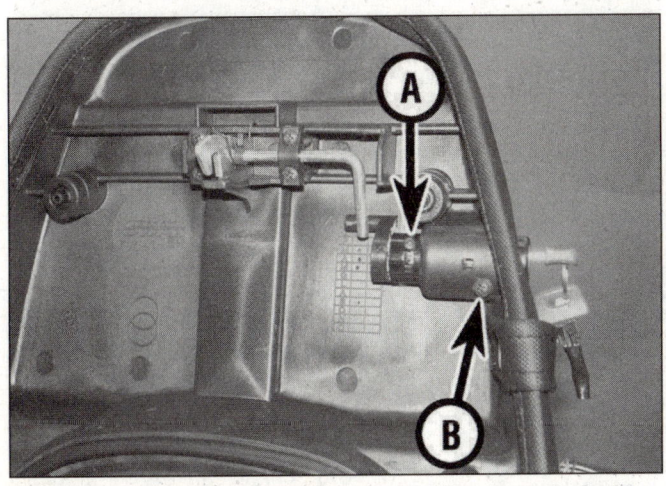

9.4 Screw (A) secures the lever, screw (B) secures the lock

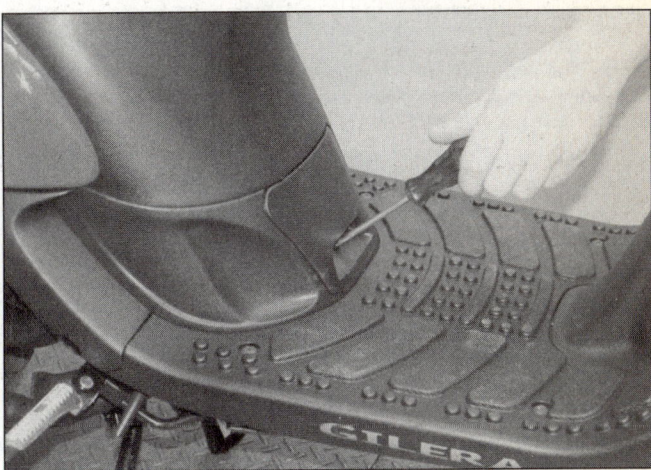

9.6 Front access panel is secured by single screw

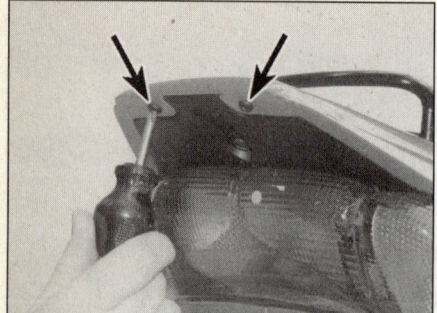

9.8a Remove the two screws (arrowed) on the underside . . .

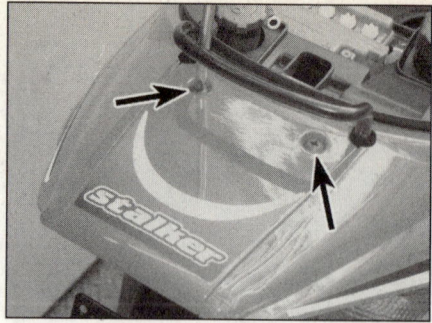

9.8b . . . and the two screws (arrowed) on the top . . .

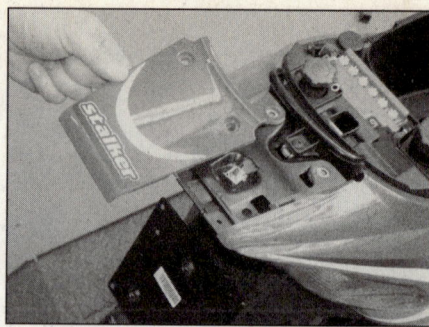

9.8c . . . then lift off the panel

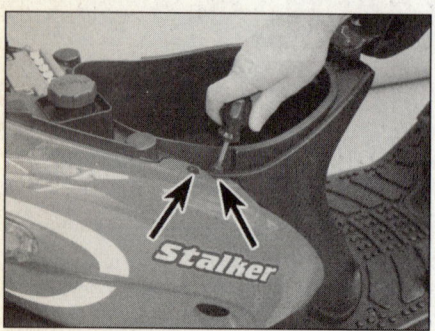

9.9a Remove the two screws on the top edge of the panel . . .

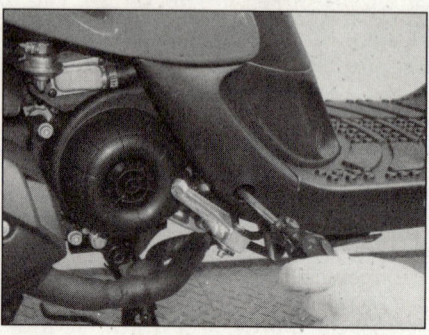

9.9b . . . the screw above the passenger footrest . . .

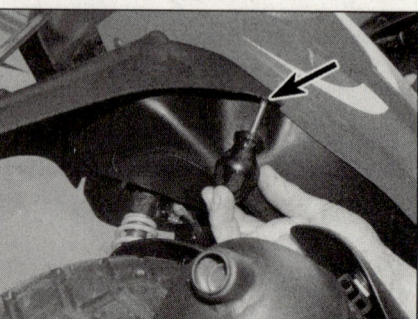

9.9c . . . the screw in the corner of the mudguard . . .

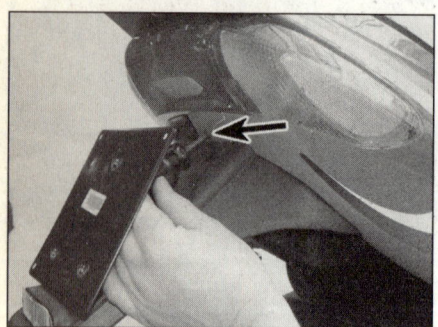

9.9d . . . and the screw behind the number plate . . .

9.9e . . . then lift the panel off . . .

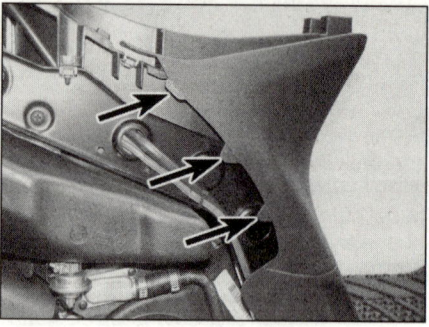

9.9f . . . noting the tabs (arrowed) on the front underseat panel

panels, first undo the four screws securing the rear centre panel and lift it off **(see illustrations)**.
9 Each side panel is secured by two screws on the top edge, one screw above the passenger footrest, and two screws at the back **(see illustrations)**. Remove the screws, then lift the panel off carefully to release it from the tabs on the back edge of the front underseat panel **(see illustrations)**.
10 Installation is the reverse of removal.

Front underseat panel

11 Remove the left and right-hand side panels (see above).
12 Remove the screw behind the seat hinge fixing point, then ease the panel forward and lift it off **(see illustrations)**.
13 Installation is the reverse of removal.

Storage compartment

14 Remove both side panels and the front underseat panel
15 Remove the battery (see Chapter 9).

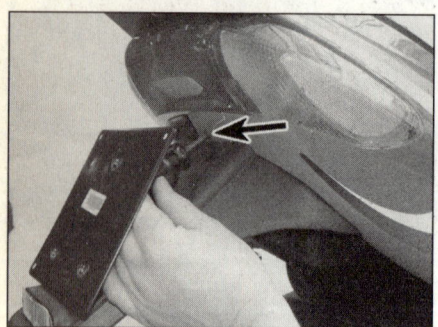

9.12a Remove the screw (arrowed) . . .

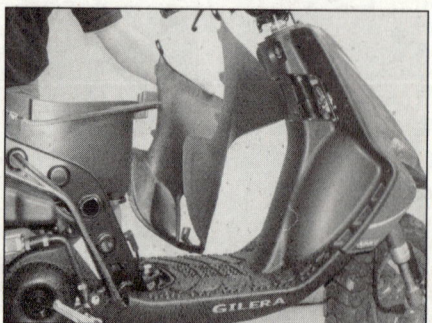

9.12b . . . then ease the panel forward and off

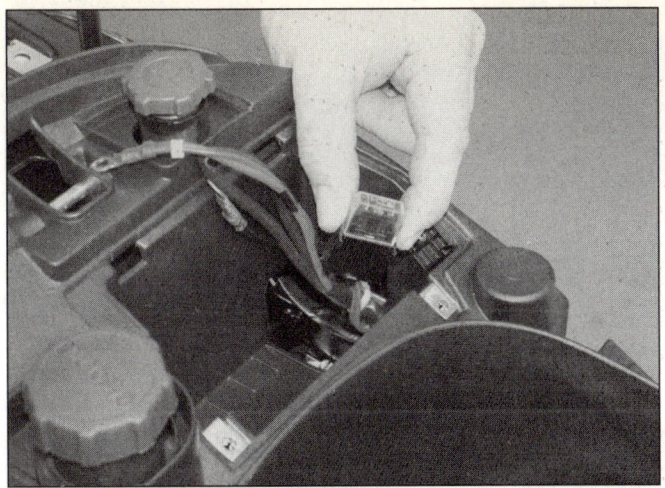

9.15 Unclip the fuseholder

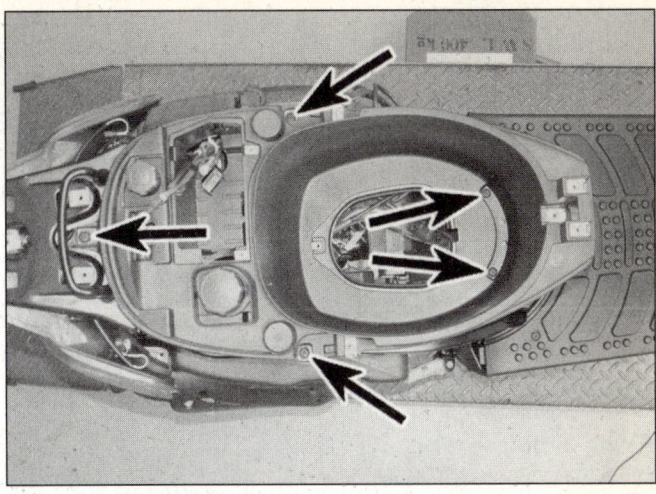

9.16a Remove the five screws (arrowed) . . .

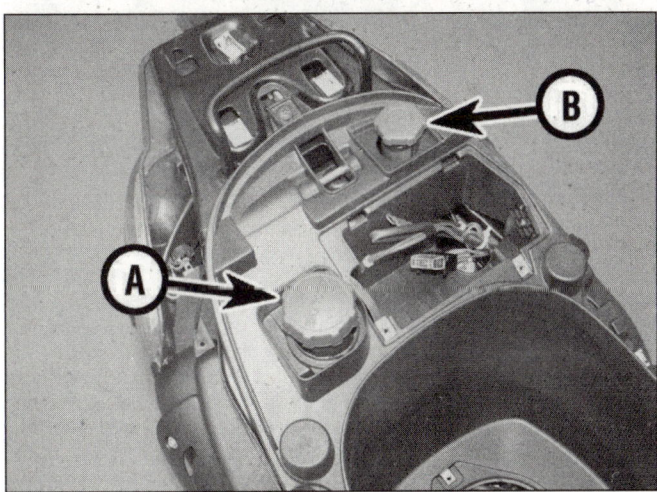

9.16b . . . then remove the fuel (A) and oil (B) filler caps . . .

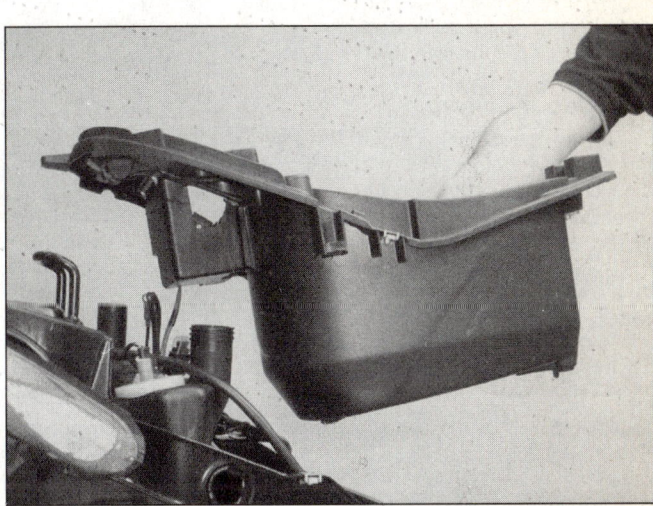

9.17 . . . and lift out the storage compartment

Unclip the fuse holder from inside the battery compartment **(see illustration)**. Refit the fuel and oil filler caps.

16 Remove the five screws securing the compartment to the frame, then remove the fuel and oil tank filler caps **(see illustrations)**.

17 Lift the storage compartment out and feed the fuse holder and the battery cables through the hole in the side of the compartment **(see illustration)**. Refit the fuel and oil filler caps.

18 Installation is the reverse of removal. Ensure no wiring is trapped between the compartment and the frame.

Rear mudguard assembly

19 Remove the side panels (see Steps 8 and 9).

20 Remove the three screws securing the assembly to the frame and lift the assembly away, then disconnect the lighting assembly wiring connector **(see illustrations)**.

21 Installation is the reverse of removal. Make sure the wiring connector is securely connected, and check the operation of the signals, brake light and tail light before riding the scooter.

9.20a Remove the three screws (arrowed) . . .

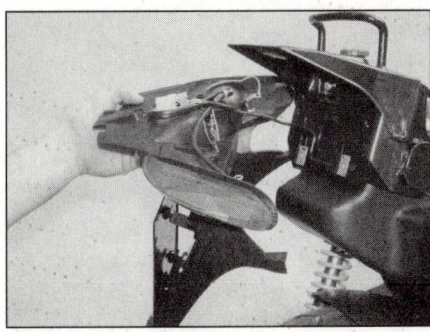

9.20b . . . then lift the mudguard assembly away . . .

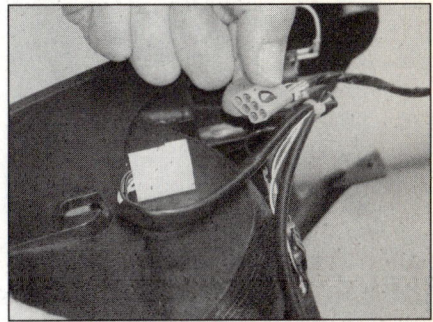

9.20c . . . and disconnect the wiring connector

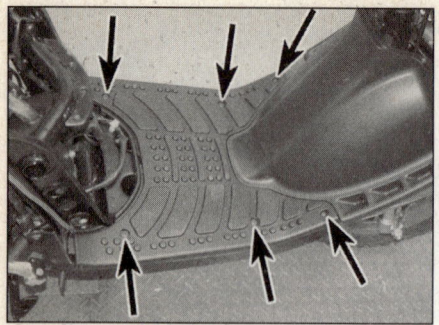

9.23 Floor panel is secured by six screws (arrowed)

9.25a Remove the three screws (arrowed) . . .

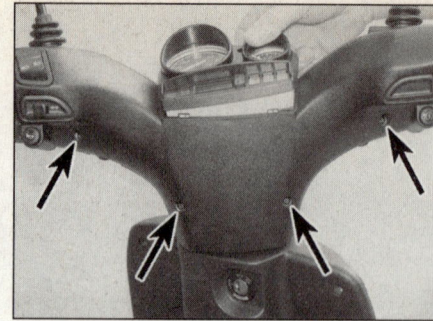

9.25b . . . and lift the instrument cluster. Note the screws (arrowed) in the rear cover

Floor panel

22 Remove both side panels and the front underseat panel (see Steps 8, 9 and 12).
23 Remove the six screws securing the floor panel and lift it off (see illustration).
24 Installation is the reverse of removal.

Handlebar covers

25 To remove the front cover, first remove the three instrument cluster screws and lift the cluster up to disengage it from the covers (see illustrations).
26 Remove the four screws from the rear cover (see illustration 9.25b). Ease the front cover away to release the clips along the joining edge, then disconnect the side light wiring connectors (see illustration).
27 If required, remove the instrument cluster (see Chapter 9).

9.26 Ease the front cover away and disconnect the wiring (arrowed)

28 To remove the rear cover, undo the four screws securing the cover to the handlebars, then lift the cover off and disconnect the wiring

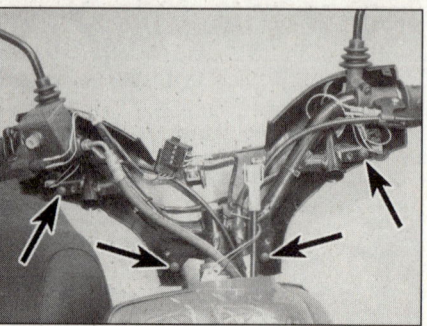

9.28a Remove the four screws (arrowed) . . .

connectors from the handlebar switches, noting where they fit (see illustrations).
29 Installation is the reverse of removal. Make sure the switch and side light wiring connectors are correctly and securely connected, and check the operation of the switches and side light before riding the scooter.

Kick panel

30 Remove the floor panel (see Steps 22 and 23).
31 Undo the two screws and remove the bag hook, then prise off the headlight access panel (see illustrations).
32 The kick panel is secured to the front panel by eight screws; remove the screws and lift the kick panel off (see illustrations).
33 Installation is the reverse of removal.

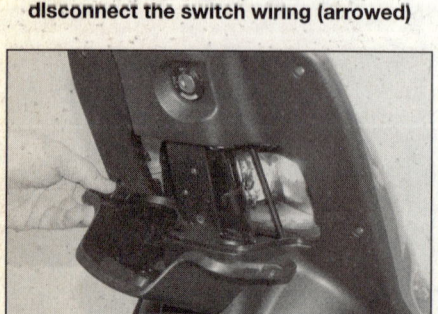

9.28b . . . then lift the cover away and disconnect the switch wiring (arrowed)

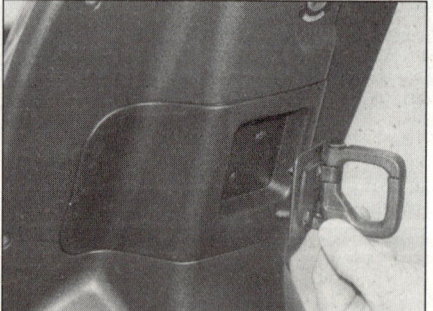

9.31a Remove the bag hook . . .

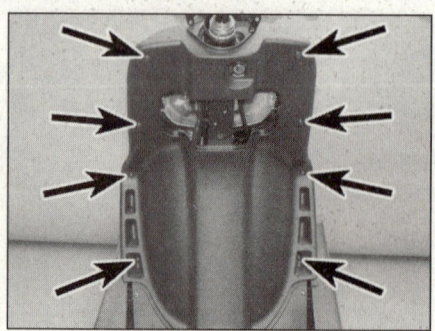

9.31b . . . and the headlight access panel

9.32a Remove the screws (arrowed) . . .

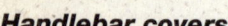

9.32b . . . and lift off the kick panel

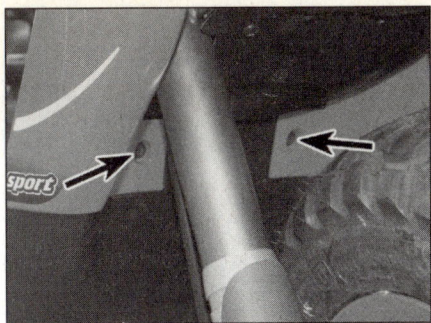

9.34a Remove the screws (arrowed) securing the panel lower edge . . .

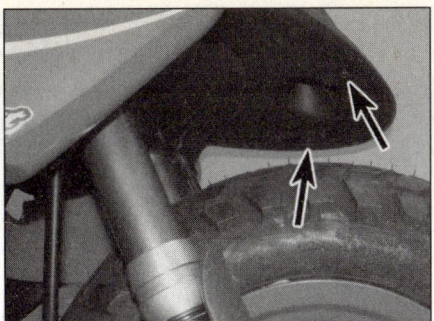

9.34b . . . and the screws (arrowed) securing the panel to the mudguard

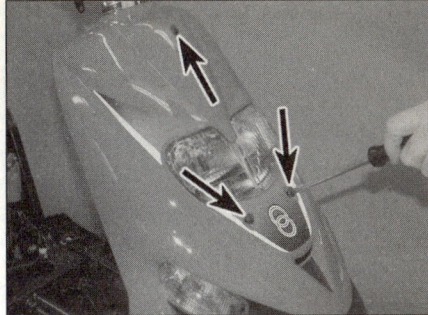

9.36 Remove the three screws (arrowed)

Front panel

34 Remove the two screws securing the lower rear edge of the panel to the belly panel, and the two screws securing the underside front edge to the mudguard **(see illustrations)**.

35 Remove the eight screws in the kick panel **(see illustration 9.32a)**.

36 Remove the three screws on the front of the panel **(see illustration)**.

37 Pull the panel forwards and disconnect the headlight and turn signal wiring connectors, noting where they fit, then lift the panel off **(see illustration)**.

38 Installation is the reverse of removal. Ensure the front edge of the mudguard locates correctly inside the lip on the lower front edge of the front panel. Make sure the headlight and turn signal wiring connectors are securely connected, and check the operation of the headlight and turn signals before riding the scooter.

Belly panel

39 Remove the floor panel (see Steps 22 and 23), kick panel and front panel (see above).

40 The belly panel is clipped over the frame supports for the floor panel; note how it fits then lift it off carefully **(see illustration)**.

41 Installation is the reverse of removal.

Ensure the belly panel is correctly positioned on the frame supports and secured by the floor panel and kick panel screws.

Front mudguard

42 Remove the steering stem (see Chapter 6).
43 Remove the front panel (see Steps 34 to 37).
44 Feed the speedometer wire up through the slot in the mudguard.
45 Disconnect one end of the front brake hose, then displace the hose grommet in the

9.37 Pull the panel away and disconnect the wiring connectors

mudguard and feed the hose through the mudguard.
46 Undo the screw securing the mudguard to the frame and lift it off **(see illustration)**.
47 Installation is the reverse of removal. Ensure the brake hose is correctly routed through the mudguard and protected by the grommet **(see illustration)**. Follow the procedure in Chapter 7 and bleed the brake.

Rear hugger

48 The hugger is secured by two screws on

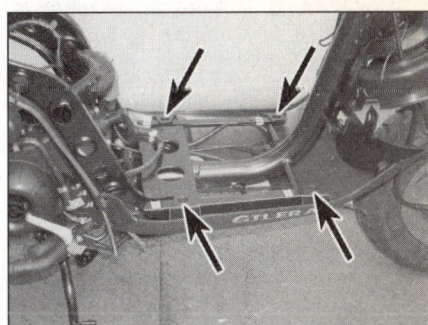

9.40 Belly panel is clipped over the frame supports

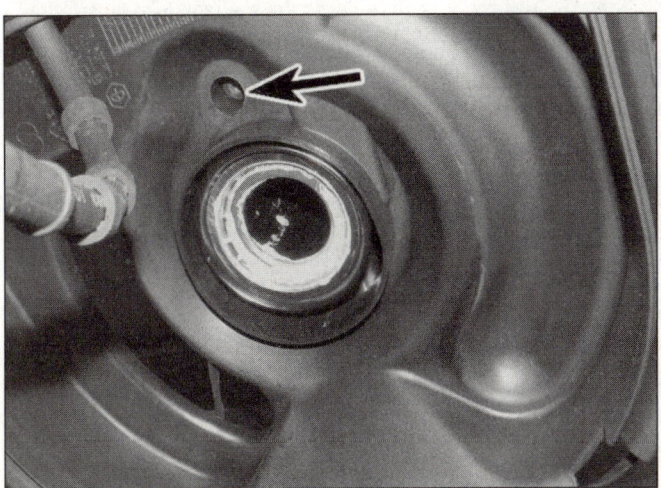

9.46 Mudguard is secured by single screw (arrowed)

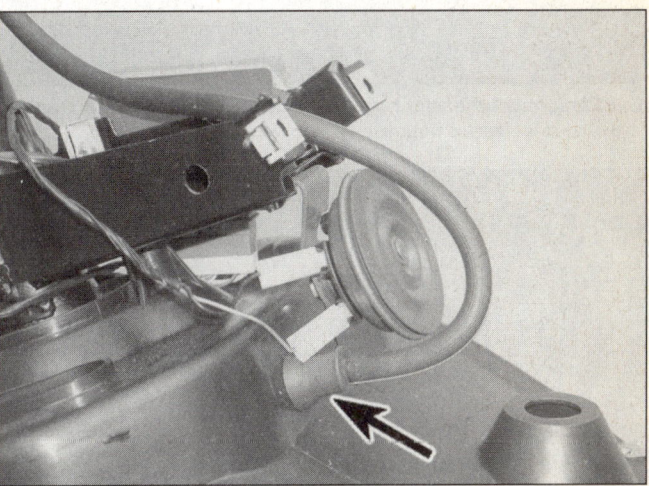

9.47 Ensure the grommet (arrowed) is correctly positioned on the brake hose

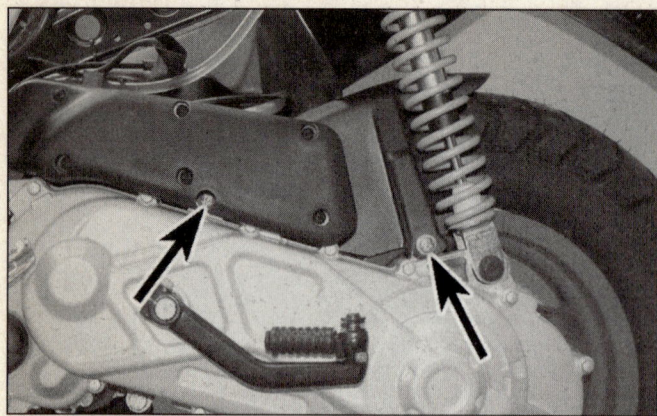

9.48a Rear hugger is secured by screws (arrowed) on left-hand side . . .

9.48b . . . and single screw (arrowed) on right-hand side

the left-hand side and one on the right-hand side **(see illustrations)**. Remove the screws and ease the hugger off backwards.

49 Installation is the reverse of removal.

10 Fuel and oil tanks

⚠️ *Warning: Refer to the precautions given in Chapter 4, Section 1 before proceeding.*

⚠️ *Warning: If the fuel tank is removed from the scooter, it should not be placed in an area where sparks or open flames could ignite the fumes*

coming out of the tank. Be especially careful inside garages where a natural gas-type appliance is located, because the pilot light could cause an explosion.

Runner fuel tank

1 The fuel tank is located at the front of the machine; refer to the procedure in Section 4 and remove both side panels, left and right-hand front side panels and the frame centre panel.

2 Disconnect the battery negative (-ve) lead and disconnect the fuel gauge sender wiring connector (see Chapter 9).

3 Disconnect the tank vent hose from the header tank **(see illustration)**.

4 Fuel flows from the tank directly to the fuel pump, therefore, unless the tank is being drained,

the fuel hose must be clamped (see **Tool tips** in Chapter 4 for hose clamping methods) to prevent spills before it is disconnected. Disconnect the fuel hose between the tank and the pump at the pump, and drain any residual fuel into a suitable container (see Chapter 4).

5 Undo the three screws securing the tank to the frame, noting the location of any washers, and lift off the tank.

6 Installation is the reverse of removal, noting the following:

• Ensure no wiring is trapped between the tank and the frame.

• Ensure any vent hoses are correctly routed.

• Tighten the fixings securely.

• Ensure the hoses are a tight fit on their unions and secure them with the clips.

Runner RST and ST fuel tank

7 The fuel tank is located at the front of the machine within the frame; refer to Section 5 (RST) or Section 6 (ST) to remove both side panels and the floor panel.

8 Remove the three screws holding the filler cap trim and three self tapping screws underneath the cover **(see illustrations)**.

9 Remove the clamp securing the flexible filler neck to the top of the tank **(see illustration)**. Note that the clamp isn't re-usable.

10 Lift the filler cap assembly out, then remove the single screw at the front of the panel and separate the two inner panels **(see illustration)**.

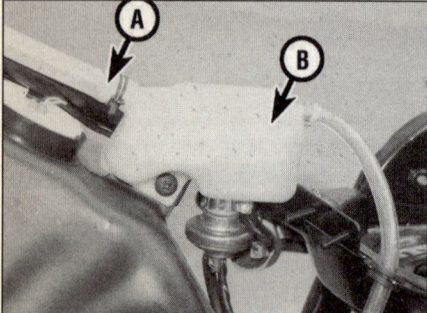

10.3 Disconnect the vent hose (A) from the header tank (B)

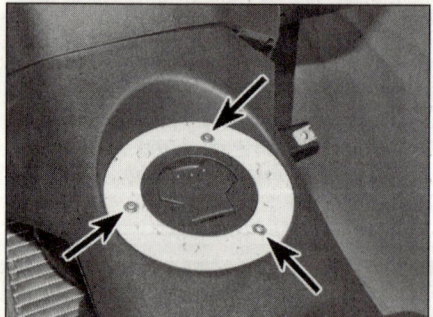

10.8a Remove the three screws from the filler cap trim (arrowed) . . .

10.8b . . . and the three self tapping screws underneath (arrowed)

10.9 Free the clamp on the flexible filler neck (arrowed)

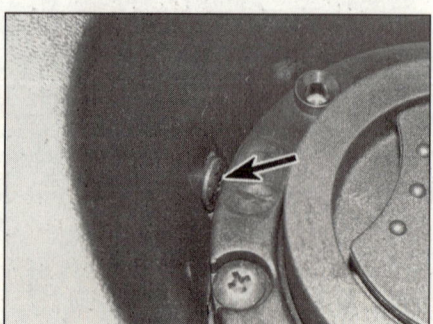

10.10 Undo the single screw at the front of the panel (arrowed)

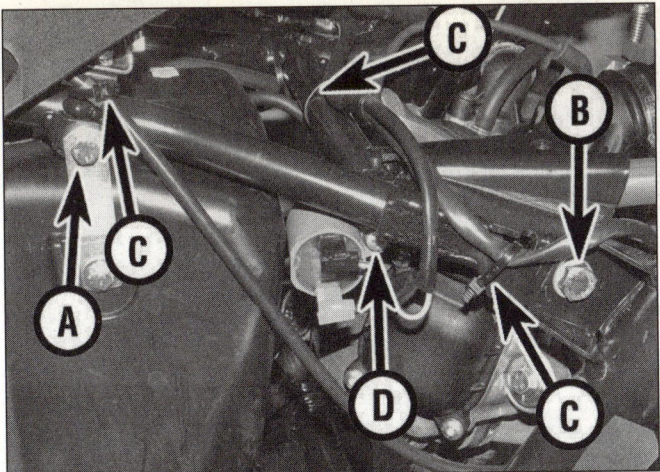

10.11a Undo the fuel tank top mounting bolt (A), the frame top rail bolt (B), cut the cable-ties (C) and free the ignition coil mounting (D)

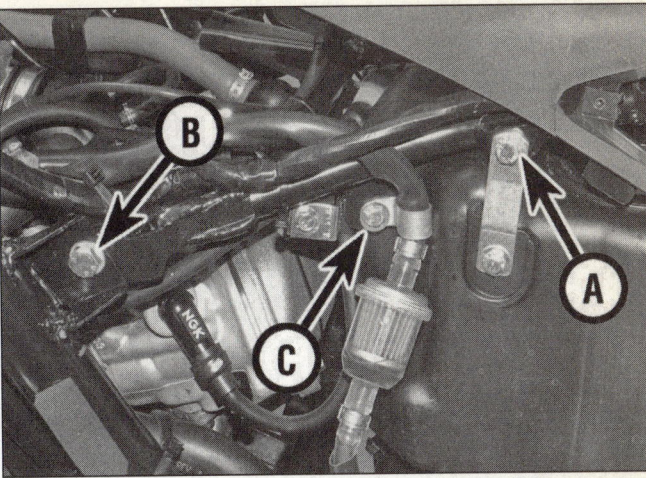

10.11b Undo the fuel tank top mounting bolt (A), the frame top rail bolt (B) and the fuel filter mounting bolt (C)

11 Disconnect the fuel tank top mounting bracket on both sides **(see illustration)**. Unbolt the frame top rails from each side, front and back **(see illustrations)**, noting the cable-ties securing the throttle cable to the frame will need to be cut and that the ignition coil and fuel filter must be freed from their mountings.

12 Disconnect the fuel level sensor wiring connector from the top of the sensor **(see illustration)**.

13 At this point, drain the fuel from the bottom of the tank by releasing the clip on the tank outlet elbow and withdrawing the outlet **(see illustration)**. Disconnect the fuel pump wiring **(see illustration)**.

14 Detach the fuel pump from the left-hand side of the tank and disconnect the hoses from it.

15 Remove the radiator (see Chapter 3).

16 Remove the fuel pump mounting bolts and pipe connections **(see illustration)**.

17 Installation is the reverse of removal, noting the following:

• Ensure that all old clips used for fuel pipes are replaced with new ones on installation. This applies particularly to the filler neck clamp.

• Always check that the hoses and pipes are secured and that there are no fuel leaks before putting the bodywork back into place.

10.11c Undo the frame top rail front mounting through-bolt and nut

Runner 50 (all models), FX125 and FXR180 oil tank

18 The oil tank is located underneath the seat. Refer to the procedure in Section 4 and remove the storage compartment.

19 Disconnect the oil level warning light sensor wiring connector (see Chapter 9).

20 Be prepared to plug the tank outlet when the oil hose is detached. Clamp the oil hose to prevent spills, then release the clip securing the hose to the tank union and detach the hose. Plug the tank outlet to prevent oil loss. Wrap a clean plastic bag around the end of the hose to prevent dirt entering the system

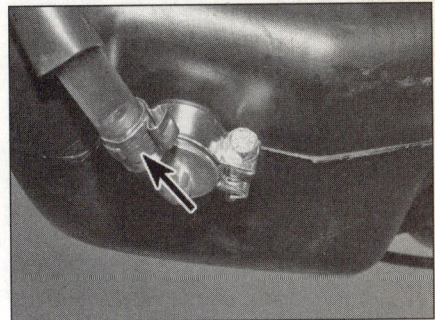

10.13a Release the clip on the tank outlet and withdraw it (arrowed) . . .

and secure the hose in an upright position to minimise oil loss.

21 Undo the two screws securing the tank to the frame, noting the location of any washers, and lift out the tank. Installation is the reverse of removal (see Step 6).

DNA fuel tank

22 The fuel tank is located at the front of the machine behind the radiator **(see illustration)**. Refer to the procedure in Section 5 and remove the side panels and displace the storage compartment and radiator panel.

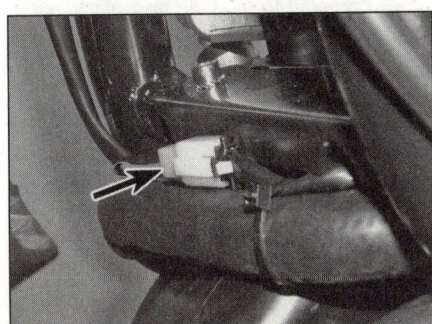

10.13b . . . and disconnect the fuel pump wiring

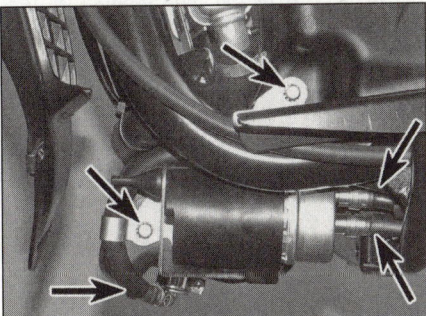

10.16 Fuel pump mounting bolts and pipe connections (arrowed)

10.22 Location of the fuel tank (arrowed) on DNA models

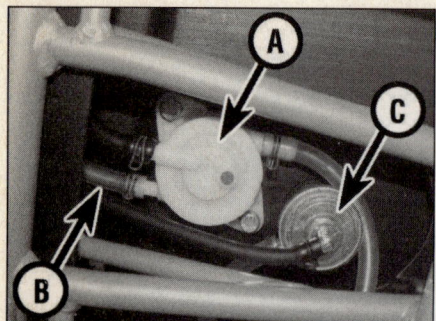

10.27 Fuel pump (A), pump outlet hose (B) and fuel tap (C)

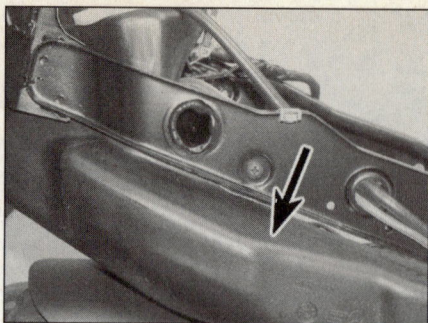

10.44 Location of the fuel tank (arrowed) on SKP/Stalker models

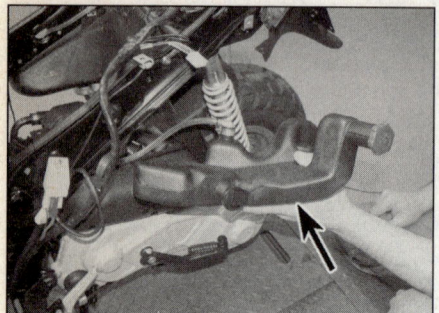

10.51 Lift out the oil tank (arrowed) . . .

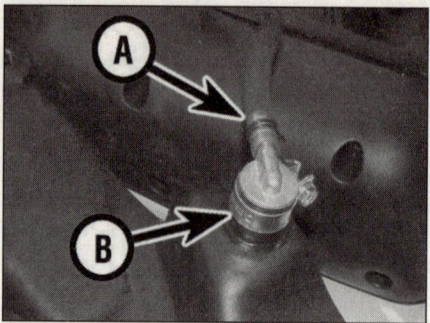

10.52 . . . then detach the hose (A) from the tank union (B)

23 Disconnect the battery negative (-ve) lead (see Chapter 9).
24 Remove the coolant reservoir and radiator (see Chapter 3).
25 Disconnect the fuel gauge sender wiring connector (see Chapter 9).
26 Disconnect the vent hose from the tank filler neck.
27 Disconnect the fuel outlet hose from the fuel pump on the underside of the fuel tank **(see illustration)**. Disconnect the vacuum hoses from the fuel pump and the fuel tap, and drain any residual fuel into a suitable container.
28 Undo the bolts securing the tank mounting brackets and lift out the tank. Installation is the reverse of removal (see Step 6).

DNA 50 oil tank

29 The oil tank is located underneath the seat. Refer to the procedure in Section 5 and remove the seat.
30 Disconnect the oil level warning light sensor wiring connector (see Chapter 9).
31 Be prepared to plug the tank outlet when the oil hose is detached. Clamp the oil hose to prevent spills, then release the clip securing the hose to the tank union and detach the hose. Plug the tank outlet to prevent oil loss. Wrap a clean plastic bag around the end of the hose to prevent dirt entering the system

and secure the hose in an upright position to minimise oil loss.
32 Undo the screw securing the tank to the frame and lift out the tank.
33 Installation is the reverse of removal (see Step 6).

Ice fuel tank

34 The fuel tank is located underneath the seat; refer to the procedure in Section 6 and remove the rear light panel and the underseat panel.
35 Disconnect the fuel gauge sender wiring connector (see Chapter 9).
36 Release the clips securing the fuel and vacuum hoses from the unions on the tap and disconnect the hoses from the tap (see Chapter 4). Drain any residual fuel in the fuel hose into a suitable container.
37 Lift the front of the tank off the mounting studs, then lift out the tank. Note how the lug on the rear of the tank locates on the frame. Note the routing of the tank vent hose. Installation is the reverse of removal (see Step 6).

Ice oil tank

38 The oil tank is located inside the main frame tube. First remove the engine/transmission unit (see Chapter 2A).
39 Remove the kick panel (see Section 6).
40 Be prepared to plug the tank outlet when

the oil hose is detached. Clamp the oil hose to prevent spills, then release the clip securing the hose to the tank union and detach the hose. Plug the tank outlet to prevent oil loss. Wrap a clean plastic bag around the end of the hose to prevent dirt entering the system and secure the hose in an upright position to minimise oil loss.
41 Undo the screw securing the oil filler neck, then unscrew the filler neck from the tank and lift out the O-ring.
42 Undo the screw securing the lower end of the tank to the frame and withdraw the tank. Disconnect the oil level warning light sensor wiring connector (see Chapter 9).
43 Installation is the reverse of removal (see Step 6).

SKP/Stalker fuel tank

44 The fuel tank is located underneath the seat on the right-hand side of the machine **(see illustration)**; refer to the procedure in Section 7 and remove the front underseat panel and the storage compartment.
45 Disconnect one end of the rear shock absorber so that the engine unit can be lowered to provide clearance to lift out the tank (see Chapter 6).
46 Disconnect the battery negative (-ve) lead and disconnect the fuel gauge sender wiring connector (see Chapter 9).
47 Release the clips securing the fuel and vacuum hoses from the unions on the tap and disconnect the hoses from the tap (see Chapter 4). Drain any residual fuel in the fuel hose into a suitable container.
48 Undo the three screws securing the tank to the frame, noting the location of any washers, and lift out the tank. Note the routing of the tank vent hose. Installation is the reverse of removal (see Step 6).

SKP/Stalker oil tank

49 The oil tank is located underneath the seat on the left-hand side of the machine. First remove the fuel tank (see above).
50 Disconnect the oil level warning light sensor wiring connector (see Chapter 9).
51 Undo the two screws securing the tank to the frame, noting the location of any washers, and lift out the tank **(see illustration)**.
52 Be prepared to plug the tank outlet when the oil hose is detached. Clamp the oil hose to prevent spills, then release the clip securing the hose to the tank union and detach the hose **(see illustration)**. Plug the tank outlet to prevent oil loss. Wrap a clean plastic bag around the end of the hose to prevent dirt entering the system and secure the hose in an upright position to minimise oil loss.
53 Installation is the reverse of removal (see Step 6).

Chapter 9
Electrical system

Refer to the beginning of Chapter 1 for model identification details

Contents

Degrees of difficulty

| **Easy**, suitable for novice with little experience |  | **Fairly easy**, suitable for beginner with some experience |  | **Fairly difficult**, suitable for competent DIY mechanic | | **Difficult**, suitable for experienced DIY mechanic | 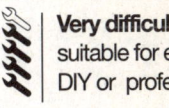 | **Very difficult**, suitable for expert DIY or professional |  |

Specifications

Battery

Capacity	
Ice	12 V, 3.6 Ah
Runner 50, DNA 50 GP, SKP/Stalker	12 V, 4 Ah
Runner Purejet 50, FX125	12 V, 9 Ah
Runner VX125, ST125, VXR180/200, ST200	12 V, 10 Ah
Runner FXR180, DNA 125/180	12 V, 12 Ah
Specific gravity when fully charged (all models)	1.26 to 1.28
Charging rate (all models)	0.5 A for 6 to 8 hrs

Alternator

Unregulated voltage output	
Runner 50 (all models), DNA 50 GP, Ice, SKP/Stalker	25 to 30 V (ac) at 3000 rpm
Runner FX125, FXR180	27 to 31 V (ac) at 2000 rpm
Stator coil resistance – Runner VX125, ST125, VXR180/200, ST200, DNA 125/180	0.7 to 0.9 ohms
Regulated current output	
Runner 50 (all models), DNA 50 GP, Ice, SKP/Stalker	1.5 to 2.0 A at 3000 rpm
Runner FX125, FXR180	8.5 A at 2000 rpm
Runner VX125, ST125, VXR180/200, ST200, DNA 125/180	8.0 A at 3000 rpm

Fuses

Runner 50, DNA 50 GP	7.5 A
Runner Purejet 50, DNA 125/180	
Main	2 x 15 A
Secondary	2 x 7.5 A
Runner Purejet 50 RST	
Main	1 x 20 A
Secondary fuses........................	2 x 5 A
Runner FX125, FXR180	
Main	1 x 25 A
Secondary	2 x 10 A, 2 x 7.5 A
Runner VX125, VXR180/200	
Main	2 x 15 A
Secondary	4 x 5 A
Runner VX125 RST, ST125, VXR200 RST and ST200	
Main	1 x 20 A
Secondary	2 x 7.5 A, 1 x 3 A

Bulbs

Headlight (main/dipped)	
Runner 50 (all models), DNA 50 GP	2 x 35 W
Runner FX125, FXR180, VX125, VXR180/200	2 x 55 W
Runner RST models and ST125/200	2 x 35 W (H8)
DNA 125/180	2 x 55/60 W
Ice, SKP/Stalker	35/35 W
Sidelight	
Ice, Runner RST and ST125/200	2 x 3 W
All others...............................	5 W
Brake/tail light	
DNA (all models).........................	10/3 W
Runner, Ice, SKP/Stalker	21/5 W
Runner RST and ST125/200 brake light.......	2 x 10 W
Runner RST and ST125/200 tail light........	2 x 3 W
Number plate light (where fitted)	5 W
Turn signals	10 W
Instrument and warning lights	1.2 and/or 2.0 W

---

1 General information

All models covered in this manual have a 12-volt electrical system charged by a three-phase alternator with a separate regulator/ rectifier.

The regulator maintains the charging system output within the specified range to prevent overcharging, and the rectifier converts the ac (alternating current) output of the alternator to dc (direct current) to power the lights and other components and to charge the battery. The alternator rotor is mounted on the right-hand end of the crankshaft.

All models are fitted with an electric starter motor. The starting system includes the motor, the battery, the relay and the various wires and switches.

Note: *Keep in mind that electrical parts, once purchased, cannot be returned. To avoid unnecessary expense, make very sure the faulty component has been positively identified before buying a replacement part.*

2 Fault finding

 Warning: To prevent the risk of short circuits, the ignition (main) switch must always be OFF and the battery negative (-ve) terminal should be disconnected before any of the bike's other electrical components are disturbed. Don't forget to reconnect the terminal securely once work is finished or if battery power is needed for circuit testing.

Tracing faults

1 A typical electrical circuit consists of an electrical component, the switches, relays, etc related to that component and the wiring and connectors that link the component to both the battery and the frame. To aid in locating a problem in any electrical circuit, refer to the wiring diagrams at the end of this Chapter.

2 Before tackling any troublesome electrical circuit, first study the wiring diagram thoroughly to get a complete picture of what makes up that individual circuit. Trouble spots, for instance, can often be narrowed down by noting if other components related to that circuit are operating properly or not. If several components or circuits fail at one time, chances are the fault lies in the fuse or earth connection.

3 Electrical problems often stem from simple causes, such as loose or corroded connections or a blown fuse. Prior to any electrical fault finding, always make a visual check of the fuse, wires and connections in the problem circuit. Intermittent failures can be especially frustrating, since you can't always duplicate the failure when it's convenient to test. In such situations, a good practice is to clean all connections in the affected circuit, whether or not they appear to be good. All of the connections and wires should also be wiggled to check for looseness which can cause intermittent failure.

4 If testing instruments are going to be utilised, use the wiring diagram to plan where you will make the necessary connections in order to accurately pinpoint the trouble spot.

Using test equipment

5 The basic tools needed for electrical fault

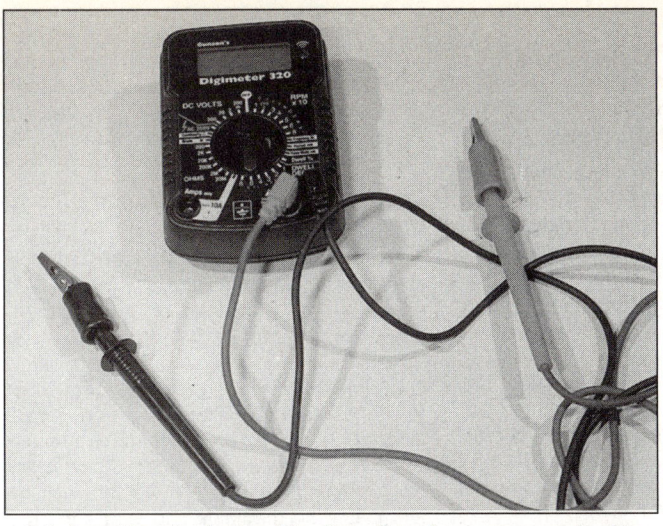

2.5 A multi-meter is capable of reading ohms, amps and volts

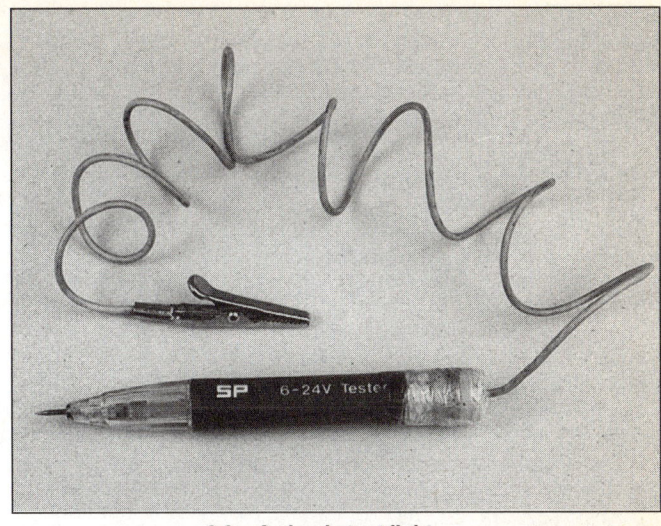

2.6a A simple test light . . .

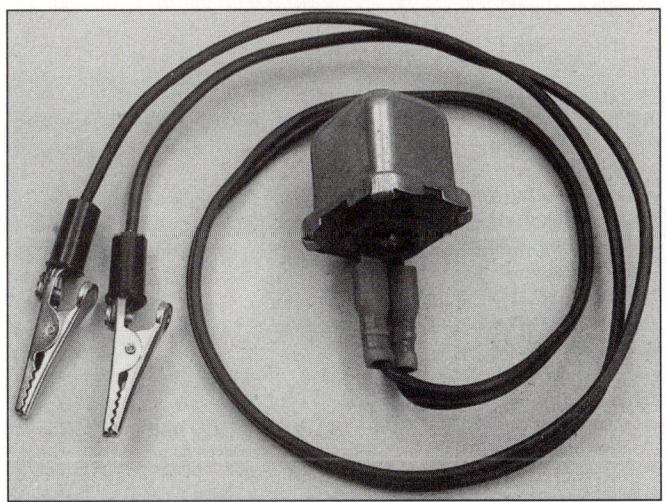

2.6b . . . or a buzzer can be used for simple voltage checks

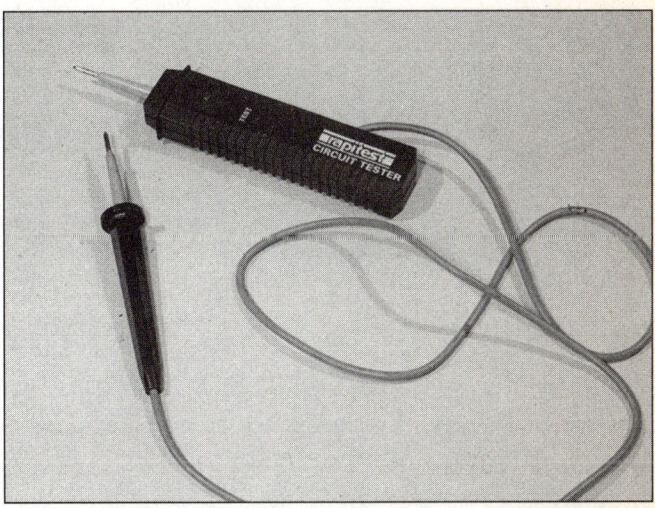

2.8a Continuity can be checked with a battery-powered tester . . .

finding include a battery and bulb test circuit, a continuity tester, a test light, and a jumper wire. A multi-meter capable of reading volts, ohms and amps is also very useful as an alternative to the above, and is necessary for performing more extensive tests and checks **(see illustration)**.

6 Voltage checks should be performed if a circuit is not functioning properly. Connect one lead of a test light or voltmeter to either the negative battery terminal or a known good earth **(see illustrations)**. Connect the other lead to a connector in the circuit being tested, preferably nearest to the battery or fuse. If the bulb lights, voltage is reaching that point, which means the part of the circuit between that connector and the battery is problem-free. Continue checking the remainder of the circuit in the same manner. When you reach a point where no voltage is present, the problem lies between there and the last good test point. Most of the time the

problem is due to a loose connection. Keep in mind that most circuits only receive voltage when the ignition is ON.

7 One method of finding short circuits is to remove the fuse and connect a test light or voltmeter in its place. There should be no load in the circuit (it should be switched off). Move the wiring harness from side-to-side while watching the test light. If the bulb lights, there is a short to earth somewhere in that area, probably where insulation has rubbed off a wire. The same test can be performed on other components in the circuit, including the switch.

8 An earth check should be done to see if a component is earthed properly. Disconnect the battery and connect one lead of a self-powered test light (continuity tester) to a known good earth **(see illustrations)**. Connect the other lead to the wire or earth connection being tested. If the bulb lights, the earth is good. If the bulb does not light, the earth is not good.

9 A continuity check is performed to see if a circuit, section of circuit or individual component is capable of passing electricity through it. Disconnect the battery and connect one lead of a self-powered test light (continuity tester) to one end of the circuit

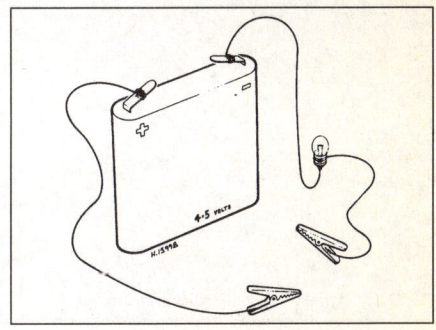

2.8b . . . or a battery and bulb circuit

being tested and the other lead to the other end of the circuit. If the bulb lights, there is continuity, which means the circuit is passing electricity through it properly. Switches can be checked in the same way.

 HAYNES HiNT *Remember that all electrical circuits are designed to conduct electricity from the battery, through the wires, switches, relays, etc. to the electrical component (light bulb, motor, etc). From there it is directed to the frame (earth) where it is passed back to the battery. Electrical problems are basically an interruption in the flow of electricity from the battery or back to it.*

3 Battery checks

Caution: Be extremely careful when handling or working around the battery.

The electrolyte is very caustic and an explosive gas (hydrogen) is given off when the battery is charging.

Removal and installation

1 On all models the battery is located under the seat. On DNA models, remove the seat (see Chapter 8), on all other models, unlock the seat and swing it upright. Remove the screw or screws securing the battery cover and lift it off **(see illustration)**. Note that on DNA models the battery is secured with a strap **(see illustration)**.
2 Unscrew the negative (-ve) terminal bolt first and disconnect the lead from the battery, then unscrew the positive (+ve) terminal bolt and disconnect the lead **(see illustration)**. Lift the battery from its holder **(see illustration)**.
3 Clean the battery terminals and lead ends with a wire brush or emery paper. Install the battery and reconnect the leads, connecting the positive (+ve) terminal first.
4 Fit the battery cover and install or lower the seat.

 HAYNES HiNT *Battery corrosion can be kept to a minimum by applying a layer of petroleum jelly to the terminals after the cables have been connected.*

Inspection – conventional battery

5 The battery fitted as standard to most models is of the conventional lead/acid type, requiring regular checks of the electrolyte level (see Chapter 1) in addition to those detailed below.
6 Check the battery terminals and leads for tightness and corrosion. If corrosion is evident, unscrew the terminal bolts and disconnect the leads from the battery, disconnecting the negative (-ve) terminal first, and clean the terminals and lead ends with a wire brush or emery paper. Reconnect the leads, connecting the negative (-ve) terminal last, and apply a thin coat of petroleum jelly to the connections to slow further corrosion.
7 The battery case should be kept clean to prevent current leakage, which can discharge

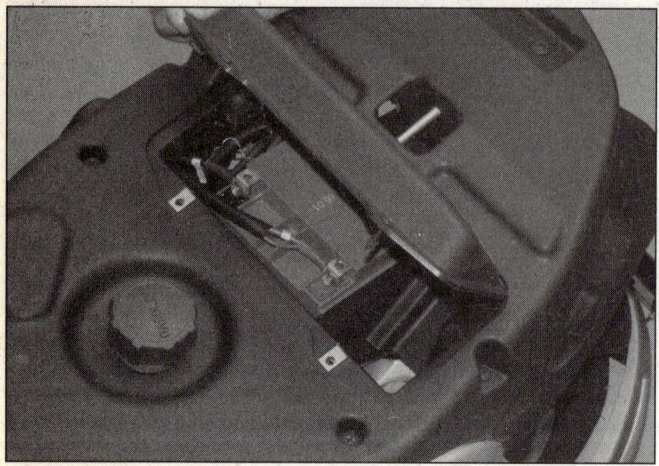
3.1a Removing the battery cover – Ice shown

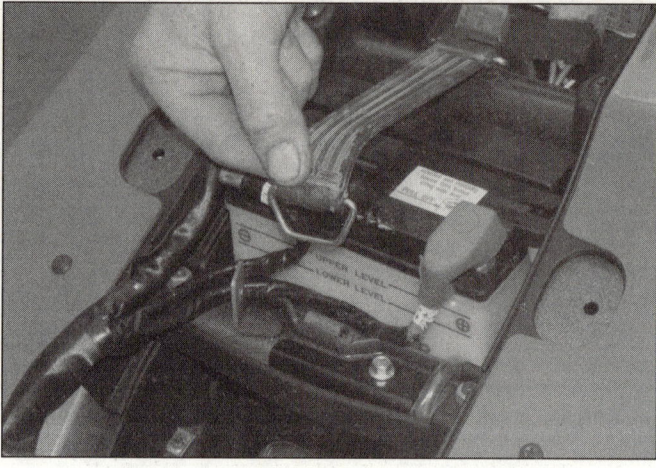
3.1b Remove the battery strap – DNA shown

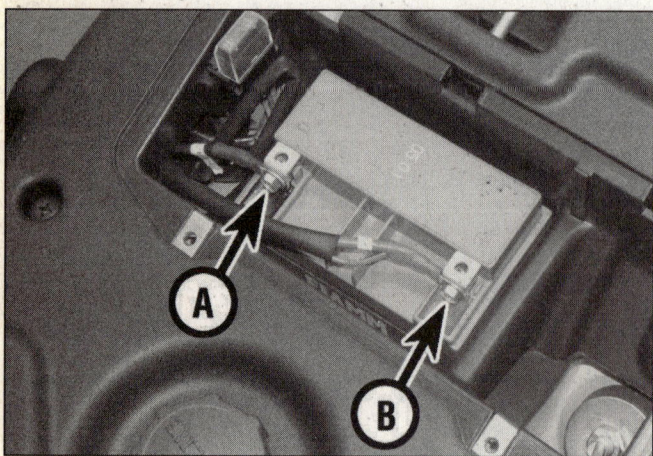
3.2a Disconnect the negative (-ve) lead (A) first, then the positive (+ve) lead (B) . . .

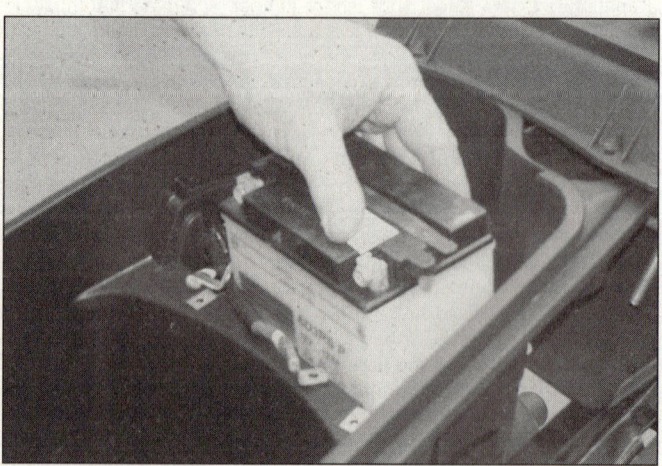
0.2b . . . and lift out the battery

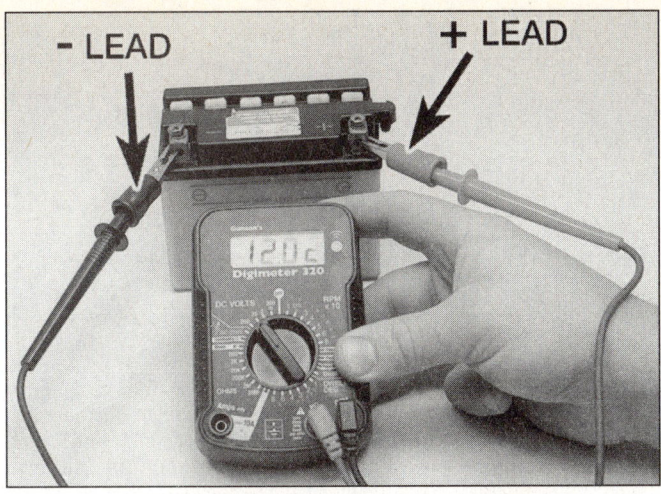

3.11 Measuring battery open-circuit voltage

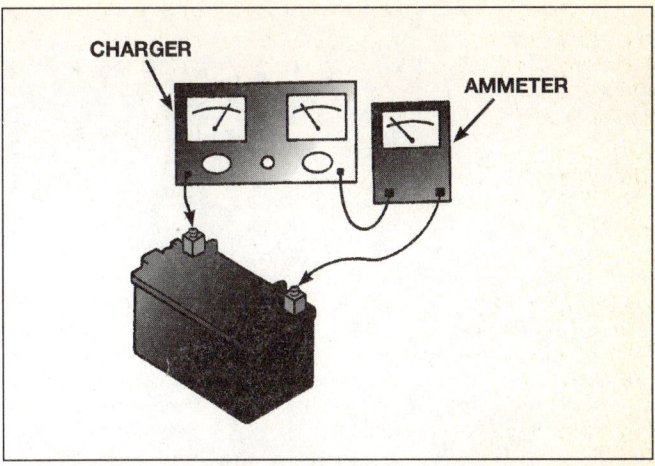

4.3 If the charger doesn't have ammeter built in, connect one in series as shown. DO NOT connect the ammeter between the battery terminals or it will be ruined

the battery over a period of time (especially when it sits unused). Wash the outside of the case with a solution of baking soda and water. Rinse the battery thoroughly, then dry it.

8 Look for cracks in the case and replace the battery if any are found. If acid has been spilled on the battery holder or surrounding frame or bodywork, neutralise it with a baking soda and water solution, dry it thoroughly, then touch up any damaged paint.

9 If the scooter sits unused for long periods of time, disconnect the cables from the battery terminals, negative (-ve) terminal first. Refer to Section 4 and charge the battery once every month to six weeks.

10 The condition of the battery can be assessed by measuring the specific gravity of the electrolyte. To do this an hydrometer is needed. Remove the cell caps from the battery. Insert the hydrometer nozzle into each cell in turn and squeeze the hydrometer pump to draw some electrolyte from the cell. Check the reading on the float at the level of the electrolyte and compare it to the Specifications at the beginning of this Chapter. If necessary, remove the battery and charge it as described below in Section 4.

11 The condition of the battery can also be assessed by measuring the voltage present at the battery terminals. Connect the voltmeter positive (+ve) probe to the battery positive (+ve) terminal, and the negative (-ve) probe to the battery negative (-ve) terminal **(see illustration)**. While Gilera provide no specifications, when fully charged there should be more than 12.5 volts present. If the voltage falls below 12.0 volts the battery must be removed and charged as described in Section 4. **Note:** *Before taking the measurement, wait at least 30 minutes after any charging has taken place (including running the engine).*

Inspection – maintenance-free (MF) battery

12 Some later models are fitted with an MF

battery as standard. MF batteries require little in the way of regular checks and are of sealed construction. All that is required is a check of terminal condition and the battery case as described in Steps 6 to 9.

13 The specific gravity cannot be measured due to its sealed construction, although voltage can be checked as described in Step 11.

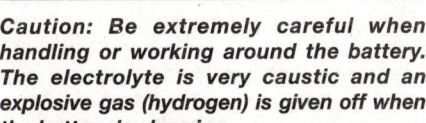

4 Battery charging

Caution: Be extremely careful when handling or working around the battery. The electrolyte is very caustic and an explosive gas (hydrogen) is given off when the battery is charging.

1 Ensure the charger is suitable for charging a 12V battery.

2 Remove the battery (see Section 3). Connect the charger to the battery **BEFORE** switching the charger ON. Make sure that the positive (+ve) lead on the charger is connected to the positive (+ve) terminal on the battery, and the negative (-ve) lead is connected to the negative (-ve) terminal.

3 Gilera recommend that the battery is charged at a maximum rate of 0.5 amps for 6 to 8 hours. Exceeding this figure can cause the battery to overheat, buckling the plates and rendering it useless. Few owners will have access to an expensive current controlled charger, so if a normal domestic charger is used check that after a possible initial peak, the charge rate falls to a safe level **(see illustration)**. If the battery becomes hot during charging **stop**. Further charging will cause damage. **Note:** *In emergencies the battery can be charged at a higher rate of around 3.0 amps for a period of 1 hour. However, this is not recommended and the*

low amp charge is by far the safer method of charging the battery.

4 When charging an MF battery, ideally use a current controlled battery charger. If using a constant voltage charger, ensure that the voltage does not exceed 14.7V otherwise the battery could be ruined.

5 If the recharged battery discharges rapidly when left disconnected it is likely that an internal short caused by physical damage or sulphation has occurred. A new battery will be required. A good battery will tend to lose its charge at about 1% per day.

6 Install the battery (see Section 3).

5 Fuses

1 The electrical system is protected by a fuse or fuses of different ratings (see Specifications at the beginning of this Chapter). On all models, the main fuse(s) is located in a holder next to the battery **(see illustration)**. On DNA 125/180 models, the secondary fuses are also located next to the battery. On Runner Purejet 50, FX125, FXR180, VX125 and VXR180/200 models, the secondary fuses are located

5.1a Location of main fuse – Ice shown

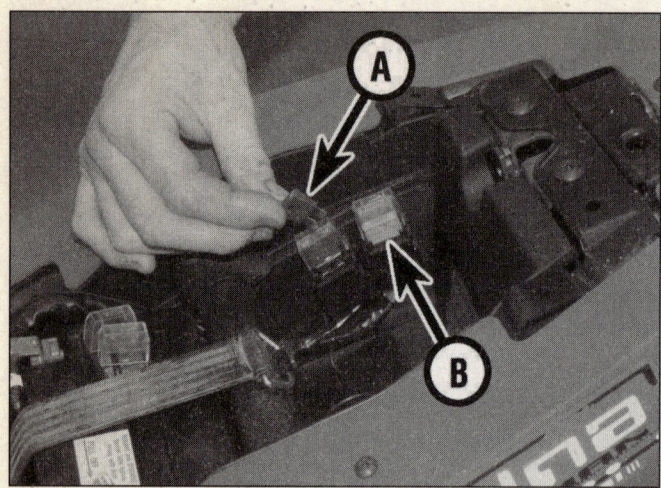

5.1b Location of main (A) and secondary fuses (B) – DNA 180 shown

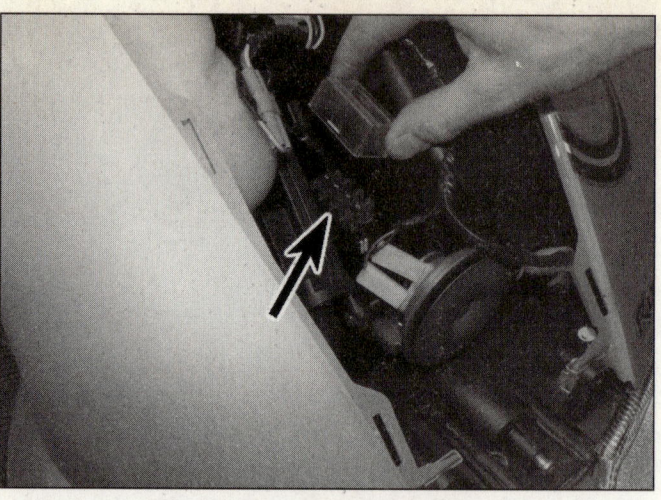

5.1c Location of secondary fuses – Runner VXR180 shown

behind the front panel (see illustrations). On Runner RST and ST models, the main and secondary fuses are located on the right-hand side of the battery compartment, under the seat (see illustration).

2 The fuses can be removed and checked visually. Remove the fuseholder cover, then pull out the fuse. If you can't pull it out with your fingers, use a pair of suitable pliers. A blown fuse is easily identified by a break in the element (see illustration). Each fuse is clearly marked with its rating and must only be replaced by a fuse of the correct rating. It is advisable to carry a spare fuse of each rating on the scooter at all times.

⚠ *Warning: Never put in a fuse of a higher rating or bridge the terminals with any other substitute, however temporary it may be. Serious damage may be done to the circuit, or a fire may start.*

3 If a fuse blows, be sure to check the wiring circuit very carefully for evidence of a short-circuit. Look for bare wires and chafed, melted or burned insulation. If a new fuse is fitted before the fault is located, it will blow immediately.

4 Occasionally a fuse will blow or cause an open-circuit for no obvious reason. Corrosion of the fuse ends and fuseholder terminals may occur and cause poor electrical contact. If this happens, remove the corrosion with a wire brush or emery paper, then spray the fuse ends and fuseholder terminals with electrical contact cleaner.

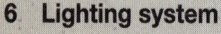

6 Lighting system

1 The battery provides power for operation of the headlight, tail light, brake light, turn signals and instrument cluster lights. If none of the lights operate, always check battery voltage before proceeding. Low battery

5.1d Location of secondary fuses – Runner VX125 RST shown

voltage indicates either a faulty battery or a defective charging system. Refer to Section 3 for battery checks and Section 26 for charging system tests. Also, on models where the lighting system is protected by a fuse, check the fuse. **Note:** *On models with a single fuse, the headlight and tail light are not protected (see Wiring diagrams at the end of this Chapter).*

Headlight

2 If the headlight fails to work, first check the fuse if applicable (see Section 5), and then the bulb (see Section 7). If they are both good,

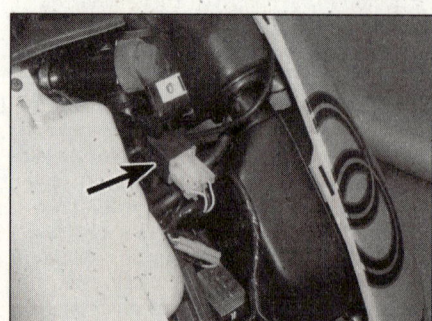

6.3a Headlight relay (arrowed) – Runner VXR180 shown

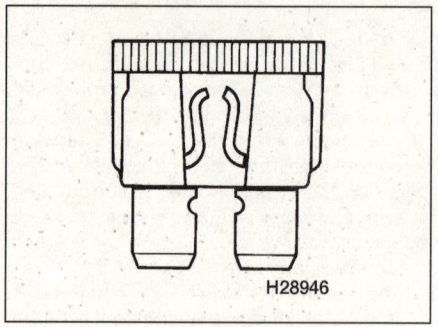

5.2 A blown fuse can be identified by a break in its element

use jumper wires to connect the bulb directly to the battery terminals. If the light comes on, the problem lies in the wiring or one of the switches in the circuit. Refer to Section 21 for the switch testing procedures, and to the *Wiring diagrams* at the end of this Chapter.

Headlight relay

3 Runner VX125 and VXR180/200 models are fitted with a headlight relay, located behind the front panel (see illustration); RST and ST models do not have a relay. DNA 125/180 models are fitted with headlight high and low (dip) beam relays, located behind the

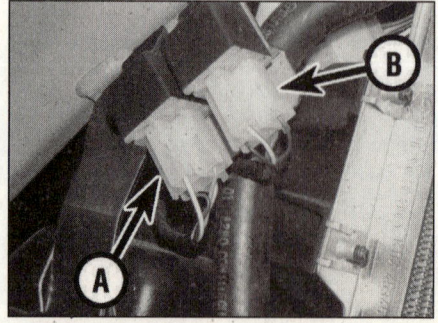

6.3b Headlight high (A) and low (B) beam relays – DNA 180 shown

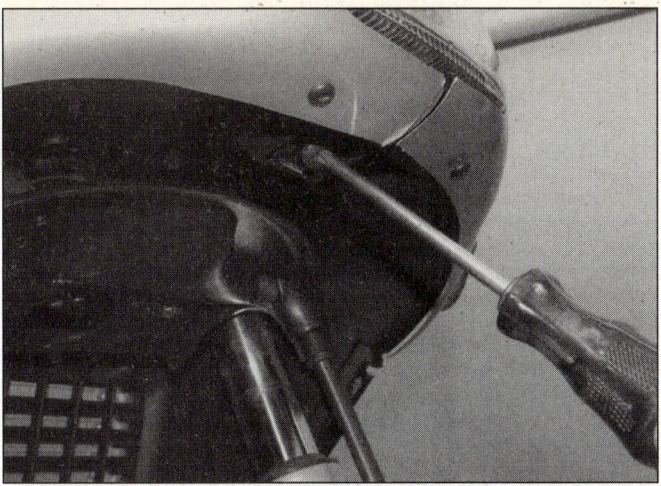

7.1a Remove the lower screw . . .

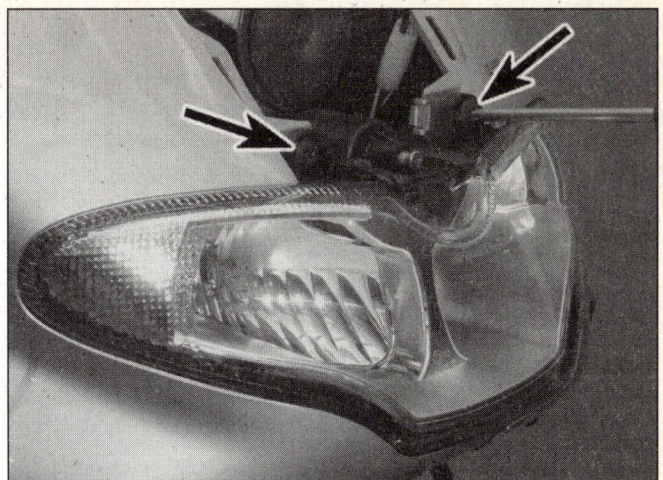

7.1b . . . and the two upper screws (arrowed) . . .

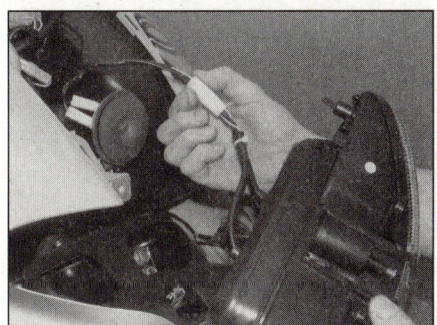

7.1c . . . then lift the headlight unit forward and disconnect the wiring

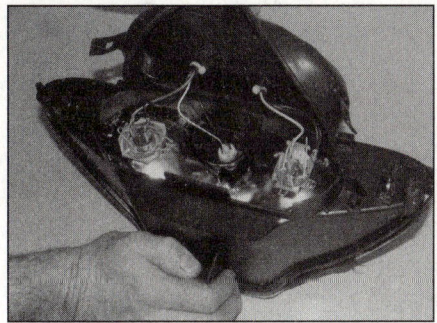

7.1d Remove the rubber cover . . .

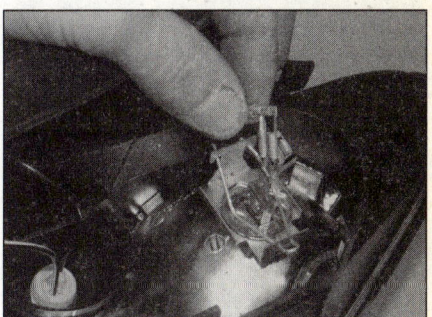

7.1e . . . and disconnect the connectors from the bulb terminals

right-hand side panel **(see illustration)**. The relay acts as a switch between the battery and the headlight circuit. Remove the appropriate panel for access to the relay (see Chapter 8).

4 Check the power supply to the relay by checking for battery voltage at the No. 30 terminal of the relay. If no voltage is present, check the wiring between the relay, the fuse and the battery (see *Wiring diagram* at the end of this Chapter).

5 If there is battery voltage at the No. 30 terminal, turn the ignition and lighting switches ON and check for voltage at the No. 87 terminal. If voltage is present, the relay is functioning correctly and any lighting fault must lie in the wiring between the relay and the dip switch, or between the dip switch and the headlight.

6 If no voltage is present at the No. 87 terminal, either the relay is faulty or there is a fault between the relay and the lighting switch or between the lighting switch and the ignition switch.

7 If available, substitute the suspect relay with a known good one and check the operation of the headlight.

Tail light

8 If the tail light fails to work, first check the bulb and the bulb terminals (see Section 9), then the fuse if applicable (see Section 5). If

the bulb and fuse are good, turn the ignition and lighting switch ON and check for battery voltage at the terminal on the supply side of the tail light. If voltage is present, check the earth circuit for an open or poor connection.

9 If no voltage is present, check the tail light wiring circuit (see *Wiring diagrams* at the end of this Chapter).

Brake light

10 If the brake light fails to work, check the bulb and the bulb terminals first (see Section 9), then the fuse (see Section 5). If the bulb and fuse are good, turn the ignition and lighting switch ON and check for battery voltage at the terminal on the supply side of the brake light, with the brake lever pulled in. If voltage is present, check the earth circuit for an open or poor connection.

11 If no voltage is present, check the brake light switches (see Section 14), then the brake light wiring circuit (see *Wiring diagrams* at the end of this Chapter).

Instrument and warning lights

12 See Section 16 for instrument and warning light bulb renewal.

Turn signals

13 See Section 11 for the turn signal circuit check.

7 **Headlight bulb and sidelight bulb**

Caution: If the headlight bulb is of the quartz-halogen type, do not touch the bulb glass as skin acids will shorten the bulb's service life. If the bulb is accidentally touched, it should be wiped carefully when cold with a rag soaked in methylated spirit and dried before fitting. Always use a paper towel or dry cloth when handling the new bulb to increase bulb life and prevent injury if it should break.

⚠ *Warning: Allow the bulb time to cool before removing it if the headlight has just been on.*

Headlight bulb

1 On Runner models, first remove the front panel (see Chapter 8). Remove the lower screw and the two upper screws securing the headlight unit and lift it forward, then disconnect the headlight wiring connector **(see illustrations)**. Remove the rubber cover and disconnect the connectors from the bulb terminals **(see illustrations)**. Release the spring clip, noting how it fits, then lift out the bulb.

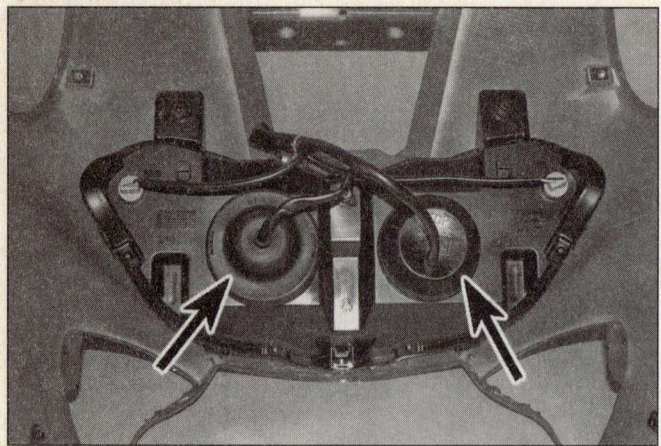

7.2a Remove the rubber cover from the back of the bulb (arrowed) . . .

7.2b . . . twist the bulbholder anti-clockwise and remove it . . .

7.2c . . . then separate the bulb from the wiring

7.3a Remove the lower screw . . .

2 On Runner RST and ST models, first remove the front panel inspection cover (see Chapter 8, Section 5). Reach inside and remove the rubber cover, from the back of the bulb **(see illustrations)** and twist the bulbholder anti-clockwise and remove it.

Separate the bulb from the wiring. **Note:** *Both headlights use an H8 halogen 35W bulb which is complete with the holder.*

3 On DNA models, first remove the front fairing (see Chapter 8). Remove the lower screw and the two upper screws securing the

headlight unit and lift it forward **(see illustrations)**. Remove the rubber cover, noting which way up it fits, and disconnect the connector from the bulb terminals **(see illustration)**. Twist the bulbholder anti-clockwise and remove it, then lift out the bulb.

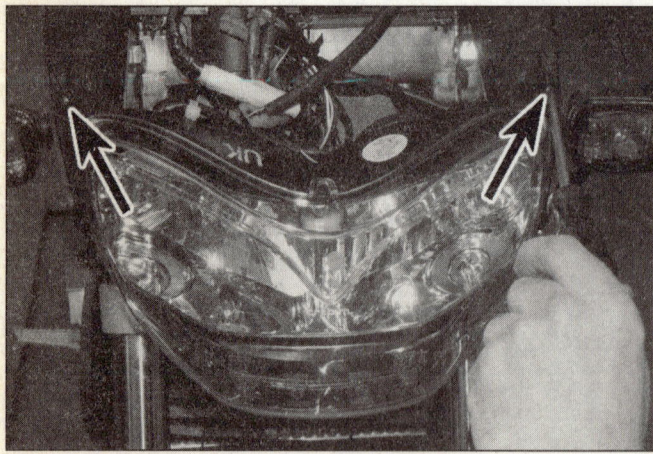

7.0b . . . and the two upper screws (arrowed)

7.3c Remove the rubber cover (arrowed) and disconnect the bulb connector

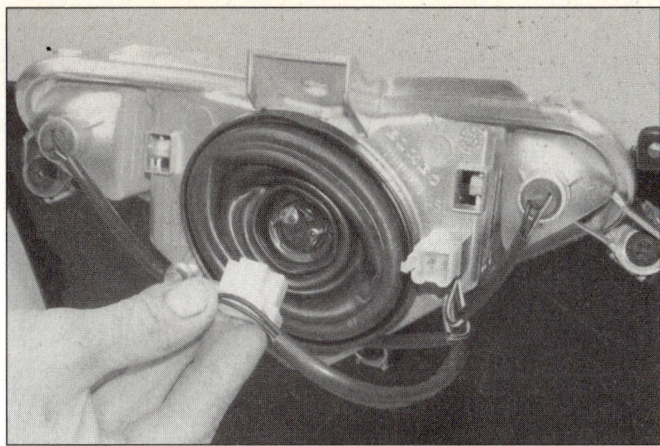

7.4a Pull off the terminal connector . . .

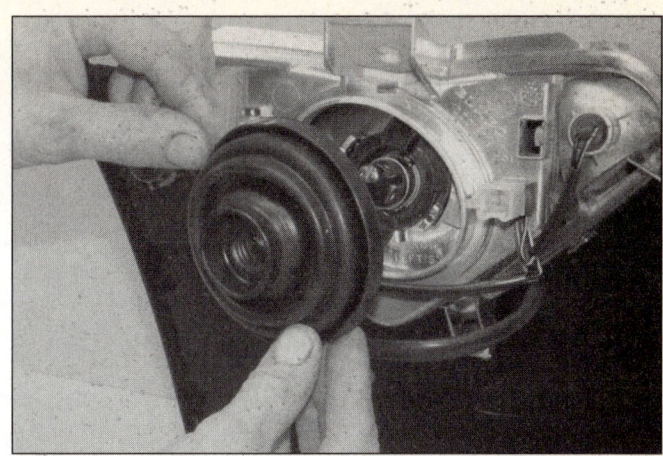

7.4b . . . then remove the rubber cover

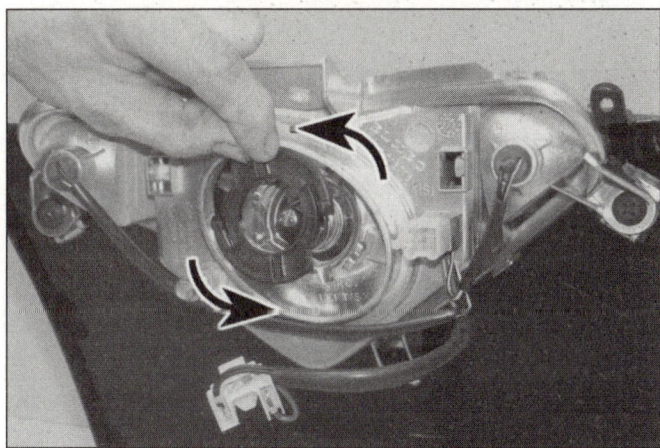

7.4c Twist the bulbholder anti-clockwise to release it . . .

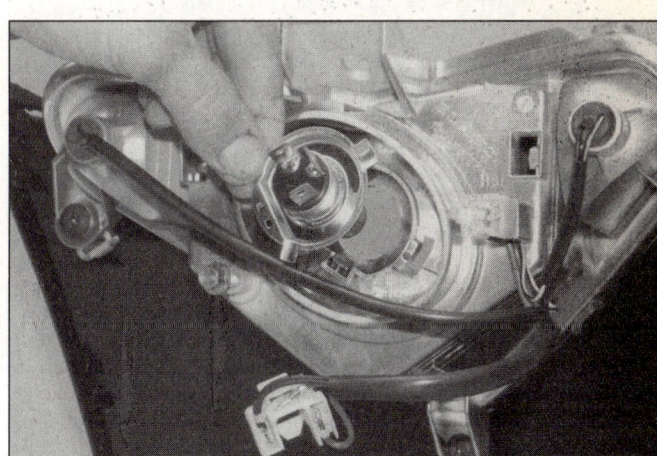

7.4d . . . then lift out the bulb

4 On Ice models, remove the front top panel and the headlight panel (see Chapter 8). Disconnect the connector from the bulb terminals and remove the rubber cover **(see illustrations)**. Twist the bulbholder anti-clockwise and remove it, then lift out the bulb **(see illustrations)**.

5 On SKP/Stalker models, remove the bag hook, then prise off the headlight access panel (see Chapter 8). Twist the bulbholder anti-clockwise and draw it out of the headlight, then push the bulb in and twist it anti-clockwise to release it from the holder **(see illustration)**.

6 Fit the new bulb bearing in mind the information in the **Note** above **(see illustration)**. Make sure the pins on the bulb fit correctly in the slots in the bulbholder. **Note:** *The bulb types and wattage ratings differ between models – refer to the Specifications*

7.5 Withdraw the bulbholder through the kick panel to access the headlight bulb

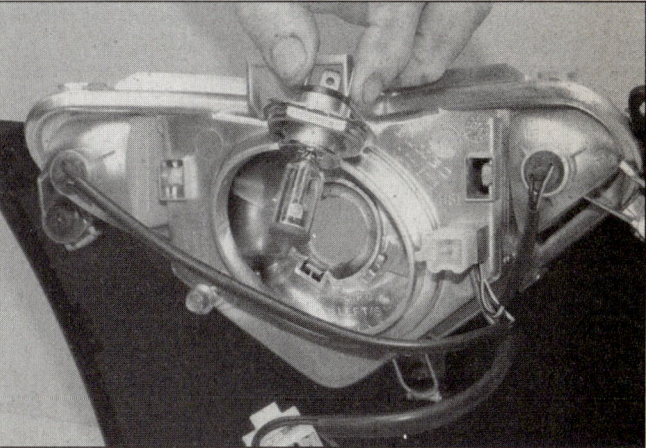

7.6 Handle quartz halogen bulbs by their wire terminals only – do not touch the glass

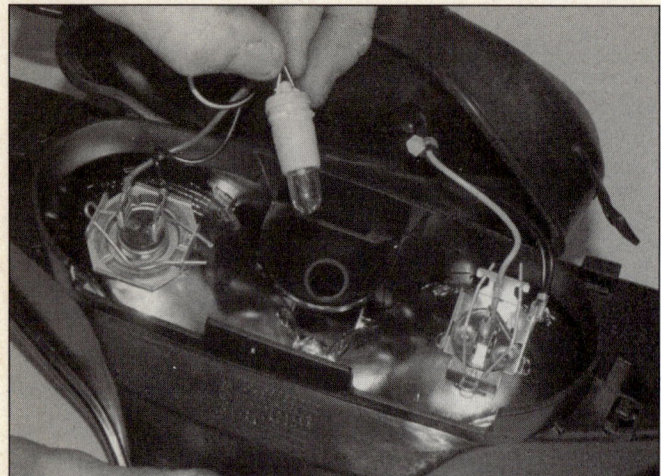

7.9a Remove the sidelight bulbholder . . .

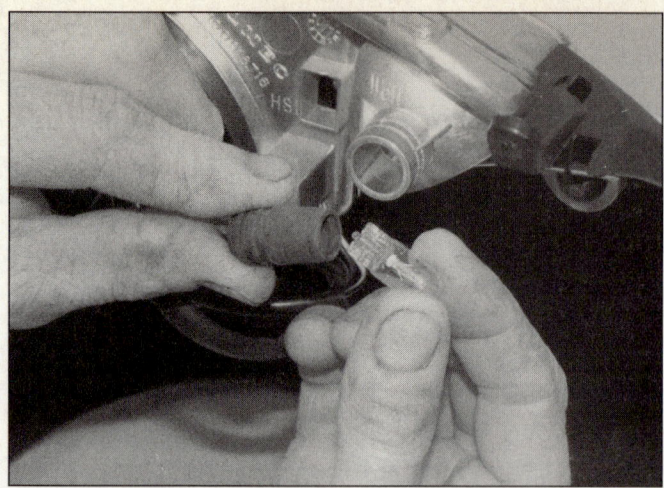

7.9b . . . and pull out the capless bulb carefully

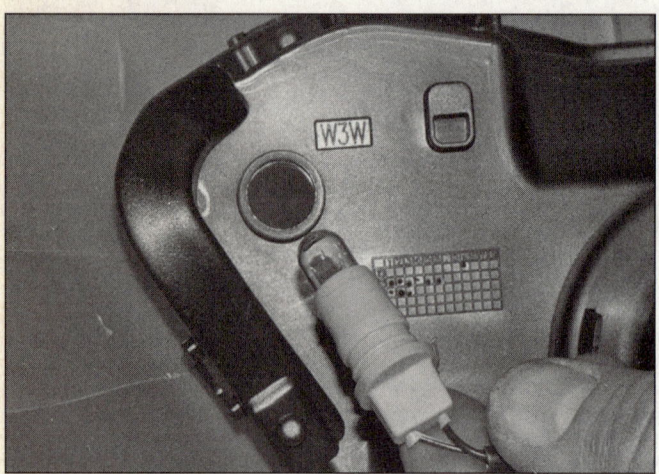

7.8c Sidelight location on Runner RST models

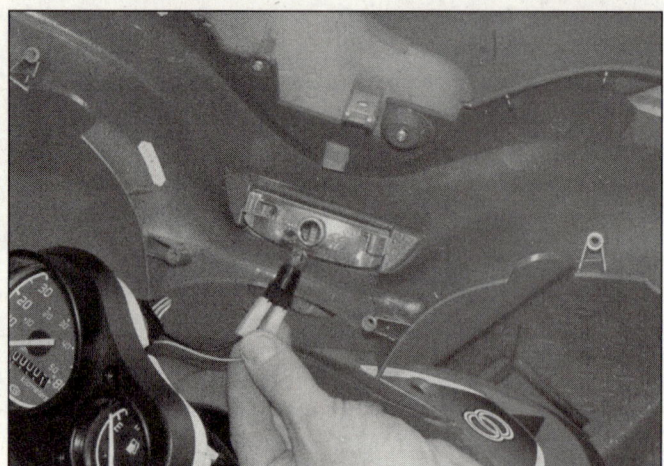

7.10a Pull the sidelight bulbholder out of its socket . . .

at the beginning of this Chapter or note the wattage marked on the cap of the original bulb, and fit a bulb of the correct type and wattage.
7 Secure the bulb with the bulbholder or the spring clip, as applicable. Install the wiring connector and rubber cover in the reverse order of removal.

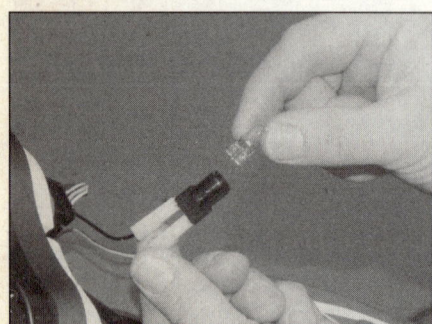

7.10b . . . then pull out the capless bulb carefully

8 If removed, install the headlight unit or headlight panel, then check the operation of the headlight. Install the remaining components in the reverse order of removal.

Sidelight bulb

9 On Runner, DNA and Ice models, follow the appropriate procedure to access the back of the headlight unit (see above). Pull the sidelight bulbholder out of its socket in the headlight, then carefully pull the bulb out of the holder **(see illustrations)**.
10 On SKP/Stalker models, first displace the front handlebar cover (see Chapter 8). Pull the bulbholder out of its socket in the back of the light, then carefully pull the bulb out of the holder **(see illustrations)**.
11 Carefully press the new bulb into the bulbholder, then install the bulbholder by pressing it in.
12 If removed, install the headlight unit or

headlight panel, then check the operation of the sidelight. Install the remaining components in the reverse order of removal.

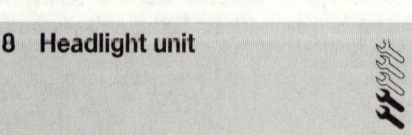

8 Headlight unit

Removal

1 On all Runner and DNA models, follow the procedure in Section 7 to remove the headlight unit.
2 On Ice models, first remove the headlight panel (see Chapter 8). The unit is secured in the panel by three screws.
3 On SKP/Stalker models, first remove the front panel (see Chapter 8). The unit is secured in the panel by two screws **(see illustration)**.

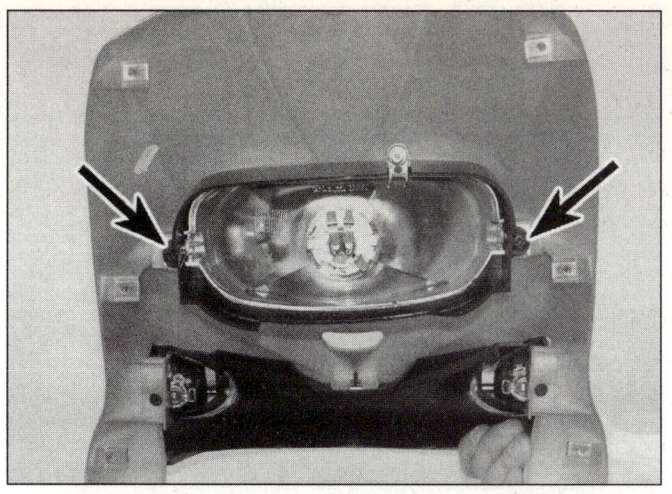

8.3 Headlight unit is retained by two screws (arrowed)

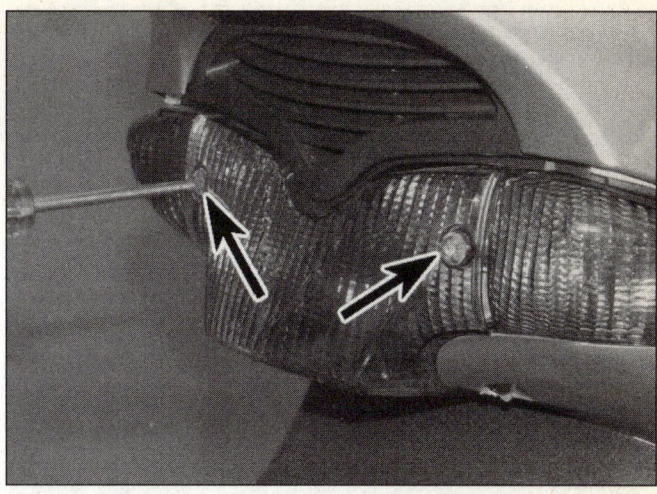

9.1a Remove the two screws (arrowed) . . .

Installation

4 Installation is the reverse of removal. Make sure all the wiring is correctly connected and secured. Check the operation of the headlight and sidelight. Check the headlight aim (see Chapter 1).

9   Brake/tail light bulb

Note: *It is a good idea to use a paper towel or dry cloth when handling new bulbs to prevent injury if the bulb should break and to increase bulb life.*

1 On Runner models, remove the two screws securing the lens and lift it off **(see illustrations)**. Push the bulb into the holder and twist it anti-clockwise to remove it.

2 On Runner RST and ST models, remove the tail panel (see Chapter 8, Section 5). Undo the two screws securing the tail light unit **(see illustration)**. Ease the unit out of the recess and disconnect the wire connector **(see illustration)**. Remove the two screws holding the bulb unit in place **(see illustrations)** and separate it from the lens. Twist and push in the bayonet type brake light bulb to release it from its socket **(see illustration)**. Pull the capless tail light bulb gently out of its socket **(see illustration)**.

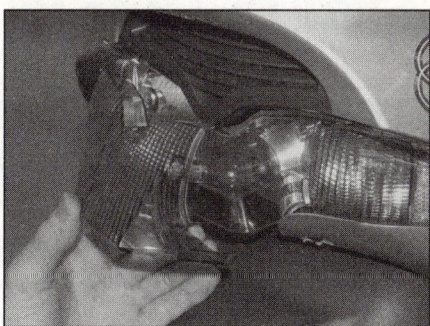

9.1b . . . and lift off the lens

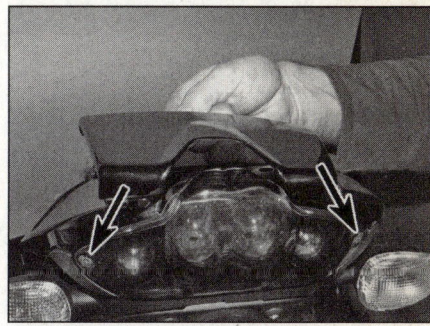

9.2a Remove the tail panel, then undo the screws securing the tail light unit (arrowed)

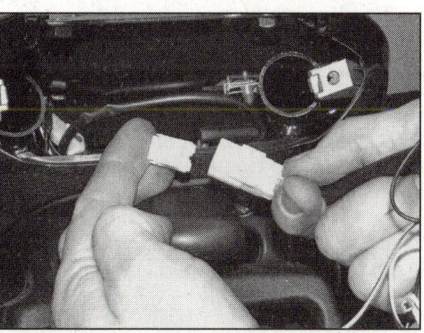

9.2b Ease the unit out of its recess and disconnect the wire connector

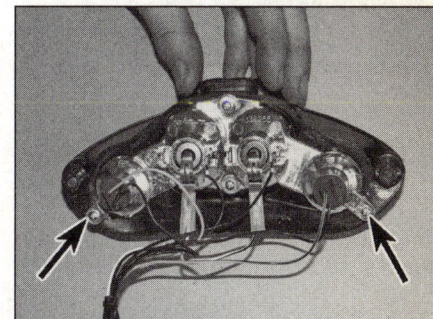

9.2c Remove the screws securing the bulb unit (arrowed) . . .

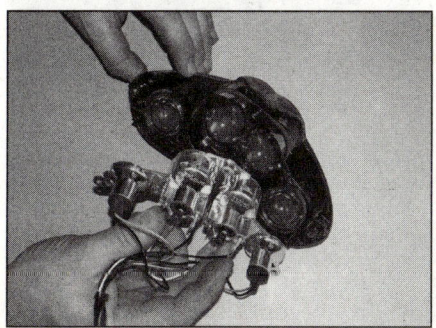

9.2d . . . and separate it from the lens

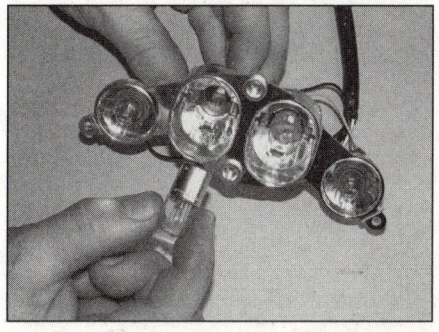

9.2e Twist and pull the bayonet brake light bulb from its socket

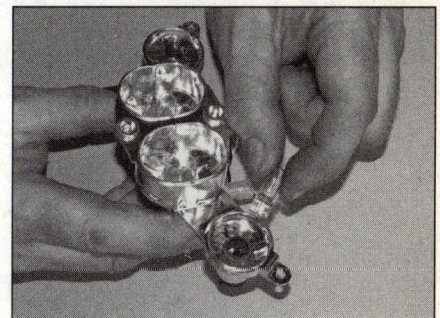

9.2f Pull the capless tail light bulb out of its socket

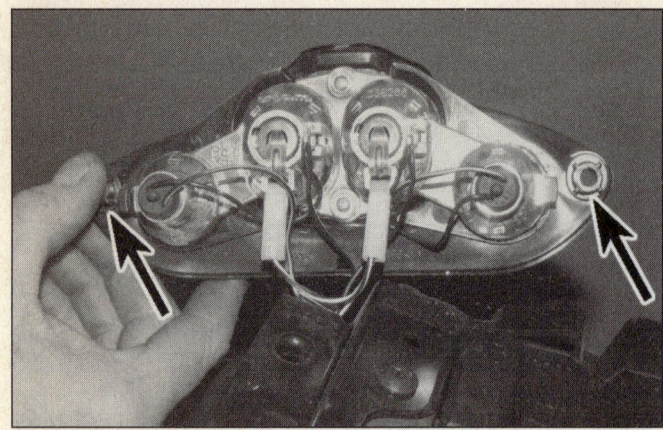

9.3a Remove the two screws (arrowed) . . .

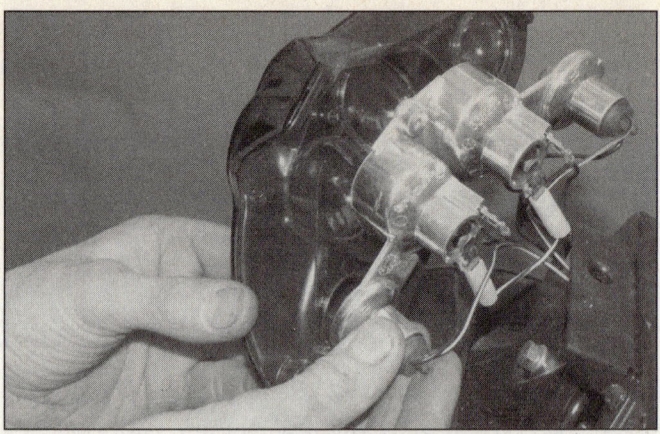

9.3b . . . and lift off the lens

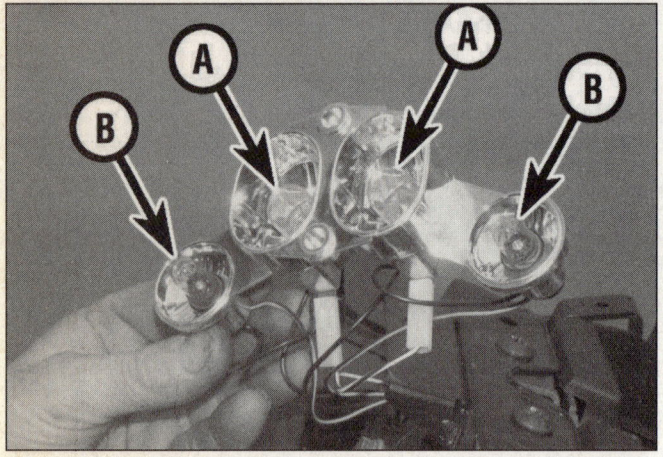

9.3c Push and twist the brake (A) and tail light bulbs (B) to remove them

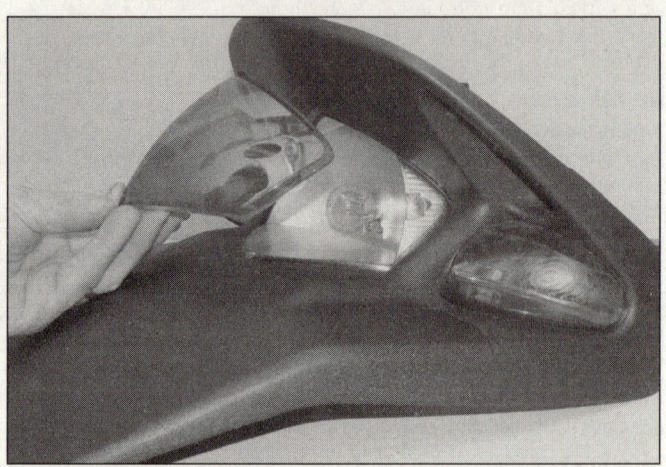

9.4a Remove the lens . . .

3 On DNA models, remove the two screws securing the light unit and lift it off. Remove the two screws on the back of the unit securing the lens and lift it off, then push the bulb into the holder and twist it anti-clockwise to remove it **(see illustrations)**.

4 On Ice models, remove the two screws securing the lens and lift it off, then push the

bulb into the holder and twist it anti-clockwise to remove it **(see illustrations)**.

5 On SKP/Stalker models, remove the two screws securing the lens and lift it off, then push the bulb into the holder and twist it anti-clockwise to remove it **(see illustration)**.

6 Check the socket terminals for corrosion and

clean them if necessary. Line up the pins of the new bulb with the slots in the socket, then push the bulb in and turn it clockwise until it locks into place. **Note:** *If the pins on the bulb are offset, the bulb can only be installed one way.*

7 Install the light unit or lens in the reverse order or removal. Note that on Runner and

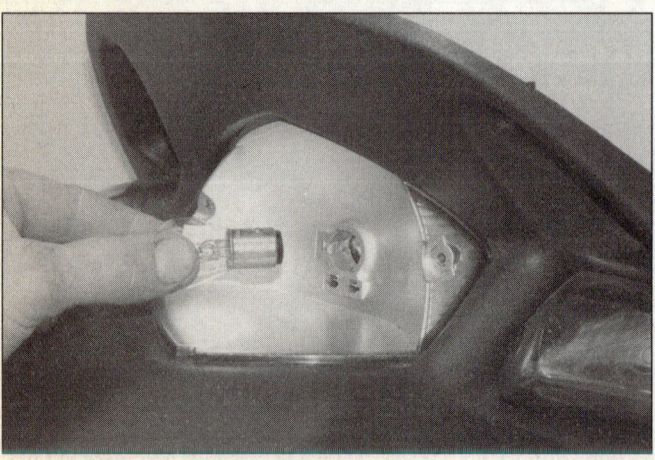

9.4b . . . then push and twist the bulb to remove it

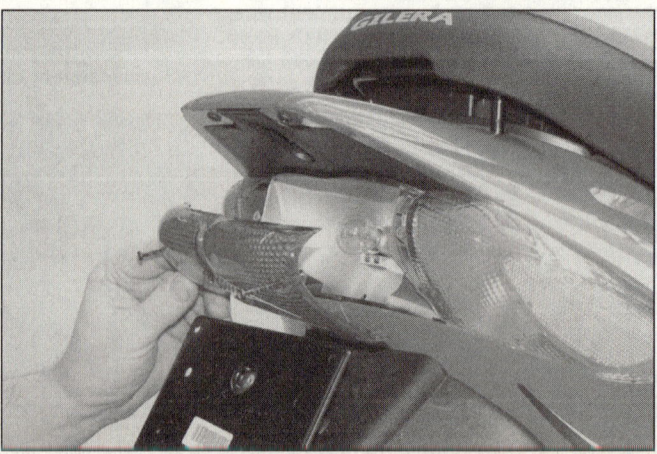

9.5 Lens is secured by two screws

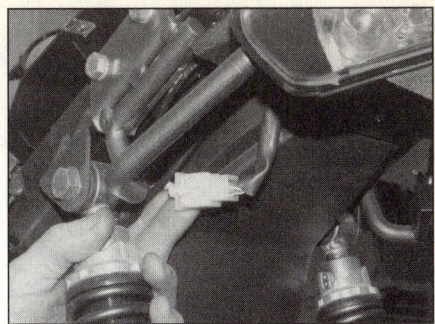

10.3 Disconnect the tail light wiring connector

SKP/Stalker models, the turn signal lenses are secured by the tail light lens – ensure the signal lenses are correctly installed before tightening the fixing screws.

8 Check the operation of the tail light and the brake light.

10 Tail light unit

1 On Runner models, remove the two screws securing the tail light lens and lift it off **(see illustration 9.1a)**. Lift off the turn signal lenses **(see illustration 12.1c)**. Ease the back of the unit out of the recess in the rear mudguard and disconnect the wiring connector.

2 On Runner RST and ST models, remove the tail panel (see Chapter 8, Section 5). Undo the two screws securing the tail light unit **(see illustration 9.2a)**. Ease the unit out of the recess and disconnect the wire connector **(see illustration 9.2b)**.

3 On DNA models, first remove the left-hand seat cowling panel (see Chapter 8). Follow the procedure in Section 9 and remove the light unit, then disconnect the brake light wiring connectors from the back of the unit. Trace the tail light wiring to the connector and disconnect it **(see illustration)**.

4 On Ice and SKP/Stalker models, the

tail light is integral with the rear mudguard assembly (see Chapter 8).

5 Installation is the reverse of removal. Check the operation of the tail light and the brake light.

11 Turn signal circuit

1 The battery provides power for operation of the turn signals, so if they do not operate, always check the battery voltage first. Low battery voltage indicates either a faulty battery or a defective charging system. Refer to Section 3 for battery checks and Section 26 for charging system tests. Also, check the fuse (see Section 5) and the switch (see Section 21).

2 Most turn signal problems are the result of a burned out bulb or corroded socket. This is especially true when the turn signals function properly in one direction, but fail to flash in the other direction. Check the bulbs and the sockets (see Section 12).

3 Note that some models use a conventional turn signal system where the turn signals are operated by a separate relay, while on others the turn signal relay is combined in either the regulator/rectifier or the ignition control unit (ICU). Establish which type is fitted by studying the appropriate wiring diagram at the end of this Chapter and test according to the relevant procedure.

Models with a turn signal relay

4 If the bulbs and sockets are good, using a multi-meter set to the 0 to 20 dc volts range, check for voltage at the B terminal on the turn signal relay with the ignition ON. Battery voltage should be shown. Turn the ignition OFF when the check is complete.

5 If no voltage is present at the relay, check the wiring from the relay to the ignition (main) switch for continuity.

6 If voltage is present at the relay, using the appropriate wiring diagram at the end of this Chapter, check the wiring between the relay,

turn signal switch and turn signal lights for continuity. If the wiring and switch are sound, fit a new relay.

Models without a turn signal relay

7 If the bulbs and sockets are good, using a multi-meter set to the 0 to 20 dc volts range, check for voltage at the input terminal of the turn signal switch with the ignition (main) switch ON. The voltage should fluctuate around 6V, although this may vary depending on the tester used. The important factor is that the voltage is supplied in pulses. Turn the ignition OFF when the check is complete.

8 If voltage is present at the switch, check the operation of the switch and the turn signal wiring.

9 If no voltage is present at the switch, check back through the wiring to the voltage regulator or ICU as appropriate.

10 If the wiring is good, refer to the appropriate wiring diagram and identify the battery voltage input terminal on the regulator or ICU, then test for battery voltage with the ignition ON.

11 If voltage is present at the input terminal, the voltage regulator or ICU is probably faulty. Have the unit checked by a Gilera dealer or substitute the unit for a known good one and check again.

12 If no voltage is present at the input terminal, check the wiring to the battery and, where appropriate, check the operation of the ignition (main) switch (see Section 20).

12 Turn signal bulbs

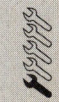

1 On Runner models, to access the front turn signal bulbs, remove the screw securing the lens and lift it off, noting how the tab on the rear edge locates in the panel **(see illustration)**. Twist the bulb cover clockwise to remove it **(see illustration)**. Push the bulb into the holder and twist it anti-clockwise to

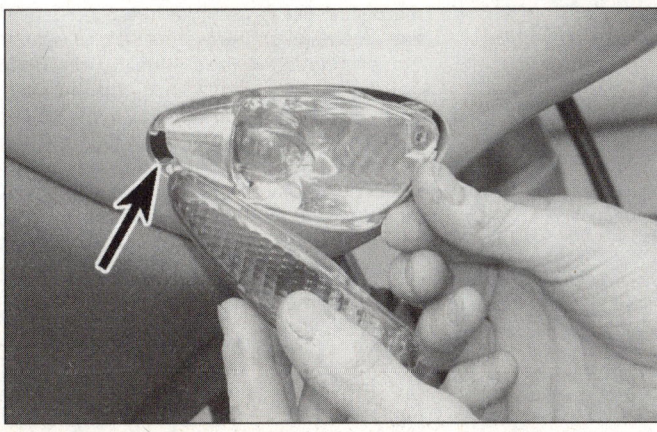

12.1a Note how the tab (arrowed) locates in the panel

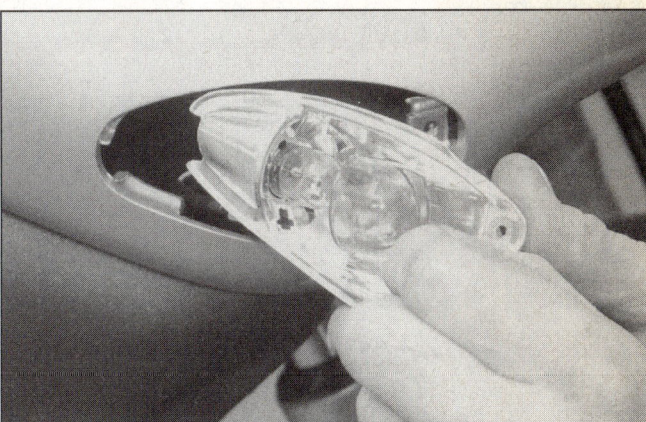

12.1b Twist the bulb cover to remove it

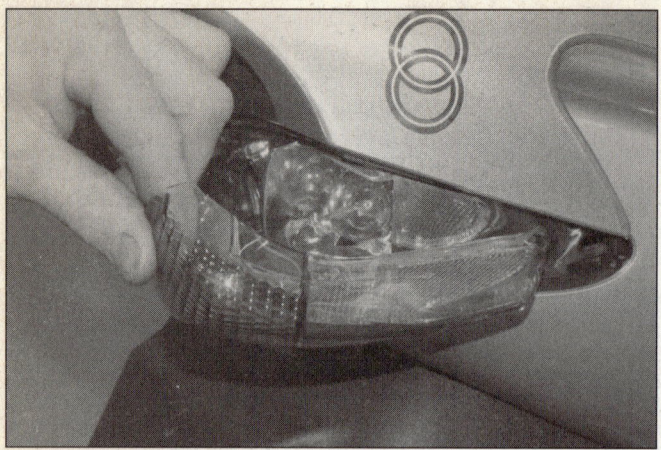

12.1c Remove the rear turn signal lens as described

12.1d Twist the bulb cover to remove it

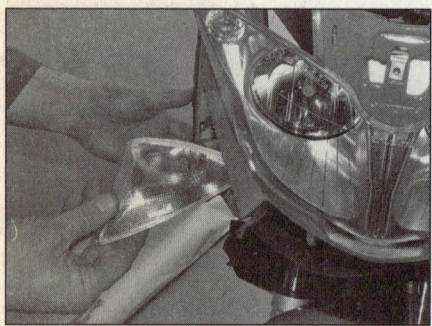

12.2a Remove the screw and manoeuvre the unit through the fairing

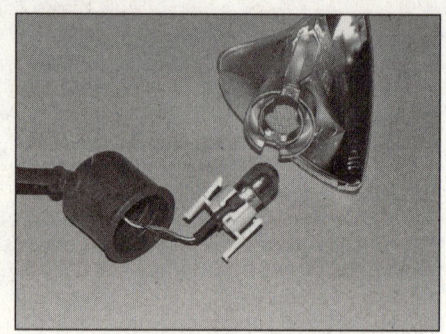

12.2b Squeeze together the ears of the bulbholder . . .

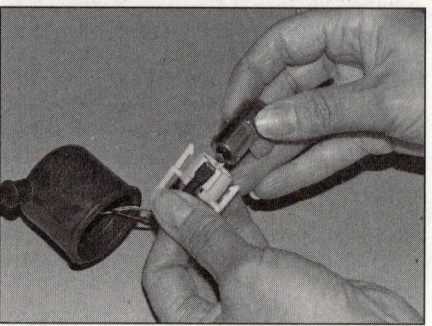

12.2c . . . and twist anti-clockwise and press inwards to remove the orange bulb

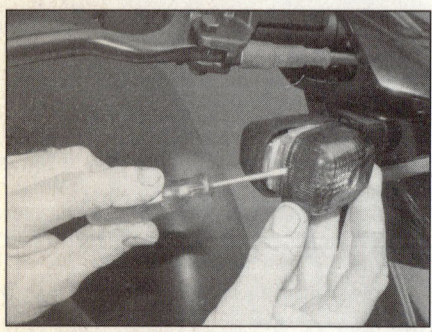

12.3a Lever the lens off carefully

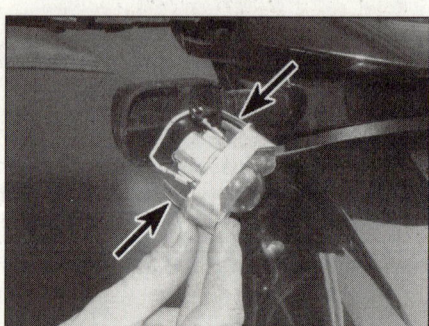

12.3b Note how the tabs (arrowed) locate

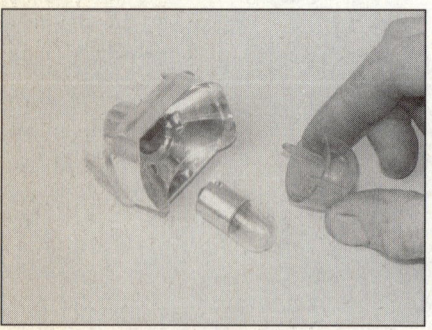

12.3c Components of the bulbholder assembly

12.3d Remove the bulbholder, then remove the bulb

remove it. To access the rear turn signal bulbs, remove the screws securing the tail light lens and remove it, then remove the turn signal lens, noting how it fits **(see illustration)**. Twist the bulb cover clockwise to remove it **(see illustration)**. Push the bulb into the holder and twist it anti-clockwise to remove it.

2 On Runner RST and ST models, to access the front turn signal bulbs, remove the screw securing the lens, then manoeuvre the unit out through the fairing aperture **(see illustration)**. Pull off the rubber boot to gain access to the bulb unit, then squeeze together the ears of the bulbholder to free it from the lens. Twist anti-clockwise and press inwards to remove the orange bulb **(see illustrations)**; on installation, note that the bulb pins are offset so it can only be fitted one way in the holder. The tab on the lens must engage the lug in the panel aperture. To change a rear turn signal bulb, remove the lens retaining screw, then twist the bulb anti-clockwise and press it in to remove it. Note that the pins are offset on the orange bulb.

3 On DNA models, to access the front turn signal bulbs, carefully lever the lens off with a small screwdriver **(see illustration)**. Note how the tabs on the bulbholder locate inside the signal body **(see illustration)**. Squeeze the sides of the bulb cover to remove it, then push the bulb into the holder and twist it anti-clockwise to remove it **(see illustration)**. To

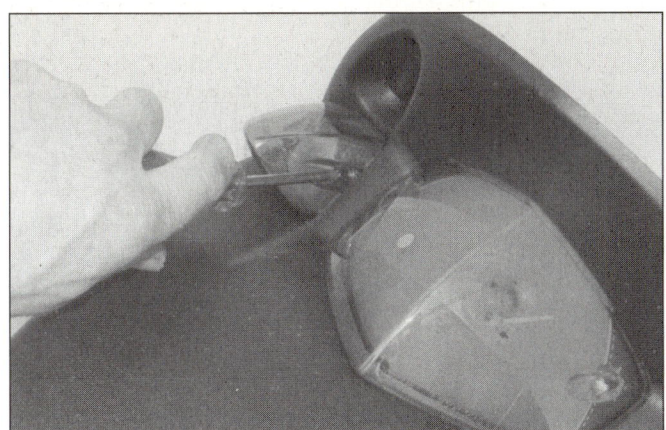

12.4a Remove the screw . . .

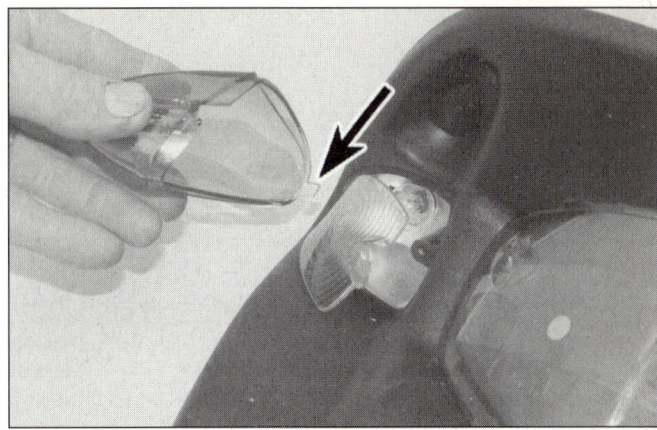

12.4b . . . then remove the lens, noting the tab (arrowed)

access the rear turn signal bulbs, first remove the boot on the bulbholder on the back of the turn signal unit, then turn the bulbholder anti-clockwise to remove it. Push the bulb into the holder and twist it anti-clockwise to remove it **(see illustration)**.

4 On Ice models, to access the front turn signal bulbs, follow the procedure for DNA models (see Step 2). To access the rear turn signal bulbs, remove the screw securing the lens and lift it off **(see illustrations)**. Squeeze the sides of the bulb cover to remove it, then push the bulb into the holder and twist it anti-clockwise to remove it.

5 On SKP/Stalker models, to access the front turn signal bulbs, remove the screw securing the lens and lift it off, noting how the tab on the front edge locates in the panel **(see illustration)**. Push the bulb into the holder and twist it anti-clockwise to remove it. To access the rear turn signal bulbs, remove the screws securing the tail light lens and remove it, then remove the turn signal lens, noting how it fits **(see illustration)**. Push the bulb into the holder and twist it anti-clockwise to remove it **(see illustration)**.

6 Check the socket terminals for corrosion

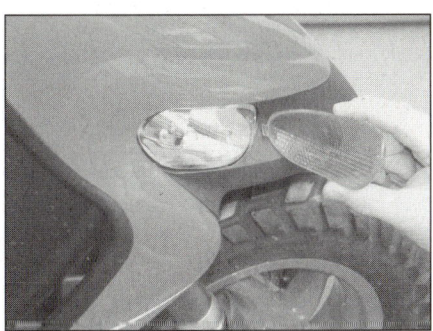

12.5a Remove the front turn signal lens, noting how it fits

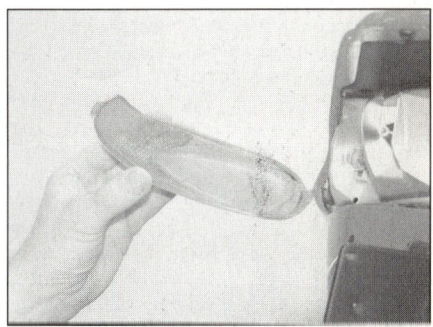

12.5b Remove the rear turn signal lens, noting how it fits

and clean them if necessary. Line up the pins of the new bulb with the slots in the socket, then push the bulb in and turn it clockwise until it locks into place.

7 Install the lens in the reverse order or removal. Note that on Runner and SKP/Stalker models, the turn signal lenses are secured by the tail light lens – ensure the signal lenses are correctly installed before tightening the fixing screws.

8 Check the operation of the turn signals.

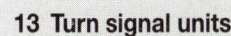

13 Turn signal units

1 On Runner models, the front turn signals are secured by the lens screw – remove the screw and lift out the signal assembly **(see illustration 12.1a)**. Disconnect the wiring connectors from the back of the assembly and remove it **(see illustration)**. The rear turn

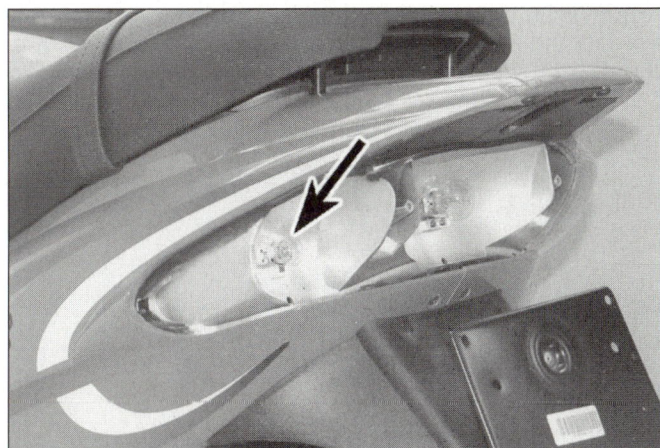

12.5c Push and twist the bulb (arrowed) to remove it

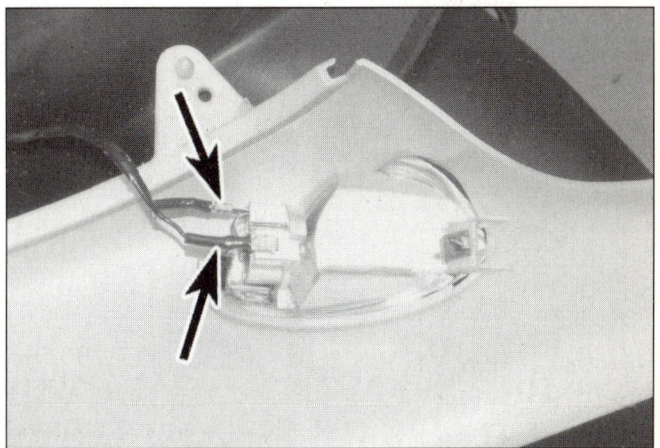

13.1 Disconnect the wiring (arrowed) from the back of the assembly

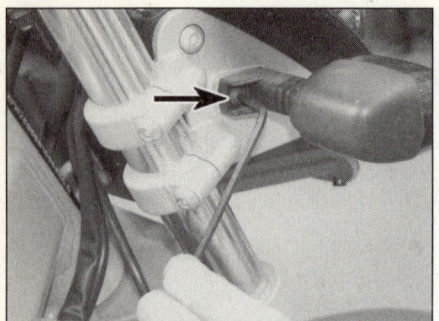

13.3a Undo the assembly bolt (arrowed) . . .

13.3b . . . then feed the wiring through the hole in the headlight bracket

13.3c Remove the screw (arrowed) . . .

signals are integral with the tail light unit (see Section 10).

2 On Runner RST and ST models, to remove the front turn signal lens, follow the procedure in Section 12. To remove a rear turn signal, follow the procedure in Chapter 8, Section 5 or 6 to remove the appropriate side panel. Detach the turn signal from the inside of the panel.

3 On DNA models, to remove the front turn signals, first remove the front fairing (see Chapter 8). Disconnect the signal wiring connectors, noting where they fit. Undo the bolt securing the assembly to the headlight bracket and lift it off, feeding the wiring carefully through the hole in the bracket **(see illustrations)**. To remove the rear turn signals, first remove the rear mudguard assembly

(see Chapter 8). Remove the bulbholder, then remove the screw **(see illustration)**. Lift off the turn signal, noting how the hook on the back locates in the mudguard **(see illustration)**.

4 On Ice models, the front turn signals are secured to the front handlebar cover (see Chapter 8). Remove the cover and disconnect the signal wiring connectors, noting where they fit **(see illustration)**. Undo the screw securing the assembly to the cover and lift it off, feeding the wiring carefully through the hole in the cover **(see illustration)**. The rear turn signals are integral with the rear mudguard assembly (see Chapter 8).

5 On SKP/Stalker models, to remove the front turn signals, first remove the kick

panel (see Chapter 8). Remove the lens (see Section 12). Disconnect the signal wiring connectors, then undo the screw securing the back of the assembly and lift it out **(see illustration)**. The rear turn signals are integral with the rear mudguard assembly (see Chapter 8).

6 Installation is the reverse of removal. Check the operation of the turn signals.

14 Brake light switches

Circuit check

Note: The brake switches are part of the safety circuit which prevents the engine from starting unless either brake lever is pulled in. If the starter circuit is faulty, follow the procedure in Steps 2 and 3 to check the switch. If the switch is good, check the starter relay (Section 23) and other components in the starter circuit as described in the relevant Sections of this Chapter. If all components are good, check the wiring between the various components (see Wiring diagrams at the end of this Chapter).

1 Before checking any electrical circuit, check the bulb (see Section 9) and fuse (see Section 5).

2 If required, remove the front handlebar

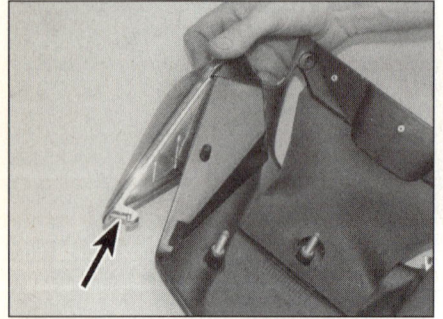

13.3d . . . the lift off the turn signal noting how the hook (arrowed) locates

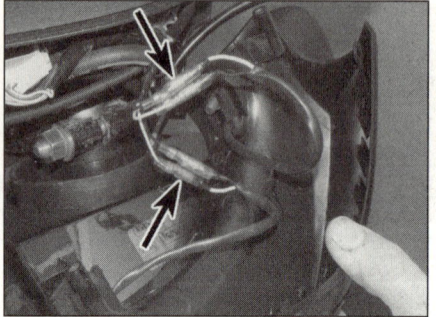

13.4a Turn signal wiring connectors (arrowed)

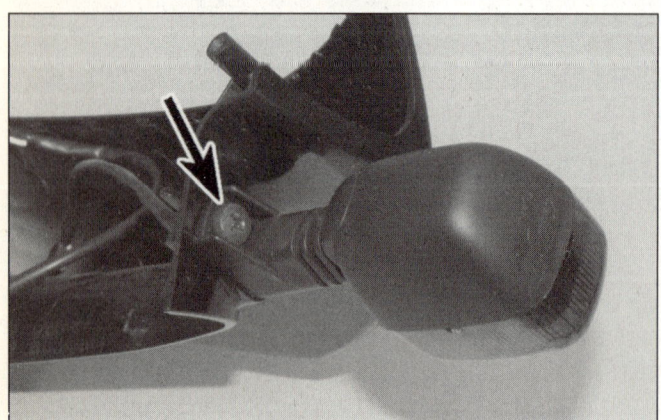

13.4b Turn signal assembly is retained by single screw (arrowed)

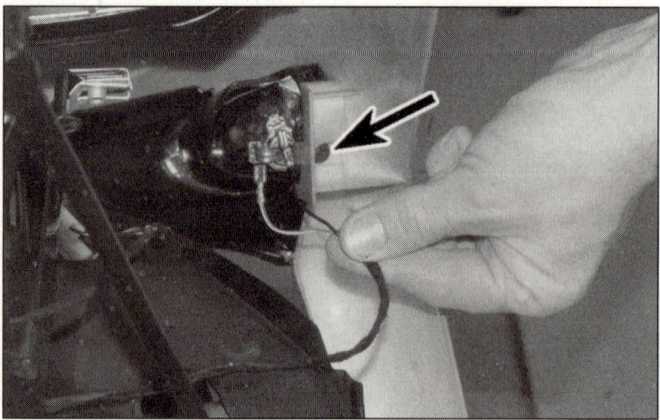

13.5 Disconnect the wiring connectors, then remove the screw (arrowed)

covers (see Chapter 8), or pull back the boot on the switch wiring connectors **(see illustration)**.

3 Disconnect the wiring connectors from the switch **(see illustration)**. Using a continuity tester, connect a probe to each terminal. With the brake lever at rest, there should be no continuity. Pull the brake lever in – there should now be continuity. If not, renew the switch.

4 If continuity is shown with the lever pulled in, the switch is functioning correctly and any fault must lie elsewhere in the circuit. Using a multi-meter or test light connected to a good earth, check for voltage at the brake light switch wiring connectors with the ignition ON (one of them should show battery voltage). If there's no voltage present, check the wire between the switch and the ignition switch (see the *Wiring diagrams* at the end of this Chapter).

5 If both continuity and voltage are obtained the switch and its power supply are proved good. Now check the wiring between the switch and the brake light bulb (see the *Wiring diagrams* at the end of this Chapter).

Switch renewal

6 The switches are mounted in the brake lever brackets **(see illustrations 14.2 and 14.3)**. Disconnect the wiring connectors from the switch, then unscrew the switch from the bracket.

7 Installation is the reverse of removal. Check the operation of the switch.

15 Instrument cluster

Check

1 Special instruments are required to check the operation of the speedometer. If it is believed to be faulty, take the scooter to a Gilera dealer for assessment, although check first that the drive cable or sensor wire is not broken (see Section 17). Refer to the relevant Sections to check the fuel gauge and warning light circuits. Individual components are not available, so if an instrument or panel display is faulty, the entire cluster must be renewed.

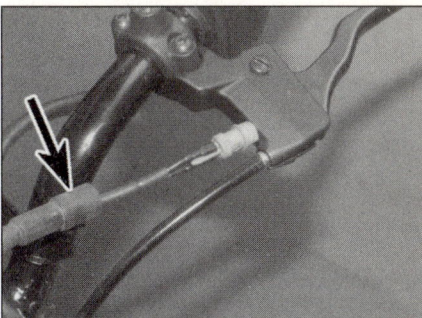

14.2 Displace the boot (arrowed) from the wiring connectors . . .

Removal

2 On Runner, Ice and SKP/Stalker models, remove the handlebar front cover (see Chapter 8). On DNA models, remove the front fairing (see Chapter 8).

3 On Runner models, detach the speedometer cable (where fitted) and displace the handlebar rear cover (see Chapter 8). Unclip the instrument cluster multi-pin wiring connectors **(see illustrations)**. Remove the

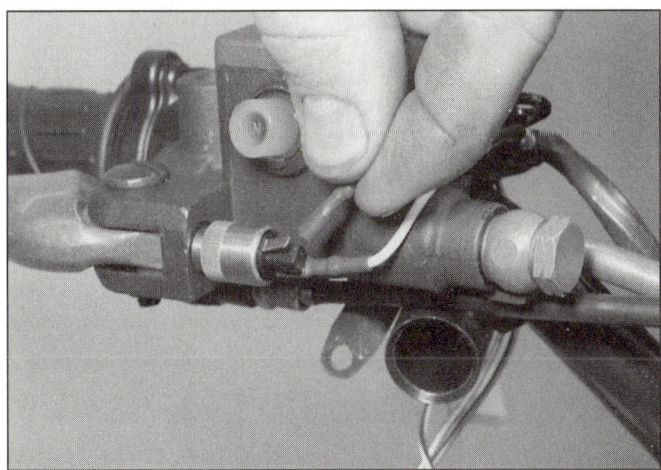

14.3 . . . then disconnect the wiring from the brake light switch

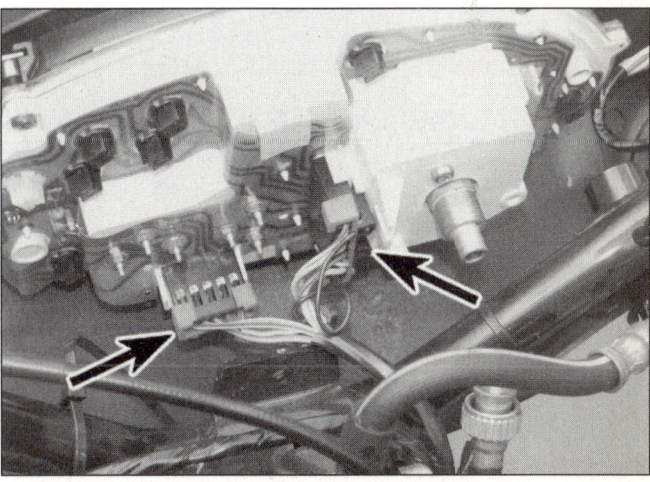

15.3a Instrument cluster wiring connectors (arrowed) on Runner models

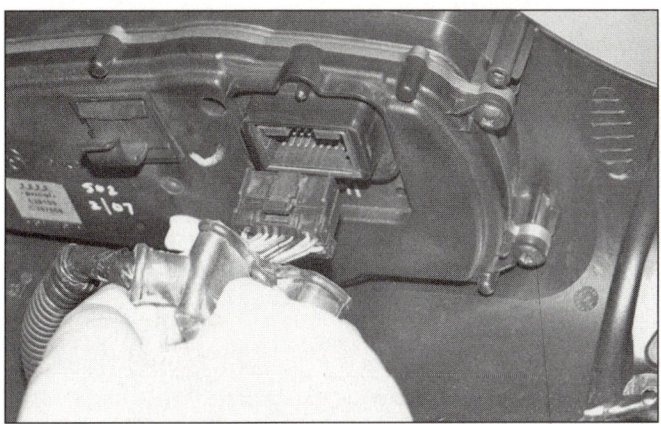

15.3b Instrument cluster wiring connector on Runner RST and ST models

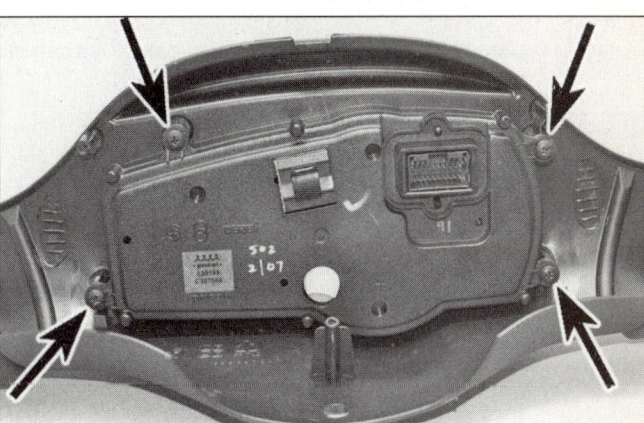

15.3c Instrument mounting screws

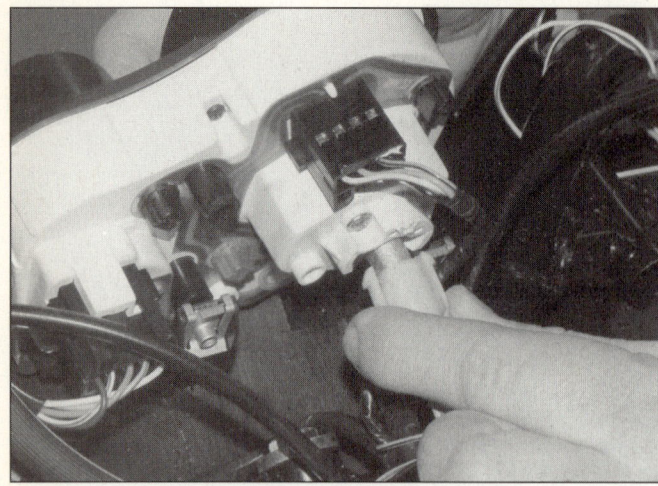

15.4a Disconnect the speedometer cable . . .

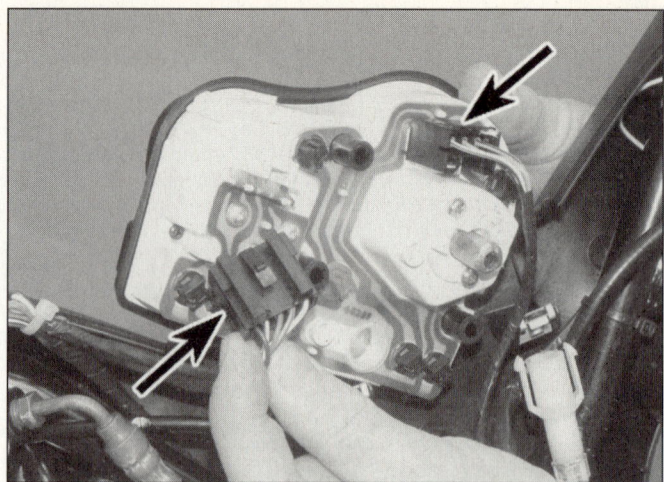

15.4b . . . and unclip the wiring connectors (arrowed)

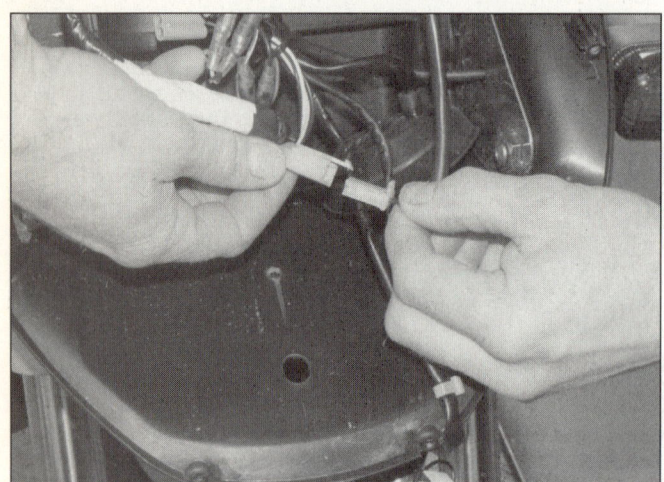

15.6a Disconnect the panel lights wiring connector . . .

15.6b . . . and the instrument cluster wiring connector (arrowed)

screws securing the instrument cluster to the cover and lift it off.

4 On SKP/Stalker models, release the clips securing the speedometer cable to the back of the speedometer and detach the cable (see illustration). Unclip the instrument cluster multi-pin wiring connectors and remove the cluster (see illustration).

5 On Ice models, remove the rear handlebar

cover, then remove the cluster from the cover (see Chapter 8).

6 On DNA models, disconnect the panel lights wiring connector, then displace the boot on the instrument cluster wiring connector and unclip the connector (see illustrations). Release the wiring from the clip on the back of the cluster. Remove three screws securing the cluster to the lower fairing half and lift it off (see illustration).

Installation

7 Installation is the reverse of removal. Make sure that the speedometer cable, where fitted, and wiring connectors are correctly routed and secured.

16 Instrument cluster bulbs and clock battery

Note: The instrument cluster on later models and all Ice models is a sealed digital display.

1 On Runner and SKP/Stalker models, remove the handlebar front cover (see Chapter 8). On DNA models, remove the front fairing (see Chapter 8).

2 On early Runner models, detach the speedometer cable and displace the handlebar rear cover (see Chapter 8). Twist the bulbholder anti-clockwise and draw it out of the instrument casing, then pull the bulb out of the bulbholder (see illustration). Check the wattage of the old bulb and make sure

15.6c Remove the screws (arrowed) and lift off the instrument cluster

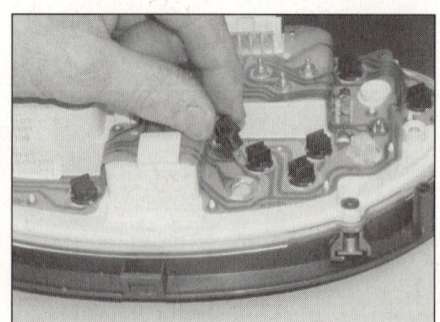

16.2 On Runner models, twist the bulbholder to remove it

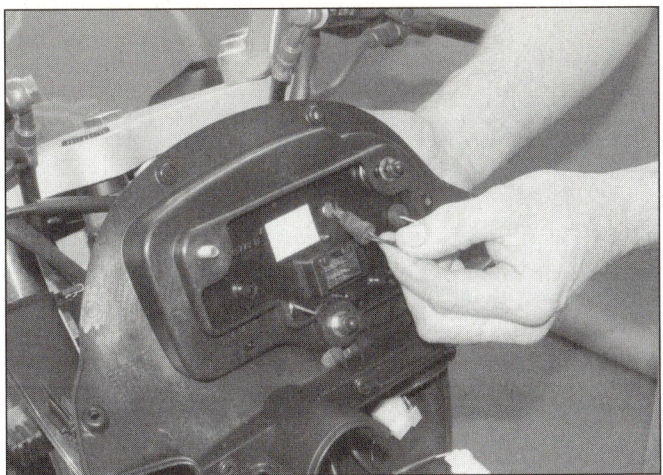

16.3 On DNA models, pull the bulbholder to remove it

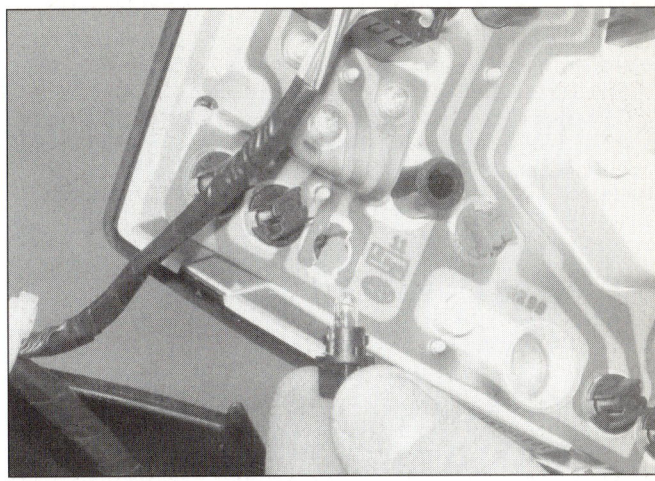

16.4a On SKP/Stalker models, twist the bulbholder to remove it . . .

that you fit a new one of the same wattage. If the socket contacts are dirty or corroded, scrape them clean and spray with electrical contact cleaner before a new bulb is installed. Carefully push the new bulb into the holder, then install the holder securely.

3 On DNA models, pull the bulbholder out of the instrument casing, then pull the bulb out of the bulbholder **(see illustration)**. Check the wattage and the socket contacts as described in Step 2, then install the new bulb.

4 On SKP/Stalker models, detach the speedometer cable and, if required, unclip the wiring connectors (see Section 15). Twist the bulbholder anti-clockwise and draw it out of the instrument casing, then pull the bulb out of the bulbholder **(see illustrations)**.

5 The clock on SKP/Stalker models is fitted with a separate battery. To access the battery, first remove the plastic plug, then turn the cap anti-clockwise using a screwdriver; remove the cap, spring and the battery, noting which way up it fits **(see illustration)**. Fit the new battery, making sure it is the correct way up, then refit the spring, cap and plug.

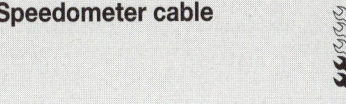

17 Speedometer cable

Removal

Note: *DNA, Ice and later Runner models are fitted with an electronically operated speedometer – the 'cable' is a wire connecting the sensor on the wheel hub to the speedometer. Do not try to disconnect the wire from the sensor.*

1 On Runner and SKP/Stalker models, follow the procedure in Section 15 and detach the speedometer cable from the back of the speedometer.

2 Pull back the boot on the bottom of the cable, then unscrew the nut and pull the inner cable out of the drive housing **(see illustration)**.

3 If required, remove the front panel to give access to the cable as it is withdrawn (see Chapter 8).

16.4b . . . then pull the bulb out

4 Pull the cable out carefully, releasing it from any guides and noting its correct routing.

5 If required, follow the procedure in Chapter 1 to remove the speedometer drive gear housing.

Installation

6 If required, follow the procedure in Chapter 1 and lubricate the inner cable and drive gear.

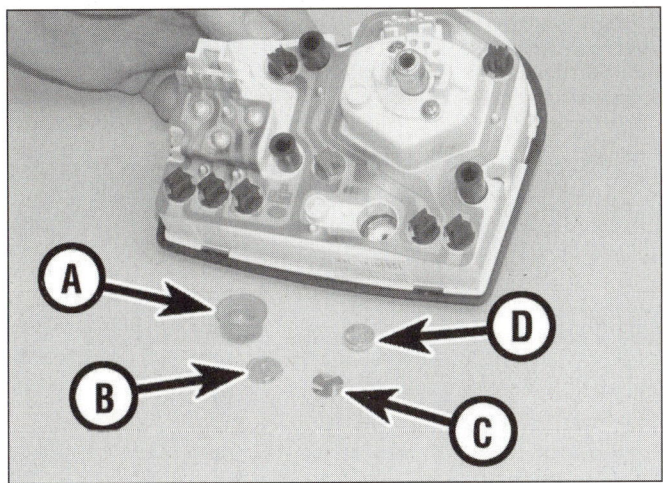

16.5 Components of the clock battery assembly – plug (A), cap (B), spring (C) and battery (D)

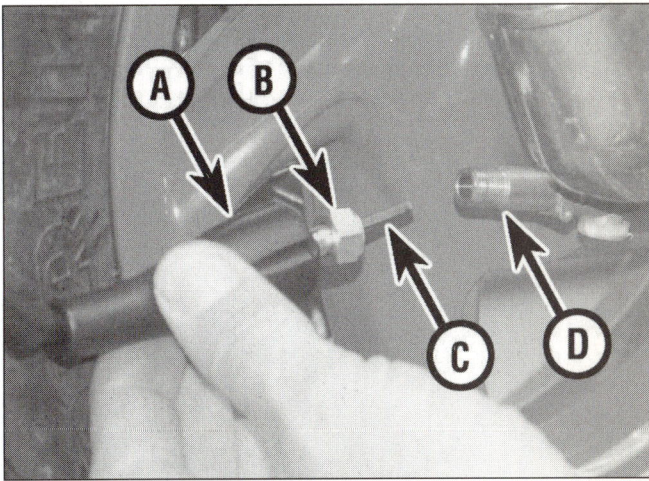

17.2 Speedometer cable boot (A), nut (B), inner cable (C) and drive housing (D)

7 Route the cable up through the bodywork to the instrument cluster and connect the upper end securely to the speedometer **(see illustration)**.

8 Connect the lower end to the drive housing and tighten the nut securely, then install the boot **(see illustration 17.2)**. Raise the front wheel clear of the ground and rotate it by hand to ensue the inner cable is correctly located.

9 Check that the cable doesn't restrict steering movement or interfere with any other components.

10 Install the remaining components in the reverse order of removal.

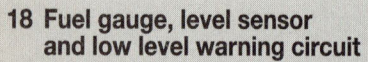

18 Fuel gauge, level sensor and low level warning circuit

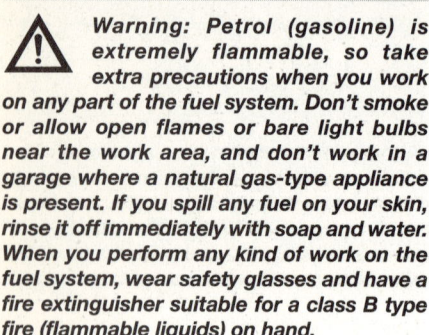

⚠️ **Warning: Petrol (gasoline) is extremely flammable, so take extra precautions when you work on any part of the fuel system. Don't smoke or allow open flames or bare light bulbs near the work area, and don't work in a garage where a natural gas-type appliance is present. If you spill any fuel on your skin, rinse it off immediately with soap and water. When you perform any kind of work on the fuel system, wear safety glasses and have a fire extinguisher suitable for a class B type fire (flammable liquids) on hand.**

Fuel gauge

Check

1 Remove the bodywork as required by your model to access the top of the fuel tank (see Chapter 8). Disconnect the wiring connector from the top of the fuel level sensor **(see illustrations)**.

2 Use the *Wiring diagrams* at the end of this Chapter to identify the earth wire and the fuel gauge wire at the connector, then connect

17.7 Connect the upper end of the cable to the speedometer – Runner shown

a jumper wire between the two terminals on the connector. With the ignition switched ON, the fuel gauge should read FULL. If it doesn't, check the fuse and the wiring between the connector and the gauge, and check for battery voltage at the switched supply terminal on the instrument cluster wiring connector. The supply terminal of the instrument cluster wiring connector can be identified either from the *Wiring diagrams* at the end of this Chapter or by its position in the connector block:

Runner 50 models – No. 1C terminal on the 3-pin connector.

Runner FX and FXR models – No. 1C terminal on the 3-pin connector.

Runner VX, VXR and ST models – No. 3 terminal on the 8-pin connector.

DNA models – No. 12 terminal.

Ice – No. 9 terminal.

SKP/Stalker – No. 1 terminal on the 5-pin connector.

If the fuse and the wiring are good, and there is voltage at the instrument cluster terminal, then the gauge is confirmed faulty.

Removal and installation

3 The fuel gauge is integral with the instrument cluster, for which no individual parts are available. If the fuel gauge is faulty,

the entire cluster must be renewed (see Section 15).

Fuel level sensor

Check

4 If the fuel gauge is confirmed good, the fault may lie in the level sensor in the fuel tank. Remove the bodywork as required by your model to access the top of the fuel tank (see Chapter 8).

5 Disconnect the wiring connector from the top of the sensor **(see illustrations 18.1a and 18.1b)**.

6 Using an ohmmeter set to the ohms x 100 scale, connect its probes to the earth and fuel gauge wire terminals on the sensor and check the resistance reading. Gilera provide no specifications, however when the tank is full, a low resistance reading should be obtained, and when the tank is empty a higher reading should be obtained.

7 If the sensor is good, check the wiring between the sensor and the gauge (see *Wiring diagrams* at the end of the Chapter).

8 No individual components are available for the sensor; if it is faulty, fit a new one.

Removal and installation

9 Disconnect the wiring connector from the top of the sensor, then turn the sensor anticlockwise and withdraw it from the tank **(see illustrations)**. Note that two types of sensor are fitted to the scooters covered by this manual. Discard the O-ring as a new one must be used.

10 Installation is the reverse of removal.

Low level warning circuit check

11 If the warning light in the instrument cluster fails to come on when the fuel is low, first check the bulb (see Section 16). If the bulb is good, remove the sensor (see Step 9).

12 Using a continuity tester, connect the probes between the earth and warning light terminals on the sensor. Start with the float

18.1a Fuel level sensor wiring connector – Ice shown

18.1b Fuel level sensor wiring connector – SKP/Stalker shown

in the full (high) position, then slowly lower it to the empty position. There should be no continuity until the float nears the empty position, when continuity should be shown. If this is not the case, renew the sensor.

13 If the sensor is good, check the wiring between the sensor and the instrument cluster (see *Wiring diagrams* at the end of the Chapter).

19 Oil level warning circuit and diode

Note: *The oil level warning circuit is fitted to all Runner 50 models, DNA 50 GP, Ice and SKP/Stalker models.*

Oil level sensor

1 If the warning light in the instrument cluster fails to come on when the oil is low, first check the bulb (see Section 16). If the bulb is good, remove the bodywork as required by your model to access the top of the oil tank (see Chapter 8).

2 Disconnect the wiring connector from the top of the sensor, then withdraw the sensor from the tank **(see illustrations)**.

3 Use the *Wiring diagrams* at the end of this Chapter to identify the oil warning light wire at the connector, and also the pair of wires that connect to the terminals on the opposite side of the sensor connector. Identify the corresponding terminals on the sensor connector.

4 Using a continuity tester, connect the probes between the warning light wire and one of the two wire terminals on the opposite side of the sensor connector. Start with the float in the full (high) position, then slowly lower it to the empty position. There should be no continuity until the float nears the empty position, when continuity should be shown. If this is not the case, renew the sensor.

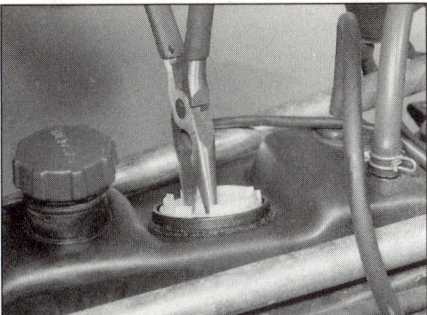

18.9a Turn the sensor anti-clockwise . . .

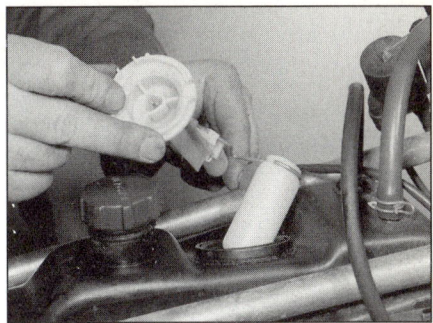

18.9b . . . and withdraw it from the tank – old type shown

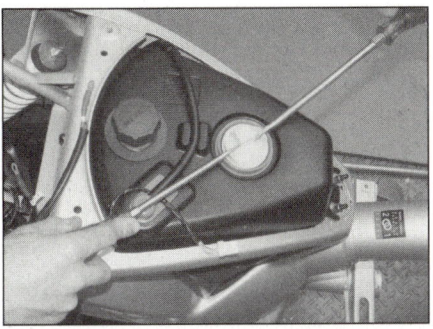

18.9c Turn the sensor anti-clockwise . . .

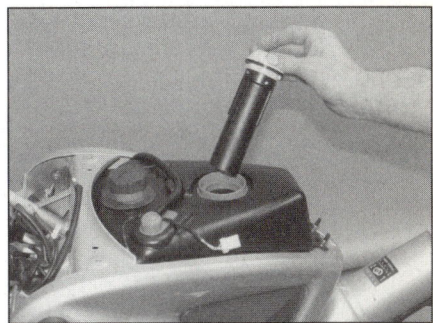

18.9d . . . and withdraw it from the tank – new type shown

5 If the sensor is good, check the wiring between the sensor and the instrument cluster, and the sensor and the other components in the warning circuit (see *Wiring diagrams* at the end of the Chapter).

Diode

6 The oil level warning light should come on for a few seconds when the ignition (main) switch is turned ON to test its operation. If the light fails to come on, first check the bulb (see Section 17). If the bulb is good, check the wiring between the various components

in the warning circuit (see *Wiring diagrams* at the end of this Chapter).

7 On some models, a diode is part of the warning light test circuit; check the *Wiring diagrams* to identify the position of the diode in the circuit

8 Disconnect the diode wiring connectors, noting which way round they fit. Using an ohmmeter or continuity tester, connect the probes to the diode terminals and note the result, then reverse the probes. The diode should show continuity in one direction and no continuity in the other direction. If it doesn't behave as stated, fit a new diode.

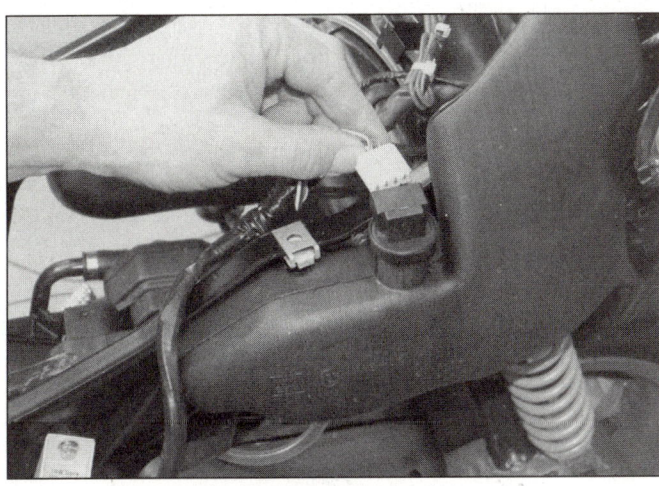

19.2a Disconnect the wiring connector . . .

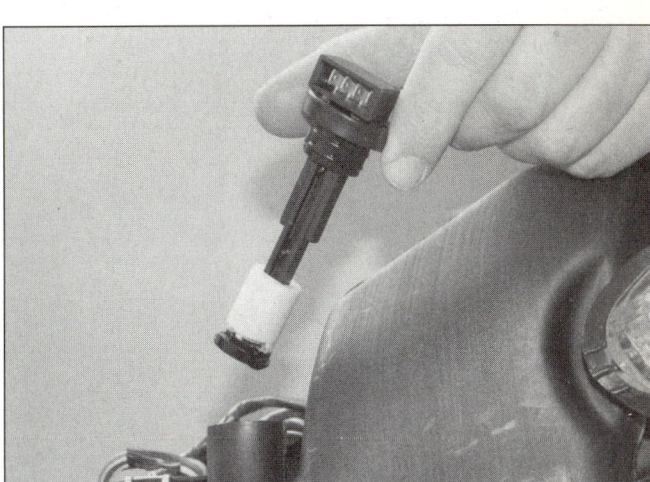

19.2b . . . and withdraw the sensor from the tank

20 Ignition (main) switch

⚠️ **Warning: To prevent the risk of short circuits, disconnect the battery negative (-ve) lead before making any ignition (main) switch checks.**

Check

1 Disconnect the battery negative (-ve) lead (see Section 3).

2 On Runner, Ice and SKP/Stalker models, the ignition (main) switch is mounted on the front frame tube; remove the front panel to access the switch (see Chapter 8). Disconnect the wiring connector from the back of the switch **(see illustrations)**.

3 On DNA models, the ignition (main) switch is mounted on the underside of the front fork top yoke; remove the front fairing panel to access the switch wiring connector (see Chapter 8). Trace the wiring back from the ignition (main) switch and disconnect it at the connector.

4 Using an ohmmeter or a continuity tester,

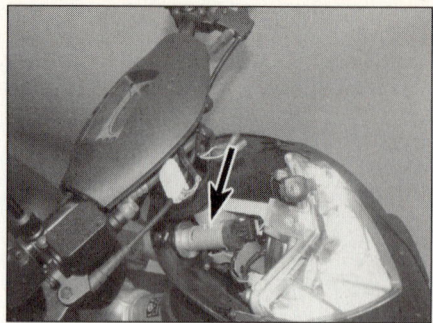

20.2a Location of the ignition (main) switch – Ice shown

check the continuity of the switch terminal pairs (see the *Wiring diagrams* at the end of this Chapter). Continuity should exist between the connected terminals when the switch is in the indicated position.

5 If the switch fails any of the tests, renew it.

Removal

6 On Runner, Ice and SKP/Stalker models, to remove the electrical switch section from the back of the steering lock, pull off the spring

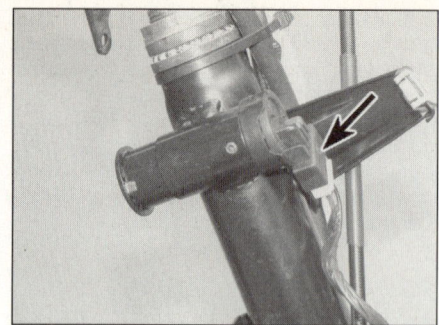

20.2b Ignition (main) switch wiring connector – SKP/Stalker shown

clip and withdraw the switch section, noting how it fits **(see illustration)**.

7 On DNA models, to remove the electrical switch section from the back of the steering lock, remove the screw and lift it off, noting how the pin in the lock locates in the switch **(see illustrations)**.

8 On Runner VX, VXR and ST models, unclip the immobiliser aerial from around the front of the switch **(see illustration)**.

9 On Runner, Ice and SKP/Stalker models, to remove the lock, insert a small screwdriver

20.6 Pull off the clip (arrowed) to detach the electrical switch

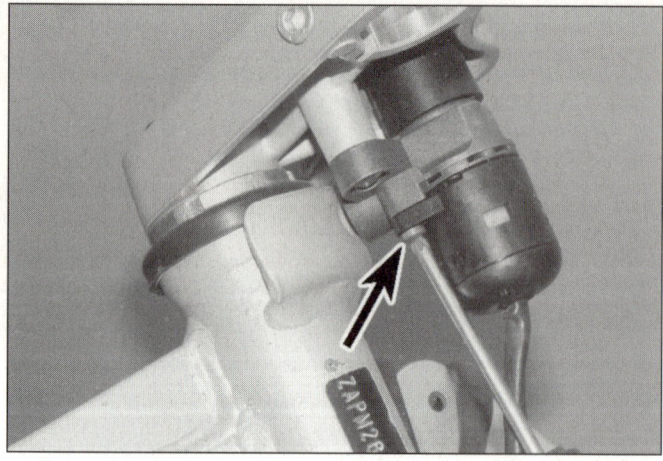

20.7a Electrical switch is secured by single screw (arrowed)

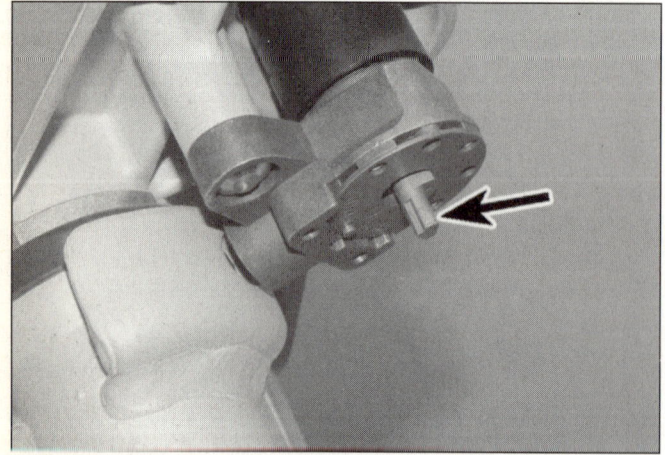

20.7b Note how the pin (arrowed) locates in the switch

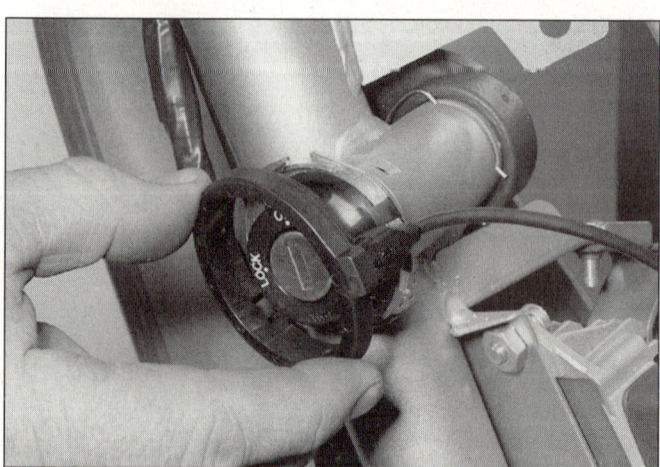

20.8 Where fitted, unclip the immobiliser aerial

into the hole in the housing behind the front bezel. Push on the retaining tongue with the screwdriver and draw the lock out of its housing.

10 On DNA models, the lock is retained by a shear-head bolt. Remove the top yoke (see Chapter 6), then support the yoke in a vice and drill off the head of the bolt. Lift off the lock and unscrew the bolt with pliers. A new bolt must be used on reassembly.

Installation

11 On Runner, Ice and SKP/Stalker models, fit the key into the lock and turn it to the ON position. Offer the lock up to its housing, making sure the anchor tang faces down. Insert the lock about half-way into the housing, then simultaneously turn the key to the OFF position and push the lock fully in until the anchor tang is felt to locate. Install the electrical switch section, making sure it locates correctly and secure it with the spring clip. Insert the key and check the operation of the switch.

12 On Runner VX, VXR and ST models, clip the immobiliser aerial to the front of the switch **(see illustration 20.8)**.

13 On DNA models, position the lock on the underside of the top yoke and install a new shear-head bolt. Tighten the bolt until the head shears off. Fit the electrical switch section over the pin in the lock, ensuring the pin locates correctly, then insert the key and check the operation of the switch. Install the fixing screw and tighten it securely.

14 Reconnect the switch wiring connector, then connect battery negative (-ve) lead. Check the operation of the ignition (main) switch.

15 Install the remaining components in the reverse order of removal.

21 Handlebar switches

Check

1 Generally speaking, the switches are reliable and trouble-free. Most troubles, when they do occur, are caused by dirty or corroded contacts, but wear and breakage is a possibility that should not be overlooked. If breakage does occur, the switch will have to be replaced with a new one.

2 The switches can be checked for continuity using an ohmmeter or a continuity test light. Always disconnect the battery negative (-ve) lead (see Section 3) to prevent the possibility of a short circuit, before making the checks.

3 Remove the handlebar front cover (see Chapter 8). Trace the wiring from the switch to be tested to the connector and disconnect it, then check for continuity between the terminals on the switch side of the connector with the switch in various positions i.e. switch OFF – no continuity, switch ON – continuity. Use the wire colours to identify the switch terminals (see the *Wiring diagrams* at the end of this Chapter).

4 On Runner and SKP/Stalker models, if the test indicates a problem exists, displace the handlebar rear cover (see Chapter 8). Check that the switch connection is good, then disconnect the wiring and repeat the continuity test on the switch terminals themselves **(see illustration)**. The switch is a sealed unit; if it is faulty, fit a new switch (see Step 6).

5 On DNA and Ice models, if the check indicates a problem exists, undo the screws securing the two halves of the switch housing and lift off the rear half **(see illustrations)**.

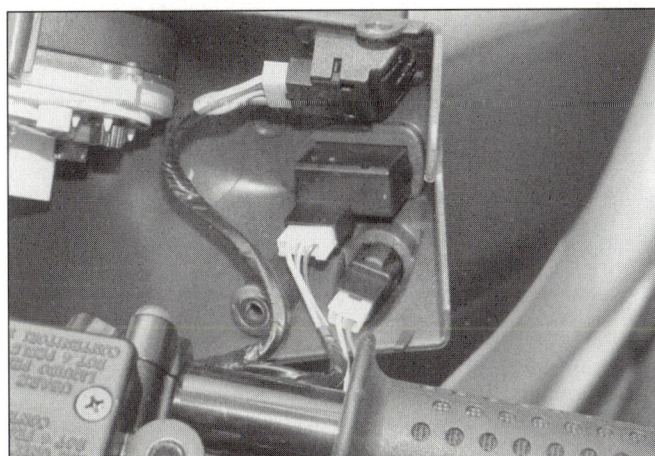

21.4 Handlebar switch wiring connectors – Runner shown

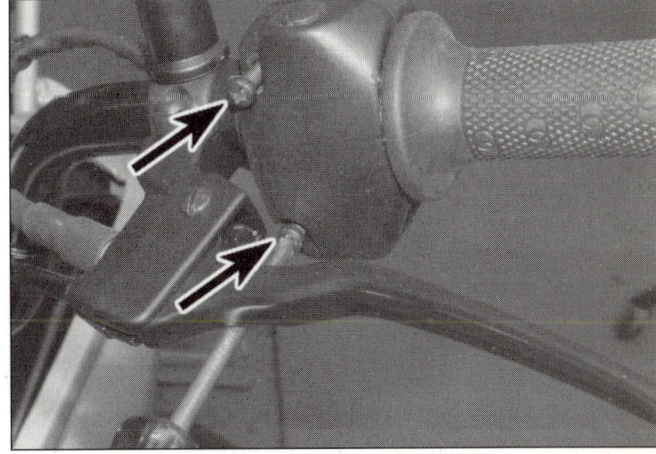

21.5a Undo the screws (arrowed) . . .

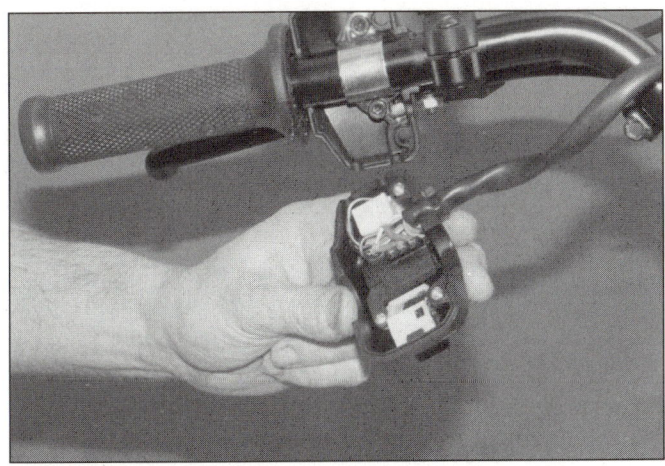

21.5b . . . and remove the rear half of the switch housing . . .

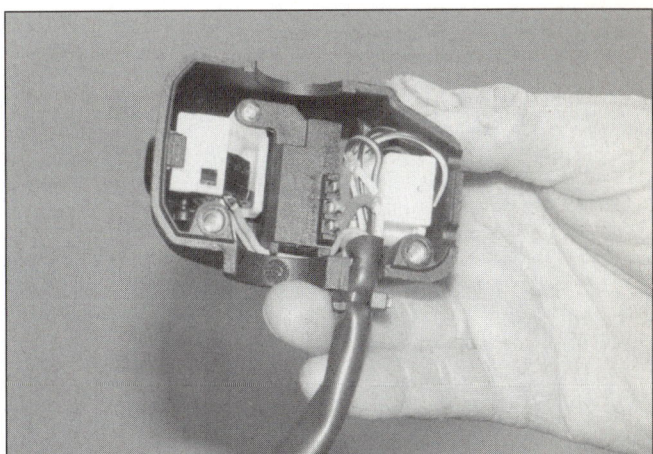

21.5c . . . then inspect the wiring connections and switch contacts

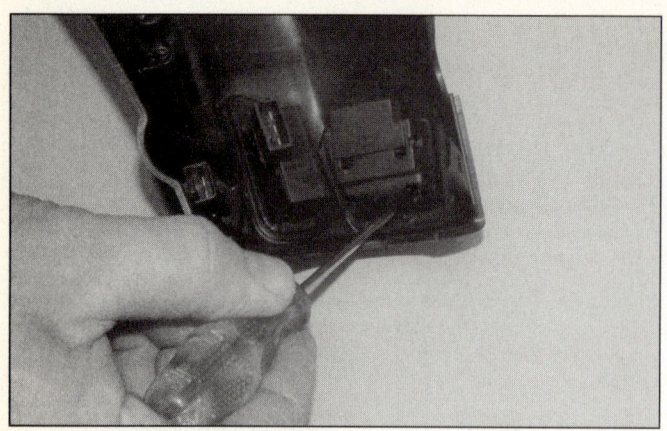

21.6a Release the clip on the switch body . . .

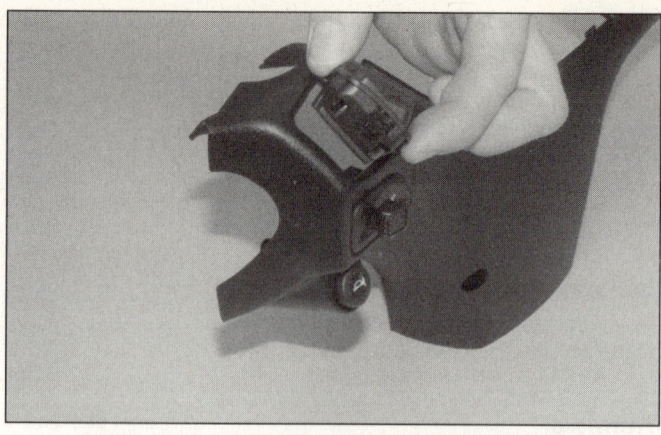

21.6b . . . and ease the switch unit out of the cover

Inspect the wiring connections and switch contacts and spray them with electrical contact cleaner. If any of the switch components are damaged or broken, fit a new switch housing (see Step 7).

Removal

6 On Runner and SKP/Stalker models, displace or remove the handlebar rear cover (see Chapter 8). If not already done, disconnect the wiring connector from the switch being removed, then release the clip on the switch body with a small screwdriver and carefully ease the switch out **(see illustrations)**.

7 On DNA and Ice models, remove the handlebar front cover (see Chapter 8). Trace the wiring from the switch housing being removed and disconnect it at the connector. Release the wiring from any clips or ties and feed it up to the housing. Undo the screws securing the two halves of the switch housing and lift off the rear half **(see illustrations 21.5a and 21.5b)**.

Installation

8 Installation is the reverse of removal. Make sure the wiring connectors are secure and test the operation of the switch.

22 Horn

Check

1 On Runner and SKP/Stalker models, the horn is mounted behind the front panel **(see illustration)**. On Runner RST and ST models, remove the inspection panel from the front panel to access the horn **(see illustration)**.

2 On DNA models, the horn is mounted above the radiator.

3 On Ice models, the horn is mounted on the right-hand side of the frame behind the headlight panel **(see illustration)**.

4 Remove the panels as necessary to access the horn (see Chapter 8).

5 Disconnect the wiring connectors from the horn **(see illustration)**. Using two jumper wires, apply battery voltage directly to the horn terminals. If the horn sounds, check the switch (see Section 21) and the wiring between the switch and the horn (see the *Wiring diagrams* at the end of this Chapter).

6 If the horn doesn't sound, renew it.

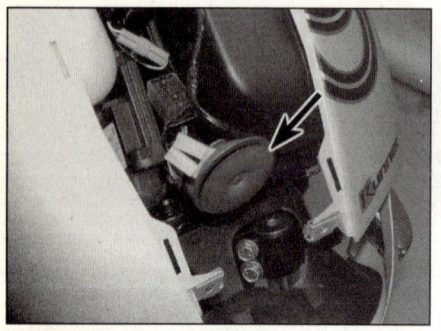

22.1a Location of the horn on Runner models

22.1b Access horn through the aperture in the front panel on Runner RST and ST

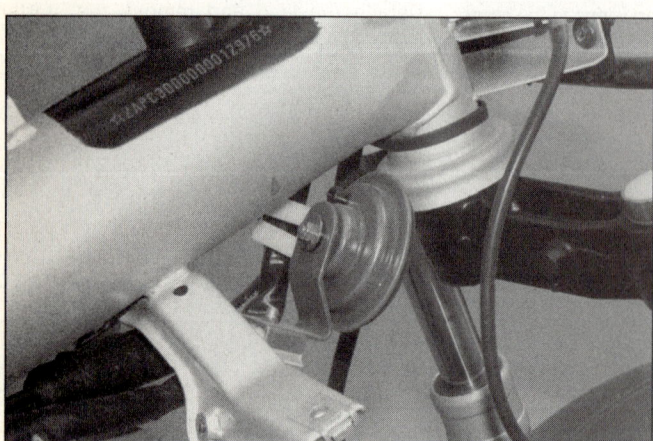

22.3 Location of the horn on Ice models

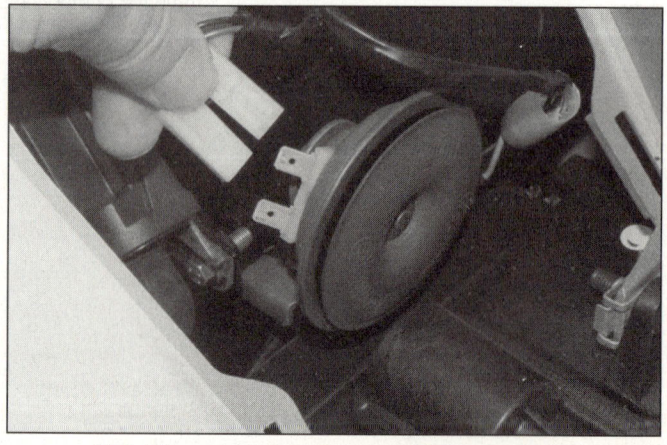

22.5 Disconnect the two horn wiring connectors

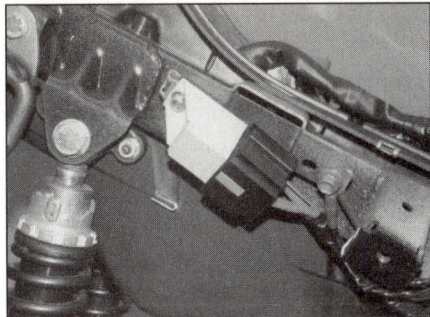

23.2a Location of the starter relay on DNA models

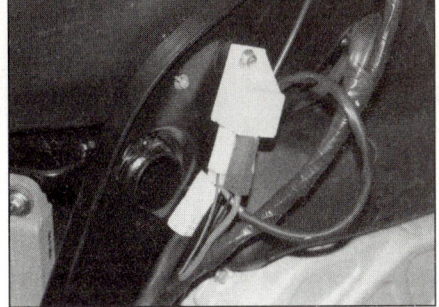

23.2b Location of the starter relay on SKP/ Stalker models

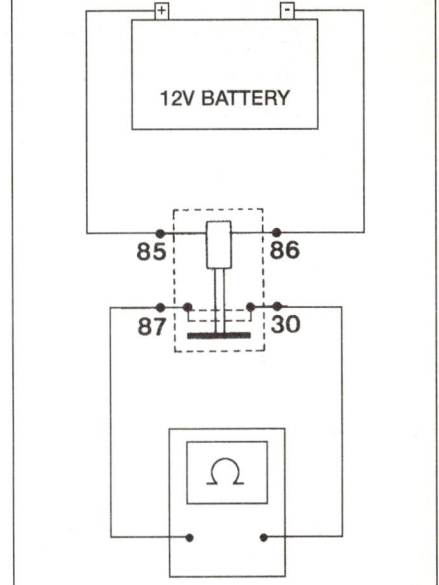

23.5 Starter relay test

Renewal

7 Remove the panels as necessary to access the horn (see above).

8 Disconnect the wiring connectors from the horn, then undo the nut or screw securing the horn and remove it.

9 Install the horn and tighten the nut or screw securely. Connect the wiring connectors and check the operation of the horn.

23 Starter relay

Check

1 If the starter circuit is faulty, first check that the battery is fully charged (see Section 3) and that the main fuse is good (see Section 5). Next check the operation of the brake light switches and the switch wiring (see Section 14). On Runner VX, VXR and ST models, if the immobiliser LED is OFF, check the immobiliser system (see Chapter 5).

2 On Runner models remove the right-hand side panel, on DNA models remove the right-hand seat cowling, on Ice models remove the underseat panel and on SKP/ Stalker models remove the front underseat panel (see Chapter 8). Locate the starter relay by tracing the lead from the positive terminal of the battery that connects to the relay (the other one connects to the ignition

switch), or trace the lead back from the starter motor to the relay **(see illustrations)**.

3 Where the relay has individual wire connectors rather than a single block connector, disconnect the battery and starter motor leads from the No. 30 and No. 87 terminals on the relay. With the ignition switched ON and either brake lever pulled in, press the starter switch. The relay should be heard to click. Switch the ignition OFF.

4 If the relay doesn't click, or if the relay has a block connector, remove the relay (see Steps 7 and 8) and test it as follows.

5 Set a multi-meter to the ohms x 1 scale and connect it across the relay's No. 30 (battery) and No. 87 (starter motor) terminals. Using a fully charged 12 volt battery and two insulated jumper wires, connect across the No. 85 and No. 86 terminals of the relay **(see illustration)**. At this point the relay should be heard to click and the multi-meter read 0 ohms (continuity) indicating the relay is good. If the relay does not click when battery voltage is applied and the multi-meter indicates infinite resistance (no continuity), the relay is faulty and must be renewed.

6 If the relay is good, check for battery voltage across the wire connectors for the No. 85 and No. 86 relay terminals with the ignition ON when the starter button is pressed. If there is no battery voltage, refer to the *Wiring diagrams* at the end of this Chapter and check the other components and wiring in the starter circuit as described in the relevant sections of this Chapter.

Renewal

7 Disconnect the battery terminals, remembering to disconnect the negative (-ve) terminal first (see Section 3).

8 Locate the starter relay (see Step 2). If the wires are connected to the relay terminals individually, make a careful note of which wire fits on which terminal (the terminals are numbered), then disconnect them. If the relay has a block connector, disconnect it **(see illustration)**. Remove the relay.

9 Installation is the reverse of removal. Connect the negative (-ve) lead last when reconnecting the battery.

24 Starter motor – removal and installation

Removal

All Runner 50 models, DNA 50 GP, Ice, SKP/Stalker and Runner FX125/FXR180

1 The starter motor is mounted underneath the engine. Disconnect the battery negative (-ve) lead (see Section 3).

2 Unscrew the two bolts securing the starter motor to the crankcase, noting the earth cable secured by the upper bolt **(see illustration)**. Slide the starter motor out from the crankcase, then peel back the terminal cover and remove the screw securing the starter lead to the motor **(see illustrations)**. Detach the lead and remove the starter motor.

23.8 Disconnect the relay from the block connector – Runner shown

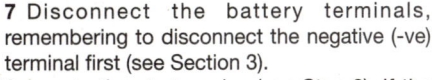

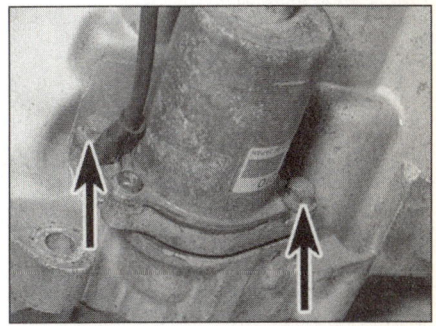

24.2a Remove the two bolts (arrowed), noting the earth cable . . .

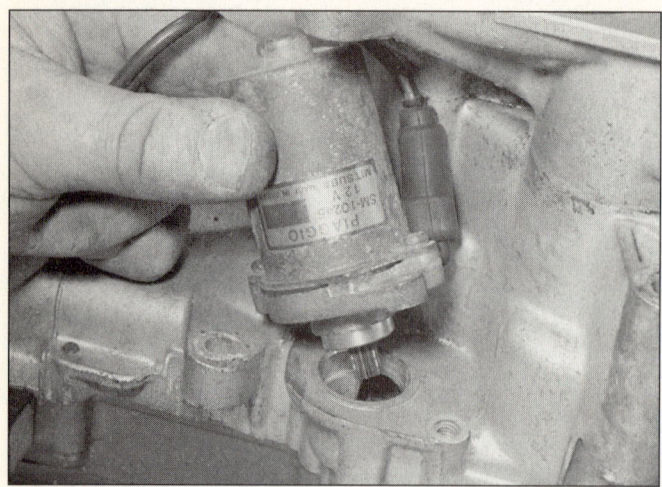

24.2b ... then remove the starter motor ...

24.2c ... and detach the lead from the terminal

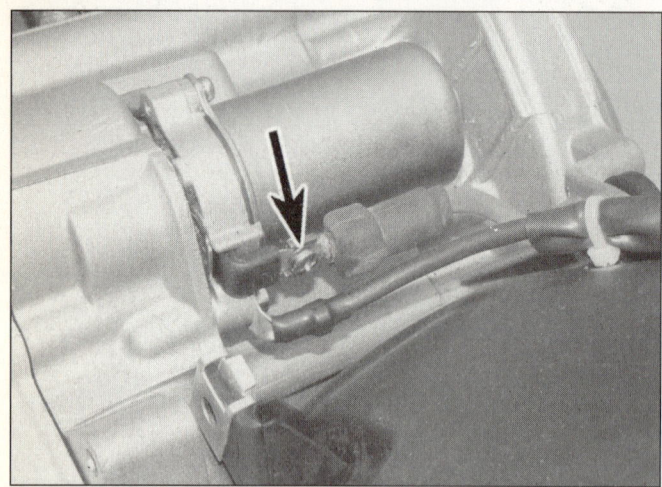

24.4 Pull back the cover and remove the screw (arrowed) securing the lead

24.5 Remove the two bolts (arrowed)

Runner VX125, ST125, VXR180/200, ST200 and DNA 125/180

3 On four-stroke engines the starter motor is mounted on top of the engine, behind the carburettor. Remove the body panels as required according to model (see Chapter 8). Disconnect the battery negative (-ve) lead (see Section 3).

4 Peel back the terminal cover, then remove the screw securing the starter lead to the motor and detach the lead **(see illustration)**.

5 Unscrew the two bolts securing the starter motor to the crankcase, noting the earth lead, then lift the starter motor out of the crankcase **(see illustration)**.

6 Remove the O-ring on the end of the starter motor and discard it as a new one must be used.

Installation

7 Installation is the reverse of removal. If applicable, fit a new O-ring on the end of the starter motor, making sure it is seated in its groove, and apply a smear of engine oil to it **(see illustration)**.

25 Starter motor – inspection

Disassembly

Note: *Several different starter motors are fitted across the range of models covered by this*

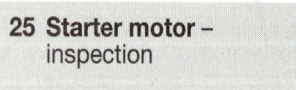

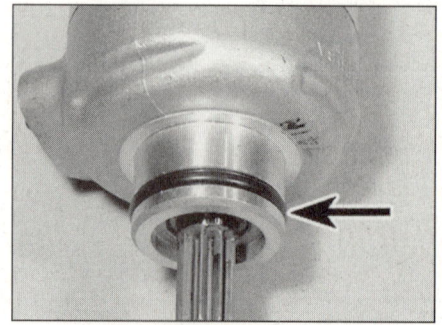

24.7 Fit a new O-ring if applicable

manual. Before disassembling the motor, note that no individual components are available, so if the motor is faulty, a new one must be fitted. It may, however, be worthwhile consulting an auto electrician before buying a new motor, as sometimes, depending on the nature of the fault, they can be repaired. When disassembling the motor, note the position of each component carefully before removing it – the procedure given below is general and does not cover the specific components of each type of motor.

1 Remove the starter motor (see Section 24).

2 Note the alignment mark between the main housing and the cover, or make your own if it isn't clear.

3 Remove the screws or bolts securing the cover to the main housing and draw the housing off, leaving the armature in place in the cover **(see illustrations)**. Remove the cover O-ring.

4 Withdraw the armature from the cover, noting any shims or washers on either or both ends of the armature shaft, and noting how the brushes locate onto the commutator **(see illustration)**.

5 Slide the brushes out from their holders, noting how they locate against the brush springs **(see illustration)**.

Inspection

6 The parts of the starter motor that are most likely to wear and require attention are the brushes. Gilera provide no specifications as to the minimum service length of the brushes – if any are excessively worn, chipped or otherwise damaged, they should be renewed. Check with a Gilera dealer or auto electrician on the availability of replacement brushes – if none are available, a new starter motor must be fitted.

7 Inspect the commutator bars on the armature for scoring, scratches and discoloration. The commutator can be cleaned and polished with crocus cloth – do not use sandpaper or emery paper. After cleaning, wipe away any residue with a cloth soaked in electrical system cleaner or denatured alcohol.

8 Using an ohmmeter or a continuity test light, check for continuity between the commutator bars **(see illustration)**. Continuity (zero

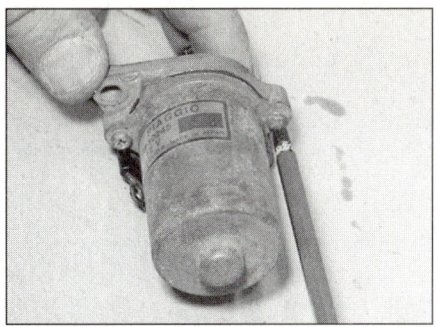

25.3a Remove the starter motor housing screws . . .

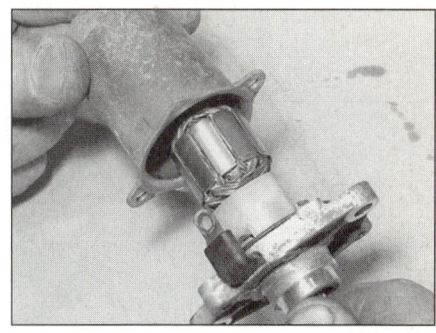

25.3b . . . and draw off the housing

resistance) should exist between each bar and all of the others. Also, check for continuity between the commutator bars and the armature shaft **(see illustration)**. There should be no continuity (infinite resistance) between the commutator and the shaft. If the checks indicate otherwise, the armature is defective.

9 Check for continuity between each brush and the terminal bolt. There should be continuity (zero resistance). Check for

continuity between the terminal bolt and the housing (when assembled). There should be no continuity (infinite resistance).

10 Check the front end of the armature shaft for worn, cracked or broken teeth. If the shaft is damaged or worn, renew the armature (or complete starter motor).

11 Inspect the end cover for signs of damages or wear. Inspect the magnets in the main housing and the housing itself for damage.

25.4 Withdraw the armature, noting how it fits

25.5 Slide the brushes out of their holders, noting how they fit

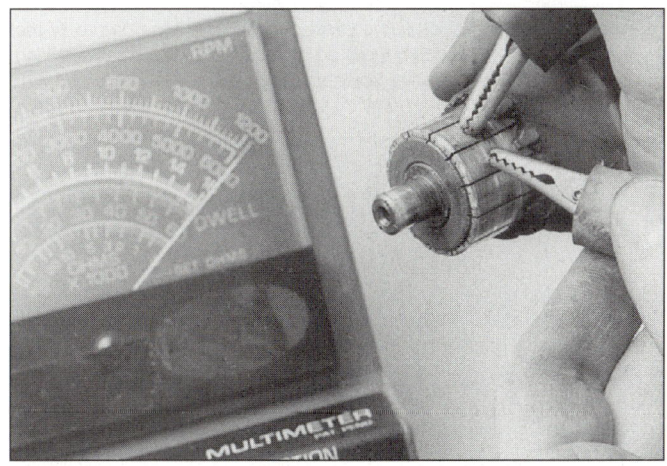

25.8a Continuity should exist between the commutator bars

25.8b There should be no continuity between the commutator bars and the armature shaft

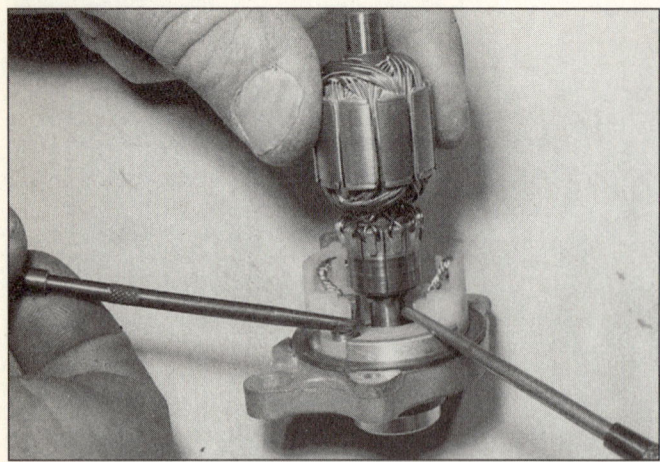

25.14a Hold the brushes back against the springs to allow the armature to be installed

25.14b Where possible, locate the spring ends (arrowed) onto the brush holders so that there is no pressure on the brushes . . .

12 Inspect the armature shaft bearing surfaces in the cover and main housing and the cover seal.

Reassembly

13 Reassemble the starter motor in the reverse order of disassembly.

14 When fitting the armature, note that it will be necessary to hold the brushes back against the pressure of their springs. There are a number of ways of doing this, all of which can be tricky, especially without the aid of an assistant. A pair of thin ended angled scribes, or something similar, can be used as shown **(see illustration)**. On some models it is possible to locate the spring end onto the top of the brush holder so that there is no pressure on the brush, which can be slid fully back into its holder while the armature is installed **(see illustration)**. Install the armature, then place the spring ends back onto the brushes so that they are pressed onto the commutator **(see illustration)**. Check that each brush is securely pressed against the commutator

by its spring and is free to move easily in its holder.

15 Renew the cover O-ring if it is damaged **(see illustration)**. Check that the armature turns freely before installing the starter motor.

26 Charging system

General information

1 If the performance of the charging system is suspect, the system as a whole should be checked first, followed by testing of the individual components. **Note:** *Before beginning the checks, make sure the battery is fully charged and that all system connections are clean and tight.*

2 Checking the output of the charging system and the performance of the various components within the charging system requires the use of a multi-meter (with voltage, current and resistance checking facilities).

3 When making the checks, follow the procedures carefully to prevent incorrect connections or short circuits, as irreparable damage to electrical system components may result if short circuits occur.

4 If a multi-meter is not available, the job of checking the charging system should be left to a Gilera dealer.

Leakage test

5 Ensure the ignition is OFF and disconnect the lead from the battery negative (-ve) terminal.

6 Set the multi-meter to the Amps function and connect its negative (-ve) probe to the battery negative (-ve) terminal, and positive (+ve) probe to the disconnected negative (-ve) lead **(see illustration)**. Always set the meter to a high amps range initially and then bring it down to the mA (milli Amps) range; if there is a high current flow in the circuit it may blow the meter's fuse.

Caution: Always connect an ammeter in series, never in parallel with the battery, otherwise it will be damaged. Do not turn the ignition ON or operate the starter motor

25.14c . . . then locate them back onto the brushes after the armature has been installed

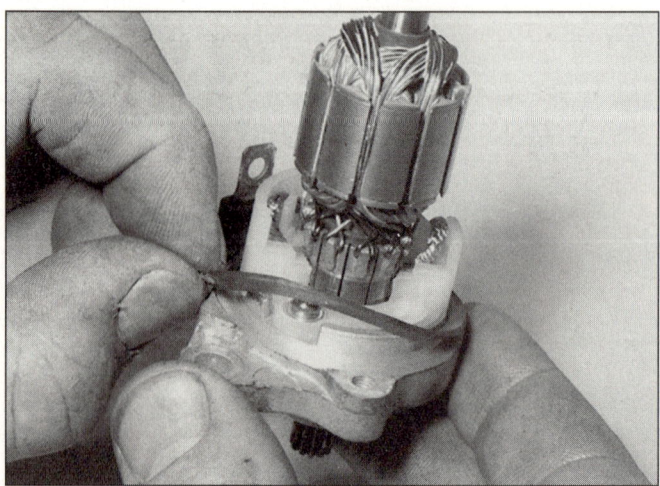

25.15 Renew the cover sealing O-ring if damaged

when the ammeter is connected – a sudden surge in current will blow the meter's fuse.

7 While Gilera do not specify an amount, if the current leakage indicated exceeds 1 mA, there is probably a short circuit in the wiring. Disconnect the meter and connect the negative (-ve) lead to the battery, tightening it securely,

8 If leakage is indicated, use the *Wiring diagrams* at the end of this Chapter to systematically disconnect individual electrical components and repeat the test until the source is identified.

 **If an alarm is fitted, take its current draw into account when measuring current leakage.**

Alternator output tests

⚠️ **Warning: The following tests require that the engine be run at a speed where the transmission may engage; it is essential that the rear tyre is well clear of the ground and does not contact any object.**

9 Specifications are given for unregulated voltage output values for all Runner 50 models, DNA 50 GP, Ice and SKP/Stalker, FX125 and FXR180 models. Support the scooter on its centre stand, start the engine and warm it up to normal operating temperature. Stop the engine and turn the ignition OFF

10 Disconnect the regulator/rectifier wiring connector (see Section 27). Connect a voltmeter set to the 0 to 50 volts ac scale between the grey/blue wire terminal in the connector and the black wire terminal (all Runner 50, DNA 50 GP, Ice and SKP/Stalker models), or between the two yellow wire terminals (Runner FX125 and FXR180 models).

11 Allow the engine to idle, then slowly increase the engine speed to 2000 or 3000 rpm according to model (see Specifications at the beginning of this Chapter) and note the reading obtained. The unregulated voltage

should be as specified. Turn the ignition OFF, disconnect the voltmeter and reconnect the regulator/rectifier connector. If the voltage is within the specified limits, follow the procedure in Step 12 and check the regulated current output.

12 Specifications are given for regulated voltage output for all models. To check the regulated current output, disconnect the battery positive (+ve) lead and connect a multi-meter set to the 0 to 20 amps dc scale (ammeter) in series between the lead and the battery positive (+ve) terminal **(see illustration)**. Connect another multi-meter set to the 0 – 20 volts dc scale (voltmeter) across the battery terminals (meter positive (+ve) probe to battery positive terminal, and meter negative (-ve) probe to battery negative terminal). Start the engine and allow it to idle, then slowly increase the engine speed to 2000 or 3000 rpm according to model (see Specifications) and note the reading obtained. The regulated current should be as specified at the beginning of this Chapter with battery voltage at 13V.

13 If the regulated current is outside these limits, yet the unregulated voltage output from the alternator is as specified (see Steps 10 and 11), renew the regulator/rectifier (see Section 27).

 Clues to a faulty regulator are constantly blowing bulbs, with brightness varying considerably with engine speed, and battery overheating.

Alternator stator coils

14 On Runner VX125, ST125, VXR180/200, ST200 models, and DNA 125/180 models, first ensure that the ignition is OFF, then locate the regulator/rectifier unit (see Section 27) and disconnect its wiring connector. Make the following continuity checks on the wire harness side of the connector.

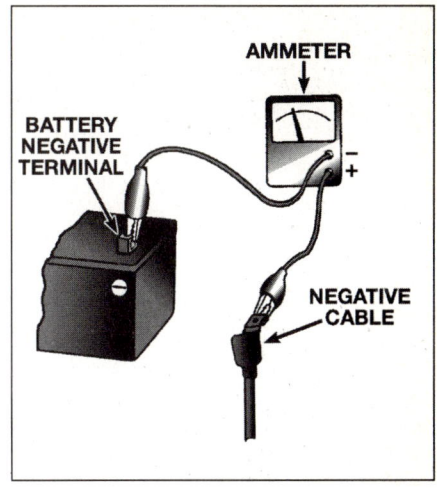

26.6 Checking the battery leakage rate – connect the meter as shown

15 Using a multi-meter set to the ohms x 10 range, connect one probe to one of the yellow wire terminals in the connector and the other probe to the black (earth) wire terminal in the connector **(see illustration)**. If the alternator stator insulation is in good condition, no continuity (infinite resistance) should be indicated. Repeat the test between the other yellow wire terminals and the black wire terminal.

16 Next measure the resistance between the yellow wire terminals in the connector. Make three tests. Very low resistance (see Specifications) should be shown.

17 If the test results indicate that the alternator stator coils are open-circuit or that there is a short to earth, have your findings confirmed by a Gilera dealer or auto electrician before fitting a new alternator stator. Check that the fault is not due to broken or shorted wiring between the alternator and regulator/rectifier connector.

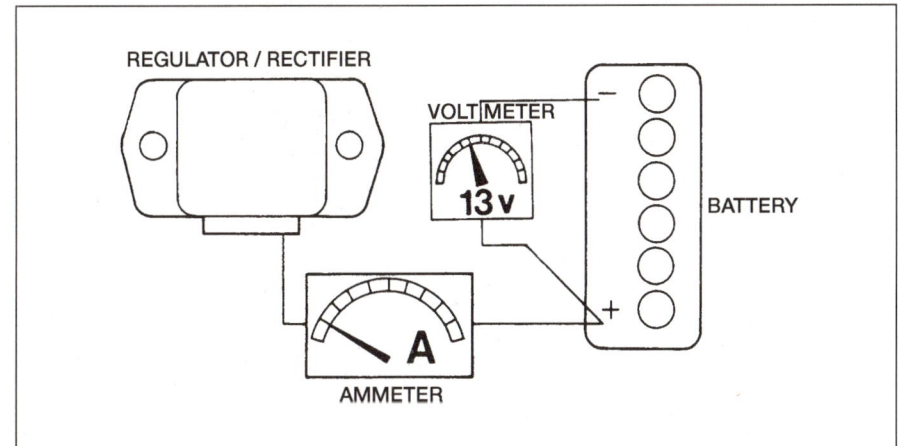

26.12 Checking the regulated current output

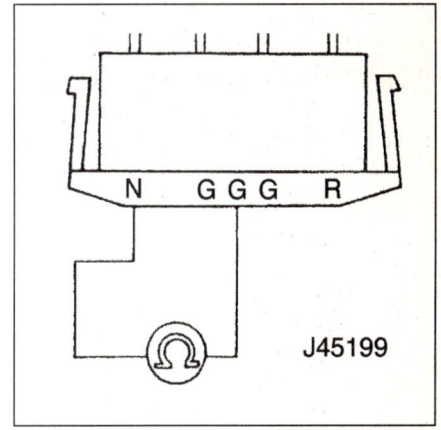

26.15 Checking the alternator coil insulation on Runner VX, VXR, ST and DNA 125/180 models

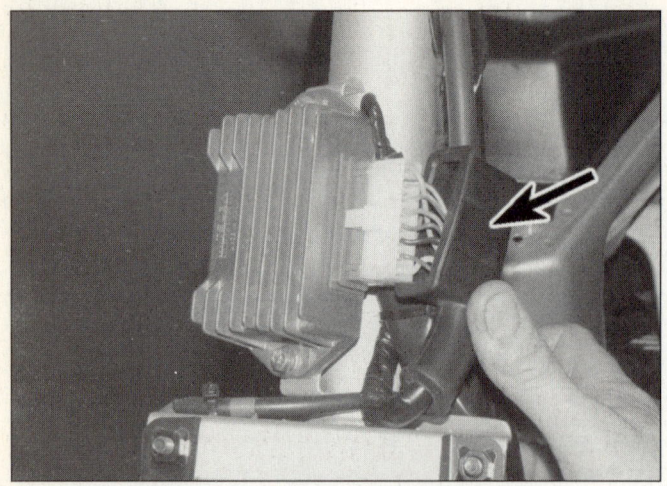

27.2a Pull off the boot (arrowed) . . .

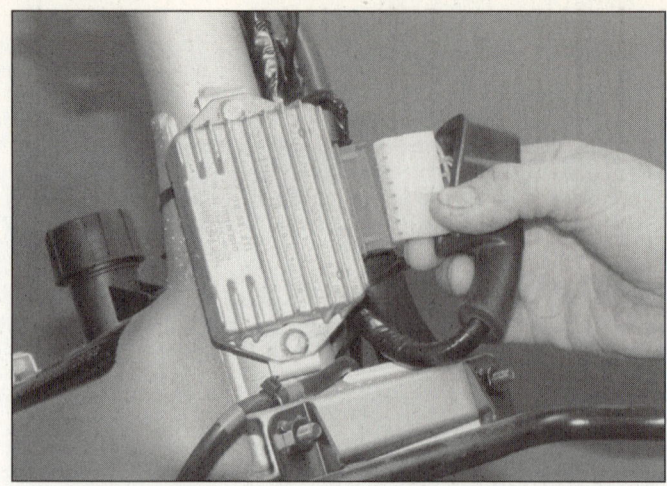

27.2b . . . and disconnect the connector – Ice shown

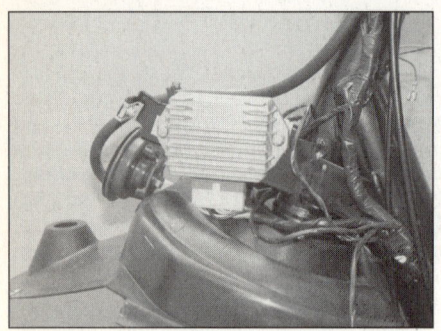

27.2c Location of the regulator/rectifier –
SKP/Stalker

27.2d Location of the regulator/rectifier –
DNA 180

27.2e Location of the regulator/rectifier –
Purejet 50

27 Regulator/rectifier

1 On Runner models remove the right-hand side panel, on DNA models remove the left-hand seat cowling, on Ice models remove the headlight panel and on SKP/Stalker models remove the front panel (see Chapter 8). On Runner RST the regulator/rectifier is mounted under the rear mudguard/undertray.

2 Disconnect the battery negative (-ve) terminal. Where fitted, pull the boot off the wiring connector, then disconnect the connector from the regulator/rectifier **(see illustrations)**.

3 Undo the two bolts securing the regulator/rectifier and remove it, noting the earth cable secured by one of the bolts on some models.

4 Install the new unit and tighten the bolts securely, not forgetting the earth cable, where fitted. Connect the wiring connector and refit the boot if applicable.

5 Install the remaining components in the reverse order of removal and reconnect the battery negative (-ve) terminal.

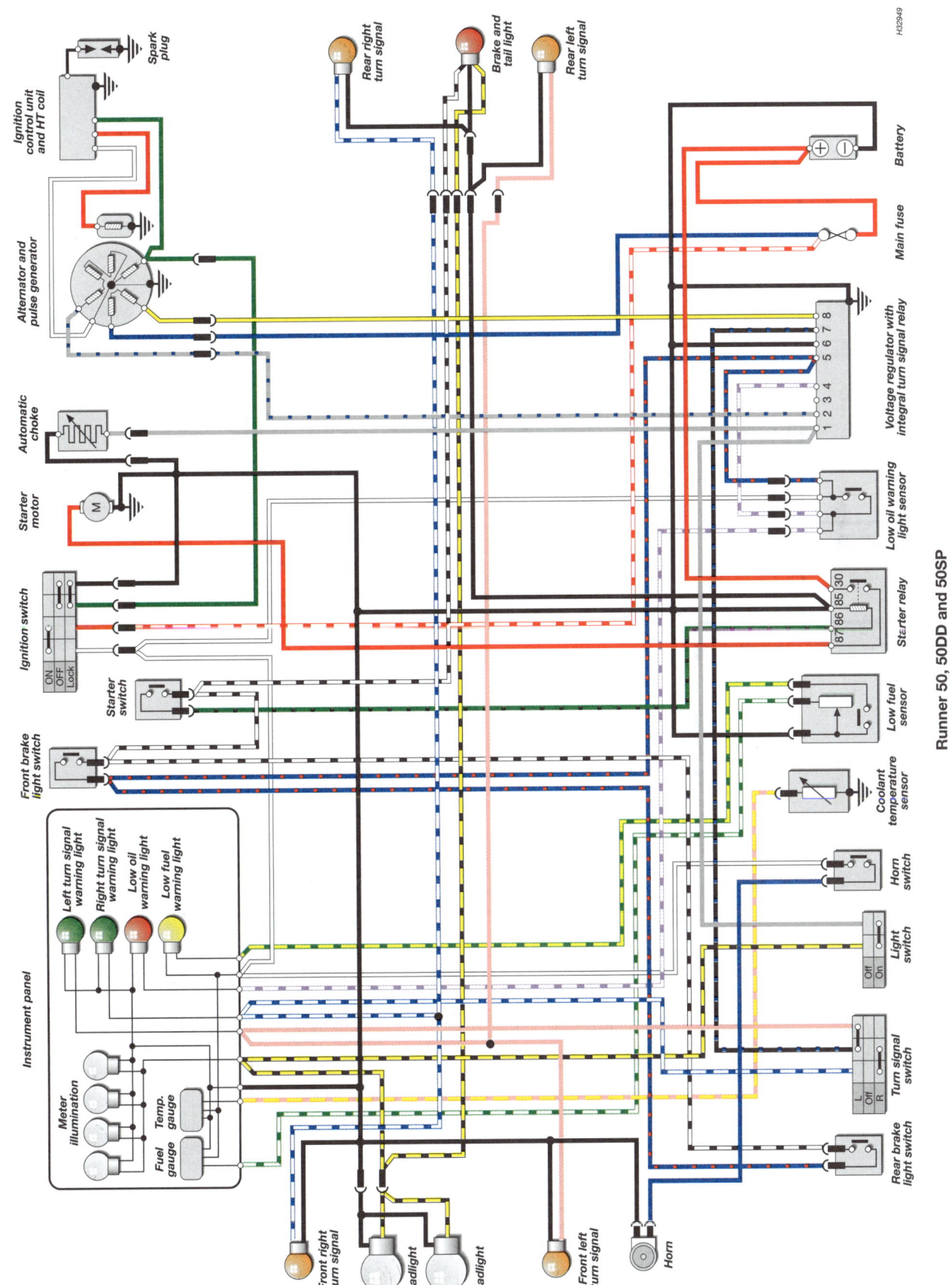

Ignition control unit and HT coil

Spark plug

Alternator and pulse generator

Automatic choke

Starter motor

Ignition switch

ON
OFF
Lock

Starter switch

Front brake light switch

Instrument panel

Left turn signal warning light

Right turn signal warning light

Low oil warning light

Low fuel warning light

Meter illumination

Temp. gauge

Fuel gauge

Front right turn signal

Headlight

Headlight

Front left turn signal

Horn

Rear right turn signal

Brake and tail light

Rear left turn signal

Battery

Main fuse

Voltage regulator with integral turn signal relay

Low oil warning light sensor

Starter relay

Low fuel sensor

Coolant temperature sensor

Horn switch

Light switch

Off
On

Turn signal switch

L
Off
R

Rear brake light switch

Runner 50, 50DD and 50SP

H32949

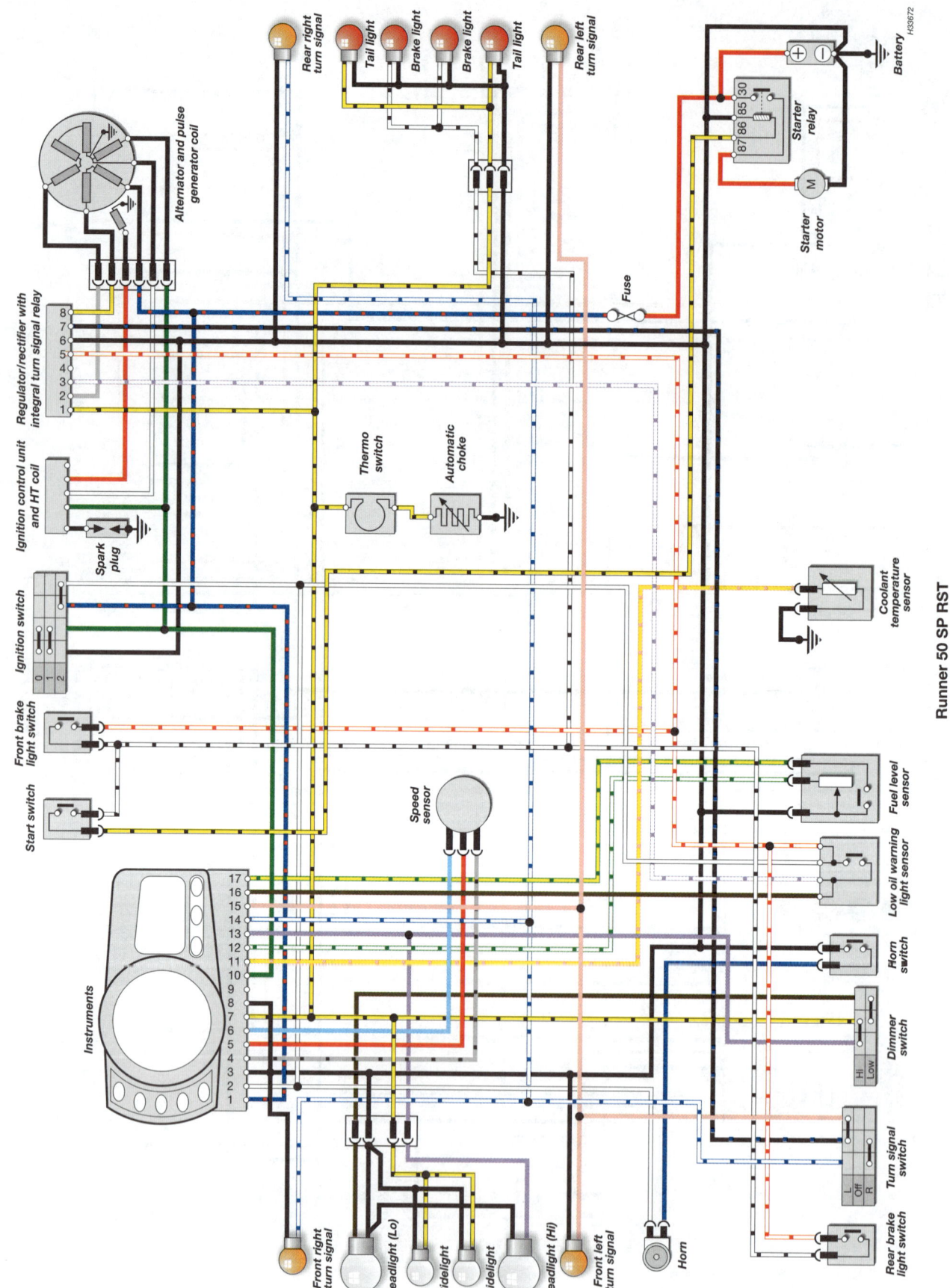

Runner 50 SP RST

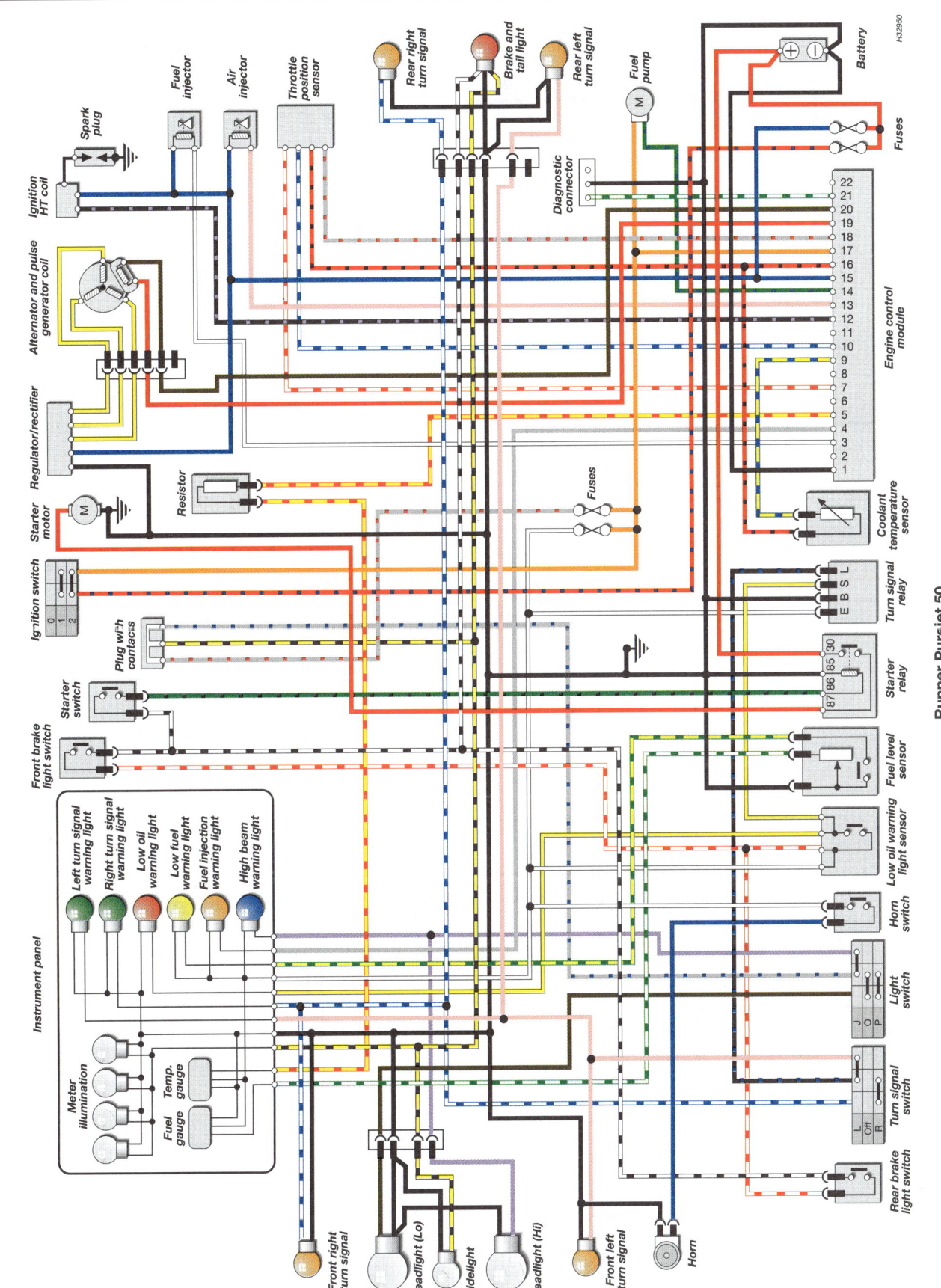

Runner Purejet 50

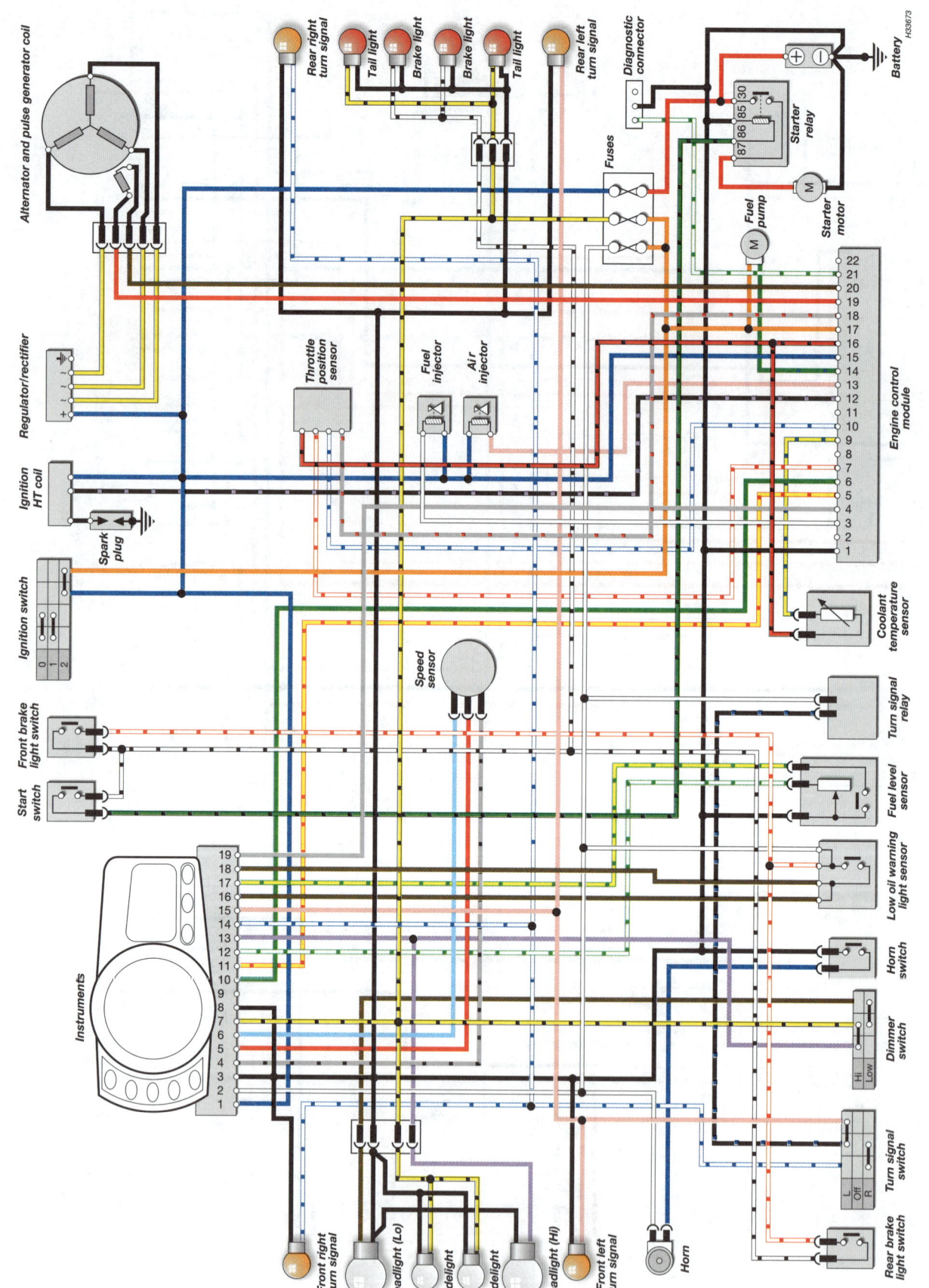

Runner Purejet 50 RST

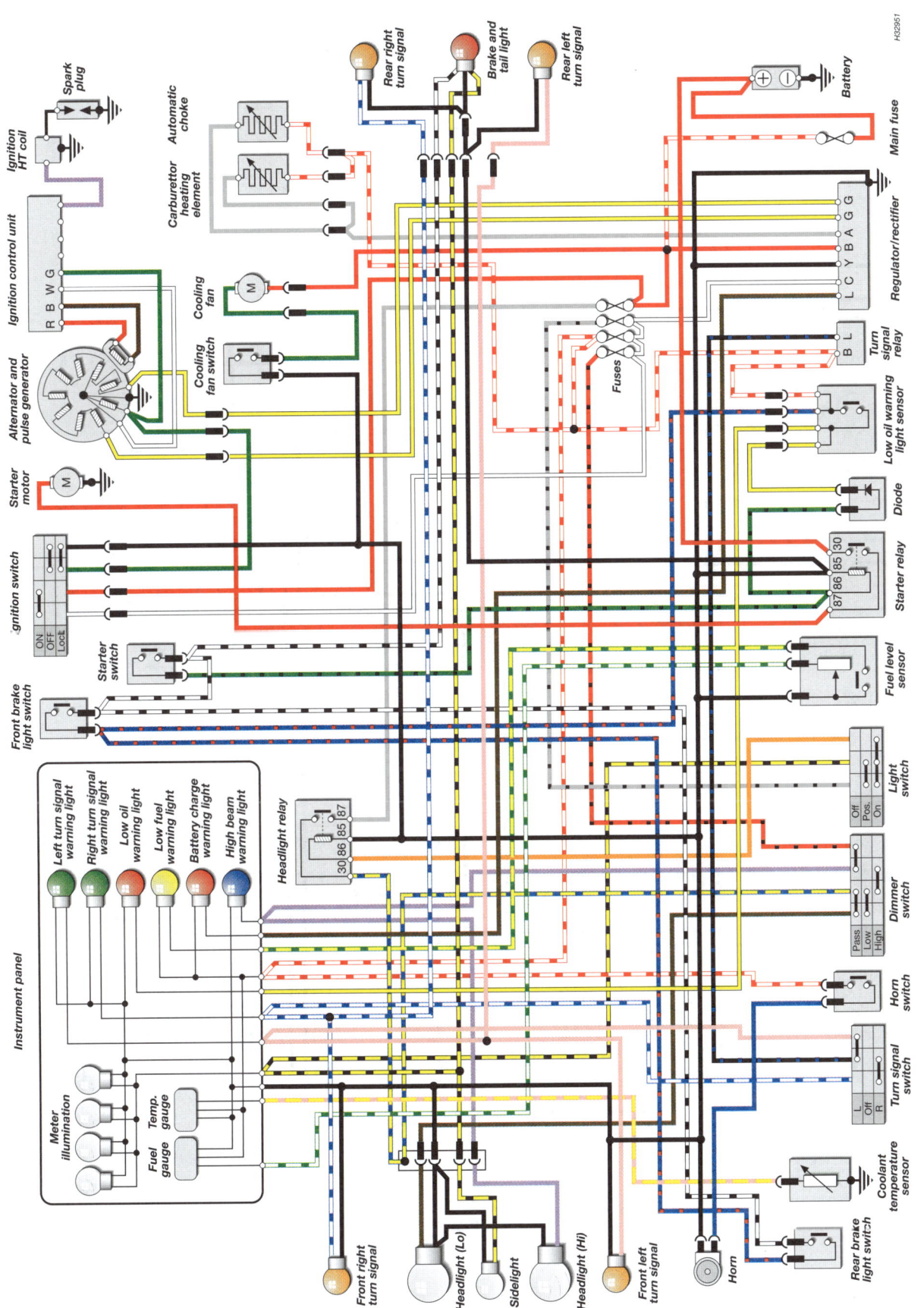

H32951

Runner FX125 and FXR180 (1998)

H32952

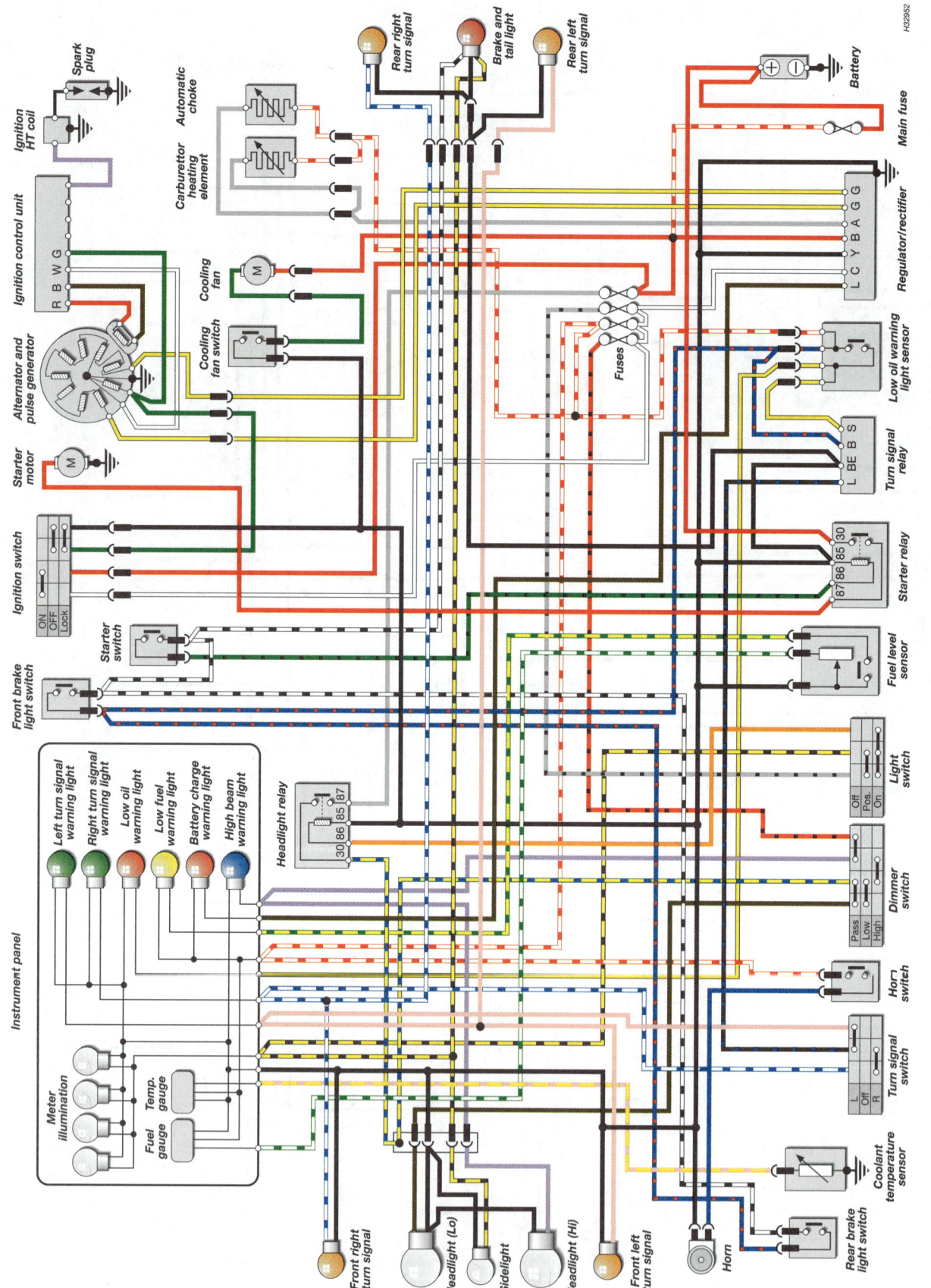

Runner FX125 and FXR180 (1999 to 2001)

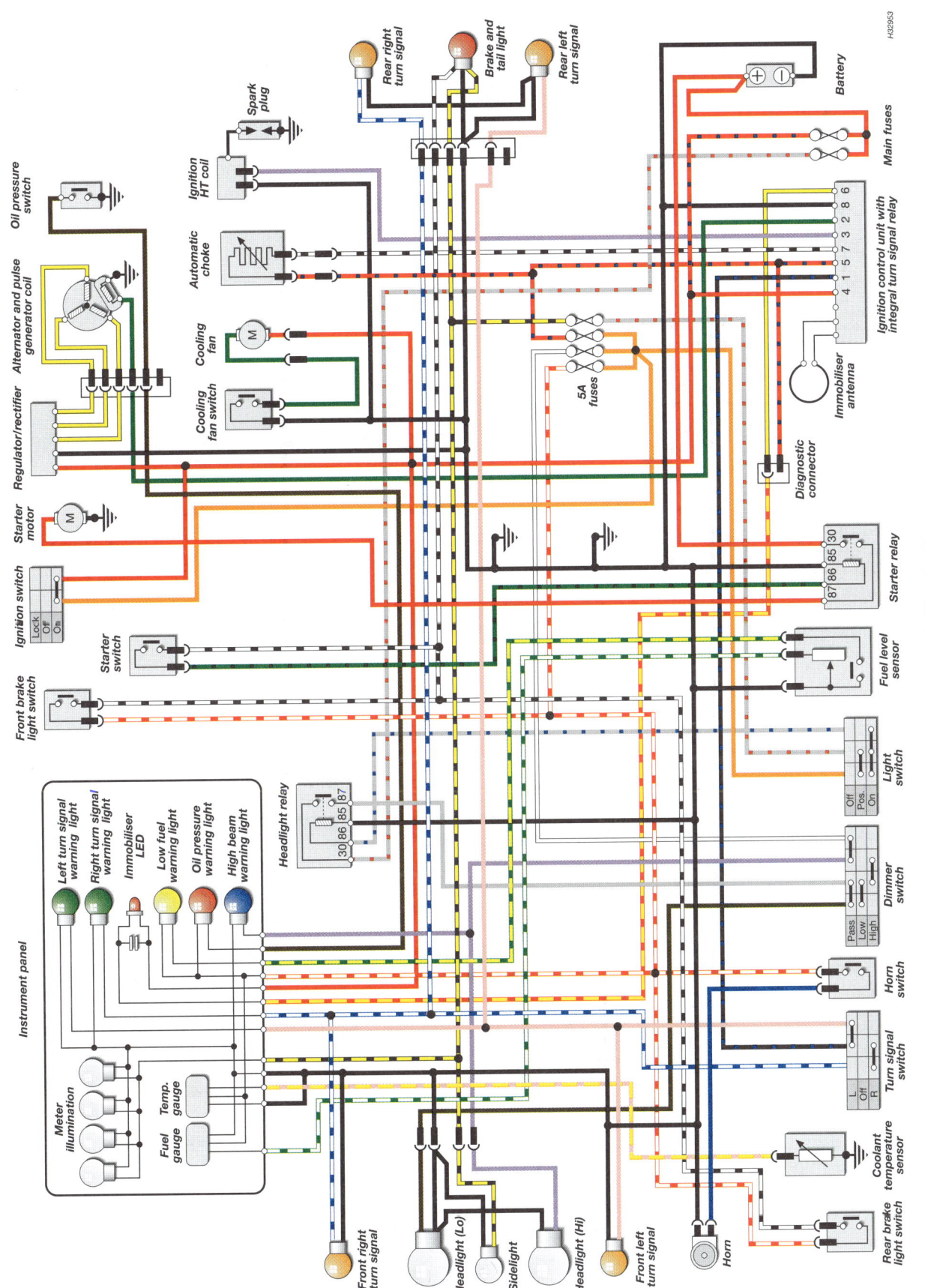

Runner VX125 and VXR180/200

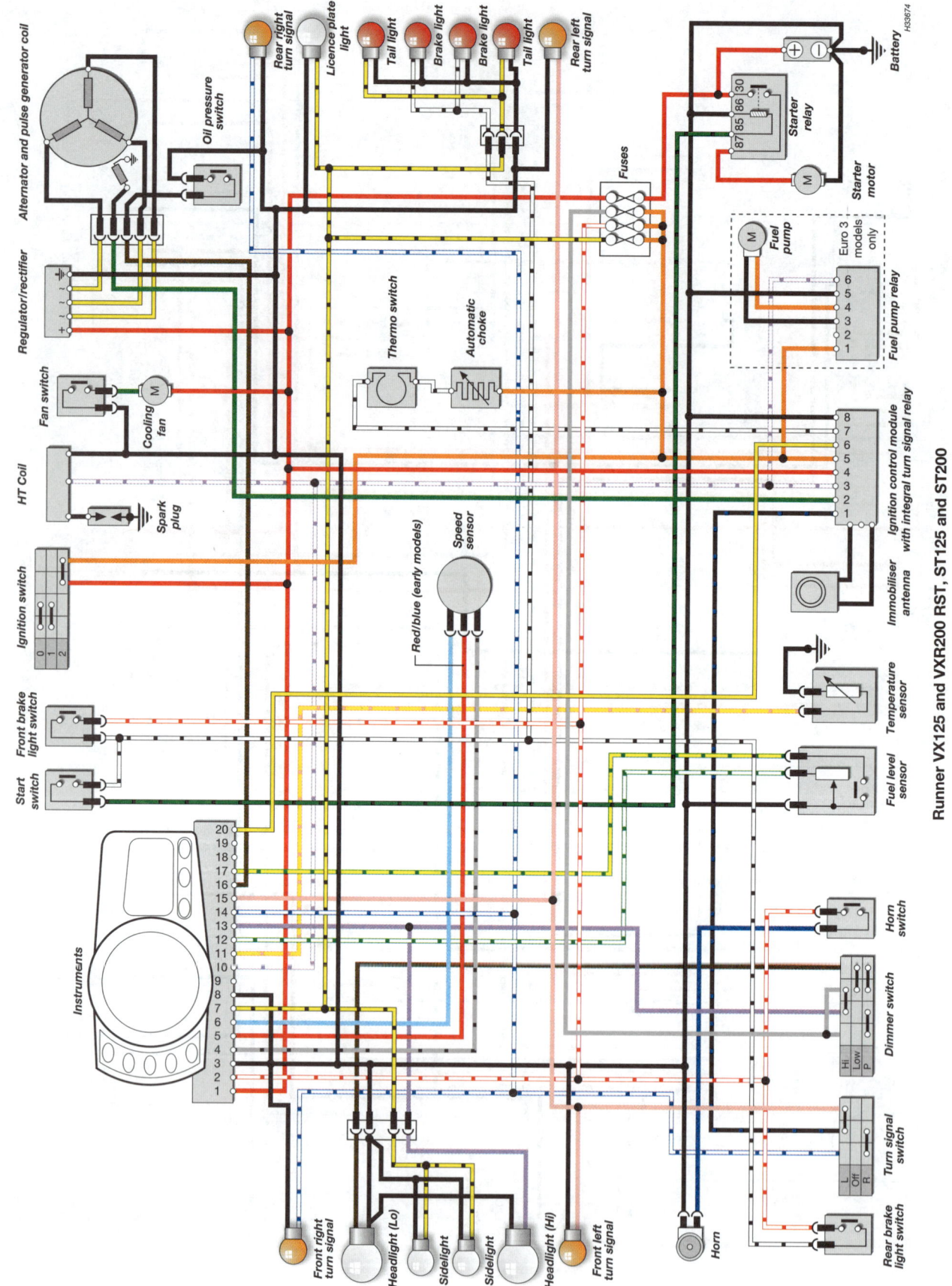

Runner VX125 and VXR200 RST, ST125 and ST200

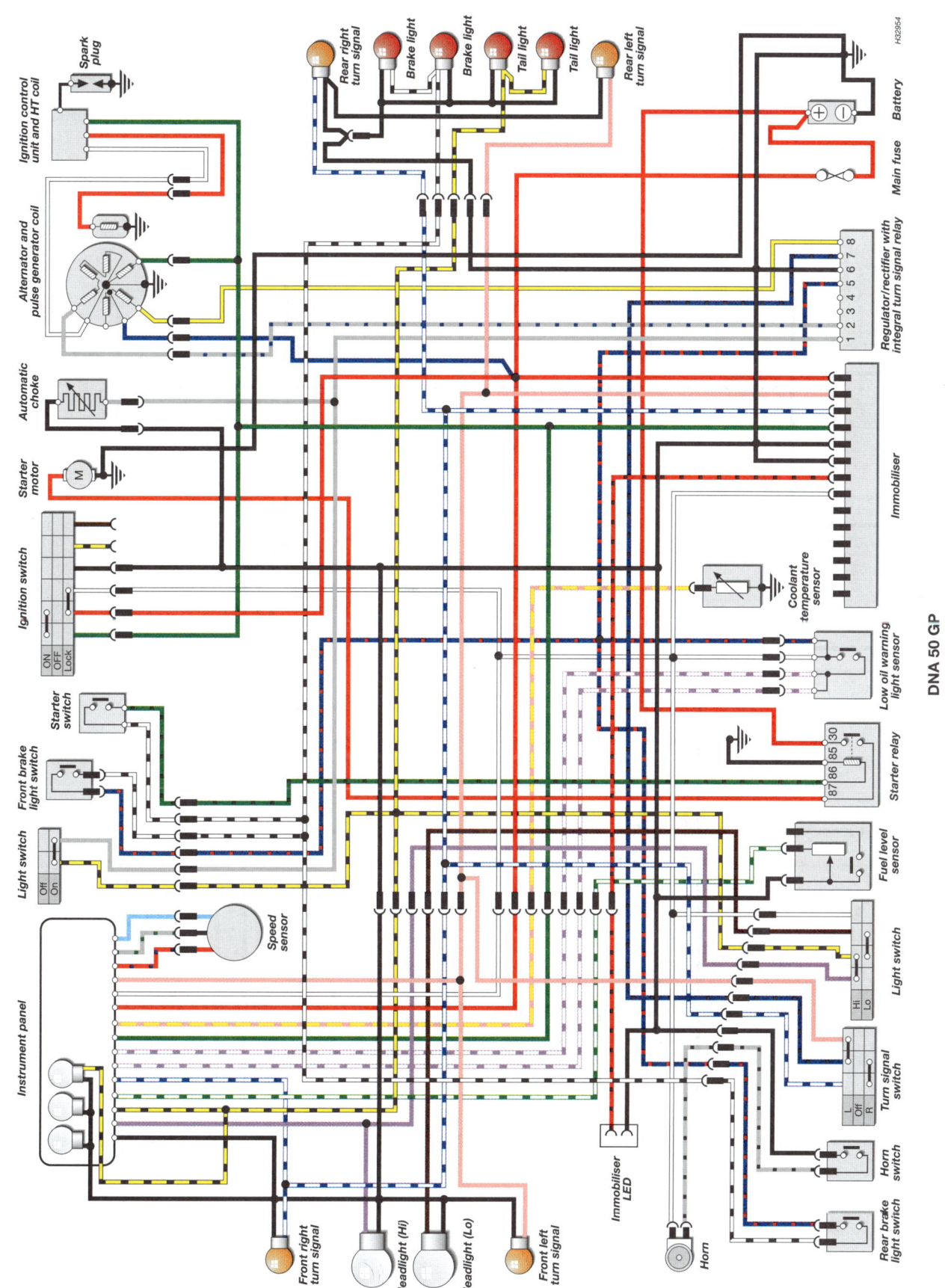

Spark plug

Ignition control unit and HT coil

Alternator and pulse generator coil

Automatic choke

Starter motor

Ignition switch

ON
OFF
Lock

Starter switch

Front brake light switch

Light switch

Off
On

Instrument panel

Speed sensor

Rear right turn signal

Brake light

Brake light

Tail light

Tail light

Rear left turn signal

Battery

Main fuse

Regulator/rectifier with integral turn signal relay

1 2 3 4 5 6 7 8

Immobiliser

Coolant temperature sensor

DNA 50 GP

Low oil warning light sensor

Starter relay

87 86 85 30

Fuel level sensor

Light switch

Hi
Lo

Turn signal switch

L
Off
R

Horn switch

Rear brake light switch

Immobiliser LED

Horn

Front right turn signal

Headlight (Hi)

Headlight (Lo)

Front left turn signal

H32954

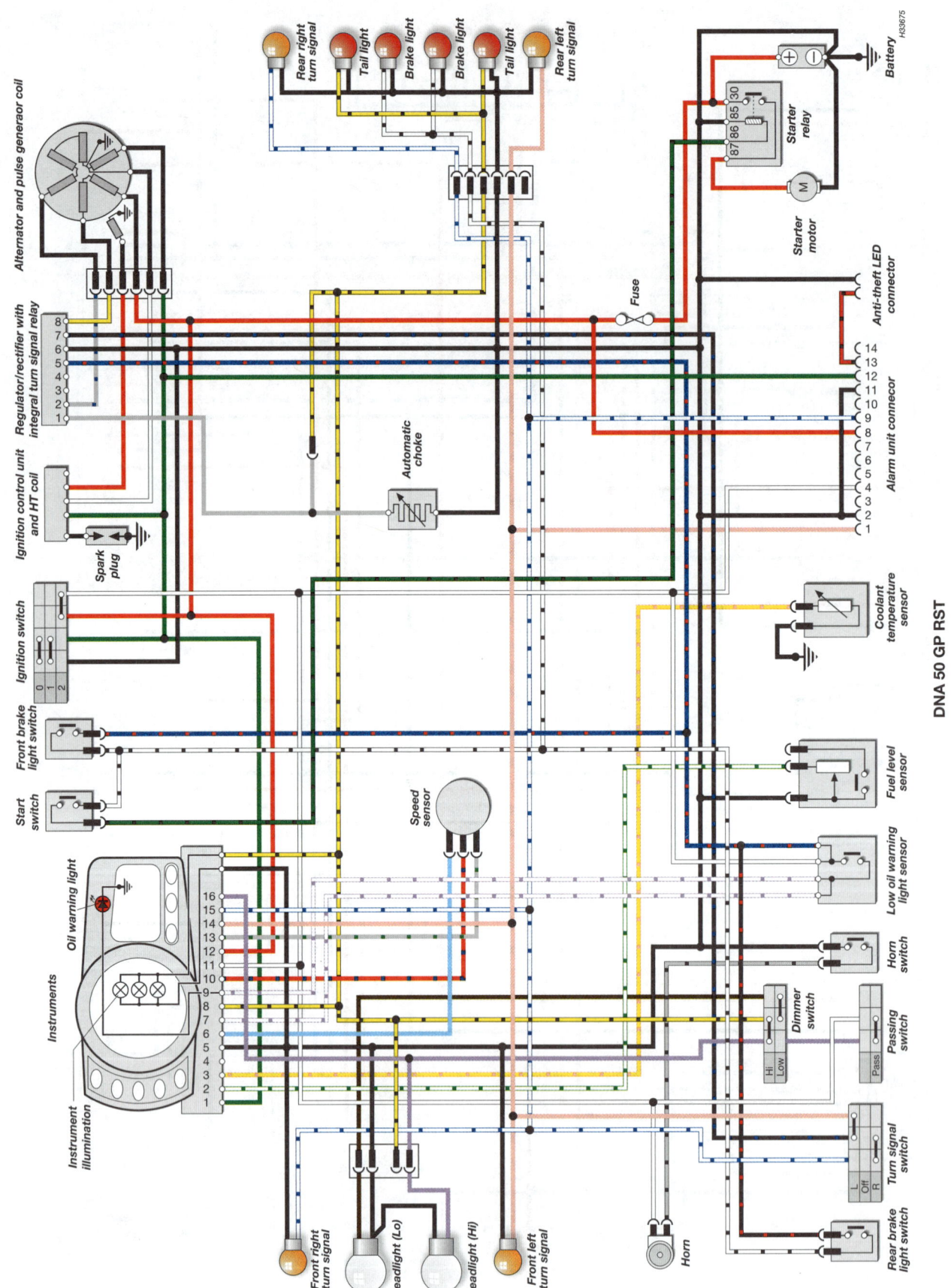

DNA 50 GP RST

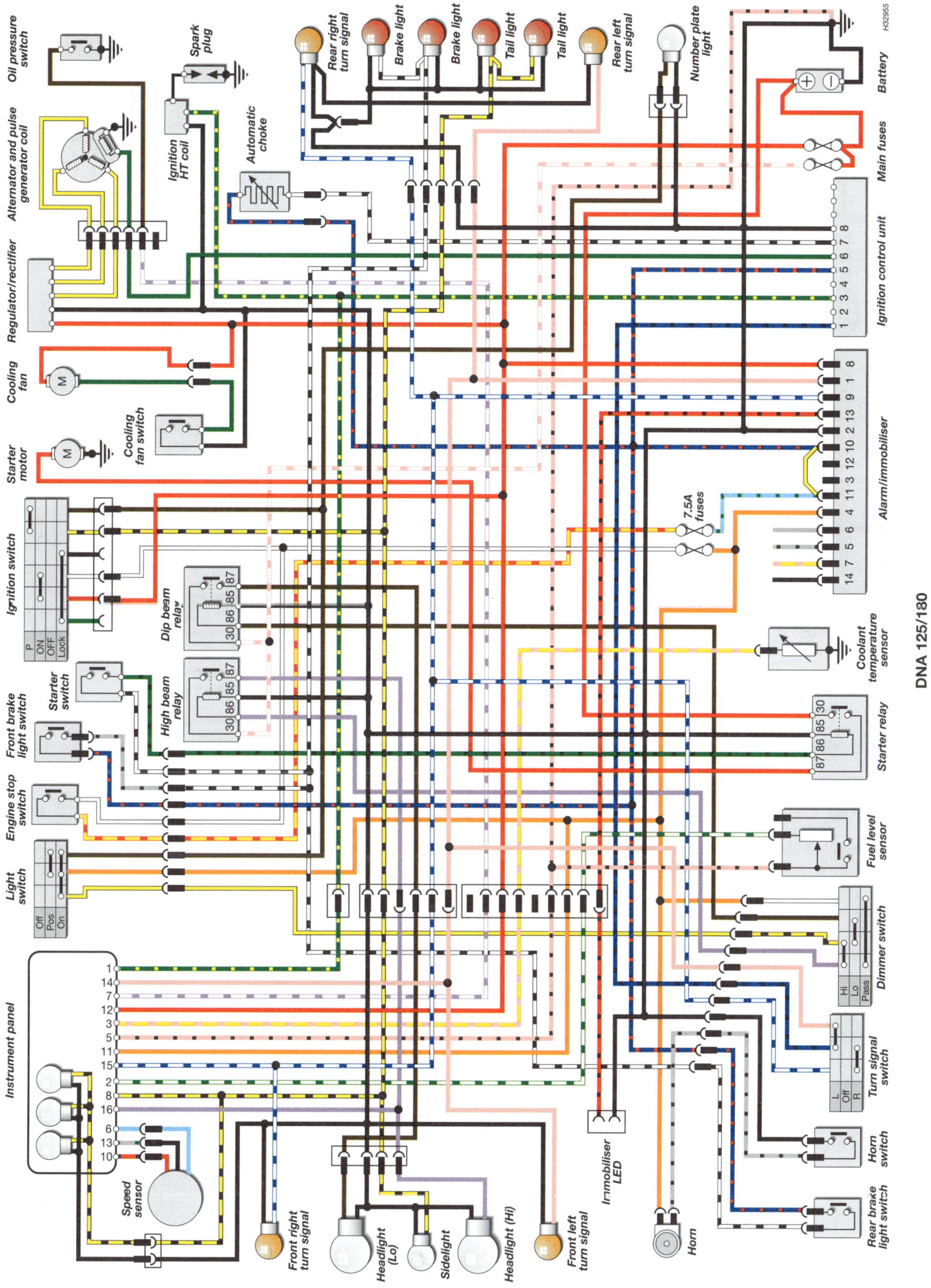

H32955

DNA 125/180

Oil pressure switch
Spark plug
Rear right turn signal
Brake light
Brake light
Tail light
Tail light
Rear left turn signal
Number plate light
Battery
Alternator and pulse generator coil
Ignition HT coil
Automatic choke
Main fuses
Regulator/rectifier
Ignition control unit
Cooling fan
Cooling fan switch
Alarm/immobiliser
Starter motor
7.5A fuses
Ignition switch
Coolant temperature sensor
Dip beam relay
High beam relay
Starter relay
Starter switch
Front brake light switch
Engine stop switch
Fuel level sensor
Light switch
Dimmer switch
Instrument panel
Turn signal switch
Immobiliser LED
Horn switch
Speed sensor
Front right turn signal
Headlight (Lo)
Sidelight
Headlight (Hi)
Front left turn signal
Horn
Rear brake light switch

P
ON
OFF
Lock

30 86 85 87

Off
Pos
On

Hi
Lo
Pass

L
Off
R

87 86 85 30

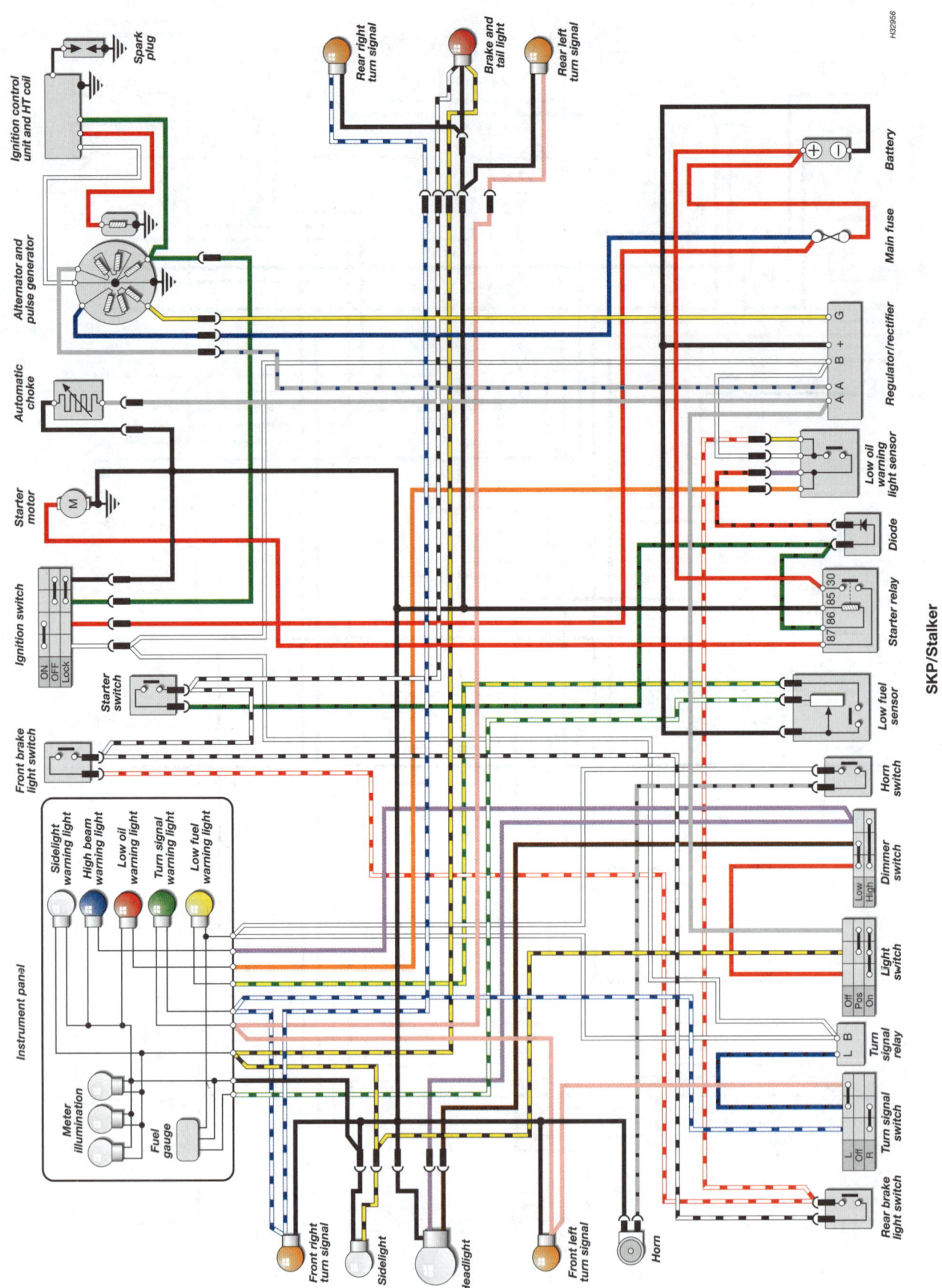

H32956

SKP/Stalker

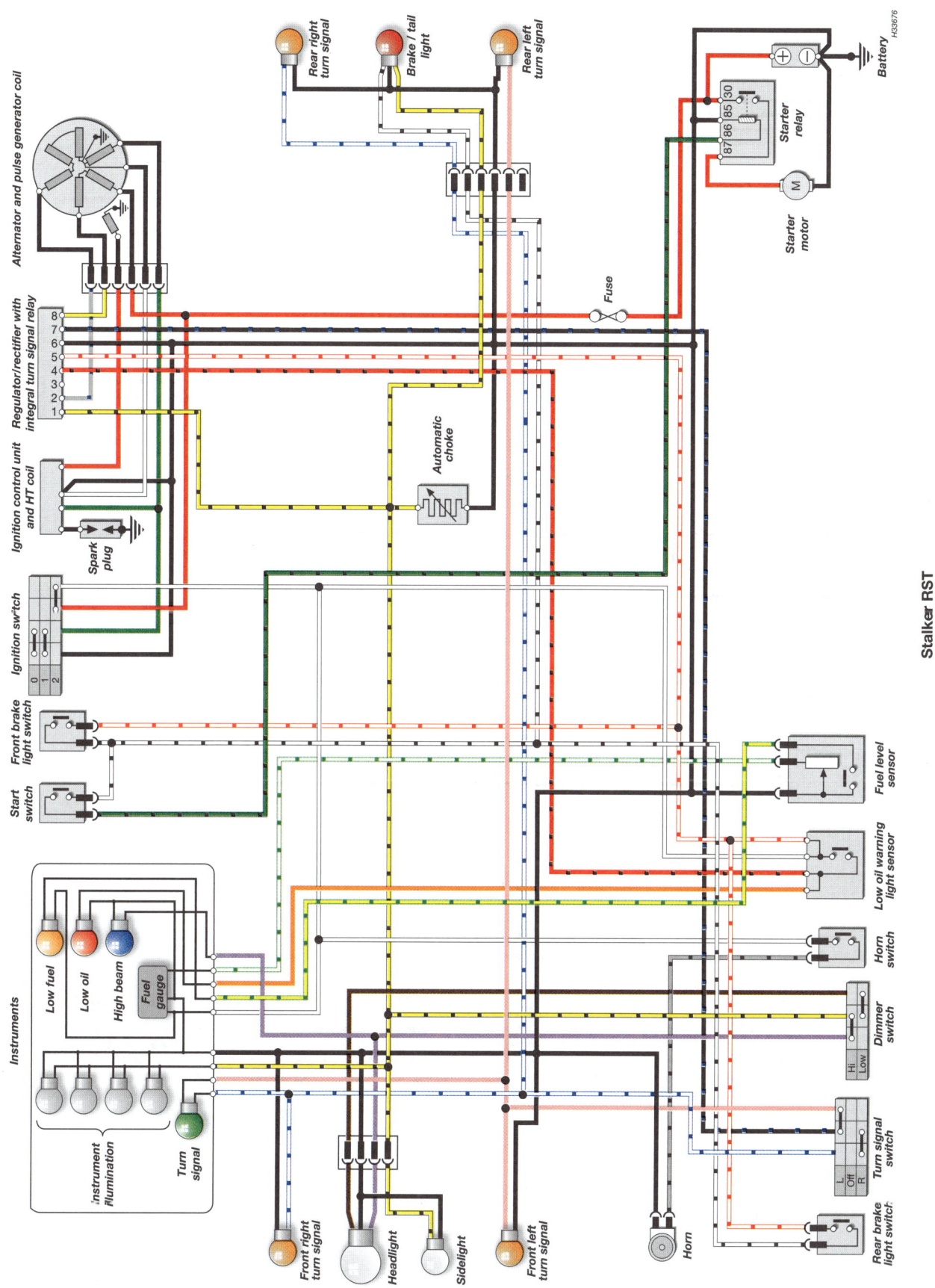

Stalker RST

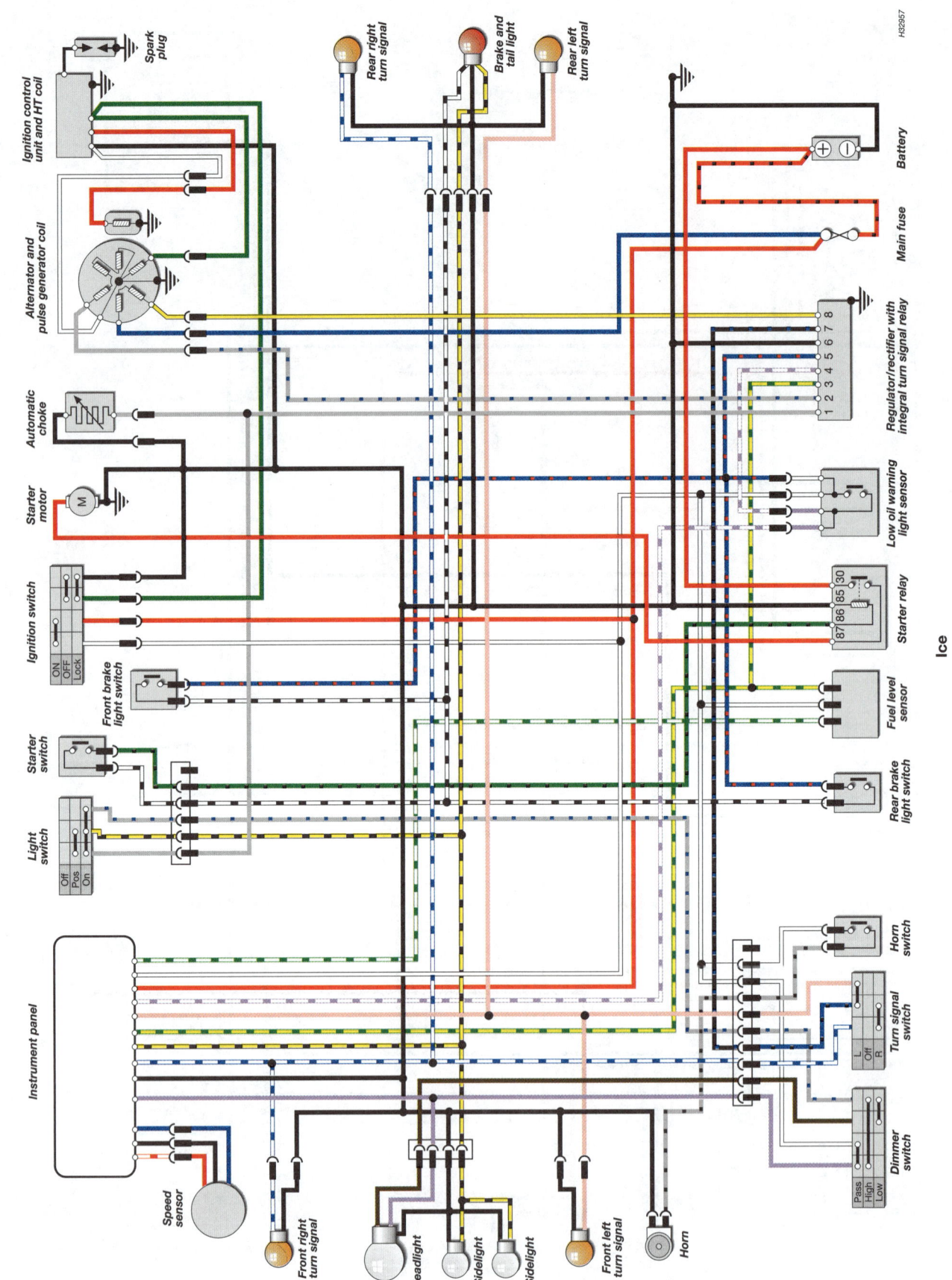

H32957

Length (distance)

Inches (in)	x 25.4	= Millimetres (mm)	x 0.0394	= Inches (in)
Feet (ft)	x 0.305	= Metres (m)	x 3.281	= Feet (ft)
Miles	x 1.609	= Kilometres (km)	x 0.621	= Miles

Volume (capacity)

Cubic inches (cu in; in³)	x 16.387	= Cubic centimetres (cc; cm³)	x 0.061	= Cubic inches (cu in; in³)
Imperial pints (Imp pt)	x 0.568	= Litres (l)	x 1.76	= Imperial pints (Imp pt)
Imperial quarts (Imp qt)	x 1.137	= Litres (l)	x 0.88	= Imperial quarts (Imp qt)
Imperial quarts (Imp qt)	x 1.201	= US quarts (US qt)	x 0.833	= Imperial quarts (Imp qt)
US quarts (US qt)	x 0.946	= Litres (l)	x 1.057	= US quarts (US qt)
Imperial gallons (Imp gal)	x 4.546	= Litres (l)	x 0.22	= Imperial gallons (Imp gal)
Imperial gallons (Imp gal)	x 1.201	= US gallons (US gal)	x 0.833	= Imperial gallons (Imp gal)
US gallons (US gal)	x 3.785	= Litres (l)	x 0.264	= US gallons (US gal)

Mass (weight)

Ounces (oz)	x 28.35	= Grams (g)	x 0.035	= Ounces (oz)
Pounds (lb)	x 0.454	= Kilograms (kg)	x 2.205	= Pounds (lb)

Force

Ounces-force (ozf; oz)	x 0.278	= Newtons (N)	x 3.6	= Ounces-force (ozf; oz)
Pounds-force (lbf; lb)	x 4.448	= Newtons (N)	x 0.225	= Pounds-force (lbf; lb)
Newtons (N)	x 0.1	= Kilograms-force (kgf; kg)	x 9.81	= Newtons (N)

Pressure

Pounds-force per square inch (psi; lbf/in²; lb/in²)	x 0.070	= Kilograms-force per square centimetre (kgf/cm²; kg/cm²)	x 14.223	= Pounds-force per square inch (psi; lbf/in²; lb/in²)
Pounds-force per square inch (psi; lbf/in²; lb/in²)	x 0.068	= Atmospheres (atm)	x 14.696	= Pounds-force per square inch (psi; lbf/in²; lb/in²)
Pounds-force per square inch (psi; lbf/in²; lb/in²)	x 0.069	= Bars	x 14.5	= Pounds-force per square inch (psi; lbf/in²; lb/in²)
Pounds-force per square inch (psi; lbf/in²; lb/in²)	x 6.895	= Kilopascals (kPa)	x 0.145	= Pounds-force per square inch (psi; lbf/in²; lb/in²)
Kilopascals (kPa)	x 0.01	= Kilograms-force per square centimetre (kgf/cm²; kg/cm²)	x 98.1	= Kilopascals (kPa)
Millibar (mbar)	x 100	= Pascals (Pa)	x 0.01	= Millibar (mbar)
Millibar (mbar)	x 0.0145	= Pounds-force per square inch (psi; lbf/in²; lb/in²)	x 68.947	= Millibar (mbar)
Millibar (mbar)	x 0.75	= Millimetres of mercury (mmHg)	x 1.333	= Millibar (mbar)
Millibar (mbar)	x 0.401	= Inches of water (inH₂O)	x 2.491	= Millibar (mbar)
Millimetres of mercury (mmHg)	x 0.535	= Inches of water (inH₂O)	x 1.868	= Millimetres of mercury (mmHg)
Inches of water (inH₂O)	x 0.036	= Pounds-force per square inch (psi; lbf/in²; lb/in²)	x 27.68	= Inches of water (inH₂O)

Torque (moment of force)

Pounds-force inches (lbf in; lb in)	x 1.152	= Kilograms-force centimetre (kgf cm; kg cm)	x 0.868	= Pounds-force inches (lbf in; lb in)
Pounds-force inches (lbf in; lb in)	x 0.113	= Newton metres (Nm)	x 8.85	= Pounds-force inches (lbf in; lb in)
Pounds-force inches (lbf in; lb in)	x 0.083	= Pounds-force feet (lbf ft; lb ft)	x 12	= Pounds-force inches (lbf in; lb in)
Pounds-force feet (lbf ft; lb ft)	x 0.138	= Kilograms-force metres (kgf m; kg m)	x 7.233	= Pounds-force feet (lbf ft; lb ft)
Pounds-force feet (lbf ft; lb ft)	x 1.356	= Newton metres (Nm)	x 0.738	= Pounds-force feet (lbf ft; lb ft)
Newton metres (Nm)	x 0.102	= Kilograms-force metres (kgf m; kg m)	x 9.804	= Newton metres (Nm)

Power

Horsepower (hp)	x 745.7	= Watts (W)	x 0.0013	= Horsepower (hp)

Velocity (speed)

Miles per hour (miles/hr; mph)	x 1.609	= Kilometres per hour (km/hr; kph)	x 0.621	= Miles per hour (miles/hr; mph)

Fuel consumption*

Miles per gallon (mpg)	x 0.354	= Kilometres per litre (km/l)	x 2.825	= Miles per gallon (mpg)

Temperature

Degrees Fahrenheit = (°C x 1.8) + 32

Degrees Celsius (Degrees Centigrade; °C) = (°F - 32) x 0.56

It is common practice to convert from miles per gallon (mpg) to litres/100 kilometres (l/100km), where mpg x l/100 km = 282

1 Engine doesn't start or is difficult to start

- ☐ Starter motor doesn't rotate
- ☐ Starter motor rotates but engine does not turn over
- ☐ Starter works but engine won't turn over (seized)
- ☐ No fuel flow
- ☐ Engine flooded
- ☐ No spark or weak spark
- ☐ Compression low
- ☐ Stalls after starting
- ☐ Rough idle

2 Poor running at low speed

- ☐ Spark weak
- ☐ Fuel/air mixture incorrect
- ☐ Compression low
- ☐ Poor acceleration

3 Poor running or no power at high speed

- ☐ Firing incorrect
- ☐ Fuel/air mixture incorrect
- ☐ Compression low
- ☐ Knocking or pinking
- ☐ Miscellaneous causes

4 Overheating

- ☐ Engine overheats
- ☐ Firing incorrect
- ☐ Fuel/air mixture incorrect
- ☐ Compression too high
- ☐ Engine load excessive
- ☐ Lubrication inadequate
- ☐ Miscellaneous causes

5 Transmission problems

- ☐ No drive to rear wheel
- ☐ Vibration
- ☐ Poor performance
- ☐ Clutch not disengaging completely

6 Abnormal engine noise

- ☐ Knocking or pinking
- ☐ Piston slap or rattling
- ☐ Valve noise
- ☐ Other noise

7 Abnormal frame and suspension noise

- ☐ Front end noise
- ☐ Shock absorber noise
- ☐ Brake noise

8 Excessive exhaust smoke

- ☐ White smoke (four-stroke engines)
- ☐ White/blue smoke (two-stroke engines)
- ☐ Black smoke
- ☐ Brown smoke

9 Poor handling or stability

- ☐ Handlebar hard to turn
- ☐ Handlebar shakes or vibrates excessively
- ☐ Handlebar pulls to one side
- ☐ Poor shock absorbing qualities

10 Braking problems – disc brakes

- ☐ Brakes are ineffective
- ☐ Brake lever pulsates
- ☐ Brakes drag

11 Braking problems – drum brakes

- ☐ Brakes are ineffective
- ☐ Brake lever pulsates
- ☐ Brakes drag

12 Electrical problems

- ☐ Battery dead or weak
- ☐ Battery overcharged

1 Engine doesn't start or is difficult to start

Starter motor doesn't rotate

- ☐ Fuse blown. Check fuse and starter circuit (Chapter 9).
- ☐ Battery voltage low. Check and recharge battery (Chapter 9).
- ☐ Starter motor defective. Make sure the wiring to the starter is secure. Make sure the starter relay clicks when the start button is pushed. If the relay clicks, then the fault is in the wiring or motor.
- ☐ Starter relay faulty. Check it (Chapter 9).
- ☐ Starter switch on handlebar not contacting. The contacts could be wet, corroded or dirty. Disassemble and clean the switch (Chapter 9).
- ☐ Wiring open or shorted. Check all wiring connections and harnesses to make sure that they are dry, tight and not corroded. Also check for broken or frayed wires that can cause a short to earth.
- ☐ Ignition (main) switch defective. Check the switch according to the procedure in Chapter 9. Renew the switch if it is defective.
- ☐ Starter safety circuit fault. Check brake light switches and wiring (Chapter 9).
- ☐ Immobiliser system fault (where fitted). See Chapter 5.
- ☐ Fuel injection system in shut-down mode (Purejet 50). See Chapter 4.

Starter motor rotates but engine does not turn over

- ☐ Starter pinion assembly defective. Inspect and repair or renew (Chapter 2A, 2B or 2C).
- ☐ Damaged pinion assembly or starter gears. Inspect and renew the damaged parts (Chapter 2A, 2B or 2C).

Starter works but engine won't turn over (seized)

- ☐ Seized engine caused by one or more internally damaged components. Failure due to wear, abuse or lack of lubrication. On all engines damage can include piston, cylinder, connecting rod, crankshaft, bearings and additionally on four-strokes, valves, camshaft, camchain. Refer to Chapter 2A, 2B or 2C for engine disassembly.

No fuel flow

- ☐ No fuel in tank.
- ☐ Fuel hose or tank vent hose trapped. Check the hoses.
- ☐ Fuel filter clogged. Remove the tap and clean the filter, or check the in-line fuel filter.
- ☐ Fuel tap vacuum hose split or detached. Check the hose.
- ☐ Fuel tap diaphragm split. Renew the tap (Chapter 4).
- ☐ Fuel hose clogged. Remove the fuel hose and carefully blow through it.
- ☐ Fuel pump defective. Renew the pump (Chapter 4).
- ☐ Float needle valve or carburettor jets clogged. The carburettor should be removed and overhauled if draining the float chamber doesn't solve the problem.

Engine flooded

- ☐ Float height or fuel level too high. Check as described in Chapter 4.
- ☐ Float needle valve worn or stuck open. A piece of dirt, rust or other debris can cause the valve to seat improperly, causing excess fuel to be admitted to the float chamber. In this case, the float chamber should be cleaned and the needle valve and seat inspected. If the needle and seat are worn, then the leaking will persist and the parts should be renewed (Chapter 4).

No spark or weak spark

- ☐ Ignition switch OFF.
- ☐ Battery voltage low. Check and recharge the battery as necessary (Chapter 9).
- ☐ Spark plug dirty, defective or worn out. Locate reason for fouled plug using spark plug condition chart at the end of this manual and follow the plug maintenance procedures (Chapter 1). Condition is especially applicable to two-stroke engines due to the oily nature of their lubrication system.
- ☐ Spark plug cap or secondary (HT) wiring faulty. Check condition. Replace either or both components if cracks or deterioration are evident (Chapter 5).
- ☐ Spark plug cap not making good contact. Make sure that the plug cap fits snugly over the plug end.
- ☐ Ignition control unit (ICU) defective. Check the unit, referring to Chapter 5 for details.
- ☐ Pick-up coil or source coil defective. Check the unit, referring to Chapter 5 for details.
- ☐ Ignition HT coil defective. Check the coil, referring to Chapter 5.
- ☐ Ignition switch shorted. This is usually caused by water, corrosion, damage or excessive wear. The switch can be disassembled and cleaned with electrical contact cleaner. If cleaning does not help, renew the switch (Chapter 9).
- ☐ Wiring shorted or broken. Make sure that all wiring connections are clean, dry and tight. Look for chafed and broken wires (Chapters 5 and 9).

Compression low

- ☐ Spark plug loose. Remove the plug and inspect its threads (Chapter 1).
- ☐ Cylinder head not sufficiently tightened down. If the cylinder head is suspected of being loose, then there's a chance that the gasket or head is damaged if the problem has persisted for any length of time. The head nuts should be tightened to the proper torque in the correct sequence (Chapter 2A, 2B or 2C).
- ☐ Low crankcase compression on two-stroke engines due to worn crankshaft oil seals. Condition will upset the fuel/air mixture. Renew the seals (Chapter 2A or 2B).

1 Engine doesn't start or is difficult to start (continued)

☐ Improper valve clearance (four-strokes). This means that the valve is not closing completely and compression pressure is leaking past the valve. Check and adjust the valve clearances (Chapter 1).

☐ Cylinder and/or piston worn. Excessive wear will cause compression pressure to leak past the rings. This is usually accompanied by worn rings as well. A top-end overhaul is necessary (Chapter 2A, 2B or 2C).

☐ Piston rings worn, weak, broken, or sticking. Broken or sticking piston rings usually indicate a lubrication or carburation problem that causes excess carbon deposits or seizures to form on the pistons and rings. Top-end overhaul is necessary (Chapter 2A, 2B or 2C).

☐ Cylinder head gasket damaged. If a head is allowed to become loose, or if excessive carbon build-up on the piston crown and combustion chamber causes extremely high compression, the head gasket may leak. Retorquing the head is not always sufficient to restore the seal, so gasket renewal is necessary (Chapter 2A, 2B or 2C).

☐ Cylinder head warped. This is caused by overheating or improperly tightened head nuts. Machine shop resurfacing or head renewal is necessary (Chapter 2A, 2B or 2C).

☐ Valve spring broken or weak (four-stroke engines). Caused by component failure or wear; the springs must be renewed (Chapter 2C).

☐ Valve not seating properly (four-stroke engines). This is caused by a bent valve (from over-revving or improper valve adjustment), burned valve or seat (improper carburation) or an accumulation of carbon deposits on the seat (from carburation or lubrication problems). The valves must be cleaned and/or renewed and the seats serviced if possible (Chapter 2C).

Stalls after starting

☐ Faulty automatic choke. Check connections and movement (Chapter 4).

☐ Ignition malfunction (Chapter 5).

☐ Carburettor malfunction (Chapter 4).

☐ Fuel contaminated. The fuel can be contaminated with either dirt or water, or can change chemically if the machine is allowed to sit for several months or more. Drain the tank and carburettor (Chapter 4).

☐ Inlet air leak. Check for loose carburettor-to-inlet manifold connection, loose carburettor top (Chapter 4).

☐ Engine idle speed incorrect. Turn idle adjusting screw until the engine idles at the specified rpm (Chapter 1).

Rough idle

☐ Ignition malfunction (Chapter 5).

☐ Idle speed incorrect (Chapter 1).

☐ Carburettor malfunction (Chapter 4).

☐ Fuel contaminated. The fuel can be contaminated with either dirt or water, or can change chemically if the machine is allowed to sit for several months or more. Drain the tank and carburettor (Chapter 4).

☐ Intake air leak. Check for loose carburettor-to-intake manifold connection, loose carburettor top (Chapter 4).

☐ Air filter clogged. Clean or renew the air filter element (Chapter 1).

2 Poor running at low speeds

Spark weak

- [ ] Battery voltage low. Check and recharge battery (Chapter 9).
- [ ] Spark plug fouled, defective or worn out. Refer to Chapter 1 for spark plug maintenance.
- [ ] Spark plug cap or HT wiring defective. Refer to Chapter 5 for details on the ignition system.
- [ ] Spark plug cap not making contact.
- [ ] Incorrect spark plug. Wrong type, heat range or cap configuration. Check and install correct plug listed in Chapter 1.
- [ ] Ignition control unit (ICU) defective. See Chapter 5.
- [ ] Pick-up coil defective. See Chapter 5.
- [ ] Ignition HT coil defective. See Chapter 5.

Fuel/air mixture incorrect

Faults listed relate to carburettor engined models. Refer to Chapter 4 for fuel injection system faults (Purejet 50).

- [ ] Pilot screw out of adjustment (Chapter 4).
- [ ] Pilot jet or air passage clogged. Remove and clean the carburettor (Chapter 4).
- [ ] Air bleed hole clogged. Remove carburettor and blow out all passages (Chapter 4).
- [ ] Air filter clogged, poorly sealed or missing (Chapter 1).
- [ ] Air filter housing poorly sealed. Look for cracks, holes or loose screws and renew or repair defective parts.
- [ ] Fuel level too high or too low. Check the float height and fuel level (Chapter 4).
- [ ] Carburettor intake manifold loose. Check for cracks, breaks, tears or loose fixings.

Compression low

- [ ] Spark plug loose. Remove the plug and inspect its threads (Chapter 1).
- [ ] Cylinder head not sufficiently tightened down. If the cylinder head is suspected of being loose, then there's a chance that the gasket or head is damaged if the problem has persisted for any length of time. The head nuts should be tightened to the proper torque in the correct sequence (Chapter 2A, 2B or 2C).
- [ ] Improper valve clearance (four-stroke engines). This means that the valve is not closing completely and compression pressure is leaking past the valve. Check and adjust the valve clearances (Chapter 1).
- [ ] Low crankcase compression on two-stroke engines due to worn crankshaft oil seals. Condition will upset the fuel/air mixture. Renew the seals (Chapter 2A or 2B).

- [ ] Cylinder and/or piston worn. Excessive wear will cause compression pressure to leak past the rings. This is usually accompanied by worn rings as well. A top-end overhaul is necessary (Chapter 2A, 2B or 2C).
- [ ] Piston rings worn, weak, broken, or sticking. Broken or sticking piston rings usually indicate a lubrication or carburation problem that causes excess carbon deposits or seizures to form on the pistons and rings. Top-end overhaul is necessary (Chapter 2A, 2B or 2C).
- [ ] Cylinder head gasket damaged. If a head is allowed to become loose, or if excessive carbon build-up on the piston crown and combustion chamber causes extremely high compression, the head gasket may leak. Retorquing the head is not always sufficient to restore the seal, so gasket renewal is necessary (Chapter 2A, 2B or 2C).
- [ ] Cylinder head warped. This is caused by overheating or improperly tightened head nuts. Machine shop resurfacing or head replacement is necessary (Chapter 2A, 2B or 2C).
- [ ] Valve spring broken or weak (four-stroke engines). Caused by component failure or wear; the springs must be replaced (Chapter 2C).
- [ ] Valve not seating properly (four-stroke engines). This is caused by a bent valve (from over-revving or improper valve adjustment), burned valve or seat (improper carburation) or an accumulation of carbon deposits on the seat (from carburation or lubrication problems). The valves must be cleaned and/or renewed and the seats serviced if possible (Chapter 2C).

Poor acceleration

- [ ] Carburettor leaking or dirty. Overhaul the carburettor (Chapter 4).
- [ ] Faulty automatic choke (Chapter4).
- [ ] Timing not advancing. The pick-up coil or the ignition control unit (ICU) may be defective (Chapter 5). If so, they must be renewed, as they can't be repaired.
- [ ] Engine oil viscosity too high (four-stroke engines). Using a heavier oil than that recommended in Chapter 1 can damage the oil pump or lubrication system and cause drag on the engine.
- [ ] Brakes dragging. On disc brakes, usually caused by debris which has entered the brake piston seals, or from a warped disc or bent axle, or cable out of adjustment where appropriate. On drum brakes, cable out of adjustment, shoe return spring broken. Repair as necessary (Chapter 7).
- [ ] Clutch slipping, drive belt worn, or variator faulty (Chapter 2D).

3 Poor running or no power at high speed

Firing incorrect

- [ ] Air filter clogged. Clean or renew filter (Chapter 1).
- [ ] Spark plug fouled, defective or worn out. See Chapter 1 for spark plug maintenance.
- [ ] Spark plug cap or HT wiring defective. See Chapter 5 for details of the ignition system.
- [ ] Spark plug cap not in good contact (Chapter 5).
- [ ] Incorrect spark plug. Wrong type, heat range or cap configuration. Check and install correct plug listed in Chapter 1.
- [ ] Ignition control unit or HT coil defective (Chapter 5).

Fuel/air mixture incorrect

Faults listed relate to carburettor engined models. Refer to Chapter 4 for fuel injection system faults (Purejet 50).

- [ ] Main jet clogged. Dirt, water or other contaminants can clog the main jet. Clean the fuel tap filter, the in-line filter, the float chamber and the jets and carburettor orifices (Chapter 4).
- [ ] Main jet wrong size. The standard jetting is for sea level atmospheric pressure and oxygen content.
- [ ] Air bleed holes clogged. Remove and overhaul carburettor (Chapter 4).
- [ ] Air filter clogged, poorly sealed, or missing (Chapter 1).
- [ ] Air filter housing or duct poorly sealed. Look for cracks, holes or loose clamps or screws, and renew or repair defective parts.
- [ ] Fuel level too high or too low. Check the float height or fuel level (Chapter 4).
- [ ] Carburettor intake manifold loose. Check for cracks, breaks, tears or loose fixings.

Compression low

- [ ] Spark plug loose. Remove the plug and inspect its threads. Reinstall and tighten to the specified torque (Chapter 1).
- [ ] Cylinder head not sufficiently tightened down. If the cylinder head is suspected of being loose, then there's a chance that the gasket or head is damaged if the problem has persisted for any length of time. The head nuts should be tightened to the proper torque in the correct sequence (Chapter 2A, 2B or 2C).
- [ ] Improper valve clearance (four-stroke engines). This means that the valve is not closing completely and compression pressure is leaking past the valve. Check and adjust the valve clearances (Chapter 1).
- [ ] Low crankcase compression on two-stroke engines due to worn crankshaft oil seals. Condition will upset the fuel/air mixture. Renew the seals (Chapter 2A or 2B).
- [ ] Cylinder and/or piston worn. Excessive wear will cause compression pressure to leak past the rings. This is usually accompanied by worn rings as well. A top-end overhaul is necessary (Chapter 2A, 2B or 2C).
- [ ] Piston rings worn, weak, broken, or sticking. Broken or sticking piston rings usually indicate a lubrication or carburation problem that causes excess carbon deposits or seizures to form on the pistons and rings. Top-end overhaul is necessary (Chapter 2A, 2B or 2C).
- [ ] Cylinder head gasket damaged. If a head is allowed to become loose, or if excessive carbon build-up on the piston crown and combustion chamber causes extremely high compression, the head gasket may leak. Retorquing the head is not always sufficient to restore the seal, so gasket replacement is necessary (Chapter 2A, 2B or 2C).
- [ ] Cylinder head warped. This is caused by overheating or improperly tightened head nuts. Cylinder head skimming or head replacement is necessary (Chapter 2A, 2B or 2C).
- [ ] Valve spring broken or weak (four-stroke engines). Caused by component failure or wear; the springs must be renewed (Chapter 2C).
- [ ] Valve not seating properly (four-stroke engines). This is caused by a bent valve (from over-revving or improper valve adjustment), burned valve or seat (improper carburation) or an accumulation of carbon deposits on the seat (from carburation or lubrication problems). The valves must be cleaned and/or renewed and the seats serviced if possible (Chapter 2C).

Knocking or pinking

- [ ] Carbon build-up in combustion chamber. Use of a fuel additive that will dissolve the adhesive bonding the carbon particles to the crown and chamber is the easiest way to remove the build-up. Otherwise, the cylinder head will have to be removed and decarbonised (Chapter 2A, 2B or 2C).
- [ ] Incorrect or poor quality fuel. Old or improper grades of fuel can cause detonation. This causes the piston to rattle, thus the knocking or pinking sound. Drain old fuel and always use the recommended fuel grade.
- [ ] Spark plug heat range incorrect. Uncontrolled detonation indicates the plug heat range is too hot. The plug in effect becomes a glow plug, raising cylinder temperatures. Install the proper heat range plug (Chapter 1).
- [ ] Improper air/fuel mixture. This will cause the cylinders to run hot, which leads to detonation. Clogged jets or an air leak can cause this imbalance. See Chapter 4.

Miscellaneous causes

- [ ] Throttle valve doesn't open fully. Adjust the throttle twistgrip freeplay (Chapter 1).
- [ ] Clutch slipping, drive belt worn, or variator faulty (Chapter 2D).
- [ ] Timing not advancing (Chapter 5).
- [ ] Engine oil viscosity too high (four-stroke engines). Using a heavier oil than the one recommended in Chapter 1 can damage the oil pump or lubrication system and cause drag on the engine.
- [ ] Brakes dragging. On disc brakes, usually caused by debris which has entered the brake piston seals, or from a warped disc or bent axle. On drum brakes, cable out of adjustment, shoe return spring broken. Repair as necessary (Chapter 7).

4 Overheating

Engine overheats – liquid-cooled engines

☐ Coolant level low. Check and add coolant (Daily (pre-ride) checks).
☐ Leak in cooling system. Check cooling system hoses and radiator for leaks and other damage. Repair or renew parts as necessary (Chapter 3).
☐ Thermostat sticking open or closed. Check and renew as described in Chapter 3.
☐ Coolant passages clogged. Drain and flush the entire system, then refill with fresh coolant.
☐ Water pump defective. Remove the pump and check the components (Chapter 3).
☐ Clogged radiator fins. Clean them by blowing compressed air through the fins from the back of the radiator.
☐ Cooling fan or fan switch fault (Chapter 3).

Engine overheats – air-cooled engines

☐ Air cooling ducts or engine cowling blocked or incorrectly fitted.
☐ Problem with cooling fan.

Firing incorrect

☐ Spark plug fouled, defective or worn out. See Chapter 1 for spark plug maintenance.
☐ Incorrect spark plug.
☐ Ignition control unit (ICU) defective (Chapter 5).
☐ Faulty ignition HT coil (Chapter 5).

Fuel/air mixture incorrect

Faults listed relate to carburettor engined models. Refer to Chapter 4 for fuel injection system faults (Purejet 50).
☐ Main jet clogged. Dirt, water or other contaminants can clog the main jet. Clean the fuel tap filter, the in-line filter, the float chamber and the jets and carburettor orifices (Chapter 4).
☐ Main jet wrong size. The standard jetting is for sea level atmospheric pressure and oxygen content.
☐ Air bleed holes clogged. Remove and overhaul carburettor (Chapter 4).
☐ Air filter clogged, poorly sealed, or missing (Chapter 1).
☐ Air filter housing or duct poorly sealed. Look for cracks, holes or loose clamps or screws, and renew or repair defective parts.
☐ Fuel level too high or too low. Check the float height or fuel level (Chapter 4).
☐ Carburettor intake manifold loose. Check for cracks, breaks, tears or loose fixings.

Compression too high

☐ Carbon build-up in combustion chamber. Use of a fuel additive that will dissolve the adhesive bonding the carbon particles to the piston crown and chamber is the easiest way to remove the build-up. Otherwise, the cylinder head will have to be removed and decarbonised (Chapter 2A, 2B or 2C).
☐ Improperly machined head surface or installation of incorrect size cylinder base gasket during engine assembly.

Engine load excessive

☐ Clutch slipping, drive belt worn, or variator faulty (Chapter 2D).
☐ Engine oil level too high (four-stroke engines). The addition of too much oil will cause pressurisation of the crankcase and inefficient engine operation. Drain to proper level (Daily (pre-ride) checks).
☐ Engine oil viscosity too high (four-stroke engines). Using a heavier oil than the one recommended in Chapter 1 can damage the oil pump or lubrication system as well as cause drag on the engine.
☐ Brakes dragging. On disc brakes, usually caused by debris which has entered the brake piston seals, or from a warped disc or bent axle. On drum brakes, cable out of adjustment, shoe return spring broken. Repair as necessary (Chapter 7).

Lubrication inadequate

☐ Engine oil level too low (four-stroke engines). Friction caused by intermittent lack of lubrication or from oil that is overworked can cause overheating. The oil provides a definite cooling function in the engine. Check the oil level (Daily (pre-ride) checks).
☐ Oil pump out of adjustment (two-stroke engines). Adjust pump cable (Chapter 1).
☐ Poor quality oil or incorrect viscosity or type. Oil is rated not only according to viscosity but also according to type. Some oils are not rated high enough for use in this engine. Check the Specifications section and change to the correct oil (Chapter 1). On two-stroke engines, make sure that you use a two-stroke oil which is suitable for oil injection engines.

Miscellaneous causes

☐ Modification to exhaust system. Most aftermarket exhaust systems cause the engine to run leaner, which make them run hotter. When installing an accessory exhaust system, always obtain advice on rejetting the carburettor.

5 Transmission problems

No drive to rear wheel

- ☐ Drive belt broken (Chapter 2D).
- ☐ Clutch not engaging (Chapter 2D).
- ☐ Clutch or drum excessively worn (Chapter 2D).

Transmission noise or vibration

- ☐ Bearings worn. Also includes the possibility that the shafts are worn. Overhaul the gearbox (Chapter 2D).
- ☐ Gears worn or chipped (Chapter 2D).
- ☐ Clutch drum worn unevenly (Chapter 2D).
- ☐ Worn bearings or bent shaft (Chapter 2D).
- ☐ Loose clutch nut or drum nut (Chapter 2D).

Poor performance

- ☐ Variator worn or insufficiently greased (Chapter 2D).
- ☐ Weak or broken driven pulley spring (Chapter 2D).
- ☐ Clutch or drum excessively worn (Chapter 2D).
- ☐ Grease on clutch friction material (Chapter 2D).
- ☐ Drive belt excessively worn (Chapter 2D).

Clutch not disengaging completely

- ☐ Weak or broken clutch springs (Chapter 2D).
- ☐ Engine idle speed too high (Chapter 1).

6 Abnormal engine noise

Knocking or pinking

- ☐ Carbon build-up in combustion chamber. Use of a fuel additive that will dissolve the adhesive bonding the carbon particles to the piston crown and chamber is the easiest way to remove the build-up. Otherwise, the cylinder head will have to be removed and decarbonised (Chapter 2A, 2B or 2C).
- ☐ Incorrect or poor quality fuel. Old or improper fuel can cause detonation. This causes the piston to rattle, thus the knocking or pinking sound. Drain the old fuel and always use the recommended grade fuel (Chapter 4).
- ☐ Spark plug heat range incorrect. Uncontrolled detonation indicates that the plug heat range is too hot. The plug in effect becomes a glow plug, raising cylinder temperatures. Install the proper heat range plug (Chapter 1).
- ☐ Improper air/fuel mixture. This will cause the cylinder to run hot and lead to detonation. Clogged jets or an air leak can cause this imbalance. See Chapter 4.

Piston slap or rattling

- ☐ Cylinder-to-piston clearance excessive. Caused by improper assembly. Inspect and overhaul top-end parts (Chapter 2A, 2B or 2C).
- ☐ Connecting rod bent. Caused by over-revving, trying to start a badly flooded engine or from ingesting a foreign object into the combustion chamber. Renew the damaged parts (Chapter 2A, 2B or 2C).
- ☐ Piston pin or piston pin bore worn or seized from wear or lack of lubrication. Renew damaged parts (Chapter 2A, 2B or 2C).
- ☐ Piston ring(s) worn, broken or sticking. Overhaul the top-end (Chapter 2A, 2B or 2C).

- ☐ Piston seizure damage. Usually from lack of lubrication or overheating. Renew the piston and where possible, rebore the cylinder, as necessary (Chapter 2A, 2B or 2C). On two-stroke engines, check that the oil pump is correctly adjusted.
- ☐ Connecting rod upper or lower end clearance excessive. Caused by excessive wear or lack of lubrication. Renew worn parts.

Valve noise – four-stroke engines

- ☐ Incorrect valve clearances. Adjust the clearances by referring to Chapter 1.
- ☐ Valve spring broken or weak. Check and renew weak valve springs (Chapter 2C).
- ☐ Camshaft bearings worn or damaged. Lack of lubrication at high rpm is usually the cause of damage. Insufficient oil or failure to change the oil at the recommended intervals are the chief causes. (Chapter 2C).

Other noise

- ☐ Exhaust pipe leaking at cylinder head connection. Caused by improper fit of pipe or loose exhaust flange. All exhaust fasteners should be tightened evenly and carefully. Failure to do this will lead to a leak.
- ☐ Crankshaft runout excessive. Caused by a bent crankshaft (from over-revving) or damage from an upper cylinder component failure.
- ☐ Engine mounting bolts loose. Tighten all engine mounting bolts (Chapter 2A, 2B or 2C).
- ☐ Crankshaft bearings worn (Chapter 2A, 2B or 2C).
- ☐ Camchain defective (four-stroke engines). Replace according to the procedure in Chapter 2C.

7 Abnormal frame and suspension noise

Front end noise

- ☐ Steering head bearings loose or damaged. Clicks when braking. Check and adjust or replace as necessary (Chapters 1 and 6).
- ☐ Bolts loose. Make sure all bolts are tightened to the specified torque (Chapter 6).
- ☐ Fork tube bent. Good possibility if machine has been in a collision. Renew the tube or the fork assembly (Chapter 6).
- ☐ Front axle nut loose. Tighten to the specified torque (Chapter 7).
- ☐ Loose or worn wheel or hub bearings. Check and renew as needed (Chapter 7).

Shock absorber noise

Note: *On models with twin rear shock absorbers the shocks must be replaced as a pair, never singly.*

- ☐ Fluid level low due to leakage from defective seal. Shock will be covered with oil. Renew the shock (Chapter 6).
- ☐ Defective shock absorber with internal damage. If replacement parts are available, the shock can be repaired, otherwise it must be replaced (Chapter 6).
- ☐ Bent or damaged shock body. Renew the shock (Chapter 6).
- ☐ Loose or worn suspension swingarm components. Check and renew as necessary (Chapter 6).

Brake noise

- ☐ Squeal caused by dust on brake pads or shoes. Usually found in combination with glazed pads or shoes. Renew the pads/shoes (Chapter 7).
- ☐ Contamination of brake pads or shoes. Oil or brake fluid causing brake to chatter or squeal. Renew pads or shoes (Chapter 7).
- ☐ Pads or shoes glazed. Caused by excessive heat from prolonged use or from contamination. Do not use sandpaper, emery cloth, carborundum cloth or any other abrasive to roughen the pad surfaces as abrasives will stay in the pad material and damage the disc or drum. A very fine flat file can be used, but pad or shoe renewal is advised (Chapter 7).
- ☐ Disc or drum warped. Can cause a chattering, clicking or intermittent squeal. Usually accompanied by a pulsating lever and uneven braking. Check the disc runout and the drum ovality (Chapter 7).
- ☐ Loose or worn wheel (front) or transmission (rear) bearings. Check and renew as needed (Chapter 7).

8 Excessive exhaust smoke

White smoke – four-stroke engines (oil burning)

- ☐ Piston oil ring worn. The ring may be broken or damaged, causing oil from the crankcase to be pulled past the piston into the combustion chamber. Renew the rings (Chapter 2C).
- ☐ Cylinder worn, or scored. Caused by overheating or oil starvation. The cylinder will have to be rebored and an oversize piston installed (125 cc models) or a new piston and cylinder purchased (180 and 200 cc models) (Chapter 2C).
- ☐ Valve stem oil seal damaged or worn. Renew oil seals (Chapter 2C).
- ☐ Valve guide worn. Inspect the valve guides and if worn seek the advice of a Gilera dealer (Chapter 2C).
- ☐ Engine oil level too high, which causes the oil to be forced past the rings. Drain oil to the proper level (Daily (pre-ride) checks).
- ☐ Head gasket broken between oil return and cylinder. Causes oil to be pulled into the combustion chamber. Renew the head gasket and check the head for warpage (Chapter 2C).
- ☐ Abnormal crankcase pressurisation, which forces oil past the rings.

White/blue smoke – two-stroke engines (oil burning)

- ☐ Oil pump cable adjustment incorrect. Check throttle cable/oil pump cable adjustment (Chapter 1).
- ☐ Accumulated oil deposits in the exhaust system. If the scooter is used for short journeys only, the oil residue from the exhaust gases will condense in the cool silencer. Take the scooter for a long run to burn off the accumulated oil residue.

Black smoke (over-rich mixture)

- ☐ Air filter clogged. Clean or renew the element (Chapter 1).
- ☐ Main jet too large or loose. Compare the jet size to the Specifications (Chapter 4).
- ☐ Automatic choke faulty (Chapter 4).
- ☐ Fuel level too high. Check and adjust the float height or fuel level as necessary (Chapter 4).
- ☐ Float needle valve held off needle seat. Clean the float chamber and fuel line and renew the needle and seat if necessary (Chapter 4).

Brown smoke (lean mixture)

- ☐ Main jet too small or clogged. Lean condition caused by wrong size main jet or by a restricted orifice. Clean float chamber and jets and compare jet size to specifications (Chapter 4).
- ☐ Fuel flow Insufficient. Float needle valve stuck closed due to chemical reaction with old fuel. Float height or fuel level Incorrect. Restricted fuel hose. Clean hose and float chamber and adjust float if necessary. Check the operation of the fuel pump (Chapter 4).
- ☐ Carburettor intake manifold clamp loose (Chapter 4).
- ☐ Air filter poorly sealed or not installed (Chapter 1).
- ☐ Ignition timing incorrect (Chapter 5).

9 Poor handling or stability

Handlebar hard to turn

☐ Steering head bearing adjuster nut too tight. Check adjustment as described in Chapter 1.

☐ Bearings damaged. Roughness can be felt as the bars are turned from side-to-side. Replace bearings and races (Chapter 6).

☐ Races dented or worn. Denting results from wear in only one position (e.g. straight ahead), from a collision or hitting a pothole or from dropping the machine. Renew races and bearings (Chapter 6).

☐ Steering stem lubrication inadequate. Causes are grease getting hard from age or being washed out by high pressure car washes. Disassemble steering head and repack bearings (Chapter 6).

☐ Steering stem bent. Caused by a collision, hitting a pothole or by dropping the machine. Renew damaged part. Don't try to straighten the steering stem (Chapter 6).

☐ Front tyre air pressure too low (Daily (pre-ride) checks and Chapter 1).

Handlebar shakes or vibrates excessively

☐ Tyres worn (Daily (pre-ride) checks and Chapter 1).

☐ Suspension worn. Renew worn components (Chapter 6).

☐ Wheel rim(s) warped or damaged. Inspect wheels for runout (Chapter 7).

☐ Wheel bearings worn. Worn wheel bearings (front) or transmission bearings (rear) can cause poor tracking. Worn front bearings will cause wobble (Chapter 7).

☐ Handlebar mountings loose (Chapter 6).

☐ Front suspension bolts loose. Tighten them to the specified torque (Chapter 6).

☐ Engine mounting bolts loose. Will cause excessive vibration with increased engine rpm (Chapter 2A, 2B or 2C).

Handlebar pulls to one side

☐ Frame bent. Definitely suspect this if the machine has been in a collision. May or may not be accompanied by cracking near the bend. Renew the frame (Chapter 6).

☐ Wheels out of alignment. Caused by improper location of axle spacers or from bent steering stem or frame (Chapter 7).

☐ Steering stem bent. Caused by impact damage or by dropping the machine. Renew the steering stem (Chapter 6).

☐ Fork tube bent. Disassemble the forks and renew the damaged parts (Chapter 6).

Poor shock absorbing qualities

Too hard:
a) Fork oil quantity excessive - conventional forks (Chapter 6).
b) Fork oil viscosity too high - conventional forks (Chapter 6).
c) Suspension bent. Causes a harsh, sticking feeling (Chapter 6).
d) Fork or front damper internal damage (Chapter 6).
e) Rear shock internal damage (Chapter 6).
f) Tyre pressure too high (Chapter 1).

Too soft:
a) Fork oil viscosity too light (Chapter 6).
b) Fork or shock spring(s) weak or broken (Chapter 6).
c) Fork or shock internal damage or leakage (Chapter 6).

10 Braking problems – disc brakes

Brake is ineffective

☐ Air in brake hose. Caused by inattention to master cylinder fluid level (Daily (pre-ride) checks) or by leakage. Locate problem and bleed brake (Chapter 7).

☐ Pads or disc worn (Chapters 1 and 7).

☐ Brake fluid leak. Locate problem and rectify (Chapter 7).

☐ Contaminated pads. Caused by contamination with oil, grease, brake fluid, etc. Renew pads. Clean disc thoroughly with brake cleaner (Chapter 7).

☐ Brake fluid deteriorated. Fluid is old or contaminated. Drain system, replenish with new fluid and bleed the system (Chapter 7).

☐ Master cylinder internal parts worn or damaged causing fluid to bypass (Chapter 7).

☐ Master cylinder bore scratched by foreign material or broken spring. Repair or renew master cylinder (Chapter 7).

☐ Disc warped. Renew disc (Chapter 7).

Brake lever pulsates

☐ Disc warped. Renew disc (Chapter 7).

☐ Axle bent. Renew axle (Chapter 7).

☐ Brake caliper bolts loose (Chapter 8).

☐ Wheel warped or otherwise damaged (Chapter 7).

☐ Wheel or hub bearings damaged or worn (Chapter 7).

Brake drags

☐ Master cylinder piston seized. Caused by wear or damage to piston or cylinder bore (Chapter 7).

☐ Lever balky or stuck. Check pivot and lubricate (Chapter 7).

☐ Brake caliper piston seized in bore. Caused by wear or ingestion of dirt past deteriorated seal (Chapter 7).

☐ Brake pads damaged. Pad material separated from backing plate. Usually caused by faulty manufacturing process or from contact with chemicals. Renew pads (Chapter 7).

☐ Caliper slider pins sticking (two piston sliding caliper). Clean the slider pins and apply a smear of silicone grease (Chapter 7).

☐ Pads improperly installed (Chapter 7).

11 Braking problems – rear drum brake

Brake is ineffective

- [ ] Cable incorrectly adjusted. Check cable (Chapter 1).
- [ ] Shoes or drum worn (Chapter 7).
- [ ] Contaminated shoes. Caused by contamination with oil, grease etc. Renew shoes. Clean drum thoroughly with brake cleaner (Chapter 7).
- [ ] Brake lever arm incorrectly positioned, or cam excessively worn (Chapter 7).

Brake lever pulsates

- [ ] Drum warped. Renew drum (Chapter 7).
- [ ] Axle bent. Renew axle (Chapter 7).
- [ ] Wheel warped or otherwise damaged (Chapter 7).
- [ ] Wheel/hub bearings (front) or transmission bearings (rear) damaged or worn (Chapter 7).

Brake drags

- [ ] Cable incorrectly adjusted or requires lubrication. Check cable (Chapter 1).
- [ ] Shoe return springs broken (Chapter 7).
- [ ] Lever balky or stuck. Check pivot and lubricate (Chapter 7).
- [ ] Lever arm or cam binds. Caused by inadequate lubrication or damage (Chapter 7).
- [ ] Brake shoe damaged. Friction material separated from shoe. Usually caused by faulty manufacturing process or from contact with chemicals. Renew shoes (Chapter 7).
- [ ] Shoes improperly installed (Chapter 7).

12 Electrical problems

Battery dead or weak

- [ ] Battery faulty. Caused by sulphated plates which are shorted through sedimentation. Also, broken battery terminal making only occasional contact (Chapter 9).
- [ ] Battery cables making poor electrical contact (Chapter 9).
- [ ] Load excessive. Caused by addition of high wattage lights or other electrical accessories.
- [ ] Ignition (main) switch defective. Switch either earths internally or fails to shut off system. Renew the switch (Chapter 9).
- [ ] Regulator/rectifier defective (Chapter 9).
- [ ] Alternator stator coil open or shorted (Chapter 9).
- [ ] Wiring faulty. Wiring either shorted to earth or connections loose in ignition, charging or lighting circuits (Chapter 9).

Battery overcharged

- [ ] Regulator/rectifier defective. Overcharging is noticed when battery gets excessively warm (Chapter 9).
- [ ] Battery defective. Renew battery (Chapter 9).
- [ ] Battery amperage too low, wrong type or size. Install manufacturer's specified amp-hour battery to handle charging load (Chapter 9).

Note: *References throughout this index are in the form - "Chapter number" • "Page number"*

Haynes Motorcycle Manuals – The Complete List

Title	Book No
APRILIA RS50 (99 - 06) & RS125 (93 - 06)	4298
Aprilia RSV1000 Mille (98 - 03) ◆	4255
Aprilia SR50	4755
BMW 2-valve Twins (70 - 96) ◆	0249
BMW F650 ◆	4761
BMW K100 & 75 2-valve Models (83 - 96) ◆	1373
BMW R850, 1100 & 1150 4-valve Twins (93 - 04) ◆	3466
BMW R1200 (04 - 06) ◆	4598
BSA Bantam (48 - 71)	0117
BSA Unit Singles (58 - 72)	0127
BSA Pre-unit Singles (54 - 61)	0326
BSA A7 & A10 Twins (47 - 62)	0121
BSA A50 & A65 Twins (62 - 73)	0155
Chinese Scooters	4768
DUCATI 600, 620, 750 and 900 2-valve V-Twins (91 - 05) ◆	3290
Ducati MK III & Desmo Singles (69 - 76) ◇	0445
Ducati 748, 916 & 996 4-valve V-Twins (94 - 01) ◆	3756
GILERA Runner, DNA, Ice & SKP/Stalker (97 - 07)	4163
HARLEY-DAVIDSON Sportsters (70 - 08) ◆	2534
Harley-Davidson Shovelhead and Evolution Big Twins (70 - 99) ◆	2536
Harley-Davidson Twin Cam 88 (99 - 03) ◆	2478
HONDA NB, ND, NP & NS50 Melody (81 - 85) ◇	0622
Honda NE/NB50 Vision & SA50 Vision Met-in (85 - 95) ◇	1278
Honda MB, MBX, MT & MTX50 (80 - 93)	0731
Honda C50, C70 & C90 (67 - 03)	0324
Honda XR80/100R & CRF80/100F (85 - 04)	2218
Honda XL/XR 80, 100, 125, 185 & 200 2-valve Models (78 - 87)	0566
Honda H100 & H100S Singles (80 - 92)	0734
Honda CB/CD125T & CM125C Twins (77 - 88)	0571
Honda CG125 (76 - 07)	0433
Honda NS125 (86 - 93) ◇	3056
Honda CBR125R (04 - 07)	4620
Honda MBX/MTX125 & MTX200 (83 - 93) ◇	1132
Honda CD/CM185 200T & CM250C 2-valve Twins (77 - 85)	0572
Honda XL/XR 250 & 500 (78 - 84)	0567
Honda XR250L, XR250R & XR400R (86 - 03)	2219
Honda CB250 & CB400N Super Dreams (78 - 84) ◇	0540
Honda CR Motocross Bikes (86 - 01)	2222
Honda CRF250 & CRF450 (02 - 06)	2630
Honda CBR400RR Fours (88 - 99) ◇ ◆	3552
Honda VFR400 (NC30) & RVF400 (NC35) V-Fours (89 - 98) ◇ ◆	3496
Honda CB500 (93 - 02) & CBF500 03 - 08 ◇	3753
Honda CB400 & CB550 Fours (73 - 77)	0262
Honda CX/GL500 & 650 V-Twins (78 - 86)	0442
Honda CBX550 Four (82 - 86)	0940
Honda XL600R & XR600R (83 - 08) ◆	2183
Honda XL600/650V Transalp & XRV750 Africa Twin (87 to 07) ◆	3919
Honda CBR600F1 & 1000F Fours (87 - 96) ◆	1730
Honda CBR600F2 & F3 Fours (91 - 98) ◆	2070
Honda CBR600F4 (99 - 06) ◆	3911
Honda CB600F Hornet & CBF600 (98 - 06) ◇ ◆	3915
Honda CBR600RR (03 - 06) ◆	4590
Honda CB650 sohc Fours (78 - 84)	0665
Honda NTV600 Revere, NTV650 and NT650V Deauville (88 - 05) ◇	3243
Honda Shadow VT600 & 750 (USA) (88 - 03)	2312
Honda CB750 sohc Four (69 - 79)	0131
Honda V45/65 Sabre & Magna (82 - 88)	0820
Honda VFR750 & 700 V-Fours (86 - 97) ◆	2101
Honda VFR800 V-Fours (97 - 01) ◆	3703
Honda VFR800 V-Tec V-Fours (02 - 05) ◆	4196
Honda CB750 & CB900 dohc Fours (78 - 84)	0535
Honda VTR1000 (FireStorm, Super Hawk) & XL1000V (Varadero) (97 - 08) ◆	3744
Honda CBR900RR FireBlade (92 - 99) ◆	2161
Honda CBR900RR FireBlade (00 - 03) ◆	4060
Honda CBR1000RR Fireblade (04 - 07) ◆	4604
Honda CBR1100XX Super Blackbird (97 - 07) ◆	3901
Honda ST1100 Pan European V-Fours (90 - 02) ◆	3384
Honda Shadow VT1100 (USA) (85 - 98)	2313
Honda GL1000 Gold Wing (75 - 79)	0309

Title	Book No
Honda GL1100 Gold Wing (79 - 81)	0669
Honda Gold Wing 1200 (USA) (84 - 87)	2199
Honda Gold Wing 1500 (USA) (88 - 00)	2225
KAWASAKI AE/AR 50 & 80 (81 - 95)	1007
Kawasaki KC, KE & KH100 (75 - 99)	1371
Kawasaki KMX125 & 200 (86 - 02) ◇	3046
Kawasaki 250, 350 & 400 Triples (72 - 79)	0134
Kawasaki 400 & 440 Twins (74 - 81)	0281
Kawasaki 400, 500 & 550 Fours (79 - 91)	0910
Kawasaki EN450 & 500 Twins (Ltd/Vulcan) (85 - 07)	2053
Kawasaki EX500 (GPZ500S) & ER500 (ER-5) (87 - 08) ◆	2052
Kawasaki ZX600 (ZZ-R600 & Ninja ZX-6) (90 - 06) ◆	2146
Kawasaki ZX-6R Ninja Fours (95 - 02) ◆	3541
Kawasaki ZX-6R (03 - 06) ◆	4742
Kawasaki ZX600 (GPZ600R, GPX600R, Ninja 600R & RX) & ZX750 (GPX750R, Ninja 750R) ◆	1780
Kawasaki 650 Four (76 - 78)	0373
Kawasaki Vulcan 700/750 & 800 (85 - 04) ◆	2457
Kawasaki 750 Air-cooled Fours (80 - 91)	0574
Kawasaki ZR550 & 750 Zephyr Fours (90 - 97) ◆	3382
Kawasaki Z750 & Z1000 (03 - 08) ◆	4762
Kawasaki ZX750 (Ninja ZX-7 & ZXR750) Fours (89 - 96) ◆	2054
Kawasaki Ninja ZX-7R & ZX-9R (94 - 04) ◆	3721
Kawasaki 900 & 1000 Fours (73 - 77)	0222
Kawasaki ZX900, 1000 & 1100 Liquid-cooled Fours (83 - 97) ◆	1681
KTM EXC Enduro & SX Motocross (00 - 07) ◆	4629
MOTO GUZZI 750, 850 & 1000 V-Twins (74 - 78)	0339
MZ ETZ Models (81 - 95) ◇	1680
NORTON 500, 600, 650 & 750 Twins (57 - 70)	0187
Norton Commando (68 - 77)	0125
PEUGEOT Speedfight, Trekker & Vivacity Scooters (96 - 08)	3920
PIAGGIO (Vespa) Scooters (91 - 06)	3492
SUZUKI GT, ZR & TS50 (77 - 90) ◇	0799
Suzuki TS50X (84 - 00) ◇	1599
Suzuki 100, 125, 185 & 250 Air-cooled Trail bikes (79 - 89)	0797
Suzuki GP100 & 125 Singles (78 - 93) ◇	0576
Suzuki GS, GN, GZ & DR125 Singles (82 - 05) ◇	0888
Suzuki GSX-R600/750 (06 - 09) ◆	4790
Suzuki 250 & 350 Twins (68 - 78)	0120
Suzuki GT250X7, GT200X5 & SB200 Twins (78 - 83) ◇	0469
Suzuki GS/GSX250, 400 & 450 Twins (79 - 85)	0736
Suzuki GS500 Twin (89 - 06) ◆	3238
Suzuki GS550 (77 - 82) & GS750 Fours (76 - 79)	0363
Suzuki GS/GSX550 4-valve Fours (83 - 88)	1133
Suzuki SV650 & SV650S (99 - 08) ◆	3912
Suzuki GSX-R600 & 750 (96 - 00) ◆	3553
Suzuki GSX-R600 (01 - 03), GSX-R750 (00 - 03) & GSX-R1000 (01 - 02) ◆	3986
Suzuki GSX-R600/750 (04 - 05) & GSX-R1000 (03 - 06) ◆	4382
Suzuki GSF600, 650 & 1200 Bandit Fours (95 - 06) ◆	3367
Suzuki Intruder, Marauder, Volusia & Boulevard (85 - 06) ◆	2618
Suzuki GS850 Fours (78 - 88)	0536
Suzuki GS1000 Four (77 - 79)	0484
Suzuki GSX-R750, GSX-R1100 (85 - 92), GSX600F, GSX750F, GSX1100F (Katana) Fours ◆	2055
Suzuki GSX600/750F & GSX750 (98 - 02) ◆	3987
Suzuki GS/GSX1000, 1100 & 1150 4-valve Fours (79 - 88)	0737
Suzuki TL1000S/R & DL1000 V-Strom (97 - 04) ◆	4083
Suzuki GSF650/1250 (05 - 09) ◆	4798
Suzuki GSX1300R Hayabusa (99 - 04) ◆	4184
Suzuki GSX1400 (02 - 07) ◆	4758
TRIUMPH Tiger Cub & Terrier (52 - 68)	0414
Triumph 350 & 500 Unit Twins (58 - 73)	0137
Triumph Pre-Unit Twins (47 - 62)	0251
Triumph 650 & 750 2-valve Unit Twins (63 - 83)	0122
Triumph Trident & BSA Rocket 3 (69 - 75)	0136
Triumph Bonneville (01 - 07) ◆	4364
Triumph Daytona, Speed Triple, Sprint & Tiger (97 - 05) ◆	3755
Triumph Triples and Fours (carburettor engines) (91 - 04) ◆	2162
VESPA P/PX125, 150 & 200 Scooters (78 - 06)	0707
Vespa Scooters (59 - 78)	0126
YAMAHA DT50 & 80 Trail Bikes (78 - 95) ◇	0800
Yamaha T50 & 80 Townmate (83 - 95) ◇	1247

Title	Book No
Yamaha YB100 Singles (73 - 91) ◇	0474
Yamaha RS/RXS100 & 125 Singles (74 - 95)	0331
Yamaha RD & DT125LC (82 - 95) ◇	0887
Yamaha TZR125 (87 - 93) & DT125R (88 - 07) ◇	1655
Yamaha TY50, 80, 125 & 175 (74 - 84) ◇	0464
Yamaha XT & SR125 (82 - 03) ◇	1021
Yamaha YBR125	4797
Yamaha Trail Bikes (81 - 00)	2350
Yamaha 2-stroke Motocross Bikes 1986 - 2006	2662
Yamaha YZ & WR 4-stroke Motocross Bikes (98 - 08)	2689
Yamaha 250 & 350 Twins (70 - 79)	0040
Yamaha XS250, 360 & 400 sohc Twins (75 - 84)	0378
Yamaha RD250 & 350LC Twins (80 - 82)	0803
Yamaha RD350 YPVS Twins (83 - 95)	1158
Yamaha RD400 Twin (75 - 79)	0333
Yamaha XT, TT & SR500 Singles (75 - 83)	0342
Yamaha XZ550 Vision V-Twins (82 - 85)	0821
Yamaha FJ, FZ, XJ & YX600 Radian (84 - 92)	2100
Yamaha XJ600S (Diversion, Seca II) & XJ600N Fours (92 - 03) ◆	2145
Yamaha YZF600R Thundercat & FZS600 Fazer (96 - 03) ◆	3702
Yamaha FZ-6 Fazer (04 - 07) ◆	4751
Yamaha YZF-R6 (99 - 02) ◆	3900
Yamaha YZF-R6 (03 - 06) ◆	4601
Yamaha 650 Twins (70 - 83)	0341
Yamaha XJ650 & 750 Fours (80 - 84)	0738
Yamaha XS750 & 850 Triples (76 - 85)	0340
Yamaha TDM850, TRX850 & XTZ750 (89 - 99) ◇ ◆	3540
Yamaha YZF750R & YZF1000R Thunderace (93 - 00) ◆	3720
Yamaha FZR600, 750 & 1000 Fours (87 - 96) ◆	2056
Yamaha XV (Virago) V-Twins (81 - 03) ◆	0802
Yamaha XVS650 & 1100 Drag Star/V-Star (97 - 05) ◆	4195
Yamaha XJ900F Fours (83 - 94) ◆	3239
Yamaha XJ900S Diversion (94 - 01) ◆	3739
Yamaha YZF-R1 (98 - 03) ◆	3754
Yamaha YZF-R1 (04 - 06) ◆	4605
Yamaha FZS1000 Fazer (01 - 05) ◆	4287
Yamaha FJ1100 & 1200 Fours (84 - 96) ◆	2057
Yamaha XJR1200 & 1300 (95 - 06) ◆	3981
Yamaha V-Max (85 - 03) ◆	4072
ATVs	
Honda ATC70, 90, 110, 185 & 200 (71 - 85)	0565
Honda Rancher, Recon & TRX250EX ATVs	2553
Honda TRX300 Shaft Drive ATVs (88 - 00)	2125
Honda Foreman (95 - 07)	2465
Honda TRX300EX, TRX400EX & TRX450R/ER ATVs (93 - 06)	2318
Kawasaki Bayou 220/250/300 & Prairie 300 ATVs (86 - 03)	2351
Polaris ATVs (85 - 97)	2302
Polaris ATVs (98 - 06)	2508
Yamaha YFS200 Blaster ATV (88 - 06)	2317
Yamaha YFB250 Timberwolf ATVs (92 - 00)	2217
Yamaha YFM350 & YFM400 (ER and Big Bear) ATVs (87 - 03)	2126
Yamaha Banshee and Warrior ATVs (87 - 03)	2314
Yamaha Kodiak and Grizzly ATVs (93 - 05)	2567
ATV Basics	10450
TECHBOOK SERIES	
Twist and Go (automatic transmission) Scooters Service and Repair Manual	4082
Motorcycle Basics TechBook (2nd Edition)	3515
Motorcycle Electrical TechBook (3rd Edition)	3471
Motorcycle Fuel Systems TechBook	3514
Motorcycle Maintenance TechBook	4071
Motorcycle Modifying	4272
Motorcycle Workshop Practice TechBook (2nd Edition)	3470

◇ = not available in the USA   ◆ = Superbike

The manuals on this page are available through good motorcycle dealers and accessory shops.
In case of difficulty, contact: **Haynes Publishing**
(UK) +44 1963 442030   (USA) +1 805 498 6703
(SV) +46 18 124016
(Australia/New Zealand) +61 3 9763 8100

Haynes Manuals – The Complete UK Car List

Title	Book No.
ALFA ROMEO Alfasud/Sprint (74 - 88) up to F *	0292
Alfa Romeo Alfetta (73 - 87) up to E *	0531
AUDI 80, 90 & Coupe Petrol (79 - Nov 88) up to F	0605
Audi 80, 90 & Coupe Petrol (Oct 86 - 90) D to H	1491
Audi 100 & 200 Petrol (Oct 82 - 90) up to H	0907
Audi 100 & A6 Petrol & Diesel (May 91 - May 97) H to P	3504
Audi A3 Petrol & Diesel (96 - May 03) P to 03	4253
Audi A4 Petrol & Diesel (95 - 00) M to X	3575
Audi A4 Petrol & Diesel (01 - 04) X to 54	4609
AUSTIN A35 & A40 (56 - 67) up to F *	0118
Austin/MG/Rover Maestro 1.3 & 1.6 Petrol (83 - 95) up to M	0922
Austin/MG Metro (80 - May 90) up to G	0718
Austin/Rover Montego 1.3 & 1.6 Petrol (84 - 94) A to L	1066
Austin/MG/Rover Montego 2.0 Petrol (84 - 95) A to M	1067
Mini (59 - 69) up to H *	0527
Mini (69 - 01) up to X	0646
Austin/Rover 2.0 litre Diesel Engine (86 - 93) C to L	1857
Austin Healey 100/6 & 3000 (56 - 68) up to G *	0049
BEDFORD CF Petrol (69 - 87) up to E	0163
Bedford/Vauxhall Rascal & Suzuki Supercarry (86 - Oct 94) C to M	3015
BMW 316, 320 & 320i (4-cyl) (75 - Feb 83) up to Y *	0276
BMW 320, 320i, 323i & 325i (6-cyl) (Oct 77 - Sept 87) up to E	0815
BMW 3- & 5-Series Petrol (81 - 91) up to J	1948
BMW 3-Series Petrol (Apr 91 - 99) H to V	3210
BMW 3-Series Petrol (Sept 98 - 03) S to 53	4067
BMW 520i & 525e (Oct 81 - June 88) up to E	1560
BMW 525, 528 & 528i (73 - Sept 81) up to X *	0632
BMW 5-Series 6-cyl Petrol (April 96 - Aug 03) N to 03	4151
BMW 1500, 1502, 1600, 1602, 2000 & 2002 (59 - 77) up to S *	0240
CHRYSLER PT Cruiser Petrol (00 - 03) W to 53	4058
CITROËN 2CV, Ami & Dyane (67 - 90) up to H	0196
Citroën AX Petrol & Diesel (87 - 97) D to P	3014
Citroën Berlingo & Peugeot Partner Petrol & Diesel (96 - 05) P to 55	4281
Citroën BX Petrol (83 - 94) A to L	0908
Citroën C15 Van Petrol & Diesel (89 - Oct 98) F to S	3509
Citroën C3 Petrol & Diesel (02 - 05) 51 to 05	4197
Citroen C5 Petrol & Diesel (01-08) Y to 08	4745
Citroën CX Petrol (75 - 88) up to F	0528
Citroën Saxo Petrol & Diesel (96 - 04) N to 54	3506
Citroën Visa Petrol (79 - 88) up to F	0620
Citroën Xantia Petrol & Diesel (93 - 01) K to Y	3082
Citroën XM Petrol & Diesel (89 - 00) G to X	3451
Citroën Xsara Petrol & Diesel (97 - Sept 00) R to W	3751
Citroën Xsara Picasso Petrol & Diesel (00 - 02) W to 52	3944
Citroen Xsara Picasso (03-08)	4784
Citroën ZX Diesel (91 - 98) J to S	1922
Citroën ZX Petrol (91 - 98) H to S	1881
Citroën 1.7 & 1.9 litre Diesel Engine (84 - 96) A to N	1379
FIAT 126 (73 - 87) up to E *	0305
Fiat 500 (57 - 73) up to M *	0090
Fiat Bravo & Brava Petrol (95 - 00) N to W	3572
Fiat Cinquecento (93 - 98) K to R	3501
Fiat Panda (81 - 95) up to M	0793
Fiat Punto Petrol & Diesel (94 - Oct 99) L to V	3251
Fiat Punto Petrol (Oct 99 - July 03) V to 03	4066
Fiat Punto Petrol (03-07) 03 to 07	4746
Fiat Regata Petrol (84 - 88) A to F	1167
Fiat Tipo Petrol (88 - 91) E to J	1625
Fiat Uno Petrol (83 - 95) up to M	0923
Fiat X1/9 (74 - 89) up to G *	0273
FORD Anglia (59 - 68) up to G *	0001

Title	Book No.
Ford Capri II (& III) 1.6 & 2.0 (74 - 87) up to E *	0283
Ford Capri II (& III) 2.8 & 3.0 V6 (74 - 87) up to E	1309
Ford Cortina Mk I & Corsair 1500 ('62 - '66) up to D*	0214
Ford Cortina Mk III 1300 & 1600 (70 - 76) up to P *0070	
Ford Escort Mk I 1100 & 1300 (68 - 74) up to N *	0171
Ford Escort Mk I Mexico, RS 1600 & RS 2000 (70 - 74) up to N *	0139
Ford Escort Mk II Mexico, RS 1800 & RS 2000 (75 - 80) up to W *	0735
Ford Escort (75 - Aug 80) up to V *	0280
Ford Escort Petrol (Sept 80 - Sept 90) up to H	0686
Ford Escort & Orion Petrol (Sept 90 - 00) H to X	1737
Ford Escort & Orion Diesel (Sept 90 - 00) H to X	4081
Ford Fiesta (76 - Aug 83) up to Y	0334
Ford Fiesta Petrol (Aug 83 - Feb 89) A to F	1030
Ford Fiesta Petrol (Feb 89 - Oct 95) F to N	1595
Ford Fiesta Petrol & Diesel (Oct 95 - Mar 02) N to 02	3397
Ford Fiesta Petrol & Diesel (Apr 02 - 07) 02 to 57	4170
Ford Focus Petrol & Diesel (98 - 01) S to Y	3759
Ford Focus Petrol & Diesel (Oct 01 - 05) 51 to 05	4167
Ford Galaxy Petrol & Diesel (95 - Aug 00) M to W	3984
Ford Granada Petrol (Sept 77 - Feb 85) up to B *	0481
Ford Granada & Scorpio Petrol (Mar 85 - 94) B to M	1245
Ford Ka (96 - 02) P to 52	3570
Ford Mondeo Petrol (93 - Sept 00) K to X	1923
Ford Mondeo Petrol & Diesel (Oct 00 - Jul 03) X to 03	3990
Ford Mondeo Petrol & Diesel (July 03 - 07) 03 to 56	4619
Ford Mondeo Diesel (93 - 96) L to N	3465
Ford Orion Petrol (83 - Sept 90) up to H	1009
Ford Sierra 4-cyl Petrol (82 - 93) up to K	0903
Ford Sierra V6 Petrol (82 - 91) up to J	0904
Ford Transit Petrol (Mk 2) (78 - Jan 86) up to C	0719
Ford Transit Petrol (Mk 3) (Feb 86 - 89) C to G	1468
Ford Transit Diesel (Feb 86 - 99) C to T	3019
Ford Transit Diesel (00-06)	4775
Ford 1.6 & 1.8 litre Diesel Engine (84 - 96) A to N	1172
Ford 2.1, 2.3 & 2.5 litre Diesel Engine (77 - 90) up to H	1606
FREIGHT ROVER Sherpa Petrol (74 - 87) up to E	0463
HILLMAN Avenger (70 - 82) up to Y	0037
Hillman Imp (63 - 76) up to R *	0022
HONDA Civic (Feb 84 - Oct 87) A to E	1226
Honda Civic (Nov 91 - 96) J to N	3199
Honda Civic Petrol (Mar 95 - 00) M to X	4050
Honda Civic Petrol & Diesel (01 - 05) X to 55	4611
Honda CR-V Petrol & Diesel (01-06)	4747
Honda Jazz (01 - Feb 08) 51 - 57	4735
HYUNDAI Pony (85 - 94) C to M	3398
JAGUAR E Type (61 - 72) up to L *	0140
Jaguar MkI & II, 240 & 340 (55 - 69) up to H *	0098
Jaguar XJ6, XJ & Sovereign; Daimler Sovereign (68 - Oct 86) up to D	0242
Jaguar XJ6 & Sovereign (Oct 86 - Sept 94) D to M	3261
Jaguar XJ12, XJS & Sovereign; Daimler Double Six (72 - 88) up to F	0478
JEEP Cherokee Petrol (93 - 96) K to N	1943
LADA 1200, 1300, 1500 & 1600 (74 - 91) up to J	0413
Lada Samara (87 - 91) D to J	1610
LAND ROVER 90, 110 & Defender Diesel (83 - 07) up to 56	3017
Land Rover Discovery Petrol & Diesel (89 - 98) G to S	3016
Land Rover Discovery Diesel (Nov 98 - Jul 04) S to 04	4606
Land Rover Freelander Petrol & Diesel (97 - Sept 03) R to 53	3929
Land Rover Freelander Petrol & Diesel (Oct 03 - Oct 06) 53 to 56	4623

Title	Book No.
Land Rover Series IIA & III Diesel (58 - 85) up to C	0529
Land Rover Series II, IIA & III 4-cyl Petrol (58 - 85) up to C	0314
MAZDA 323 (Mar 81 - Oct 89) up to G	1608
Mazda 323 (Oct 89 - 98) G to R	3455
Mazda 626 (May 83 - Sept 87) up to E	0929
Mazda B1600, B1800 & B2000 Pick-up Petrol (72 - 88) up to F	0267
Mazda RX-7 (79 - 85) up to C *	0460
MERCEDES-BENZ 190, 190E & 190D Petrol & Diesel (83 - 93) A to L	3450
Mercedes-Benz 200D, 240D, 240TD, 300D & 300TD 123 Series Diesel (Oct 76 - 85)	1114
Mercedes-Benz 250 & 280 (68 - 72) up to L *	0346
Mercedes-Benz 250 & 280 123 Series Petrol (Oct 76 - 84) up to B *	0677
Mercedes-Benz 124 Series Petrol & Diesel (85 - Aug 93) C to K	3253
Mercedes-Benz A-Class Petrol & Diesel (98-04) S to 54	4748
Mercedes-Benz C-Class Petrol & Diesel (93 - Aug 00) L to W	3511
Mercedes-Benz C-Class (00-06)	4780
MGA (55 - 62) *	0475
MGB (62 - 80) up to W	0111
MG Midget & Austin-Healey Sprite (58 - 80) up to W *	0265
MINI Petrol (July 01 - 05) Y to 05	4273
MITSUBISHI Shogun & L200 Pick-Ups Petrol (83 - 94) up to M	1944
MORRIS Ital 1.3 (80 - 84) up to B	0705
Morris Minor 1000 (56 - 71) up to K	0024
NISSAN Almera Petrol (95 - Feb 00) N to V	4053
Nissan Almera & Tino Petrol (Feb 00 - 07) V to 56	4612
Nissan Bluebird (May 84 - Mar 86) A to C	1223
Nissan Bluebird Petrol (Mar 86 - 90) C to H	1473
Nissan Cherry (Sept 82 - 86) up to D	1031
Nissan Micra (83 - Jan 93) up to K	0931
Nissan Micra (93 - 02) K to 52	3254
Nissan Micra Petrol (03-07) 52 to 57	4734
Nissan Primera Petrol (90 - Aug 99) H to T	1851
Nissan Stanza (82 - 86) up to D	0824
Nissan Sunny Petrol (May 82 - Oct 86) up to D	0895
Nissan Sunny Petrol (Oct 86 - Mar 91) D to H	1378
Nissan Sunny Petrol (Apr 91 - 95) H to N	3219
OPEL Ascona & Manta (B Series) (Sept 75 - 88) up to F *	0316
Opel Ascona Petrol (81 - 88)	3215
Opel Astra Petrol (Oct 91 - Feb 98)	3156
Opel Corsa Petrol (83 - Mar 93)	3160
Opel Corsa Petrol (Mar 93 - 97)	3159
Opel Kadett Petrol (Nov 79 - Oct 84) up to B	0634
Opel Kadett Petrol (Oct 84 - Oct 91)	3196
Opel Omega & Senator Petrol (Nov 86 - 94)	3157
Opel Rekord Petrol (Feb 78 - Oct 86) up to D	0543
Opel Vectra Petrol (Oct 88 - Oct 95)	3158
PEUGEOT 106 Petrol & Diesel (91 - 04) J to 53	1882
Peugeot 205 Petrol (83 - 97) A to P	0932
Peugeot 206 Petrol & Diesel (98 - 01) S to X	3757
Peugeot 206 Petrol & Diesel (02 - 06) 51 to 06	4613
Peugeot 306 Petrol & Diesel (93 - 02) K to 02	3073
Peugeot 307 Petrol & Diesel (01 - 04) Y to 54	4147
Peugeot 309 Petrol (86 - 93) C to K	1266
Peugeot 405 Petrol (88 - 97) E to P	1559
Peugeot 405 Diesel (88 - 97) E to P	3198
Peugeot 406 Petrol & Diesel (96 - Mar 99) N to T	3394
Peugeot 406 Petrol & Diesel (Mar 99 - 02) T to 52	3982

* Classic reprint

Title	Book No.
Peugeot 505 Petrol (79 - 89) up to G	0762
Peugeot 1.7/1.8 & 1.9 litre Diesel Engine (82 - 96) up to N	0950
Peugeot 2.0, 2.1, 2.3 & 2.5 litre Diesel Engines (74 - 90) up to H	1607
PORSCHE 911 (65 - 85) up to C	0264
Porsche 924 & 924 Turbo (76 - 85) up to C	0397
PROTON (89 - 97) F to P	3255
RANGE ROVER V8 Petrol (70 - Oct 92) up to K	0606
RELIANT Robin & Kitten (73 - 83) up to A *	0436
RENAULT 4 (61 - 86) up to D *	0072
Renault 5 Petrol (Feb 85 - 96) B to N	1219
Renault 9 & 11 Petrol (82 - 89) up to F	0822
Renault 18 Petrol (79 - 86) up to D	0598
Renault 19 Petrol (89 - 96) F to N	1646
Renault 19 Diesel (89 - 96) F to N	1946
Renault 21 Petrol (86 - 94) C to M	1397
Renault 25 Petrol & Diesel (84 - 92) B to K	1228
Renault Clio Petrol (91 - May 98) H to R	1853
Renault Clio Diesel (91 - June 96) H to N	3031
Renault Clio Petrol & Diesel (May 98 - May 01) R to Y	3906
Renault Clio Petrol & Diesel (June '01 - '05) Y to 55	4168
Renault Espace Petrol & Diesel (85 - 96) C to N	3197
Renault Laguna Petrol & Diesel (94 - 00) L to W	3252
Renault Laguna Petrol & Diesel (Feb 01 - Feb 05) X to 54	4283
Renault Mégane & Scénic Petrol & Diesel (96 - 99) N to T	3395
Renault Mégane & Scénic Petrol & Diesel (Apr 99 - 02) T to 52	3916
Renault Megane Petrol & Diesel (Oct 02 - 05) 52 to 55	4284
Renault Scenic Petrol & Diesel (Sept 03 - 06) 53 to 06	4297
ROVER 213 & 216 (84 - 89) A to G	1116
Rover 214 & 414 Petrol (89 - 96) G to N	1689
Rover 216 & 416 Petrol (89 - 96) G to N	1830
Rover 211, 214, 216, 218 & 220 Petrol & Diesel (Dec 95 - 99) N to V	3399
Rover 25 & MG ZR Petrol & Diesel (Oct 99 - 04) V to 54	4145
Rover 414, 416 & 420 Petrol & Diesel (May 95 - 98) M to R	3453
Rover 45 / MG ZS Petrol & Diesel (99 - 05) V to 55	4384
Rover 618, 620 & 623 Petrol (93 - 97) K to P	3257
Rover 75 / MG ZT Petrol & Diesel (99 - 06) S to 06	4292
Rover 820, 825 & 827 Petrol (86 - 95) D to N	1380
Rover 3500 (76 - 87) up to E *	0365
Rover Metro, 111 & 114 Petrol (May 90 - 98) G to S	1711
SAAB 95 & 96 (66 - 76) up to R *	0198
Saab 90, 99 & 900 (79 - Oct 93) up to L	0765
Saab 900 (Oct 93 - 98) L to R	3512
Saab 9000 (4-cyl) (85 - 98) C to S	1686
Saab 9-3 Petrol & Diesel (98 - Aug 02) R to 02	4614
Saab 9-3 Petrol & Diesel (02-07) 52 to 57	4749
Saab 9-5 4-cyl Petrol (97 - 04) R to 54	4156
SEAT Ibiza & Cordoba Petrol & Diesel (Oct 93 - Oct 99) L to V	3571
Seat Ibiza & Malaga Petrol (85 - 92) B to K	1609
SKODA Estelle (77 - 89) up to G	0604
Skoda Fabia Petrol & Diesel (00 - 06) W to 06	4376
Skoda Favorit (89 - 96) F to N	1801
Skoda Felicia Petrol & Diesel (95 - 01) M to X	3505
Skoda Octavia Petrol & Diesel (98 - Apr 04) R to 04	4285
SUBARU 1600 & 1800 (Nov 79 - 90) up to H *	0995

Title	Book No.
SUNBEAM Alpine, Rapier & H120 (67 - 74) up to N *	0051
SUZUKI SJ Series, Samurai & Vitara (4-cyl) Petrol (82 - 97) up to P	1942
Suzuki Supercarry & Bedford/Vauxhall Rascal (86 - Oct 94) C to M	3015
TALBOT Alpine, Solara, Minx & Rapier (75 - 86) up to D	0337
Talbot Horizon Petrol (78 - 86) up to D	0473
Talbot Samba (82 - 86) up to D	0823
TOYOTA Avensis Petrol (98 - Jan 03) R to 52	4264
Toyota Carina E Petrol (May 92 - 97) J to P	3256
Toyota Corolla (80 - 85) up to C	0683
Toyota Corolla (Sept 83 - Sept 87) A to E	1024
Toyota Corolla (Sept 87 - Aug 92) E to K	1683
Toyota Corolla Petrol (Aug 92 - 97) K to P	3259
Toyota Corolla Petrol (July 97 - Feb 02) P to 51	4286
Toyota Hi-Ace & Hi-Lux Petrol (69 - Oct 83) up to A	0304
Toyota RAV4 Petrol & Diesel (94-06) L to 55	4750
Toyota Yaris Petrol (99 - 05) T to 05	4265
TRIUMPH GT6 & Vitesse (62 - 74) up to N *	0112
Triumph Herald (59 - 71) up to K *	0010
Triumph Spitfire (62 - 81) up to X	0113
Triumph Stag (70 - 78) up to T *	0441
Triumph TR2, TR3, TR3A, TR4 & TR4A (52 - 67) up to F *	0028
Triumph TR5 & 6 (67 - 75) up to P *	0031
Triumph TR7 (75 - 82) up to Y *	0322
VAUXHALL Astra Petrol (80 - Oct 84) up to B	0635
Vauxhall Astra & Belmont Petrol (Oct 84 - Oct 91) B to J	1136
Vauxhall Astra Petrol (Oct 91 - Feb 98) J to R	1832
Vauxhall/Opel Astra & Zafira Petrol (Feb 98 - Apr 04) R to 04	3758
Vauxhall/Opel Astra & Zafira Diesel (Feb 98 - Apr 04) R to 04	3797
Vauxhall/Opel Astra Petrol (04 - 08)	4732
Vauxhall/Opel Astra Diesel (04 - 08)	4733
Vauxhall/Opel Calibra (90 - 98) G to S	3502
Vauxhall Carlton Petrol (Oct 78 - Oct 86) up to D	0480
Vauxhall Carlton & Senator Petrol (Nov 86 - 94) D to L	1469
Vauxhall Cavalier Petrol (81 - Oct 88) up to F	0812
Vauxhall Cavalier Petrol (Oct 88 - 95) F to N	1570
Vauxhall Chevette (75 - 84) up to B	0285
Vauxhall/Opel Corsa Diesel (Mar 93 - Oct 00) K to X	4087
Vauxhall Corsa Petrol (Mar 93 - 97) K to R	1985
Vauxhall/Opel Corsa Petrol (Apr 97 - Oct 00) P to X	3921
Vauxhall/Opel Corsa Petrol & Diesel (Oct 00 - Sept 03) X to 53	4079
Vauxhall/Opel Corsa Petrol & Diesel (Oct 03 - Aug 06) 53 to 06	4617
Vauxhall/Opel Frontera Petrol & Diesel (91 - Sept 98) J to S	3454
Vauxhall Nova Petrol (83 - 93) up to K	0909
Vauxhall/Opel Omega Petrol (94 - 99) L to T	3510
Vauxhall/Opel Vectra Petrol & Diesel (95 - Feb 99) N to S	3396
Vauxhall/Opel Vectra Petrol & Diesel (Mar 99 - May 02) T to 02	3930
Vauxhall/Opel Vectra Petrol & Diesel (June 02 - Sept 05) 02 to 55	4618
Vauxhall/Opel 1.5, 1.6 & 1.7 litre Diesel Engine (82 - 96) up to N	1222
VW 411 & 412 (68 - 75) up to P *	0091
VW Beetle 1200 (54 - 77) up to S	0036
VW Beetle 1300 & 1500 (65 - 75) up to P	0039

Title	Book No.
VW 1302 & 1302S (70 - 72) up to L *	0110
VW Beetle 1303, 1303S & GT (72 - 75) up to P	0159
VW Beetle Petrol & Diesel (Apr 99 - 07) T to 57	3798
VW Golf & Jetta Mk 1 Petrol 1.1 & 1.3 (74 - 84) up to A	0716
VW Golf, Jetta & Scirocco Mk 1 Petrol 1.5, 1.6 & 1.8 (74 - 84) up to A	0726
VW Golf & Jetta Mk 1 Diesel (78 - 84) up to A	0451
VW Golf & Jetta Mk 2 Petrol (Mar 84 - Feb 92) A to J	1081
VW Golf & Vento Petrol & Diesel (Feb 92 - Mar 98) J to R	3097
VW Golf & Bora Petrol & Diesel (April 98 - 00) R to X	3727
VW Golf & Bora 4-cyl Petrol & Diesel (01 - 03) X to 53	4169
VW Golf & Jetta Petrol & Diesel (04 - 07) 53 to 07	4610
VW LT Petrol Vans & Light Trucks (76 - 87) up to E	0637
VW Passat & Santana Petrol (Sept 81 - May 88) up to E	0814
VW Passat 4-cyl Petrol & Diesel (May 88 - 96) E to P	3498
VW Passat 4-cyl Petrol & Diesel (Dec 96 - Nov 00) P to X	3917
VW Passat Petrol & Diesel (Dec 00 - May 05) X to 05	4279
VW Polo & Derby (76 - Jan 82) up to X	0335
VW Polo (82 - Oct 90) up to H	0813
VW Polo Petrol (Nov 90 - Aug 94) H to L	3245
VW Polo Hatchback Petrol & Diesel (94 - 99) M to S	3500
VW Polo Hatchback Petrol (00 - Jan 02) V to 51	4150
VW Polo Petrol & Diesel (02 - May 05) 51 to 05	4608
VW Scirocco (82 - 90) up to H *	1224
VW Transporter 1600 (68 - 79) up to V	0082
VW Transporter 1700, 1800 & 2000 (72 - 79) up to V *	0226
VW Transporter (air-cooled) Petrol (79 - 82) up to Y *	0638
VW Transporter (water-cooled) Petrol (82 - 90) up to H	3452
VW Type 3 (63 - 73) up to M *	0084
VOLVO 120 & 130 Series (& P1800) (61 - 73) up to M *	0203
Volvo 142, 144 & 145 (66 - 74) up to N *	0129
Volvo 240 Series Petrol (74 - 93) up to K	0270
Volvo 262, 264 & 260/265 (75 - 85) up to C *	0400
Volvo 340, 343, 345 & 360 (76 - 91) up to J	0715
Volvo 440, 460 & 480 Petrol (87 - 97) D to P	1691
Volvo 740 & 760 Petrol (82 - 91) up to J	1258
Volvo 850 Petrol (92 - 96) J to P	3260
Volvo 940 petrol (90 - 98) H to R	3249
Volvo S40 & V40 Petrol (96 - Mar 04) N to 04	3569
Volvo S40 & V50 Petrol & Diesel (Mar 04 - Jun 07) 04 to 07	4731
Volvo S60 Petrol & Diesel (01-08)	4793
Volvo S70, V70 & C70 Petrol (96 - 99) P to V	3573
Volvo V70 / S80 Petrol & Diesel (98 - 05) S to 55	4263

DIY MANUAL SERIES

Title	Book No.
The Haynes Air Conditioning Manual	4192
The Haynes Car Electrical Systems Manual	4251
The Haynes Manual on Bodywork	4198
The Haynes Manual on Brakes	4178
The Haynes Manual on Carburettors	4177
The Haynes Manual on Diesel Engines	4174
The Haynes Manual on Engine Management	4199
The Haynes Manual on Fault Codes	4175
The Haynes Manual on Practical Electrical Systems	4267
The Haynes Manual on Small Engines	4250
The Haynes Manual on Welding	4176

* Classic reprint

CL24.08/09

Preserving Our Motoring Heritage

< *The Model J Duesenberg Derham Tourster. Only eight of these magnificent cars were ever built – this is the only example to be found outside the United States of America*

Almost every car you've ever loved, loathed or desired is gathered under one roof at the Haynes Motor Museum. Over 300 immaculately presented cars and motorbikes represent every aspect of our motoring heritage, from elegant reminders of bygone days, such as the superb Model J Duesenberg to curiosities like the bug-eyed BMW Isetta. There are also many old friends and flames. Perhaps you remember the 1959 Ford Popular that you did your courting in? The magnificent 'Red Collection' is a spectacle of classic sports cars including AC, Alfa Romeo, Austin Healey, Ferrari, Lamborghini, Maserati, MG, Riley, Porsche and Triumph.

A Perfect Day Out

Each and every vehicle at the Haynes Motor Museum has played its part in the history and culture of Motoring. Today, they make a wonderful spectacle and a great day out for all the family. Bring the kids, bring Mum and Dad, but above all bring your camera to capture those golden memories for ever. You will also find an impressive array of motoring memorabilia, a comfortable 70 seat video cinema and one of the most extensive transport book shops in Britain. The Pit Stop Cafe serves everything from a cup of tea to wholesome, home-made meals or, if you prefer, you can enjoy the large picnic area nestled in the beautiful rural surroundings of Somerset.

John Haynes O.B.E., Founder and Chairman of the museum at the wheel of a Haynes Light 12. >

< *The 1936 490cc sohc-engined International Norton – well known for its racing success*

The Museum is situated on the A359 Yeovil to Frome road at Sparkford, just off the A303 in Somerset. It is about 40 miles south of Bristol, and 25 minutes drive from the M5 intersection at Taunton.

Open 9.30am - 5.30pm (10.00am - 4.00pm Winter) 7 days a week, *except Christmas Day, Boxing Day and New Years Day*

Special rates available for schools, coach parties and outings Charitable Trust No. 292048